Algebra $\frac{1}{2}$

An Incremental Development

Third Edition

Algebra $\frac{1}{2}$

An Incremental Development

Third Edition

John H. Saxon, Jr.

SAXON PUBLISHERS, INC.

Saxon Publishers gratefully acknowledges the contributions of the following individuals in the completion of this project:

Author: John Saxon

Editorial: Brian E. Rice, Matt Maloney, R. Clint Keele

Editorial Support Services: Christopher Davey, Jenifer Sparks, Jack Day, Shelley Turner

Production: Adriana Maxwell, Brenda Lopez

Printed in the United States of America

ISBN: 978-1-56577-149-9
ISBN: 1-56577-149-4

Manufacturing Code: 29 0868 21
                            4500819581

Contents

Preface

The third edition of John Saxon's *Algebra $\frac{1}{2}$*, a widely used, classic textbook, was originally published in the year 2000. This copyright update is a minor revision of that publication. We have reproduced geometric formulas, abbreviations, and unit conversion facts inside the back cover, and we have corrected the few errors discovered since its original publication.

The *Algebra $\frac{1}{2}$* course focuses on introductory algebra topics. It is designed to facilitate your transition from the concrete concepts of arithmetic to the abstract concepts of algebra. One feature of *Algebra $\frac{1}{2}$* that you will find particularly useful is the lesson reference numbers in the problem sets. Beneath each problem number in the problem sets is a number in parentheses; this number refers to the lesson where the concepts and skills required to solve the problem are introduced. Should you have difficulty solving a particular problem, refer to the appropriate lesson for assistance.

To help you understand John Saxon and his vision for this text, I give you what can best be described as his exhortation to students. In the section below, Mr. Saxon addresses students like you and explains his philosophy about learning. I urge you to carefully read what Mr. Saxon says. I also hope that you will join the ranks of many thousands of students who have used the Saxon program and, as a result, have achieved success in mathematics.

John Saxon's exhortation to students

Algebra is not difficult. Algebra is just different. Time is required in order for things that are different to become things that are familiar. In this book, we provide the necessary time by reviewing all the concepts in every problem set. Also, the parts of a particular concept are introduced in small increments so that they may be practiced for a period of time before the next part of the same concept is introduced. Understanding the first part makes it easier to understand the second part. If you find that a particular problem is troublesome, get help at once because the problem won't go away. It will appear again and again in future problem sets.

The problem sets contain all the review that is necessary. **Your task is to work all the problems in every problem set.** The answers to odd-numbered problems are in the back of the book. You will have to check the answers to even-numbered problems with a classmate. Don't be discouraged if you continue to make mistakes. Everyone makes mistakes, often for a long period of time. A large part of learning algebra is devising defense mechanisms to protect you from yourself. If you work at it, you can find ways to prevent these mistakes. Your teacher is an expert because he or she has made the same mistakes many times and has finally found ways to prevent them. You must do the same. Each person must devise his or her own defense mechanisms.

The repetition in the problem sets in this book is needed to allow students the opportunity to master all the concepts. Application of the concepts must be practiced for a long time to ensure retention. This practice has an element of drudgery to it, but it has been demonstrated that people who are not willing to practice fundamentals often find success elusive. Ask any athlete, musician, or artist about the necessity of practicing fundamental skills.

This book will prove to you that mathematics is reasonable and that mathematics is not hard. If you do every problem in every problem set, you will be amazed at how easy it will all become. Let me say again: algebra is not **difficult.** Algebra is just **different.** Things that are different become familiar only after you have been exposed to them for a long time.

acknowledgments   In closing, I would like to thank the staff who contributed to the revision of this textbook. In particular, I thank editors Brian Rice, Matt Maloney, and Clint Keele; copy editors Chris Davey and Jenifer Sparks; accuracy checkers Karen Bottoms, Kara Chiodo, and Julia Suggs; production team leader Carrie Brown; production team members Sariah Adams, Eric Atkins, Wendy Chitwood, Jane Claunch, David LeBlanc, Chad Morris, Tonea Morrow, Dan O'Conner, Nancy Rimassa, Debra Sullivan, Jean Van Vleck, Sunnie Wagner, and Loren White; and production coordinator Angela Johnson. I also thank Travis Southern, who led Jeremy Eiken, Larry Gilchrist, Sherri Little, and Erin McCain in the editorial work during its formative stages. Finally, I thank Julie Webster, editor-in-chief, and Travis Rose, production manager, for their leadership of the editorial and production departments during the project.

Most important, I thank all the teachers who gave us input during the revision of this textbook. Without feedback from teachers, our textbooks would be less effective. As John Saxon liked to say, teachers are the ones "in the trenches." In particular, I thank teacher Etan Savir of Baltimore, Maryland. Mr. Savir surveyed many longtime users of the program and helped write an early draft of the revision based on teachers' suggestions. Most notably, he wrote additional topics A–I. Similarly, I would like to thank teacher Frank Stone of Lubbock, Texas. I appreciate the time he spent testing the book and the insights he shared.

Frank Y. H. Wang, Ph.D.
Norman, Oklahoma

LESSON 1 *Whole Number Place Value • Expanded Notation • Reading and Writing Whole Numbers • Addition*

1.A

whole number place value

We use the **Hindu-Arabic system** to write our numbers. This system is a base 10 system and thus has ten different symbols. The symbols are called **digits,** or **numerals,** and they are

$$0, 1, 2, 3, 4, 5, 6, 7, 8, 9$$

The numbers we say when we count are called **counting numbers,** or **natural numbers.** We may show the set of counting numbers this way:

$$\{1, 2, 3, 4, 5, \ldots\}$$

The three dots, called an *ellipsis*, mean that the list continues without end. The symbols, { }, are called braces and are sometimes used to designate a set. If we include zero with the set of counting numbers, then we form the set of **whole numbers.**

$$\{0, 1, 2, 3, 4, \ldots\}$$

When we write whole numbers, we can write the **decimal point** at the end of the number, or we can leave it off. Both of these

$$427. \qquad 427$$

represent the same number. In the right-hand number, the decimal point is assumed to be after the 7.

The value of a digit in a number depends on where the digit appears in the number. The first place to the left of the decimal point is the ones' place. We also call this place the **units' place,** which has a **place value** of 1. The next place to the left of the units' place is the **tens' place,** with a place value of 10, followed by the **hundreds' place,** with a place value of 100, and then the **thousands' place,** with a place value of 1,000. Each place to the left has one more zero.

Whole Number Place Values

hundred trillions	ten trillions	trillions		hundred billions	ten billions	billions		hundred millions	ten millions	millions		hundred thousands	ten thousands	thousands		hundreds	tens	units		decimal point
100,000,000,000,000	10,000,000,000,000	1,000,000,000,000	,	100,000,000,000	10,000,000,000	1,000,000,000	,	100,000,000	10,000,000	1,000,000	,	100,000	10,000	1,000	,	100	10	1	.

To find the value of a digit in a number, multiply the digit times the place value. For example, the 5 in the left-hand number below

415,623   701,586   731,235

has a value of 5 × 1000, or 5000, because it is in the thousands' place. The value of the 5 in the center number is 5 × 100, or 500, because it is in the hundreds' place. The value of the 5 in the right-hand number is 5 × 1, or 5, because it is in the units' (ones') place.

example 1.1   In the number 46,235:

(a) What is the value of the digit 5?

(b) What is the value of the digit 2?

(c) What is the value of the digit 4?

solution   First we write the decimal point at the end of the number.

46,235.

(a) The 5 is one place to the left of the decimal point. This is the units' place. This digit has a value of 5 × 1, or **5.**

(b) The 2 is three places to the left of the decimal point. This is the hundreds' place. This digit has a value of 2 × 100, or **200.**

(c) The 4 is five places to the left of the decimal point. This is the ten-thousands' place. This digit has a value of 4 × 10,000, or **40,000.**

1.B

expanded notation   Writing a number in **expanded notation** is a good way to practice the idea of place value. When we write a number in expanded notation, we consider the value of every digit in the number individually. To write a number in expanded notation, we write each of the nonzero digits multiplied by the place value of the digit. We use parentheses to enclose each of these multiplications and put a plus sign between each set of parentheses.

To write 5020 in expanded notation, we write

(5 × 1000) + (2 × 10)

because this number contains five thousands and two tens.

example 1.2   Write the following number in standard notation: (4 × 10,000) + (6 × 100) + (5 × 1)

solution   Standard notation is our usual way of writing numbers. The number has four ten thousands, no thousands, six hundreds, no tens, and five ones. The number is **40,605.**

example 1.3   Write the number 6,305,126 in expanded notation.

solution

There are six millions,   three hundred thousands,
(6 × 1,000,000)   (3 × 100,000)

five thousands,   one hundred,   two tens,   and six ones.
(5 × 1000)   (1 × 100)   (2 × 10)   (6 × 1)

If we add them all together, we get

(6 × 1,000,000) + (3 × 100,000) + (5 × 1000) + (1 × 100) + (2 × 10) + (6 × 1)

1.C

reading and writing whole numbers

We begin by noting that all numbers between 20 and 100 that do not end in zero are hyphenated words when we write them out.

23 is written twenty-three	64 is written sixty-four
35 is written thirty-five	79 is written seventy-nine
42 is written forty-two	86 is written eighty-six
51 is written fifty-one	98 is written ninety-eight

The hyphen is also used in whole numbers when the whole number is used as a modifier. The words

ten thousand

are not hyphenated. But when we use these words as a modifier, as when we say

ten-thousands' place,

the words are hyphenated. Other examples of this rule are

hundred-millions' digit

ten-billions' place

hundred-thousands' place

The word *and* is not used when we write out whole numbers.

501	is written	five hundred one
	not	five hundred and one
370	is written	three hundred seventy
	not	three hundred and seventy
422	is written	four hundred twenty-two
	not	four hundred and twenty-two

Do not think of this as a useless exercise! Knowing how to correctly and accurately write numbers is necessary when writing a check, for example. Before we read whole numbers, we place a comma after every third digit beginning at the decimal point and moving to the left.[†] The commas divide the numbers into groups of three digits.

Place Value

Trillions			Billions			Millions			Thousands			Units (Ones)			· Decimal point
Hundreds	Tens	Ones	Hundreds	Tens	Ones	Hundreds	Tens	Ones	Hundreds	Tens	Ones	Hundreds	Tens	Ones	· Decimal point

To read the number 4125678942, we begin on the right-hand end, write a decimal point, and separate the number into groups of three by writing commas.

4,125,678,942.

Then we read the number, beginning with the leftmost group. First we read the number in the group, and then we read the name of the group. Then we move to the right and repeat the procedure.

four billion, one hundred twenty-five million, six hundred seventy-eight thousand, nine hundred forty-two

---

[†]It is our convention to usually write four-digit whole numbers without commas.

example 1.4 Use words to write this number: 51723642

solution We write the decimal point on the right-hand end. Then we move to the left and place a comma after each group of three digits.

$$51{,}723{,}642.$$

The leftmost group is the millions' group. We read it as

fifty-one million,

and write the comma after the word *million*. The next three-digit group is the thousands' group. We read it as

seven hundred twenty-three thousand,

and we write the comma after the word *thousand*. The last three-digit group is the units' group. We do not say "units" but just read the three-digit number as

six hundred forty-two

Note that the words *fifty-one*, *twenty-three*, and *forty-two* are hyphenated. Also note that we do not use the word *and* between the groups. Now we put the parts together and read the number as

fifty-one million, seven hundred twenty-three thousand, six hundred forty-two

Note that the commas appear in the same places the commas appeared when we used digits to write the number.

example 1.5 Use digits to write the number fifty-one billion, twenty-seven thousand, five hundred twenty.

solution The first group is the billions' group. It contains the number fifty-one.

$$51{,} \qquad {,}$$

All the groups after the first group must have three digits. There are no millions, so we use three 0's.

$$51{,}000{,} \qquad {,}$$

There are twenty-seven thousands. We write 027 in the next group so that the group will contain three digits.

$$51{,}000{,}027{,}$$

Now we finish by writing 520 in the last group.

51,000,027,520

1.D

addition When we add numbers, we call each of the numbers **addends,** and we call the answer a **sum.**

```
  523   addend
  619   addend
+ 512   addend
 1654   sum
```

To add whole numbers, we write the numbers so that the units' places of the numbers are aligned vertically. Then we add in columns.

example 1.6   Add: $4 + 407 + 3526$

solution   We write the numbers so that the units' places of the numbers are aligned vertically. Then we add.

$$
\begin{array}{r}
4 \\
407 \\
+\ 3526 \\
\hline
\mathbf{3937}
\end{array}
$$

To add money, we write each amount of money with a dollar sign, and with two places to the right of the decimal point. Then we align the decimal points and add.

example 1.7   Add: $\$2.54 + \$5 + 9¢$

solution   We write the numbers so that there are two places to the right of each decimal point and align the decimal points. We include dollar signs, and then we add.

$$
\begin{array}{r}
\$2.54 \\
\$5.00 \\
+\ \$0.09 \\
\hline
\mathbf{\$7.63}
\end{array}
$$

This book is designed to permit the reader to automate the upper-level skills of arithmetic while the concepts of algebra are being introduced. The addition, subtraction, multiplication, and division problems in the practice and problem sets are designed to provide paper-and-pencil practice in the four basic operations of arithmetic. **Throughout this book, do not use a calculator unless you are instructed to do so by your teacher.**

practice   **a.**   In the number 152068, what is the value of the 2?

b.   Write in standard notation: $(6 \times 1000) + (4 \times 10) + (3 \times 1)$

c.   Write 85,020 in expanded notation.

d.   Use digits to write this number: ten billion, two hundred five million, forty-one thousand, five hundred

e.   Use words to write this number: 36025103

**problem set
1**

1.   In the number 5062973, what is the value of each of these digits?

(a) 6   (b) 9   (c) 3

2.   Write the six-digit number that has the digit 4 in the thousands' place, with each of the remaining digits being 3.

3.   Write the seven-digit number that has the digit 3 in the millions' place and the digit 7 in the hundreds' place, with each of the remaining digits being 6.

4.   A number has eight digits. Every digit is 9 except the ten-millions' digit, which is 3, the ten-thousands' digit, which is 5, and the units' digit, which is 2. Use digits to write the number.

5.   Use digits to write this number: forty-one billion, two hundred thousand, five hundred twenty

6. Use digits to write this number: five hundred seven billion, six hundred forty million, ninety thousand, forty-two

7. Use digits to write this number: four hundred seven trillion, ninety million, seven hundred forty-two thousand, seventy-two

8. Use digits to write this number: nine hundred eighty million, four hundred seventy

Use words to write each number:

9. 517236428

10. 90807060

11. 32000000652

12. 3250009111

13. 6040000

14. 99019900

Write each number in standard notation:

15. $(3 \times 100,000) + (4 \times 1000) + (2 \times 10)$

16. $(7 \times 10,000) + (8 \times 100) + (6 \times 10)$

17. $(9 \times 1000) + (4 \times 100) + (5 \times 1)$

18. $(7 \times 1,000,000) + (2 \times 10,000) + (6 \times 1000)$

Write each number in expanded notation:

19. 5280   **20.** 408

21. 70,600   **22.** 21,000

23. 4005   **24.** 9080

Add:

25.
```
   43
   76
   84
 + 91
```

26.
```
  4628
  5734
+ 8416
```

27.
```
  $53.58
+ $52.78
```

28. 9056 + 4708 + 9076   **29.** 432 + 846 + 943 + 721

30. $3.64 + 52¢ + $9

LESSON 2   *The Number Line and Ordering • Rounding Whole Numbers*

2.A

the number line and ordering

A **number line** can be used to help us arrange numbers in order. Each number corresponds to a unique point on the number line. The zero point of a number line is called the **origin.** The numbers to the right of the origin are called **positive numbers,** and they are all greater than zero. Every positive number has an **opposite** that is the same distance to the left of the origin. The numbers to the left of the origin are called **negative numbers.** The negative numbers are all less than zero. Zero is neither positive nor negative.

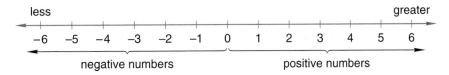

On this number line, the tick marks indicate the location of **integers.** The set of integers includes all of the counting numbers as well as their opposites and the number zero.

$$\{\dots, -3, -2, -1, 0, 1, 2, 3, \dots\}$$

Notice that the negative numbers are written with a negative sign. For -5 we say "negative five." Positive numbers may be written with or without a positive sign. Both $+5$ and 5 are positive and equal to each other.

As we move to the right on a number line, the numbers become greater and greater. As we move to the left on a number line, the numbers become less and less. A number is greater than another number if it is farther to the right on a number line.

When we put a dot on a number line to mark the location of a number, we call the dot the **graph** of the number. The number associated with a point on the number line is called the **coordinate** of the point. Any group of numbers can be arranged in order from the least to the greatest. If we graph the numbers 3, -4, and 7 on a number line, we get this figure:

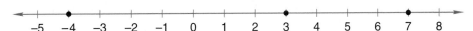

When we graph these numbers, we see that the least number is on the left and the greatest number is on the right.

example 2.1   Use a number line to arrange these integers in order from least to greatest:

$$3, -4, 0, 1, -2$$

solution   To arrange these numbers in order, we first graph each of the numbers on a number line.

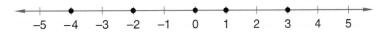

We arrange the numbers in the order they appear from left to right on the number line.

$-4, -2, 0, 1, 3$

example 2.2   Arrange the following numbers in order from least to greatest: 465, 654, -546, 456, and 564

solution   Negative numbers are always less than positive numbers, so -546 is the least number. Since all the positive numbers have three digits, the number with the least value among these is the one with the digit of least value in the hundreds' place. We have 2 numbers that begin with 4:

465   and   456

Now we look at the second digits (those in the tens' place) and see that 456 is the lesser of the two numbers because 5 is less than 6. So the two positive numbers with the least value are, in order,

456   and   465

This leaves 654 and 564. Of course, 564 is less than 654 because it has the lesser value in the hundreds' place. So our answer is

–546, 456, 465, 564, 654

If we graphed these numbers on a number line, this is the order in which they would appear.

2.B

rounding whole numbers

We often use the **rounded** form of a number. We round because some numbers, such as multiples of 10 and of 100, are easier to say and to think about than others, and in many situations approximations are as useful as more exact values. If the distance to a barn is 209 yards, a farmer might say that it is about 200 yards to the barn. If so, we could say the farmer rounded 209 to the nearest hundred because 209 is closer to 200 than it is to any other multiple of 100.

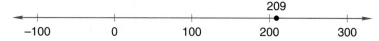

If it is 246 yards to the barn, the farmer would say that it is about 250 yards to the barn. In this case, we could say the farmer rounded 246 to the nearest 10 because 246 is closer to 250 than it is to any other multiple of 10.

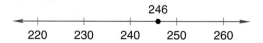

Rather than draw a number line, we will use a circle and an arrow to help us round numbers. To demonstrate, we will round 24,374 to the nearest thousand using three steps.

1. Circle the digit in the place to which we are rounding and mark the digit to its right with an arrow.

2. Leave the circled digit unchanged or increase it one unit as determined by the following rules:
   (a) If the arrow-marked digit is less than 5, do not change the circled digit.
   (b) If the arrow-marked digit is 5 or greater, increase the circled digit by one unit.

   Rule (a) applies in this problem, so we leave the circled digit unchanged.

3. Change the arrow-marked digit and all digits to its right to zero.

Our answer is 24,000.

example 2.3   Round 471,326,502 to the nearest ten thousand.

solution   First we circle the ten-thousands' digit and mark the digit to its right with an arrow.

Since the arrow-marked digit is greater than 5, we increase the circled digit from 2 to 3.

$$\downarrow$$

471,3③6,502

Next change the arrow-marked digit and all digits to its right to zero.

$$\downarrow$$

471,3③0,000

So our answer is **471,330,000.**

example 2.4   Round 83,752,914,625 to the nearest ten million.

solution   First we circle the ten-millions' digit and mark the digit to its right with an arrow.

$$\downarrow$$

83,7⑤2,914,625

Since the arrow-marked digit is less than 5, we leave the circled digit unchanged. Now we change the arrow-marked digit and all digits to its right to zero.

83,750,000,000

practice   **a.**   Use a number line to arrange these numbers in order: $-1, 4, -7, 0, 7, 5$

b.   Arrange the following numbers in order from least to greatest: $736, -637, 367, 376, 673$

c.   Round 914,471,752 to the nearest ten thousand.

d.   Round 83,625,502 to the nearest thousand.

**problem set
2**   **†1.**
(2)   Use a number line to arrange these numbers in order from least to greatest:
$2, 19, -11, 6, -5$

Arrange the following numbers in order from least to greatest:

2.   514, 154, 145, −415, 451
(2)

3.   942, 249, 924, 294, 429
(2)

4.   Round 4,185,270 to the nearest hundred.
(2)

5.   Round 83,721,525 to the nearest thousand.
(2)

6.   Round 415,237,842 to the nearest hundred thousand.
(2)

7.   A number has nine digits. All the digits are 7 except the ten-thousands' digit, which is
(1)   2, and the tens' digit, which is 5. Write the number.

8.   A number has seven digits. All the digits are 3 except the hundred-thousands' digit,
(1)   which is 6, the thousands' digit, which is 4, and the hundreds' digit, which is 7. Write
the number.

---

†The italicized numbers within parentheses below each problem number refer to the lesson in which
the concepts for that problem are discussed.

9. Use digits to write one hundred seven million, forty-seven thousand, twenty.
(1)

10. Use digits to write ninety-three billion, four hundred sixty-two million, forty-seven.
(1)

Use words to write each number:

11. 731284006
(1)

12. 903721625
(1)

13. 9003001256
(1)

14. 7234000052
(1)

Write in standard notation:

15. $(7 \times 10{,}000) + (6 \times 100) + (5 \times 10) + (4 \times 1)$
(1)

16. $(3 \times 100{,}000) + (9 \times 1000) + (7 \times 100) + (6 \times 10) + (3 \times 1)$
(1)

17. $(9 \times 1000) + (6 \times 100) + (9 \times 1)$
(1)

Write in expanded notation:

18. 109,326
(1)

19. 68,312
(1)

20. 903,162
(1)

Add:

21. $93.17
(1) $45.26
       + $90.15

22.   7316
(1)   4582
       + 9143

23.   88,871
(1)   40,012
       + 90,375

24.   78,524
(1)   91,325
       70,026
       + 91,358

25.   42,715
(1)   90,826
       41,222
       + 39,057

26. $37{,}251 + 81{,}432 + 90{,}256 + 21{,}312$
(1)

27. $14 + 32 + 16 + 21 + 932 + 21$
(1)

28. $1 + 2 + 21 + 12 + 122 + 1222$
(1)

29. $33¢ + \$3 + \$13.99$
(1)

30. $4 + 314 + 134 + 13{,}245$
(1)

LESSON 3   *Subtraction • Addition and Subtraction Patterns*

3.A
subtraction

In subtraction, we subtract the **subtrahend** from the **minuend.** The result is the **difference.** For example, the difference between 47 and 21 is 26.

$$
\begin{array}{r r}
47 & \text{minuend} \\
-\ 21 & \text{subtrahend} \\
\hline
26 & \text{difference}
\end{array}
$$

example 3.1   Subtract: $432 - 257$

solution   First we align the digits in the units' place. We must follow the correct order of subtraction by writing the minuend above the subtrahend. This time we must borrow twice.

$$
\begin{array}{r}
\overset{3}{\cancel{4}}\,\overset{12}{\cancel{3}}\,\overset{1}{2} \\
-\ 2\,5\,7 \\
\hline
\mathbf{1\,7\,5}
\end{array}
$$

example 3.2   Subtract: $\$4 - 35\cent$

solution   We write money as in the addition problems, converting to dollar form and aligning the decimal points.

$$
\begin{array}{r}
\$ \overset{3}{4}.\overset{9}{0}\,\overset{1}{0} \\
-\ \$0.3\,5 \\
\hline
\mathbf{\$3.6\,5}
\end{array}
$$

3.B
addition and subtraction patterns

If one operation will undo another operation, we say that the operations are **inverse operations.** Adding 5 and 8 gives us 13.

$$5 + 8 = 13$$

This addition can be undone by subtracting one of the addends from the sum

$$13 - 8 = 5$$

$$13 - 5 = 8$$

Thus, **addition and subtraction are inverse operations.**

Consider the pattern of the following addition problem:

$$
\begin{array}{r l}
465 & \text{addend} \\
+\ 357 & \text{addend} \\
\hline
822 & \text{sum—the greatest number}
\end{array}
$$

Three numbers are involved. When we know two of them, we can find the missing number. If the sum is missing, we add the addends; but if an addend is missing, we find the missing addend by subtracting the known addend from the sum. We can use a letter to represent a missing number.

example 3.3   Find the missing number:
$$\begin{array}{r} 472 \\ + \quad A \\ \hline 628 \end{array}$$

solution   The missing number is an addend, the difference between 628 and 472. **This is an addition pattern, but we need to subtract to find the missing number.**

$$\begin{array}{r} \overset{5}{\cancel{6}}\overset{1}{}2\,8 \\ -\,4\,7\,2 \\ \hline 1\,5\,6 \end{array}$$

Now we check by adding.

$$\begin{array}{r} 472 \\ +\,156 \\ \hline 628 \end{array} \quad \text{check}$$

The value of A is **156.**

example 3.4   Find the missing number: $M + 257 = 493$

solution   What number added to 257 equals 493? To find the number, an addend, we will subtract 257 from 493.

$$\begin{array}{r} 4\,\overset{8}{\cancel{9}}\overset{1}{}3 \\ -\,2\,5\,7 \\ \hline 2\,3\,6 \end{array}$$

Now we check.

$$\begin{array}{r} 236 \\ +\,257 \\ \hline 493 \end{array} \quad \text{check}$$

The value of M is **236.**

Consider the pattern of the following subtraction problem:

$$\begin{array}{r} 822 \\ -\,357 \\ \hline 465 \end{array} \quad \begin{array}{l} \text{minuend—the greatest number} \\ \text{subtrahend} \\ \text{difference} \end{array}$$

Again three numbers are involved. When we know two of them, we can find the third number. If the difference is missing, we subtract; if the subtrahend is missing, we subtract the difference from the minuend; and if the minuend is missing, we add the subtrahend and difference.

example 3.5   Find the missing number:
$$\begin{array}{r} 526 \\ -\quad X \\ \hline 329 \end{array}$$

solution   To find X, the subtrahend, we subtract 329 from 526.

$$\begin{array}{r} \overset{4}{\cancel{5}}\overset{1}{2}\overset{1}{6} \\ -\,3\,2\,9 \\ \hline 1\,9\,7 \end{array}$$

Now we check using our subtraction pattern.

$$\begin{array}{r} 526 \\ -\,197 \\ \hline 329 \end{array} \quad \text{check}$$

The value of X is **197.**

example 3.6   Find the missing number: $P - 423 = 287$

solution   The first number in a subtraction pattern, the minuend, always equals the sum of the subtrahend and the difference. So we add the subtrahend and difference to find P.

$$\begin{array}{r} 423 \\ +\ 287 \\ \hline 710 \end{array}$$

Now we check using our subtraction pattern.

$$\begin{array}{r} 710 \\ -\ 423 \\ \hline 287 \end{array} \quad \text{check}$$

The value of P is **710**.

practice   **a.**   Subtract: $54.85 - $27.68

Find the missing numbers:

b. $\begin{array}{r} 563 \\ +\quad A \\ \hline 912 \end{array}$ **c.** $K + 123 = 522$

d. $\begin{array}{r} M \\ -\ 364 \\ \hline 376 \end{array}$ **e.** $741 - F = 372$

problem set 3

1. *(1)* A number has six digits. Every digit is a 2 except the thousands' digit, which is 5, and the units' digit, which is 3. What is the number?

2. *(1)* A number has five digits. Every digit is a 7 except the thousands' digit, which is 0. What is the number?

3. *(1)* A number has seven digits. Every digit is a 4 except the hundred-thousands' digit, which is 1. What is the number?

4. *(1)* Use digits to write fourteen million, seven hundred five thousand, fifty-two.

5. *(1)* Use digits to write five hundred billion, four hundred sixty-five thousand, one hundred eighty-two.

Write in expanded notation:

6. *(1)* 64,030

7. *(1)* 79,003

8. *(1)* 123,419

Add or subtract as indicated:

9. *(3)* $\begin{array}{r} 551 \\ -\ 174 \end{array}$ **10.** *(3)* $\begin{array}{r} 853 \\ -\ 284 \end{array}$ **11.** *(1)* $\begin{array}{r} 936 \\ +\ 474 \end{array}$ **12.** *(1)* $\begin{array}{r} 839 \\ +\ 472 \end{array}$

13. *(3)* $60 - $49.49   **14.** *(3)* $4017 - 3952$

Find the missing numbers:

15.
(3)

$$
\begin{array}{r}
X \\
-\ 245 \\
\hline
276
\end{array}
$$

16. $800 - M = 436$
(3)

17.
(3)

$$
\begin{array}{r}
735 \\
+\ \ A \\
\hline
1211
\end{array}
$$

18. $925 + F = 1111$
(3)

Write in standard notation:

19. $(8 \times 10{,}000) + (5 \times 1000) + (3 \times 100) + (2 \times 10) + (5 \times 1)$
(1)

20. $(6 \times 1000) + (6 \times 100) + (6 \times 1)$
(1)

21. $(3 \times 100{,}000) + (2 \times 10{,}000) + (9 \times 100) + (7 \times 1)$
(1)

22. Use words to write 5803125702.
(1)

Add:

23. $295 + 486 + 588 + 714$
(1)

24. $\$2 + \$9.37 + 86¢$
(1)

25.
(1)

$$
\begin{array}{r}
90{,}125 \\
40{,}061 \\
30{,}627 \\
+\ 95{,}132 \\
\end{array}
$$

26.
(1)

$$
\begin{array}{r}
1125 \\
986 \\
139 \\
+\ 2364 \\
\end{array}
$$

27. Round 716,487,250 to the nearest ten million.
(2)

28. Round 716,487,250 to the nearest ten thousand.
(2)

29. Use a number line to arrange these numbers from least to greatest: 6, –2, 1, 0, –4
(2)

30. Arrange the following numbers in order from least to greatest:
(2) 321, –213, 123, 231, 132

LESSON 4 *Multiplication • Division • Multiplication and Division Patterns*

4.A

multiplication

Multiplication is a shorthand notation we use to denote repeated addition. If we wish to add 7 twelve times, we could write

$$7 + 7 + 7 + 7 + 7 + 7 + 7 + 7 + 7 + 7 + 7 + 7 = 84$$

or we could write

$$7 \times 12 = 84$$

which also means, "twelve sevens is eighty-four." If we wish to add 12 seven times, we could write

$$12 + 12 + 12 + 12 + 12 + 12 + 12 = 84$$

or we could write

$$12 \times 7 = 84$$

which is the more compact way of saying, "seven twelves is eighty-four." Because the sum of twelve 7's is the same as the sum of seven 12's, we could write for either addition problem

$$7 \times 12 \qquad \text{or} \qquad 12 \times 7$$

Here we use a cross to indicate multiplication. In algebra, we often use a center dot instead of a cross. The dot also indicates multiplication. We can write the multiplications above as

$$7 \cdot 12 \qquad \text{or} \qquad 12 \cdot 7$$

When we multiply two numbers, the order of the numbers does not affect the result.

In multiplication, we call numbers that are multiplied together **factors.** We call the answer the **product.**

$$
\begin{array}{r r l}
 & 12 & \text{factor} \\
\times & 7 & \text{factor} \\
\hline
 & 84 & \text{product}
\end{array}
$$

example 4.1

Multiply: 164×23

solution

We usually write the number with the most digits on top. We first multiply by the 3 of 23, then by the 20 of 23. We add the partial products and find the final product.

$$
\begin{array}{r}
164 \\
\times \quad 23 \\
\hline
492 \\
328 \\
\hline
\mathbf{3772}
\end{array}
$$

example 4.2

Multiply: $\$5.79 \times 29$

solution

We multiply as usual and then write the product with a dollar sign and two decimal places.

$$
\begin{array}{r}
\$5.79 \\
\times \quad 29 \\
\hline
52\,11 \\
115\,8 \\
\hline
\mathbf{\$167.91}
\end{array}
$$

4.B

division

When we divide, we divide the **dividend** by the **divisor.** The result of the division is the **quotient.** Division can be indicated by either a division sign (÷), a division box ($\overline{)}$), or a division bar (–). Proper placement of the dividend and divisor must be maintained to arrive at the quotient.

$$\text{dividend} \div \text{divisor} = \text{quotient} \qquad \text{divisor}\overline{)\text{dividend}}^{\text{quotient}}$$

$$\frac{\text{dividend}}{\text{divisor}} = \text{quotient}$$

Here are three ways to indicate the division of 20 by 4.

$$20 \div 4 \qquad 4\overline{)20} \qquad \frac{20}{4}$$

It is sometimes helpful to think of division as a process of separating the dividend into a number of equal groups. For instance, if we wish to divide 12 by 4, we may write

$$\frac{12}{4}$$

The primary question we are asking is, "If we divide twelve objects into four equal groups, how many will be in each group?" Some people find it easier to visualize the equivalent question, "Into how many groups of four can we divide twelve objects?" We can display the solution visually by using twelve dots and arranging them in groups of four.

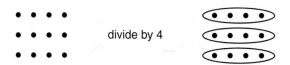

We see that twelve dots can be divided into three groups of four, so we may say that

$$\frac{12}{4} = 3$$

An **algorithm** is a step-by-step process to solve a particular type of problem. When mathematicians speak of a division algorithm, they are merely describing a procedure for solving a division problem.

example 4.3 Divide: $\dfrac{\$13.70}{5}$

solution We will use the common division algorithm. The quotient is written with a dollar sign, and the decimal point in the answer is directly above the decimal point in the dividend.

$$
\begin{array}{r}
\$2.74 \\
5\overline{)\$13.70} \\
\underline{10} \\
3\,7 \\
\underline{3\,5} \\
20 \\
\underline{20} \\
0
\end{array}
$$

Thus,

$$\frac{\$13.70}{5} = \mathbf{\$2.74}$$

example 4.4   Divide: $2183 \div 47$

solution   We use the same algorithm.

$$
\begin{array}{r}
46 \\
47\overline{)2183} \\
\underline{188} \\
303 \\
\underline{282} \\
21 \quad \text{remainder}
\end{array}
$$

Thus,

$$2183 \div 47 = \mathbf{46\ r\ 21}$$

4.C
multiplication and division patterns

Remember that addition and subtraction are inverse operations because either one of these operations will "undo" the other operation. **Multiplication and division are also inverse operations.** To demonstrate, we begin with the number 5, and then multiply by 4 to get 20.

$$5 \times 4 = 20$$

Now if we divide 20 by 4, we will undo the multiplication by 4 and be back at 5 again.

$$20 \div 4 = 5$$

Thus, multiplication and division are inverse operations.

Consider the pattern of the following multiplication problem:

$$
\begin{array}{rl}
8 & \text{factor} \\
\times\ 9 & \text{factor} \\
\hline
72 & \text{product}
\end{array}
$$

Three numbers are involved. When we know two of them, we can find the missing number. If the product is missing, we multiply the factors; but if a factor is missing, we find the missing factor by dividing the product by the known factor.

example 4.5   Find the missing number: $12 \cdot N = 168$

solution   The missing number is one of the two factors, so we divide the product by the known factor.

$$
\begin{array}{r}
14 \\
12\overline{)168} \\
\underline{12} \\
48 \\
\underline{48} \\
0
\end{array}
$$

Now we check by multiplying.

$$
\begin{array}{r}
12 \\
\times\ 14 \\
\hline
48 \\
12 \\
\hline
168 \quad \text{check}
\end{array}
$$

The value of N is **14.**

Consider the pattern of the following division problem:

$$\frac{56}{7} = 8 \quad \text{or} \quad \frac{\text{dividend}}{\text{divisor}} = \text{quotient}$$

Again three numbers are involved. When we know two of them, we can find the third number. If the quotient is missing, we divide; if the divisor is missing, we divide the dividend by the quotient; and if the dividend is missing, we multiply the divisor and quotient.

example 4.6   Find the missing number: $\dfrac{64}{A} = 4$

solution   To find a missing divisor, we divide the dividend by the quotient.

$$\begin{array}{r} 16 \\ 4\overline{)64} \\ 4 \\ \hline 24 \\ 24 \\ \hline 0 \end{array}$$

Now we check by dividing.

$$\begin{array}{r} 4 \quad \text{check} \\ 16\overline{)64} \\ 64 \\ \hline 0 \end{array}$$

The value of A is **16.**

example 4.7   Find the missing number: $B \div 3 = 15$

solution   To find a missing dividend, we multiply the divisor and the quotient.

$$\begin{array}{r} 15 \\ \times \ 3 \\ \hline 45 \end{array}$$

Now we check by dividing.

$$\begin{array}{r} 15 \\ 3\overline{)45} \\ 3 \\ \hline 15 \\ 15 \\ \hline 0 \end{array}$$

The value of B is **45.**

practice   Multiply or divide as indicated:

a. $300 \times \$1.25$

b. $778 \cdot 563$

c. $\dfrac{261}{30}$

d. $12\overline{)\$49.08}$

Find the missing numbers:

e. $15 \cdot C = 180$

f. $\dfrac{x}{3} = 56$

g. $\dfrac{368}{B} = 92$

**problem set
4**

1. A number has four digits. All the digits are 3 except for the thousands' digit, which is 7.
(1) What is the number?

2. A number has seven digits. All the digits are 3 except for the hundreds' digit and the
(1) thousands' digit, both of which are 9. What is the number?

3. Use digits to write forty-seven million, fourteen.
(1)

4. Use digits to write fourteen billion, forty-two thousand, seven hundred fifty-five.
(1)

5. Round 716,487,250 to the nearest million.
(2)

6. Arrange the following numbers in order from least to greatest:
(2) 671, –76, 167, –176, 617

7. Write 7650 in expanded notation.
(1)

8. Write $(5 \times 1000) + (6 \times 10) + (7 \times 1)$ in standard notation.
(1)

Divide:

9. $\dfrac{\$25.11}{9}$
(4)

10. $2800 \div 50$
(4)

11. $45\overline{)50{,}217}$
(4)

12. $\dfrac{9114}{7}$
(4)

13. $4165 \div 40$
(4)

14. $21\overline{)30{,}215}$
(4)

Multiply:

15. $\begin{array}{r} 285 \\ \times\ 321 \end{array}$
(4)

16. $\begin{array}{r} \$5.06 \\ \times\ \ \ 75 \end{array}$
(4)

17. $\begin{array}{r} 512 \\ \times\ 320 \end{array}$
(4)

18. $25 \times 40 \times 100$
(4)

19. 500×420
(4)

20. $6 \times 12 \times 24$
(4)

Find the missing numbers:

21. $\begin{array}{r} 943 \\ -\ \ X \\ \hline 274 \end{array}$
(3)

22. $\begin{array}{r} 605 \\ +\ \ M \\ \hline 927 \end{array}$
(3)

23. $\begin{array}{r} K \\ -\ 2257 \\ \hline 925 \end{array}$
(3)

24. $25 \times N = 400$
(4)

25. $625 \div W = 25$
(4)

26. $\dfrac{X}{54} = 7$
(4)

Add:

27. $\begin{array}{r} 408{,}627 \\ 915{,}634 \\ 589{,}062 \\ +\ 113{,}093 \\ \hline \end{array}$
(1)

28. $\begin{array}{r} 957{,}125 \\ 826{,}015 \\ 902{,}121 \\ +\ 313{,}947 \\ \hline \end{array}$
(1)

29. $73 + 816 + 92 + 47 + 321 + 5432$
(1)

30. $92¢ + \$31.82 + \$21$
(1)

LESSON 5 *Addition and Subtraction Word Problems*

The key to working word problems that have an addition pattern or a subtraction pattern is recognizing that the problem has a particular pattern.

ADDITION PATTERN	SUBTRACTION PATTERN

$$\begin{array}{r} 4 \\ +\ 5 \\ \hline \text{largest number} \longrightarrow \quad 9 \end{array} \qquad \begin{array}{r} 9 \longleftarrow \text{largest number} \\ -\ 4 \\ \hline 5 \end{array}$$

Both patterns have three numbers. Word problems that have one of these patterns will give us two of the numbers. We put the given numbers in the pattern and add or subtract as required to find the third number in the pattern.

If a problem makes us think **some and some more,** the pattern is an addition pattern. If a problem makes us think **some went away,** the pattern is a subtraction pattern. The words **how much greater** or **how much less** also indicate a subtraction pattern.

example 5.1   The Duke counted 5260 people. Then the Duchess counted 4720 people. How much greater was the Duke's count?

solution   The words *how much greater* tell us that the pattern is a subtraction pattern. We remember that the bottom number in a subtraction pattern is the difference. The greatest number is the minuend (top number).

$$\begin{array}{r} 5260 \quad \text{Duke} \\ -\ 4720 \quad \text{Duchess} \\ \hline 540 \quad \text{difference} \end{array}$$

The Duke's count was **540** greater than the Duchess's count.

example 5.2   Four hundred seventeen birds were in the trees at eight o'clock. By nine o'clock the number had increased to nine hundred forty-two. How many birds arrived between eight and nine o'clock?

solution   This problem makes us think *some and some more*. This means that the problem has an addition pattern. We know one addend and the sum.

$$\begin{array}{r} 417 \quad \text{at eight o'clock} \\ +\quad B \quad \text{birds arrived} \\ \hline 942 \quad \text{at nine o'clock} \end{array}$$

This pattern is an addition pattern, but we must subtract the known addend from the sum to find the missing number.

$$\begin{array}{r} 942 \\ -\ 417 \\ \hline 525 \end{array} \quad \text{check} \quad \begin{array}{r} 417 \quad \text{at eight o'clock} \\ +\ 525 \quad \text{birds arrived} \\ \hline 942 \quad \text{at nine o'clock} \end{array}$$

We find that **525 birds** arrived between eight and nine o'clock.

example 5.3   At sunrise many ducks were on the pond. Then four hundred twenty-five ducks flew away. Six hundred forty-two ducks remained on the pond. How many ducks were on the pond at sunrise?

solution A problem with the premise *some went away* has a subtraction pattern. This problem says some ducks flew away, so the pattern is a subtraction pattern.

$$
\begin{array}{rl}
D & \text{ducks on the pond at sunrise} \\
-\ 425 & \text{flew away} \\
\hline
642 & \text{ducks remaining}
\end{array}
$$

This is an easy pattern to solve because the minuend (top number) is the sum of the other two numbers.

check

$$
\begin{array}{rl}
425 & \\
+\ 642 & \\
\hline
1067 &
\end{array}
\qquad
\begin{array}{rl}
1067 & \text{ducks on the pond at sunrise} \\
-\ 425 & \text{flew away} \\
\hline
642 & \text{ducks remaining}
\end{array}
$$

There were **1067 ducks** on the pond at sunrise.

example 5.4 George had five dollars and forty-two cents. Then his mom gave him some money. Now he has nine dollars and sixty-five cents. How much money did his mom give him?

solution This problem makes us think *some and some more*. This means the pattern is an addition pattern.

$$
\begin{array}{rl}
\$5.42 & \text{George had} \\
+\quad M & \text{money his mom gave him} \\
\hline
\$9.65 & \text{total}
\end{array}
$$

This is an addition pattern, but we must subtract to find the missing number. Then we check.

check

$$
\begin{array}{rl}
\$9.65 & \\
-\ \$5.42 & \\
\hline
\$4.23 &
\end{array}
\qquad
\begin{array}{rl}
\$5.42 & \text{George had} \\
+\ \$4.23 & \text{money his mom gave him} \\
\hline
\$9.65 & \text{total}
\end{array}
$$

George's mom gave him **$4.23.**

practice   a. Hundreds of knights came to the tournament. Then four hundred twenty knights went home. Seven hundred fifty-six knights remained. How many knights came to the tournament?

   b. Rita had nine thousand, thirty-five items in her basement. Then she found some more items. Now she has ten thousand, eighty-one items. How many items did she find?

problem set 5

1. When the major estimated the crowd, she estimated 6190 people. Then the captain
(5) estimated the crowd and got 5320 people. How much greater was the major's estimate?

2. At nine o'clock there were five hundred thirty dancers in the meadow. By eleven
(5) o'clock the number had increased to seven hundred seventy-eight. How many dancers came to the meadow between nine and eleven o'clock?

3. The estimated world population in the year 1650 was 550,000,000. The estimated
(5) world population in 1750 was 725,000,000. By how many people did the world's population increase between 1650 and 1750?

4. Zechariah brought $25.17 with him to the fifth annual carnival of finger painting. He
(5) left with $8.56. How much money did he spend at the carnival?

5. A number has eight digits. All of them are 8 except the ten-thousands' digit, which is 3, the units' digit, which is 7, and the millions' digit, which is 6. What is the number?
(1)

6. A number has seven digits. All the digits are 5 except for the hundreds' digit and the millions' digit, both of which are 1. What is the number?
(1)

Divide:

7. $\dfrac{9300}{7}$
(4)

8. $41.63 \div 23$
(4)

9. $16\overline{)41{,}725}$
(4)

Multiply:

10. $\begin{array}{r} \$7.89 \\ \times\quad 9 \\ \hline \end{array}$
(4)

11. $\begin{array}{r} 506 \\ \times\quad 27 \\ \hline \end{array}$
(4)

12. $\begin{array}{r} 512 \\ \times\; 632 \\ \hline \end{array}$
(4)

Find the missing numbers:

13. $\begin{array}{r} A \\ -\; 526 \\ \hline 437 \end{array}$
(3)

14. $\begin{array}{r} 743 \\ -\quad N \\ \hline 188 \end{array}$
(3)

15. $F - 123 = 289$
(3)

16. $\begin{array}{r} K \\ +\; 325 \\ \hline 1001 \end{array}$
(3)

17. $\begin{array}{r} 643 \\ +\quad X \\ \hline 1112 \end{array}$
(3)

18. $S + 727 = 915$
(3)

19. $\begin{array}{r} 32 \\ \times\; W \\ \hline 224 \end{array}$
(4)

20. $D \div 26 = 7$
(4)

21. $\dfrac{990}{P} = 45$
(4)

22. Write in standard notation: $(7 \times 10{,}000) + (4 \times 100) + (3 \times 10)$
(1)

23. Write 2109 in expanded notation.
(1)

24. Use digits to write forty-seven million, fourteen.
(1)

25. Use digits to write fourteen billion, forty-two thousand, seven hundred fifty-five.
(1)

26. Write these numbers in order from least to greatest: 916, 169, −619, 961, 196, −691
(2)

27. Use words to write 5021.
(1)

28. Round 716,487,250 to the nearest thousand.
(2)

Add:

29. 408,627 + 915,634
(1)

30. $9.99 + 33¢ + $1.07
(1)

LESSON 6   *Reading and Writing Decimal Numbers •*
Adding and Subtracting Decimal Numbers •
Rounding Decimal Numbers

6.A

**reading and
writing
decimal
numbers**

We have noted that whole numbers have a decimal point just after the last digit in the number. Sometimes the decimal point is written. Many times it is not written but is understood to be there. Thus, the two notations

$$615. \qquad \text{and} \qquad 615$$

both designate the number six hundred fifteen.

Some numbers have digits to the right of the decimal point. We often call these numbers **decimal numbers.** Some people call these numbers **decimal fractions** because they can be written as whole numbers divided by 10, 100, 1000, 10,000, or some other multiple of 10, as shown here.

$$61.23 = \frac{6123}{100}$$

The first place to the right of the decimal in a decimal fraction is the tenths' place, which has a place value of $\frac{1}{10}$. The next place is the hundredths' place, with a place value of $\frac{1}{100}$, followed by the thousandths' place, with a place value of $\frac{1}{1000}$, and so on. The value of a digit is the digit times the place value. Thus, the 6 in

$$0.0006724$$

has a value of 6 times $\frac{1}{10,000}$, or 6 ten-thousandths, because it is in the ten-thousandths' place. When a whole number does not precede the decimal number, a zero is placed before the decimal point.

Decimal Place Values

millions	hundred thousands	ten thousands	thousands	hundreds	tens	units	decimal point	tenths	hundredths	thousandths	ten-thousandths	hundred-thousandths	millionths
1,000,000	, 100,000	10,000	1,000	, 100	10	1	.	$\frac{1}{10}$	$\frac{1}{100}$	$\frac{1}{1,000}$	$\frac{1}{10,000}$	$\frac{1}{100,000}$	$\frac{1}{1,000,000}$

To read a decimal number, we begin on the left-hand end and read according to the following procedure:

1. Read the digits to the left of the decimal point in the same way you would read a whole number.

2. Read the decimal point as *and*.

3. Read the digits to the right of the decimal point as if they formed a whole number; then name the *place value* of the last digit in the number.

When writing out the decimal part of a number with words, place the commas in the same places you would when writing out whole numbers. Note, however, that commas are *not* used in the numerical representation of decimals.

We will demonstrate by reading several decimal fractions.

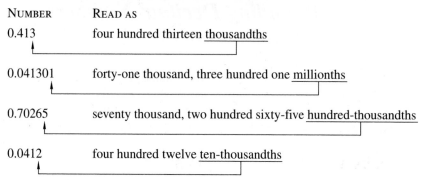

NUMBER	READ AS
0.413	four hundred thirteen <u>thousandths</u>
0.041301	forty-one thousand, three hundred one <u>millionths</u>
0.70265	seventy thousand, two hundred sixty-five <u>hundred-thousandths</u>
0.0412	four hundred twelve <u>ten-thousandths</u>

In the following example we will read two decimal numbers that have nonzero digits on both sides of the decimal point.

example 6.1   Read the numbers, then write them with words: (a) 4165.0162   (b) 7108000.21578

solution   (a) 4165.0162   **Four thousand, one hundred sixty-five *and* one hundred sixty-two ten-thousandths**

(b) 7,108,000.21578   **Seven million, one hundred eight thousand *and* twenty-one thousand, five hundred seventy-eight hundred-thousandths**

To write a decimal number using digits and a decimal point:

1. Write the whole number part as usual.
2. Represent *and* with a decimal point.
3. Find the place value of the first digit by looking at the final word.
4. Fill in the decimal part of the number by writing that part after *and* so that its final digit has the correct place value.
5. If necessary, fill in any blank places between the decimal point and the number just written with zeros.

example 6.2   Use digits and a decimal point to write each number:

(a) Fifteen and thirty-one hundredths

(b) Two hundred three and twenty-five thousandths

solution   (a) Fifteen   15
            and   15.
            ... hundredths   15._ _
            thirty-one   15.<u>3</u><u>1</u>
                             15.31

(b) Two hundred three   203
            and   203.
            ... thousandths   203._ _ _
            twenty-five   203._<u>2</u><u>5</u>
                                 203.025

6.B

adding and subtracting decimal numbers

We add and subtract decimal numbers just as we do whole numbers. When we add and subtract decimal numbers, we must remember to write the numbers so that the decimal points are aligned one above the other, just as we vertically align the digits in the units' place in whole number addition.

example 6.3   Simplify: (a) 6.231 + 0.04   (b) 6.23 − 0.044

solution   To begin, we write the numbers with the decimal points one above the other. In these examples, we write place-holding zeros to the right of a decimal number to make the arithmetic easier. Then we add or subtract as indicated.

(a)   6.231   (b)   6 . 2̶ 3̶ 0
      + 0.040   − 0 . 0 4 4
      ───────   ───────────
       6.271   **6 . 1 8 6**

6.C
rounding decimal numbers

The number line can help us understand the process of rounding decimal numbers. If we graph 0.0423,

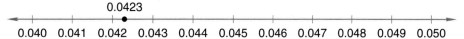

we can see that this number is closer to 0.042 than it is to 0.043. If we round 0.0423 to the nearest thousandth, we get

0.042

Since 0.0423 is closer to 0.04 than it is to 0.05, we can also round 0.0423 to the nearest hundredth, or

0.04

We find that a circle and an arrow can also be used to explain how we round decimal numbers. The procedure is the same as the procedure we use for whole numbers.

example 6.4   Round 212.0165725 to the nearest ten-thousandth.

solution   First we circle the digit in the ten-thousandths' place. Then we mark the digit to its right with an arrow.

$$\downarrow$$
212.016⑤725

The arrow-marked digit is greater than 5, so we increase the circled digit by 1.

$$\downarrow$$
212.016⑥725

Next we change the arrow-marked digit and the digits to its right to zero.

$$\downarrow$$
212.016⑥000

Zeros at the end of the number and to the right of the decimal point have no value, so we can omit them.

212.0166

example 6.5   Round 4057.2138362 to two decimal places.

solution   We begin by circling the second digit to the right of the decimal point and marking the next digit to its right with an arrow.

Since the arrow-marked digit is less than 5, we do not change the circled digit. Now we change the arrow-marked digit and the digits to its right to 0. We discard the terminal zeros and get

4057.21

When using a calculator, it is common to have an answer result in many decimal places. It is important to know how to accurately round decimal numbers.

practice   Use digits and a decimal point to write each number:

a.   Five thousand and seven hundred forty-two ten-thousandths

b.   Six hundred forty-two and seventy-five thousandths

Use words to write each number:

c.   7000.065   **d.**   42.000617

Add or subtract as indicated:

e.   44.016 – 0.1422   **f.**   5.228 + 6.759

g.   Round 416.042737 to the nearest hundred-thousandth.

h.   Round 2837.065248 to the nearest ten-thousandth.

problem set 6

1.
(5)   Thirty-seven million, nine hundred eighteen thousand, five hundred is how much greater than nineteen million, ninety-nine thousand, nine?

2.
(5)   The estimated population of the world in 1750 was 725,000,000 people. During the next 100 years the population increased by 475,000,000 people. What was the world's population in 1850?

3.
(5)   Exactly 10,000 runners began the marathon. If only 5420 runners finished the marathon, how many dropped out along the way?

4.
(1)   A number has seven digits. All the digits are 6 except the hundred-thousands' digit, which is 2, and the thousands' digit, which is 4. What is the number?

5.
(1)   A number has six digits. All the digits are 3 except the ten-thousands' digit, which is 7, and the thousands' digit, which is 2. What is the number?

Subtract. Add to check.

6.
(6)   14.03 – 0.0132   **7.**
                                   (6)   941.2 – 14.23

Divide:

8.
(4) $\dfrac{3624}{23}$ **9.**
                                   (4) $12.75 ÷ 17$ **10.**
                                                                (4) $51\overline{)41,362}$

11.
(4) $27\overline{)2189}$ **12.**
                                   (4) $2546 ÷ 41$ **13.**
                                                                (4) $\dfrac{92,438}{51}$

14.
(6)   Round 0.020532 to the nearest thousandth.

15.
(6)   Round 14.11931627 to the nearest hundred-thousandth.

Use words to write each number:

16.
(6)   3178.0285   **17.**
                                   (6)   504327.001510512

18. Use digits and a decimal point to write the number sixty-three thousand and two
(6) hundred fourteen ten-thousandths.

19. Use digits and a decimal point to write the number twenty-nine millionths.
(6)

Find the missing numbers:

20. $\quad$ 625 $\qquad\qquad$ **21.** $\quad$ 921 $\qquad\qquad$ **22.** $X - 763 = 189$
(3) $\underline{+ \quad Z}$ $\qquad\qquad\quad$ (3) $\underline{- \quad Y}$ $\qquad\qquad\quad$ (3)
$\qquad\quad$ 913 $\qquad\qquad\qquad\quad$ 199

23. $\qquad W$ $\qquad\qquad$ **24.** $N \div 18 = 15$ $\qquad\qquad$ **25.** $\dfrac{945}{V} = 45$
(4) $\underline{\times \; 8}$ $\qquad\qquad\quad$ (4) $\qquad\qquad\qquad\qquad\quad$ (4)
$\qquad$ \$50.00

Add:

26. $0.005 + 21.62 + 9.035 + 5165.2$ $\qquad$ **27.** $70.02 + 0.0013 + 9.062 + 0.142$
(6) $\qquad\qquad\qquad\qquad\qquad\qquad\qquad\qquad$ (6)

28. Write 3917 in expanded notation.
(1)

29. Write in standard notation:
(1)
$$(9 \times 10,000) + (4 \times 1000) + (5 \times 100) + (7 \times 10) + (9 \times 1)$$

30. Multiply: $\quad$ 703
(4) $\qquad\qquad\quad \underline{\times \; 579}$

LESSON 7 *Multiplying Decimal Numbers • Dividing Decimal Numbers • Estimation*

7.A
multiplying decimal numbers

Multiplication of decimal numbers is similar to multiplication of whole numbers. When we multiply decimal numbers, we do not need to align the decimal points. We first do the multiplication as if the decimal points were not present. Then we add the number of decimal places in both factors to find the position of the decimal point in the product.

example 7.1 Multiply: 4.12×63.2

solution We multiply just as if the decimal points were not present.

$$
\begin{array}{r}
4.12 \\
\times \, 63.2 \\
\hline
824 \\
1236 \quad\ \\
2472 \quad\quad\ \\
\hline
260384
\end{array}
$$

The first factor has two decimal places, and the second factor has one decimal place. Two plus one equals three, so the product has three decimal places.

260.384

example 7.2   Multiply: 6.78×0.0537

solution   Again we multiply just as if the decimal points were not present.

$$
\begin{array}{r}
0.0537 \\
\times \quad 6.78 \\
\hline
4296 \\
3759 \\
3222 \\
\hline
364086
\end{array}
$$

There are four plus two decimal places in the factors, so we need six decimal places in the product.

0.364086

7.B

dividing decimal numbers

To divide by a decimal number, we first move the decimal point in the divisor to the right to make the divisor a whole number. Then the decimal point in the dividend must be moved to the right the same number of places. The decimal point in the answer is placed just above the decimal point in the dividend.

This procedure makes the division easier to do and also makes the division easier to think about. For example, what might $6.4328 \div 0.04$ mean? This problem is difficult to visualize, but the equivalent problem, $643.28 \div 4$, could be imagined to represent \$643.28 divided among four students or 643.28 liters of a solution poured in four vats. Notice that a decimal in the dividend is okay, but we must have a whole number in the divisor.

example 7.3   Divide: $0.084 \div 0.35$

solution   First we record the numbers using a division box.

$$0.35\overline{)0.084}$$

Next we move the decimal point in the divisor to the right so that the divisor is a whole number. We will illustrate this with an arrow.

$$035.\overline{)0.084}$$

Now we must move the decimal point in the dividend the same number of places and write the decimal point for the quotient just above it.

$$35.\overline{)008.\overset{.}{4}}$$

We will now copy this result, omitting all the arrows and the extra zeros. This gives us an equivalent division problem, $8.40 \div 35$, which is easier to think about than $0.084 \div 0.35$. Now we divide.

$$
\begin{array}{r}
0.24 \\
35\overline{)8.40} \\
\underline{7\ 0} \\
1\ 40 \\
\underline{1\ 40} \\
0
\end{array}
$$

example 7.4   Divide: $21 \div 0.5$

solution   Again we record the numbers using a division box.

$$0.5\overline{)21}$$

Now we move the decimal point in 0.5 one place to the right. Since the decimal point in 21 is to the right of the 1, it is necessary to add a zero to the right of the number. We then shift the decimal point one place to the right forming the equivalent division problem, $210 \div 5$.

$$
\begin{array}{r}
\mathbf{42.} \\
05.\overline{)210.} \\
\underline{20} \\
10 \\
\underline{10} \\
0
\end{array}
$$

example 7.5   Divide: $31 \div 8$. Write the quotient as a decimal number.

solution   Up to this point, we have written answers to these types of problems with remainders. Now we can write the quotient as a decimal number. We write the decimal point to the right of the 31 and insert zeros to find the quotient.

$$
\begin{array}{r}
\mathbf{3.875} \\
8\overline{)31.000} \\
\underline{24} \\
7\,0 \\
\underline{6\,4} \\
60 \\
\underline{56} \\
40 \\
\underline{40} \\
0
\end{array}
$$

example 7.6   Divide and round to two decimal places: $0.004415 \div 0.032$

solution   First we record the numbers.

$$0.032\overline{)0.004415}$$

Next we move the decimal point in the divisor to the right so that the divisor is a whole number.

$$0032.\overline{)0.004415}$$

Now we must move the decimal point in the dividend the same number of places and write the decimal point for the answer just above it.

$$32.\overline{)0004.415}$$

Now we divide.

$$
\begin{array}{r}
0.137 \\
32\overline{)4.415} \\
\underline{3\,2} \\
1\,21 \\
\underline{96} \\
255 \\
\underline{224} \\
31
\end{array}
$$

Now we have three decimal places in the quotient. If we round 0.137 to two decimal places, we get

$$0.14$$

7.C

estimation   Estimation is a technique that is used to check whether an answer is reasonable. Estimation can be done with both whole numbers and decimals. The idea is to round the numbers so the arithmetic can be done mentally. For both whole numbers and decimals this involves rounding the first nonzero digit. When working with decimals, estimation helps us quickly check that we have placed the decimal point correctly. For example, in the subtraction problem 912.0039 – 8.93 = 903.0739, we can round first to 900 – 9 = 891. This quick estimation would alert us to an error in aligning the decimal points if the exact calculation were very different.

When multiplying decimals, estimation helps us quickly check that we have placed the decimal point correctly. For instance, 4.12×63.2 is about 4×60, which we can mentally calculate as 240; so our placement of the decimal in 260.384 was correct in example 7.1. In example 7.2, 6.78×0.0537 is about 7×0.05, which is 0.35; so again our placement of the decimal point in 0.364086 was correct. The symbol ~ indicates an approximation, not an exact value.

$$6.78 \cdot 0.0537 = \sim 0.35$$

practice   Estimate, and then evaluate (find the value of):

   a. 44.612×2.14 **b.** 5.22×0.064

Divide. Round to two decimal places.

   c. $\dfrac{43.24}{0.027}$ **d.** $52 \div 18$

problem set 7

1. $_{(5)}$ Hercules performed 1569 heroic acts, while Theseus performed only 1237. How many heroic acts did they perform in all?

2. $_{(5)}$ Saturday's football game was attended by 35,264 Tiger fans and 17,927 Eagle fans. How many more Tiger fans than Eagle fans attended the game?

3. $_{(5)}$ Seventy-two thousand delegates attended the convention. By the fourth day, only thirty-nine thousand, four hundred remained. How many delegates left before the fourth day began?

4. $_{(1)}$ A number has 12 digits. All of them are 7 except the ten-billions' digit, which is 4, the hundred-thousands' digit, which is 6, and the hundreds' digit, which is 2. What is the number?

Subtract. Add to check.

5. $_{(6)}$ $1.416 - 0.0168$ 6. $_{(6)}$ $23.41 - 2.666$ 7. $_{(6)}$ $38.04 - 1.6$

Estimate, and then evaluate:

8. $_{(7)}$ 14.13×21.6 9. $_{(7)}$ 914.23×0.0132 10. $_{(7)}$ 0.00413×0.312

11. $_{(4)}$ Divide: $\$90.16 \div 23$

Divide. Round to two decimal places.

12. $_{(7)}$ $41\overline{)74{,}316}$ 13. $_{(7)}$ $\dfrac{90.327}{0.08}$

14. $_{(7)}$ $42 \div 0.009$

15. $_{(6)}$ Round 91.648573 to the nearest ten-thousandth.

16. $_{(6)}$ Round 0.84165839 to the nearest millionth.

17. Write these numbers in order from least to greatest: 12, –10, –13, 0 –2, 6
(2)

18. Use digits and a decimal point to write the number four thousand, seven and nine
(6)   thousand, seven hundred forty-two hundred-thousandths.

19. Use digits and a decimal point to write the number seven hundred two and nine hundred
(6)   forty-two hundred-thousandths.

Use words to write the following numbers:

20. 14372.015264   **21.** 9001.321
(6)   (6)

Find the missing numbers:

22.   *X*   **23.** *S* + 473 = 1151   **24.**   126
(3)   – 493   (3)   (3)   + *A*
         ――――   ――――――
          409   1152

25. 276 ÷ *X* = 12   **26.** $\dfrac{N}{7}$ = 27   **27.** 13 × *P* = 117
(4)   (4)   (4)

Add:

28. $15 + 54¢ + $31.62
(1)

29. 3.164 + 75.236 + 4328.914
(6)

30. 3.0624 + 9053.216
(6)

LESSON 8   *Multiplying and Dividing by Powers of 10 •*
Ordering Decimal Numbers

8.A

**multiplying
and dividing
by powers
of 10**

When we use 10 as a factor two times, the product is 100.

$$10 \times 10 = 100$$

When we use 10 as a factor three times, the product is 1000.

$$10 \times 10 \times 10 = 1000$$

When we use 10 as a factor four times, the product is 10,000.

$$10 \times 10 \times 10 \times 10 = 10,000$$

From this we can see that the number of zeros in each product equals the number of times 10 is used as a factor. The product is called a **power of 10.** Thus, we see that the number

$$100,000,000$$

has eight 0's and must be the eighth power of 10. This is the product we get if 10 is used as a factor eight times.

$$10 \times 10 \times 10 \times 10 \times 10 \times 10 \times 10 \times 10 = 100,000,000 \qquad \text{eighth power of 10}$$

   When we multiply a number by a power of 10, all we do is move the decimal point to the right. The number of places the decimal point is moved equals the number of zeros in the power of 10.

example 8.1   Multiply: $47{,}162.314 \times 100$

solution   When we multiply by a power of 10, the digits will not change. The only change is in the
position of the decimal point.

$$\begin{array}{r} 47{,}162.314 \\ \times \qquad 100 \\ \hline 4{,}716{,}231.400 \end{array}$$

The decimal point moved two places *to the right*. Zeros located at the end of a number and
to the right of the decimal point do not change the value of the number and can be omitted.

4,716,231.4

example 8.2   Multiply: $0.031652 \times 10{,}000$

solution   We see that 10,000 has four zeros. Thus, if we multiply a number by 10,000, all we do is
move the decimal point four places *to the right*. This time we will not show the multiplication
but will just write the answer.

316.52

**When we divide a number by a power of 10, we move the decimal point to the left.
The number of places we move the decimal point equals the number of zeros in the
power of 10.**

example 8.3   Divide: $41.32 \div 1000$

solution   We will do the division this time.

$$\begin{array}{r} 0.04132 \\ 1000\overline{)41.32000} \\ \underline{40\ 00} \\ 1\ 320 \\ \underline{1\ 000} \\ 3200 \\ \underline{3000} \\ 2000 \\ \underline{2000} \\ 0 \end{array}$$

All that happened was that the decimal point was moved three places *to the left*.

example 8.4   Divide: $48.512 \div 10{,}000$

solution   This time we will just write the answer. The number 10,000 has four zeros, so dividing by
10,000 will move the decimal point four places *to the left*. When we get to the left-most digit
and still have more places to move the decimal point, we add zeros to the left of the number.

0.0048512

8.B

ordering decimal numbers

The number line can be used to help us understand the way decimal numbers are arranged in
order. If we want to order the numbers 4.36, 4.22, 4.65, and 4.56, we could graph the
numbers on the number line.

Whenever we graph numbers on a number line, the figure will show the numbers arranged **in
order** from least to greatest.

Another method of ordering decimal numbers is to compare corresponding place
values.

example 8.5   Order the numbers 0.426, 0.0732, 0.732, and 0.0426 from least to greatest.

solution   The digit to the left of the decimal point in all the numbers is zero. Next we consider the digits to the right of the decimal point. There are two numbers that begin with a zero to the right of the decimal point. They are

$$0.0732 \quad \text{and} \quad 0.0426$$

When we consider the second digits, we see that the number 0.0732 is greater, so we reverse the positions of the numbers.

$$0.0426 \quad \text{and} \quad 0.0732$$

Next, we look at the remaining numbers: 0.426 and 0.732. When we consider the digits to the right of the decimal point, we see that the number on the left is smaller than the number on the right. This information lets us determine the final ordering of these numbers. We get

0.0426, 0.0732, 0.426, 0.732

practice   Do each multiplication or division problem mentally:

a. $4162 \cdot 100$

b. $4162 \div 100$

c. $73.426 \cdot 10{,}000$

d. $73.416 \div 10{,}000$

e.   Graph these numbers on a number line: 0.453, 0.445, 0.423, 0.460

f.   Order from least to greatest: 0.321, 0.0945, 0.095, 0.3199

problem set 8

1.
(5)   The first measurement was fourteen million, six hundred forty-two light-years. The second measurement was thirty-two million, fifteen thousand, thirty-two light-years. How much greater was the second measurement?

2.
(5)   Plato delivered 1743 orations, whereas Aristotle delivered only 1234. How many orations did they deliver in all?

Simplify mentally:

3.
(8) $\dfrac{41{,}362.68}{100}$

4.
(8) 305.2165×100

5.
(8) $9315.21 \div 1000$

6.
(8) $32.1652 \times 10{,}000$

Multiply:

7.
(7) 0.00526×3.14

8.
(7) 2.315×413

9.
(7) 0.00312×0.642

10.
(7) 313.65×0.9

Subtract. Add to check.

11.
(6) $392.163 - 4.077$

12.
(6) $3.2421 - 1.363$

Find the missing numbers:

13.
(3,6)
$$\begin{array}{r} A \\ +\ 13.4 \\ \hline 28.9 \end{array}$$

14.
(3,6) $116.04 - X = 107.06$

15.
(4,7) $\dfrac{Q}{12.2} = 6$

16.
(4,7) $9 \times R = 587.7$

17.
(4,7) $58.8 \div M = 4.9$

Divide. Round to two decimal places.

18.
(7) $\dfrac{59.329}{0.4}$

19.
(7) $52 \div 7$

20.
(7) $\dfrac{321.4}{0.071}$

21.
(7) $3.22 \div 0.0022$

22.
(6) Round 42.12345678 to the nearest millionth.

23.
(6) Round 31.6372052 to two decimal places.

24.
(6) Use digits and a decimal point to write the number forty-seven billion, sixty-seven thousand and four hundred seventeen hundred-thousandths.

25.
(6) Use digits and a decimal point to write the number one thousand, three and four thousand, seven hundred forty-two hundred-thousandths.

Use words to write each number:

26.
(6) 0.00006184

27.
(6) 4000062.013

28.
(8) Order these decimal numbers from least to greatest: 0.0426, 0.0164, 0.0461, 0.0614

Add:

29.
(6) $7186.132 + 185.62$

30.
(6) $42.16 + 0.0032 + 3.165$

LESSON 9 *Points, Lines, Rays, and Line Segments • Angles • Perimeter*

9.A

points, lines, rays, and line segments

Here we show a series of dots, each one smaller than the one to its left.

If we continue drawing dots with each one smaller than the one to its left, we would finally have a dot so small that it could not be seen without magnification. This dot would still be larger than a mathematical point because a mathematical point is so small that it has no size at all. A **point** is an exact location in space. We represent points with dots and usually name them with uppercase letters. Here we show point *A*.

A
•

A **curve** is an endless connection of mathematical points. A **line** is a straight curve. Because a line is made of mathematical points, a line has no width. However, a line does have one dimension, length. When we draw a line with a pencil, the line we draw is a graph of the mathematical line and marks the location of the mathematical line. We sometimes put arrowheads on the ends of lines to emphasize that the lines continue without end in both directions.

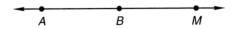

Any two points on a line can be used to name a line. We use an overbar with two arrowheads to indicate a line. Any of the following notations designate the line shown above:

$$\overleftrightarrow{AB} \qquad \overleftrightarrow{BA} \qquad \overleftrightarrow{AM} \qquad \overleftrightarrow{MA} \qquad \overleftrightarrow{BM} \qquad \overleftrightarrow{MB}$$

These notations are read as "line *AB*," "line *BA*," "line *AM*," "line *MA*," "line *BM*," and "line *MB*," respectively. All these notations name the same line.

A **ray** is sometimes called a **half line.** A ray begins at one point and continues without end through another point.

We use a single arrowhead overbar is used to name a ray. We could call the ray from the preceding figure either

$$\overrightarrow{PQ} \qquad \text{or} \qquad \overrightarrow{PX}$$

These notations are read "ray *PQ*" and "ray *PX*." The first letter is the endpoint and the second letter is any other point on the ray. This ray cannot be designated $\overrightarrow{QX}$, since *Q* is not an endpoint.

A **line segment** is the portion of a line between two of its points.

We use the overbar with no arrowheads to name a line segment. We could use either

$$\overline{AB} \qquad \text{or} \qquad \overline{BA}$$

to name the line segment between points *A* and *B*. These notations are read "line segment *AB*" and "line segment *BA*."

A line segment has a specific length. We can refer to the length of a line segment by writing two letters without an overbar. Thus, *AB* is the length of $\overline{AB}$. We use this notation in the figure below to state that the sum of the lengths of the shorter segments equals the length of the longest segment.

$$AB + BC = AC$$

example 9.1   In this figure, *AB* is 3 units and *AC* is 7 units. Find *BC*.

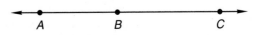

solution   *BC* means the length of $\overline{BC}$. We are given that *AB* is 3 units and *AC* is 7 units. From the figure above we see that $AB + BC = AC$. Therefore, we find that *BC* is **4 units.**

9.B

angles   An **angle** is formed by two rays that have a common endpoint. The **vertex** of an angle is the common endpoint of two rays.

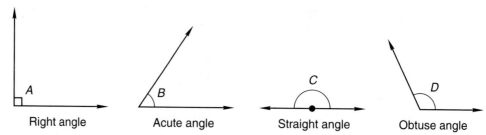

| Right angle | Acute angle | Straight angle | Obtuse angle |

Angle *A* is formed by two **perpendicular** rays. We say angle *A* is a **right angle.** The little square drawn in this angle tells us that the angle is a right angle, or a 90° angle. Angles smaller than right angles are called **acute angles.** Angle *B* is an acute angle. If the two rays point in opposite directions, we say that the angle formed is a **straight angle.** Angle *C* is a straight angle. An angle, such as angle *D*, that is greater than a right angle but less than a straight angle is an **obtuse angle.**

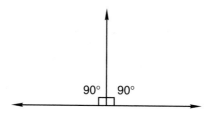

From the figure, we note that a straight angle can be formed when two 90° angles share one ray. From this we see that a straight angle is a 180° angle.

9.C

perimeter   The word **perimeter** comes from the Greek prefix *peri-*, which means "around," and the Greek word *metron*, which means "measure." Thus, the perimeter of a figure means the measure around or the distance around the figure. To find perimeter, we add the lengths of the sides of the figure.

example 9.2   Find the perimeter of this figure. Dimensions are in meters (m).

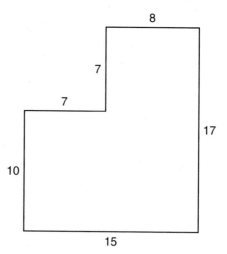

solution   Perimeter is the sum of the lengths of the sides. We make sure that we include units in our answer. The standard abbreviation for meters is m.

$$\text{Perimeter} = 10\,m + 7\,m + 7\,m + 8\,m + 17\,m + 15\,m$$
$$= \textbf{64 meters}$$

example 9.3   Find the perimeter of this figure. The dimensions are in feet (ft). All angles are right angles.

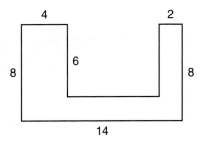

solution   Two lengths are not given. We will name these lengths *N* and *M* as shown below.

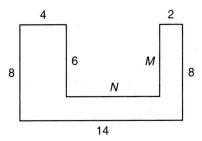

Since all angles are right angles, we can determine the missing lengths. Because eight feet is the vertical distance on both the right and left sides, 6 and *M* will have the same measure. Thus, we will have the following figure:

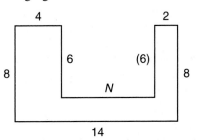

Again using the fact that all the angles are right angles, we can say the distance across the top is 14 feet because the distance across the bottom is 14 feet. So we can write

$$4 + N + 2 = 14 \quad \text{or} \quad N + 6 = 14$$

Thus, $N = 8$.

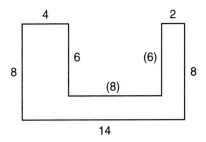

The perimeter is the distance around the figure, or the sum of all these lengths.

Perimeter = 8 ft + 4 ft + 6 ft + 8 ft + 6 ft + 2 ft + 8 ft + 14 ft = **56 feet**

practice   **a.**   For this figure use symbols to name a line, two rays, and a segment.

b.   In this figure *XY* is 12.3 inches (in.) and *XZ* is 20.1 in. Find *YZ*.

c. Draw an example of an acute angle, a right angle, an obtuse angle, and a straight angle.

d. Find the perimeter of this figure. All angles are right angles. Dimensions are in centimeters (cm).

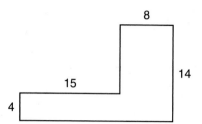

**problem set
9**

1.
(5)
Thousands of people attended the music conference. If 35,000 people attended the conference and 19,763 were not musicians, how many musicians attended the conference?

2.
(5)
Bosch prepared 23,215 canvases, whereas Picasso prepared only 16,219. How many more canvases did Bosch prepare?

Simplify mentally:

3.
(8)
$\dfrac{3164.215}{100}$

4.
(8)
3164.215×100

5.
(8)
$\dfrac{417,365.20}{1000}$

6.
(8)
$2.15 \times 10,000$

Multiply:

7.
(7)
0.0316×2.4

8.
(7)
2.862×61

9.
(7)
8.123×0.9

Subtract. Add to check.

10.
(6)
$43.24 - 0.000613$

11.
(6)
$3.065 - 0.21$

12.
(9)
In this figure, PR is 3.065 units and QR is 1.423 units. Find PQ.

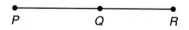

Find the perimeter of each figure. Dimensions are in inches. All angles are right angles.

13.
(9)

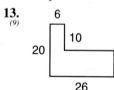

14.
(9)

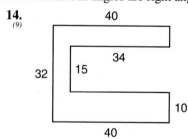

Divide. Round all decimal answers to two decimal places.

15.
(7)
$0.002215 \div 0.042$

16.
(7)
$\dfrac{16.032}{0.024}$

17.
(7)
$\dfrac{416.5}{0.07}$

18.
(6)
Round 61.373737842 to the nearest ten-millionth.

19. Round 433.6851472 to five decimal places.
(6)

20. Use digits and a decimal point to write the number seven hundred forty-two million,
(6) five hundred thirty-seven and ten thousand, nine hundred forty-eight millionths.

21. Use digits and a decimal point to write the number one thousand, seven hundred forty-
(6) eight ten-millionths.

Use words to write each number:

22. 0.00128647
(6)

23. 27000316.081
(6)

24. Order these decimal numbers from least to greatest:
(8) 2.04285, 2.00321, 2.0155, 2.01465

Add:

25. 904.682 + 513.976 + 214.685
(6)

26. 2172.062 + 5091.799
(6)

Find the missing numbers:

27.
(3,6)
$$\begin{array}{r} 204.63 \\ -\quad\ \ A \\ \hline 39.67 \end{array}$$

28. 88.762 + L = 89.8
(3,6)

29. $\dfrac{Z}{9} = 0.52$
(4,7)

30. 0.8 × R = 1.44
(4,7)

---

*LESSON **10*** *Divisibility*

The number 2 will divide into the number 30 with no remainder.

$$\frac{30}{2} = 15$$

Thus, we say that 2 is a factor of 30 and also that 30 is divisible by 2. Other factors of 30 are 3, 5, 6, 10, and 15.

$$\frac{30}{3} = 10 \qquad \frac{30}{5} = 6 \qquad \frac{30}{6} = 5 \qquad \frac{30}{10} = 3 \qquad \frac{30}{15} = 2$$

To be called a factor, a number must be a whole number. If we list all the factors of 30, we get

1, 2, 3, 5, 6, 10, 15, and 30

The capability of a whole number to be divided by another whole number with no remainder is called **divisibility.**

It is often helpful to know if a whole number is divisible by 2, 3, 5, or 10. There are rules that we can use to find out if a number is a factor without actually dividing.

RULES FOR DIVISIBILITY

1. A whole number is divisible by 2 if its last digit is 0, 2, 4, 6, or 8.
2. A whole number is divisible by 3 if the sum of its digits is divisible by 3.
3. A whole number is divisible by 5 if its last digit is either 5 or 0.
4. A whole number is divisible by 10 if its last digit is 0.

example 10.1   Which of the following numbers are divisible by 3?

(a) 99   (b) 1239   (c) 1561

solution   We will add the digits in each number and divide the sum by 3.

(a) 99 $9 + 9 = 18$ $\dfrac{18}{3} = 6$

(b) 1239 $1 + 2 + 3 + 9 = 15$ $\dfrac{15}{3} = 5$

(c) 1561 $1 + 5 + 6 + 1 = 13$ $\dfrac{13}{3} = 4\,r\,1$

The numbers (a) **99** and (b) **1239** are divisible by 3. The number (c) 1561 is not divisible by 3 because the sum of its digits, 13, is not divisible by 3. For confirmation, we check for divisibility using the standard division algorithm below.

$$
\begin{array}{r}
33 \\
3\overline{)99} \\
9 \\
\hline
09 \\
9 \\
\hline
0
\end{array}
\qquad
\begin{array}{r}
413 \\
3\overline{)1239} \\
12 \\
\hline
03 \\
3 \\
\hline
09 \\
9 \\
\hline
0
\end{array}
\qquad
\begin{array}{r}
520 \\
3\overline{)1561} \\
15 \\
\hline
06 \\
6 \\
\hline
01 \\
0 \\
\hline
1
\end{array}
$$

example 10.2   Which of the following numbers are divisible by: (a) 2?   (b) 5?   (c) 10?

4   32   75   99   4165   4020

solution   (a) The number 2 is a divisor of **4, 32,** and **4020** because the last digit of each of these numbers is an even digit.

(b) The numbers that are divisible by 5 have either a 5 or a 0 as their last digit. These numbers are **75, 4165,** and **4020.**

(c) To be divisible by 10, the last digit must be 0. Thus, **4020** is the only number that is divisible by 10.

practice   Which of the following numbers are divisible by: (a) 3?   (b) 5?   (c) 10?

47,285   45,285   305,961   235,725   84,603   72,840

problem set 10

1. In all, there were two million, three hundred thousand, six hundred nineteen people in
(5) the city. If one million, two hundred nineteen thousand, three hundred twelve of them were adolescents, how many were not adolescents?

2. Aristotle was called the peripatetic philosopher because he walked as he talked. He
(5) walked 1627 meters the first week and 2941 meters the second week. How much farther did he walk the second week?

3. Use digits and a decimal point to write the number seven hundred sixty-two million,
(6) four hundred forty-two and twelve thousand, seven hundred ninety-two hundred-thousandths.

4. Use digits and a decimal point to write the number fourteen thousand, seven hundred
(6) two millionths.

Find the perimeter of each figure. Dimensions are in meters. All angles are right angles.

5.
(9)

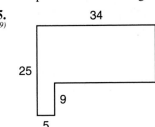

6.
(9)

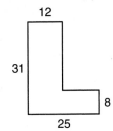

Multiply:

7. 0.0352 × 2.24
(7)

8. 305 × 2.42
(7)

9. 3.062 × 410
(7)

10. 0.9 × 70
(7)

Subtract. Add to check.

11. 4.016 − 3.217
(6)

12. 23.21 − 0.0034
(6)

Find the missing numbers:

13.   2.049
(3,6)   − $\underline{\quad N \quad}$
          0.684

14. $F + 963.09 = 1750.24$
(3,6)

15. $\dfrac{14.28}{X} = 0.51$
(4,7)

16. $M \cdot 5 = 8.5$
(4,7)

Divide. Round each answer to two decimal places.

17. 0.0030 ÷ 0.031
(7)

18. $\dfrac{18.034}{0.04}$
(7)

19. 2.77 ÷ 0.0055
(7)

20. $\dfrac{50.93}{9}$
(7)

21. Which of the following numbers are divisible by:
(10)
  (a) 2?   (b) 3?   (c) 5?   (d) 10?

            235   300   4888   9132   72,654

22. Round 4283.52162 to the nearest hundred.
(6)

23. Round 478.64385 to three decimal places.
(6)

Simplify mentally:

24. 47,123 ÷ 1000
(8)

25. 40.265 × 1000
(8)

26. $\dfrac{0.00143}{100}$
(8)

27. Use words to write this number: 472.058
(6)

28. Order from least to greatest: 0.417, 0.341, 0.471, 0.714, 0.704
(8)

29. In this figure, *MN* is 7.43 cm and *MR* is 11 cm. Find *NR*.
(9)

M   N   R

Add:

30. 416.52 + 3.006 + 215.006
(6)

LESSON *11* *Word Problems about Equal Groups*

Some word problems are about equal groups and can be solved by either multiplying or dividing. The key to working these problems is to recognize that the problems are about equal groups. To illustrate the pattern, we will show three stacks of pancakes. Each stack has 4 pancakes, so there are 12 pancakes in all.

If we use addition for this problem, we write

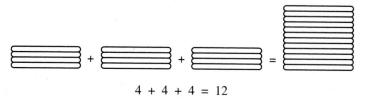

$$4 + 4 + 4 = 12$$

We can also use multiplication and write

$$4 \times 3 = 12$$

This is a multiplication/division pattern. The first factor is the number in each equal group. The second factor is the number of groups. The product is the total.

Number in each group $\times$ number of groups $=$ total

If we know the factors, we multiply to find the total. If we know the total and one of the factors, we divide to find the other factor.

example 11.1 Forty-two students can ride on each bus. If there are 12 buses, how many students can ride to the game?

solution If we recognize that the problem is about equal groups, the problem is easy to solve. All we have to do is use the multiplication/division pattern. Forty-two students are in each equal group. There are twelve equal groups. We have

$$\begin{array}{ccc} 42 & \times & 12 & = \text{total} \\ \text{Number in one} & & \text{number of} \\ \text{equal group} & & \text{equal groups} \end{array}$$

We multiply 42 by 12 to find the total.

$$\begin{array}{r} 42 \\ \times\ 12 \\ \hline 84 \\ 42 \\ \hline 504 \quad \text{total} \end{array}$$

Therefore **504 students** can ride to the game.

"Equal" refers to the fact that the number of items is "equally" distributed through the number of groups—there may be a remainder, however. The answer will not always come out evenly.

example 11.2 Forty-two students can ride on each bus. There are 1264 students who want to go to the game. How many buses are needed to take all the students to the game?

solution Aha! This is an equal groups problem. All we have to do is put the numbers into the multiplication/division pattern. There are 42 in each group, and there are 1264 total students.

$$42 \times N = 1264$$

We divide to find *N*, which is the number of equal groups.

$$
\begin{array}{r}
30 \text{ buses} \\
42\overline{)1264} \\
\underline{126} \\
4
\end{array}
$$

We can fill 30 buses completely. However, we need **31 buses** because we cannot leave the extra four students behind.

example 11.3   Five hundred sixty students will be as evenly divided as possible between 34 buses. How many students will ride on each bus?

solution   We see that this is an equal groups problem. All we have to do is apply the multiplication/division pattern.

$$N \times 34 = 560$$

To find the number of students on each bus, we divide 560 by 34.

$$
\begin{array}{r}
16 \text{ students} \\
34\overline{)560} \\
\underline{34} \\
220 \\
\underline{204} \\
16
\end{array}
$$

We cannot put an equal number on each bus. If we put 16 on each bus, there will be 16 left over. So we put one extra student on 16 of the buses.

16 buses will have 17 students	=	272 students
18 buses will have 16 students	=	288 students
34 buses		560 students

practice   **a.** Forty kids stood patiently in each line. There were 35 lines of kids. How many kids were standing patiently in all the lines?

b. Forty kids could crawl into one space. If there were 1600 kids, how many spaces would it take to hold them all?

c. There were 148 kids that had to be crowded as evenly as possible into 8 spaces. How many kids were in each space?

problem set 11   **1.** Fifty players could ride each bus. If there were 15 buses, how many players could ride to the tournament?
(11)

2. Six hundred sixty students will be evenly distributed between 15 classes. How many students will be in each class?
(11)

3. On the first jump, the frog jumped nineteen and eight hundred sixty-three ten-thousandths inches. On the next jump, the frog jumped twenty-four and four thousand, five hundred six ten-thousandths inches. How far did the frog jump in all?
(6)

4. Of the forty-three thousand, two hundred nineteen delegates who attended, twenty-six thousand, three hundred fourteen were multilingual. How many delegates were not multilingual?
(5)

Find the perimeter of each figure. Dimensions are in inches. All angles are right angles.

5.
(9)

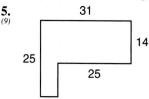

31
14
25
25

6.
(9)

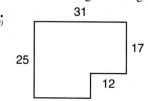

31
17
25
12

Simplify mentally:

7. 132,116 ÷ 10,000
(8)

8. 136.13 × 1000
(8)

9. $\dfrac{123.6}{1000}$
(8)

Multiply:

10. 162 × 2.25
(7)

11. 1.811 × 20.1
(7)

12. 19 × 0.91
(7)

Subtract. Add to check.

13. 61.81 − 0.0012
(6)

14. 129.631 − 2.48
(6)

15. 2.11 − 1.031
(6)

16. Which of the following numbers are divisible by:
(10)

(a) 2? (b) 3? (c) 5? (d) 10?

6132 6325 9130 6111 6130

Divide. Round each answer to two decimal places.

17. $\dfrac{411.23}{61}$
(7)

18. 0.0016 ÷ 0.011
(7)

19. $\dfrac{11.031}{3.1}$
(7)

20. Round 223.092870 to the nearest hundredth.
(6)

21. Round 1621.32161 to the nearest hundred.
(6)

22. Use digits and a decimal point to write the number one trillion, six hundred twenty-five
(6) billion, two hundred fifty thousand, twenty-five and one hundred twenty-three
thousandths.

Use words to write each number:

23. 123.9621
(6)

24. 223092870
(1)

25. Add: 1135.62 + 32.61
(6)

26. What is an acute angle?
(9)

27. In this figure, *DF* is 6.32 cm and *DE* is 3.12 cm. What is *EF*?
(9)

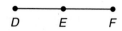

D E F

Find the missing numbers:

28. $A - 22.49 = 68.73$
(3,6)

29. $x \cdot 0.3 = 116.91$
(4,7)

30. $\dfrac{0.0768}{D} = 0.48$
(4,7)

LESSON 12 *Prime Numbers and Composite Numbers • Products of Prime Numbers*

12.A
prime numbers and composite numbers

The number 6 can be composed by multiplying the two whole numbers 3 and 2, or 1 and 6.

$$3 \times 2 = 6 \qquad 1 \times 6 = 6$$

The number 6 has four factors: 1, 2, 3, and 6. We say that 6 is a **composite number.** A composite number is a whole number that has 3 or more whole number factors. The number 21 is also a composite number. We can compose 21 by multiplying 3 and 7, or 1 and 21.

$$3 \times 7 = 21 \qquad 1 \times 21 = 21$$

The number 11 can be composed in only one way. That way is to multiply 11 by 1.

$$11 \times 1 = 11$$

There are many other numbers whose only factors are the numbers themselves and the number 1. Some are

$$5 \times 1 = 5 \qquad 23 \times 1 = 23 \qquad 31 \times 1 = 31$$

There is no other way to compose 5, 23, or 31 by multiplying. We call these numbers **prime numbers.**

PRIME NUMBER

A prime number is a whole number greater than 1 whose only whole number factors are 1 and the number itself.

---

example 12.1   Find the prime numbers from 1 to 40.

solution   First let us write all the numbers from 1 to 40.

$$
\begin{array}{cccccccccc}
1 & 2 & 3 & 4 & 5 & 6 & 7 & 8 & 9 & 10 \\
11 & 12 & 13 & 14 & 15 & 16 & 17 & 18 & 19 & 20 \\
21 & 22 & 23 & 24 & 25 & 26 & 27 & 28 & 29 & 30 \\
31 & 32 & 33 & 34 & 35 & 36 & 37 & 38 & 39 & 40
\end{array}
$$

To find the prime numbers we will eliminate those which are not prime. Since 1 is not a prime number, we will cross it off. The number 2 is a prime number, but all other even numbers are not because they have 2 as a factor. The number 3 is also prime, but any number divisible by 3 is not prime. The number 5 is a prime number, but any number divisible by 5 is not prime. We cross off all of the numbers that are not prime. Now we have

$$
\begin{array}{cccccccccc}
\cancel{1} & 2 & 3 & \cancel{4} & 5 & \cancel{6} & 7 & \cancel{8} & \cancel{9} & \cancel{10} \\
11 & \cancel{12} & 13 & \cancel{14} & \cancel{15} & \cancel{16} & 17 & \cancel{18} & 19 & \cancel{20} \\
\cancel{21} & \cancel{22} & 23 & \cancel{24} & \cancel{25} & \cancel{26} & \cancel{27} & \cancel{28} & 29 & \cancel{30} \\
31 & \cancel{32} & \cancel{33} & \cancel{34} & \cancel{35} & \cancel{36} & 37 & \cancel{38} & \cancel{39} & \cancel{40}
\end{array}
$$

Now we check the remaining numbers to make sure they are prime. Each number remaining is only divisible by 1 and the number itself. Therefore, the prime numbers from 1 to 40 are **2, 3, 5, 7, 11, 13, 17, 19, 23, 29, 31,** and **37.**

12.B

products of prime numbers

Sometimes it is necessary to write a composite number as a product of prime numbers. We can write 12 as a product of prime numbers as

$$2 \times 2 \times 3$$

Here we found the prime factors of 12 by inspection. However, if we wish to write large numbers such as 84 or 1260 as products of prime numbers, it is nice to have a procedure to follow. A procedure often used is to divide the given number by the prime numbers 2, 3, 5, etc., until the prime factors are found. To find the prime factors of 84, we begin by dividing by the smallest prime number, 2.

$$\frac{84}{2} = 42$$

Now 42 can be divided by 2, so we divide again.

$$\frac{42}{2} = 21$$

Since 21 is not divisible by 2, we try dividing by the next smallest prime number, 3.

$$\frac{21}{3} = 7$$

The number 7 is prime, so we stop dividing. If we string these steps together, we get

$$\frac{84}{2} = 42 \quad\longrightarrow\quad \frac{42}{2} = 21 \quad\longrightarrow\quad \frac{21}{3} = 7$$

So we can write 84 as a product of prime numbers as

$$2 \times 2 \times 3 \times 7$$

Many people use the following division format to find the prime factors of a number.

$$
\begin{array}{r|r}
2 & 84 \\ \hline
2 & 42 \\ \hline
3 & 21 \\ \hline
  & 7
\end{array}
\quad \text{so } 84 = 2 \times 2 \times 3 \times 7
$$

We did the same divisions as before, but this time we used a more compact format.

example 12.2　Write 1260 as a product of prime numbers.

solution　We will work the problem twice to demonstrate both formats.

$$\frac{1260}{2} = 630 \;\longrightarrow\; \frac{630}{2} = 315 \;\longrightarrow\; \frac{315}{3} = 105 \;\longrightarrow\; \frac{105}{3} = 35 \;\longrightarrow\; \frac{35}{5} = 7$$

Now we use the other format.

$$
\begin{array}{r|r}
2 & 1260 \\ \hline
2 & 630 \\ \hline
3 & 315 \\ \hline
3 & 105 \\ \hline
5 & 35 \\ \hline
  & 7
\end{array}
$$

Both formats yield the same answer.

$$1260 = \mathbf{2 \times 2 \times 3 \times 3 \times 5 \times 7}$$

practice　Write each number as a product of prime numbers:

a.　120　　　　　　　　**b.**　640　　　　　　　　**c.**　2520

**problem set
12**

1.
(6)
The circumference of the great wheel was twelve thousand and forty-one thousandths inches. The circumference of the lesser wheel was only one thousand, twenty-one and two hundred-thousandths inches. How much larger was the great wheel?

2.
(6)
When the smoke cleared, the judges found that on the first try Roger had covered fourteen million, seven hundred sixty-two and seventy-five ten-thousandths units. The second try was only eight hundred forty-two thousand, fifteen and seven thousandths units. What was the sum of both tries?

3.
(11)
Five pounds of beans will fit in each container. How many containers are needed for 740 pounds of beans?

4.
(11)
Six hundred two fanatic fans wish to travel to the game on 25 buses. If the fans are divided as evenly as possible, how many fanatic fans will travel on each bus?

5.
(10)
Which of the following numbers are divisible by:

(a) 2?   (b) 3?   (c) 5?   (d) 10?

625   302   9172   3132   62,120

Find the perimeter of each figure. Dimensions are in feet. All angles are right angles.

6.
(9)

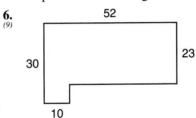

7.
(9)

Simplify mentally:

8. 91,865 ÷ 100
(8)

9. 36.8211 × 1000
(8)

10. What is the sum of the prime numbers that are greater than 3 and less than 28?
(12)

11. What is the sum of the eight smallest prime numbers?
(12)

Multiply:

12. 913 × 0.19
(7)

13. 0.0316 × 8.9
(7)

14. Write each number as a product of prime numbers: (a) 95   (b) 720   (c) 2862
(12)

Subtract. Add to check.

15. 162.133 − 0.0123
(6)

16. 1.329 − 0.999
(6)

Find the missing numbers:

17.
(3)
$$\begin{array}{r} A \\ -\ \$41.29 \\ \hline \$9.93 \end{array}$$

18. 25 × D = 1953
(4,7)

19. $\dfrac{N}{3.1} = 200.32$
(4,7)

Divide. Round each answer to two decimal places.

20. $\dfrac{3012.3}{12}$
(7)

21. $\dfrac{32.631}{0.03}$
(7)

22. 18.621 ÷ 6.1
(7)

23. Round 4692.83215 to the nearest hundred.
(6)

24. Round 4113.62185 to two decimal places.
(6)

25. Use digits to write the number nine hundred sixty-one billion, three hundred thirteen
(1)   million, twenty-five.

Use words to write the following numbers:

26. 0.001621   **27.** 16.0562
(6)   (6)

28. What is an obtuse angle?
(9)

Add:

29. 931.62 + 621.73 + 631.81
(6)

30. 0.721 + 4.3906
(6)

LESSON 13   *Common Factors and the Greatest Common Factor • Multiplication Word Problems*

13.A

common factors and the greatest common factor

The factors of 12 are 1, 2, 3, 4, 6, and 12. The factors of 15 are 1, 3, 5, and 15. So the shared or **common factors** of 12 and 15 are 1 and 3, and we can call 3 the **greatest common factor (GCF)** of 12 and 15. The compact notation for this is

$$GCF\,(12,\,15)\,=\,3$$

example 13.1   Find all the common factors and the greatest common factor of the following pairs of numbers:

(a) 24 and 30   (b) 24 and 7   (c) 24 and 6

solution   (a) The factors of 24 are 1, 2, 3, 4, 6, 8, 12, and 24. The factors of 30 are 1, 2, 3, 5, 6, 10, 15, and 30. So the common factors are **1, 2, 3,** and **6,** and the greatest common factor is **6.**

(b) The factors of 24 are 1, 2, 3, 4, 6, 8, 12, and 24. The factors of 7 are just 1 and 7. So the only common factor is **1,** and **1** is also the greatest common factor. Note that two numbers whose GCF is 1 are said to be **relatively prime.**

(c) The factors of 24 are 1, 2, 3, 4, 6, 8, 12, and 24. The factors of 6 are 1, 2, 3, and 6. So the common factors are **1, 2, 3,** and **6,** and **6** is the greatest common factor. Notice that when one number is a factor of the other, as 6 is a factor of 24, the GCF of the two must be the smaller number.

When the numbers have many factors, listing them can be time-consuming. An alternative approach is to write each number as the product of prime numbers. Then the GCF is formed by multiplying the greatest number of common (or shared) prime factors. When there are no shared prime factors, the GCF is 1, since 1 is a factor of every whole number.

We can find GCF (24, 30) by this method:

$$24 = ② \times 2 \times 2 \times ③$$
$$30 = ② \times ③ \times 5$$

The common prime factors of the two numbers are 2 and 3. The greatest number of 2's in both is 1 and the greatest number of 3's in both is 1. So the GCF is $2 \cdot 3 = 6$.

example 13.2   Find GCF (72, 90).

solution
$$72 = ② \times 2 \times 2 \times ③ \times ③$$
$$90 = ② \times ③ \times ③ \times 5$$
$$\text{GCF (72, 90)} = 2 \times 3 \times 3 = \mathbf{18}$$

13.B
multiplication word problems

Some word problems require that numbers be multiplied to find the answer. These word problems sometimes contain the word *product*. Many of them contain the word *times* used in a phrase such as "5 times as many."

example 13.3   Harriet's score in the second game was the product of her first game's score and 25. If Harriet had scored 14,025 points in the first game, how many points did she score in the second game?

solution   The word *product* tells us to multiply.

$$25 \times 14,025 \text{ points} = \mathbf{350,625 \ points}$$

example 13.4   Roger scored 26,142 points in the first game. He scored 7 times this many points in the second game. How many points did he score in all?

solution   The word *times* tells us to multiply, and the words *in all* tell us to add.

$$\begin{array}{r} 26,142 \\ \times \quad\quad 7 \\ \hline 182,994 \end{array} \qquad \begin{array}{rl} 26,142 & \text{first game} \\ +\ 182,994 & \text{second game} \\ \hline 209,136 & \text{in all} \end{array}$$

He scored **209,136 points** in all.

practice   **a.**   List all the common factors of 12 and 30.

b.   Find the greatest common factor of 18 and 60.

c.   Inflation caused the price of everything to increase. The price of an item after inflation was 4 times the price before inflation. If an item cost $5.67 before inflation, what did it cost after inflation?

problem set 13

1.
(13)   The pinball wizard set a new record on a pinball machine. Her new record score was 26 times the previous high score of 79,864 points. What was her new record score?

2.
(13)   Because Edgar was sedulous, he turned into a boy genius and scored 2.53 times better than he did on his last calculus test. His last test score was 38 percent. What did he score on his latest test?

3.
(11)   If 100 pounds of pinto beans fit in one bag, how many bags are needed to hold 26,000 pounds of pinto beans?

4. The first field measured fourteen million, seven hundred forty-two thousand and
(6) seventeen hundred-thousandths hectares. The second field measured only eight
hundred thousand and forty-two millionths hectares. By how much was the first
field larger?

5. Find the sum of the prime numbers that are between 12 and 42.
(12)

6. Which of the following numbers are divisible by:
(10)
   (a) 2?   (b) 3?   (c) 5?   (d) 10?
            1020   125   130   1332   185   132

Find the perimeter of each figure. Dimensions are in centimeters. All angles are right angles.

7.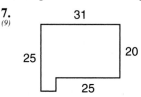
(9)

8.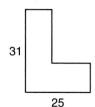
(9)

Simplify mentally:

9. 31,621 ÷ 1000
(8)

10. 311.836152 × 10,000
(8)

Multiply:

11. 621 × 8.11
(7)

12. 2.28 × 22.4
(7)

13. Write each number as a product of prime numbers: (a) 360   (b) 720   (c) 1440
(12)

List all the common factors of each pair of numbers:

14. 15 and 18
(13)

15. 36 and 45
(13)

16. 9 and 10
(13)

Find the missing numbers:

17. $643.28
(3) $\underline{-\qquad N}$
        $257.29

18.   1019.05
(3,6) $\underline{+\qquad S}$
       2364.41

19. 245 ÷ V = 9.8
(4,7)

Find the following greatest common factors:

20. GCF (8, 36)
(13)

21. GCF (50, 75)
(13)

Divide. Round each answer to two decimal places.

22. $\dfrac{311.12}{1.2}$
(7)

23. $\dfrac{621}{0.31}$
(7)

24. Round 1231.62567 to three decimal places.
(6)

25. Use digits and a decimal point to write the number three hundred twenty-one million,
(6) six hundred seventeen thousand, two hundred twelve and two hundred thirty-one
thousandths.

26. What angle is formed by two right angles who have exactly one ray in
(9) common?

Use words to write each number:

27. 161.016
(6)

28. 613.162
(6)

29. Add: 621.81 + 31.62
(6)

30. Order from least to greatest: 1.119, 1.191, 1.911, 1.091, 0.901
(8)

LESSON *14* *Fractions • Expanding and Reducing Fractions*

14.A
fractions

When we write two numbers vertically and draw a line between them, we have written a **fraction.** Thus 3 over 4, written as follows,

$$\text{Numerator} \longrightarrow \frac{3}{4} \longleftarrow \text{Fraction bar}$$
$$\text{Denominator} \longrightarrow$$

is a fraction. We call the top number the **numerator** of the fraction. We call the bottom number the **denominator** of the fraction. We call the line between the numbers a **fraction bar.**

Fractions are numbers used to designate parts of a whole. The denominator (bottom of the fraction) tells us how many equal parts there are in all. The numerator (top of the fraction) tells us how many of these parts we are considering. Here we show what we mean when we write $\frac{1}{4}$, $\frac{2}{4}$, $\frac{3}{4}$, and $\frac{4}{4}$.

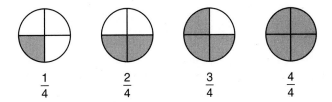

$$\frac{1}{4} \qquad \frac{2}{4} \qquad \frac{3}{4} \qquad \frac{4}{4}$$

If two fractions have the same value, we say that the fractions are **equivalent fractions.** The two fractions

$$\frac{1}{2} \qquad \text{and} \qquad \frac{2}{4}$$

are equivalent fractions. We can show this by drawing a picture that represents each of these fractions. First, we draw two circles that are the same size. We divide the first circle into two equal parts, or halves. Then we divide the second circle into four equal parts, or fourths.

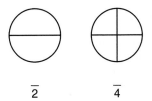

$$\overline{2} \qquad \overline{4}$$

On the left we will shade one of the halves to represent $\frac{1}{2}$, and on the right we will shade two of the fourths to represent $\frac{2}{4}$.

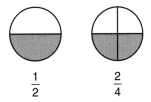

$$\frac{1}{2} \qquad \frac{2}{4}$$

We see that we have shaded equal parts of each whole. We say that $\frac{1}{2}$ and $\frac{2}{4}$ are equivalent fractions because they represent equal parts of the whole and thus have the same value. Therefore, one half and two fourths are different names for the same number.

14.B

**expanding
and reducing
fractions**

We can change the name of any fraction by multiplying or dividing both the numerator and the denominator by the same number. We will call this rule the **denominator-numerator rule for fractions.** Let us examine why this rule makes sense. If we take the fraction $\frac{2}{5}$ and multiply both the numerator and the denominator by 3, we get the fraction $\frac{6}{15}$.

$$\frac{2}{5} = \frac{2 \cdot 3}{5 \cdot 3} = \frac{6}{15}$$

Now we see if $\frac{2}{5}$ and $\frac{6}{15}$ are equivalent fractions by drawing and shading circles.

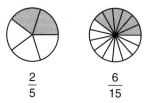

$$\frac{2}{5} \qquad \frac{6}{15}$$

The rule makes sense because $\frac{2}{5}$ and $\frac{6}{15}$ represent equivalent parts of a whole.

DENOMINATOR-NUMERATOR RULE FOR FRACTIONS

The denominator and numerator of a fraction can be multiplied or divided by the same number (except zero) without changing the value of the fraction.

When we change the name of a fraction by making the denominator greater, we say that we have **expanded** the fraction. When we change the name of a fraction by making the denominator less, we say we have **reduced** the fraction. When we have reduced a fraction so that no prime number will divide into both the numerator and denominator evenly, we say that we have reduced the fraction to its **lowest terms.**

example 14.1   Expand the fraction $\frac{3}{4}$ so that the denominator is 24.

solution   If we multiply 4 by 6, we get 24. The denominator-numerator rule says we must also multiply 3 by 6.

$$\frac{3}{4} = \frac{3 \cdot 6}{4 \cdot 6} = \mathbf{\frac{18}{24}}$$

The number 18 over 24 is another way to write the number 3 over 4. Both fractions have the same value, so they represent the same number.

All whole numbers may be written as fractions with denominators of 1, because this does not change the value of the number. Changing whole numbers to fractions allows them to be manipulated by the denominator-numerator rule for fractions.

example 14.2   Write each number with a denominator of 20:   (a) 5   (b) $\dfrac{3}{5}$

solution   (a) Five can be written as 5 over 1. We will multiply the numerator and denominator by 20.

$$5 = \frac{5}{1} = \frac{5 \cdot 20}{1 \cdot 20} = \mathbf{\frac{100}{20}}$$

(b) We will multiply both 3 and 5 by 4.

$$\frac{3}{5} = \frac{3 \cdot 4}{5 \cdot 4} = \mathbf{\frac{12}{20}}$$

example 14.3   Reduce $\frac{30}{45}$ to lowest terms.

solution   As the first step, we see that 5 is a common factor of 30 and 45. We divide both the numerator and denominator of the fraction by 5.

$$\frac{30}{45} = \frac{30 \div 5}{45 \div 5} = \frac{6}{9}$$

Next we see that 3 is a common factor of 6 and 9. We divide both the numerator and denominator of the new fraction by 3.

$$\frac{6}{9} = \frac{6 \div 3}{9 \div 3} = \frac{2}{3}$$

This fraction is an equivalent fraction to the original fraction. The fraction is now in lowest terms because 2 and 3 do not have a common prime factor.

Notice that although 5 and 3 are both common factors of 30 and 45, neither one is the greatest common factor of 30 and 45. If we divide the numerator and denominator of $\frac{30}{45}$ by the greatest common factor of 30 and 45, which is 15, we reduce the fraction to $\frac{2}{3}$ in one step.

example 14.4   Reduce $\frac{16}{32}$ using GCF (16, 32).

solution   GCF (16, 32) = 16

$$\frac{16}{32} = \frac{16 \div 16}{32 \div 16} = \frac{1}{2}$$

practice   Write each number with a denominator of 18:

a. 3   **b.** $\frac{1}{6}$ **c.** $\frac{4}{9}$

Reduce each fraction to lowest terms:

d. $\frac{18}{24}$ **e.** $\frac{36}{72}$ **f.** $\frac{15}{25}$

problem set 14

1.
(11) The Ramirez Restaurant has 5282 taco shells. If each "family meal" holds 12 tacos, how many complete family meals can be sold?

2.
(11) The fairy queen found that 14 dryads could sit comfortably on one toadstool. If 780 dryads were coming to the forest convocation, how many toadstools would she have to provide so that they could all sit comfortably?

3.
(6) The first microbe had a measure of one hundred sixty-two ten-millionths meter. The measure of the second microbe was four hundred twenty-three hundred-millionths meter. By how much was the first microbe larger?

4.
(5) In the flang-flung contest, Jesse Lee flang his fourteen million, six hundred forty-two units. When Jethroe tried, he flung his thirty-two million, fifteen thousand, thirty-two units. How much farther did Jethroe flung than Jesse Lee flang?

5.
(13) Heidi ran 14 times as far after she got her second wind. If she ran three thousand and seven hundred eighty-seven millionths feet on her first wind, how far did she run in all?

6.
(10) Which of the following numbers are divisible by:

(a) 10?   (b) 5?   (c) 2?   (d) 3?

120   135   122   1332   1620

Find the perimeter of each figure. Dimensions are in kilometers (km). All angles are right angles.

7.
(9)

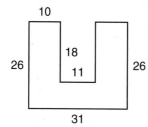

8.
(9)

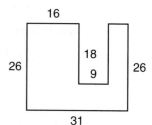

9. Reduce each fraction to lowest terms:
(14)

     (a) $\dfrac{45}{60}$ (b) $\dfrac{30}{75}$ (c) $\dfrac{80}{220}$ (d) $\dfrac{16}{80}$

10. Write each as a fraction with a denominator of 20:
(14)

     (a) $\dfrac{1}{2}$ (b) 7

Simplify mentally:

11. $12.361 \div 1000$ **12.** 11.3×1000
(8)   *(8)*

Multiply:

13. 113×0.009 **14.** 2.14×11.6
(7)   *(7)*

15. Write each number as a product of prime numbers: (a) 1800   (b) 900   (c) 450
(12)

Subtract. Add to check.

16. $131.61 - 11.87$ **17.** $181.811 - 6.329$
(6)   *(6)*

Find the missing numbers:

18.
(3)
$$\begin{array}{r} M \\ +\ \$463.12 \\ \hline \$657.06 \end{array}$$

19.
(3)
$$\begin{array}{r} \$653.28 \\ -\qquad S \\ \hline \$468.29 \end{array}$$

20. $\dfrac{24.455}{N} = 6.7$
(4,7)

21. Find GCF (40, 60).   **22.** Find GCF (7, 42).
(13)   *(13)*

Divide. Round each answer to two decimal places.

23. $6111.12 \div 7.5$ **24.** $\dfrac{611.21}{0.2}$
(7)   *(7)*

25. Round 1612.316289 to four decimal places.
(6)

Use words to write the following numbers:

26. 1231.161   **27.** 3.121
(6)   *(6)*

28. List all the common factors of 48 and 72.
(13)

Add:

29. $1093.06 + 113.1016 + 915.09$
(6)

30. $647.112 + 9158.0109$
(6)

LESSON 15   *Fractions and Decimals • Fractions to Decimals • Rounding Repeaters • Decimals to Fractions*

15.A

fractions and decimals

Both fractions and decimal numbers can be used to represent the parts of a whole.

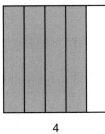   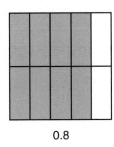

$$\frac{4}{5}$$ 0.8

On the left we have divided the whole figure into five equal parts and shaded four of them to represent $\frac{4}{5}$. On the right we have divided the same figure into ten equal parts and shaded eight of them to represent 0.8, which is eight tenths. We see that the shaded areas are equal. This is a picture that shows us that

$$\frac{4}{5} \qquad \text{equals} \qquad 0.8$$

15.B

fractions to decimals

To write a fraction of a whole number as a decimal number, we divide the numerator by the denominator.

example 15.1   Write each fraction as a decimal number: (a) $\frac{3}{8}$ (b) $\frac{1}{30}$

solution   (a) We divide 3 by 8.

$$
\begin{array}{r}
0.375 \\
8\overline{)3.000} \\
\underline{2\,4} \\
60 \\
\underline{56} \\
40 \\
\underline{40} \\
0
\end{array}
$$

(b) We divide 1 by 30.

$$
\begin{array}{r}
0.0333 \\
30\overline{)1.0000} \\
\underline{90} \\
100 \\
\underline{90} \\
100 \\
\underline{90} \\
10
\end{array}
$$

In (a), the number terminates. In (b), the 3 repeats, so we put a bar over it. Thus, our answers are

(a) **0.375**   (b) **0.0\overline{3}**

The repeating digits of a decimal number are called the **repetend.** The bar we use over the repetend is called a **vinculum.**

If the denominator of the fraction is a power of 10, we do not really need to divide. We can just "say the number," then write the decimal form. So $\frac{8}{10}$ is "eight tenths," which written as a decimal is 0.8. And $\frac{9}{100}$ is "nine hundredths," which written as a decimal is 0.09.

example 15.2   Write each fraction as a decimal number: (a) $\dfrac{3}{10}$ (b) $\dfrac{2}{5}$ (c) $\dfrac{3}{20}$

solution   (a) $\dfrac{3}{10}$ = "three tenths" = **0.3**

(b) $\dfrac{2}{5} = \dfrac{2 \cdot 2}{5 \cdot 2} = \dfrac{4}{10}$ = "four tenths" = **0.4**

(c) $\dfrac{3}{20} = \dfrac{3 \cdot 5}{20 \cdot 5} = \dfrac{15}{100}$ = "fifteen hundredths" = **0.15**

If we had not noticed that multiplying the denominator of $\frac{3}{20}$ by 5 turned it into a power of 10, the long division $20\overline{)3}$ would have given the answer 0.15 also.

Every fraction can be written as a decimal number. To write a fraction of a whole number as a decimal number, we divide the denominator into the numerator. The answer will always be either a **terminating decimal number** or a **repeater,** a decimal number that repeats in a definite pattern. Sometimes it is easy to see whether the digits terminate or repeat. Other times there are a large number of repeating digits in the pattern, and the pattern is not easy to see. When this happens, we just round to a convenient number of digits. When writing a fraction as a decimal number, it is important to remember that if the number does not terminate, the repeating pattern is always there, even if we do not immediately see it. We show several examples here.

(a) $\dfrac{1}{8}$ = 0.125   (b) $\dfrac{3}{7}$ = 0.4285714285714285714…

(c) $\dfrac{21}{99}$ = 0.2121212121…   (d) $\dfrac{5}{6}$ = 0.8333333333…

Here we use vincula as necessary to rewrite the repeating answers.

(b) $0.\overline{428571}$ (c) $0.\overline{21}$ (d) $0.8\overline{3}$

15.C
rounding repeaters

To round repeating decimal numbers, it is helpful to write out the repeating pattern several times.

example 15.3   Round $42.\overline{617}$ to the nearest millionth.

solution   We begin by writing the repeating digits until the millionths' place is passed.

$$42.617617617617…$$

Then we circle the digit in the millionths' place and mark the digit to its right with an arrow.

$$\downarrow$$
$$42.61761\textcircled{7}617617…$$

Since the arrow-marked digit is greater than 5, we increase the circled digit by 1 and get

$$\downarrow$$
$$42.61761\textcircled{8}617617…$$

Then we change the arrow-marked digit and the digits to its right to zero.

$$\downarrow$$
$$42.61761\textcircled{8}000000…$$

Terminal zeros to the right of the decimal point have no value. Thus, we can omit these zeros and write the answer as

42.617618

15.D

decimals to fractions

Both terminating and repeating decimal numbers can be written as fractions of whole numbers. The method of writing repeaters as fractions is rather complicated and will be taught in a subsequent course. We will discuss terminating decimals now.

Remember how we have learned to convert $\frac{3}{10}$ to a decimal by saying its name and writing the decimal form? We can use this same method with any terminating decimal to write it as a fraction. So $0.7 =$ "seven tenths" $= \frac{7}{10}$. Of course, by "say the number" we mean for you to follow the rules of reading decimal numbers from Lesson 6. Using the expression "point seven" will not help!

example 15.4 Write 0.041 as a fraction.

solution
$$0.041 = \text{"forty-one thousandths"} = \frac{\mathbf{41}}{\mathbf{1000}}$$

example 15.5 Write 0.35 as a fraction.

solution
$$0.35 = \text{"thirty-five hundredths"} = \frac{35}{100}$$
$$\text{Now we reduce the fraction: } \frac{35}{100} = \frac{\mathbf{7}}{\mathbf{20}}$$

practice   **a.** Round $4.6\overline{13}$ to the nearest millionth.

b. Round $1.4\overline{16}$ to five decimal places.

Write each fraction as a decimal number:

c. $\dfrac{1}{3}$ 　　　　　　　　　　　　　**d.** $\dfrac{1}{12}$

Write each decimal number as a fraction reduced to lowest terms:
e. 0.0031 　　　　　　　　　　**f.** 0.6

problem set 15

1.
(5)
Their approach was inexorable, and there were fourteen million, seven thousand, nine hundred twenty hungry locusts in the first wave. In the second wave, there were only nine hundred thousand, sixty-seven. How many hungry locusts were there in all?

2.
(13)
Ward 4 reported 8 times as many votes as Ward 7 reported. Ward 6 reported 12 times as many votes as Ward 7 reported. If Ward 7 reported nine thousand, forty-three votes, how many votes did the three wards report in all?

3.
(11)
The ladybugs grouped themselves into bunches of 20. If there were nine thousand, forty-two ladybugs, how many bunches did they form?

4.
(10)
Which of the following numbers are divisible by: (a) 3?　　(b) 2?
　　　　　　　212　　　　2133　　　　312　　　　610　　　　630

5.
(12)
Find the sum of the prime numbers that are between 30 and 42.

6.
(9)
Find the perimeter of this figure. Dimensions are in feet. All angles are right angles.

Write each fraction as a decimal number.

7. $\dfrac{5}{9}$ **8.** $\dfrac{1}{20}$
(15)   (15)

9. Write $\frac{3}{14}$ with a denominator of 42.
(14)

10. Reduce each fraction to lowest terms: (a) $\dfrac{70}{60}$ (b) $\dfrac{16}{24}$ (c) $\dfrac{24}{36}$
(14)

Simplify mentally:

11. $169{,}211 \div 10{,}000$ **12.** 123.61311×100
(8)   (8)

Multiply:

13. 89.21×62.1 **14.** 2.16×32.8
(7)   (7)

15. Write each number as a product of prime numbers: (a) 3600   (b) 450   (c) 4500
(12)

Subtract. Add to check.

16. $1131.13 - 131.98$ **17.** $192.68 - 6.321$
(6)   (6)

Find the missing numbers:

18. $N - 364.82 = 59.69$ **19.** $\begin{array}{r} 16.0375 \\ +\quad\quad A \\ \hline 17.0094 \end{array}$
(3,6)   (3,6)

20. $\dfrac{2.76}{F} = 12$
(4,7)

21. Find GCF (34, 51).   **22.** Find GCF (26, 117).
(13)   (13)

Divide. Round each answer to two decimal places.

23. $7.81 \div 3.1$ **24.** $\dfrac{2310}{13}$
(7)   (7)

25. Round $4017.3\overline{36}$ to the nearest millionth.
(15)

26. Round $946.0\overline{54}$ to eight decimal places.
(15)

Write each decimal number as a fraction reduced to lowest terms:

27. 0.85   **28.** 0.76
(15)   (15)

29. Add: $613.1 + 7214.6 + 11.2 + 3.1$
(6)

30. Order from least to greatest: 0.0119, 0.091, 0.0191, 0.9
(8)

LESSON 16 *Exponents*

Often it is necessary to indicate that a number is to be multiplied by itself a given number of times. If we wish to indicate that 7 is to be used as a factor six times, we could write

$$7 \cdot 7 \cdot 7 \cdot 7 \cdot 7 \cdot 7$$

We can also designate repeated multiplication of a number by using **exponential notation.** Exponential notation lets us express the same thought in a more concise form. To indicate the same multiplication by using exponential notation, we write

base $\longrightarrow 7^6 \longleftarrow$ exponent or power

The lower number is called the **base** and the upper number is called the **exponent.** The exponent tells how many times the base is used as a factor. The whole expression is called an **exponential expression.** Sometimes we call the exponent the power.

$$3^4 = 3 \cdot 3 \cdot 3 \cdot 3 \qquad \text{The base is 3 and the exponent is 4.}$$
$$4^3 = 4 \cdot 4 \cdot 4 \qquad \text{The base is 4 and the exponent is 3.}$$
$$\left(\frac{2}{3}\right)^3 = \frac{2}{3} \cdot \frac{2}{3} \cdot \frac{2}{3} \qquad \text{The base is } \frac{2}{3} \text{ and the exponent is 3.}$$

The following examples show how we read exponential expressions:

4^2 "four squared" or "four to the second power"
2^3 "two cubed" or "two to the third power"
5^4 "five to the fourth power"
10^5 "ten to the fifth power"

example 16.1 Evaluate the following exponential expressions:
(a) 4^2 (b) 3^4 (c) 2^3

solution (a) $4^2 = 4 \cdot 4 = \mathbf{16}$

(b) $3^4 = 3 \cdot 3 \cdot 3 \cdot 3 = \mathbf{81}$

(c) $2^3 = 2 \cdot 2 \cdot 2 = \mathbf{8}$

example 16.2 Write 7056 as a product of prime numbers using exponents.

solution Using the methods taught in Lesson 12, we can write 7056 as

$$2 \cdot 2 \cdot 2 \cdot 2 \cdot 3 \cdot 3 \cdot 7 \cdot 7$$

We can write $2 \cdot 2 \cdot 2 \cdot 2$ as 2^4, $3 \cdot 3$ as 3^2, and $7 \cdot 7$ as 7^2. Thus, 7056 written as a product of prime numbers using exponents is

$$\mathbf{2^4 \cdot 3^2 \cdot 7^2}$$

practice Simplify:
a. 2^6 **b.** 1^3 **c.** 5^4

d. Write 3240 as a product of prime numbers using exponents.

problem set 16

1. Only fourteen pigeons could be housed in a single space. If three thousand, eight
(11) hundred eight had to be sheltered, how many spaces were necessary?

2. Gene could muster up a total of fourteen and seven hundred forty-two ten-thousandths
(13) units. Mary could muster up 7 times that much. How much could the two of them muster up altogether?

3. When the final calculations were processed, Roberto found that he had sequenced
(5) ninety-one thousand, forty-two genes. Raul was chagrined because this exceeded his
total by twelve thousand, fifteen genes. What was Raul's total?

4. Each box would hold 142 apples. If the crew filled 432 boxes one shift and had 5 apples
(11) left over, how many apples were there in all?

5. Which of the following numbers are divisible by: (a) 5?   (b) 10?
(10)
650   625   15   20   30

6. What are the prime numbers that are greater than 40 but less than 64?
(12)

7. Find the perimeter of this figure.
(9) Dimensions are in yards (yd). All
angles are right angles.

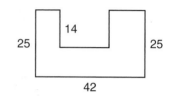

Write each fraction as a decimal number. Round to two decimal places.

8. $\dfrac{19}{25}$ **9.** $\dfrac{4}{7}$
(15)   *(15)*

Reduce each fraction to lowest terms:

10. $\dfrac{36}{42}$ **11.** $\dfrac{72}{120}$
(14)   *(14)*

12. Write $\frac{9}{27}$ with a denominator of 243.
(14)

Simplify:

13. $(0.5)^2$ **14.** 9^3
(16)   *(16)*

15. Multiply: 13.61×71.3
(7)

16. Simplify mentally: $12,389.32 \div 100$
(8)

17. Subtract. Add to check: $181,131.62 - 1.9876$
(6)

18. Divide, and round to two decimal places: $\dfrac{613.15}{3.1}$
(7)

19. List the common factors of 20 and 30.
(13)

20. Find GCF (20, 30).
(13)

Write each number as a product of prime numbers using exponents:

21. 288   **22.** 1080   **23.** 10,800
(16)   *(16)*   *(16)*

24. Round 87,621.32178939 to the nearest millionth.
(6)

25. Round 437.00$\overline{621}$ to the nearest hundred-millionth.
(15)

26. Use words to write the number 172.312.
(6)

27. Add: $1361.31 + 21.14 + 112.17 + 1.18$
(6)

28. Write the decimal number 0.65 as a fraction reduced to lowest terms.
(15)

Find the missing number:

29.   14,392.091   **30.** $\dfrac{321}{B} = 0.04$
(3,6) $\underline{+\qquad\quad A}$ *(4,7)*
            107,072.060

LESSON 17 Areas of Rectangles

Area is the amount of surface of a figure. The diagram on the left represents a surface that is 4 feet long and 3 feet wide. On the right we show how this surface can be divided into twelve squares. All the sides of the squares are 1 foot long.

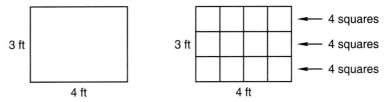

There are four squares in each row and three rows, so there are twelve squares.

$$4 \text{ squares} \times 3 = 12 \text{ squares}$$

Therefore, twelve 1-foot squares cover the surface.

If there were six rows of four squares each, then there would be a total of twenty-four squares.

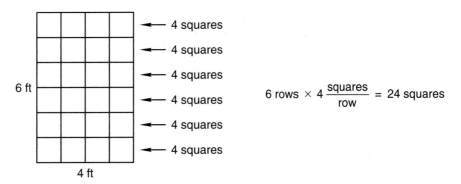

$$6 \text{ rows} \times 4 \frac{\text{squares}}{\text{row}} = 24 \text{ squares}$$

The length of the first column tells us the number of rows and the width tells us the number of squares in each row. Thus,

$$\text{Number of squares} = \text{length} \times \text{width}$$

Each square could be covered by a tile that is 1 foot long on each side. It is helpful to think of tiles when we hear the word *area*. Tiles can be touched and manipulated and are easily understood, while area is more abstract.

example 17.1 How many 1-inch-square tiles would it take to cover this figure?

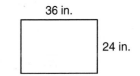

solution Each row will have 36 tiles, and there will be 24 rows. Now we multiply.

$$36 \frac{\text{tiles}}{\text{row}} \times 24 \text{ rows} = \textbf{864 tiles}$$

From this we see that the area of a rectangle equals the length times the width.

> Area of a rectangle = length × width

Area is measured in square units. We may use exponents to indicate that units have been multiplied. Recall that when we add or subtract measures with like units, the units *do not* change.

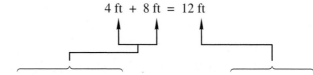

$$4 \text{ ft} + 8 \text{ ft} = 12 \text{ ft}$$

The units of the addends are the same as the units of the sum.

However, when we multiply or divide measures, the units *do* change.

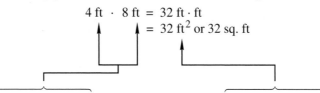

$$4 \text{ ft} \cdot 8 \text{ ft} = 32 \text{ ft} \cdot \text{ft}$$
$$= 32 \text{ ft}^2 \text{ or } 32 \text{ sq. ft}$$

The units of the factors are multiplied to form the units of the product.

The result of multiplying feet by feet is square feet, which we may abbreviate sq. ft or ft^2. Square feet is one of the units used to measure area. Both dimensions (length and width) *must* be expressed in the same units to determine the area. We cannot, for example, multiply feet by inches, but must convert either one or the other (feet to inches or inches to feet), so that both are the same unit of measure.

example 17.2   Find the area of this figure in square centimeters. Dimensions are in centimeters. All angles are right angles.

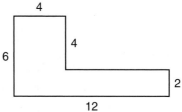

solution   We will divide the given figure into rectangles and find the area of each rectangle. Then we will add the areas. Two ways are shown.

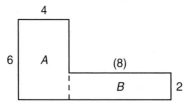   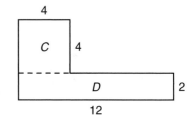

$$\begin{array}{ll} \text{Area } A = 6 \text{ cm} \times 4 \text{ cm} = 24 \text{ cm}^2 \\ + \text{ Area } B = 2 \text{ cm} \times 8 \text{ cm} = 16 \text{ cm}^2 \\ \hline \qquad\qquad\quad \text{Total area} = 40 \text{ cm}^2 \end{array}$$

$$\begin{array}{ll} \text{Area } C = 4 \text{ cm} \times 4 \text{ cm} = 16 \text{ cm}^2 \\ + \text{ Area } D = 2 \text{ cm} \times 12 \text{ cm} = 24 \text{ cm}^2 \\ \hline \qquad\qquad\quad \text{Total area} = 40 \text{ cm}^2 \end{array}$$

The area of the figure is **40 cm^2.** Thus, forty tiles, each 1-centimeter square, would be required to cover the figure.

practice   Find the area of each figure. Dimensions are in feet. All angles are right angles.

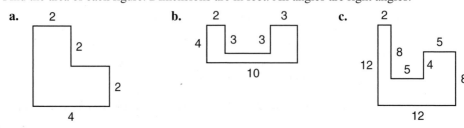

problem set 17

1. During an eleven year period, the Garber Dunns drove their combine 10,802 miles
(11) through the wheat fields. If they drove an equal amount each year, how many miles did
they drive their combine each year?

2. There were four thousand, eight hundred forty-two ants in each anthill. If there were
(11) three hundred thirty anthills, how many ants were there in all?

3. In the next valley, the anthills each contained one hundred eight thousand, fifteen ants.
(5) How many more ants lived in one of these anthills than lived in one anthill from
Problem 2?

4. Which of the following numbers are divisible by: (a) 3? (b) 5?
(10)
135   1050   335   4145   1010

5. Find the sum of the first 13 prime numbers.
(12)

6. Find the perimeter of this figure.   **7.** Find the area of this figure.
(9) Dimensions are in meters. All angles   (17) Dimensions are in centimeters. All
are right angles.   angles are right angles.

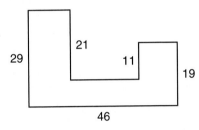

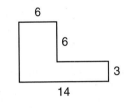

8. How many 1-inch-square tiles would
(17) cover this figure? Dimensions are in
inches. All angles are right angles.

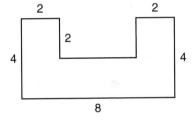

Write each fraction as a decimal number. Write the number as a repeating decimal or round
to two decimal places if necessary.

9. $\dfrac{3}{17}$ **10.** $\dfrac{7}{11}$ **11.** $\dfrac{7}{500}$
(15)   (15)   (15)

Write each number as a product of prime numbers using exponents:

12. 540   **13.** 30   **14.** 210
(16)   (12)   (12)

15. Find GCF (36, 216).
(13)

Reduce each fraction to lowest terms:

16. $\dfrac{21}{49}$ **17.** $\dfrac{36}{48}$
(14)   (14)

18. Write $\frac{3}{7}$ with a denominator of 210.
(14)

19. Multiply: 62.13 × 7.8
(7)

20. Simplify mentally: 625.3 × 100
(8)

21. Subtract (add to check): 185.3617 − 17.3169
(6)

Find the missing numbers:

22.
(3,6)
$$179.3622$$
$$-\qquad Z$$
$$\overline{57.4643}$$

23.
(4,7)
$$\frac{V}{0.6} = 44.4$$

24. Divide, and round to two decimal places: $\dfrac{231.2}{0.048}$
(7)

25. Round 3.141592654 to the nearest ten-millionth.
(6)

26. Round $2.\overline{07}$ to seven decimal places.
(15)

Write each decimal number as a fraction reduced to lowest terms:

27. 0.134
(15)

28. 0.025
(15)

Simplify:

29. $(0.8)^3$
(16)

30. 1^{24}
(16)

LESSON 18 *Multiplying Fractions and Whole Numbers • Fractional Part of a Number*

18.A

**multiplying
fractions and
whole
numbers**

When we multiply two fractions, we multiply the numerators of the factors to get the numerator of the product. We multiply the denominators of the factors to get the denominator of the product.

$$\frac{1}{4} \cdot \frac{3}{5} = \frac{1 \cdot 3}{4 \cdot 5} = \frac{3}{20}$$

Every whole number can be written as a fraction by writing a 1 as the denominator. Thus, both of these

$$\frac{4}{1} \qquad 4$$

are ways to write the number 4. To multiply 4 by $\frac{2}{9}$, we write the 1 under the 4 and multiply the fractions.

$$\frac{2}{9} \cdot \frac{4}{1} = \frac{8}{9}$$

With practice you will see that when you have both a fraction and a whole number as factors, you can simply multiply the numerator of the fraction by the whole number to get the numerator of the product. Thus, we can write the multiplication of $\frac{2}{9}$ by 4 as

$$\frac{2}{9} \cdot 4 = \frac{8}{9}$$

If you have trouble deciding whether to multiply the numerator or denominator by the whole number, change the whole number to a fraction to make the multiplication clear.

18.B

fractional part of a number

When we multiply a whole number by a fraction, the answer is a part of the whole number. In (a), we show the number 15. In (b), we see that if we divide 15 into five equal parts each part is 3. Each of these parts is $\frac{1}{5}$ of 15.

15		3 3 3 3 3		3 3 3 3 3		3 3 3 3 3
(a)		(b)		(c)		(d)

$$\frac{1}{5} \times 15 = 3 \qquad \frac{2}{5} \times 15 = 6 \qquad \frac{4}{5} \times 15 = 12$$

In (c), we show that $\frac{2}{5} \times 15$ means two of the parts, and the answer is 6. In (d), we show that $\frac{4}{5} \times 15$ means four of the parts, and the answer is 12.

We use the word *of* to designate multiplication. Thus,

$$\frac{2}{5} \text{ of } 15 \qquad \text{means} \qquad \frac{2}{5} \times 15$$

$$\frac{4}{5} \text{ of } 15 \qquad \text{means} \qquad \frac{4}{5} \times 15$$

example 18.1   Find $\frac{3}{7}$ of 42.

solution   The word *of* means to multiply. So we multiply 42 by $\frac{3}{7}$.

$$\frac{3}{7} \times \frac{42}{1} = \frac{3 \times 42}{7 \times 1} = \frac{126}{7} = \mathbf{18}$$

example 18.2   What number is $\frac{5}{7}$ of 12?

solution   The word *of* means to multiply.

$$\frac{5}{7} \cdot 12 = \frac{\mathbf{60}}{\mathbf{7}}$$

practice   **a.**   Find $\frac{2}{3}$ of 30.

b.   What number is $\frac{3}{4}$ of 15?

c.   What number is $\frac{5}{7}$ of 3?

problem set 18

1.
(13)
Paul picked 5482 peaches. Peter picked four times as many as Paul picked. Penny picked twice as many as Peter picked. How many peaches did they pick altogether?

2.
(6)
Nineteen million and forty-seven hundred-thousandths centimeters was Ahab's first guess. His second guess was seventeen thousand, five and two hundred thirty-seven ten-thousandths centimeters greater than his first guess. What was his second guess?

3.
(11)
Even with a pry bar, Judy could not force more than sixty-three rocks into each container. If she had seven hundred thousand, thirty-three containers, how many rocks did she need to fill all the containers?

4.
(11)
When Judy came to work the next day, she was delighted because four hundred sixteen thousand, nine hundred forty-three containers had been delivered. How many rocks (see problem 3) would fill all the new containers?

5.
(12)
What prime numbers are less than 50 but greater than 25?

6. Find the perimeter of this figure.
(9) Dimensions are in centimeters. All angles are right angles.

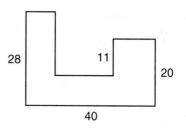

Find the area of each figure. Dimensions are in centimeters. All angles are right angles.

7.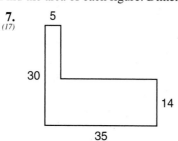
(17)

8.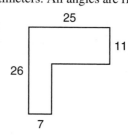
(17)

Reduce each fraction to lowest terms:

9. $\dfrac{480}{1000}$
(14)

10. $\dfrac{66}{104}$
(14)

11. $\dfrac{210}{294}$
(14)

12. $\dfrac{738}{882}$
(14)

Write each fraction as a decimal number. Round to three decimal places.

13. $\dfrac{16}{17}$
(15)

14. $\dfrac{7}{250}$
(15)

15. $\dfrac{11}{13}$
(15)

Expand each fraction so that the denominator is 90:

16. $\dfrac{3}{10}$
(14)

17. $\dfrac{14}{15}$
(14)

18. Multiply: 62.13×11.31
(7)

19. Simplify mentally: $621.1378 \div 10,000$
(8)

Simplify:

20. 4^3
(16)

21. 13^2
(16)

22. Subtract (add to check): $183.1782 - 1.8999$
(6)

23. What number is $\frac{2}{3}$ of 15?
(18)

24. What number is $\frac{5}{9}$ of 10?
(18)

25. Find $\frac{3}{5}$ of 100.
(18)

26. Find $\frac{4}{7}$ of 12.
(18)

Find the missing numbers:

27. $0.11111 - K = 0.01121$
(3,6)

28. $P \times 78 = 43.68$
(4,7)

29. Write the decimal number 0.095 as a fraction, and simplify.
(15)

30. Find GCF (121, 132).
(13)

LESSON 19   *Symbols for Multiplication • Multiplying Fractions • Dividing Fractions*

19.A
symbols for multiplication

Thus far, we have used a cross or a center dot to designate multiplication. To write 4 times 3, we have written

$$4 \times 3 \quad \text{or} \quad 4 \cdot 3$$

In algebra, the lowercase letter x is a commonly used variable. The symbol for the letter x is similar to the cross ($\times$) used to indicate multiplication. Therefore, in algebra we usually do not use the cross but designate multiplication in other ways. (We will still use the cross when it is convenient.) Parentheses may also be used to indicate multiplication. All the following indicate that 4 and 3 are to be multiplied:

$$4 \cdot 3 \qquad 4(3) \qquad (4)3 \qquad (4)(3)$$

None of these forms is necessarily a preferred form, and all of them have the same meaning.

19.B
multiplying fractions

To multiply fractions, we multiply the numerators to get the new numerator and multiply the denominators to get the new denominator.

example 19.1   Simplify: $\dfrac{4}{9} \cdot \dfrac{5}{7}$

solution   We get the new numerator by multiplying 4 and 5 and the new denominator by multiplying 9 and 7.

$$\frac{4}{9} \cdot \frac{5}{7} = \frac{20}{63}$$

example 19.2   Simplify: $\left(\dfrac{2}{3}\right)^3$

solution   We multiply the numerators, then we multiply the denominators.

$$\frac{2}{3} \cdot \frac{2}{3} \cdot \frac{2}{3} = \frac{8}{27}$$

If the numerators and denominators contain common factors, it is helpful to simplify (reduce) before multiplying. The terms of fractions may be reduced before they are multiplied. Consider this multiplication:

$$\frac{3}{8} \cdot \frac{2}{3} = \frac{6}{24} \qquad \frac{6}{24} \text{ reduces to } \frac{1}{4}$$

We see that neither $\frac{3}{8}$ nor $\frac{2}{3}$ can be reduced individually, but their product, $\frac{6}{24}$, can be reduced. We can avoid reducing after we multiply by reducing before we multiply. This is also known as **canceling.** To cancel, any numerator may be paired with any denominator. Below we have paired 3 with 3 and 2 with 8.

Then we reduce the pairs: $\frac{3}{3}$ reduces to $\frac{1}{1}$, and $\frac{2}{8}$ reduces to $\frac{1}{4}$, as we show below. Then we multiply the reduced terms.

$$\overset{1}{\underset{4}{\cancel{\frac{3}{8}}}} \cdot \overset{1}{\underset{1}{\cancel{\frac{2}{3}}}} = \frac{1 \cdot 1}{4 \cdot 1} = \frac{1}{4}$$

Canceling *only* applies to the multiplication of fractions.

example 19.3   Simplify: $\dfrac{4}{9} \cdot \dfrac{18}{30}$

solution   By inspection, we see that we can reduce before we multiply. We can pair the 4 with the 30 and the 18 with the 9. Then we multiply the reduced terms.

$$\overset{2}{\underset{1}{\cancel{\frac{4}{9}}}} \cdot \overset{2}{\underset{15}{\cancel{\frac{18}{30}}}} = \frac{4}{15}$$

19.C

dividing fractions

"Divide" means the same thing as "multiply by the reciprocal." The product of a number and its **reciprocal** is 1. So

$$\frac{3}{4} \cdot \frac{4}{3} = 1 \qquad \text{and} \qquad 2 \cdot \frac{1}{2} = 1.$$

From this you can see that to find the reciprocal of a fraction you turn it upside down (switch the numerator and denominator) and to find the reciprocal of a whole number you make the fraction $\frac{1}{\text{the whole number}}$. When it comes to whole numbers, $10 \div 5$ and $10 \cdot \frac{1}{5}$ have the same meaning and are equally easy. But when it comes to fractions, division is hard to understand (as was the case with decimals). So we always convert a fraction division problem to multiplication by the reciprocal. Then we never have to divide by a fraction!

We divide fractions by inverting the divisor (forming its reciprocal) and multiplying. Both of these expressions indicate that $\frac{5}{7}$ is to be divided by $\frac{4}{5}$.

$$\frac{\frac{5}{7}}{\frac{4}{5}} \qquad \text{or} \qquad \frac{5}{7} \div \frac{4}{5}$$

Thus, in both expressions, the divisor is $\frac{4}{5}$. We simplify both expressions in the same way— by inverting the divisor and multiplying.

$$\frac{5}{7} \div \frac{4}{5} = \frac{5}{7} \cdot \frac{5}{4} = \frac{25}{28}$$

example 19.4   Simplify: $\dfrac{21}{6} \div \dfrac{27}{4}$

solution   First we invert the divisor. Then we cancel and multiply.

$$\frac{21}{6} \div \frac{27}{4} = \frac{21}{6} \cdot \frac{4}{27} = \overset{7}{\underset{3}{\cancel{\frac{21}{6}}}} \cdot \overset{2}{\underset{9}{\cancel{\frac{4}{27}}}} = \frac{14}{27}$$

practice   Simplify:

a. $\left(\dfrac{4}{9}\right)\left(\dfrac{3}{12}\right)$ b. $\dfrac{\frac{3}{8}}{\frac{4}{6}}$ c. $\dfrac{4}{5} \div \dfrac{10}{5}$

problem set 19

1.
(6) The prize was for the closest guess. The exact answer was 14,016.2163 kilograms. Charles guessed thirteen thousand, forty-one and six ten-thousandths kilograms. Mary guessed fourteen thousand, nine hundred ninety-one and twenty-three hundredths kilograms. By how much did each of them miss the exact answer? Whose guess was closer?

2.
(13) Mice scampered in until 51,416 had arrived. Then 4 times this number scampered in on the next day. How many mice scampered in altogether?

3.
(5) Five thousand, seven hundred fifteen Romans stood and roared their approval. Nineteen thousand, seven remained seated and were discontented. How many more Romans were discontented than approved?

4.
(11) The fire department had rules that occupancy by more than 315 in a room was unlawful. If 14,321 attended, what is the minimum number of rooms needed to hold them lawfully?

5.
(12) What is the smallest prime number that is at least 14 greater than 21?

Simplify. If possible, cancel before multiplying.

6.
(19) $\dfrac{5}{8} \cdot \dfrac{4}{7}$

7.
(19) $\left(\dfrac{5}{9}\right)\dfrac{15}{20}$

8.
(19) $\dfrac{3}{8} \div \dfrac{2}{3}$

9.
(19) $\dfrac{9}{4} \div \dfrac{14}{3}$

10.
(9) Find the perimeter of this figure. Dimensions are in meters. All angles are right angles.

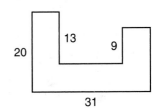

Find the area of each figure. Dimensions are in yards. All angles are right angles.

11.
(17)

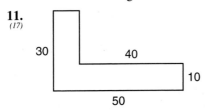

12.
(17)

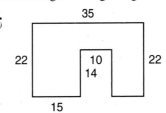

Reduce each fraction to lowest terms:

13.
(14) $\dfrac{360}{540}$

14.
(14) $\dfrac{196}{360}$

15.
(14) $\dfrac{256}{720}$

Write each fraction as a decimal number. Round to two decimal places.

16.
(15) $\dfrac{17}{23}$

17.
(15) $\dfrac{5}{17}$

Write each number as a product of prime numbers using exponents:

18.
(16) 4200

19.
(16) 10,080

20.
(7) Multiply: 1.28×62.1

Simplify:

21. $(1.2)^2$
(16)

22. $\left(\dfrac{3}{8}\right)^2$
(19)

Divide. Round to two decimal places.

23. $\dfrac{7.32}{0.12}$
(7)

24. $\dfrac{61.31}{3.1}$
(7)

25. Round $28.30\overline{57}$ to the nearest ten-millionth.
(15)

26. Convert 0.362 to a fraction reduced to lowest terms.
(15)

27. Find $\frac{3}{7}$ of 140.
(18)

28. What is $\frac{2}{9}$ of 81?
(18)

Find the missing numbers:

29. $18.32 + A = 1921.761$
(3,6)

30. $\dfrac{4.5}{M} = 3$
(4,7)

LESSON 20   *Multiples • Least Common Multiple*

20.A

multiples   **Multiples,** factors, and products are words that go together. We know that 3 times 2 equals 6.

$$3 \cdot 2 = 6$$

In this example, the factors are 3 and 2 and the product is 6. Because we can multiply 3 by 2 and get 6, we say that 6 is a multiple of 3 and that 6 is also a multiple of 2. The numbers 3, 6, 9, 12, 15, and 18 are multiples of 3 because they can be composed by multiplying 3 by a counting number.

$$3 \cdot 1 = 3$$
$$3 \cdot 2 = 6$$
$$3 \cdot 3 = 9$$
$$3 \cdot 4 = 12$$
$$3 \cdot 5 = 15$$
$$3 \cdot 6 = 18$$

Similarly, the numbers 2, 4, 6, 8, 10, 12, and 14 are all multiples of 2 because they can be composed by multiplying 2 by a counting number, as shown here.

$$2 \cdot 1 = 2$$
$$2 \cdot 2 = 4$$
$$2 \cdot 3 = 6$$
$$2 \cdot 4 = 8$$
$$2 \cdot 5 = 10$$
$$2 \cdot 6 = 12$$
$$2 \cdot 7 = 14$$

The words *multiple*, *factor*, and *product* are not difficult. Solving problems that use these words will help us remember what they mean.

example 20.1   The number 8 is a multiple of which numbers?

solution   We can compose 8 by multiplying 2 and 4 or by multiplying 1 and 8.

$$2 \cdot 4 = 8 \qquad 1 \cdot 8 = 8$$

So 8 is a multiple of **1, 2, 4,** and **8.** Note that we say that 8 is a multiple of itself and also of 1.

example 20.2   Find all multiples of 9 that are less than 50.

solution   A multiple of 9 is the product of 9 and a counting number.

$$9 \cdot 1 = 9$$
$$9 \cdot 2 = 18$$
$$9 \cdot 3 = 27$$
$$9 \cdot 4 = 36$$
$$9 \cdot 5 = 45$$
$$9 \cdot 6 = 54$$

Thus, the multiples of 9 that are less than 50 are **9, 18, 27, 36,** and **45.**

20.B
least common multiple

The multiples of 2 are

$$2, 4, 6, 8, 10, 12, 14, 16, 18, 20, \ldots$$

The multiples of 3 are

$$3, 6, 9, 12, 15, 18, 21, \ldots$$

So we can say the shared or **common multiples** of 2 and 3 are 6, 12, 18, ... Common multiples are the numbers that appear in both lists. The smallest of these common multiples is 6, so we say the **least common multiple (LCM)** of 2 and 3 equals 6, or LCM (2, 3) = 6. We can always find the LCM of two or more numbers by examining their lists of multiples, but it is nice to have a special procedure to use if some of the numbers are large numbers. The procedure is as follows:

1. Write each number as a product of prime numbers.
2. Compute the LCM by using each factor as a factor in the LCM the greatest number of times it is a factor in any of the given numbers.

To demonstrate this procedure, we will find the LCM of 18, 81, and 500. First we write each number as a product of prime factors.

$$18 = 2 \cdot 3 \cdot 3 \qquad 81 = 3 \cdot 3 \cdot 3 \cdot 3 \qquad 500 = 2 \cdot 2 \cdot 5 \cdot 5 \cdot 5$$

Now we find the LCM by using the procedure in step 2. The number 2 is a factor of both 18 and 500. It appears most in 500 where it is a factor twice, so it will appear twice in the LCM.

$$2 \cdot 2$$

The number 3 is a factor of both 18 and 81. It appears 4 times in 81, so it will appear 4 times in the LCM.

$$2 \cdot 2 \cdot 3 \cdot 3 \cdot 3 \cdot 3$$

The number 5 is the other factor. It appears 3 times in 500 so it will appear 3 times in the LCM.

$$\text{LCM } (18, 81, 500) = 2 \cdot 2 \cdot 3 \cdot 3 \cdot 3 \cdot 3 \cdot 5 \cdot 5 \cdot 5 = 40{,}500$$

example 20.3   Find LCM (24, 55, 80).

solution   First we write the numbers as products of prime factors.

$$24 = 2 \cdot 2 \cdot 2 \cdot 3 \qquad 55 = 5 \cdot 11 \qquad 80 = 2 \cdot 2 \cdot 2 \cdot 2 \cdot 5$$

To compute the LCM, we use each factor the greatest number of times it is a factor of any of the numbers.

$$\text{LCM } (24, 55, 80) = 2 \cdot 2 \cdot 2 \cdot 2 \cdot 3 \cdot 5 \cdot 11 = \mathbf{2640}$$

example 20.4   Below we show three numbers expressed as products of prime factors.

$$\text{first number} = 2 \cdot 2 \cdot 3 \cdot 7 \cdot 7$$
$$\text{second number} = 2 \cdot 2 \cdot 2 \cdot 2 \cdot 5 \cdot 7$$
$$\text{third number} = 2 \cdot 5 \cdot 5 \cdot 5 \cdot 5$$

(a) What are the numbers?

(b) What is the LCM of the numbers?

solution   (a) We multiply to find the numbers.

$$\text{first number} = 2 \cdot 2 \cdot 3 \cdot 7 \cdot 7 = \mathbf{588}$$
$$\text{second number} = 2 \cdot 2 \cdot 2 \cdot 2 \cdot 5 \cdot 7 = \mathbf{560}$$
$$\text{third number} = 2 \cdot 5 \cdot 5 \cdot 5 \cdot 5 = \mathbf{1250}$$

(b) LCM $(588, 560, 1250) = 2 \cdot 2 \cdot 2 \cdot 2 \cdot 3 \cdot 5 \cdot 5 \cdot 5 \cdot 5 \cdot 7 \cdot 7 = \mathbf{1,470,000}$

Thus, we find that the smallest number that is evenly divisible by 588, 560, and 1250 is 1,470,000.

practice   a.   Find all multiples of 7 that are less than 56.

b.   Find all multiples of 6 that are greater than 29 and are also less than 50.

Use products of prime numbers to find the LCM of each group of numbers:

c.   18 and 250   d.   35, 60, and 90

problem set   1.   Seven thousand, forty-two volksmarchers wore red hats. Ninety-three thousand, nine
20   *(5)*   hundred seventy-five wore blue hats. If one hundred thirty-seven thousand, eight
hundred forty-two attended the walking festival, how many did not wear either red hats
or blue hats?

2.   When the first box was opened, the chapeaux inside totaled one thousand, nine hundred
(11)   three. If 47,300 students were expected to attend, how many boxes of chapeaux would
be required so that every student could have one?

3.   When the first frost came, nineteen thousand, two ragweed plants shriveled and died.
(13)   If 5 times this number survived the frost, how many had there been before the frost
came?

4.   Eloise drove 636.57 miles on the first day. Elvira drove 3 times as far on the second
(13)   day. On the third day, Noni drove twice as far as Eloise drove. What was the total
distance driven by the three women?

5.   Find all multiples of 4 that are less than 42.
(20)

Simplify. If possible, cancel before multiplying.

6.
(19) $\dfrac{42}{15} \cdot \dfrac{3}{7}$

7.
(19) $\dfrac{5}{18} \cdot \dfrac{90}{120}$

8.
(19) $\dfrac{5}{8} \div \dfrac{7}{4}$

9.
(19) $\dfrac{7}{18} \div \dfrac{14}{9}$

10. Find the perimeter of this figure.
(9)   Dimensions are in feet. All angles are
    right angles.

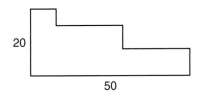

Find the area of each figure. Dimensions are in meters. All angles are right angles.

11.
(17)

12.
(17)

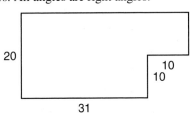

Reduce each fraction to lowest terms:

13.
(14) $\dfrac{540}{720}$

14.
(14) $\dfrac{144}{360}$

15. Simplify: $\left(\dfrac{7}{13}\right)^2$
(19)

Write each fraction as a decimal number. Round to two decimal places.

16.
(15) $\dfrac{21}{23}$

17.
(15) $\dfrac{6}{13}$

18. Find which of the following numbers is divisible by both 2 and 3:
(10)
    A. 1215   B. 572   C. 1111   D. 9924

19. Order from least to greatest: 0.04, 0.0049, 0.1, 0.0096
(8)

Find the missing numbers:

20. $\dfrac{2}{7} \cdot C = \dfrac{4}{21}$
(4,19)

21. $87(M) = 28.71$
(4,7)

Find the least common multiple of each group of numbers:

22. 75 and 180
(20)

23. 22, 121, and 200
(20)

Convert each decimal to a fraction reduced to lowest terms:

24. 0.024
(15)

25. 0.00064
(15)

26. Round 194,591,014.62 to the nearest million.
(6)

27. Use words to write the number 111546435.
(1)

28. Simplify mentally: 8361.2361 ÷ 100
(8)

Multiply. Reduce the fraction to lowest terms.

29. $\frac{3}{4} \cdot 42$
(18)

30. $\frac{4}{7} \cdot 4$
(18)

LESSON 21   *Average*

The **average** of a set of numbers is the sum of the numbers divided by the number of numbers in the set.

$$\text{Average} = \frac{\text{sum of numbers}}{\text{number of numbers}}$$

The average of the four numbers 1, 2, 4, and 5 is 3.

$$\text{Average} = \frac{1 + 2 + 4 + 5}{4} = \frac{12}{4} = 3$$

If we have 4 stacks of pancakes as shown here,

the average is the number in each stack if we distribute the pancakes evenly.

If we know the average of a set of numbers, we can determine the sum of the numbers. **The sum is the average times the number of numbers in the set.**

example 21.1   Find the average of 1765, 93, 742, and 21,050.

solution   We add the four numbers and divide the sum by 4.

$$\text{Average} = \frac{1765 + 93 + 742 + 21,050}{4} = \frac{23,650}{4} = \textbf{5912.5}$$

example 21.2   Find the average of 8, 17, 14, 10, 18, 6, 13, and 12.

solution   We add the eight numbers and divide the sum by 8.

$$\text{Average} = \frac{8 + 17 + 14 + 10 + 18 + 6 + 13 + 12}{8} = \frac{98}{8} = \textbf{12.25}$$

example 21.3   The average of four numbers is 10. Three of the four numbers are 2, 14, and 7. What is the fourth number?

solution   If the average of four numbers is 10, the sum of the numbers is 10 times 4, or 40. We will call the missing number X.

$$2 + 14 + 7 + X = 40$$

We find X in this missing-number problem by first adding the numbers we know on the left side of the equals sign.

$$\underbrace{2 + 14 + 7}_{23} + X = 40$$

$$23 + X = 40$$

We subtract to find the fourth number.

$$\begin{array}{r} 40 \\ -\ 23 \\ \hline 17 \end{array}$$

practice

a. Find the average of 74.2, 87.3, and 106.5.

b. The average of four numbers is 100.1. Three of the numbers are 24.2, 13.5, and 48.7. What is the fourth number?

c. At four different stores, Stacy found that air filters cost an average of $7.63. If the first three stores priced air filters at $5.21, $7.42, and $9.15, what was the cost of the fourth air filter?

problem set 21

1. *(6)* Jed guessed ten billion, four hundred seventy-five thousand, fifteen and nine hundred twenty-three ten-thousandths. Ned guessed eight billion, four hundred seventy-three million, forty-two and seventy-five thousandths. How much greater was Jed's guess than Ned's guess?

2. *(6)* On the first day, the measurements were 4012.06 and 0.00418 meters. On the next day, the measurements were 732.05 and 9.016 meters. What was the total for both days?

3. *(11)* Only 243 bats could squeeze through at one time. If 416,202 bats came, how many times would it take for all of them to squeeze through?

4. *(10)* Which of the following numbers are divisible by: (a) 3?   (b) 5?

          11,682   10,517   2193   4200

5. *(12)* List the prime numbers that are greater than 30 and less than 50.

6. *(21)* Find the average of 1242, 87, 521, and 169,810.

7. *(21)* The average cost of five items is $316.05. The first four items cost $48.20, $40.60, $63.75, and $70.15. Find the cost of the fifth item.

Simplify. If possible, cancel before multiplying.

8. *(19)* $\dfrac{36}{28} \cdot \dfrac{7}{6}$ **9.** *(19)* $\dfrac{21}{32} \cdot \dfrac{4}{7}$ **10.** *(19)* $\dfrac{5}{7} \div \dfrac{15}{21}$ **11.** *(19)* $\dfrac{9}{25} \div \dfrac{27}{15}$

12. *(9)* Find the perimeter of the following figure. Dimensions are in meters. All angles are right angles.

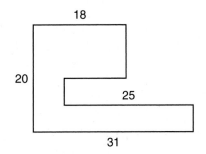

13. *(17)* Find the area of the following figure. Dimensions are in centimeters. All angles are right angles.

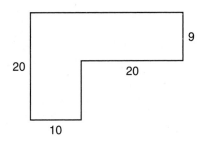

Reduce each fraction to lowest terms:

14. $\dfrac{270}{360}$
(14)

15. $\dfrac{35}{42}$
(14)

16. Find all the multiples of 3 that are less than 50.
(20)

Write each fraction as a decimal number. Round to two decimal places.

17. $\dfrac{11}{17}$
(15)

18. $\dfrac{5}{13}$
(15)

Write each number as a product of prime numbers using exponents:

19. 2520
(16)

20. 8400
(16)

21. Multiply: 66.12×1.7
(7)

22. Simplify: $\left(\dfrac{3}{4}\right)^3$
(19)

23. Convert 0.95 to a fraction reduced to lowest terms.
(15)

Find the missing numbers:

24.
(3,6)
$$\begin{array}{r} 12.876 \\ -N \\ \hline 3.0931 \end{array}$$

25. $x \div \dfrac{1}{4} = \dfrac{5}{6}$
(4,19)

Divide. Round to two decimal places.

26. $\dfrac{6.25}{0.87}$
(7)

27. $\dfrac{71.3}{3.7}$
(7)

28. Find LCM (45, 50, 60).
(20)

29. Find GCF (45, 50, 60).
(13)

30. Find $\frac{3}{8}$ of 64.
(18)

LESSON 22 *Multiple Fractional Factors*

There is no change in the procedure when a problem has three or more fractions to be multiplied. First we cancel common factors, and then we multiply.

example 22.1   Simplify: $\dfrac{56}{27} \cdot \dfrac{14}{21} \cdot \dfrac{15}{22}$

solution   As our first step, we should cancel. We can pair any numerator with any denominator. Our goal is to pair numbers with common factors. By inspection, we can pair 56 and 21, 14 and 22, and 15 and 27. We see that 7 is a common factor of 56 and 21, 2 is a common factor of 14 and 22, and 3 is a common factor of 27 and 15. Now we reduce these pairs: $\frac{56}{21}$ reduces to $\frac{8}{3}$, $\frac{14}{22}$ reduces to $\frac{7}{11}$, and $\frac{15}{27}$ reduces to $\frac{5}{9}$. Then we multiply the reduced terms.

$$\dfrac{\overset{8}{\cancel{56}}}{\underset{9}{\cancel{27}}} \cdot \dfrac{\overset{7}{\cancel{14}}}{\underset{3}{\cancel{21}}} \cdot \dfrac{\overset{5}{\cancel{15}}}{\underset{11}{\cancel{22}}} = \dfrac{8}{9} \cdot \dfrac{7}{3} \cdot \dfrac{5}{11} = \dfrac{\mathbf{280}}{\mathbf{297}}$$

example 22.2 Simplify: $\dfrac{26}{30} \cdot \dfrac{21}{39} \div \dfrac{4}{15}$

solution First we change division by a fraction into multiplication by the reciprocal.

$$\frac{26}{30} \cdot \frac{21}{39} \div \frac{4}{15} = \frac{26}{30} \cdot \frac{21}{39} \cdot \frac{15}{4}$$

Now we cancel. By inspection, we can pair 26 with 30 and 21 with 39.

$$\overset{13}{\underset{15}{\cancel{26}}} \cdot \overset{7}{\underset{13}{\cancel{21}}} \cdot \frac{15}{4} = \frac{13}{15} \cdot \frac{7}{13} \cdot \frac{15}{4}$$

Now we see that we can cancel the 13's and 15's (really we are dividing both the numerator and the denominator by 13 and by 15), so

$$\overset{1}{\underset{1}{\cancel{13}}} \cdot \frac{7}{\underset{1}{\cancel{13}}} \cdot \overset{1}{\underset{1}{\cancel{15}}} = \frac{1}{1} \cdot \frac{7}{1} \cdot \frac{1}{4} = \frac{7}{4}$$

practice Simplify:

a. $\dfrac{12}{105} \cdot \dfrac{14}{30} \cdot \dfrac{15}{14}$

b. $\dfrac{4}{15} \cdot \dfrac{3}{16} \cdot \dfrac{6}{18}$

c. $\dfrac{6}{21} \cdot \dfrac{14}{30} \div \dfrac{6}{15}$

d. $\dfrac{10}{35} \cdot \dfrac{14}{28} \div \dfrac{12}{45}$

problem set 22

1. *(6)* Ninety million, four thousand and sixty-two millionths is a big number. By how much is it greater than eighty-six million, four hundred twenty-seven thousand and fourteen ten-thousandths?

2. *(5)* In the first wave there were 742,000 grains of sand. The second and third waves contained 96,016 and 1,001,892 grains. How many grains were there in all?

3. *(21)* The average time for the three downhill runs was 49.8 seconds. If the first run took only 45.2 seconds and the second run slowed to 51.8 seconds, what was the time for the third run?

4. *(13)* Harry cornered 146 Komodo dragons in the backyard. Jennet cornered 5 times that number in the side yard. How many Komodo dragons did they corner altogether?

5. *(21)* Find the average of 1862, 1430, and 276.

6. *(12,20)* (a) What are the prime numbers between 80 and 90?
(b) List the multiples of 3 that are greater than 80 and less than 90.

Simplify:

7. *(22)* $\dfrac{63}{54} \cdot \dfrac{21}{35} \cdot \dfrac{15}{22}$

8. *(22)* $\dfrac{26}{90} \cdot \dfrac{24}{25} \div \dfrac{4}{15}$

9. *(22)* $\dfrac{36}{24} \cdot \dfrac{8}{6} \div \dfrac{3}{6}$

10. *(9)* Find the perimeter of the following figure. Dimensions are in inches. All angles are right angles.

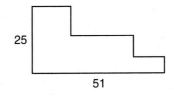

11. *(17)* Find the area of the following figure. Dimensions are in feet. All angles are right angles.

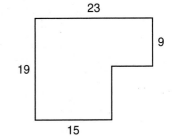

12. Find LCM (100, 14, 20).   **13.** Find GCF (10, 15, 20).
(20)   (13)

Write each fraction as a decimal number. Round to two decimal places.

14. $\dfrac{13}{17}$ **15.** $\dfrac{3}{11}$ **16.** $\dfrac{7}{20}$
(15)   (15)   (15)

Reduce each fraction to lowest terms:

17. $\dfrac{540}{1440}$ **18.** $\dfrac{128}{360}$ **19.** $\dfrac{720}{840}$ **20.** $\dfrac{240}{256}$
(14)   (14)   (14)   (14)

21. Simplify: $(0.4)^3$ **22.** Multiply: 581×0.163
(16)   (7)

23. Subtract (add to check): $6854.32 - 1.871$
(6)

Find the missing numbers:

24. $4.56 + F = 12.3$ **25.** $\dfrac{1}{4}(D) = 16$
(3,6)   (4,19)

Divide. Round to two decimal places.

26. $\dfrac{11.7}{3.1}$ **27.** $\dfrac{1132.1}{0.7}$
(7)   (7)

28. Round 0.301029996 to the nearest hundredth.
(6)

29. What is $\frac{3}{11}$ of 132?
(18)

30. Convert 0.015 to a fraction reduced to lowest terms.
(15)

LESSON 23   *U.S. Customary System • Unit Multipliers*

23.A

U.S. Customary System

When we attach words to numbers, as in

      4 feet   13 inches   27 yards   42 miles

we call each combination a **denominate number,** and we call the words **units.** We say that the units of the denominate number

      4 feet

are feet. In the denominate number

      32 miles per hour

we say that the units are miles per hour. The basic units of length in the **U.S. Customary System** are the inch (in.), foot (ft), yard (yd), and mile (mi). They are related by the following equivalences:

LENGTH EQUIVALENTS

12 inches = 1 foot	3 feet = 1 yard	5280 feet = 1 mile

The basic units of weight in the U.S. Customary System are the ounce (oz), pound (lb), and ton. They are related by the following equivalences:

WEIGHT EQUIVALENTS

16 ounces = 1 pound   2000 pounds = 1 ton

23.B

unit multipliers
If we multiply a number by a fraction that equals 1, we do not change the value of the number. We do change the name of the fraction. If we multiply 5 by 3 over 3, we get 15 over 3.

$$5 \times \frac{3}{3} = \frac{15}{3}$$

Fifteen divided by 3 has a value of 5 and thus is another way to write 5. Each of these fractions

$$\frac{12 \text{ in.}}{1 \text{ ft}} \qquad \frac{1 \text{ yd}}{3 \text{ ft}} \qquad \frac{5280 \text{ ft}}{1 \text{ mi}}$$

has a value of 1 because the denominators and the numerators have equal values. We call these fractions **unit multipliers** because the value of each is 1. We can use these fractions as well as their reciprocals as multipliers to change the units of denominate numbers without changing their values.

For example, to convert 5 feet to inches, we use the first unit multiplier given above. We are able to cancel units before we multiply.

$$\frac{5 \text{ ft}}{1} \times \frac{12 \text{ in.}}{1 \text{ ft}} = 60 \text{ in.}$$

In this instance, we performed the division 5 ft ÷ 1 ft, which means "how many feet are in 5 feet?" The answer is simply 5. Then we multiplied 5 × 12 in.

example 23.1   Use a unit multiplier to convert 420 feet to yards.

solution   The two unit multipliers that we can use are

$$\text{(a)} \quad \frac{3 \text{ ft}}{1 \text{ yd}} \qquad \text{and} \qquad \text{(b)} \quad \frac{1 \text{ yd}}{3 \text{ ft}}$$

We want to cancel the unit "ft" and keep the unit "yd," so we select the unit multiplier that has a numerator of yd and a denominator of ft. Then we multiply and cancel units.

$$420 \text{ ft} \times \frac{1 \text{ yd}}{3 \text{ ft}} = \frac{420}{3} \text{ yd} = \textbf{140 yd}$$

What would have happened if we had used unit multiplier (a) instead of (b)?

$$420 \text{ ft} \times \frac{3 \text{ ft}}{1 \text{ yd}} = 420 \cdot 3 \frac{\text{(ft)(ft)}}{1 \text{ yd}}$$

Aha! The mistake is obvious because "ft" did not cancel and the desired unit "yd" is not in the numerator.

example 23.2   Use a unit multiplier to convert 72 inches to feet.

solution   We have a choice of two unit multipliers.

$$\text{(a)} \quad \frac{12 \text{ in.}}{1 \text{ ft}} \qquad \text{and} \qquad \text{(b)} \quad \frac{1 \text{ ft}}{12 \text{ in.}}$$

We want to change the name of 72 inches to feet, so we choose (b) because it has "in." in the denominator and "ft" in the numerator. We will multiply 72 inches by 1 foot over 12 inches and cancel the inches.

$$72 \text{ in.} \times \frac{1 \text{ ft}}{12 \text{ in.}} = \frac{72}{12} \text{ ft} = \textbf{6 ft}$$

example 23.3   Use a unit multiplier to convert 4.6 miles to feet.

solution   There are two unit multipliers that we can use.

$$(a) \quad \frac{5280 \text{ ft}}{1 \text{ mi}} \quad \text{and} \quad (b) \quad \frac{1 \text{ mi}}{5280 \text{ ft}}$$

We decide to use (a) because it has "mi" in the denominator and "ft" in the numerator.

$$4.6 \text{ mi} \times \frac{5280 \text{ ft}}{1 \text{ mi}} = \textbf{24,288 ft}$$

example 23.4   Use a unit multiplier to convert 4 tons to pounds.

solution   The two possible unit multipliers are

$$(a) \quad \frac{2000 \text{ lb}}{1 \text{ ton}} \quad \text{and} \quad (b) \quad \frac{1 \text{ ton}}{2000 \text{ lb}}$$

We use (a) so that the tons will cancel out, leaving pounds in the answer.

$$4 \text{ ton} \times \frac{2000 \text{ lb}}{1 \text{ ton}} = \textbf{8000 lb}$$

practice   Use unit multipliers to convert:

a. 412 feet to yards   **b.** 17,200 feet to inches   **c.** 412 feet to inches

d. 48 ounces to pounds   **e.** 40,000 pounds to tons

problem set 23

1. Hortense ran nineteen thousand, seven and four hundred twenty-three thousandths
(6) centimeters in the allotted time. Then Jim ran eight thousand, forty-two and seven hundred sixty-five ten-thousandths centimeters in the allotted time. What was the sum of the distances they ran?

2. At first there were only 2,046,021 microbes. Then Muzowbe added 3 times this many
(13) microbes. How many microbes were there in all?

3. The first factory could produce 243 cars in an allotted work period. If 19,197 cars were
(11) required, how many work periods had to be allotted?

4. From the following list, Kunta selected the numbers that were divisible by 3: 40,225;
(10) 90,663; 72,205; 20,163. What was the sum of the numbers he selected?

5. (a) List the prime numbers between 60 and 70.
(12,20)
(b) Write the multiple of 9 between 60 and 70.

6. The average of four numbers is 638.4. The first three numbers are 216, 159.8, and
(21) 301.25. Find the fourth number.

Use unit multipliers to convert:

7. 120 inches to feet   **8.** 999 feet to yards   **9.** 336 ounces to pounds
(23)   (23)   (23)

Simplify:

10. $\dfrac{42}{12} \cdot \dfrac{36}{14} \div \dfrac{18}{2}$ **11.** $\dfrac{12}{16} \cdot \dfrac{4}{3} \div \dfrac{5}{6}$ **12.** $\dfrac{16}{24} \cdot \dfrac{12}{4} \cdot \dfrac{1}{2}$
(22)   (22)   (22)

13. Find the perimeter of the following
(9) figure. Dimensions are in yards. All
angles are right angles.

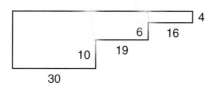

14. Find the area of the following figure.
(17) Dimensions are in meters. All angles
are right angles.

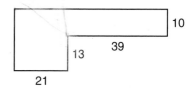

Write each number as a product of prime numbers using exponents:

15. 2880
(16)

16. 6750
(16)

Write each fraction as a decimal number. Round to two decimal places.

17. $\dfrac{13}{19}$
(15)

18. $\dfrac{17}{20}$
(15)

Reduce each fraction to lowest terms:

19. $\dfrac{180}{256}$
(14)

20. $\dfrac{240}{600}$
(14)

21. $\dfrac{540}{2160}$
(14)

Multiply:

22. 71.2×0.173
(7)

23. 61.7×11.2
(7)

24. Find LCM (18, 81, 270).
(20)

25. List the first three common multiples of 10, 15, and 20.
(20)

Divide. Write the answer as a repeating decimal if necessary.

26. $\dfrac{713.7}{2.5}$
(7)

27. $\dfrac{7181.3}{0.3}$
(7,15)

28. Multiply: $\dfrac{3}{4} \cdot 400$
(18)

Find the missing numbers:

29. $71.161 - Q = 0.8121$
(3,6)

30. $\dfrac{2}{3} \cdot B = \dfrac{3}{8}$
(4,19)

LESSON 24 *Metric System*

The advantage to the metric system, or International System (SI), is its simplicity. All you
have to do to convert from one metric unit to another is to multiply or divide by a power of
ten. Thus, you simply move the decimal point. The base unit of length in the metric system
is the meter (m). A meter is just a little longer than a yard.

Mass is the amount of matter in an object. Measurements of mass are compared to the
standard kilogram. (The standard is a platinum-iridium alloy kept at the International Bureau
of Weights and Measures in France.) Thus, the base unit of mass in the metric system is the
kilogram and the root unit is the gram. A kilogram is about 2.2 pounds.

Units larger or smaller than the root unit are indicated by prefixes that are consistent across the categories of measurement. Some of these prefixes are shown in the table below with their numerical meanings and their usages in length and mass.

METRIC PREFIXES

Prefix	Abbreviation	Power of 10	Length	Mass
kilo-	k	1000	kilometer (km)	kilogram (kg)
hecto-	h	100	hectometer (hm)	hectogram (hg)
deka-	dk	10	dekameter (dkm)	dekagram (dkg)
–	–	1	meter (m)	gram (g)
deci-	d	$\frac{1}{10}$	decimeter (dm)	decigram (dg)
centi-	c	$\frac{1}{100}$	centimeter (cm)	centigram (cg)
milli-	m	$\frac{1}{1000}$	millimeter (mm)	milligram (mg)

From this chart we can derive equivalences and form unit multipliers. For example,

$$1 \text{ cm} = \frac{1}{100} \text{ m}$$

From this we find the equivalence

$$100 \text{ cm} = 1 \text{ m}$$

Similarly, we can derive that

$$1000 \text{ g} = 1 \text{ kg}$$

The four unit multipliers that we can form from these equivalences are

$$\frac{100 \text{ cm}}{1 \text{ m}} \qquad \frac{1 \text{ m}}{100 \text{ cm}} \qquad \frac{1000 \text{ g}}{1 \text{ kg}} \qquad \frac{1 \text{ kg}}{1000 \text{ g}}$$

example 24.1   Convert 528 centimeters to meters.

solution   We may choose either

$$\text{(a)} \quad \frac{100 \text{ cm}}{1 \text{ m}} \qquad \text{or} \qquad \text{(b)} \quad \frac{1 \text{ m}}{100 \text{ cm}}$$

We will use (b) because "cm" is in the denominator and "m" is in the numerator.

$$528 \text{ cm} \times \frac{1 \text{ m}}{100 \text{ cm}} = \frac{528}{100} \text{ m} = \textbf{5.28 m}$$

Note that 528 cm equals 5.28 m. All we had to do was move the decimal point!

example 24.2   Convert 486 kilograms to grams.

solution   We will use the unit multiplier that has "kg" in the denominator and "g" in the numerator.

$$486 \text{ kg} \times \frac{1000 \text{ g}}{1 \text{ kg}} = \textbf{486,000 g}$$

We simply move the decimal point.

example 24.3   Convert 350 decimeters to meters.

solution   We may choose either

$$\text{(a)} \quad \frac{10 \text{ dm}}{1 \text{ m}} \qquad \text{or} \qquad \text{(b)} \quad \frac{1 \text{ m}}{10 \text{ dm}}$$

We choose (b) because "dm" is in the denominator and "m" is in the numerator.

$$350 \text{ dm} \times \frac{1 \text{ m}}{10 \text{ dm}} = 35 \text{ m}$$

Once again, the answer has the same digits, and we simply moved the decimal point.

practice Use unit multipliers to convert:

    a. 58 meters to centimeters

    b. 100 meters to kilometers

    c. 48,000 milligrams to grams

problem set 24

1. At the turn of the century, fourteen thousand, seven items were on the proscribed list. Thirty years later only seven thousand, nine hundred forty-two remained on this list. How many had been removed?
(5)

2. Mary measured it first. She got one hundred forty-seven and nine hundred twenty-three millionths inches. Then Jim tried. He got one hundred forty-six and three thousand, one hundred forty-two ten-thousandths inches. By how much was Mary's measurement greater?
(6)

3. Each slot could hold only 47 balls. If there were 1982 balls, how many slots were needed to hold them all?
(11)

4. Which of the following numbers are divisible by: (a) 2? (b) 10?
(10)
    40,613   90,528   71,423   4020

5. (a) List the prime numbers between 20 and 30.
(12,20)
    (b) List the multiples of 4 between 20 and 30.

6. Find the average of 98, 142, 76, 81, and 6.
(21)

Use unit multipliers to convert:

7. 859 centimeters to meters
(24)

8. 6400 kilometers to meters
(24)

9. 204 inches to feet
(23)

10. 17 tons to pounds
(23)

11. 50,000 centigrams to grams
(24)

Simplify:

12. $\dfrac{16}{24} \cdot \dfrac{12}{4} \cdot \dfrac{1}{3}$
(22)

13. $\dfrac{18}{24} \cdot \dfrac{8}{9} \cdot \dfrac{3}{2}$
(22)

14. $\dfrac{14}{21} \cdot \dfrac{7}{2} \div \dfrac{14}{6}$
(22)

15. Find the perimeter of the following figure. Dimensions are in feet. All angles are right angles.
(9)

16. Find the area of the following figure. Dimensions are in inches. All angles are right angles.
(17)

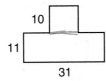

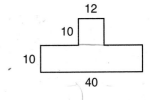

17. List the first three common multiples of 5 and 15.
(20)

18. List all the common factors of 12 and 18.
(13)

Write each fraction as a decimal. Round to two decimal places.

19. $\dfrac{3}{14}$ **20.** $\dfrac{19}{25}$ **21.** $\dfrac{81}{135}$
(15)   (15)   (15)

Reduce each fraction to lowest terms:

22. $\dfrac{24}{72}$ **23.** $\dfrac{18}{24}$
(14)   (14)

24. Find GCF (180, 300).
(13)

25. Convert 0.035 to a fraction reduced to lowest terms.
(15)

26. Find the missing number: $\dfrac{X}{0.7} = 10.23$
(4,7)

27. Write each fraction with a denominator of 42:
(14)

   (a) $\dfrac{3}{14}$ (b) $\dfrac{4}{7}$ (c) $\dfrac{33}{126}$

28. Round $218.0\overline{97}$ to the nearest millionth.
(15)

29. Find LCM (20, 25, 36).
(20)

30. What is $\frac{3}{10}$ of 35?
(18)

LESSON 25 *Area as a Difference*

We have been finding the areas of figures by adding rectangular areas. Sometimes we can find the total area by finding the difference of rectangular areas.

example 25.1 Use the difference of areas to find the area of this figure. Dimensions are in meters. All angles are right angles.

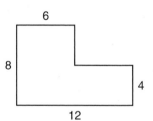

solution We add dashed lines to complete the whole rectangle. The dimensions of the small rectangle *B* are found by subtracting 6 m from 12 m and 4 m from 8 m.

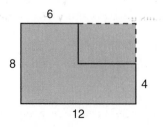
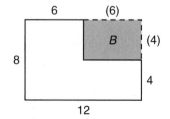

Then we can find the area of the whole rectangle and subtract from it the area of the small rectangle *B*.

Area of whole rectangle: Area of rectangle *B*:

$8 \text{ m} \times 12 \text{ m} = 96 \text{ m}^2$ $6 \text{ m} \times 4 \text{ m} = 24 \text{ m}^2$

Thus, the area of the figure is

$$96 \text{ m}^2 - 24 \text{ m}^2 = \textbf{72 m}^2$$

example 25.2   Use the difference of areas to find the area of this figure. Dimensions are in feet. All angles are right angles.

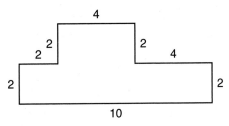

solution   We use dashed lines to complete the whole rectangle. Then we find the area of the whole rectangle, and from this we subtract the areas of the two small rectangles *A* and *B*.

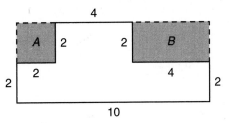

Area of whole rectangle: $4 \text{ ft} \times 10 \text{ ft} = 40 \text{ ft}^2$

Area of rectangle *A*: $2 \text{ ft} \times 2 \text{ ft} = 4 \text{ ft}^2$

Area of rectangle *B*: $2 \text{ ft} \times 4 \text{ ft} = 8 \text{ ft}^2$

Area of figure $= 40 \text{ ft}^2 - 4 \text{ ft}^2 - 8 \text{ ft}^2 = \textbf{28 ft}^2$

practice   Use the difference of areas to find the area of each figure. All angles are right angles.

    a.   Dimensions are in centimeters.   **b.**   Dimensions are in feet.

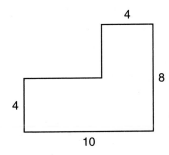 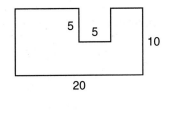

problem set 25

1. In the first month, ten thousand, forty-two students used the library. In the second
   ⁽¹³⁾ month, 4 times this number used the library. In the third month, only four thousand, seventy-five students used the library. How many students used the library in all?

2. The flowers proliferated until they numbered 17,842. Then the first frost killed 9085.
   ⁽⁵⁾ How many flowers were still alive?

3. The first night 482 monkeys came. Five times this number came on the second night.
   ⁽¹³⁾ On the third night only 392 came. How many came in all?

4. Which of the following numbers are divisible by 3?
(10)

             315,234   906,185   21,387   4072

5. (a) List the prime numbers between 40 and 50.
(12,20)
    (b) List the multiples of 3 between 40 and 50.

6. The average of six numbers is 48.6. The first five numbers are 6.2, 5.1, 9.8, 8.8, and 10.
(21)
    Find the sixth number.

Use unit multipliers to convert:

7. 46.31 meters to centimeters   **8.** 48 miles to feet
(24)   (23)

9. 416 grams to kilograms   **10.** 2.54 centimeters to meters
(24)   (24)

Simplify:

11. $\dfrac{42}{24} \cdot \dfrac{6}{7} \cdot \dfrac{2}{3}$ **12.** $\dfrac{72}{48} \cdot \dfrac{8}{9} \cdot \dfrac{3}{4}$ **13.** $\dfrac{2}{3} \cdot \dfrac{27}{64} \div \dfrac{3}{16}$
(22)   (22)   (22)

14. Find the perimeter of the following   **15.** Use the difference of areas to find the
(9) figure. Dimensions are in feet. All   (25) area of this figure. Dimensions are in
    angles are right angles.   meters. All angles are right angles.

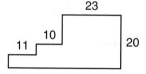
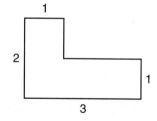

Write each number as a product of prime numbers using exponents:

16. 288   **17.** 630
(16)   (16)

Write each fraction as a decimal. Round to two decimal places.

18. $\dfrac{3}{19}$ **19.** $\dfrac{8}{23}$
(15)   (15)

Reduce each fraction to lowest terms:

20. $\dfrac{39}{72}$ **21.** $\dfrac{210}{420}$ **22.** $\dfrac{125}{360}$
(14)   (14)   (14)

23. Find GCF (42, 63).
(13)

24. Convert 0.18 to a fraction reduced to lowest terms.
(15)

25. What is $\frac{7}{8}$ of 32?
(18)

Find the missing numbers:

26. M **27.** $\dfrac{7}{20} \div Z = \dfrac{6}{5}$
(3,6) $\underline{- \ 1.38}$ (4,19)
       9.93

Divide. Round to two decimal places.

28. $\dfrac{625.8}{1.7}$ **29.** $\dfrac{1361.4}{0.4}$
(7)   (7)

30. Find LCM (24, 100).
(20)

LESSON 26   Mode, Median, Mean, and Range • Average in Word Problems

26.A
mode, median, mean, and range

In statistics, three words that are used to describe the central tendency of a set of numbers are **mode, median,** and **mean.** In this set of numbers

2, 2, 2, 2, 2, 7, 8, 8, 9, 10, and 784

the number 2 appears more than any other number. We say that the number that appears the most often is the mode of a set of numbers. If a set of numbers has no number that appears two or more times, then the set of numbers has no mode. In a set of numbers arranged from least to greatest, we call the middle number the median. In this set, the number 7 is the median, or the middle number. If we add the numbers and divide this sum by the number of numbers in the set, we find what is called the mean of a set of numbers.

$$\text{Mean} = \frac{2 + 2 + 2 + 2 + 2 + 7 + 8 + 8 + 9 + 10 + 784}{11} = 76$$

One other measure in statistics that is easy to find is the **range,** which is the numerical difference between the least and greatest numbers in the set. The range of the set above is $784 - 2 = 782$.

Beginners often have difficulty remembering that *mean* and *average* are two words with the same meaning. We will use the word *mean* often in the problem sets so that this word becomes familiar.

example 26.1   A high school counselor administered a math test to twelve eighth-grade students for their high school placement. The students had the following scores:

40, 30, 43, 48, 26, 50, 55, 40, 34, 42, 47, 50

Find the (a) range, (b) mode, (c) median, and (d) mean of this set of scores. Round any decimal results to two decimal places.

solution   We begin by arranging the scores in order from least to greatest.

26, 30, 34, 40, 40, 42, 43, 47, 48, 50, 50, 55

(a)   The greatest score is 55 and the least score is 26. The range of the scores is the difference between these two scores.

$$55 - 26 = \mathbf{29}$$

(b)   In this set of scores, 40 and 50 both appear twice in the list, and no number appears more than twice. Thus, there are two modes, **40** and **50.** Sets of numbers with two modes are called **bimodal.**

(c)   There are twelve numbers in our set. Therefore there is no middle number. The median of an even number of scores is the mean—the average—of the two middle scores. Our two middle scores are 42 and 43, thus the median is

$$\frac{42 + 43}{2} = \mathbf{42.5}$$

(d)   We add the twelve numbers and divide the sum by 12 to find the mean.

$$\frac{26 + 30 + 34 + 40 + 40 + 42 + 43 + 47 + 48 + 50 + 50 + 55}{12} = \frac{505}{12}$$

$$\approx \mathbf{42.08}$$

26.B

**average in
word problems**

Many word problems require that we find the average, or the mean, of a set of numbers.

example 26.2 When the boys measured the distance three times, they got three different answers. If the measurements were 4.017 meters, 4.212 meters, and 3.996 meters, what was the mean of the three measurements?

solution We add the three numbers and then divide the sum by 3.

$$
\begin{array}{r}
4.017 \text{ m} \\
4.212 \text{ m} \\
+\ 3.996 \text{ m} \\
\hline
12.225 \text{ m}
\end{array}
\qquad
\text{Mean} = \frac{12.225 \text{ m}}{3} = \textbf{4.075 m}
$$

example 26.3 When Athena sprang in full armor from the head of Zeus, two other gods guessed the weight of her panoply. One guess was 41.802 kilograms, and the other guess was 37.408 kilograms. What was the mean of the two guesses?

solution We add the two numbers and then divide the sum by 2.

$$
\begin{array}{r}
41.802 \text{ kg} \\
+\ 37.408 \text{ kg} \\
\hline
79.210 \text{ kg}
\end{array}
\qquad
\text{Mean} = \frac{79.21 \text{ kg}}{2} = \textbf{39.605 kg}
$$

example 26.4 The mean weight of the three pigs was 320 pounds. The first pig weighed 220 pounds and the second pig weighed 240 pounds. How much did the third pig weigh?

solution If the mean of the three weights is 320 pounds, the sum of the weights is 320 pounds times 3, or 960 pounds. We will call our missing weight P.

$$220 \text{ lb} + 240 \text{ lb} + P = 960 \text{ lb}$$

This is a missing-addend problem. We find P by first adding the weights on the left side of the equals sign.

$$460 \text{ lb} + P = 960 \text{ lb}$$

We subtract to find the weight of the third pig.

$$P = 960 \text{ lb} - 460 \text{ lb} = \textbf{500 lb}$$

practice **a.** Find the (a) range, (b) mode, (c) median, and (d) mean of the following numbers: 9, 8, 2, 4, 5, 4, 6. Round any decimal results to two places.

b. The height of the first of the three buildings was 420 ft. The height of the second building was 380 ft. What was the height of the third building if the mean height of the three buildings was 430 ft?

**problem set
26**

1.
(26) The mean weight of the four trucks was 3700 pounds. The first truck weighed 3250 pounds, the second truck weighed 3890 pounds, and the third truck weighed 3640 pounds. How much did the fourth truck weigh?

2.
(26) Members initially estimated that the club's first rocketry experiment would reach an altitude of 214.063 meters. Later, club members estimated that the rocket would reach an altitude of at least 435.09 meters. What was the mean of their estimations?

3.
(26) Find the mean of the first eight prime numbers.

4. (a) Which of the following numbers are divisible by 3?
(10,26)

$$41,625 \quad 9081 \quad 20,733 \quad 10,662$$

(b) What is the mean of the numbers that are divisible by 3?

5. There were 325 pellets in every beanbag. The shipment contained 495,625 pellets. This
(11) would be enough pellets to make how many beanbags?

6. The first toss was 60,152.035 meters. The second toss was 82,006.012 meters. By how
(6) many meters was the second toss greater?

Use unit multipliers to convert:

7. 136.15 centimeters to meters
(24)

8. 12 miles to feet
(23)

9. 1899 meters to kilometers
(24)

Simplify:

10. $\dfrac{21}{36} \cdot \dfrac{12}{14} \cdot \dfrac{2}{3}$
(22)

11. $\dfrac{36}{42} \cdot \dfrac{21}{9} \cdot \dfrac{1}{2}$
(22)

12. $\dfrac{28}{36} \cdot \dfrac{8}{21} \div \dfrac{16}{27}$
(22)

13. Find the area. Dimensions are in
(17) meters. All angles are right angles.

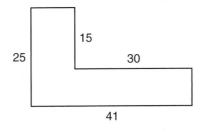

14. Use the difference of areas to find the
(25) area of this figure. Dimensions are in
feet. All angles are right angles.

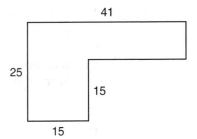

15. Simplify: $\left(\dfrac{8}{3}\right)^3$
(16)

16. Find LCM (12, 26, 39).
(20)

Write each fraction as a decimal. Round to two decimal places.

17. $\dfrac{7}{13}$
(15)

18. $\dfrac{11}{17}$
(15)

Reduce each fraction to lowest terms:

19. $\dfrac{24}{28}$
(14)

20. $\dfrac{240}{300}$
(14)

21. $\dfrac{144}{256}$
(14)

22. Convert 0.004 to a fraction reduced to lowest terms.
(15)

23. Find $\frac{4}{11}$ of 132.
(18)

Subtract. Add to check.

24. 1361.78 − 31.921
(6)

25. 789.891 − 77.892
(6)

Divide. Round to two decimal places.

26. $\dfrac{7621.1}{2.1}$
(7)

27. $\dfrac{3.623}{0.02}$
(7)

28. Find the (a) range, (b) mode, (c) median, and (d) mean of the following set of
(26)   numbers: 6, 4, 6, 1, 7, 2, 6. Round any decimal results to two places.

29. Find the missing number: $\dfrac{B}{0.556} = 32$
(4,7)

30. Find GCF (48, 60, 78).
(13)

LESSON 27   *Areas of Triangles*

An **altitude,** or a **height,** of a triangle is the perpendicular distance from the base of the
triangle or extension of the base to the opposite vertex, or corner. Any one of the three sides
can be designated as the base. Thus, a triangle has a different height relative to each side.

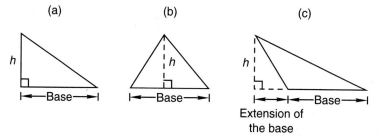

The altitude, h, can be one of the sides of the triangle (a), fall inside the triangle (b), or fall
outside the triangle (c). When the altitude falls outside the triangle, we have to extend the
base so that the altitude can be drawn. This extension of the base is not part of the length of
the base. The formula for the area of any triangle is the product of the base and height
divided by 2.

$$\text{Area of a triangle} = \frac{\text{base} \times \text{height}}{2}$$

example 27.1   Find the areas of these triangles. Dimensions are in inches.

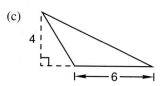

solution   The base of each triangle is 6 in. and the height of each triangle is 4 in. Thus, all the triangles
have the same area.

$$\text{Area} = \frac{\text{base} \times \text{height}}{2} = \frac{6 \text{ in.} \times 4 \text{ in.}}{2} = \textbf{12 in.}^2$$

practice   Find the area of each triangle. Dimensions are in feet.

a.
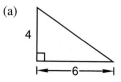

b.
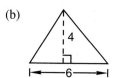

c.
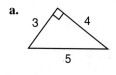

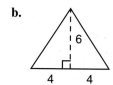

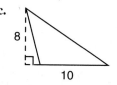

problem set 27

1. The first shift produced 14,782 units. The second shift produced 18,962 units. The third shift produced only 2085 units. By how many units did the production of the second shift exceed the sum of the production of the first and third shifts?
(5)

2. Seven thousand, four hundred eight hundred-thousandths was Mary's guess. Tom guessed six thousand, five hundred eighty-two ten-thousandths. Whose guess was larger and by how much?
(6)

3. Nine hundred eighty-four was increased by one hundred forty-seven thousand, seventeen. Then this sum was doubled. What was the final result?
(13)

4. Find the average of the prime numbers that are greater than 20 but less than 42.
(26)

5. The first number was 743. The second number was 486. The third number was twice the sum of the first two. What was the mean of the three numbers?
(26)

6. Which of the following numbers are divisible by 5?
(10)

$$41,320 \qquad 90,183 \qquad 76,142 \qquad 9405 \qquad 50,172$$

Use unit multipliers to convert:

7. 45 pounds to ounces
(23)

8. 81 feet to yards
(23)

9. 4899 meters to centimeters
(24)

Simplify:

10. $\dfrac{20}{24} \cdot \dfrac{6}{15} \cdot \dfrac{2}{3}$
(22)

11. $\dfrac{16}{20} \cdot \dfrac{5}{8} \div \dfrac{1}{4}$
(22)

12. $\dfrac{18}{20} \cdot \dfrac{5}{3} \div \dfrac{6}{9}$
(22)

13. Find the perimeter of this figure. Dimensions are in feet. All angles are right angles.
(9)

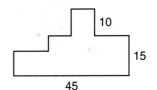

Find the area of each figure. Dimensions are in feet.

14.
(27)

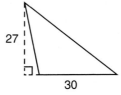

15.
(27)

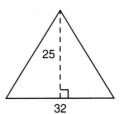

Write each number as a product of prime numbers using exponents:

16. 324
(16)

17. 2916
(16)

Write each fraction as a decimal. Round to two decimal places.

18. $\dfrac{7}{17}$
(15)

19. $\dfrac{7}{13}$
(15)

20. $\dfrac{7}{200}$
(15)

Reduce each fraction to lowest terms:

21. $\dfrac{72}{120}$
(14)

22. $\dfrac{280}{360}$
(14)

23. Write 0.125 as a fraction reduced to lowest terms.
(15)

24. Find the (a) range, (b) mode, (c) median, and (d) mean of the following list of
(26)   numbers: 9, 9, 23, 2, 10, 3, 9, 3

25. What is $\frac{4}{9}$ of 270?
(18)

26. Order from least to greatest: 112.091, 112.9, 1129.0, 112.00956
(8)

Divide. Round each answer to two decimal places.

27. $\dfrac{611.32}{0.04}$ **28.** $\dfrac{0.0062}{0.07}$
(7)   (7)

29. Find LCM (10, 14, 25).
(20)

30. Find the missing number: $\left(\dfrac{3}{2}\right)F = \dfrac{67}{4}$
(4,19)

LESSON 28 *Improper Fractions, Mixed Numbers, and Decimal Numbers*

improper fractions and mixed numbers

If the numerator of the fraction is less than the denominator of the fraction, the fraction represents a number less than 1 and is called a **proper fraction.** The fraction $\frac{2}{3}$ has a numerator that is less than the denominator and is therefore a proper fraction.

$\dfrac{2}{3}$ designates a number less than 1, as we see in the figure

1

If the numerator of a fraction is greater than or equal to the denominator of the fraction, the fraction represents a number greater than or equal to 1, and the fraction is called an **improper fraction.** Thus, the number

$$\frac{10}{3}$$

can be called an improper fraction. To illustrate this improper fraction, we note that the denominator is 3 and draw a circle divided into three equal parts.

The fraction $\frac{10}{3}$ tells us that we are considering 10 of these parts, each of which is $\frac{1}{3}$ of a whole.

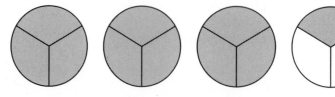

Each of the first three circles has 3 shaded parts equal to $\frac{1}{3}$ of a whole. The last circle has 1 shaded part for a total of 10 shaded parts. From this we can see that the number represented by $\frac{10}{3}$ is the same number as the number represented by $3\frac{1}{3}$.

$$\frac{10}{3} \quad \text{equals} \quad 3\frac{1}{3}$$

The number $3\frac{1}{3}$ has two parts. One part is the number 3, which is a whole number. The other part is the fraction $\frac{1}{3}$. We call a number that has both a whole number part and a fractional part a **mixed number.** We note that $3\frac{1}{3}$ really means

$$\text{three plus one third} \quad \text{or} \quad 3 + \frac{1}{3}$$

Because we use mixed numbers so often, we omit the plus sign to make the number easier to write. But we must remember that

$$3\frac{1}{3} \quad \text{means} \quad 3 + \frac{1}{3}$$

improper fraction to mixed number

To change an improper fraction to a mixed number, we divide the denominator into the numerator. The whole number part of the answer is the whole number part of the mixed number. The remainder will be the numerator of the fraction of the mixed number, and the denominator remains the same.

To convert the improper fraction $\frac{10}{3}$ to a mixed number, we divide the 3 into the 10.

$$3\overline{)10} = 3 \text{ r } 1$$
$$\underline{9}$$
$$1$$

This tells us that $\frac{10}{3}$ represents 3 wholes, with a remainder of 1. So

$$\frac{10}{3} = 3\frac{1}{3}$$

example 28.1 Convert the following improper fractions to mixed numbers:

(a) $\dfrac{14}{5}$ (b) $\dfrac{21}{8}$ (c) $\dfrac{30}{4}$

solution In each case we divide the denominator into the numerator to find the number of wholes represented by the fraction. The remainder will be the numerator of the fraction of the mixed number, and the denominator will remain the same. We must remember to reduce the fractional part to lowest terms.

(a) $\dfrac{14}{5} \longrightarrow 5\overline{)14}$ so $\dfrac{14}{5} = 2 \text{ r } 4$ Thus, $\dfrac{14}{5}$ can be written as $2\dfrac{4}{5}$.
$\phantom{(a) \dfrac{14}{5} \longrightarrow 5)}\underline{10}$
$\phantom{(a) \dfrac{14}{5} \longrightarrow 5)}4$

(b) $\dfrac{21}{8} \longrightarrow 8\overline{)21}$ so $\dfrac{21}{8} = 2 \text{ r } 5$ Thus, $\dfrac{21}{8}$ can be written as $2\dfrac{5}{8}$.
$\phantom{(b) \dfrac{21}{8} \longrightarrow 8)}\underline{16}$
$\phantom{(b) \dfrac{21}{8} \longrightarrow 8)}5$

(c) $\dfrac{30}{4} \longrightarrow 4\overline{)30}$ so $\dfrac{30}{4} = 7 \text{ r } 2$ Thus, $\dfrac{30}{4}$ can be written as $7\dfrac{2}{4} = 7\dfrac{1}{2}$.
$\phantom{(c) \dfrac{30}{4} \longrightarrow 4)}\underline{28}$
$\phantom{(c) \dfrac{30}{4} \longrightarrow 4)}2$

mixed number to improper fraction

In the preceding section we found that $\frac{10}{3}$ and $3\frac{1}{3}$ were equal numerals,

$$\frac{10}{3} = 3\frac{1}{3}$$

and we found that the mixed number that is equal to $\frac{10}{3}$ can be found by dividing 10 by 3.

$$3\overline{)10} \qquad \text{so} \qquad \frac{10}{3} = 3\frac{1}{3}$$
$$\underline{9}$$
$$1$$

To go the other way and find the improper fraction represented by the mixed number $3\frac{1}{3}$, we will use our picture of $3\frac{1}{3}$ again.

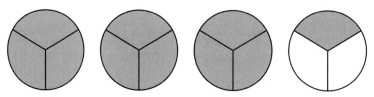

We see here that the number $3\frac{1}{3}$ is composed of ten parts, each with a size of $\frac{1}{3}$. Nine of these one thirds come from the whole number 3, and one of them comes from the fraction $\frac{1}{3}$. We can say, therefore, that the mixed number $3\frac{1}{3}$ is the same as the improper fraction $\frac{10}{3}$.

For another example, we will write $2\frac{1}{8}$ as an improper fraction. To do this, we must find out how many $\frac{1}{8}$'s there are in 2 and then add one more $\frac{1}{8}$.

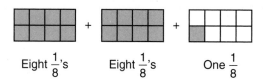

Eight $\dfrac{1}{8}$'s   Eight $\dfrac{1}{8}$'s   One $\dfrac{1}{8}$

Eight $\dfrac{1}{8}$'s plus eight $\dfrac{1}{8}$'s plus one $\dfrac{1}{8}$ equals seventeen $\dfrac{1}{8}$'s, or $\dfrac{17}{8}$.

Thus, the procedure for finding the improper fraction represented by a mixed number is to (1) find the number of fractional parts in the whole number, and then (2) add to this the number of fractional parts designated by the fraction. We can do this in two steps:

1. Multiply the denominator of the fraction by the whole number.
2. Add this product to the numerator of the fraction and record the sum over the denominator of the fraction.

Thus, to write $5\frac{3}{11}$ as an improper fraction, we write

$$5\frac{3}{11} = \frac{11 \times 5 + 3}{11} = \frac{58}{11}$$

Some people find it helpful to remember the procedure by thinking of it as a semi-circular process.

$$5\frac{3}{11} = 5\overset{+}{\underset{\times}{\frac{3}{11}}} = \frac{11 \times 5 + 3}{11} = \frac{55 + 3}{11} = \frac{58}{11}$$

We begin at the bottom with 11, multiply by 5, add 3, and record the sum over 11.

example 28.2   Write $7\frac{4}{9}$ as an improper fraction.

solution   We multiply 9 by 7 to get 63 and then add 4 to get the numerator of 67. Then we record this over the denominator of 9.

$$7\frac{4}{9} = 7\overset{+}{\underset{\times}{\frac{4}{9}}} = \frac{9 \times 7 + 4}{9} = \frac{63 + 4}{9} = \mathbf{\frac{67}{9}}$$

mixed number to decimal To change a mixed number to a decimal, let the whole number part of the mixed number be the whole number part of the decimal number (i.e., to the left of the decimal point), and convert the fractional part to a decimal number as we did in Lesson 15.

example 28.3 Convert the following mixed numbers to decimals: (a) $3\frac{1}{8}$ (b) $32\frac{1}{5}$

solution (a)
$$\begin{array}{r} 0.125 \\ 8\overline{)1.000} \\ \underline{8} \\ 20 \\ \underline{16} \\ 40 \\ \underline{40} \\ 0 \end{array}$$
Since $\frac{1}{8} = 0.125$, $3\frac{1}{8} = \textbf{3.125}$

(b) $\frac{1}{5} = \frac{2}{10} = 0.2$ Since $\frac{1}{5} = 0.2$, $32\frac{1}{5} = \textbf{32.2}$

decimal to mixed number This is easy. Just "say the number" as in Lesson 15. For example, 3.1 = "three and one tenth" = $3\frac{1}{10}$. Caution: Do not forget to reduce the fraction to lowest terms, if possible!

practice Convert each mixed number to an improper fraction:

a. $5\frac{2}{3}$ b. $6\frac{7}{8}$

Convert each improper fraction to a mixed number:

c. $\frac{14}{3}$ d. $\frac{23}{5}$

e. Write $157\frac{1}{6}$ as a decimal number rounded to two decimal places.

f. Write 5.09 as a mixed number.

problem set 28

1. *(6)* Four hundred seventeen ten-thousandths is how much greater than four hundred seventeen hundred-thousandths?

2. *(13)* The first flock contained 5283 birds. The second flock contained 5 times as many birds. The third flock had twice as many birds as the second flock. How many birds were there in all?

3. *(1,4)* Seven times 4,820,718 is a very large number. Write this number in words.

4. *(26)* Find the average of the prime numbers that are greater than 10 and less than 25.

Convert each improper fraction to a mixed number:

5. *(28)* $\frac{17}{9}$ 6. *(28)* $\frac{24}{7}$

7. *(28)* Draw a diagram that shows why $4\frac{1}{4}$ equals $\frac{17}{4}$.

Convert each mixed number to an improper fraction reduced to lowest terms:

8. $6\frac{2}{9}$
(28)

9. $8\frac{4}{7}$
(28)

10. $5\frac{2}{8}$
(28)

Use unit multipliers to convert:

11. 192.72 centimeters to meters
(24)

12. 17 miles to feet
(23)

Simplify. If possible, cancel as the first step.

13. $\frac{28}{36} \cdot \frac{24}{21} \cdot \frac{3}{16}$
(22)

14. $\frac{18}{24} \cdot \frac{36}{28} \cdot \frac{14}{27}$
(22)

15. $\frac{16}{18} \cdot \frac{16}{12} \div \frac{8}{9}$
(22)

16. Find the area of the following figure
(17,27) (total area = area of rectangle + area of triangle). Dimensions are in feet. All angles that look like right angles are right angles.

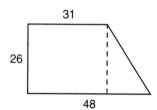

31

26

48

17. Express the perimeter of the following
(9,24) figure in centimeters. Dimensions are in meters. All angles are right angles.

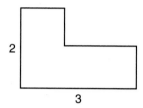

2

3

18. Write 1440 as a product of prime numbers using exponents.
(16)

Write each mixed number as a decimal. Round to two decimal places.

19. $5\frac{16}{23}$
(28)

20. $9\frac{7}{19}$
(28)

Reduce each fraction to lowest terms:

21. $\frac{36}{42}$
(14)

22. $\frac{280}{320}$
(14)

23. $\frac{125}{175}$
(14)

24. List the multiples of 3 that are greater than 15 and less than 30.
(20)

25. Find LCM (9, 18, 60).
(20)

26. Subtract (add to check): 172.325 − 61.89
(6)

27. Divide. Round to two decimal places: $\frac{7811.3}{0.03}$
(7)

28. Find the missing number: 21.1101 − H = 0.1001
(3,6)

29. Janet scored 82, 100, 85, 92, 86, 72, 85, and 97. Find the (a) range, (b) mode,
(26) (c) median, and (d) mean of her scores.

30. Write 531.25 as a mixed number.
(28)

LESSON *29* *Graphs*

Graphs are used to present numerical information in picture form. Two common forms of graphs are **bar graphs** and **broken-line graphs.** The two graphs shown here present the same information.

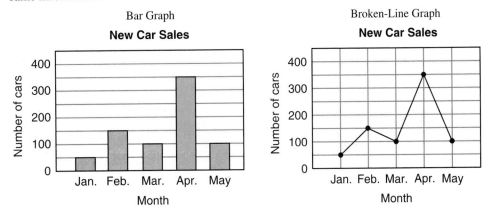

Both graphs show sales of new cars each month from January through May. Some people believe that the bar graph is easier to interpret, whereas others prefer broken-line graphs. Note that exact information cannot be obtained from either kind of graph.

Good graphs contain several important components. Every graph must have a title, so that people reading the graph know immediately what the graph illustrates. The quantities plotted vertically and horizontally should be clearly labeled and should have subtitles to explain what they represent. Also, care should be taken when choosing the scale. Whenever possible, the major divisions on a scale should be divisible by 2 or by 5. Scales in which the major divisions are numbers such as 3 or 7 are often difficult to read. Major divisions should also be spaced equally both horizontally and vertically.

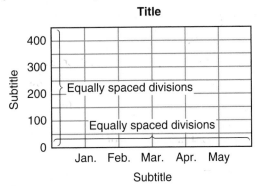

example 29.1   Based on the following graph, how many more cars were sold in April than were sold in January?

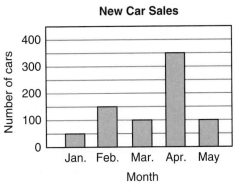

solution   We cannot read the graph exactly, but it appears that 350 cars were sold in April, whereas only 50 were sold in January.

$$350 - 50 = \textbf{300 more cars} \text{ were sold in April}$$

example 29.2   The daily high temperatures recorded during the week were as follows: Monday, 86°F; Tuesday, 80°F; Wednesday, 75°F; Thursday, 82°F; Friday, 88°F; Saturday, 74°F; and Sunday, 84°F. Make a bar graph and a broken-line graph that present this information.

solution   It is not necessary to show the full vertical scale. We will use a vertical scale that goes between 70°F and 100°F.

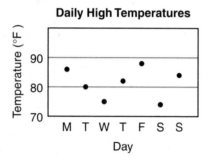

In the figure on the left below, we draw bars of proper heights to make a bar graph, and in the figure on the right, we connect the points with straight lines to make a broken-line graph.

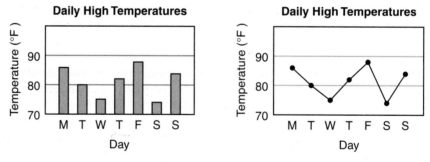

Another type of graph is the **pie graph.** As with bar graphs and broken-line graphs, it is important to use descriptive labels on pie graphs so that they can be easily understood.

example 29.3   Based on the following pie graph, how much more money did Juan spend on meats, fruits, vegetables, breads, and dairy products than on entertainment and junk food?

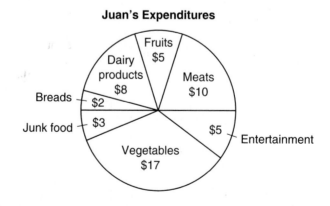

solution   First we find how much Juan spent on meats, fruits, vegetables, breads, and dairy products.

$$\$10 + \$5 + \$17 + \$2 + \$8 = \$42$$

Now we find how much he spent on entertainment and junk food.

$$\$5 + \$3 = \$8$$

Since the question is "how much more," we find the difference.

$$\$42 - \$8 = \mathbf{\$34}$$

practice   **a.**   In this graph, what is the average number of type B cars sold in the 3 years shown?

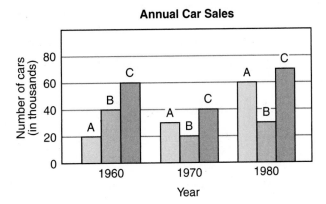

Annual Car Sales

problem set   **1.**   The lowest temperature recorded on Monday was 71°F; Tuesday, 68°F; Wednesday,
29   (29)   60°F; Thursday, 66°F; and Friday, 73°F. Make a broken line graph that presents this
information.

2.   The first try flew nineteen thousand and seventy-five millionths feet. The second try
(6)   flew twenty-one thousand and one thousand, three millionths feet. What was the sum
of the distances in the two tries?

3.   In the first hour, fourteen thousand, nine hundred eighty-two visitors entered the theme
(13)   park. Then, during the rest of the day, 10 times this number came. How many came in
all?

4.   What is the mean of the prime numbers greater than 30 but less than 45?
(26)

5.   One truck could carry 840 toasters. If 19,420 toasters had to be transported, how many
(11)   trucks were required?

6.   In the preceding problem, if only 18 trucks could be located, how many toasters had to
(11)   be left on the loading dock?

7.   Find $\frac{5}{6}$ of 48.   **8.**   Find $\frac{6}{7}$ of 35.
(18)   (18)

Convert each improper fraction to a mixed number:

9. $\dfrac{15}{7}$ **10.** $\dfrac{21}{5}$
(28)   (28)

11.   Draw a diagram that shows why $2\frac{1}{4}$ equals $\frac{9}{4}$.
(28)

Convert each mixed number to an improper fraction reduced to lowest terms:

12. $7\dfrac{3}{8}$ **13.** $6\dfrac{2}{3}$ **14.** $5\dfrac{7}{11}$
(28)   (28)   (28)

Use unit multipliers to convert:

15.   199.62 decigrams to grams   **16.**   18 miles to feet
(24)   (23)

Simplify. If possible, cancel as the first step.

17.
(22) $\dfrac{42}{48} \cdot \dfrac{32}{14} \cdot \dfrac{3}{4}$

18.
(22) $\dfrac{18}{20} \cdot \dfrac{16}{8} \div \dfrac{27}{2}$

19.
(17,27) Convert centimeter measures to meters, and then find the area of this figure in square meters. All angles that look like right angles are right angles.

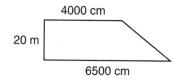

20.
(4,19) Find the missing number: $\dfrac{2}{5} R = \dfrac{2}{5}$

Write each mixed number as a decimal. Round to two decimal places.

21.
(28) $8\dfrac{16}{25}$

22.
(28) $1\dfrac{8}{13}$

Reduce each fraction to lowest terms:

23.
(14) $\dfrac{183}{270}$

24.
(14) $\dfrac{360}{420}$

Multiply:

25.
(7) 31.25×0.0012

26.
(7) 17.01×0.12

27.
(6) Subtract (add to check): $61.892 - 9.299$

28.
(28) Write 5.85 as a mixed number reduced to lowest terms.

29.
(26) Find the (a) range, (b) mode, (c) median, and (d) mean of the following numbers: 8, 7, 9, 9, 7, 5, 4

30.
(20) Find LCM (12, 30, 50).

LESSON 30   *Adding and Subtracting Fractions • Adding and Subtracting Fractions with Unequal Denominators*

30.A

adding and subtracting fractions

The denominator of a fraction tells us into how many equal parts the whole is divided. The numerator of a fraction indicates how many of these parts we are considering. Since the fractions $\frac{1}{5}$ and $\frac{3}{5}$ both have 5 in the denominator, we know that each of the wholes has been divided into five parts. In one of the fractions we are considering 1 of the parts, and in the other we are considering 3 of the parts.

$\dfrac{1}{5}$ $\dfrac{3}{5}$

If we add the fractions $\frac{1}{5}$ and $\frac{3}{5}$, we get $\frac{4}{5}$

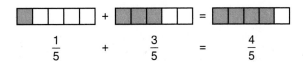

$$\frac{1}{5} \quad + \quad \frac{3}{5} \quad = \quad \frac{4}{5}$$

because we have one $\frac{1}{5}$ from the first fraction and three $\frac{1}{5}$'s from the second fraction for a total of four $\frac{1}{5}$'s. This gives us a picture of why we add the numerators when we add fractions whose denominators are equal.

> **FRACTIONS WITH EQUAL DENOMINATORS**
>
> To add or subtract fractions whose denominators are equal, the numerators are added or subtracted as indicated by the + and − signs, and the result is recorded over the same denominator.

30.B
adding and subtracting fractions with unequal denominators

When we wish to add fractions whose denominators are not equal,

$$\frac{1}{4} + \frac{1}{2}$$

we must first transform one or both fractions as necessary so that the fractions will have equal denominators. If we multiply the numerator and denominator of the second fraction above by 2,

$$\frac{1}{4} + \frac{1(2)}{2(2)} = \frac{1}{4} + \frac{2}{4}$$

we change $\frac{1}{2}$ to $\frac{2}{4}$. Now both denominators are equal, and we add.

$$\frac{1}{4} + \frac{2}{4} = \frac{3}{4}$$

In this problem, the original denominators were 2 and 4. The new denominator for both fractions is 4 because 4 is the smallest number that is evenly divisible by both 2 and 4. Thus, 4 is the LCM of 2 and 4. When we use the least common multiple of several numbers as the new denominator, we call it the **least common denominator,** which we abbreviate as **LCD.**

Remember that the rule we used to change $\frac{1}{2}$ to $\frac{2}{4}$ is the denominator-numerator rule for fractions.

> **DENOMINATOR-NUMERATOR RULE FOR FRACTIONS**
>
> Both the denominator and the numerator of a fraction can be multiplied or divided by the same number (except zero) without changing the value of the fraction.

We will use four steps to add or subtract fractions with unequal denominators:

1. Find the least common denominator of the fractions.

2. Write all fractions with this new denominator.

3. Find the new numerators.

4. Add or subtract the fractions.

example 30.1 Simplify: $\dfrac{5}{11} - \dfrac{1}{5}$

solution Both of these denominators are prime numbers so the least common denominator is 5×11, or 55. We write the fractions with this new denominator:

$$\frac{5}{11} - \frac{1}{5} = \frac{}{55} - \frac{}{55}$$

In the first fraction, we have multiplied the old denominator of 11 by 5 to get 55, so we must multiply the old numerator by 5. We get

$$\frac{5}{11} - \frac{1}{5} = \frac{25}{55} - \frac{}{55}$$

The old denominator of the second fraction was 5. Now it is 55. We have multiplied the old denominator by 11. Thus, we must multiply the old numerator by 11. Now we have

$$\frac{5}{11} - \frac{1}{5} = \frac{25}{55} - \frac{11}{55} = \mathbf{\frac{14}{55}}$$

example 30.2 Simplify: $\dfrac{1}{4} + \dfrac{5}{9} + \dfrac{2}{3}$

solution First we find the LCD of the fractions using the prime factorization of each denominator.

$$2 \cdot 2 \quad \text{and} \quad 3 \cdot 3 \quad \text{and} \quad 3 \quad \longrightarrow \quad 2 \cdot 2 \cdot 3 \cdot 3 = 36$$

Now we use 36 as the new denominator for each fraction.

$$\frac{1}{4} + \frac{5}{9} + \frac{2}{3} = \frac{}{36} + \frac{}{36} + \frac{}{36}$$

In the leftmost fraction, we have multiplied the old denominator by 9 to get 36, so we also multiply the old numerator by 9.

$$\frac{1}{4} + \frac{5}{9} + \frac{2}{3} = \frac{9}{36} + \frac{}{36} + \frac{}{36}$$

In the center fraction, we have multiplied the old denominator by 4 to get 36, so we must also multiply the old numerator by 4.

$$\frac{1}{4} + \frac{5}{9} + \frac{2}{3} = \frac{9}{36} + \frac{20}{36} + \frac{}{36}$$

In the rightmost fraction, we have multiplied the old denominator by 12 to get 36, so we must also multiply the old numerator by 12. Then we add.

$$\frac{1}{4} + \frac{5}{9} + \frac{2}{3} = \frac{9}{36} + \frac{20}{36} + \frac{24}{36} = \frac{53}{36} = 1\frac{17}{36}$$

You may choose to write your answer as an improper fraction or as a mixed number. Just remember to reduce your answers to lowest terms.

practice Simplify:

a. $\dfrac{3}{4} - \dfrac{2}{5}$

b. $\dfrac{5}{3} + \dfrac{1}{2} - \dfrac{1}{4}$

c. $\dfrac{5}{8} - \dfrac{1}{2} + \dfrac{1}{4}$

d. $\dfrac{2}{3} + \dfrac{3}{4} - \dfrac{1}{5}$

problem set 30

1. On the graph shown, how many fewer cars were sold in February than were sold in April?
(29)

New Car Sales

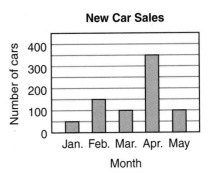

2. The highest temperature on Monday was 80°F, the highest temperature on Wednesday was 60°F, and the highest temperature on Friday was 70°F. Make a bar graph that displays this information.
(29)

3. Hamilcar saw an average of 12 elephants daily for the 3-day period. He saw 8 elephants on the first day and 7 elephants on the second day. How many elephants did he see on the third day?
(26)

4. When Hannibal opened the boxes, he found that each box contained 53 spear points. If 5062 spears needed new points, how many boxes did he have to open?
(11)

5. The first batch contained 5142 red marbles and 7821 green marbles. The second batch had twice as many red marbles and 3 times as many green marbles. How many total red marbles and green marbles were there in both batches?
(13)

6. Coach McCain's basketball team scored the following points in the first six games of the season: 53, 58, 46, 62, 58, 54. Find the (a) range, (b) mode, (c) median, and (d) mean of their scores in the first six games. Round to 2 decimal places.
(26)

7. Find $\frac{3}{8}$ of 42.
(18)

8. Find $\frac{6}{7}$ of 49.
(18)

Convert each improper fraction to a mixed number:

9. $\dfrac{17}{8}$
(28)

10. $\dfrac{22}{5}$
(28)

11. Draw a diagram that shows why $3\frac{1}{5}$ equals $\frac{16}{5}$.
(28)

Convert each mixed number to an improper fraction reduced to lowest terms:

12. $7\dfrac{2}{3}$
(28)

13. $7\dfrac{6}{7}$
(28)

Simplify:

14. $\dfrac{4}{5} - \dfrac{3}{4}$
(30)

15. $\dfrac{2}{3} + \dfrac{5}{8} - \dfrac{3}{4}$
(30)

16. $\dfrac{3}{8} + \dfrac{5}{6} - \dfrac{1}{4}$
(30)

17. $\dfrac{2}{3} + \dfrac{5}{8} + \dfrac{3}{4}$
(30)

Use unit multipliers to convert:

18. 721 yards to feet
(23)

19. 19,262 centimeters to meters
(24)

Simplify:

20. $\dfrac{28}{32} \cdot \dfrac{24}{21} \cdot \dfrac{3}{4}$
(22)

21. $\dfrac{16}{18} \cdot \dfrac{20}{24} \div \dfrac{10}{9}$
(22)

22. Convert meter measures to centi-
(24,27)   meters, and then express the area of
this figure in square centimeters.

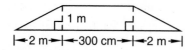

23. Convert centimeter measures to
(9,24)   meters, and then express the perimeter
of this figure in meters. All angles are
right angles.

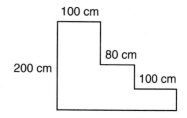

Reduce each fraction to lowest terms:

24. $\dfrac{180}{200}$
(14)

25. $\dfrac{256}{720}$
(14)

Write each mixed number as a decimal. Round to two decimal places.

26. $5\dfrac{16}{21}$
(28)

27. $2\dfrac{9}{17}$
(28)

28. Write 2450 as a product of prime numbers using exponents.
(16)

29. Write 301.008 as a mixed number reduced to lowest terms.
(28)

30. Find the missing number: $\dfrac{4}{5} + G = \dfrac{8}{5}$
(3,30)

LESSON 31   *Order of Operations*

There seem to be two ways that the following expression can be simplified.

$$4 + 3 \times 5$$

It looks as though we could add first and then multiply (a), or multiply first and then add (b).

(a) ADD FIRST	(b) MULTIPLY FIRST
$4 + 3 \times 5$	$4 + 3 \times 5$
7×5	$4 + 15$
35	19

Thus, there seem to be two possible answers to this problem. Since two answers to the same problem would cause considerable confusion, mathematicians have had to agree on one way or the other. They have agreed to always multiply before adding or subtracting.

> **ORDER OF OPERATIONS**
>
> 1. Multiply in order from left to right.
> 2. Add and subtract in order from left to right.

Therefore, the value of the expression above is 19 and is not 35.

example 31.1 Simplify: $41 - 3 \cdot 5 + 4 \cdot 6$

solution Two multiplications are indicated. We do these first and then move from left to right, performing the additions and subtractions in the order we encounter them.

$41 - 15 + 24$	multiplied $3 \cdot 5$ and $4 \cdot 6$
$26 + 24$	subtracted 15 from 41
50	added 26 and 24

example 31.2 Simplify: $4 + 5 \cdot 3 - 2 \cdot 4 + 6 \cdot 3$

solution We do the multiplications first. We finish by doing the additions and subtractions from left to right.

$4 + 15 - 8 + 18$	multiplied $5 \cdot 3$, $2 \cdot 4$, and $6 \cdot 3$
$19 - 8 + 18$	added 4 and 15
$11 + 18$	subtracted 8 from 19
29	added 11 and 18

practice Simplify:

a. $4 + 3 \cdot 6 - 2 \cdot 3$

b. $2 + 3 \cdot 6 - 4 \cdot 3$

problem set 31

1.
(13) Mildred bought 20 show tickets for $2.50 each. If she gave the agent a $100 bill, how much change did she receive?

2.
(29) How many more type B cars were sold in 1980 than were sold in 1970?

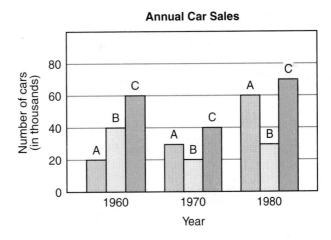

Annual Car Sales

3.
(11) Try as he might, Waltersheid found that he could do only 175 in an hour. If he had to do 2975 in all, how many hours would it take him?

4.
(26) The average cost of 5 kits was $9.50. The first kit cost $11.25, the second kit cost $8.75, the third kit cost $9.35, and the fourth kit cost $8.90. Find the cost of the fifth kit.

5.
(23) In Saudi Arabia it takes 20 kursh to equal 1 riyal.

(a) Write the two unit multipliers implied by this relationship.

(b) Use one of the unit multipliers to convert 16,000 kursh to riyals.

6.
(18) What number is $\frac{5}{6}$ of 960?

7.
(18) What number is $\frac{11}{5}$ of 55?

Convert each improper fraction to a mixed number:

8. $\dfrac{41}{3}$
(28)

9. $\dfrac{52}{16}$
(28)

10. Draw a diagram that shows why $4\frac{1}{3}$ equals $\frac{13}{3}$.
(28)

Find the least common multiple of:

11. 14, 94, and 300
(20)

12. 27, 66, and 90
(20)

13. Write $15\frac{2}{3}$ as an improper fraction.
(28)

14. Use one unit multiplier to convert 14,780,000 milligrams to grams.
(24)

Simplify:

15. $\dfrac{15}{18} \cdot \dfrac{6}{30} \div \dfrac{3}{2}$
(22)

16. $\dfrac{160}{180} \cdot \dfrac{10}{12} \div \dfrac{20}{18}$
(22)

17. $\dfrac{8}{9} + \dfrac{5}{6}$
(30)

18. $\dfrac{5}{8} + \dfrac{11}{16} + \dfrac{1}{2}$
(30)

19. $\dfrac{7}{27} + \dfrac{1}{3} - \dfrac{1}{9}$
(30)

20. $\dfrac{1}{4} + \dfrac{2}{3} - \dfrac{6}{7}$
(30)

21. $7 + 5 \times 9$
(31)

22. $5 \cdot 8 - 2 \cdot 7 + 5$
(31)

23. $4 \cdot 8 - 8 \cdot 2$
(31)

24. $6 \cdot 7 + 6 - 2 \cdot 9$
(31)

25. Convert meter measures to centi-
(24,27) meters, and then find the area of this figure in square centimeters.

26. Convert meter measures to centi-
(17,24) meters, and then find the area of this figure in square centimeters. All angles are right angles.

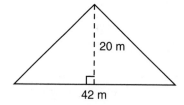

20 m

42 m

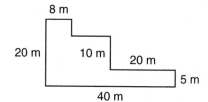

8 m

20 m   10 m   20 m

5 m

40 m

27. Find the missing number: $x - \dfrac{5}{17} = \dfrac{10}{17}$
(3,30)

Write each fraction as a decimal number. Round to two decimal places.

28. $\dfrac{42}{17}$
(15)

29. $\dfrac{40}{25}$
(15)

30. Write as a mixed number: 12.12
(28)

LESSON 32 *Variables and Evaluation*

In algebra, we often use letters as **variables** to stand for or to take the places of numbers. The letters themselves have no value. The expression

$$x + 4$$

means "a number plus 4" or "the sum of a number and 4" or "4 more than a number." The value of the whole expression depends upon the value of x. For example, if we replace x with 11, the value of the expression is 15.

$$11 + 4 = 15$$

When two variables are written together side-by-side, such as

$$xy$$

the notation means that x and y are to be multiplied. This also applies to a number written just before a letter. The expression

$$3x$$

means 3 and x are to be multiplied.

example 32.1 Evaluate: $xy + x$ if $x = 2$ and $y = 4$

solution The word **evaluate** means "find the value of." We replace x with 2 and y with 4.

$$xy + x = 2 \cdot 4 + 2$$

We remember to multiply before we add. Thus we get

$$8 + 2 = \mathbf{10}$$

example 32.2 Evaluate: $xmy - xy$ if $x = 2$, $m = 5$, and $y = 4$

solution We replace x with 2, m with 5, and y with 4.

$$xmy - xy = 2 \cdot 5 \cdot 4 - 2 \cdot 4$$

We multiply before we subtract and get

$$40 - 8 = \mathbf{32}$$

example 32.3 Evaluate: $mx + 4m$ if $x = \dfrac{2}{3}$ and $m = \dfrac{9}{11}$

solution First we replace m and x with $\frac{9}{11}$ and $\frac{2}{3}$, respectively.

$$mx + 4m = \frac{9}{11} \cdot \frac{2}{3} + 4 \cdot \frac{9}{11} = \frac{\overset{3}{\cancel{9}}}{11} \cdot \frac{2}{\underset{1}{\cancel{3}}} + \frac{36}{11}$$

Now we multiply and then add.

$$\frac{6}{11} + \frac{36}{11} = \frac{42}{11} = \mathbf{3\dfrac{9}{11}}$$

practice Evaluate:

a. $xy + yx$ if $x = 2$ and $y = 4$

b. $mpx + mx$ if $x = 3$, $p = 4$, and $m = 6$

problem set
32

1. *(26)* The mean cost of four items was $39.96. The first item cost $28.50, the second item cost $41.25, and the third item cost $50. Find the cost of the fourth item.

2. *(29)* The attendance at the first six home games was 10,400; 8000; 14,600; 7000; 12,000; 15,700. Make a broken-line graph that presents this information.

3. *(26)* Find the (a) range, (b) mode, (c) median, and (d) mean of the attendance figures in problem 2. Round any decimal results to two places.

4. *(26)* In the first cache, Hazel uncovered 1481 dull tokens. The next cache held 1300 shiny tokens, and the last cache had 300 tokens that were both shiny and dull. What was the average number of tokens per cache?

5. *(11)* Four thousand, fifty-seven screaming football fans could be seated in each section of the stadium. If the stadium had 17 sections, how many screaming football fans would it hold?

6. *(18)* What number is $\frac{4}{13}$ of 39?

7. *(18)* What number is $\frac{11}{5}$ of 500?

Convert each improper fraction to a mixed number:

8. *(28)* $\dfrac{93}{13}$

9. *(28)* $\dfrac{41}{7}$

Evaluate:

10. *(32)* $p + gp$ if $p = 1$ and $g = 22$

11. *(32)* $xyz + yz$ if $x = 3$, $y = 4$, and $z = 5$

12. *(20)* Find the least common multiple of 200, 120, and 180.

13. *(3,30)* Find the missing number: $\dfrac{14}{31} + x = \dfrac{21}{31}$

Simplify:

14. *(30)* $\dfrac{2}{3} + \dfrac{5}{8} + \dfrac{1}{2}$

15. *(30)* $\dfrac{6}{7} - \dfrac{4}{5}$

16. *(30)* $\dfrac{3}{5} + \dfrac{4}{7} - \dfrac{1}{3}$

17. *(22)* $\dfrac{4}{5} \cdot \dfrac{20}{40} \div \dfrac{5}{10}$

18. *(22)* $\dfrac{2}{8} \cdot \dfrac{16}{24} \div \dfrac{15}{8}$

19. *(7)* $(0.0023)(1.047)$

20. *(28)* Write $15\frac{2}{25}$ as a decimal.

21. *(28)* Write 16.16 as a mixed number.

22. *(23)* Twenty shillings equals 1 pound.

(a) Write the two unit multipliers implied by this comparison.

(b) Use one of these unit multipliers to convert 1000 pounds to shillings.

23. *(27)* Find the area of this figure. Dimensions are in feet.

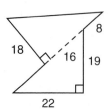

24. *(9)* Find the perimeter of this figure. Dimensions are in centimeters. All angles are right angles.

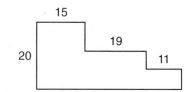

25. Simplify this fraction: $\dfrac{260}{305}$
₍₁₄₎

Write each fraction as a decimal number. Round to two decimal places.

26. $\dfrac{52}{63}$ **27.** $\dfrac{14}{19}$
₍₁₅₎   ₍₁₅₎

Simplify:

28. $8 \cdot 10 - 2 - 10 \cdot 6$ **29.** $\dfrac{1}{8} + \dfrac{3}{4} \cdot \dfrac{1}{6}$
₍₃₁₎   ₍₃₁₎

30. $3 \cdot 8 - 6 \cdot 4 + 24 \cdot 1 - 12 \cdot 2$
₍₃₁₎

LESSON 33   *Multiple Unit Multipliers • Conversion of Units of Area*

33.A
multiple unit multipliers

We may repeatedly multiply a number by 1 without changing the number.

$$5 \cdot 1 = 5$$
$$5 \cdot 1 \cdot 1 = 5$$
$$5 \cdot 1 \cdot 1 \cdot 1 = 5$$
$$5 \cdot 1 \cdot 1 \cdot 1 \cdot 1 = 5$$

Unit multipliers are used to convert from one unit of measure to another. Since unit multipliers are forms of 1, we may multiply a measure by several unit multipliers to convert the units without changing the measurement. For example, to convert from inches to yards, we could remember that 1 yard equals 36 inches. However, memorizing this fact is unnecessary. We prefer to convert inches to yards by first converting inches to feet. Then we convert feet to yards.

example 33.1   Convert 360 inches to yards.

solution   We will use one unit multiplier to convert from inches to feet. Then we will use another to convert from feet to yards.

$$360 \text{ in.} \cdot \frac{1 \text{ ft}}{12 \text{ in.}} \cdot \frac{1 \text{ yd}}{3 \text{ ft}} = \frac{360}{(12)(3)} \text{ yd} = \mathbf{10 \text{ yd}}$$

example 33.2   Use two unit multipliers to convert 1.4 kilometers to centimeters.

solution   We will go from kilometers to meters to centimeters.

$$1.4 \text{ km} \cdot \frac{1000 \text{ m}}{1 \text{ km}} \cdot \frac{100 \text{ cm}}{1 \text{ m}} = \frac{1.4(1000)(100)}{1} \text{ cm} = \mathbf{140{,}000 \text{ cm}}$$

We might have remembered that 1 kilometer equals 100,000 centimeters, but attempting shortcuts like this often leads to errors.

example 33.3   Use two unit multipliers to convert 24 miles to inches.

solution   We will go from miles to feet to inches.

$$24 \text{ mi} \cdot \frac{5280 \text{ ft}}{1 \text{ mi}} \cdot \frac{12 \text{ in.}}{1 \text{ ft}} = \textbf{24(5280)(12) in.} = \textbf{1,520,640 in.}$$

Using a calculator, we find the answer multiplied out is 1,520,640 in. Either answer is acceptable.

33.B

conversion of units of area

Two unit multipliers are required to convert units of area, as shown in the next three examples.

example 33.4   Use two unit multipliers to convert 4 square feet to square inches.

solution   First we write 4 square feet as

$$4 \text{ ft}^2$$

Since "ft^2" means "ft" times "ft," we can write this as

$$4 \text{ ft} \cdot \text{ft}$$

Two unit multipliers are required because a separate unit multiplier is needed to change each "ft" to "in."

$$4 \text{ ft} \cdot \text{ft} \times \frac{12 \text{ in.}}{1 \text{ ft}} \times \frac{12 \text{ in.}}{1 \text{ ft}} = \textbf{4(12)(12) in.}^2 = \textbf{576 in.}^2$$

Again, using a calculator, the answer multiplied out is 576 in.^{2}

example 33.5   Use two unit multipliers to convert 4 square meters to square centimeters.

solution   This time, instead of writing 4 m^2 as 4 m $\cdot$ m, we will simply keep it in mind and cancel using two unit multipliers.

$$4 \text{ m}^2 \times \frac{100 \text{ cm}}{1 \text{ m}} \times \frac{100 \text{ cm}}{1 \text{ m}} = \textbf{4(100)(100) cm}^2 = \textbf{40,000 cm}^2$$

example 33.6   Use two unit multipliers to convert 400 square inches to square feet.

solution   Since square inches means inches times inches, we use two unit multipliers so we can cancel in.^{2}.

$$400 \text{ in.}^2 \times \frac{1 \text{ ft}}{12 \text{ in.}} \times \frac{1 \text{ ft}}{12 \text{ in.}} = \frac{\textbf{400}}{\textbf{(12)(12)}} \text{ ft}^2 \approx \textbf{2.78 ft}^2$$

We rounded our answer to two decimal places, so we used the approximately equals sign ($\approx$) in our answer.

practice   Use two unit multipliers to convert:

a.   6 miles to inches

b.   20 square feet to square inches

problem set 33

1. For every 37 tickets she sold, Martine was given a free ticket for one of the children. If
(11) 175 children wanted to go, how many tickets did Martine have to sell?

2. By how many pounds was the weight in April less than the weight in January? There
(29) are 2000 pounds in 1 ton.

Tons Per Month

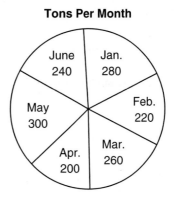

3. Ralph's average score for the 5 tests was 82. On four of the tests his scores were 85, 73,
(26) 92, and 66. What was his score on the other test?

4. Nineteen million, four hundred eighty-four thousand and seventy-five thousandths is a
(6) big number. Twenty-two million, thirteen and nine hundred eighty-four ten-
thousandths is even bigger. What is the difference between these big numbers?

5. Red ones cost $5 each, and Don bought 7 red ones. Blue ones were $3.40 each, and he
(13) bought 9 of these. Green ones were only $1.30 each, so he bought 20 of these. How
much money did Don spend?

6. What number is $\frac{5}{16}$ of 128?   **7.** What number is $\frac{14}{3}$ of 30?
(18)   (18)

Write each improper fraction as a mixed number:

8. $\dfrac{93}{12}$ **9.** $\dfrac{40}{7}$
(28)   (28)

Evaluate:

10. $e + g + fg$ if $e = 0.08$, $g = 1.7$, and $f = 0.5$
(32)

11. $\dfrac{x}{y} + xy$ if $x = 6$ and $y = 2$
(32)

Simplify:

12. $\dfrac{3}{7} + \dfrac{2}{5} - \dfrac{3}{10}$ **13.** $\dfrac{5}{8} + \dfrac{3}{5} - \dfrac{1}{4}$
(30)   (30)

14. $\dfrac{7}{11} - \dfrac{1}{3}$ **15.** $32 - 2 \cdot 5 + 3 \cdot 6$
(30)   (31)

16. $7 + 5 \cdot 3 - 2 \cdot 4 + 5 \cdot 3$ **17.** $3 + 3 \cdot 5 - 4 \cdot 2$
(31)   (31)

18. $\dfrac{4}{5} \cdot \dfrac{25}{20} \div \dfrac{5}{10}$
(22)

19. Find the missing number: $\dfrac{7}{12} + w = \dfrac{3}{4}$
(3,30)

20. Simplify: 0.016×0.0023
(7)

21. Write 50.05 as a mixed number.
(28)

22. There are 16 ounces in 1 pint of liquid.
(23)

    (a) Write the two unit multipliers implied by this relationship.

    (b) Use one of these unit multipliers to convert 640 ounces to pints.

23. Use two unit multipliers to convert 90 yards to inches.
(33)

24. Use two unit multipliers to convert 7.5 ft^2 to in.^{2}.
(33)

25. Use two unit multipliers to convert 450 ft^2 to yd^2.
(33)

26. Find the area of this figure. Dimensions are in feet.
(17,27)

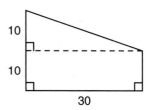

27. Write 4160 as a product of prime numbers using exponents.
(16)

Write each fraction as a decimal number:

28. $\dfrac{13}{5}$ **29.** $\dfrac{17}{4}$
(28)   *(28)*

30. Write $\frac{7}{18}$ as a decimal number. Round to two decimal places.
(15)

LESSON 34 *Adding Mixed Numbers • Rate*

34.A
adding mixed
numbers

To add mixed numbers, we add the whole numbers together and the fractions together:

$$2\frac{1}{5} + 9\frac{2}{5} = 11\frac{3}{5}$$

When there are unequal denominators or when the sum of the fractions is improper, there are more steps.

example 34.1   Add: $2\dfrac{3}{4} + 3\dfrac{1}{8} + 7\dfrac{1}{2}$

solution   We add the whole numbers as usual and add the fractions using a common denominator.

$$2\frac{3}{4} + 3\frac{1}{8} + 7\frac{1}{2} = 2\frac{6}{8} + 3\frac{1}{8} + 7\frac{4}{8} = 12\frac{11}{8}$$

Now we need to make $\frac{11}{8}$ a mixed number and add.

$$12\frac{11}{8} = 12 + 1\frac{3}{8} = \mathbf{13\frac{3}{8}}$$

When the whole numbers are large numbers, it may be convenient to add the whole numbers and the fractions in a vertical format.

example 34.2   Add: $528\frac{1}{3} + 7142\frac{3}{4}$

solution   We rewrite the problem in a vertical format. Then we rewrite the fractions with a common denominator and add.

$$528\frac{1}{3} = 528\frac{4}{12} \qquad \text{renamed}$$

$$+\ 7142\frac{3}{4} = 7142\frac{9}{12} \qquad \text{renamed}$$

$$= 7670\frac{13}{12} \qquad \text{added}$$

$$\mathbf{= 7671\frac{1}{12}} \qquad \text{simplified}$$

34.B

rate   A **rate** is a ratio. A **ratio** is a comparison of two numbers. A ratio can be written several different ways, but in this lesson we will concentrate on the fractional form. If two apples can be purchased for 16 cents, we can write either

$$\frac{2 \text{ apples}}{16 \text{ cents}} \qquad \text{or} \qquad \frac{16 \text{ cents}}{2 \text{ apples}}$$

Often we use the word *per* instead of writing the units as a fraction.

$$\frac{2 \text{ apples}}{16 \text{ cents}} = \frac{1}{8} \text{ apple per cent} \qquad \text{or} \qquad \frac{16 \text{ cents}}{2 \text{ apples}} = 8 \text{ cents per apple}$$

Other examples of rate include speed, which is distance per time, and mileage, which is distance per quantity of fuel used.

example 34.3   Waldo bought 5 toys for 40 dollars.

(a) What was the rate (ratio) in dollars per toy?

(b) What was the rate (ratio) in toys per dollar?

solution   (a) The first denominate number goes in the numerator. So for dollars per toy, we write

$$\frac{40 \text{ dollars}}{5 \text{ toys}} = \frac{8 \text{ dollars}}{1 \text{ toy}} = \textbf{8 dollars per toy}$$

(b) For the rate in toys per dollar, the number of toys goes in the numerator.

$$\frac{5 \text{ toys}}{40 \text{ dollars}} = \frac{1 \text{ toy}}{8 \text{ dollars}} = \frac{1}{8} \textbf{ toy per dollar}$$

practice   Add:

a. $2\frac{1}{5} + 3\frac{1}{10}$ **b.** $472\frac{2}{5} + 312\frac{3}{4}$

c. Roger could travel 48 yards in 6 seconds. What was his rate in yards per second and what was his rate in seconds per yard?

d. Eight apples can be purchased for 2 dollars. What is the rate in apples per dollar and what is the rate in dollars per apple?

problem set **1.** Silicon chips were packed 420 to the box. If 130,420 chips were to be shipped, how
        34   (11) many boxes would be needed?

2. In the catalogue, apple trees were $15.95 each, so Sam bought 3 apple trees. He also
(13) bought 7 nectarine trees for $17.75 each and 4 peach trees for $11.95 each. How much
money did he spend for fruit trees?

3. What was the average of the car sales for the five months listed on this broken-
(21,29) line graph?

New Car Sales

4. The weights of the first four loads were 14,000 pounds, 12,000 pounds, 18,200 pounds,
(26) and 16,280 pounds. What was the (a) range, (b) mode, (c) median, and
(d) mean of the weights of the four loads?

5. Heidi could travel 64 feet in 8 seconds. What was her rate in feet per second, and what
(34) was her rate in seconds per foot?

6. Bernard stepped on 6 locusts in 30 minutes. What was his rate in locusts per minute and
(34) in minutes per locust?

7. Find the missing number: $0.375 + P = 1.2$
(3,6)

8. What number is $\frac{5}{17}$ of 136?
(18)

Write each improper fraction as a mixed number:

9. $\dfrac{37}{3}$ **10.** $\dfrac{421}{5}$
(28)   (28)

11. Find the least common multiple of 60, 84, and 120.
(20)

Simplify:

12. $\dfrac{3}{4} + \dfrac{5}{8} + \dfrac{2}{3} - \dfrac{1}{6}$ **13.** $\dfrac{5}{8} + \dfrac{1}{16} + \dfrac{1}{2} - \dfrac{1}{4}$
(30)   (30)

14. $3 + 2 \cdot 6 - 4 \cdot 3$ **15.** $5 \cdot 2 - 3 \cdot 2 + 4 \cdot 3$
(31)   (31)

16. $\dfrac{16}{25} \times \dfrac{15}{8} \div \dfrac{3}{2}$ **17.** $\dfrac{30.03}{0.0021}$
(22)   (7)

18. $\dfrac{4}{3} - \dfrac{7}{10}$ **19.** $8\dfrac{1}{2} + 2\dfrac{5}{6}$
(30)   (34)

20. $57\dfrac{5}{13} + 13\dfrac{2}{3}$
(34)

21. Write 15.15 as a mixed number.
(28)

22. There are 40 gallons in 1 barrel.
(23)
(a) Write the two unit multipliers implied by this relationship.

(b) Use one of these unit multipliers to convert 2500 barrels to gallons.

23. Use two unit multipliers to convert 132 square meters to square centimeters.
(33)

Evaluate:

24. $xy + 2m$ if $x = 2$, $y = 4$, and $m = 3$
(32)

25. $xym + xy$ if $x = 3$, $m = 4$, and $y = 6$
(32)

26. $mx + 4m$ if $x = \dfrac{2}{3}$ and $m = 5$
(32)

27. Find the area of this figure. Dimen-
(17,27) sions are in feet.

28. Find the perimeter of this figure.
(9) Dimensions are in meters. All angles are right angles.

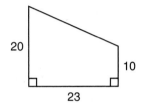

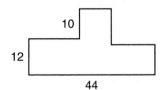

Write each mixed number as a decimal:

29. $4\dfrac{3}{5}$
(28)

30. $301\dfrac{3}{8}$
(28)

LESSON 35 *Subtracting Mixed Numbers*

When we calculate $54 - 23$, we subtract the tens' and units' places separately. We can subtract mixed numbers the same way.

example 35.1 Subtract: $4\dfrac{1}{2} - 1\dfrac{1}{8}$

solution We subtract the fractions using common denominators. Then we subtract the whole numbers.

$$4\frac{1}{2} - 1\frac{1}{8} = 4\frac{4}{8} - 1\frac{1}{8} = \mathbf{3\frac{3}{8}}$$

When we calculate $72 - 35$, however, we cannot subtract 5 from 2, so we must borrow 1 ten (10 ones), and subtract

$$\begin{array}{r} \overset{6}{\cancel{7}}\overset{1}{2} \\ -\ 3\ 5 \\ \hline 3\ 7 \end{array}$$

Similarly, with mixed numbers it is sometimes necessary to borrow before we can subtract.

example 35.2   Subtract: $5\dfrac{1}{10} - 1\dfrac{14}{15}$

solution   Our first step is to rewrite the fractions with common denominators.

$$5\dfrac{1}{10} - 1\dfrac{14}{15} = 5\dfrac{3}{30} - 1\dfrac{28}{30}$$

We cannot subtract $\frac{28}{30}$ from $\frac{3}{30}$, so we borrow 1 unit $\left(\frac{30}{30}\right)$ from 5 and add the 1 unit $\left(\frac{30}{30}\right)$ to $\frac{3}{30}$.

$$5\dfrac{1}{10} = \overset{4}{\cancel{5}}\,\dfrac{\overset{33}{\cancel{3}}}{30}$$

$$-\ 1\dfrac{14}{15} = 1\dfrac{28}{30}$$

$$\rule{3cm}{0.4pt}$$

$$= 3\dfrac{5}{30} = \mathbf{3\dfrac{1}{6}}$$

practice   Subtract:

a. $7\dfrac{1}{5} - 4\dfrac{2}{3}$ **b.** $316\dfrac{1}{5} - 42\dfrac{7}{8}$

**problem set
35**

1.
(6)   The first measurement was four hundred seventeen ten-thousandths meter. The second measurement was forty-five thousandths meter. Which measurement was larger and by how much?

2.
(29)   A company divides its employees into classes based on years of employment. How much more does a class A employee make in 2 years than a class D employee makes in 2 years?

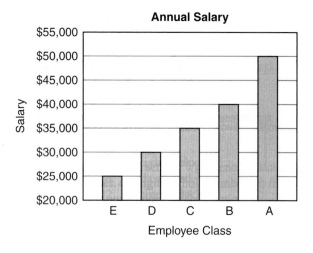

3.
(11)   The legal limit for the number of cars in a parade was 450 cars. If 9000 drivers wanted to be in a parade, how many parades were required to accommodate all of them?

4.
(21)   The lions weighed 417 lb, 832 lb, and 619 lb. The tigers weighed only 148 lb, 212 lb, and 184 lb. What was the average weight of the six lions and tigers?

5.
(3,30) $\dfrac{105}{112} - x = \dfrac{98}{112}$ **6.**
(18)   What number is $\frac{5}{12}$ of 48?

Write each improper fraction as a mixed number:

7.
(28)
$\dfrac{214}{5}$

8.
(28)
$\dfrac{47}{2}$

9. Find the least common multiple of 50, 60, and 72.
(20)

Simplify:

10. $\dfrac{3}{4} + \dfrac{5}{8} + \dfrac{3}{16}$
(30)

11. $\dfrac{13}{15} - \dfrac{1}{5}$
(30)

12. $3 \cdot 12 - 4 \cdot 2 + 3 \cdot 5$
(31)

13. $2 \cdot 5 \cdot 2 - 3 \cdot 5 + 2 - 5$
(31)

14. $\dfrac{4}{6} \times \dfrac{9}{14} \div \dfrac{2}{5}$
(22)

15. $52\dfrac{3}{8} + 19\dfrac{2}{3}$
(34)

16. $5\dfrac{1}{2} - 2\dfrac{4}{5}$
(35)

17. $9\dfrac{2}{14} - 3\dfrac{15}{21}$
(35)

18. $600\dfrac{2}{9} - 311\dfrac{3}{7}$
(35)

19. Write $5\frac{2}{3}$ as an improper fraction.
(28)

Evaluate:

20. $xy - y$ if $x = 5$ and $y = 4$
(32)

21. $m - xy$ if $m = 10$, $x = 2$, and $y = 3$
(32)

22. $xym - m$ if $x = \dfrac{1}{2}$, $y = 4$, and $m = 2$
(32)

Use two unit multipliers to convert:

23. 400 inches to yards
(33)

24. 3.6 kilometers to centimeters
(33)

25. 4 square miles to square feet
(33)

26. Twenty-four apricots can be purchased for $2. What is the rate in apricots per dollar and
(34) dollars per apricot?

27. Express the area of this figure in
(24,27) square centimeters. Begin by changing
0.4 meters to centimeters.

28. Express the perimeter of this figure in
(9,24) centimeters. Begin by changing 0.1
meters to centimeters. All angles are
right angles.

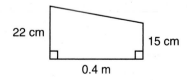

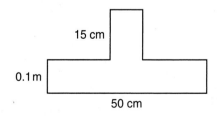

29. Write $12\frac{7}{8}$ as a decimal number.
(28)

30. Round $5.\overline{5}$ to the nearest hundred-thousandth.
(15)

LESSON 36   *Rate Word Problems*

Rate word problems are equal group problems. The rate is the number in an equal group. Suppose 20 apples cost 10 dollars. The two rates (ratios) are

$$\text{(a)} \quad \frac{20 \text{ apples}}{10 \text{ dollars}} \qquad \text{(b)} \quad \frac{10 \text{ dollars}}{20 \text{ apples}}$$

If we multiply (a) by 8 dollars, we get apples because the dollars will cancel.

$$\frac{20 \text{ apples}}{10 \text{ dollars}} \times 8 \text{ dollars} = 16 \text{ apples}$$

If we multiply (b) by 8 apples, we get dollars because the apples will cancel.

$$\frac{10 \text{ dollars}}{20 \text{ apples}} \times 8 \text{ apples} = 4 \text{ dollars}$$

When the problem asks "how many apples," we will use the rate that has apples in the numerator. When the problem asks "how many dollars" or "what will be the cost," we will use the rate that has dollars in the numerator. When we solve rate problems, we can always multiply to find the answer. This is because we have our choice of two rates.

Note that rates, like fractions, can be reduced. Rates (a) and (b) can be reduced to

(a) 2 apples per dollar

(b) 1 dollar per 2 apples

However, rates can be used to solve problems without reducing them first.

example 36.1   Twenty apples cost 5 dollars. How many apples can we buy for 80 dollars?

solution   The pattern is

$$\text{Rate} \times \text{number} = \text{total}$$

The two rates (ratios) for this problem are

$$\text{(a)} \quad \frac{20 \text{ apples}}{5 \text{ dollars}} \qquad \text{(b)} \quad \frac{5 \text{ dollars}}{20 \text{ apples}}$$

We want to know the number of apples, so we use rate (a) because it has apples in the numerator.

$$\frac{20 \text{ apples}}{5 \text{ dollars}} \times 80 \text{ dollars} = \textbf{320 apples}$$

example 36.2   Twenty apples cost 5 dollars. What is the cost of 40 apples?

solution   The pattern is

$$\text{Rate} \times \text{number} = \text{total}$$

The two rates (ratios) for this problem are

$$\text{(a)} \quad \frac{20 \text{ apples}}{5 \text{ dollars}} \qquad \text{(b)} \quad \frac{5 \text{ dollars}}{20 \text{ apples}}$$

We want to know the cost, so we want to know the number of dollars. We will use rate (b) because it has dollars in the numerator.

$$\frac{5 \text{ dollars}}{20 \text{ apples}} \times 40 \text{ apples} = \textbf{10 dollars}$$

practice Chestnuts cost 40 cents for 2 ounces.

    a. Write the two rates (ratios) implied by this statement.

    b. How many ounces of chestnuts can Joan buy for $1.20?

    c. What would be the cost of 50 ounces of chestnuts?

problem set 36

1. (26) The mean weight of the seven linebackers was 236 pounds. The first six linebackers weighed 215 lb, 305 lb, 265 lb, 196 lb, 221 lb, and 236 lb, respectively. What was the weight of the seventh linebacker?

2. (29) The values of the crops sold each year were as follows: $700,000 in 1940; $800,000 in 1945; $1,400,000 in 1950; $2,000,000 in 1955; and $3,000,000 in 1960. Draw a bar graph that presents this information.

3. (13) The children bought 7 notebooks for $5.40 each, 200 pencils for 30 cents each, and 40 reams of paper for $22.50 a ream. How much did they spend in all?

4. (11) Four hundred sixty quarts could be packaged in one shift. If 10,120 quarts were needed, how many shifts would be required?

5. (36) Marco Polo bought 40 skins for 8 liras.
    (a) Write the two rates (ratios) implied by this statement.
    (b) How many skins could Marco Polo buy for 200 liras?
    (c) What would be the cost of 200 skins?

6. (36) Andrea exchanged three books for seven CDs.
    (a) What are the two rates (ratios) implied by this statement?
    (b) How many CDs could she have exchanged at the same rate for 9 books?

7. (3,6) Find the missing number: $713.891 - x = 712.9993$

8. (18) What number is $\frac{4}{5}$ of 200?

Write each improper fraction as a mixed number:

9. (28) $\dfrac{21}{4}$

10. (28) $\dfrac{86}{11}$

11. (20) Find the least common multiple of 40, 50, and 70.

Simplify:

12. (30) $\dfrac{3}{5} - \dfrac{1}{15}$

13. (30) $\dfrac{1}{10} + \dfrac{3}{5} - \dfrac{1}{20}$

14. (31) $3 + 5 - 2 \cdot 4 + 3 \cdot 5$

15. (31) $4 + 3(2) + 5 \cdot 4$

16. (34) $2\dfrac{1}{4} + 3\dfrac{1}{8}$

17. (34) $429\dfrac{1}{5} + 8162\dfrac{4}{15}$

18. (34) $534\dfrac{3}{8} + 371\dfrac{1}{40}$

19. (35) $7\dfrac{3}{7} - 4\dfrac{3}{4}$

20. (35) $79\dfrac{2}{7} - 55\dfrac{1}{3}$

21. (7) $\dfrac{716.2}{0.008}$

22. (22) $\dfrac{3}{8} \times \dfrac{24}{9} \div \dfrac{3}{7}$

23. Write 40.04 as a mixed number.
(28)

Evaluate:

24. $zy - z$ if $z = 3$ and $y = 4$
(32)

25. $xyz + yz$ if $x = \dfrac{1}{3}$, $y = 9$, and $z = 2$
(32)

Use two unit multipliers to convert:

26. 540 inches to yards
(33)

27. 187,625.8 centigrams to kilograms
(33)

28. Find the area of this figure. Dimen-
(17,27) sions are in inches.

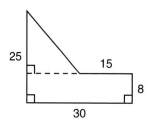

29. Find the perimeter of this figure.
(9) Dimensions are in centimeters. All angles are right angles.

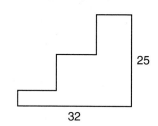

30. (a) List the prime numbers between 20 and 36.
(12,20)
   (b) List the multiples of 7 between 20 and 36.

LESSON 37 *Equations: Answers and Solutions*

If we connect two meaningful arrangements of numbers, or of numbers and variables, with an equals sign, we have written an **equation.** Some equations are *true* equations, and some equations are *false* equations.

$$\text{(a)} \quad 4 + 2 = 6 \qquad \text{true}$$
$$\text{(b)} \quad 4 + 2 = 3 \qquad \text{false}$$

Equation (a) is a true equation because 4 plus 2 equals 6. Equation (b) is a false equation because 4 plus 2 does not equal 3. Some equations that contain variables are called **conditional equations.**

$$\text{(c)} \quad x + 4 = 7 \qquad \text{conditional}$$

Equation (c) is a conditional equation because it is neither a true equation nor a false equation. Its truth or falsity depends on the number we use to replace x. If we replace x with 5, the equation becomes a false equation.

$$5 + 4 = 7 \qquad \text{false}$$

But if we replace x with 3, the equation becomes a true equation.

$$3 + 4 = 7 \qquad \text{true}$$

If replacing x with a number turns a conditional equation into a true equation, we say that the number is a **solution** of the equation or an answer to the equation. We also say that the number *satisfies the equation.* Many times we can look at a conditional equation and tell by inspection what number will satisfy the equation.

example 37.1   Solve: $x + 4 = 10$

solution   *Solve* means to find the number that will make this conditional equation a true equation. Since $6 + 4 = 10$, the solution is **6.**

example 37.2   Solve: $x - 4 = 10$

solution   The equation tells us that 4 subtracted from some number equals 10. The number must be 14 because

$$14 - 4 = 10$$

So the solution is **14.**

Notice that in both examples the problems looked like missing number problems, which they are. We solve them just like we did the missing number problems.

practice   Solve:

a. $x + 6 = 12$ **b.** $x - 6 = 12$ **c.** $x - 14 = 6$

problem set
37

1.
(36)   Winifred paid $180 for the first 10 items.

(a) Write the two rates (ratios) implied by this statement.

(b) How much would 25 items at the same rate cost?

(c) How many items can Winifred buy for $900 at the same rate?

2.
(26)   The mean daily rate of production for 5 days at the bottling plant was 1 million bottles of Big Pop per day. The totals for the first 4 days were 998,163 bottles, 899,989 bottles, 1,200,316 bottles, and 987,900 bottles. How many bottles of Big Pop were produced on the fifth day?

3.
(29)   By how much did the income in 1950 exceed the income in 1910?

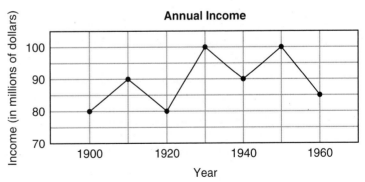

4.
(11)   If 415 came in each unit and if 29,050 were required, how many units had to be obtained?

5.
(18)   What number is $\frac{5}{16}$ of 32?

Solve:

6.
(37) $x - 17 = 20$

7.
(37) $x + 4 = 10$

8.
(6,37) $x - 0.0009 = 513.0011$

9.
(30,37) $\frac{2}{7} + x = \frac{5}{7}$

Write each improper fraction as a mixed number:

10. $\dfrac{31}{5}$ **11.** $\dfrac{93}{7}$
(28)   (28)

Simplify:

12. $\dfrac{3}{5} - \dfrac{2}{10}$ **13.** $\dfrac{3}{8} + \dfrac{1}{2} - \dfrac{1}{4}$ **14.** $4 + 3 \cdot 2 - 5$
(30)   (30)   (31)

15. $3\dfrac{1}{8} + 2\dfrac{1}{4} + 5\dfrac{1}{2}$ **16.** $428\dfrac{1}{11} + 22\dfrac{1}{44}$ **17.** $3\dfrac{2}{5} + 748\dfrac{2}{10}$
(34)   (34)   (34)

18. $4\dfrac{4}{10} - 1\dfrac{1}{5}$ **19.** $548\dfrac{6}{8} - 31\dfrac{1}{16}$ **20.** $991\dfrac{1}{3} - 791\dfrac{17}{18}$
(35)   (35)   (35)

21. 71.82×8.01 **22.** $\dfrac{936.7}{0.04}$ **23.** $\dfrac{21}{8} \times \dfrac{4}{14} \div \dfrac{9}{2}$
(7)   (7)   (22)

24. Convert 250.025 to a mixed number.
(28)

Evaluate:

25. $xy + yz - z$ if $x = 1$, $y = 7$, and $z = 2$
(32)

26. $xyz - xy$ if $x = 2$, $y = 3$, and $z = 3$
(32)

27. Use two unit multipliers to convert 10 miles to inches.
(33)

28. Find the area of this figure. Dimensions are in yards.
(17,27)

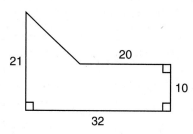

29. Write $\frac{11}{13}$ as a decimal number. Round to two decimal places.
(15)

30. Reduce to lowest terms: $\dfrac{102}{170}$
(14)

LESSON 38 *Rectangular Coordinates*

Here we show two number lines. The lines are perpendicular and intersect at the origin of both lines. We call the vertical line the **y-axis** and the horizontal line the **x-axis.** The whole figure is called a **rectangular coordinate system** or **Cartesian coordinate system.** Still other times, the figure is simply called a **coordinate plane.**

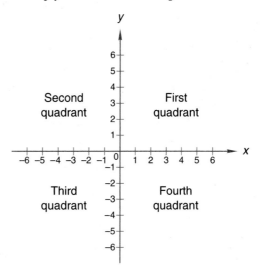

The number lines (axes) divide the plane into four quarters, or **quadrants.** The upper right quadrant is called the first quadrant. The others are numbered in a counterclockwise direction.

Any point on the plane can be designated by saying how far it is to the right or left of the y-axis and how far up or down it is from the x-axis. Two numbers are associated with every point on the plane. The first number tells how far the point is to the right (+) or to the left (–) of the y-axis. This number is called the **x-coordinate** of the point. The second number tells how far the point is above (+) or below (–) the x-axis. This is called the **y-coordinate** of the point. We name a point by referring to its coordinates. We write its coordinates as follows:

(*x*-coordinate, *y*-coordinate)

example 38.1 Four points are graphed on this rectangular coordinate system. What are the *x*- and *y*-coordinates of the points?

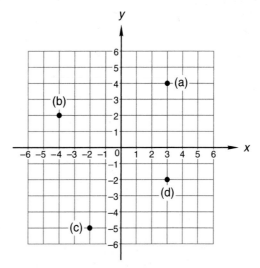

solution   Point (a) is 3 units to the right of the *y*-axis and 4 units above the *x*-axis.

(a) $x = 3$, $y = 4$ or **(3, 4)**

Point (b) is 4 units to the left of the *y*-axis and 2 units above the *x*-axis.

(b) $x = -4$, $y = 2$ or **(−4, 2)**

Point (c) is 2 units to the left of the *y*-axis and 5 units below the *x*-axis.

(c) $x = -2$, $y = -5$ or **(−2, −5)**

Point (d) is 3 units to the right of the *y*-axis and 2 units below the *x*-axis.

(d) $x = 3$, $y = -2$ or **(3, −2)**

example 38.2   Graph the following points: (a) (4, 2)   (b) (4, −3)   (c) (−4, −3)

solution   The first number is always the *x*-coordinate, and the second number is always the *y*-coordinate. Thus,

(a) is 4 units to the right of the *y*-axis and 2 units above the *x*-axis

(b) is 4 units to the right of the *y*-axis and 3 units below the *x*-axis

(c) is 4 units to the left of the *y*-axis and 3 units below the *x*-axis

Now we graph the points.

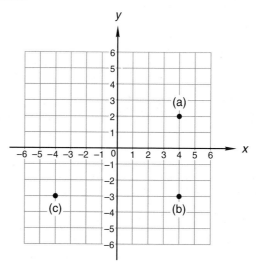

example 38.3   Make a sketch of a rectangular coordinate system, and graph the points (−3, 2) and (4, −1).

solution   A quick sketch is all we need. We do not even need to put numbers on the axes.

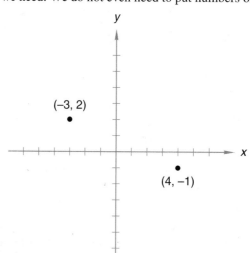

example 38.4   The vertices of a rectangle are (–2, –3), (4, 2), (4, –3), and (–2, 2). Draw the rectangle and find its perimeter and area.

solution   We graph each point and draw the rectangle.

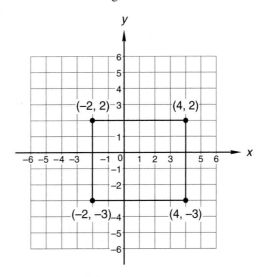

We see that the rectangle is 6 units long and 5 units wide. So,

$$\text{Perimeter} = 6 \text{ units} + 5 \text{ units} + 6 \text{ units} + 5 \text{ units} = \textbf{22 units}$$

$$\text{Area} = 6 \text{ units} \times 5 \text{ units} = \textbf{30 sq. units}$$

practice   Make a sketch of a rectangular coordinate system. Graph these points:

    a. (–4, –3)   **b.** (–4, 2)   **c.** (3, –2)   **d.** (3, 5)

**problem set
38**

1.
(36)   Rubella was paid $56 for working 7 hours. Write the two rates (ratios) implied by this statement. How much was she paid for a 40-hour week?

2.
(26)   The four weights were 4016 tons, 7132 tons, 9831 tons, and 6253 tons. What was the (a) range, (b) mode, (c) median, and (d) mean of the four weights?

3.
(13)   If 942 tries were permitted and John averaged 462 points on each try, how many points did John get if he used all his tries?

4.
(18)   What number is $\frac{5}{17}$ of 34?

Solve:

5. $3x = 12$
(37)

6. $\frac{x}{2} = 57$
(37)

7. $\frac{2}{5} + x = \frac{3}{5}$
(30,37)

Write each improper fraction as a mixed number:

8. $\frac{428}{17}$
(28)

9. $\frac{521}{3}$
(28)

10.   Find the least common multiple of 50, 47, and 120.
(20)

Simplify:

11.
(30) $\dfrac{15}{17} - \dfrac{2}{34}$

12.
(34) $\dfrac{3}{8} + 1\dfrac{1}{5} - \dfrac{1}{10}$

13.
(31) $4 + 13 - 5 \cdot 2 + 7$

14.
(31) $2 \cdot 8 - 3 \cdot 1 + 2 \cdot 4$

15.
(34) $3\dfrac{1}{5} + 2\dfrac{1}{8}$

16.
(34) $376\dfrac{4}{5} + 142\dfrac{3}{10}$

17.
(35) $42\dfrac{7}{8} - 15\dfrac{3}{4}$

18.
(35) $513\dfrac{11}{20} - 21\dfrac{4}{5}$

19.
(7) $\dfrac{13.62}{0.05}$

20.
(22) $\dfrac{14}{16} \cdot \dfrac{24}{21} \div \dfrac{2}{3}$

21.
(10) The number 5970 is divisible by which of the following numbers: 2, 3, 5, 10?

22.
(24) How many centimeters is 241.36 meters?

Evaluate:

23.
(32) $xz - yz$ if $x = 7$, $y = 1$, and $z = 3$

24.
(32) $xyz + yz - y$ if $x = 6$, $y = 3$, and $z = \dfrac{1}{3}$

25.
(33) Use two unit multipliers to convert 400 square inches to square feet. Round any decimal answer to two places.

26.
(17,27) Find the area of this figure in square centimeters.

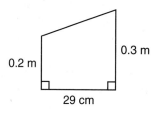

0.2 m   0.3 m

29 cm

27.
(9) Find the perimeter of this figure. Dimensions are in yards. All angles are right angles.

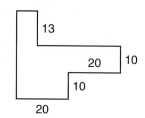

13

20   10

10

20

28.
(28) Convert 92.45 to a mixed number.

29.
(38) Make a sketch of a rectangular coordinate system, and graph the points (3, 5), (–3, 1), (5, –4), and (–5, –5).

30.
(27,38) The vertices of a triangle are (–4, –4), (2, 3), and (–4, 3). Draw the triangle, and find its area.

LESSON *39*   *Equivalent Equations • Addition-Subtraction Rule for Equations*

39.A
equivalent equations

The five equations shown here are different equations.

$$\text{(a) } x = 6 \qquad \text{(b) } x + 3 = 9 \qquad \text{(c) } x - 3 = 3$$

$$\text{(d) } 3x = 18 \qquad \text{(e) } \frac{x}{3} = 2$$

The number 6 is a solution to all five equations, because if we replace x with 6, each of the equations becomes a true equation.

$$\text{(a) } 6 = 6 \qquad \text{(b) } 6 + 3 = 9 \qquad \text{(c) } 6 - 3 = 3$$
$$\qquad\qquad\qquad\qquad\quad 9 = 9 \qquad\qquad\qquad 3 = 3$$

$$\text{(d) } 3(6) = 18 \qquad \text{(e) } \frac{6}{3} = 2$$
$$\qquad\quad 18 = 18 \qquad\qquad\qquad 2 = 2$$

Equation (a) was the easiest because it told us that the answer was 6. We did not even have to think. We say that all five equations are **equivalent equations** because equivalent equations are equations that have the same solutions (answers).

39.B
addition-subtraction rule for equations

Some equations are very easy to solve. We can mentally calculate the numbers that are solutions to the simple equations (b) through (e).

$$\text{(b) } x + 3 = 9 \qquad \text{(c) } x - 3 = 3 \qquad \text{(d) } 3x = 18 \qquad \text{(e) } \frac{x}{3} = 2$$

However, many equations are not easy to solve mentally. It is helpful to have rules that can be used to solve difficult equations. The first rule is the **addition-subtraction rule for equations.**

ADDITION-SUBTRACTION RULE FOR EQUATIONS

1. The same number can be added to both sides of an equation without changing the solution to the equation.
2. The same number can be subtracted from both sides of an equation without changing the solution to the equation.

Part 1 of this rule is often called the **Addition Property of Equality** and part 2 the **Subtraction Property of Equality.** The essential idea, when we simplify equations with this rule, is that we perform the same operation on both sides of the equation.

We will begin by using this rule to solve some equations.

example 39.1   Solve: $x - 3 = 7$

solution   We can undo the subtraction of 3 by adding 3. So we add 3 to both sides of the equation.

$$\begin{array}{ll} x - 3 = 7 & \text{equation} \\ x - 3 + 3 = 7 + 3 & \text{added 3 to both sides} \\ x = 10 & \text{simplified} \end{array}$$

As our final step, we need to check our solution.

$$x - 3 = 7 \qquad \text{equation}$$
$$(10) - 3 = 7 \qquad \text{substituted 10 for } x$$
$$7 = 7 \qquad \text{check}$$

So, $x = \mathbf{10}$.

example 39.2   Solve: $n + 3 = 7$

solution   This time we must undo the addition of 3 by subtracting 3. We subtract 3 from both sides of the equation.

$$n + 3 = 7 \qquad \text{equation}$$
$$n + 3 - 3 = 7 - 3 \qquad \text{subtracted 3 from both sides}$$
$$n = 4 \qquad \text{simplified}$$

Now we check our answer.

$$n + 3 = 7 \qquad \text{equation}$$
$$(4) + 3 = 7 \qquad \text{substituted 4 for } n$$
$$7 = 7 \qquad \text{check}$$

So, $n = \mathbf{4}$.

example 39.3   Solve: $y + \dfrac{3}{4} = \dfrac{9}{11}$

solution   We can undo the addition of $\frac{3}{4}$ by subtracting $\frac{3}{4}$. We subtract $\frac{3}{4}$ from both sides of the equation.

$$y + \frac{3}{4} = \frac{9}{11} \qquad \text{equation}$$

$$y + \frac{3}{4} - \frac{3}{4} = \frac{9}{11} - \frac{3}{4} \qquad \text{subtracted } \frac{3}{4} \text{ from both sides}$$

$$y = \frac{9}{11} - \frac{3}{4} \qquad \text{simplified}$$

$$y = \frac{36}{44} - \frac{33}{44} \qquad \text{found common denominator}$$

$$y = \frac{3}{44} \qquad \text{simplified}$$

Now we check our answer.

$$y + \frac{3}{4} = \frac{9}{11} \qquad \text{equation}$$

$$\left(\frac{3}{44}\right) + \frac{3}{4} = \frac{9}{11} \qquad \text{substituted } \frac{3}{44} \text{ for } y$$

$$\frac{3}{44} + \frac{33}{44} = \frac{9}{11} \qquad \text{found common denominator}$$

$$\frac{36}{44} = \frac{9}{11} \qquad \text{simplified}$$

$$\frac{9}{11} = \frac{9}{11} \qquad \text{check}$$

So, $y = \frac{3}{44}$.

example 39.4 Solve: $z - \dfrac{3}{5} = \dfrac{2}{10}$

solution We can undo the subtraction of $\frac{3}{5}$ by adding $\frac{3}{5}$. We add $\frac{3}{5}$ to both sides of the equation.

$$z - \frac{3}{5} = \frac{2}{10} \qquad \text{equation}$$

$$z - \frac{3}{5} + \frac{3}{5} = \frac{2}{10} + \frac{3}{5} \qquad \text{added } \frac{3}{5} \text{ to both sides}$$

$$z = \frac{2}{10} + \frac{3}{5} \qquad \text{simplified}$$

$$z = \frac{1}{5} + \frac{3}{5} \qquad \text{reduced } \frac{2}{10} \text{ to } \frac{1}{5}$$

$$z = \frac{4}{5} \qquad \text{simplified}$$

Now we check our solution.

$$z - \frac{3}{5} = \frac{2}{10} \qquad \text{equation}$$

$$\frac{4}{5} - \frac{3}{5} = \frac{2}{10} \qquad \text{substituted } \frac{4}{5} \text{ for } z$$

$$\frac{1}{5} = \frac{2}{10} \qquad \text{simplified}$$

$$\frac{2}{10} = \frac{2}{10} \qquad \text{check}$$

So, $z = \frac{4}{5}$.

practice Solve. Check your answer.

    a. $a + 4 = 6$ **b.** $x - 2 = 4$

    c. $x + \dfrac{1}{2} = \dfrac{3}{4}$ **d.** $x - \dfrac{1}{3} = \dfrac{11}{12}$

problem set 39

1. The squirrel could store 48 nuts in a hiding place. If there were 768 nuts to hide, how
(11) many hiding places did the squirrel need?

2. The squirrel could store 48 nuts per hour. Write the two rates (ratios) implied by this
(36) statement. How many nuts could the squirrel store in 20 hours?

3. When the engineers measured the distance 6 times, they found six different
(26) measurements. The measurements were 5.6 meters, 5.4 meters, 5.3 meters, 5.7 meters,
5.2 meters, and 5.6 meters. What was the (a) range, (b) mode, (c) median, and
(d) mean of the six measurements? Round any decimal answers to two places.

4. The average of the first five numbers drawn was 2499. The first four numbers were
(26) 4165, 320, 7142, and 64. What was the fifth number?

5. What number is $\frac{3}{5}$ of 40?
(18)

Write each improper fraction as a mixed number:

6.
(28)　$\dfrac{316}{13}$

7.
(28)　$\dfrac{428}{5}$

8.
(20)　Find the least common multiple of 8, 12, and 72.

Simplify:

9.
(30)　$\dfrac{14}{15} - \dfrac{1}{5}$

10.
(34)　$4\dfrac{2}{5} + 3\dfrac{5}{10}$

11.
(31)　$3 + 2 + 2 \cdot 5 - 3 \cdot 2$

12.
(31)　$3 - 2 \cdot 1 + 4 \cdot 7$

13.
(34)　$3\dfrac{2}{7} + 5\dfrac{20}{21}$

14.
(34)　$420\dfrac{3}{5} + 262\dfrac{1}{40}$

15.
(35)　$43\dfrac{5}{7} - 12\dfrac{2}{14}$

16.
(35)　$210\dfrac{5}{8} - 17\dfrac{3}{40}$

17.
(7)　611.2×0.0061

18.
(7)　$\dfrac{0.8136}{0.008}$

19.
(22)　$\dfrac{18}{20} \cdot \dfrac{24}{16} \div \dfrac{9}{10}$

20.
(38)　Sketch a rectangular coordinate system, and graph the points (0, 3) and (2, –3).

Solve:

21.
(39)　$x - 9 = 10$

22.
(39)　$x + \dfrac{4}{5} = \dfrac{8}{9}$

23.
(39)　$x - 3.5 = 4$

Evaluate:

24.
(32)　$x + xy + xyz$ 　　if $x = 1$, $y = 2$, and $z = 3$

25.
(32)　$xy + x - y$ 　　if $x = 5$ and $y = 1$

26.
(33)　Use two unit multipliers to convert 625.611 centimeters to kilometers.

27.
(17,27)　Find the area of this figure. Dimensions are in feet.

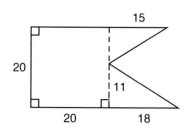

28.
(15)　Write $\frac{20}{23}$ as a decimal number. Round to two decimal places.

29. Convert 14.145 to a mixed number.
(28)

30. Name the *x*- and *y*-coordinates of
(38) point (a) and point (b).

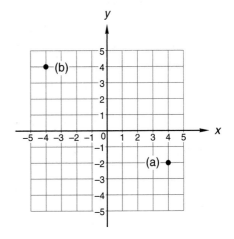

LESSON 40   *Reciprocals • Multiplication Rule • Division Rule*

40.A

reciprocals   Remember that when we invert a fraction, we say that we have written the reciprocal of the fraction. Thus,

$$\frac{2}{5} \quad \text{is the reciprocal of} \quad \frac{5}{2}$$

$$\frac{5}{2} \quad \text{is the reciprocal of} \quad \frac{2}{5}$$

$$\frac{3}{7} \quad \text{is the reciprocal of} \quad \frac{7}{3}$$

$$\frac{7}{3} \quad \text{is the reciprocal of} \quad \frac{3}{7}$$

Since whole numbers can be written with a denominator of 1, all whole numbers, except zero, have a reciprocal.

$$\frac{1}{4} \quad \text{is the reciprocal of} \quad 4$$

$$4 \quad \text{is the reciprocal of} \quad \frac{1}{4}$$

$$\frac{1}{16} \quad \text{is the reciprocal of} \quad 16$$

$$16 \quad \text{is the reciprocal of} \quad \frac{1}{16}$$

The number 0 can be written with a denominator of 1

$$\frac{0}{1}$$

and this still means zero. When we turn it upside down, we get

$$\frac{1}{0}$$

We say that this expression has no meaning because we cannot divide by 0. For this reason we say that the number 0 does not have a reciprocal. **The number 0 is the only number that does not have a reciprocal.**

The reciprocal of 4 is $\frac{1}{4}$. If we multiply 4 by its reciprocal, the answer is 1.

$$\frac{4}{1} \cdot \frac{1}{4} = \frac{4}{4} = 1$$

The reciprocal of $\frac{1}{3}$ is 3. If we multiply $\frac{1}{3}$ by its reciprocal, the answer is 1.

$$\frac{1}{3} \cdot \frac{3}{1} = \frac{3}{3} = 1$$

The reciprocal of $\frac{2}{5}$ is $\frac{5}{2}$. If we multiply $\frac{2}{5}$ by its reciprocal, the answer is 1.

$$\frac{2}{5} \cdot \frac{5}{2} = \frac{10}{10} = 1$$

> The product of any number and its reciprocal is the number 1.

We can use this property of reciprocals to help us solve equations.

40.B
multiplication rule

If a variable is multiplied by a number, we say that the number is the **coefficient** of the variable. In the expression

$$4x$$

we say that 4 is the coefficient of x. The **multiplication rule for equations** can help us solve equations in which the variable has a coefficient.

> MULTIPLICATION RULE FOR EQUATIONS
>
> Both sides of an equation can be multiplied by the same number (except zero) without changing the solution to the equation.

This rule is often called the **Multiplication Property of Equality.** To use this rule, we multiply both sides of the equation by the reciprocal of the coefficient of the variable in order to solve for the variable.

example 40.1   Solve: $4x = 12$

solution   To "get rid of" the 4, we will multiply by the reciprocal of 4, $\frac{1}{4}$. We must remember to multiply *both sides* of the equation by $\frac{1}{4}$.

$$4x = 12 \qquad \text{equation}$$

$$\frac{1}{\overset{1}{\cancel{4}}} \cdot \overset{1}{\cancel{4}}x = \overset{3}{\cancel{12}} \cdot \frac{1}{\underset{1}{\cancel{4}}} \qquad \text{multiplied both sides by } \frac{1}{4}$$

$$x = 3 \qquad \text{simplified}$$

Since $\frac{1}{4} \cdot 4 = 1$, $\frac{1}{4} \cdot 4x = 1x$. But it is simpler to write x than $1x$. We can check our solution by using 3 for x in the original equation.

$$
\begin{array}{ll}
4x = 12 & \text{equation} \\
4(3) = 12 & \text{substituted 3 for } x \\
12 = 12 & \text{check}
\end{array}
$$

Thus, the value of x is **3**.

example 40.2   Solve: $\dfrac{2}{3}y = \dfrac{1}{5}$

solution   To "get rid of" the $\frac{2}{3}$, we will multiply both sides of the equation by $\frac{3}{2}$.

$$\frac{2}{3}y = \frac{1}{5} \qquad \text{equation}$$

$$\frac{\overset{1}{\cancel{3}}}{\underset{1}{\cancel{2}}} \cdot \frac{\overset{1}{\cancel{2}}}{\underset{1}{\cancel{3}}}y = \frac{1}{5} \cdot \frac{3}{2} \qquad \text{multiplied both sides by } \frac{3}{2}$$

$$y = \frac{3}{10} \qquad \text{simplified}$$

Now we use $\frac{3}{10}$ in the original equation to check our answer.

$$\frac{2}{3}y = \frac{1}{5} \qquad \text{equation}$$

$$\frac{\overset{1}{\cancel{2}}}{\underset{1}{\cancel{3}}} \cdot \frac{\overset{1}{\cancel{3}}}{\underset{5}{\cancel{10}}} = \frac{1}{5} \qquad \text{substituted } \frac{3}{10} \text{ for } y$$

$$\frac{1}{5} = \frac{1}{5} \qquad \text{check}$$

Thus, the value of y is $\frac{3}{10}$.

example 40.3   Solve: $\dfrac{m}{3} = 6$

solution   Since the coefficient of m is $\frac{1}{3}$, we multiply both sides of the equation by 3 to "get rid of" the $\frac{1}{3}$.

$$\frac{m}{3} = 6 \qquad \text{equation}$$

$$\overset{1}{\cancel{3}} \cdot \frac{m}{\underset{1}{\cancel{3}}} = 6 \cdot 3 \qquad \text{multiplied both sides by 3}$$

$$m = 18 \qquad \text{simplified}$$

Now we check our answer by using 18 for m in the original equation.

$$\frac{m}{3} = 6 \qquad \text{equation}$$

$$\frac{18}{3} = 6 \qquad \text{substituted 18 for } m$$

$$6 = 6 \qquad \text{check}$$

Thus, the value of m is **18**.

40.C

division rule If we divide 20 by 4, we get the same answer that we get if we multiply 20 by $\frac{1}{4}$.

$$\frac{20}{4} = 5 \qquad 20 \cdot \frac{1}{4} = 5$$

Thus, dividing by a number and multiplying by the reciprocal of the same number produce the same result. We know that we can solve equations by multiplying both sides of the equation by the reciprocal of the coefficient of the variable. We can also solve equations by dividing both sides of the equation by the coefficient of the variable. This procedure is called the **division rule for equations.**

> **DIVISION RULE FOR EQUATIONS**
>
> Both sides of an equation can be divided by the same number (except zero) without changing the solution to the equation.

This rule is often called the **Division Property of Equality.**

example 40.4 Solve by dividing: $4x = 3$

solution Of course, we could solve this equation by multiplying both sides by $\frac{1}{4}$.

$$4x = 3 \qquad \text{equation}$$

$$\left(\frac{1}{4}\right)4x = 3\left(\frac{1}{4}\right) \qquad \text{multiplied both sides by } \frac{1}{4}$$

$$x = \frac{3}{4} \qquad \text{simplified}$$

However, we were told to divide. When we solve by dividing, the answer will be exactly the same.

$$4x = 3 \qquad \text{equation}$$

$$\frac{4x}{4} = \frac{3}{4} \qquad \text{divided both sides by 4}$$

$$x = \frac{3}{4} \qquad \text{simplified}$$

Now we check our solution.

$$4x = 3 \qquad \text{equation}$$

$$4\left(\frac{3}{4}\right) = 3 \qquad \text{substituted } \frac{3}{4} \text{ for } x$$

$$3 = 3 \qquad \text{check}$$

Thus, the value of x is $\frac{3}{4}$.

example 40.5 Solve by dividing: $N \times 0.04 = 28$

solution The coefficient of N is 0.04. So we divide both sides by 0.04.

$$N \times 0.04 = 28 \qquad \text{equation}$$

$$\frac{N \times 0.04}{0.04} = \frac{28}{0.04} \qquad \text{divided both sides by 0.04}$$

$$N = 700 \qquad \text{simplified}$$

Now we check our solution.

$$N \times 0.04 = 28 \qquad \text{equation}$$
$$(700) \times 0.04 = 28 \qquad \text{substituted 700 for } N$$
$$28 = 28 \qquad \text{check}$$

Thus, the value of N is **700.**

When we need to "get rid of" a coefficient, how should we decide which rule to use—multiplication or division? Choose whichever looks easier! To solve $\frac{1}{3}x = \frac{4}{5}$, it is easier to multiply by the reciprocal, 3, than to divide by the coefficient, $\frac{1}{3}$. To solve $6x = 54$, most students think division by 6 is easier than multiplication by $\frac{1}{6}$. It is really a matter of style, since division by a number and multiplication by that number's reciprocal are exactly the same. These rules are often combined into one rule, the **Multiplication-Division Rule for Equations.**

practice Solve each equation by multiplying both sides of the equation by the reciprocal of the coefficient of x or by dividing both sides by the coefficient of x. Check each answer.

a. $\dfrac{5}{11}x = 7$ **b.** $3x = 15$ **c.** $\dfrac{x}{3} = 5$ **d.** $4x = \dfrac{1}{3}$

problem set 40

1.
(26) Sandra counted skiers as they slid around the corner. The first hour she counted 415, and the second hour she counted 478. If she counted 526 in the third hour, what was the average number of skiers for the 3 hours?

2.
(36) Watonga picked up 420 cans in the first 6 minutes. Write the two rates (ratios) implied by this statement. How many cans could Watonga pick up in 48 hours at the same rate?

3.
(11) Nineteen thousand, four hundred forty came to see the spectacle. If 32 could be seated in a bus, how many buses were required to haul them all away?

4.
(38) Sketch a rectangular coordinate system, and graph the points $(-4, -1)$ and $(3, 1)$.

Write each improper fraction as a mixed number:

5.
(28) $\dfrac{41}{3}$

6.
(28) $\dfrac{93}{21}$

7.
(20) Find the least common multiple of 27, 28, and 30.

Simplify:

8.
(30) $\dfrac{5}{16} - \dfrac{1}{8}$

9.
(34) $2\dfrac{1}{5} + 3\dfrac{1}{3} - \dfrac{2}{10}$

10.
(31) $14 - 2 \cdot 3 + 4 \cdot 5$

11.
(31) $2 \cdot 5 - 2 \cdot 2 + 3$

12.
(34) $7\dfrac{1}{8} + 3\dfrac{2}{5}$

13.
(35) $674\dfrac{2}{5} - 13\dfrac{7}{10}$

14.
(34) $2\dfrac{1}{4} + 3\dfrac{1}{8} + 4\dfrac{5}{12}$

15.
(35) $461\dfrac{3}{4} - 65\dfrac{7}{8}$

16.
(7) 117.1×2.01

17.
(7) $\dfrac{171.6}{0.006}$

18.
(6) $6132.81 - 621.981$

19.
(22) $\dfrac{6}{21} \cdot \dfrac{24}{3} \div \dfrac{8}{14}$

20.
(33) Use two unit multipliers to convert 1 mile to inches.

Solve:

21. $v - 8 = 9$ **22.** $x + \dfrac{3}{8} = \dfrac{9}{14}$ **23.** $w - \dfrac{3}{7} = \dfrac{5}{14}$
₍₃₉₎   ₍₃₉₎   ₍₃₉₎

24. $\dfrac{2}{19}x = 6$ **25.** $7q = 35$ **26.** $8r = \dfrac{1}{9}$
₍₄₀₎   ₍₄₀₎   ₍₄₀₎

27. Write 51.785 as a mixed number.
₍₂₈₎

28. Evaluate: $xyz + xy + yz - z$ if $x = \dfrac{1}{3}$, $y = 12$, and $z = 2$
₍₃₂₎

29. Find the area of this figure.
_(17,27) Dimensions are in inches.

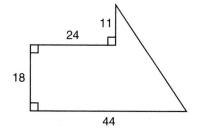

30. (a) List the prime numbers between 37 and 46.
_(12,20)
     (b) List the multiples of 6 between 37 and 46.

LESSON 41   *Overall Average*

The average of the averages is seldom the **overall average.** Suppose we have ten numbers and the first three numbers are the numbers 3, 4, and 5. The average of the first three numbers is 4.

$$\frac{3 + 4 + 5}{3} = \frac{12}{3} = 4$$

Suppose the last seven numbers are 7, 8, 8, 8, 8, 8, and 9. The average of these numbers is 8.

$$\frac{7 + 8 + 8 + 8 + 8 + 8 + 9}{7} = \frac{56}{7} = 8$$

The average of the first three numbers is 4. The average of the other seven numbers is 8. When we average 4 and 8 we get 6.

$$\frac{4 + 8}{2} = \frac{12}{2} = 6$$

Now we will compute the overall average of the original ten numbers by dividing their sum by the number of numbers.

$$\text{Overall average} = \frac{3 + 4 + 5 + 7 + 8 + 8 + 8 + 8 + 8 + 9}{10} = \frac{68}{10} = 6.8$$

We see that the average of the averages is 6 and the overall average of the ten numbers is 6.8. They are not equal. **Therefore, we cannot find the overall average of a set of numbers by finding the average of the averages.** The overall average must be some number between the average of the first group, 4, and the average of the second group, 8. We cannot assume it is 6, which is halfway between 4 and 8. The overall average of 6.8 is closer to 8 than it is to 4 because there are more numbers in the group whose average is 8.

example 41.1 The average of the first two numbers was 6. The average of the next 8 numbers was 20. What was the overall average of the 10 numbers?

solution We compute the overall average the same way we compute any average. *The average is always the sum of the numbers divided by the number of numbers.* The average of the first two numbers was 6, so their sum was 2×6, or 12. The average of the next eight numbers was 20, so their sum was 8×20, or 160. The total number of numbers was 10.

$$\text{Overall average} = \frac{(2 \times 6) + (8 \times 20)}{2 + 8} = \frac{172}{10} = \mathbf{17.2}$$

practice **a.** The average price of the first four items was $40. The average price of the next six items was $80. What was the overall average price?

problem set 41

1. (26) The average rainfall for 5 days was 3 inches per day. It rained 1 inch on the first day, 4.5 inches on the second day, 2.9 inches on the third day, and 4 inches on the fourth day. How many inches did it rain on the fifth day?

2. (36) Ronald paid $600 and got 30 hanging plants. Write the two rates (ratios) implied by this statement. How much would he have had to pay for 70 hanging plants at the same rate?

3. (11) If 47 could be crammed into each compartment and if 2820 were waiting patiently in line, how many compartments would it take for all of them?

4. (21,29) What was the average rainfall for the first 5 months of the year as indicated by this graph?

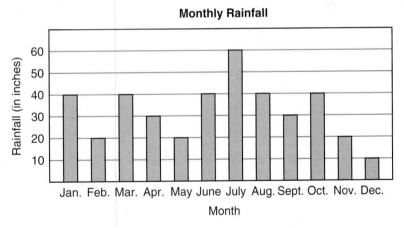

Monthly Rainfall

5. (41) The average weight of the three largest lynx was 38 pounds. The average weight of the other 7 lynx was 31 pounds. What was the overall average weight of the lynx?

6. (41) Twelve narwhals had tusks an average of 91 centimeters long. Four other narwhals had tusks an average of 110 centimeters long. What was the overall average length of the tusks of the sixteen narwhals?

Write each improper fraction as a mixed number:

7. (28) $\dfrac{82}{5}$ **8.** (28) $\dfrac{121}{15}$

9. Find the least common multiple of 35, 40, and 120.
(20)

Solve:

10. $x + \dfrac{3}{4} = \dfrac{7}{8}$　　　　**11.** $x - \dfrac{1}{2} = \dfrac{5}{6}$　　　　**12.** $6x = 18$
(39)　　　　　　　　　　　(39)　　　　　　　　　　　(40)

13. $\dfrac{x}{4} = 15$　　　　　**14.** $5x = 20$　　　　　**15.** $\dfrac{x}{7} = 5$
(40)　　　　　　　　　　　(40)　　　　　　　　　　　(40)

Simplify:

16. $\dfrac{7}{15} - \dfrac{1}{5}$　　　　　　　　**17.** $3 \cdot 8 - 2 \cdot 6 + 1 \cdot 7$
(30)　　　　　　　　　　　　　　　(31)

18. $36\dfrac{3}{4} - 21\dfrac{7}{8}$　　　　　　　**19.** $\dfrac{171.6}{0.6}$
(35)　　　　　　　　　　　　　　　(7)

20. 112.4×0.071　　　　　　　**21.** $6781.8 - 179.89$
(7)　　　　　　　　　　　　　　　　(6)

22. $\dfrac{16}{18} \cdot \dfrac{24}{36} \div \dfrac{8}{9}$　　　　　　　**23.** $5\dfrac{1}{5} + 4\dfrac{4}{9}$
(22)　　　　　　　　　　　　　　　(34)

Evaluate:

24. $x + zx - y$　　if $x = 10$, $y = 3$, and $z = 2$
(32)

25. $xy + xz + yz$　　if $x = 2$, $y = 4$, and $z = 6$
(32)

26. Use two unit multipliers to convert 5280 inches to yards. Round any decimal answer to
(33) two places.

27. Find the area of this figure. Dimen-
(17,27) sions are in meters. Angles that look
like right angles are right angles.

28. Find the perimeter of this figure. Di-
(9) mensions are in centimeters. All angles are right angles.

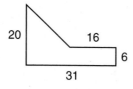

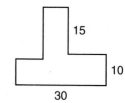

29. Write $\frac{19}{24}$ as a decimal number. Round to two decimal places.
(15)

30. Sketch a rectangular coordinate system, and graph the points $(0, -2)$ and $(3, 2)$.
(38)

LESSON *42*   *Symbols of Inclusion • Division in Order of Operations*

42.A
symbols of inclusion

Thus far we have been using parentheses to indicate multiplication. Each of the following indicate that 4 and 5 are to be multiplied:

(a) (4)(5)   (b) 4(5)   (c) (4)5

Multiplication is indicated when there is no plus or minus sign between parentheses, as in (a). Multiplication is also indicated when there is no plus or minus sign between a number and parentheses, as in (b) and (c).

Parentheses can also be used to group numbers together. When we see parentheses we always simplify within the parentheses first. Then we multiply, and finally we add and subtract.

example 42.1   Simplify: $4 + (3 \cdot 5)2 + 2(15 - 3)$

solution   We begin by simplifying within the two sets of parentheses.

$$4 + (15)2 + 2(12)$$

Now we perform all the multiplication.

$$4 + 30 + 24$$

We finish by adding the numbers.

58

example 42.2   Simplify: $8(20 - 3) - (17 - 11 + 3)2 + 5$

solution   We begin by simplifying within the two sets of parentheses.

$$8(17) - (9)2 + 5$$

Now we multiply.

$$136 - 18 + 5$$

We finish by adding and subtracting from left to right.

$118 + 5$ subtracted 18 from 136

123   added

Parentheses are called **symbols of inclusion.** We also use brackets as symbols of inclusion.

(parentheses)   [brackets]

When an expression contains more than one symbol of inclusion, we begin by simplifying within the innermost symbols of inclusion.

example 42.3   Simplify: $24 - 2[(5 - 2)(14 - 12) + 3]$

solution   We begin by simplifying within the parentheses.

$$24 - 2[(3)(2) + 3]$$

Now we simplify within the brackets. We remember to multiply before we add.

$$24 - 2[6 + 3]$$
$$24 - 2[9]$$

Again we multiply first and then subtract.

$$24 - 18 = \mathbf{6}$$

example 42.4   Simplify: $33 - 2[3(3 + 12) - (5 \cdot 2)3]$

solution   We begin by simplifying within the parentheses.

$$33 - 2[3(15) - (10)3]$$

Now we simplify within the brackets.

$$33 - 2[45 - 30]$$
$$33 - 2[15]$$

Next we multiply and then subtract.

$$33 - 30 = \mathbf{3}$$

42.B

**division in
order of
operations**

The rules for the order of operations when we have addition, subtraction, multiplication, and division are as follows:

ORDER OF OPERATIONS

1. Simplify within the symbols of inclusion.
2. Multiply and divide in order from left to right.
3. Add and subtract in order from left to right.

---

example 42.5   Simplify: $5 + 12 \div 2 + 3 \cdot 4 - 2(5 - 2)$

solution   First we simplify within the parentheses and get

$$5 + 12 \div 2 + 3 \cdot 4 - 2(3)$$

We must always multiply and divide before we add or subtract. Thus, we skip the first operation, which is addition. The next operation is division. We divide 12 by 2 and get 6. Now we have

$$5 + 6 + 3 \cdot 4 - 2(3)$$

The next multiplication or division is $3 \cdot 4$. We multiply and get

$$5 + 6 + 12 - 2(3)$$

Now we do the last multiplication and finish by adding and subtracting from left to right.

$$5 + 6 + 12 - 6 = \mathbf{17}$$

practice   Simplify:

a. $4 + 10 \div 2 - 3(6 - 4)$ **b.** $5 + 10 \cdot 6 - 2(3 \cdot 2) - 2$

c. $55 - 3[(4 - 1)(10 - 6) + 2]$ **d.** $2[3(6 - 3)(4 - 2) + 2] - 2$

**problem set
42**

1. The first shift lasted 4 hours and produced 800 units per hour. The second shift was a
(41) 6-hour shift that produced 600 units per hour. The third shift was a 4-hour shift that produced 400 units per hour. What was the average number of units per hour for the entire period?

2. Ashanti averaged 89 points per test. Write the two rates (ratios) implied by this
(36) statement. How many points would she score if she took 22 tests and maintained the same average?

3.
(29,41)
Seventy people had been employed for 20 years. Thirty other people had been employed for 10 years. Using the information in the graph below, what was the overall average salary of the one hundred given employees?

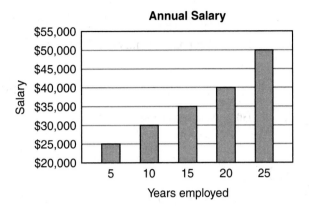

Annual Salary

4.
(23)
Four quarts equal 1 gallon.

(a) Write the two unit multipliers implied by this statement.

(b) Use one of the unit multipliers to convert 1,000,000 gallons to quarts.

5.
(38)
Sketch a rectangular coordinate system, and graph the points (–2, 3) and (–3, –1).

6.
(18)
What number is $\frac{6}{14}$ of 126?

Write each improper fraction as a mixed number:

7.
(28)
$\dfrac{94}{7}$

8.
(28)
$\dfrac{289}{12}$

Solve:

9.
(39)
$x + \dfrac{5}{8} = \dfrac{11}{16}$

10.
(39)
$x - \dfrac{1}{4} = \dfrac{5}{12}$

11.
(40)
$14x = 56$

12.
(40)
$\dfrac{x}{4} = 9$

13.
(40)
$9x = 81$

14.
(40)
$\dfrac{x}{13} = 6$

Simplify:

15.
(30)
$\dfrac{11}{12} - \dfrac{5}{6}$

16.
(35)
$19\dfrac{1}{8} - 8\dfrac{3}{4}$

17.
(7)
$\dfrac{195.8}{1.1}$

18.
(22)
$\dfrac{14}{16} \cdot \dfrac{6}{32} \div \dfrac{3}{4}$

19.
(6)
$9876.5 - 643.99$

20.
(7)
163.09×0.063

21.
(34)
$5\dfrac{2}{9} + 3\dfrac{5}{6}$

22.
(42)
$5(4) \div 2 \times (9 - 4)$

23.
(42)
$[(15 - 3)(2 + 3) - 15] + 2$

24.
(42)
$6[8 - (10 - 4) \div 3] - 28 \div 4$

25.
(42)
$13 + (2 - 1)[5 + (7 - 2)]$

Evaluate:

26.
(32)
$mn + zy - y$ if $m = 4$, $n = 3$, $z = 2$, and $y = 1$

27. $ax + bx - ab$ if $a = 2$, $b = 3$, and $x = 2$
(32)

28. Use two unit multipliers to convert 628 kilometers to centimeters.
(33)

29. Find the area of this figure. Dimensions
(17,27) are in feet. Angles that look like right
angles are right angles.

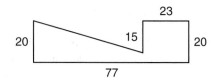

30. Write $\frac{5}{8}$ as a decimal number.
(15)

LESSON 43   *Multiplying Mixed Numbers • Dividing Mixed Numbers*

43.A

multiplying mixed numbers

The easiest way to multiply mixed numbers is to convert them to improper fractions and then multiply the improper fractions.

example 43.1   Multiply: $4\frac{1}{3} \cdot \frac{6}{5}$

solution   We first write $4\frac{1}{3}$ as an improper fraction.

$$\frac{13}{3} \cdot \frac{6}{5}$$

We always cancel if we can. Then we multiply.

$$\frac{13}{\overset{}{\underset{1}{3}}} \cdot \frac{\overset{2}{6}}{5} = \frac{26}{5}$$

This answer can be written as $5\frac{1}{5}$ if desired.

example 43.2   Multiply: $2\frac{1}{4} \times 3\frac{1}{3} \times 5\frac{1}{12}$

solution   First we convert each mixed number to an improper fraction.

$$\frac{9}{4} \times \frac{10}{3} \times \frac{61}{12}$$

Now we cancel where possible and then multiply.

$$\frac{\overset{3}{\underset{}{\cancel{9}}}}{4} \times \frac{\overset{5}{\cancel{10}}}{\underset{1}{\cancel{3}}} \times \frac{61}{\underset{\underset{2}{6}}{\cancel{12}}} = \frac{305}{8}$$

In arithmetic, we usually convert all improper fractions to mixed numbers. In algebra and other advanced courses, the improper fraction form is preferred by many. We will leave this answer as an improper fraction. In future lessons, we will sometimes use the improper fraction form, and other times we will use the mixed number form. Either form is correct.

43.B
dividing mixed numbers

To divide mixed numbers, we first write the mixed numbers as improper fractions. Then we invert the divisor and multiply.

example 43.3 Simplify: $\dfrac{2\frac{1}{8}}{3\frac{2}{3}}$

solution First we write both mixed numbers as improper fractions.

$$\dfrac{\frac{17}{8}}{\frac{11}{3}}$$

Now we invert and multiply.

$$\frac{17}{8} \cdot \frac{3}{11} = \frac{51}{88}$$

example 43.4 Simplify: $4\frac{1}{8} \div 2\frac{1}{5} \cdot 3\frac{1}{4} \div 5\frac{1}{2}$

solution First we write each mixed number as an improper fraction.

$$\frac{33}{8} \div \frac{11}{5} \cdot \frac{13}{4} \div \frac{11}{2}$$

Next we invert the divisors and change every division sign to a multiplication sign. Then we cancel and multiply.

$$\frac{\overset{3}{\cancel{33}}}{\underset{4}{\cancel{8}}} \cdot \frac{5}{\underset{1}{\cancel{11}}} \cdot \frac{13}{4} \cdot \frac{\overset{1}{\cancel{2}}}{11} = \frac{195}{176}$$

practice Simplify:

a. $4\frac{1}{4} \times \frac{8}{9}$

b. $2\frac{1}{4} \times 1\frac{1}{2} \times 3\frac{1}{3}$

c. $\dfrac{3\frac{1}{4}}{2\frac{1}{5}}$

d. $4\frac{2}{3} \div 1\frac{1}{6} \cdot 2\frac{1}{3} \div 1\frac{2}{3}$

problem set 43

1. Nineteen thousand, one hundred forty-two millionths was the first guess. The second
  (6) guess was eight thousand, five hundred forty-one hundred-thousandths. Which guess was greater and by how much?

2. They were happy because 80 of the people could be seated comfortably in each vehicle.
  (11) If there were 1420 vehicles in the parking lot, how many people could be seated comfortably?

3. Pavo bought 20 bunches at $40 a bunch. Write the two rates (ratios) implied by this
  (36) statement. How much would he have to pay for 100 bunches?

4. Fran did 42 steps a minute for the first hour. For the next 30 minutes she did 20 steps a
(13) minute, and for the last 50 minutes she did only 10 steps every minute. How many did
she do in all?

5. The first go contained 40 astronauts. The second go contained twice that many. The
(13) third go contained four times the number the second go contained. By how many
astronauts did the third go exceed the sum of the first go and the second go?

6. Sketch a rectangular coordinate system, and graph the points $(4, -1)$ and $(2, 4)$.
(38)

7. Write $\frac{271}{15}$ as a mixed number.
(28)

8. Find the least common multiple of 12, 22, and 40.
(20)

Solve:

9. $\frac{2}{3}x = 3$ **10.** $\frac{3}{7}x = \frac{2}{9}$ **11.** $\frac{x}{5} = 60$
(40)   (40)   (40)

12. $5x = 60$ **13.** $x + \frac{1}{8} = \frac{1}{2}$ **14.** $x - \frac{1}{4} = \frac{1}{2}$
(40)   (39)   (39)

Simplify:

15. $61\frac{11}{15} - 15\frac{3}{5}$ **16.** $\frac{5}{8} + 2\frac{1}{4} - \frac{1}{10}$
(35)   (34)

17. $2362.8 - 189.87$ **18.** $\frac{612.5}{0.07}$
(6)   (7)

19. $\frac{12}{16} \cdot \frac{12}{21} \div \frac{6}{14}$ **20.** $7 + (6 \cdot 3) \div 2 + 3(11 - 2)$
(22)   (42)

21. $6(17 - 5) - (15 - 13 + 4)4 + 6$ **22.** $41 - 4[(6 - 2) + 3(5 - 3)]$
(42)   (42)

23. $2\frac{1}{3} \times \frac{2}{7}$ **24.** $5\frac{5}{7} \times 1\frac{1}{2} \times 3\frac{2}{3}$
(43)   (43)

25. $\dfrac{9\frac{3}{8}}{5\frac{3}{4}}$ **26.** $4\frac{1}{6} \div 8\frac{3}{4} \times 2\frac{1}{6} \div 6\frac{1}{2}$
(43)   (43)

Evaluate:

27. $xy + yz - z$ if $x = \frac{1}{5}$, $y = 20$, and $z = 3$
(32)

28. $xyz - x$ if $x = 6$, $y = 16$, and $z = \frac{1}{12}$
(32)

29. Express the perimeter of this figure in
(9,24) centimeters. All angles are right
angles.

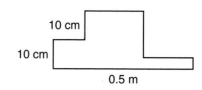

10 cm

10 cm

0.5 m

30. Convert 59.850 to a mixed number.
(28)

LESSON 44   Roots • Order of Operations with Exponents and Roots

44.A
roots

The inverse operation of raising to a power is called taking the **root.** If we use 2 as a factor 4 times, the answer is 16.

$$2^4 = 16$$

If we wish to undo this, we can ask, "What number used as a factor 4 times equals 16?" We would write

$$\sqrt[4]{16}$$

The answer is 2 because

$$2 \cdot 2 \cdot 2 \cdot 2 = 16$$

so we write

$$\sqrt[4]{16} = 2$$

We read this by saying "the fourth root of sixteen equals two." We say that 16 is the **radicand,** 4 is the **index,** and 2 is the **root.** We call the symbol

the **radical sign.** If the index is not written, it is understood to be 2. We call the whole expression a **radical expression** or just a **radical.** The following examples show how to read radical expressions:

$$\sqrt{16} \qquad \text{"the square root of 16"}$$
$$\sqrt[3]{27} \qquad \text{"the cube root of 27"}$$
$$\sqrt[5]{32} \qquad \text{"the fifth root of 32"}$$

For the present, we will restrict our attention to radicals that represent whole numbers. In later lessons, we will investigate radicals that represent decimal numbers.

example 44.1   Simplify: (a) $\sqrt[4]{81}$ (b) $\sqrt[3]{27}$ (c) $\sqrt{16}$ (d) $\sqrt[3]{8}$

solution   (a) Since $3 \cdot 3 \cdot 3 \cdot 3 = 81$, $\sqrt[4]{81} = \mathbf{3}$

(b) Since $3 \cdot 3 \cdot 3 = 27$, $\sqrt[3]{27} = \mathbf{3}$

(c) Since $4 \cdot 4 = 16$, $\sqrt{16} = \mathbf{4}$

(d) Since $2 \cdot 2 \cdot 2 = 8$, $\sqrt[3]{8} = \mathbf{2}$

example 44.2   Simplify: (a) 1^5 (b) $\sqrt[3]{1}$

solution   (a) If we use 1 as a factor 5 times, the answer is 1.

$$1 \cdot 1 \cdot 1 \cdot 1 \cdot 1 = \mathbf{1}$$

We see that **1 raised to any power equals 1.**

(b) When we write

$$\sqrt[3]{1}$$

we are asking "what number used as a factor 3 times equals 1?" Of course, the answer is 1.

$$\sqrt[3]{1} = \mathbf{1}$$

The fourth root of 1 is 1. The fifth root of 1 is 1. **Any root of 1 is 1.**

44.B

**order of
operations
with exponents
and roots**

When we simplify expressions containing symbols of inclusion, we always begin by simplifying within these symbols. Then we simplify exponents and roots. Lastly, we remember to multiply and divide before we add or subtract.

ORDER OF OPERATIONS

1. Simplify within the symbols of inclusion.
2. Simplify exponents and roots.
3. Multiply and divide in order from left to right.
4. Add and subtract in order from left to right.

---

example 44.3   Simplify: $4(3 - 2 + 8) + 2^2 - \sqrt[3]{27} + 12 \div 2$

solution   First we simplify within the parentheses.

$$4(9) + 2^2 - \sqrt[3]{27} + 12 \div 2$$

Then we simplify the exponents and roots.

$$4(9) + 4 - 3 + 12 \div 2$$

Now we multiply and divide as indicated.

$$36 + 4 - 3 + 6$$

We finish by adding and subtracting from left to right.

$$40 - 3 + 6 \qquad \text{added 36 and 4}$$
$$37 + 6 \qquad \text{subtracted 3 from 40}$$
$$\mathbf{43} \qquad \text{added 37 and 6}$$

practice   Simplify:

a. $\sqrt[4]{625}$ **b.** $\sqrt[3]{64}$

c. $\sqrt{81}$ **d.** $5(4 - 1 + 7) + 5^2 - \sqrt[3]{64}$

**problem set
44**

1. Lucas bought 78 pots for \$312. Write the two rates (ratios) implied by this statement. What would he have had to pay for 400 pots at the same rate?
(36)

2. What was the average number of tons of recycled aluminum per month for the first 4 months of the year?
(21,29)

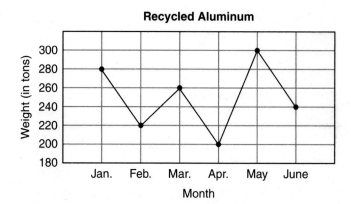

Recycled Aluminum

3. During the first hour, twenty-two million, forty rabbits were born. During the second
(5) hour, only fourteen million, eight hundred sixty-five thousand, nine hundred thirty-two
rabbits were born. How many more rabbits were born during the first hour?

4. The average number of pills in each of the 10 small containers was 1100. The average
(41) number of pills in each of the 20 big containers was 1400. What was the average
number of pills in all the containers?

5. Sketch a rectangular coordinate system, and graph the points (–1, –1) and (–2, 3).
(38)

6. Write $7\frac{5}{16}$ as an improper fraction.
(28)

7. Find the least common multiple of 14, 21, and 49.
(20)

Solve:

8. $\frac{7}{8}x = 4$ **9.** $4x = 80$ **10.** $\frac{x}{7} = 84$
(40)   (40)   (40)

11. $x - \frac{3}{7} = \frac{9}{14}$ **12.** $x + \frac{3}{11} = \frac{9}{22}$
(39)   (39)

Simplify:

13. $3 + (2 \cdot 5)3 + 4(8 \div 2)$ **14.** $10 + 2[5(6 - 4) - 3]$
(42)   (42)

15. $\sqrt{36}$ **16.** $\sqrt[3]{216}$
(44)   (44)

17. $5\frac{1}{2} \times \frac{12}{7}$ **18.** $3\frac{1}{5} \times 1\frac{3}{8} \times 1\frac{1}{11}$
(43)   (43)

19. $\dfrac{1\frac{2}{5}}{2\frac{1}{7}}$ **20.** $1\frac{1}{6} \div 3 \cdot 6\frac{3}{4} \div 1\frac{1}{2}$
(43)   (43)

21. $\frac{5}{6} + 1\frac{5}{12} - \frac{3}{4}$ **22.** $17\frac{7}{12} - 12\frac{3}{4}$
(34)   (35)

23. $117.89 - 112.341$ **24.** $\dfrac{7812}{0.003}$
(6)   (7)

25. $14 + 3\big[(5 - 1)(8 - 6) - \sqrt[3]{8}\big] + 1$
(44)

26. Evaluate: $xz + yz - xy$ if $x = 4$, $y = \frac{1}{2}$, and $z = 8$
(32)

27. Use two unit multipliers to convert 3 miles to inches.
(33)

28. Find the area of this figure. Dimensions
(17,27) are in feet. Angles that look like right
angles are right angles.

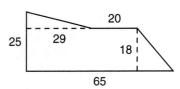

29. If we use 10 as a factor twice, we get 100 as the product. How many times must we use
(13) 10 as a factor to get 1,000,000 as the product?

30. Use two unit multipliers to convert 5 square meters to square centimeters.
(33)

LESSON 45 *Volume*

We use the word area to describe the size of a surface. When we tell how large an area is, we describe how many squares of a certain size can be drawn on the surface. Area has only length and width.

We use the word **volume** to describe a space or a solid that has depth as well as length and width. Volume is not flat. Volume describes how many cubes of a certain size something will hold. A **cube** is an object that has six identical square faces.

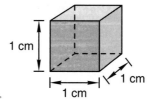

If each of the edges is 1 centimeter long, we say that the cube has a volume of 1 cubic centimeter. If each of the edges is 1 foot long, the volume is 1 cubic foot. If each of the edges is 1 mile long, the volume is 1 cubic mile, etc. We use exponents to help us abbreviate the units for volume.

$$1 \text{ cubic centimeter } = 1 \text{ cm}^3 \qquad 1 \text{ cubic foot } = 1 \text{ ft}^3 \qquad 1 \text{ cubic mile } = 1 \text{ mi}^3$$

If we have a rectangular region that measures 4 centimeters by 2 centimeters, it has an area of 8 square centimeters.

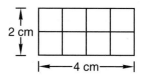

We can use sugar cubes to help us think about volume. One sugar cube with a volume of 1 cubic centimeter can be set on each of the squares shown. If we place one cube on each square, we will use eight cubes. If we stack the cubes two deep, we will use sixteen cubes.

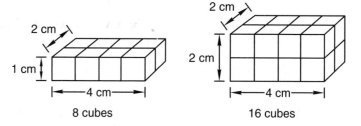

8 cubes   16 cubes

The figure on the left has a volume of 8 cm^3, and the figure on the right has a volume of 16 cm^3. If we stack the cubes three deep, we would have three layers of eight cubes; and if we stack them four deep, we would have four layers of 8 cubes.

$$3 \text{ layers of 8 cubes } = 24 \text{ cubes}$$

$$4 \text{ layers of 8 cubes } = 32 \text{ cubes}$$

We call a geometric figure that occupies a space a **geometric solid.** We call the region on which we stack cubes a **base.** If the sides of the solid go straight up from a base to a uniform height, the sides make a right angle where they contact the base. We call these geometric solids **right geometric solids** or just **right solids.** From the discussion about sugar cubes above, we see that the volume of a right solid equals the area of a base times the height.

Volume of right solid = area of base × height

example 45.1 The rectangle shown is a base of a right solid whose sides are 4 centimeters tall. Dimensions are in centimeters. Find the volume of the solid.

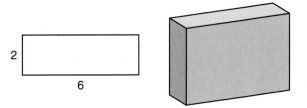

solution The base measures 6 cm by 2 cm so the area of the base is 12 cm^2.

Area of base = 6 cm × 2 cm = 12 cm^2

This means that twelve one-centimeter cubes will cover the base to a depth of 1 centimeter. The height of the solid is 4 centimeters, so we will stack the cubes four deep.

$$\text{Volume} = \text{area of base} \times \text{height}$$
$$= \left(12 \text{ cm}^2\right) \times (4 \text{ cm}) = \textbf{48 cm}^3$$

This tells us that forty-eight one-centimeter cubes will completely fill the space occupied by this right solid.

example 45.2 The two-dimensional drawing shows a base of a right solid that is 6 feet tall. Find the volume of the solid. Dimensions are in feet.

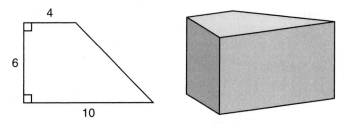

solution First we find the area of the base. We divide the two-dimensional figure into two regions, as shown on the right below.

$$\text{Area of base} = \text{Area } A + \text{Area } B$$
$$= (6 \text{ ft} \times 4 \text{ ft}) + \frac{(6 \text{ ft} \times 6 \text{ ft})}{2}$$
$$= 24 \text{ ft}^2 + 18 \text{ ft}^2$$
$$= 42 \text{ ft}^2$$

Now we know that the base can be covered to a depth of 1 foot with forty-two one-cubic-foot cubes. Of course, we would have to cut the cubes to fit into the corners. If we stack the cubes 6 feet deep, we get a volume of 252 cubic feet.

$$\text{Volume} = \text{area of base} \times \text{height} = \left(42 \text{ ft}^2\right) \times (6 \text{ ft}) = \textbf{252 ft}^3$$

It will take 252 one-foot cubes to completely fill the space occupied by this right solid.

practice   **a.**   Find the number of 1-centimeter cubes that can be placed in a rectangular box measuring 4 cm by 6 cm by 10 cm.

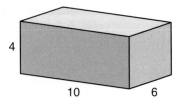

b.   On the left we show a base of a right solid whose height is 12 meters. Dimensions are in meters. Find the volume of the solid.

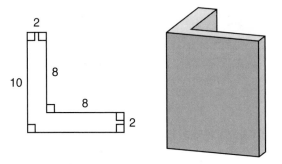

c.   On the left we show a base of a right solid whose height is 2 meters. Dimensions are in meters. Find the volume of the solid.

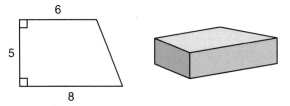

problem set 45

1.   The average number of teachers in each of the 40 small towns was 116. The average number of teachers in each of the 60 large towns was 216. What was the average number of teachers in all the towns?
(41)

2.   Sheila went to court 12 times a month for the first year. For the next 10 years, she went to court twice a month. For the last year, she went to court 3 times a month. How many times did she go to court in all in the twelve years?
(13)

3.   The grocer sold avocados for 79 cents each. Write the two rates (ratios) implied by this statement. How many avocados would the grocer sell for $23.70?
(36)

4.   Antigone's estimate of 16,319.06 cm exceeded the actual measurement by three hundred nine and twelve thousandths cm. What was the actual measurement?
(6)

5.   Sketch a rectangular coordinate system, and graph the points (4, 1) and (–3, 1).
(38)

6.   On the left we show a base of a right solid whose height is 3 feet. Dimensions are in feet. Find the volume of the solid.
(45)

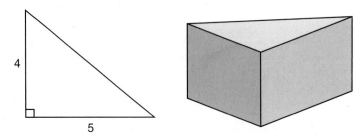

7. On the left we show a base of a right solid whose height is 7 feet. Dimensions are in
(45) feet. Find the volume of the solid.

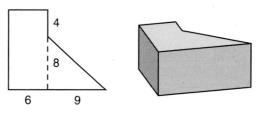

Solve:

8. $\dfrac{3}{8}x = 1$ **9.** $5x = 90$ **10.** $\dfrac{x}{4} = 35$
(40)   (40)   (40)

11. $x - \dfrac{2}{5} = \dfrac{1}{100}$ **12.** $x + \dfrac{3}{13} = \dfrac{9}{26}$
(39)   (39)

Simplify:

13. $5 + [(3 \cdot 2)3 - (10 - 2)]$ **14.** $5 + \sqrt[4]{16}(1^2 + 5) + 15 \div 3$
(42)   (44)

15. $4\dfrac{1}{3} \times \dfrac{7}{5}$ **16.** $2\dfrac{1}{4} \times 1\dfrac{2}{5} \times 1\dfrac{3}{14}$
(43)   (43)

17. $\dfrac{2\dfrac{1}{3}}{3\dfrac{2}{7}}$ **18.** $\dfrac{6}{5} \div \dfrac{3}{2} \cdot \dfrac{15}{8} \div \dfrac{9}{8}$
(43)   (22)

19. $\dfrac{7}{8} + 1\dfrac{3}{16} - \dfrac{1}{2}$ **20.** $14\dfrac{3}{16} - 1\dfrac{1}{2}$
(34)   (35)

21. $12\dfrac{4}{9} + 10\dfrac{7}{30}$ **22.** 23.04×0.00012
(34)   (7)

23. $\dfrac{9663}{0.0006}$
(7)

24. Evaluate: $km + zm - kz$ if $k = 3$, $m = 6$, and $z = \dfrac{1}{3}$
(32)

25. Use two unit multipliers to convert 17 kilometers to centimeters.
(33)

26. Find the area of this figure. Dimensions
(17,27) are in meters. Angles that look like
right angles are right angles.

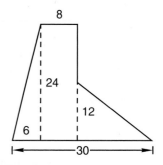

27. The number 10 is used as a factor how many times to get a product of 100,000,000?
(13)

28. (a) List the prime numbers that are greater than 41 but less than 67.
$\overset{}{\scriptstyle(12,20)}$
(b) List the multiples of 3 that are greater than 41 but less than 67.

29. Use two unit multipliers to convert 120 square miles to square feet.
$\overset{}{\scriptstyle(33)}$

30. How much more did the teacher spend for foil and paper than she spent for scissors?
$\overset{}{\scriptstyle(29)}$

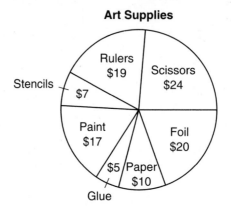

Art Supplies

LESSON 46 *Order of Operations with Fractions*

Thus far, we have restricted order of operations problems to those containing whole numbers. The procedure is the same for fractions and mixed numbers. Unless otherwise indicated, we always multiply and divide before adding and subtracting.

example 46.1 Simplify: $\dfrac{3}{20} + \dfrac{3}{2} \div \dfrac{5}{2}$

solution We skip the addition because we must divide first. We invert the divisor, change the division sign to a multiplication sign, and then multiply.

$$\frac{3}{20} + \frac{3}{2} \cdot \frac{2}{5} = \frac{3}{20} + \frac{3}{5}$$

Now we find the least common denominator and add.

$$\frac{3}{20} + \frac{3}{5} = \frac{3}{20} + \frac{12}{20} = \frac{15}{20} = \frac{3}{4}$$

example 46.2 Simplify: $\dfrac{5}{7} - \dfrac{1}{10} \cdot \dfrac{4}{5}$

solution We skip the subtraction and do the multiplication first.

$$\frac{5}{7} - \frac{1}{10} \cdot \frac{4}{5} = \frac{5}{7} - \frac{2}{25}$$

Now we find the least common denominator and subtract.

$$\frac{5}{7} - \frac{2}{25} = \frac{125}{175} - \frac{14}{175} = \frac{111}{175}$$

practice   Simplify:

    a. $\dfrac{9}{7} - \dfrac{3}{7} \cdot \dfrac{5}{2}$ **b.** $4\dfrac{1}{5} + 2\dfrac{1}{3} \cdot 5$

**problem set
46**

1. Four large ones cost $40. Write the two rates (ratios) implied by this statement. How
(36) much would the customer have to pay for 120 large ones?

2. The order was for 4 bunches of asparagus at 50 cents a bunch, 9 bushels of okra at $5.50
(13) a bushel, and 4 pecks of beans at $7.50 a peck. What was the total cost of the order?

3. The average elapsed time for the first 10 time trials was 26 minutes. The average
(41) elapsed time for the remaining 90 time trials was 30 minutes. Find the overall average
of the time trials. (Express the result as a decimal number.)

4. William has 42 boxes and 5040 items to put in the boxes. If he divides the items evenly,
(11) how many will go in each box?

5. Find the least common multiple of 18, 42, and 50.
(20)

Solve:

6. $\dfrac{5}{3}x = 20$ **7.** $4x = 2$ **8.** $\dfrac{x}{4} = 7$ **9.** $x - 7 = 2$
(40)   (40)   (40)   (39)

Simplify:

10. $3^3 + 4^4 + 2^5$ **11.** $\sqrt[5]{243}$ **12.** $\sqrt[3]{125}$
(16)   (44)   (44)

13. $\dfrac{3}{4} + 7\dfrac{11}{12} - \dfrac{5}{6}$ **14.** $321\dfrac{7}{12} - 123\dfrac{3}{4}$ **15.** $(6)(3) + 4(2 + 12)$
(34)   (35)   (42)

16. 111.8×0.007 **17.** $\dfrac{179.32}{0.004}$ **18.** $7\dfrac{1}{8} \div 2\dfrac{1}{4} \times 3\dfrac{1}{6}$
(7)   (7)   (43)

19. $2\dfrac{1}{4} \times 6\dfrac{3}{4} \div 3\dfrac{1}{8}$ **20.** $\dfrac{7\dfrac{2}{3}}{6\dfrac{5}{6}}$ **21.** $\dfrac{4}{5} - \dfrac{1}{2} \div \dfrac{5}{6}$
(43)   (43)   (46)

22. $5(9 - 7 + 4) + 3^2 - \sqrt[3]{27} + 3 \cdot 2$ **23.** $\dfrac{3}{5}\left(\dfrac{7}{10} - \dfrac{1}{3}\right)$
(44)   (46)

24. $1\dfrac{1}{2} + 7\dfrac{1}{2} \times \dfrac{2}{9}$
(46)

25. Evaluate: $xyz + y + x + z$ if $x = 3$, $y = 4$, and $z = 5$
(32)

26. Express the perimeter of this figure in
(9,24) meters. Dimensions are in centimeters. All angles are right angles.

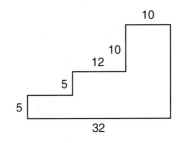

27. Find the volume in cubic centimeters of a right solid whose height is 5 cm and whose
(45)   base is shown in problem 26.

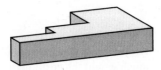

28. The coordinates of a triangle are $(-2, 2)$, $(-2, -3)$, and $(4, -3)$. Draw the triangle and find
(27,38)   its area.

29. Factor 1,000,000,000 in multiples of 10.
(13)

30. Use two unit multipliers to convert 5 square yards to square feet.
(33)

LESSON 47   *Evaluation of Exponential Expressions and Radicals*

Recall that exponential expressions designate a base and tell us how many times the base is
to be used as a factor. The expression 5^3 means

$$5 \cdot 5 \cdot 5$$

When the base is a variable, the exponent tells us how many times the variable is to be used
as a factor. Thus, the expression x^3 means

$$x \cdot x \cdot x$$

When we evaluate exponential and radical expressions that contain variables, we replace the
variables with the proper numbers.

example 47.1   Evaluate: m^2 if $m = 9$

solution   We replace m with 9 and get

$$9^2$$

and 9^2 means 9 times 9, so we get

$$9^2 = 9 \cdot 9 = \textbf{81}$$

example 47.2   Evaluate: 4^x if $x = 3$

solution   We replace x with 3 and get

$$4^3$$

This means to use 4 as a factor 3 times.

$$4^3 = 4 \cdot 4 \cdot 4 = \textbf{64}$$

example 47.3   Evaluate: $\sqrt[n]{64}$ if $n = 3$

solution   We replace n with 3 and get

$$\sqrt[3]{64}$$

The cube root of 64 is 4 because $4 \cdot 4 \cdot 4 = 64$.

$$\sqrt[3]{64} = \textbf{4}$$

example 47.4   Evaluate: $\sqrt[3]{n}$ if $n = 27$

solution   We replace n with 27 and get

$$\sqrt[3]{27}$$

The third root of 27 is 3 because $3 \cdot 3 \cdot 3 = 27$.

$$\sqrt[3]{27} = 3$$

practice   Evaluate:

    a. 2^x if $x = 4$ **b.** x^3 if $x = 5$

    c. $\sqrt[n]{27}$ if $n = 3$ **d.** $\sqrt[n]{81}$ if $n = 2$

problem set 47

1.
(13) There were 3 times as many castles as there were kings. There were 7 times as many princesses as kings. If there were 12 kings, what is the sum of the number of kings, castles, and princesses?

2.
(41) Joe tossed 4 into the pot. Their average weight was 6 lb. Then he tossed in 5 more whose average weight was 7 lb. Then he threw in a big one. The overall average weight of all of them was 7 lb. What did the big one weigh?

3.
(5) The number of red frogs exceeded the number of blue frogs by 80. The number of green frogs was 20 less than the number of blue frogs. If there were 120 blue frogs, what was the sum of the reds, the blues, and the greens?

4.
(36) Spinach Pop could be produced at 640 bottles per hour. Write the two rates (ratios) implied by this statement. How many hours would it take to produce 9600 bottles of Spinach Pop?

5.
(45) On the left we show a base of a right solid whose height is 6 inches. Dimensions are in inches, and all angles are right angles. Find the volume of the solid.

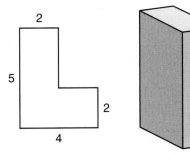

6.
(45) On the left we show a base of a right solid whose height is 15 meters. Dimensions are in meters. Find the volume of the solid.

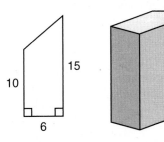

7. Find the least common multiple of 16, 24, and 36.
(20)

Solve:

8. $\dfrac{4}{3}x = 160$ **9.** $x + 6 = 12$ **10.** $x - 5 = 13$
(40)   (39)   (39)

Simplify:

11. $2^2 + 3^3 + 4^2$ **12.** $\sqrt[4]{16}$
(16)   (44)

13. $7(2 + 6 - 4) + 2^3 - \sqrt[3]{8}$ **14.** $\dfrac{4}{5} + 6\dfrac{3}{10} - \dfrac{6}{15}$
(44)   (34)

15. $615\dfrac{3}{8} - 138\dfrac{3}{4}$ **16.** $7(8 - 3) + 4 + (6)(2)$
(35)   (42)

17. $725.89 - 62.871$ **18.** $\dfrac{381.42}{0.006}$
(6)   (7)

19. $7(6 - 4) + 2(4 + 2) - 7 \cdot 2$ **20.** $3\dfrac{3}{5} \times 3\dfrac{1}{2} \div 6\dfrac{3}{4}$
(42)   (43)

21. $\dfrac{3\dfrac{4}{5}}{2\dfrac{7}{8}}$ **22.** $6\dfrac{2}{9} \div 5\dfrac{1}{9} - \dfrac{7}{8}$
(43)   (46)

23. $4\dfrac{1}{10} - 2\dfrac{7}{8} \times 1\dfrac{1}{3}$
(46)

Evaluate:

24. $xyz + yz - y$ if $x = \dfrac{1}{6}$, $y = 3$, and $z = 2$
(32)

25. 6^x if $x = 3$
(47)

26. $\sqrt[x]{144}$ if $x = 2$
(47)

27. 0.5^y if $y = 4$
(47)

28. Use two unit multipliers to convert 6200 centimeters to kilometers.
(33)

29. Write 0.0035 as a fraction.
(15)

30. Express the perimeter of this figure in feet. Dimensions are in inches. All angles are
(9,23)   right angles.

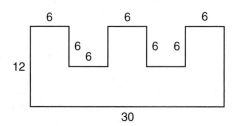

LESSON 48 Fractional Part of a Number • Fractional Equations

48.A
fractional part of a number

We remember that a fraction designates a part of a whole. On the left we show a rectangle that represents the number 1 or the whole thing. On the right, we divide the whole thing into five equal parts and shade two of the parts. This is what we mean by the fraction $\frac{2}{5}$.

If the whole is a number greater than 1, then $\frac{2}{5}$ of the number means two of the five equal parts of the number. For example, if the number is 150, each of the five equal parts is 30.

Then two of these parts equal $30 + 30 = 60$.

$$\frac{2}{5} \times 150 = 60$$

48.B
fractional equations

The equation above is read as

Two fifths of 150 is 60.

This statement contains a fraction and two numbers. Notice that "of" corresponds to "×" or "·" and "is" corresponds to "=".

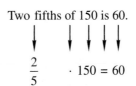

The general equation for the fractional part is very important. It is, in words,

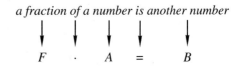

F is a fraction, and A and B are numbers.

example 48.1   What fraction of 75 is 25?

solution   We translate this question directly into an equation by replacing *what fraction* with F, replacing *of* with a multiplication symbol, and replacing *is* with an equals sign.

What fraction of 75 is 25?   question

$$F \quad \cdot 75 = 25 \qquad \text{equation}$$

$$\frac{F \cdot \cancel{75}}{\cancel{75}} = \frac{25}{75} \qquad \text{divided both sides by 75}$$

$$F = \frac{1}{3} \qquad \text{simplified}$$

Thus, $\frac{1}{3}$ of 75 is 25.

example 48.2   Five sevenths of what number is $\frac{5}{2}$?

solution   We translate this question directly into an equation by replacing *what number* with A.

Five sevenths of what number is $\frac{5}{2}$?   question

$$\frac{5}{7} \qquad \cdot \quad A \quad = \frac{5}{2} \qquad \text{equation}$$

To solve, we multiply both sides of the equation by the reciprocal of $\frac{5}{7}$.

$$\frac{\cancel{7}}{\cancel{5}} \cdot \frac{\cancel{5}}{\cancel{7}} \cdot A = \frac{\cancel{5}}{2} \cdot \frac{7}{\cancel{5}} \qquad \text{multiplied both sides by } \frac{7}{5}$$

$$A = \frac{7}{2} \qquad \text{simplified}$$

Thus, $\frac{5}{7}$ of $\frac{7}{2}$ is $\frac{5}{2}$.

example 48.3   Five sevenths of $\frac{5}{2}$ is what number?

solution   We make a direct translation.

Five sevenths of $\frac{5}{2}$ is what number?   question

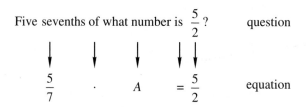

$$\frac{5}{7} \qquad \cdot \frac{5}{2} = \quad B \qquad \text{equation}$$

To solve, we multiply.

$$B = \frac{25}{14} \qquad \text{multiplied}$$

Thus, $\frac{5}{7}$ of $\frac{5}{2}$ is $\frac{25}{14}$.

example 48.4   What number is $\frac{7}{9}$ of 450?

solution   Once again we make a direct translation.

$$\text{What number is } \frac{7}{9} \text{ of 450?}$$

$$B \quad = \quad \frac{7}{9} \cdot 450$$

To solve, we multiply.

$$B = 350$$

Thus, **350** is $\frac{7}{9}$ of 450.

practice   **a.**   What fraction of 20 is 140?

b.   Seven fifths of what number is $\frac{3}{8}$?

c.   Five thirteenths of 26 is what number?

problem set 48

1.
(11)   The cheerleaders could put 44 pompons in one box. If there were 1760 pompons that had to be packed, how many boxes did the cheerleaders need?

2.
(11)   When the boxes came, a count revealed an overshipment. They had received 62 boxes. Given the information in problem 1, now how many pompons were required to fill all the boxes?

3.
(36)   Ronk bought 14 games for $70. Write the two rates (ratios) for this statement. How many games could he buy for $200 at the same rate?

4.
(26)   The times for the race came down with practice. The average time for the 5 racers in the first race was 57 seconds. The average time for the second race was 55 seconds. For the third race, the average time was 52 seconds. What was the average time for all three races?

5.
(48)   Two fifths of what number is 10?

6.
(48)   What fraction of 72 is 96?

7.
(48)   Six sevenths of 217 is what number?

8.
(48)   What number is $\frac{6}{7}$ of 217?

9.
(28)   Write $\frac{316}{25}$ as a mixed number.

10.
(20)   Find the least common multiple of 8, 21, and 24.

Solve:

11.
(40) $\dfrac{6}{7}x = 18$ **12.**
(39) $x + \dfrac{5}{13} = \dfrac{18}{26}$ **13.**
(40) $7x = 315$

Simplify:

14. $3[4 - (5 - 4) + 2] + 14$
(42)

15. $6(3 - 1) + 2(3 - 1) - 4$
(42)

16. $\dfrac{4}{9} + \dfrac{5}{4} \cdot \dfrac{1}{6}$
(46)

17. $4\dfrac{2}{5} \cdot \dfrac{3}{7} - \dfrac{4}{7}$
(46)

18. $4^2 + 3^3 - 2^3$
(16)

19. $\sqrt[3]{8} + \sqrt[3]{27}$
(44)

20. $\dfrac{7}{8} + 5\dfrac{5}{16} - \dfrac{3}{4}$
(34)

21. $117\dfrac{9}{10} - 12\dfrac{3}{5}$
(35)

22. $6\dfrac{3}{8} \times 2\dfrac{4}{5} \div 2\dfrac{1}{2}$
(43)

23. $\dfrac{8\dfrac{6}{7}}{3\dfrac{5}{14}}$
(43)

24. $4\dfrac{3}{4} \div 2\dfrac{1}{3} \times 3\dfrac{1}{3} \div 1\dfrac{1}{4}$
(43)

Evaluate:

25. $\sqrt[x]{243}$ if $x = 5$
(47)

26. x^3 if $x = 8$
(47)

27. $y + xyz - z$ if $x = 24$, $y = \dfrac{1}{4}$, and $z = 2$
(32)

28. Sketch a rectangular coordinate system, and graph the points $(-2, -1)$ and $(3, 3)$.
(38)

29. On the left we show a base of a right solid whose height is 17 centimeters. Dimensions
(45) are in centimeters, and all angles are right angles. Find the volume of the solid.

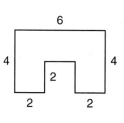
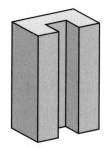

30. Use two unit multipliers to convert 360 yards to inches.
(33)

LESSON 49 *Surface Area*

The **surface area** of a solid is the total area of all the exposed surfaces of the solid. A rectangular box has six surfaces. It has a top and a bottom, a front and a back, and two sides. The surface area is the sum of these six areas.

example 49.1   Find the surface area of this rectangular box. All dimensions are in meters.

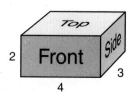

solution   Since the box is rectangular, the areas of the top and the bottom are equal. The area of the front equals the area of the back, and the areas of the two sides are equal.

$$
\begin{aligned}
\text{Area of front} &= 4\,\text{m} \times 2\,\text{m} = 8\,\text{m}^2 \\
\text{Area of back} &= 4\,\text{m} \times 2\,\text{m} = 8\,\text{m}^2 \\
\text{Area of top} &= 4\,\text{m} \times 3\,\text{m} = 12\,\text{m}^2 \\
\text{Area of bottom} &= 4\,\text{m} \times 3\,\text{m} = 12\,\text{m}^2 \\
\text{Area of side} &= 3\,\text{m} \times 2\,\text{m} = 6\,\text{m}^2 \\
+ \quad \text{Area of side} &= 3\,\text{m} \times 2\,\text{m} = 6\,\text{m}^2 \\
\hline
\text{Total surface area} & \phantom{= 3\,\text{m} \times 2\,\text{m}} = \mathbf{52\,m^2}
\end{aligned}
$$

example 49.2   Find the surface area of this right solid. All dimensions are in centimeters.

solution   The solid has two ends that are triangles and three faces that are rectangles.

$$
\begin{aligned}
\text{Area of one end} &= \frac{4\,\text{cm} \times 3\,\text{cm}}{2} = 6\,\text{cm}^2 \\[4pt]
\text{Area of one end} &= \frac{4\,\text{cm} \times 3\,\text{cm}}{2} = 6\,\text{cm}^2 \\[4pt]
\text{Area of bottom} &= 3\,\text{cm} \times 6\,\text{cm} = 18\,\text{cm}^2 \\
\text{Area of back} &= 4\,\text{cm} \times 6\,\text{cm} = 24\,\text{cm}^2 \\
+ \quad \text{Area of front} &= 5\,\text{cm} \times 6\,\text{cm} = 30\,\text{cm}^2 \\
\hline
\text{Total surface area} & \phantom{= 5\,\text{cm} \times 6\,\text{cm}} = \mathbf{84\,cm^2}
\end{aligned}
$$

practice   **a.** Find the surface area of this rectangular solid. Dimensions are in feet.

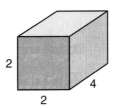

b. Find the surface area of this right solid. Dimensions are in centimeters.

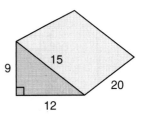

problem set 49

1.
(36)
Sarah sold whortleberries after school. She sold 40 pecks for $640. Write the two rates (ratios) implied by this statement. How much money would she get for 100 pecks at the same rate?

2.
(6)
Irwin stretched but could only reach seventy-one and one thousand, four hundred three ten-millionths inches. He lost because Eisel could reach seventy-two and one thousand, six hundred forty-two hundred-thousandths inches. How much farther could Eisel reach?

3.
(13)
Knapp hid the flowers in discrete bunches of 48. Some bunches were under the front porch. In all, he hid 1305 discrete bunches of flowers. How many flowers did he hide in all?

4. Find the volume of this right solid.
(45) Dimensions are in feet. First find the
area of one triangular end. Remember
that the area of a triangle is one half
the base times the height.

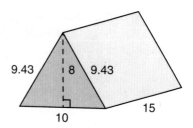

5. Find the surface area of the right prism in problem 4.
(49)

6. Five twelfths of what number is $\frac{7}{3}$?
(48)

7. What fraction of 26 is 65?
(48)

8. What number is $\frac{3}{8}$ of 256?
(48)

9. Write $\frac{213}{8}$ as a mixed number.
(28)

10. Find the least common multiple of 16, 24, and 30.
(20)

Solve:

11. $\dfrac{7}{8}x = 14$ **12.** $x - \dfrac{1}{8} = \dfrac{3}{16}$ **13.** $x + \dfrac{5}{8} = \dfrac{14}{5}$
(40) (39) (39)

Simplify:

14. $6 \cdot 3 + (3 \cdot 2)5 - 4(2 \cdot 2)$ **15.** $4(6 - 2 + 1) + 3^2 - \sqrt[3]{8}$
(42) (44)

16. $\dfrac{7}{20} + \dfrac{4}{5} \cdot \dfrac{2}{3}$ **17.** $3\dfrac{1}{6} \cdot \dfrac{1}{8} - \dfrac{4}{12}$
(46) (46)

18. $3^2 + 4^2 - 5^2$ **19.** $\dfrac{3}{4} + 7\dfrac{1}{16} - \dfrac{5}{8}$
(16) (34)

20. $113\dfrac{4}{7} - 32\dfrac{1}{14}$ **21.** 31.62×0.08
(35) (7)

22. $3\dfrac{2}{3} \times 2\dfrac{3}{4} \div 3\dfrac{1}{2}$ **23.** $\dfrac{6\dfrac{3}{4}}{7\dfrac{11}{12}}$
(43) (43)

24. $89.265 - 6.898$
(6)

Evaluate:

25. 3^x if $x = 5$ **26.** $\sqrt[p]{8}$ if $p = 3$
(47) (47)

27. $xyz - x + xy$ if $x = 12$, $y = \dfrac{1}{4}$, and $z = 6$
(32)

28. Find the area of this figure.
(27) Dimensions are in meters.

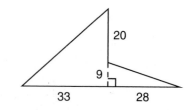

29. Use two unit multipliers to convert 250,001 centimeters to kilometers.
(33)

30. Susie Q had an average of 83 on her first four tests but an average of 90 on her other
(41)   three tests. What was her overall test average?

LESSON 50   *Scientific Notation for Numbers Greater Than Ten • Scientific Notation for Numbers Between Zero and One*

50.A
scientific notation for numbers greater than ten

When we multiply 0.0534 by 1000, we move the decimal point three places to the right.

$$0.0534 \times 1000 = 53.4$$

Because 10^3 equals 1000, when we multiply 0.0534 by 10^3, we also move the decimal point three places to the right.

$$0.0534 \times 10^3 = 53.4$$

When we multiply a number by a positive power of 10, we move the decimal point to the right the number of places indicated by the exponent.

We can use this fact to write numbers in a special way that makes very large numbers easy to handle. We call this special way **scientific notation.** When we write a number greater than or equal to ten in scientific notation, we use three steps:

1. Place the decimal point just to the right of the first nonzero digit.
2. Count the number of places the decimal point moved to the left.
3. Multiply the number in step one by 10^b (*b* is the number of places the decimal point moved) to indicate where the decimal point should be.

example 50.1 Write 7,024,000 in scientific notation.

solution First we rewrite the number by removing the commas and placing the new decimal point just to the right of the 7, the first nonzero digit.

$$7.024000$$

Now we count the number of places the decimal point moved.

$$7.024000$$

The decimal point moved six places, so we multiply by 10^6 and get

$$\mathbf{7.024 \times 10^6}$$

The 10^6 tells us that the decimal point *is really* six places to the right of where it is written.

example 50.2 Write 476.23 in scientific notation.

solution We put the decimal point just to the right of the 4. Then we count the number of places the decimal point moved.

$$4.7623$$

The decimal point moved two places, so we write

$$\mathbf{4.7623 \times 10^2}$$

The 10^2 tells us that the decimal point *is really* two places to the right of where it is written.

50.B

scientific notation for numbers between zero and one

We write large numbers (numbers greater than 10) in scientific notation using a positive exponent. We can also write small numbers (numbers between 0 and 1) in scientific notation. For these numbers, we use a negative exponent. We use 10 with a negative exponent to show that the decimal point should be moved **to the left.** The notation

$$4.76 \times 10^{-3}$$

tells us that the decimal point *is really* three places to the left of where we have written it. Thus

$$4.76 \times 10^{-3} \quad \text{means} \quad 0.00476$$

When we write a number between zero and one in scientific notation, we use three steps:

1. Place the decimal point just to the right of the first nonzero digit.
2. Count the number of places the decimal point moved to the right.
3. Multiply the number in step one by 10^{-b} (b is the number of places the decimal point moved) to indicate where the decimal point should be.

example 50.3   Write 0.0652 in scientific notation.

solution   We begin by writing all of the digits in the number. We place the new decimal point just to the right of the first nonzero digit, which is 6.

$$006.52$$

We see that the true position of the decimal point is two places *to the left* of where we have written it. Now we must choose an exponent for 10 that tells us what the true location of the decimal point is, so we write

$$\mathbf{6.52 \times 10^{-2}}$$

The 10^{-2} tells us that the true position of the decimal point *is really* two places to the left of where it is written.

example 50.4   Write these numbers in standard notation: (a) 4.6×10^{-4} (b) 4.6×10^{4}

solution   (a) The negative exponent tells us to move the decimal point four places to the left.

$$4.6 \times 10^{-4} = \mathbf{0.00046}$$

(b) The positive exponent tells us to move the decimal point four places to the right.

$$4.6 \times 10^{4} = \mathbf{46,000}$$

practice   Write each number in scientific notation:

   a.   476,000   **b.**   0.000476   **c.**   30,560,000   **d.**   0.000003056

Write each number in standard notation:

   e. 4.06×10^{5} **f.** 4.72×10^{-6}

problem set 50

1. *(11)*   Jeremoth put all his money in gilt-edged stock certificates. If he invested $64,000 and paid $40 for each certificate, how many certificates did Jeremoth buy?

2. *(6)*   Marsha guessed forty-one thousand, fifteen millionths. Then Kevin guessed twenty-seven ten-thousandths. What was the sum of their guesses?

3. *(36)*   Forty good ones cost $12. Write the two rates (ratios) implied by this statement. How many good ones could be purchased for $3.40?

4. The sum of the weights of the first four contestants was 760 pounds. The first three
(26) contestants weighed 210 pounds, 185 pounds, and 220 pounds. What was the average weight of the four contestants?

5. Five sevenths of what number is $\frac{7}{3}$?
(48)

6. Three fifths of what number is $\frac{3}{7}$?
(48)

7. What number is $\frac{4}{7}$ of 210?
(48)

8. Find the volume of a rectangular box which measures 3 ft by 4 ft by 6 ft.
(45)

9. Write each number in scientific notation:
(50)
(a) 4,203,742   (b) 0.0056305

10. Write each number in standard notation:
(50)
(a) 9.277×10^5 (b) 2.132×10^{-6}

Solve:

11. $\frac{8}{9}x = 16$
(40)

12. $x - 3\frac{1}{4} = \frac{1}{2}$
(39)

Simplify:

13. $7 \cdot 2 + (3 \cdot 2)4 - 3(2 \cdot 1)$
(42)

14. $6(3 - 2 + 1) + 3^2 - \sqrt[3]{8}$
(44)

15. $\frac{3}{20} + \frac{4}{5} \cdot \frac{3}{4}$
(46)

16. $4\frac{2}{3} \cdot \frac{3}{4} - \frac{7}{12}$
(46)

17. $137\frac{5}{7} - 16\frac{1}{14}$
(35)

18. $\frac{4}{5} + 3\frac{1}{10} - \frac{14}{25}$
(34)

19. $3^2 - \sqrt{9} + \sqrt[3]{8}$
(44)

20. 21.32×0.06
(7)

21. $\frac{6111.2}{0.005}$
(7)

22. $\frac{6\frac{4}{5}}{5\frac{3}{4}}$
(43)

Evaluate:

23. $xyz + yz - xy$ if $x = 20$, $y = \frac{1}{5}$, and $z = 5$
(32)

24. y^2 if $y = 3$
(47)

25. $\sqrt[p]{27}$ if $p = 3$
(47)

26. Find the volume of this rectangular
(45) solid. Dimensions are in feet.

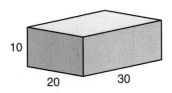

10   20   30

27. Find the surface area of the rectangular solid in problem 26.
(49)

28. Use two unit multipliers to convert 3,059,000 miles to inches.
(33)

29. Add: $3\dfrac{1}{18} + 9\dfrac{7}{20} + 12\dfrac{5}{24}$
(34)

30. Sketch a rectangular coordinate system, and graph the points (3, −4) and (2, 1).
(38)

LESSON 51   *Decimal Part of a Number*

The equation for the fractional part of a number is *a fraction of a number is another number* or

$$F \cdot A = B$$

where *F* is a fraction and *A* and *B* are numbers. The equation for the decimal part of a number is exactly the same, except that we use *D* to stand for a decimal.

a decimal part of a number is another number

$$D \cdot A = B$$

example 51.1   What decimal part of 240 is 90?

solution   We translate this question directly into an equation by replacing *what decimal part* with *D*, *of* with a multiplication symbol, and *is* with an equals sign.

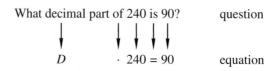

To solve, we divide both sides of the equation by 240.

$$\frac{D \cdot \cancel{240}}{\cancel{240}} = \frac{90}{240} \qquad \text{divided both sides by 240}$$

$$D = 0.375 \qquad \text{simplified}$$

Thus, **0.375** of 240 is 90.

example 51.2   Four tenths of what number is 72?

solution   We make a direct translation.

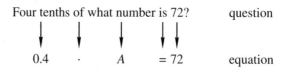

To solve, we divide both sides by 0.4.

$$A = \frac{72}{0.4} = 180$$

Thus, 0.4 of **180** is 72.

The equation for the decimal part of a number is always present when we translate these questions, as we see in the next example.

example 51.3 Four tenths of 72 is what number?

solution First we write the equation.

$$D \cdot A = B$$

Next we replace D with 0.4 and A with 72.

$$0.4 \cdot 72 = B$$

We multiply to find the answer.

$$B = 28.8$$

Thus, 0.4 of 72 is **28.8.**

practice **a.** Seven tenths of what number is 0.14?

b. Seven hundredths of 86 is what number?

c. What decimal part of 72 is 30.24?

problem set 51

1. On one hand, there were one hundred forty-two thousand, seven hundred sixty-three. On the other hand, there were two hundred twenty-eight thousand, fourteen. How many more were there on the other hand?
(5)

2. The whole batch cost $28,000 and contained 140 items. Write the two rates (ratios) implied by this statement. What would be the price for 200 items?
(36)

3. What was the average number of tons of bricks sold during the 4-month period of March, April, May, and June?
(21,29)

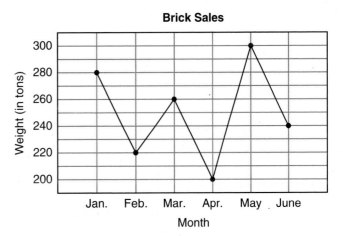

Brick Sales

4. The average time for the four races was 10.2 seconds. If the times for the first three races were 10.1, 10.6, and 10.3 seconds, what was the time for the fourth race?
(26)

5. Find the surface area of this rectangular solid. Dimensions are in meters.
(49)

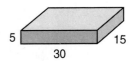

6. Find the volume of this right solid.
(45) Dimensions are in centimeters. First find the area of one end and then multiply by the length.

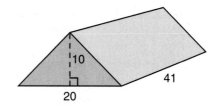

7. What number is $\frac{5}{8}$ of 168?
(48)

8. Four fifths of what number is $\frac{7}{2}$?
(48)

9. Five sixths of what number is $4\frac{1}{3}$?
(48)

10. Four tenths of what number is 5?
(51)

11. Forty-four hundredths of 75 is what number?
(51)

12. What decimal part of 33 is 0.0066?
(51)

13. Write $\frac{167}{7}$ as a mixed number.
(28)

Solve:

14. $\frac{4}{9}x = 16$
(40)

15. $x - \frac{3}{5} = 2\frac{3}{10}$
(39)

Simplify:

16. $6 \cdot 2 + (6 \cdot 3)7 - 4(3 \cdot 1)$
(42)

17. $5(6 - 3 + 1) + 6^2 - \sqrt{100}$
(44)

18. $\frac{11}{14} + \frac{3}{7} \cdot \frac{3}{4}$
(46)

19. $6\frac{2}{3} \cdot \frac{1}{4} - \frac{3}{4}$
(46)

20. $117\frac{3}{8} - 14\frac{7}{16}$
(35)

21. $\frac{3}{5} + 3\frac{4}{15} - \frac{7}{30}$
(34)

22. $3^2 + \sqrt[3]{27} - \sqrt[3]{8}$
(44)

23. $118.321 - 81.34$
(6)

24. $4\frac{2}{3} \times 2\frac{3}{4} \div 1\frac{5}{12}$
(43)

25. $\dfrac{7\frac{2}{3}}{2\frac{5}{6}}$
(43)

Evaluate:

26. $x + xy + xyz$ if $x = 1$, $y = 10$, and $z = \frac{1}{5}$
(32)

27. p^3 if $p = 2$
(47)

28. Use two unit multipliers to convert 6 miles to inches.
(33)

29. (a) Write 98,213,000 in scientific notation.
(50)
(b) Write 3.207×10^{-5} in standard notation.

30. Use two unit multipliers to convert 12 square kilometers to square meters.
(33)

LESSON 52 *Fractions and Symbols of Inclusion*

We have restricted our practice with symbols of inclusion to problems that have whole numbers. Symbols of inclusion can also be used in the simplification of expressions that contain fractions or mixed numbers.

example 52.1 Simplify: $\dfrac{3}{2}\left(\dfrac{1}{4} + \dfrac{7}{16}\right) - \dfrac{1}{8}$

solution First we simplify within the parentheses by finding a common denominator and adding.

$$\frac{3}{2}\left(\frac{4}{16} + \frac{7}{16}\right) - \frac{1}{8} = \frac{3}{2}\left(\frac{11}{16}\right) - \frac{1}{8}$$

Next we multiply.

$$\frac{33}{32} - \frac{1}{8}$$

Now we find a common denominator and subtract.

$$\frac{33}{32} - \frac{4}{32} = \mathbf{\frac{29}{32}}$$

example 52.2 Simplify: $\dfrac{1}{3}\left(3\dfrac{1}{4} - \dfrac{1}{8}\right) + \dfrac{1}{48}$

solution First we simplify within the parentheses.

$$\frac{1}{3}\left(3\frac{2}{8} - \frac{1}{8}\right) + \frac{1}{48} = \frac{1}{3}\left(3\frac{1}{8}\right) + \frac{1}{48}$$

Next we multiply and find a common denominator. Then we add and simplify the result.

$$\frac{1}{3}\left(\frac{25}{8}\right) + \frac{1}{48} = \frac{25}{24} + \frac{1}{48} = \frac{25}{24} + \frac{1}{48} = \frac{51}{48} = \mathbf{\frac{17}{16}}$$

example 52.3 Simplify: $\dfrac{2}{5}\left[\left(\dfrac{2}{3} - \dfrac{1}{6}\right) + \left(\dfrac{1}{3} + \dfrac{5}{6}\right)\right]$

solution First we simplify within the parentheses.

$$\frac{2}{5}\left[\left(\frac{4}{6} - \frac{1}{6}\right) + \left(\frac{2}{6} + \frac{5}{6}\right)\right] = \frac{2}{5}\left[\left(\frac{3}{6}\right) + \left(\frac{7}{6}\right)\right]$$

Now we simplify within the brackets.

$$\frac{2}{5}\left[\frac{10}{6}\right]$$

Then we multiply.

$$\frac{2}{5}\left[\frac{10}{6}\right] = \mathbf{\frac{2}{3}}$$

practice Simplify:

a. $\dfrac{3}{4}\left[\left(\dfrac{4}{5} - \dfrac{1}{2}\right) + \left(\dfrac{1}{6} + \dfrac{1}{3}\right)\right]$

b. $\dfrac{1}{4}\left(2\dfrac{1}{2} - \dfrac{1}{7}\right) + \dfrac{1}{28}$

problem set 52

1. On the first day the attendance was forty-seven thousand, three hundred sixty-four. On the second day the attendance was fifty-three thousand, seven. How many more attended on the second day?
   (5)

2. Each bin held 14 uniforms. Write the two rates (ratios) implied by this statement. If there were 140 bins in all, how many uniforms did they hold?
   (36)

3. Fifteen could be purchased for only $315. Write the two rates (ratios) implied by this statement. How much would 140 cost?
   (36)

4. The bulls weighed 2153 lb, 1491 lb, 1840 lb, 2396 lb, and 1432 lb. What was the (a) range, (b) mode, (c) median, and (d) mean weight of the bulls?
   (26)

5. Find the volume of this right solid. Dimensions are in feet. First find the area of the triangle, and then multiply by the length of the solid.
   (45)

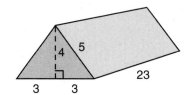

6. Find the surface area of the right solid given in problem 5.
   (49)

7. Write 2.15 as a mixed number.
   (28)

8. Five eighths of what number is 100?
   (48)

9. What fraction of 64 is 56?
   (48)

10. What decimal part of 507 is 441.09?
    (51)

11. Fifty-two hundredths of what number is 104?
    (51)

Solve:

12. $\dfrac{4}{7}x = 112$
    (40)

13. $x + \dfrac{7}{12} = 3\dfrac{5}{12}$
    (39)

Simplify:

14. $28 - 2[(6 - 2) \div (10 - 9) + 3]$
    (42)

15. $4[(3 - 1)(3 + 2) - 1] + 25$
    (42)

16. $7\dfrac{3}{4} \cdot \dfrac{2}{3} - \dfrac{5}{12}$
    (46)

17. $\dfrac{13}{14} + \dfrac{2}{7} \cdot \dfrac{3}{4}$
    (46)

18. $62.891 - 18.812$
    (6)

19. $2^3 + 3^3 - \sqrt[3]{8}$
    (44)

20. $36\dfrac{6}{7} - 14\dfrac{3}{14}$
    (35)

21. $\dfrac{7}{9}\left(3\dfrac{1}{6} + \dfrac{1}{3}\right) + \dfrac{5}{6}$
    (52)

22. $\dfrac{11}{20} - \left[\left(\dfrac{1}{25} + \dfrac{7}{10}\right) - \dfrac{3}{5}\right]$
    (52)

23. $\dfrac{4}{5} + 2\dfrac{7}{10} - \dfrac{3}{20}$
    (34)

24. $\dfrac{17.025}{0.003}$
    (7)

25. $4\dfrac{1}{8} \div 2\dfrac{1}{4} \times 3\dfrac{1}{2} \div 1\dfrac{1}{16}$
    (43)

26.
(43)
$$\dfrac{8\frac{1}{2}}{4\frac{1}{7}}$$

Evaluate:

27. $xyz + yz - x$ if $x = 16$, $y = \dfrac{1}{8}$, and $z = 24$
(32)

28. $p^3 + p + q$ if $p = 2$ and $q = 3$
(47)

29. Use two unit multipliers to convert 2162.18 centigrams to kilograms.
(33)

30. (a) Write 6,657,000,000 in scientific notation.
(50)
(b) Write 3.209×10^{-7} in standard notation.

LESSON 53 *Percent*

The language spoken by the ancient Romans was Latin. The Latin word for *by* is *per* and the word for *one hundred* is *centum*. We put these words together in English to form the word **percent.** From this we see that percent means *by 100*. The symbol for percent is %.

One percent of a number is one hundredth of the number. To demonstrate we will use the number 256. If we divide 256 into one hundred equal parts, each part is 2.56.

Thus, 2.56 is 1 percent of 256 because 1 percent is exactly the same thing as one hundredth. If we want 5 percent of 256, we must use five of these parts.

$$5 \text{ percent of } 256 = 5(2.56) = 12.8$$

One hundred sixty percent of 256 would be 160 of these parts.

$$160 \text{ percent of } 256 = 160(2.56) = 409.6$$

From this we see that we can find a given percent of a number if we first divide the number into 100 equal parts. Each of these parts is 1 percent of the number.

example 53.1   (a) What is 1 percent of 7500?

(b) What is 34 percent of 7500?

solution   (a) To find 1 percent of 7500, we divide 7500 by 100.

$$1 \text{ percent of } 7500 = \frac{7500}{100} = \mathbf{75}$$

(b) Thirty-four percent is 34 times the value of 1 percent.

$$34 \times 75 = \mathbf{2550}$$

example 53.2   (a) What is 1% of 67?

(b) What is 140% of 67?

solution   (a) To find 1% of 67, we divide 67 by 100.

$$1\% \text{ of } 67 = \frac{67}{100} = \mathbf{0.67}$$

(b) One hundred forty percent is 140 of these parts.

$$140 \times 0.67 = \mathbf{93.8}$$

practice   a. What is 1 percent of 64?   b. What is 40 percent of 64?

c. What is 1% of 5?   d. What is 35% of 5?

problem set 53

1.
(6)
The original diameter of the microbe was one thousand, four hundred seventy-five millionths inch. Later the diameter increased to one hundred three ten-thousandths inch. By how much did the diameter increase?

2.
(36)
Jimmy bought 1900 oscillators for $38,000. Write the two rates (ratios) implied by this statement. How much would he have to pay for 5000 oscillators?

3.
(41)
The team averaged 86 points in the first 2 games, 92 points in the following 8 games, 80 points in the next 8 games, and 70 points in the final 2 games. What was their overall average of points scored per game?

4.
(50)
(a) Write in standard notation: 6.3×10^9

(b) Write in scientific notation: 0.00000047

5.
(45)
Find the volume of this rectangular box. Dimensions are in yards.

6.
(49)
Find the surface area of the rectangular box.

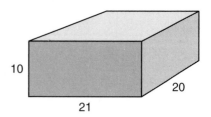

10

20

21

7.
(48)
Three fourths of what number is 51?

8.
(48)
Three sevenths of 91 is what number?

9.
(51)
Three thousandths of what number is 18?

10.
(51)
What decimal part of 94 is 68.62?

11.
(53)
(a) What is 1% of 24?

(b) What is 56% of 24?

12. (a) What is 1 percent of 3200?
(53)
    (b) What is 101 percent of 3200?

13. Write $7\frac{3}{22}$ as an improper fraction.
(28)

Solve:

14. $\dfrac{5}{4}x = 120$
(40)

15. $x + \dfrac{3}{11} = \dfrac{51}{22}$
(39)

Simplify:

16. $17 - 2[(6 - 4)(7 - 3) - 7]$
(42)

17. $3^2 + 2[(7 + 1)(7 - 5) - 12]$
(44)

18. $6\dfrac{2}{3} \cdot \dfrac{1}{4} - \dfrac{5}{12}$
(46)

19. $\dfrac{5}{6} + 1\dfrac{7}{12} - \dfrac{2}{3}$
(34)

20. $\left(2\dfrac{1}{7} - \dfrac{5}{9}\right)\dfrac{3}{8} - \dfrac{25}{42}$
(52)

21. $\left[\dfrac{1}{8} + \dfrac{1}{2}\left(\dfrac{7}{9} - \dfrac{1}{4}\right)\right] + \dfrac{2}{3}$
(52)

22. $\sqrt[3]{27} - \sqrt{9} + 3$
(44)

23. $16\dfrac{3}{5} - 5\dfrac{1}{10}$
(35)

24. $\dfrac{181.02}{0.006}$
(7)

25. $7\dfrac{1}{4} \div 3\dfrac{1}{3} \times 1\dfrac{2}{3} \times 1\dfrac{1}{6}$
(43)

26. $\dfrac{3\frac{2}{7}}{2\frac{1}{14}}$
(43)

Evaluate:

27. $xyzt + xyz + yzt$ if $x = \dfrac{1}{6}$, $y = 3$, $z = 4$, and $t = 5$
(32)

28. $\sqrt[x]{8} + y$ if $x = 3$ and $y = 8$
(47)

29. Use four unit multipliers to convert 625 square yards to square inches.
(33)

30. Three points are graphed on this rectangular coordinate system. What are the x- and
(38) y-coordinates of the points?

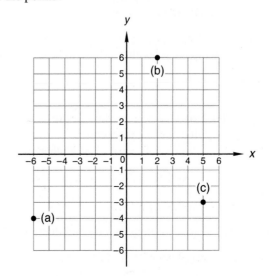

LESSON 54   *Ratio and Proportion • P^Q and $\sqrt[Q]{P}$*

54.A

ratio and proportion

Remember that a ratio is a comparison of two numbers. We can write a ratio as a fraction. If we write

$$\frac{3}{4}$$

we can say that we have written the fraction three fourths. We can also say that we have written the ratio of 3 to 4. There are many equivalent forms of this ratio (fraction).

$$\frac{3}{4} \qquad \frac{6}{8} \qquad \frac{15}{20} \qquad \frac{90}{120} \qquad \frac{150}{200} \qquad \frac{450}{600}$$

All these ratios have the same value.

When we write an equation that consists of two ratios connected by an equals sign, such as

$$\frac{3}{4} = \frac{6}{8}$$

we say that we have written a **proportion.** Proportions can be either true proportions or false proportions.

$$\frac{1}{2} = \frac{5}{10} \qquad \text{true} \qquad\qquad \frac{1}{2} = \frac{7}{10} \qquad \text{false}$$

The proportion on the left is a true proportion, and the proportion on the right is a false proportion.

We find it helpful to note that the **cross products** of a true proportion are equal to each other. The cross product can be found by multiplying the upper term (numerator) of one ratio by the lower term (denominator) of the other ratio. We call this process **cross multiplication.**

$$4 \cdot 6 = 24$$
$$\frac{3}{4} \diagdown\!\!\!\!\diagup \frac{6}{8}$$
$$3 \cdot 8 = 24$$

Here one cross product is 4 times 6, and the other cross product is 3 times 8. Both cross products equal 24.

When one part of a proportion is a variable, the proportion is a **conditional proportion.** Conditional proportions can also be called **conditional equations.**

$$\frac{20}{15} = \frac{4}{x}$$

This proportion is a conditional proportion and is neither true nor false. There is a value of x that will make this proportion a true proportion. To find this value of x, we begin by setting the cross products equal to each other, as we show in the following two examples.

example 54.1   Solve: $\dfrac{20}{15} = \dfrac{4}{x}$

solution   We begin by setting the cross products equal to each other.

$$20x = 4 \cdot 15$$

To solve, we divide both sides by 20.

$$\frac{\cancel{20}x}{\cancel{20}} = \frac{4 \cdot 15}{20} \qquad \text{divided both sides by 20}$$

$$x = \mathbf{3} \qquad \text{simplified}$$

Students sometimes think of cross multiplication as some special form of multiplication. When we cross multiply, we have really multiplied both sides of the equation by the product of the denominators to eliminate the fractions.

$$\frac{20}{15} = \frac{4}{x} \qquad \text{equation}$$

$$\cancel{15} \cdot x \cdot \frac{20}{\cancel{15}} = \frac{4}{\cancel{x}} \cdot 15 \cdot \cancel{x} \qquad \text{multiplied both sides by } 15 \cdot x$$

$$20x = 4 \cdot 15 \qquad \text{simplified}$$

Cross multiplication is a convenient shortcut.

example 54.2 Solve: $\dfrac{4}{5} = \dfrac{p}{7}$

solution First we set the cross products equal to each other.

$$4 \cdot 7 = 5p$$

Then we divide both sides by 5.

$$\frac{4 \cdot 7}{5} = \frac{\cancel{5}p}{\cancel{5}} \qquad \text{divided both sides by 5}$$

$$\frac{\mathbf{28}}{\mathbf{5}} = p \qquad \text{simplified}$$

We decide to leave the answer in the form of an improper fraction.

54.B

P^Q and $\sqrt[Q]{P}$ We have been evaluating exponential expressions where one of the numbers is represented by a variable. We know how to find the value of

$$\sqrt[3]{P} \qquad \text{if } P = 8$$

and the value of

$$P^3 \qquad \text{if } P = 2$$

Sometimes both numbers are represented by variables.

example 54.3 Evaluate: x^y if $x = 4$ and $y = 3$

solution We replace x with 4 and replace y with 3 and get

$$(4)^3 = \mathbf{64}$$

example 54.4 Evaluate: $\sqrt[P]{Q}$ if $P = 3$ and $Q = 64$

solution We replace P with 3 and replace Q with 64 and get

$$\sqrt[3]{64} = \mathbf{4}$$

practice Solve:

a. $\dfrac{4}{p} = \dfrac{7}{2}$ **b.** $\dfrac{s}{5} = \dfrac{4}{3}$

Evaluate:

c. x^y if $x = 4$ and $y = 2$ **d.** $\sqrt[x]{y}$ if $x = 4$ and $y = 16$

problem set 54

1. Willikin hid one hundred forty million, fourteen in the boscage of the weald. The next
   (5) week he hid an additional fifteen million, nine hundred eighty-two thousand. How many did Willikin hide in all?

2. Wilhelmina bought 80 horses at the auction. She paid 320 guineas for them. Write the
   (36) two rates (ratios) implied by this statement. How much would she have had to pay for 320 horses at the same rate?

3. Richard the Lion-Hearted counted his troops on the outskirts of Accra. He counted
   (5) seven thousand, nine hundred forty-two. If this was two hundred forty-two more than he counted yesterday, what was yesterday's count?

4. Six tenths of what number is 72?
   (51)

5. What decimal part of 360 is 60?
   (51)

6. Use two unit multipliers to convert 1000 square centimeters to square meters.
   (33)

7. Find the volume of this right solid.
   (45) Dimensions are in meters. First find the area of a triangular end.

8. Find the surface area of the right solid.
   (49)

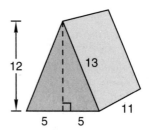

9. What fraction of 56 is 21?
   (48)

10. Eight thirteenths of what number is 16?
    (48)

11. (a) What is 1% of 77.2?
    (53) (b) What is 500% of 77.2?

12. (a) What is 1% of 90?
    (53) (b) What is 77% of 90?

Solve:

13. $\dfrac{8}{7}x = 104$
    (40)

14. $x - \dfrac{5}{12} = \dfrac{15}{4}$
    (39)

15. $\dfrac{t}{11} = \dfrac{9}{44}$
    (54)

16. $\dfrac{5}{6} = \dfrac{2}{y}$
    (54)

Simplify:

17. $24 + 2[6(3 - 1) \div (7 - 3) + 6]$
    (42)

18. $2^3 + 2[(8 + 1)(6 - 5) - 3]$
    (44)

19. $5\dfrac{6}{7} \cdot \dfrac{3}{2} - 1\dfrac{1}{14}$
    (46)

20. $\dfrac{5}{6} + 1\dfrac{5}{12} - 1\dfrac{1}{3}$
    (35)

21. $\sqrt[3]{8} + \sqrt[3]{27} - 5$
    (44)

22. $23\dfrac{4}{5} - 6\dfrac{1}{15}$
    (35)

23. $\dfrac{182.101}{0.0006}$
    (7)

24. $8\dfrac{3}{4} \div 1\dfrac{1}{3} \times 1\dfrac{3}{4} \div \dfrac{1}{12}$
    (43)

25.
(52) $\dfrac{5}{69}\left[\dfrac{1}{7}(4 + 3) + \dfrac{11}{2}\right]$

26.
(52) $\dfrac{1}{6}\left(2\dfrac{1}{3} + \dfrac{1}{2}\right) + \dfrac{2}{3}$

Evaluate:

27. m^n if $m = 6$ and $n = 3$
(54)

28. $xyt - yt + x$ if $x = 6$, $y = \dfrac{1}{3}$, and $t = 12$
(32)

29. $\sqrt[x]{y}$ if $x = 3$ and $y = 125$
(54)

30. (a) Write 100,000 in scientific notation.
(50)
     (b) Write 0.0072 in scientific notation.

     (c) Write 3.2×10^5 in standard notation.

     (d) Write 3.2×10^{-5} in standard notation.

LESSON 55   *Fractions, Decimals, and Percents • Reference Numbers*

55.A
fractions, decimals, and percents

We can designate equivalent amounts of a whole by using a fraction, a decimal number, or by using a percent.

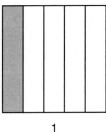   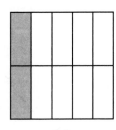   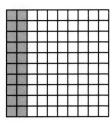

$\dfrac{1}{5}$ 0.2   20 percent

In the figure on the left, we have shaded one of the five equal parts to represent $\frac{1}{5}$. The center figure has ten equal parts, and we have shaded two of them to represent two tenths, which is 0.2. The figure on the right has been divided into one hundred equal parts; twenty of these parts have been shaded to represent 20 percent. All three shaded areas are equal. From these diagrams we see that

$$\dfrac{1}{5} \quad\text{and}\quad 0.2 \quad\text{and}\quad 20\text{ percent}$$

are three ways of saying the same thing. That is because $\frac{1}{5}$, 0.2, and 20 percent are just equivalent fractions in disguise:

$$\dfrac{1}{5} = \dfrac{2}{10} = \dfrac{20}{100}$$

example 55.1   (a) Find the decimal equivalent of $\frac{51}{100}$.

(b) Find the percent equivalent of $\frac{51}{100}$.

solution   (a) To find the decimal equivalent of $\frac{51}{100}$, we divide.

$$\frac{51}{100} = \mathbf{0.51}$$

In this case the denominator is a power of ten, so we could also "say the number":

$$\frac{51}{100} = \text{"fifty-one hundredths"} = 0.51$$

(b) To change a decimal to a percent, we move the decimal point two places to the right.

$$0.51 = \mathbf{51 \text{ percent}}$$

55.B

reference numbers   Many people understand how to change from one of the three previously mentioned forms to the others but still make mistakes. The mistake made most often is moving the decimal point the wrong way. To prevent mistakes, it is helpful to memorize one set of numbers that is correct. Then we use these numbers as reference numbers. In this book, we will use the numbers from the preceding example as reference numbers. Thus, the fraction reference number is always $\frac{51}{100}$, the decimal reference number is always 0.51, and the percent reference number is always 51%.

example 55.2   Complete the table. Begin by inserting the reference numbers.

FRACTION	DECIMAL	PERCENT
		25%

solution   First we write the reference numbers.

FRACTION	DECIMAL	PERCENT
$\frac{51}{100}$	0.51	51%
		25%

The reference numbers remind us to move the decimal point two places to the left to get the decimal form. Thus,

25 percent is equivalent to the decimal number 0.25

To change 0.25 to a fraction, we write it as twenty-five hundredths and then simplify.

$$\frac{25}{100} = \frac{1}{4}$$

Thus we have

FRACTION	DECIMAL	PERCENT
$\frac{51}{100}$	0.51	51%
$\frac{1}{4}$	**0.25**	25%

example 55.3   Complete the table. Begin by inserting the reference numbers.

FRACTION	DECIMAL	PERCENT
$\frac{1}{16}$		

solution   Three blank spaces are provided for the reference numbers. We write them in these spaces.

FRACTION	DECIMAL	PERCENT
$\frac{51}{100}$	0.51	51%
$\frac{1}{16}$		

To find the decimal form equivalent to $\frac{1}{16}$, we divide.

$$
\begin{array}{r}
0.0625 \\
16\overline{)1.0000} \\
\underline{96} \\
40 \\
\underline{32} \\
80 \\
\underline{80} \\
0
\end{array}
$$

The reference numbers show us that we move the decimal point two places to the right to find the percent form. Thus, 0.0625 is equivalent to 6.25 percent.

FRACTION	DECIMAL	PERCENT
$\frac{51}{100}$	0.51	51%
$\frac{1}{16}$	**0.0625**	**6.25%**

practice   Complete the table. Begin by inserting the reference numbers.

FRACTION	DECIMAL	PERCENT
$\frac{1}{8}$	a.	b.
c.	0.22	d.

problem set 55

1. Bill's funds were limited; he bought only 70 items, for which he paid $3500. Write the two rates (ratios) implied by this statement. What would he have had to pay for 720 items at the same rate?
   (36)

2. The fishmonger sold 40 codfish at 10 shillings each, 59 salmon at 30 shillings each, and 1 grouper for 300 shillings. What was the average price paid per fish?
   (41)

3. The crones and the curmudgeons forced their way in until 900,062 had arrived. This was 202,020 more than had come last time. How many came last time?
   (5)

4. Three tenths of what number is 36?
   (51)

5. What decimal part of 480 is 60?
   (51)

6. (a) Write 0.000387 in scientific notation.
(50)

(b) Write 8.69×10^{11} in standard notation.

7. (a) What is 1 percent of 37?
(53)

(b) What is 132 percent of 37?

8. Complete the table. Begin by inserting
(55) the reference numbers.

Fraction	Decimal	Percent
$\frac{3}{40}$	(a)	(b)
(c)	(d)	42%

9. What is the volume of a right solid whose base is the figure shown below and whose
(45) height is 10 centimeters? Dimensions are in centimeters.

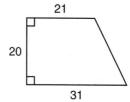 

10. Find the least common multiple of 10, 15, and 25.
(20)

11. Six sevenths of 98 is what number?
(48)

12. What fraction of 64 is 48?
(48)

Solve:

13. $\frac{12}{13}x = 60$
(40)

14. $x + \frac{3}{7} = \frac{29}{14}$
(39)

15. $\frac{14}{15} = \frac{3}{v}$
(54)

16. $\frac{6}{x} = \frac{4}{9}$
(54)

Simplify:

17. $\sqrt{144} - 3[(11 - 3) \div (3 - 1) - 4]$
(44)

18. $2^2 + 2[2(3 + 1)(3 - 2) - 1]$
(44)

19. $4\frac{3}{5} \cdot \frac{2}{3} - \frac{14}{15}$
(46)

20. $5\frac{2}{3} - 3\frac{5}{6} + \frac{5}{18}$
(35)

21. $3^2 + 2^2 - 3 + \sqrt[3]{8}$
(44)

22. 197.3×0.013
(7)

23. $6211.89 - 8.987$
(6)

24. $\frac{192.03}{0.05}$
(7)

25. $\dfrac{1\frac{3}{4}}{2\frac{1}{5}}$
(43)

26. $\frac{5}{3}\left(\frac{1}{7} + \frac{3}{8}\right) - \frac{1}{4}$
(52)

27. $\frac{1}{4}\left(2\frac{1}{4} - \frac{1}{8}\right) + \frac{3}{16}$
(43)

Evaluate:

28.
(32) $xyz + xz - z$ if $x = \dfrac{1}{3}$, $y = 9$, and $z = 12$

29.
(47) $\sqrt[z]{y} + x^2$ if $x = 2$, $y = 8$ and $z = 3$

30.
(38) The vertices of a square are $(-4, 2)$, $(-4, -4)$, $(2, -4)$, and $(2, 2)$. Draw the square, and find its perimeter and area.

LESSON 56 *Equations with Mixed Numbers*

When equations contain mixed numbers, it is often helpful if we convert the mixed numbers to improper fractions as the first step.

example 56.1   Solve: $2\dfrac{1}{3}m = 5$

solution   As the first step, we write $2\frac{1}{3}$ as an improper fraction.

$$\frac{7}{3}m = 5$$

Now we solve by multiplying both sides by $\frac{3}{7}$.

$$\frac{\cancel{3}}{\cancel{7}} \cdot \frac{\cancel{7}}{\cancel{3}}m = 5 \cdot \frac{3}{7} \qquad \text{multiplied both sides by } \frac{3}{7}$$

$$m = \frac{15}{7} \qquad \text{simplified}$$

example 56.2   Solve: $3\dfrac{1}{2}k = 4\dfrac{1}{5}$

solution   This time there are two mixed numbers. As the first step, we write them both as improper fractions.

$$\frac{7}{2}k = \frac{21}{5}$$

To solve, we multiply both sides by $\frac{2}{7}$.

$$\frac{\cancel{2}}{\cancel{7}} \cdot \frac{\cancel{7}}{\cancel{2}}k = \frac{21}{5} \cdot \frac{2}{7} \qquad \text{multiplied both sides by } \frac{2}{7}$$

$$k = \frac{6}{5} \qquad \text{simplified}$$

practice   Solve:

a. $2\dfrac{1}{4}p = 8\dfrac{1}{2}$

b. $4\dfrac{1}{5}x = 3\dfrac{1}{2}$

problem set 56

1.
(36) The shipment of new tires cost \$780, and for this price the dealer got 10 tires.
(a) Write the two rates (ratios) implied by this statement.
(b) What would the dealer have to pay for 58 tires at the same rate?
(c) How many tires could the dealer get for \$156 at the same rate?

2. Two numbers were proposed. The first number was nine million, forty-seven. The
(5)   second number was eight million, seven hundred ninety-three thousand, two hundred
fifteen. By how much was the first number greater?

3. The first four cows through the chute were nice and fat. The first one weighed 1200 lb,
(26)   the second one weighed 900 lb, and the third one weighed 840 lb. What did the last cow
weigh if the average weight of all four cows was 998 lb?

4. By how much did Rio de Janeiro's rainfall in July exceed the total rainfall of May and
(29)   December combined?

Rainfall in Rio de Janeiro

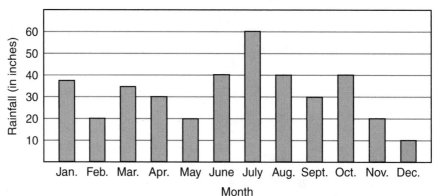

5. Complete the table. Begin by inserting
(55)   the reference numbers.

FRACTION	DECIMAL	PERCENT
$\frac{3}{8}$	(a)	(b)
(c)	(d)	38%

6. (a) What is 1 percent of 52?
(53)
(b) What is 140 percent of 52?

7. Three fourths of what number is 60?
(48)

8. Six tenths of what number is 42?
(51)

9. What fraction of 57 is 45?
(48)

10. What decimal part of 280 is 70?
(51)

11. Four ninths of 99 is what number?
(48)

12. What is the volume of a solid whose base is the figure shown on the left and whose
(45)   height is 5 centimeters? Dimensions are in centimeters.

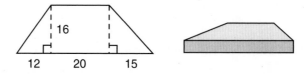

13. Write $6\frac{16}{17}$ as an improper fraction.
(28)

Solve:

14.
(54)
$$\frac{x}{9} = \frac{5}{6}$$

15.
(54)
$$\frac{5}{x} = \frac{2}{3}$$

16.
(56)
$$3\frac{1}{5}x = 8$$

17.
(56)
$$x + 1\frac{3}{5} = 3\frac{7}{10}$$

Simplify:

18.
(42)
$$72 - 3[(14 - 4) \div (3 - 1) - 4]$$

19.
(44)
$$3^3 + 2^2[2(2 + 1)(2 - 1) - 5]$$

20.
(35)
$$4\frac{4}{5} - 3\frac{2}{3} + \frac{7}{15}$$

21.
(44)
$$2^3 + 3^2 - \sqrt[3]{27}$$

22.
(7)
$$132.7 \times 0.012$$

23.
(6)
$$18{,}251.3 - 62.982$$

24.
(7)
$$\frac{135.06}{0.003}$$

25.
(43)
$$2\frac{1}{3} \div 1\frac{1}{6} \times 3\frac{1}{4} \div 1\frac{1}{3}$$

26.
(52)
$$\frac{1}{3}\left(\frac{1}{6} + \frac{5}{12}\right) - \frac{1}{36}$$

27.
(52)
$$\frac{1}{4}\left(3\frac{1}{3} - \frac{1}{6}\right) + \frac{1}{12}$$

Evaluate:

28.
(32)
$$xy + x + xyz - z \quad \text{if } x = 24, \ y = \frac{1}{6}, \text{ and } z = 3$$

29.
(54)
$$\sqrt[p]{q} + pq \quad \text{if } p = 3 \text{ and } q = 8$$

30.
(50)
(a) Write 16,000,000,000 in scientific notation.
(b) Write 1.6×10^{-8} in standard notation.

LESSON 57 *Mixed Number Problems*

We can write any mixed number as an improper fraction. We can write $2\frac{1}{3}$ as the improper fraction $\frac{7}{3}$.

$$2\frac{1}{3} \text{ equals } \frac{7}{3}$$

When we encounter word problems that contain mixed numbers, we will rewrite the mixed numbers as improper fractions.

example 57.1   Two and one half of what number is $7\frac{1}{3}$?

solution   We will translate the question keeping in mind the fractional part of a number equation.

A fraction of a number is another number.
$$F \cdot A = B$$

Two and one half of what number is $7\dfrac{1}{3}$?

$$2\frac{1}{2} \qquad \cdot \qquad A \qquad = 7\frac{1}{3}$$

Now we rewrite the mixed numbers as their improper fraction equivalents.

$$\frac{5}{2} \cdot A = \frac{22}{3}$$

We solve by multiplying both sides by $\frac{2}{5}$.

$$\frac{\cancel{2}}{\cancel{5}} \cdot \frac{\cancel{5}}{\cancel{2}} \cdot A = \frac{22}{3} \cdot \frac{2}{5} \qquad \text{multiplied both sides by } \frac{2}{5}$$

$$A = \frac{44}{15} \qquad \text{simplified}$$

Thus, $2\frac{1}{2}$ of $\frac{44}{15}$ is $7\frac{1}{3}$.

example 57.2   Two and one fifth of $8\frac{1}{8}$ is what number?

solution   This time we rewrite the problem using improper fractions.

$$\frac{11}{5} \text{ of } \frac{65}{8} \text{ is what number?}$$

Now we write the fractional part of a number equation.

A fraction of a number is another number.

$$F \cdot A = B$$

$$\frac{11}{5} \cdot \frac{65}{8} = B \qquad \text{substituted}$$

Now we cancel and multiply.

$$\frac{11}{\cancel{5}} \cdot \frac{\overset{13}{\cancel{65}}}{8} = B \qquad \text{canceled}$$
$$\underset{1}{}$$

$$\frac{143}{8} = B \qquad \text{simplified}$$

Thus, $2\frac{1}{5}$ of $8\frac{1}{8}$ is $\frac{143}{8}$.

practice   **a.**   Three and one half of $6\frac{1}{4}$ is what number?

b.   Three and one fourth of what number is $6\frac{1}{8}$?

c.   What fraction of $3\frac{2}{5}$ is $9\frac{7}{8}$?

problem set   **1.**   Jimmy bought 80 small trees and paid \$3520. Write the two rates (ratios) implied by
57   *(36)*   this statement. What would he have to pay for just 10 small trees at the same rate?

2.   The average weight of the first two dogs was 43 pounds. The average weight of the next
(41)   three dogs was 58 pounds. What was the overall average weight of all five dogs?

3.   The first try resulted in 1436. The second try resulted in 1892. The third try was the big
(5)   one, as it came to 4400. By how much did the third try exceed the sum of the first two?

4.   Ninety-seven was a bad guess. However, 5 times this number increased by six hundred
(13)   forty-two was the correct number. What was the correct number?

5.
(55)
Complete the table. Begin by inserting the reference numbers.

FRACTION	DECIMAL	PERCENT
(a)	(b)	76%
(c)	0.6	(d)

6.
(53)
(a) What is 1% of 3600?

(b) What is 16% of 3600?

7.
(33)
Use two unit multipliers to convert 10,000 square inches to square feet. Round any decimal answer to two places.

8.
(51)
Eight tenths of what number is 48?

9.
(48)
What fraction of 60 is 48?

10.
(51)
What decimal part of 350 is 70?

11.
(57)
What fraction of $2\frac{7}{9}$ is $8\frac{1}{3}$?

12.
(57)
Five and five eighths of what number is $4\frac{1}{4}$?

13.
(45)
What is the volume of a right solid whose base is the figure shown on the left and whose height is 2 feet? Dimensions are in feet.

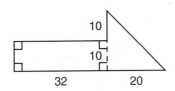
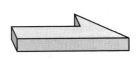

14.
(49)
Find the surface area of this triangular solid. Dimensions are in meters.

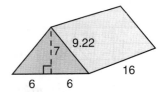

15.
(38)
Make a sketch of a rectangular coordinate system, and graph the points (3, –5) and (0, 3).

Solve:

16.
(54)
$\dfrac{15}{7} = \dfrac{4}{x}$

17.
(54)
$\dfrac{5}{6} = \dfrac{p}{4}$

18.
(56)
$3\dfrac{7}{15}x = 3$

19.
(56)
$x + 3\dfrac{3}{14} = 4\dfrac{5}{28}$

Simplify:

20.
(42)
$64 - 2[(3 - 1)(5 - 2) + 1]$

21.
(44)
$2^3 + 2^2[3(2 - 1)(2 + 2) - 7]$

22.
(46)
$2\dfrac{1}{3} \cdot 1\dfrac{3}{4} - \dfrac{7}{12}$

23.
(35)
$6\dfrac{2}{5} - 2\dfrac{1}{4} + \dfrac{3}{40}$

24. $2^4 + 3^3 - 2^3 + \sqrt[3]{8}$
(44)

25. $9218.821 - 61.872$
(6)

26. $\frac{1}{5}\left(3\frac{1}{4} - 2\frac{1}{3}\right) + \frac{7}{15}$
(52)

27. $\dfrac{2\frac{3}{4}}{1\frac{7}{8}}$
(43)

28. $6\frac{2}{3} \div 1\frac{1}{6} \times 3\frac{1}{3} \div 2\frac{4}{5}$
(43)

29. (a) Write 1.3×10 in standard notation.
(50)   (b) Write 0.0392 in scientific notation.

30. Evaluate:
(54)
 (a) x^y if $x = 3$ and $y = 3$
 (b) $\sqrt[x]{y}$ if $x = 3$ and $y = 125$

LESSON 58 *The Distance Problem*

Jimmy can drive 60 miles (mi) in 1 hour (hr). This statement gives us two rates (ratios).

$$\frac{60 \text{ miles}}{1 \text{ hour}} \quad \text{and} \quad \frac{1 \text{ hour}}{60 \text{ miles}}$$

If we want to know how far he could drive in 2 hours, we use the rate with miles on top (in the numerator).

$$\text{Distance} = \frac{60 \text{ miles}}{1 \text{ hour}} \times 2 \text{ hours} = 120 \text{ miles}$$

Whenever you see the equation

$$(1) \ \text{Distance} = \text{rate} \times \text{time}$$

the rate used has time on the bottom (in the denominator). This rate is called **speed.** If we want to know how long it would take to drive 300 miles, we use the rate with time on top.

$$\text{Time} = \frac{1 \text{ hour}}{60 \text{ miles}} \times 300 \text{ miles} = \frac{300 \text{ hours}}{60} = 5 \text{ hours}$$

This equation tells us that

$$(2) \ \text{Time} = \text{rate} \times \text{distance}$$

If we use the rate with time in the numerator, we can multiply to find the time required. Most books teach only equation (1). If we only use equation (1), we must divide to find the time required. Remember that the two equations use different rates. Equation (1) solves for distance and uses a rate with units of distance on top. Equation (2) solves for time and uses a rate with units of time on top.

example 58.1 Helen could travel 40 miles per hour. How long would it take her to travel 600 miles?

solution First we write the two rates.

$$\text{(a)} \ \frac{40 \text{ miles}}{1 \text{ hour}} \qquad \text{(b)} \ \frac{1 \text{ hour}}{40 \text{ miles}}$$

If we use rate (a), then we can use equation (1).

$$\text{Distance} = \text{rate} \times \text{time}$$

We replace rate with $\frac{40 \text{ miles}}{1 \text{ hour}}$ and replace distance with 600 miles. We get

$$600 \text{ miles} = \frac{40 \text{ miles}}{1 \text{ hour}} \times \text{time}$$

To solve, we multiply both sides of the equation by the reciprocal of $\frac{40 \text{ miles}}{1 \text{ hour}}$.

$$600 \text{ mi} \times \frac{1 \text{ hr}}{40 \text{ mi}} = \frac{1 \text{ hr}}{40 \text{ mi}} \cdot \frac{40 \text{ mi}}{1 \text{ hr}} \cdot \text{time}$$

$$\mathbf{15 \text{ hr}} = \text{time}$$

If we use rate (b), we can use equation (2) and find the same answer by multiplying.

$$\text{Time} = \text{rate} \times \text{distance}$$

$$\text{Time} = \frac{1 \text{ hr}}{40 \text{ mi}} \times 600 \text{ mi} = \mathbf{15 \text{ hr}}$$

In this case, we see that using equation (2) is much easier because we do not have to manipulate the equation to solve for time. However, we must learn how to use equation (1), because this general relationship may be used in other problems.

example 58.2 Harry could travel 350 miles in 7 hours.

(a) What was his speed?

(b) How long would it take him to travel 800 miles?

(c) At the same speed, how far could he travel in 12 hours?

solution (a) First we write the two rates.

$$\text{(a)} \quad \frac{350 \text{ miles}}{7 \text{ hours}} = \frac{50 \text{ miles}}{1 \text{ hr}} \qquad \text{(b)} \quad \frac{7 \text{ hours}}{350 \text{ miles}} = \frac{1 \text{ hour}}{50 \text{ miles}}$$

Speed is the rate with time in the denominator, so

$$\text{Speed} = \mathbf{50 \text{ miles per hour (mph)}}$$

(b) Now we write rate equation (2) to solve for time.

$$\text{Time} = \text{rate} \times \text{distance}$$

We replace rate with $\frac{1 \text{ hour}}{50 \text{ miles}}$ and replace distance with 800 miles. To solve, we multiply

$$\text{Time} = \frac{1 \text{ hr}}{50 \text{ mi}} \times 800 \text{ mi}$$

$$\text{Time} = \mathbf{16 \text{ hr}}$$

(c) To solve for distance, we use rate equation (1).

$$\text{Distance} = \text{rate} \times \text{time}$$

We replace rate with $\frac{50 \text{ miles}}{1 \text{ hour}}$ and time with 12 hours. To solve, we multiply.

$$\text{Distance} = \frac{50 \text{ mi}}{1 \text{ hr}} \times 12 \text{ hr}$$

$$\text{Distance} = \mathbf{600 \text{ mi}}$$

practice Mildred traveled the first 120 miles in 3 hours.

a. What was her speed?

b. How long would it take her to travel 400 miles at the same speed? Work the problem two ways.

problem set 58

1. *(6)* The first guess was sixty-nine thousand and seven hundred forty-one hundred-thousandths. The second guess was only forty-two thousand and seventy-five hundred-thousandths. By how much was the first guess greater?

2. *(5)* While new ideas abounded, there was a dearth of suggestions as to how they were to be used. There were one hundred forty-three thousand new ideas but only nine thousand, six hundred fourteen suggestions for their use. How many more new ideas were there than suggestions for their use?

3. *(36)* Jill could buy 53 new ones for only $742. Write the two rates (ratios) implied by this statement. How much would Jill have to pay for only 25 new ones?

4. *(13)* One hundred forty-five thousand came on the first day. On the second day, 5 times this many came. How many came in all?

5. *(58)* Sherri traveled 195 miles in 3 hours.

   (a) What was her speed?

   (b) How long would it take her to travel 520 miles at the same speed?

6. *(55)* Complete the table. Begin by inserting the reference numbers.

FRACTION	DECIMAL	PERCENT
(a)	0.24	(b)
$\frac{1}{2}$	(c)	(d)

7. *(50)* (a) Write 106,000,000 in scientific notation.

   (b) Write 4.13×10^{-8} in standard notation.

8. *(51)* Seven tenths of what number is 42?

9. *(48)* What fraction of 72 is 64?

10. *(51)* What decimal part of 420 is 273?

11. *(57)* Two and two sevenths of $8\frac{1}{2}$ is what number?

12. *(57)* Three and one third of what number is $\frac{65}{3}$?

13. *(45)* What is the volume of a right solid whose base is the figure shown on the left and whose height is 3 inches? Dimensions are in inches. Angles that look like right angles are right angles.

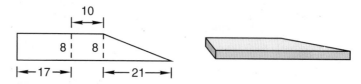

Solve:

14. *(54)* $\dfrac{16}{5} = \dfrac{3}{x}$

15. *(54)* $\dfrac{6}{7} = \dfrac{p}{14}$

16. *(56)* $2\dfrac{5}{12}x = 9$

17. *(56)* $x - 2\dfrac{3}{14} = 1\dfrac{1}{21}$

Simplify:

18. $38 - 2[(6 - 5)(4 - 1) + 1]$
(42)

19. $2^3 + 3^2[(7 - 2)(3 - 1)3 - 25]$
(44)

20. $1\dfrac{1}{3} \cdot 2\dfrac{3}{4} - \dfrac{7}{12}$
(46)

21. $5\dfrac{3}{5} - 1\dfrac{3}{4} + \dfrac{7}{20}$
(35)

22. $2^3 + 3^2 - 2^2 + \sqrt{16}$
(44)

23. 16.82×0.013
(7)

24. $\dfrac{618.21}{0.004}$
(7)

25. $\dfrac{1}{5}\left(\dfrac{2}{3} + \dfrac{1}{2}\right) - \dfrac{2}{15}$
(52)

26. $\dfrac{1}{4}\left(2\dfrac{3}{4} - 1\dfrac{1}{8}\right) + \dfrac{3}{16}$
(52)

27. $\dfrac{1\dfrac{4}{7}}{2\dfrac{3}{4}}$
(43)

28. (a) What is 1% of 19.5?
(53)
     (b) What is 31% of 19.5?

Evaluate:

29. $x^2 + 2xy + y^x$ if $x = 2$ and $y = 3$
(54)

30. p^q if $p = 2$ and $q = 3$
(54)

LESSON 59 *Proportions with Fractions*

There is no change in the method of solving conditional proportions when they contain fractions or mixed numbers. The first step is to cross multiply. Then we divide or multiply as required to complete the solution.

example 59.1 Solve: $\dfrac{\dfrac{2}{3}}{x} = \dfrac{\dfrac{5}{8}}{\dfrac{1}{5}}$

solution As the first step, we cross multiply.

$$\dfrac{2}{3} \cdot \dfrac{1}{5} = \dfrac{5}{8}x \qquad \text{cross multiplied}$$

$$\dfrac{2}{15} = \dfrac{5}{8}x \qquad \text{simplified}$$

We finish by multiplying both sides by $\frac{8}{5}$.

$$\dfrac{8}{5} \cdot \dfrac{2}{15} = \dfrac{\cancel{5}}{\cancel{8}}x \cdot \dfrac{\cancel{8}}{\cancel{5}} \qquad \text{multiplied both sides by } \dfrac{8}{5}$$

$$\dfrac{16}{75} = x \qquad \text{simplified}$$

example 59.2   Solve: $\dfrac{\frac{x}{3}}{\frac{3}{4}} = \dfrac{\frac{1}{3}}{\frac{2}{5}}$

solution   As the first step, we cross multiply.

$$\frac{2}{5}x = \frac{1}{\cancel{3}} \cdot \frac{\cancel{3}}{4} \qquad \text{cross multiplied}$$

$$\frac{2}{5}x = \frac{1}{4} \qquad \text{simplified}$$

We finish by multiplying both sides by $\frac{5}{2}$.

$$\frac{\cancel{5}}{\cancel{2}} \cdot \frac{\cancel{2}}{\cancel{5}}x = \frac{1}{4} \cdot \frac{5}{2} \qquad \text{multiplied both sides by } \frac{5}{2}$$

$$x = \frac{5}{8} \qquad \text{simplified}$$

practice   Solve:

a. $\dfrac{\frac{3}{2}}{\frac{1}{5}} = \dfrac{\frac{1}{4}}{x}$

b. $\dfrac{\frac{y}{2}}{\frac{2}{3}} = \dfrac{\frac{1}{5}}{\frac{1}{6}}$

c. $\dfrac{\frac{1}{2}}{\frac{1}{8}} = \dfrac{2}{x}$

d. $\dfrac{\frac{1}{3}}{x} = \dfrac{\frac{1}{5}}{7}$

problem set 59

1. The average of the first three numbers was 42. The average of the next seven numbers
(41) was only 12. What was the average of all ten numbers?

2. Seven big ones cost $280,000. Write the two rates (ratios) implied by this statement.
(36) How many big ones could be purchased for $120,000?

3. The first one weighed one hundred forty thousand, twenty-six pounds. The second
(5) weighed only one hundred thirty-two thousand, seven hundred eighty-one pounds. The
first one weighed how many pounds more than the second one?

4. Carolyn could walk 10 miles in 3 hours.
(58)
(a) What was her speed?

(b) How long would it take her to walk 25 miles at the same speed?

5. Complete the table. Begin by inserting
(55) the reference numbers.

Fraction	Decimal	Percent
(a)	(b)	16%
$\frac{4}{5}$	(c)	(d)

6. (a) Write 0.093 in scientific notation.
(50)
(b) Write 1.2×10^{6} in standard notation.

7. Nine tenths of what number is 72?
(51)

8. What fraction of $6\frac{1}{2}$ is $8\frac{1}{4}$?   **9.** What decimal part of 630 is 441?
(56)   (51)

10. Eight and one fourth of what number is $7\frac{1}{3}$?
(56)

11. One and one fourth of $8\frac{2}{3}$ is what number?
(56)

12. What is the volume of a right solid whose base is the figure shown on the left
(45) and whose height is 4 inches? Dimensions are in inches.

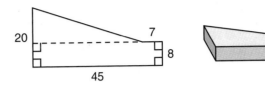

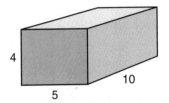

13. (a) What is 1% of 192?
(53) (b) What is 45% of 192?

14. Find the surface area of this
(49) rectangular solid. Dimensions are in
meters.

Solve:

15. $\dfrac{\frac{1}{5}}{\frac{1}{4}} = \dfrac{\frac{9}{10}}{x}$ **16.** $\dfrac{\frac{2}{3}}{\frac{2}{5}} = \dfrac{p}{\frac{7}{12}}$
(59)   (59)

17. $1\frac{3}{5}x = 6$ **18.** $3\frac{1}{4}p = 5$
(56)   (56)

Simplify:

19. $49 - 2\left[(5 - 2^2)(4 + 2) - 5\right]$ **20.** $\sqrt[3]{8} + 2^3\left[2^2(2^3 - 5) - 4\right]$
(44)   (44)

21. $2\frac{1}{3} \cdot 3\frac{1}{4} - \dfrac{11}{12}$ **22.** $14\frac{2}{3} - 12\frac{7}{8} + \dfrac{11}{48}$
(46)   (35)

23. 171.6×0.007 **24.** $1171.61 - 13.321$
(7)   (6)

25. $\dfrac{611.51}{0.03}$ **26.** $\dfrac{1}{6}\left(\dfrac{1}{3} + \dfrac{1}{2}\right) - \dfrac{5}{36}$
(7)   (52)

27. $\dfrac{1}{5}\left(\dfrac{1}{4} - \dfrac{1}{8}\right) + 2\frac{7}{8}$ **28.** $\dfrac{6\frac{2}{3}}{2\frac{1}{4}}$
(52)   (43)

29. $6\frac{1}{4} \div 3\frac{2}{3} \times 2\frac{1}{4} \div \dfrac{1}{8}$
(43)

30. Evaluate: $x^y + 3xy^2 + 3x^2y + y^x$ if $x = 1$ and $y = 2$
(54)

LESSON 60 *Circles*

Every point on a circle is the same distance from the center of the circle. We call this distance the **radius** of the circle. We call a line that connects two points on a circle a **chord** of the circle. A **diameter** of a circle is a chord that passes through the center of the circle. From the circles shown here, we see that a diameter of a circle is twice the radius of the same circle. The **circumference** of a circle is the total distance around the circle.

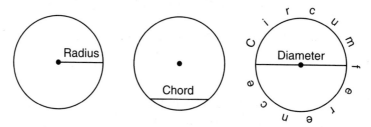

Many ancients thought that the circle was the perfect geometric figure. They were especially interested in the relationship between the diameter of a circle and the circumference of the same circle. They found that three diameters (*d*) would not go all the way around the circle. There is a little extra left over no matter how large or how small the circle is.

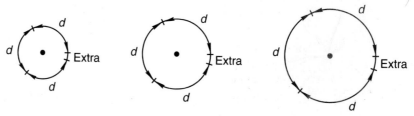

Now we know that the number of times the diameter will go around a circle is approximately

3.141592654 times

This is not exact because the exact numeral for this number has more digits than can ever be counted. We use the Greek character π to represent this number. (This character is written as *pi* and pronounced like pie.) We will use 3.14 as an approximation of π. If we multiply the diameter *d* by π, we can find the circumference of a circle. If we multiply the square of the radius *r* by π, we can find the area of a circle.

$$\boxed{\text{Circumference} = \pi d} \qquad \boxed{\text{Area of a circle} = \pi r^2}$$

example 60.1 The radius of a circle is 5 centimeters (cm).

(a) What is the circumference of the circle?

(b) What is the area of the circle?

solution (a) If the radius is 5 cm, the diameter is 10 cm. So

$$\text{Circumference} = \pi d$$
$$= \pi(10 \text{ cm})$$
$$\approx 3.14(10 \text{ cm})$$
$$\approx \mathbf{31.4 \text{ cm}}$$

(b) The area is π times the radius squared. So

$$\begin{aligned} \text{Area} &= \pi r^2 \\ &= \pi(5 \text{ cm})^2 \\ &\approx 3.14 \cdot 25 \text{ cm}^2 \\ &\approx \textbf{78.5 cm}^2 \end{aligned}$$

practice   The radius of a big circle is 100 meters.

a. What is the diameter of the circle?

b. What is the circumference of the circle?

c. What is the area of the circle?

problem set 60

1. Eudemonia bought 560 red ones for 7 pesos. Write the two rates (ratios) implied by this
(36) statement. How many red ones could she buy with 60 pesos at the same rate?

2. The Prince reined in after traveling 56 miles in 8 hours. If he traveled at the same rate
(58) on the next day, how far could he go in 14 hours?

3. Eau de Vapid meandered 40 miles in 5 hours. Then he sauntered 60 miles in 10 hours.
(58) By how much did his first rate exceed his second rate?

4. On the next leg of the trip, Eau de Vapid covered 40 miles in 20 hours. What was his
(41) average speed for all three legs of the trip? (*Reminder*: Averages cannot be averaged
to determine the overall average. Thus, to find the average speed for all three legs of
the trip, the total distance must be divided by the total time.)

5. Complete the table. Begin by inserting
(55) the reference numbers.

FRACTION	DECIMAL	PERCENT
(a)	0.72	(b)
$\frac{3}{5}$	(c)	(d)

6. The radius of a circle is 8 feet. Use 3.14 to approximate π.
(60)
    (a) What is the diameter of the circle?

    (b) What is the circumference of the circle?

    (c) What is the area of the circle?

7. Seven tenths of what number is 490?
(51)

8. What fraction of $3\frac{1}{9}$ is $\frac{24}{5}$?
(57)

9. What decimal part of 720 is 420?
(51)

10. Three and one third of what number is $4\frac{1}{2}$?
(57)

11. Two and one fourth of $2\frac{1}{3}$ is what number?
(57)

12. What is the volume of a right solid whose base is the figure shown on the left and whose
(45) height is 6 feet? Dimensions are in feet.

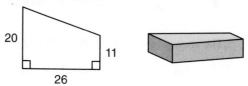

20   11

26

13. (a) What is 1% of 5.3?
(53) (b) What is 25% of 5.3?

14. Use two unit multipliers to convert 8000 square kilometers to square meters. Write
(33,50) the result in scientific notation.

Solve:

15. $\dfrac{\frac{3}{16}}{\frac{3}{5}} = \dfrac{8}{x}$
(59)

16. $\dfrac{\frac{3}{5}}{\frac{1}{4}} = \dfrac{\frac{5}{6}}{p}$
(59)

17. $2\dfrac{4}{5}x = 5$
(56)

18. $4\dfrac{1}{5}p = 6$
(56)

Simplify:

19. $54 - 2\left[\left(6 - 2^2\right)(3 + 1) - \sqrt{25}\right]$
(44)

20. $\sqrt{16} + 2^2\left[2\left(3^2 - 2^2\right) - 5\right]$
(44)

21. $3\dfrac{1}{3} \cdot 2\dfrac{1}{4} - \dfrac{5}{12}$
(46)

22. $15\dfrac{6}{7} - 3\dfrac{3}{14} + \dfrac{9}{14}$
(35)

23. 621.8×0.018
(7)

24. $2612.81 - 14.313$
(6)

25. $\dfrac{1821.5}{0.7}$
(7)

26. $\dfrac{1}{5}\left(\dfrac{1}{2} + 2\dfrac{1}{3}\right) - \dfrac{4}{15}$
(52)

27. $\dfrac{1}{4}\left(\dfrac{1}{6} + 1\dfrac{1}{4}\right) - \dfrac{1}{4}$
(52)

28. $3\dfrac{1}{2} \times 6\dfrac{1}{3} \div 2\dfrac{1}{3} \times 1\dfrac{1}{3}$
(43)

29. What are the x- and y-coordinates of the three points on this graph?
(38)

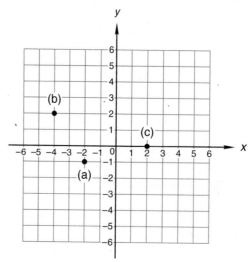

30. Evaluate: $xyz + z^z + y^z - y^z$ if $x = \dfrac{1}{3}$, $y = 6$, and $z = 2$
(54)

LESSON 61 *Solving Equations in Two Steps*

The answer to all four of these equations is 6.

(a) $\dfrac{x}{3} = 2$ (b) $3x = 18$ (c) $x + 2 = 8$ (d) $x - 3 = 3$

We use the multiplication-division rule to solve (a) and (b), and we use the addition-subtraction rule to solve (c) and (d).

(a) $3 \cdot \dfrac{x}{3} = 2 \cdot 3$ (b) $\dfrac{3x}{3} = \dfrac{18}{3}$

$\quad\quad x = 6$ $\quad\quad x = 6$

(c) $x + 2 - 2 = 8 - 2$ (d) $x - 3 + 3 = 3 + 3$

$\quad\quad\quad x = 6$ $\quad\quad\quad\quad x = 6$

Often it is necessary to use both rules to solve an equation. In this lesson, we show how to solve equations in which it is easier to use the addition-subtraction rule before the multiplication-division rule.

example 61.1   Solve: $3x + 2 = 7$

solution   First we subtract 2 from both sides of the equation.

$$3x + 2 - 2 = 7 - 2 \quad\quad \text{subtracted 2 from both sides}$$
$$3x = 5 \quad\quad\quad\quad \text{simplified}$$

Now we divide both sides of the equation by 3.

$$\dfrac{3x}{3} = \dfrac{5}{3} \quad\quad \text{divided both sides by 3}$$

$$x = \dfrac{5}{3} \quad\quad \text{simplified}$$

example 61.2   Solve: $\dfrac{2}{3}x - \dfrac{1}{2} = \dfrac{10}{3}$

solution   First we add $\frac{1}{2}$ to both sides of the equation.

$$\dfrac{2}{3}x - \dfrac{1}{2} + \dfrac{1}{2} = \dfrac{10}{3} + \dfrac{1}{2} \quad\quad \text{added } \dfrac{1}{2} \text{ to both sides}$$

$$\dfrac{2}{3}x = \dfrac{23}{6} \quad\quad\quad \text{simplified}$$

Now we multiply both sides of the equation by $\frac{3}{2}$.

$$\dfrac{3}{2} \cdot \dfrac{2}{3}x = \dfrac{23}{6} \cdot \dfrac{3}{2} \quad\quad \text{multiplied both sides by } \dfrac{3}{2}$$
$$\quad\quad\quad\quad 2$$

$$x = \dfrac{23}{4} \quad\quad\quad \text{simplified}$$

example 61.3   Solve: $2\dfrac{1}{3}x - 1\dfrac{1}{5} = \dfrac{23}{10}$

solution   This equation can be solved using the same two steps as in the previous two examples. However, for convenience we recast the equation by writing the mixed numbers as improper fractions.

$$\dfrac{7}{3}x - \dfrac{6}{5} = \dfrac{23}{10}$$

Now we proceed as in the last two examples. First we add $\frac{6}{5}$ to both sides of the equation.

$$\frac{7}{3}x - \frac{6}{5} + \frac{6}{5} = \frac{23}{10} + \frac{6}{5} \qquad \text{added } \frac{6}{5} \text{ to both sides}$$

$$\frac{7}{3}x = \frac{7}{2} \qquad \text{simplified}$$

Now we multiply both sides of the equation by $\frac{3}{7}$.

$$\frac{3}{7} \cdot \frac{7}{3}x = \frac{7}{2} \cdot \frac{3}{7} \qquad \text{multiplied both sides by } \frac{3}{7}$$

$$x = \frac{3}{2} \qquad \text{simplified}$$

practice Solve:

a. $\dfrac{2}{3}x - \dfrac{1}{6} = \dfrac{1}{2}$

b. $2\dfrac{1}{2}x + \dfrac{1}{8} = \dfrac{1}{4}$

c. $1\dfrac{1}{4}x - \dfrac{1}{3} = \dfrac{3}{5}$

d. $\dfrac{2}{7}x + \dfrac{1}{5} = 2\dfrac{1}{10}$

problem set 61

1.
(54) The knight found that his warhorse could run 6900 feet in 230 seconds. Write the two rates (ratios) implied by this statement. At this rate, how long would it take his warhorse to run 100,000 feet?

2.
(58) Ethelred the Unready was not ready, yet he covered the 480 miles in 4 hours.
(a) Write the two rates (ratios) implied by this statement.
(b) What was his speed?
(c) At this rate, how long would it take him to go 1440 miles?

3.
(58) The last leg of the journey was 1200 miles, so the tour group got an early start. If their speed was 60 miles per hour, how long did it take them to finish the last leg of the journey?

4.
(36) Hadrian's men increased their efforts and built 430 feet of wall in 1 day. At this rate, how long would it take to build 7310 feet of wall?

5.
(55) Complete the table. Begin by inserting the reference numbers.

FRACTION	DECIMAL	PERCENT
(a)	0.22	(b)
$\frac{21}{25}$	(c)	(d)

6.
(50) (a) Write 0.639 in scientific notation.
(b) Write 7.01×10^4 in standard notation.

7.
(51) Eight tenths of what number is 96?

8.
(48) What fraction of 52 is 30?

9.
(51) What decimal part of 700 is 581?

10.
(57) Three and one fifth of what number is $7\frac{1}{3}$?

11.
(57) Two and one tenth of $1\frac{3}{4}$ is what number?

12. What is the volume of a right solid whose base is the figure shown on the left and whose
(45) height is 3 feet? Dimensions are in feet. Angles that look like right angles are right
angles.

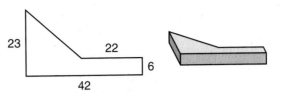

13. Find the surface area of this right
(49) solid. Dimensions are in inches.

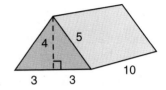

14. The diameter of a circle is 32 centimeters.
(60)
    (a) What is the radius of the circle?

    (b) What is the circumference of the circle?

    (c) What is the area of the circle?

Solve:

15. $\dfrac{\frac{5}{2}}{\frac{3}{4}} = \dfrac{12}{x}$
(59)

16. $\dfrac{\frac{4}{7}}{\frac{3}{8}} = \dfrac{x}{\frac{7}{15}}$
(59)

17. $\dfrac{3}{7}x + 2 = 7\dfrac{1}{4}$
(61)

18. $5x + 6\dfrac{3}{14} = 12\dfrac{2}{7}$
(61)

19. $7x - 2 = 11$
(61)

Simplify:

20. $\sqrt{9} + \sqrt{25}[3(3 - 1) - 2]$
(44)

21. 6111×0.0013
(7)

22. $2\dfrac{1}{3} \cdot 3\dfrac{1}{4} - \dfrac{5}{6}$
(46)

23. $14\dfrac{4}{5} - 4\dfrac{3}{4} + \dfrac{9}{10}$
(35)

24. $\dfrac{1}{3}\left(\dfrac{1}{2} + 2\dfrac{1}{3}\right) - \dfrac{7}{18}$
(52)

25. $2\dfrac{1}{2} \times 3\dfrac{2}{3} \div 1\dfrac{5}{6} \times \dfrac{1}{3}$
(43)

26. $\dfrac{1}{4}\left(\dfrac{1}{6} + 3\dfrac{1}{2}\right) - \dfrac{4}{5}$
(52)

27. $\dfrac{4\frac{1}{3}}{5\frac{5}{6}}$
(43)

28. $96 - 4\left[\left(7 - 2^2\right) \div (1 + 2) + \sqrt{36}\right]$
(44)

29. (a) What is 1% of 31.2?
(53)
    (b) What is 50% of 31.2?

30. Evaluate: $x^2 + xy + xyz + \sqrt[z]{x}$ if $x = 9$, $y = \dfrac{1}{3}$, and $z = 2$
(54)

LESSON 62   *Fractional Part Word Problems*

The equation

A fraction of a number is another number

or

$$F \cdot A = B$$

is an important equation in mathematics. This equation is used to solve many problems that are encountered in everyday life. (This equation is also the same as the percent equation, as we will see in a later lesson.)

example 62.1   Five eighths of the gnomes who lived in the magic forest had happy faces. If 840 gnomes had happy faces, how many gnomes lived in the magic forest?

solution   We can change the wording of this problem to

$$\frac{5}{8} \text{ of what number is 840?}$$

which we can solve by using the equation for a fractional part of a number, remembering that "of" corresponds to "·" and "is" corresponds to "=". We substitute and solve.

$$\frac{5}{8} \cdot A = 840 \qquad \text{equation}$$

$$\frac{8}{5} \cdot \frac{5}{8} \cdot A = 840 \cdot \frac{8}{5} \qquad \text{multiplied both sides by } \frac{8}{5}$$

$$A = 1344 \qquad \text{simplified}$$

So **1344 gnomes** lived in the forest. If 840 had happy faces, then 504 did not have happy faces.

example 62.2   On Monday $2\frac{4}{5}$ times the acceptable number of rock badgers took refuge in the mountain caves. If 640 was the acceptable number, how many rock badgers took refuge in the mountain caves on Monday?

solution   We can restate the problem as

$$2\frac{4}{5} \text{ of 640 is what number?}$$

We will change $2\frac{4}{5}$ to an improper fraction. Then we will use the fractional part of a number equation, substitute, and solve.

$$\frac{14}{5} \cdot 640 = B \qquad \text{equation}$$

$$1792 = B \qquad \text{simplified}$$

Thus, a total of **1792 rock badgers** took refuge in the mountain caves on Monday.

example 62.3   When the fog lifted, 400 ghosts were spied skulking near the outskirts. If 240 ghosts were not spied, what fraction of the ghosts was not spied?

solution   Since there are 640 ghosts in all, we can restate the problem as

What fraction of 640 is 240?

We use the fractional part of a number equation, substitute, and solve.

$$F \cdot 640 = 240 \qquad \text{equation}$$

$$\frac{F \cdot \cancel{640}}{\cancel{640}} = \frac{240}{640} \qquad \text{divided both sides by 640}$$

$$F = \frac{3}{8} \qquad \text{simplified}$$

Thus, $\frac{3}{8}$ of the ghosts were not spied.

practice **a.** When the gun sounded, only two fifths of the racers began to run. If 460 racers began to run, how many racers were there in all?

problem set **1.** Fourteen big ones could be purchased for 9 crowns. Write the two rates (ratios) implied
62 (36) by this statement. How many big ones could be purchased for 360 crowns?

2. Forty-three bottles could be filled in 2 minutes. Write the two rates (ratios) implied by
(36) this statement. How long would it take to fill 860 bottles?

3. When daylight came, 640 crickets were seen outside the school. If the other 160
(62) crickets were not seen, what fraction of the crickets were not seen?

4. The speaker used 62 of the author's sentences verbatim. What fraction of the author's
(62) 80 sentences were used verbatim?

5. There were $2\frac{1}{3}$ times as many intrepid students as expected. If 30 were expected to be
(62) intrepid, what was the total number of intrepid students?

6. (a) What is 1% of 0.031?
(53)
      (b) What is 92% of 0.031?

7. Complete the table. Begin by inserting
(55) the reference numbers.

Fraction	Decimal	Percent
(a)	0.12	(b)
$\frac{5}{6}$	(c)	(d)

8. Jodie ran a mile in 8 minutes.
(58)
      (a) Write the two rates (ratios) implied by this statement.

      (b) What was her speed?

      (c) At this rate, how far would she run in half an hour?

9. Four tenths of what number is 316?   **10.** What fraction of $\frac{45}{6}$ is $7\frac{1}{4}$?
(51)   (57)

11. What decimal part of 640 is 560?
(51)

12. Two and one fourth of what number is $6\frac{1}{3}$?
(57)

13. Three and one half of $1\frac{1}{10}$ is what number?
(57)

14. What is the volume of a right solid whose base is the figure shown on the left and whose
(45) height is 2 meters? Dimensions are in meters.

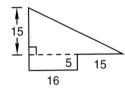

15. What is the circumference and area of a wrestling mat with a radius of 14 ft?
(60)

16. Use two unit multipliers to convert 16,000 square inches to square feet. Round any
(33) decimal answer to two places.

Solve:

17.
(59) $\dfrac{\frac{1}{3}}{\frac{2}{5}} = \dfrac{6}{x}$

18.
(59) $\dfrac{\frac{2}{3}}{\frac{3}{4}} = \dfrac{\frac{5}{12}}{p}$

19.
(61) $3\frac{5}{6}x + 4 = 7\frac{1}{2}$

20.
(61) $3\frac{2}{5}p - \frac{1}{6} = 1\frac{2}{5}$

21.
(61) $7r - 1\frac{3}{7} = 5$

Simplify:

22.
(44) $64 - 3\left[\left(6 - 2^2\right)\left(3^2 - 2^2\right) + 1\right]$

23.
(44) $\sqrt[3]{8} + \sqrt{16}[2(3 - 1) + 7]$

24.
(46) $2\frac{1}{4} \cdot 3\frac{2}{3} - \frac{5}{6}$

25.
(35) $14\frac{3}{4} - 4\frac{1}{5} + \frac{7}{20}$

26.
(43) $\dfrac{4\frac{2}{3}}{2\frac{1}{6}}$

27.
(52) $\frac{1}{4}\left(\frac{1}{2} + 3\frac{1}{4}\right) - \frac{5}{8}$

28.
(52) $\frac{1}{3}\left(\frac{1}{2} + 3\frac{1}{3}\right) - \frac{5}{6}$

29.
(50)   (a) Write 3.09×10^{-5} in standard notation.

       (b) Write 19,000 in scientific notation.

30.
(54)   Evaluate: $x^2 + y^2 + 2xy + \sqrt[x]{z}$ if $x = 3$, $y = 5$, and $z = 27$

LESSON 63   *Changing Rates*

We know that a rate is a ratio. Either number can be on top. If thirty jars can be filled in one minute, we can write two rates.

$$\frac{30 \text{ jars}}{1 \text{ minute}} \quad \text{and} \quad \frac{1 \text{ minute}}{30 \text{ jars}}$$

If the number of jars per minute were doubled, the two new rates would be

$$\frac{60 \text{ jars}}{1 \text{ minute}} \quad \text{and} \quad \frac{1 \text{ minute}}{60 \text{ jars}}$$

If the original rate were increased by seven jars per minute, the two new ratios would be

$$\frac{37 \text{ jars}}{1 \text{ minute}} \quad \text{and} \quad \frac{1 \text{ minute}}{37 \text{ jars}}$$

In everyday usage the word *rate* means speed, which is the number per unit of time. This is the ratio with the time in the denominator.

example 63.1 Prince Charming traveled 60 leagues in 2 days. Then he doubled his rate. How long would it take him to go 300 leagues at this new speed?

solution The given ratios are

$$\frac{60 \text{ leagues}}{2 \text{ days}} = \frac{30 \text{ leagues}}{1 \text{ day}} \quad \text{and} \quad \frac{2 \text{ days}}{60 \text{ leagues}} = \frac{1 \text{ day}}{30 \text{ leagues}}$$

If he doubles his rate, he doubles the ratio with time in the denominator, which means he doubles the distance he can travel in one day. Thus, the new ratios are

$$\frac{(2 \times 30) \text{ leagues}}{1 \text{ day}} = \frac{60 \text{ leagues}}{1 \text{ day}} \quad \text{and} \quad \frac{1 \text{ day}}{(2 \times 30) \text{ leagues}} = \frac{1 \text{ day}}{60 \text{ leagues}}$$

To find the time required to go 300 leagues at the new rate, we choose the ratio with time in the numerator.

$$\frac{1 \text{ day}}{60 \text{ leagues}} \cdot 300 \text{ leagues} = \frac{300 \text{ days}}{60} = \textbf{5 days}$$

example 63.2 The machine could cap 500 bottles in 2 hours. If the rate of the machine were tripled, how many bottles could be capped in 10 hours at the new rate?

solution The given ratios are

$$\frac{500 \text{ bottles}}{2 \text{ hours}} = \frac{250 \text{ bottles}}{1 \text{ hour}} \quad \text{and} \quad \frac{2 \text{ hours}}{500 \text{ bottles}} = \frac{1 \text{ hour}}{250 \text{ bottles}}$$

If the rate were tripled, the machine could cap three times the number of bottles in the same time. The new ratios would be

$$\frac{(3 \times 250) \text{ bottles}}{1 \text{ hour}} \quad \text{and} \quad \frac{1 \text{ hour}}{(3 \times 250) \text{ bottles}}$$

To find the number of bottles, we choose the ratio with bottles in the numerator.

$$\frac{750 \text{ bottles}}{1 \text{ hour}} \times 10 \text{ hours} = \textbf{7500 bottles}$$

example 63.3 Raul ran 6 miles in 2 hours. Then he ran 20 miles in 4 hours. By how much did his rate increase?

solution Unless otherwise specified, rate means speed, and it is understood that time is in the denominator.

$$\text{Initial rate} = \frac{6 \text{ mi}}{2 \text{ hr}} = \frac{3 \text{ mi}}{1 \text{ hr}} \qquad \text{Second rate} = \frac{20 \text{ mi}}{4 \text{ hr}} = \frac{5 \text{ mi}}{1 \text{ hr}}$$

His rate increased from 3 miles per hour to 5 miles per hour. His rate increased by **2 miles per hour.**

practice **a.** Jim drove the 120 miles to Grandmother's house in 3 hours. He increased his speed by 10 miles per hour on the way home. How long did it take him to drive home?

b. Margot could pickle 500 cucumbers in 2 hours. She got tired and reduced her rate by one half. How long would it take her to pickle 2000 cucumbers at the new rate?

problem set 63 **1.** The bus labored up the mountain at 40 yards per minute. If it was 2800 yards to the top, (58) how long would it take the bus to get there?

2. The skiers could traverse 7,000 feet of rough terrain in 20 minutes. How long would it take (58) take them to traverse 26,950 feet of rough terrain?

3.
(63) The machine bottled 8,000 bottles in 4 hours. If the rate of the machine were doubled, how long would it take the machine to bottle 40,000 bottles?

4.
(63) The tram could cover 400 centimeters in 50 seconds. If the rate of the tram were reduced by one half during the thunderstorm, how far could the tram go in 20,000 seconds?

5.
(62) Sia deleted $\frac{9}{10}$ of her e-mail messages. If she deleted 72 e-mail messages, how many did she originally have?

6.
(55) Complete the table. Begin by inserting the reference numbers.

Fraction	Decimal	Percent
(a)	0.16	(b)
$\frac{2}{5}$	(c)	(d)

7.
(50) (a) Write 3.09×10^{-4} in standard notation.
      (b) Write 6,103,000 in scientific notation.

8.
(51) What decimal part of 720 is 80?

9.
(48) What fraction of 625 is 75?

10.
(57) Six and two fifths of what number is $6\frac{1}{4}$?

11.
(57) Three and one fifth of $1\frac{1}{2}$ is what number?

12.
(60) The radius of a circle is 10 centimeters.
      (a) What is the circumference of the circle?
      (b) What is the area of the circle?

13.
(45) The base of a right solid is shown on the left. If the sides of the solid are 5 inches tall, what is the volume of the solid? Dimensions are in inches.

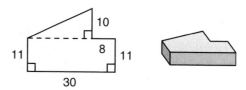

14.
(33) Use two unit multipliers to convert 28,000 square miles to square feet.

Solve:

15.
(59) $\dfrac{\frac{3}{4}}{\frac{2}{5}} = \dfrac{6}{x}$

16.
(59) $\dfrac{\frac{5}{12}}{\frac{5}{3}} = \dfrac{\frac{5}{2}}{k}$

17.
(61) $6\frac{2}{7}x + \frac{1}{2} = 2\frac{1}{3}$

18.
(61) $\frac{6}{7}x + 3\frac{6}{7} = 7\frac{16}{21}$

19.
(61) $3x + 6 = 28$

Simplify:

20.
(44) $56 - 3\left[3(3 - 1)(2^2 - 2) - 5\right]$

21.
(44) $\sqrt{4} + 5\left[3 \div (2 - 1) + \sqrt{9}\right]$

22.
(46) $\frac{4}{5} + 2\frac{1}{5} \cdot 1\frac{3}{4}$

23.
(35) $13\frac{7}{10} - 3\frac{2}{5} + \frac{4}{15}$

24. 621.3×0.0014 **25.** $21.62 - 18.9261$
₍₇₎   ₍₆₎

26. $3\frac{6}{7} \times 2\frac{1}{3} \div 4\frac{1}{2} \div \frac{1}{3}$ **27.** $\frac{1}{2}\left(6\frac{2}{3} + \frac{1}{4}\right) - \frac{5}{24}$
₍₄₃₎   ₍₅₂₎

28. (a) What is 1% of 22?
₍₅₃₎ (b) What is 100% of 22?

29. Evaluate: $xyz + x^y + \sqrt[y]{x} - x$ if $x = 16$, $y = 2$, and $z = \frac{1}{4}$
₍₅₄₎

30. Round 41,190,364 to the hundred-thousands' place, and write the rounded number in
_(2,50) scientific notation.

LESSON 64 *Semicircles*

Half a circle is called a **semicircle**. An **arc** is a part of the circumference of a circle. The length of the arc or **arc length** of a semicircle is one half the circumference of a whole circle. The area of a closed semicircle is one half the area of a whole circle.

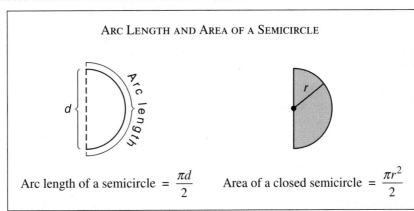

ARC LENGTH AND AREA OF A SEMICIRCLE

Arc length of a semicircle $= \dfrac{\pi d}{2}$ Area of a closed semicircle $= \dfrac{\pi r^2}{2}$

Sometimes it is necessary to find the perimeter or the area of a figure that contains one or more semicircles.

example 64.1   Find (a) the perimeter and (b) the area of this figure. Dimensions are in meters.

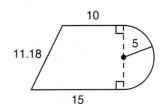

solution   (a)   The perimeter includes the arc length of the semicircle. Remember that the approximate value of π is 3.14.

$$\text{Perimeter} = 15\,\text{m} + 11.18\,\text{m} + 10\,\text{m} + \frac{\pi d}{2}$$

$$\approx 15\,\text{m} + 11.18\,\text{m} + 10\,\text{m} + \frac{3.14(10\,\text{m})}{2}$$

$$\approx 15\,\text{m} + 11.18\,\text{m} + 10\,\text{m} + 15.7\,\text{m}$$

$$\approx \mathbf{51.88\,m}$$

(b)   The area is the sum of the areas of a triangle, a rectangle, and a semicircle.

$$\text{Area} = \frac{(5\text{ m})(10\text{ m})}{2} + (10\text{m} \cdot 10\text{m}) + \frac{\pi r^2}{2}$$

$$\approx \frac{(5\text{ m})(10\text{ m})}{2} + (10\text{ m} \cdot 10\text{ m}) + \frac{3.14(5\text{ m})^2}{2}$$

$$\approx 25\text{ m}^2 + 100\text{ m}^2 + 39.25\text{ m}^2$$

$$\approx \textbf{164.25 m}^2$$

example 64.2   Find (a) the perimeter and (b) the area of this figure. Dimensions are in centimeters.

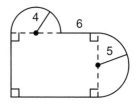

solution   (a) The perimeter includes two semicircles.

$$\text{Perimeter} \approx 14\text{ cm} + 10\text{ cm} + \frac{3.14(8\text{ cm})}{2} + 6\text{ cm} + \frac{3.14(10\text{ cm})}{2}$$

$$\approx 14\text{ cm} + 10\text{ cm} + 12.56\text{ cm} + 6\text{ cm} + 15.7\text{ cm}$$

$$\approx \textbf{58.26 cm}$$

(b) The area includes a rectangle and two semicircles.

$$\text{Area} \approx (10\text{ cm} \cdot 14\text{ cm}) + \frac{3.14(4\text{ cm})^2}{2} + \frac{3.14(5\text{ cm})^2}{2}$$

$$\approx 140\text{ cm}^2 + 25.12\text{ cm}^2 + 39.25\text{ cm}^2$$

$$\approx \textbf{204.37 cm}^2$$

practice   **a.**   Find the perimeter of this figure. Dimensions are in centimeters.

b.   Find the area of this figure.

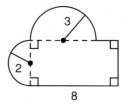

problem set 64

1.   Roland heard the clarion from afar and increased the speed of the column to 4 miles per hour. How far could the column go in 16 hours?
(58)

2.   Charlemagne's column covered the first 12 miles in 4 hours. He then increased the speed by 2 miles per hour. If the total distance of the trip was 52 miles, how long did it take to finish the trip?
(63)

3.   Alison traveled at 5 miles per hour for 12 hours. Then she traveled at 8 miles per hour for 8 hours. How far did she go in all?
(63)

4.   The roses had to be packed 48 to a shipping box. If 4800 boxes were available, how many roses could be shipped?
(13)

5.   Deva ate $\frac{11}{15}$ of the $7\frac{1}{2}$ kielbasas with spicy mustard. Zach ate the rest with sauerkraut. How many kielbasas did Zach eat?
(62)

6.   Complete the table. Begin by inserting the reference numbers.
(55)

Fraction	Decimal	Percent
(a)	(b)	60%

7. (a) Write 10,300 in scientific notation.
(50)
    (b) Write 6.019×10^8 in standard notation.

8. What decimal part of 240 is 160?   **9.** What fraction of 576 is 36?
(51)   (48)

10. Five and two thirds of what number is $3\frac{1}{4}$?
(57)

11. The radius of a circle is 7 feet.
(60)
    (a) What is the circumference of the circle?
    (b) What is the area of the circle?

12. Find (a) the perimeter and (b) the
(64) area of the figure. Dimensions are in meters.

13. The base of a right solid is shown on the left. If the sides of the solid are 1 foot tall, what is
(45) the volume of the solid in cubic feet? Dimensions are in feet.

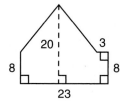 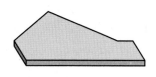

14. Find the surface area of a cube whose edges are 7 meters long.
(49)

Solve:

15. $\dfrac{\frac{1}{5}}{\frac{3}{10}} = \dfrac{5}{x}$
(59)
                                            16. $\dfrac{\frac{7}{12}}{\frac{5}{24}} = \dfrac{5}{y}$
                                                (59)

17. $4\frac{1}{2}x - 1\frac{1}{3} = \dfrac{17}{12}$
(61)
                                          18. $2\frac{1}{2}x - 2\frac{1}{4} = 3\frac{2}{5}$
                                                (61)

19. $3x + 7 = 25$
(61)

Simplify:

20. $2^2 + 2\left[2^2\left(4^2 - 3^2\right) - 3^3\right]$
(44)
                                       21. $\dfrac{3}{7} + 3\frac{1}{2} \cdot \dfrac{2}{3}$
                                            (46)

22. $6\frac{7}{10} - 4\frac{4}{15} + \dfrac{7}{30}$
(35)
                                       23. $\dfrac{2\frac{1}{3}}{3\frac{1}{5}}$
                                                (43)

24. $178.22 - 19.621$
(6)
                                       25. $\dfrac{192.61}{0.005}$
                                              (7)

26. $\dfrac{1}{3}\left(2\frac{1}{3} + 6\frac{1}{2}\right) - \dfrac{7}{24}$
(52)

27. Sketch a rectangular coordinate system, and graph the points (3, −3) and (−2, 2).
(38)

28. (a) What is 1% of 1.34?   (b)   What is 110% of 1.34?
(53)

29. Evaluate: $xy + \sqrt[y]{z} + xyz + x^y$ if $x = 3$, $y = 3$, and $z = 1$
(54)

30. Round 109,376 to the ten-thousands' place, and express the answer in scientific notation.
(2,50)

LESSON 65   *Proportions with Mixed Numbers •*
Using Proportions with Similar Triangles

65.A

proportions with mixed numbers

To solve conditional proportions that contain mixed numbers, the first step is to write the mixed numbers as improper fractions. We do this because multiplying fractions is easier than multiplying mixed numbers.

example 65.1   Solve: $\dfrac{\frac{4}{9}}{x} = \dfrac{2\frac{1}{5}}{1\frac{3}{4}}$

solution   As the first step, we change the mixed numbers to improper fractions. Then we have

$$\dfrac{\frac{4}{9}}{x} = \dfrac{\frac{11}{5}}{\frac{7}{4}}$$

Now we cross multiply and get

$$\dfrac{\cancel{4}}{9} \cdot \dfrac{7}{\cancel{4}} = \dfrac{11}{5}x \qquad \text{cross multiplied}$$

$$\dfrac{7}{9} = \dfrac{11}{5}x \qquad \text{simplified}$$

Now we will solve by multiplying both sides by $\frac{5}{11}$.

$$\dfrac{5}{11} \cdot \dfrac{7}{9} = \dfrac{\cancel{11}}{\cancel{5}}x \cdot \dfrac{\cancel{5}}{\cancel{11}} \qquad \text{multiplied both sides by } \dfrac{5}{11}$$

$$\dfrac{35}{99} = x \qquad \text{simplified}$$

65.B

using proportions with similar triangles

If two triangles have angles with equal measures, the triangles are similar triangles. We say they are similar because they have the same shape, but one of the triangles might be larger than the other triangle.

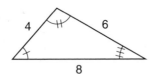

We use tick marks to denote angles with equal measures. Angles with the same number of tick marks have equal measures. Sides opposite angles of equal measure are called **corresponding sides.** Notice that corresponding sides of similar triangles all have the same ratio:

$$\dfrac{4}{2} = \dfrac{6}{3} = \dfrac{8}{4}$$

We say that corresponding sides are **in proportion,** and we can use proportions to find missing lengths.

example 65.2   Find *x* and *y*.

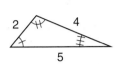 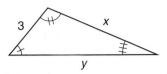

solution   The triangles are similar because the angles in one triangle have the same measure as the angles in the other triangle. The sides labeled 2 and 3 are corresponding sides because they are opposite angles of equal measure. Likewise, 4 and *x* correspond, as do 5 and *y*. We write the proportions

$$\frac{2}{3} = \frac{4}{x} \quad \text{and} \quad \frac{2}{3} = \frac{5}{y}$$

and solve by cross multiplying.

$$2x = 12 \qquad 2y = 15$$

$$x = \mathbf{6} \qquad y = \frac{\mathbf{15}}{\mathbf{2}}$$

Note that though the proportion

$$\frac{4}{x} = \frac{5}{y}$$

is true, we cannot use it because it is an equation with two variables. We should write proportions with only one variable.

practice   Solve:

a. $\dfrac{1\frac{3}{4}}{\frac{2}{3}} = \dfrac{5\frac{1}{4}}{x}$

b. $\dfrac{3\frac{1}{4}}{p} = \dfrac{2\frac{1}{6}}{3\frac{2}{10}}$

c. Find *m* and *p*. Write two proportions and solve.

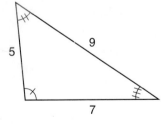 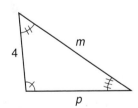

problem set
65

1. Four fifths of the pixies in the kingdom had sad faces. If 840 pixies had sad faces, how
(62) many pixies lived in the kingdom?

2. When the siren sounded, 440 were seen walking in the forest. If the other 360 were not
(62) seen, what fraction of the total was seen?

3. The cutters cut out 400 jigsaw puzzles in 8 hours. They got tired and could only cut $\frac{1}{5}$
(63) as fast as before. At the slower rate, how many jigsaw puzzles could they cut out in the next 160 hours?

4. The platoon advanced 5 kilometers in $1\frac{1}{2}$ hours. During the rain they advanced 4
(63) kilometers in 2 hours. By how much did the platoon's rate decrease?

5. Complete the table. Begin by inserting
(55) the reference numbers.

FRACTION	DECIMAL	PERCENT
(a)	0.18	(b)

6. Johnny galloped with glee for two hours and covered six whole miles! At this rate, how
(58) far could he gallop with glee in nine hours?

7. What decimal part of 360 is 300?
(51)

8. What fraction of 360 is 300?
(48)

9. Two and one third of $3\frac{1}{4}$ is what number?
(57)

10. The radius of a circle is 3 inches.
(60)
  (a) What is the circumference of the circle?
  (b) What is the area of the circle?

11. Find (a) the perimeter and (b) the
(64) area of this figure. Dimensions are in
dekameters.

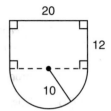

12. The base of a right solid is shown on the left. If the solid is 20 centimeters tall, what is
(45) the volume of the solid in cubic centimeters? Dimensions are in centimeters.

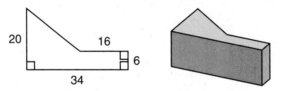

13. Find the surface area of a cube whose edges are 16 inches long.
(49)

14. Find x and y.
(65)

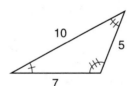

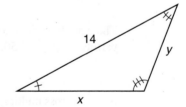

Solve:

15. $\dfrac{2\frac{1}{3}}{\dfrac{7}{10}} = \dfrac{6}{x}$
(65)

16. $\dfrac{2\frac{6}{7}}{4\frac{12}{21}} = \dfrac{4\frac{2}{3}}{x}$
(65)

17. $3\frac{1}{4}x - 2\frac{1}{3} = \dfrac{17}{12}$
(61)

18. $3\frac{1}{6}x - \dfrac{3}{8} = 1\dfrac{17}{24}$
(61)

19. $17x - 12 = 19$
(61)

Simplify:

20. $3^2 + 2^3\left[2\left(3^2 - 4\right) - 3\right]$
(44)

21. $\dfrac{2}{7} + 2\frac{1}{3} \cdot \dfrac{1}{2}$
(46)

22. $13\frac{2}{3} - 4\frac{1}{2} + 2\frac{5}{6}$
(35)

23. 181.2×0.013
(7)

24. $1921.61 - 19.897$

(6)

25. $\dfrac{175.61}{0.7}$

(7)

26. $\dfrac{1}{4}\left(3\dfrac{1}{5} + 2\dfrac{1}{2}\right) - \dfrac{3}{10}$

(52)

27. $3\dfrac{1}{3} \times 2\dfrac{1}{2} \div \dfrac{2}{3} \div 2\dfrac{5}{6}$

(43)

28. Evaluate: $xyz + \sqrt{y} + x^z$ if $x = 1$, $y = 36$, and $z = 2$

(54)

29. (a) What is 1% of 40.3?   (b)   What is 120% of 40.3?

(53)

30. Round 61,237,899,721.2 to the nearest thousand, and write the number in scientific

(2,50) notation.

LESSON 66   Ratio Word Problems

Often it is desirable to maintain a fixed ratio between two quantities. The conditions are stated in ratio word problems. Three of the four parts are usually given. We use the statement of the problem to help us write a conditional proportion. Then we solve the conditional proportion to find the missing part.

example 66.1   The ratio of the number of parrots to the number of macaws was 5 to 7. How many macaws were there when the parrots numbered 750?

solution   The two ratios are between P for parrots and M for macaws. **If P is in the numerator (on top) in one ratio, P must be in the numerator (on top) in the other ratio.** We decide to put P in the numerator. This gives us

$$\frac{P}{M} = \frac{P}{M}$$

We were told that the ratio of the number of parrots to the number of macaws was 5 to 7. The first number given (5) goes with the first word (parrots), and the second number given (7) goes with the second word (macaws). Thus, we write

$$\frac{5}{7} = \frac{P}{M}$$

These numbers are the ratio numbers. The other numbers are the problem numbers. Since the parrots numbered 750, we replace the remaining P with 750.

$$\frac{5}{7} = \frac{750}{M}$$

Now we cross multiply and solve for M.

$$5M = 7 \cdot 750 \qquad \text{cross multiplied}$$
$$\frac{\cancel{5}M}{\cancel{5}} = \frac{7 \cdot 750}{5} \qquad \text{divided both sides by 5}$$
$$M = 1050 \qquad \text{simplified}$$

Thus, when the parrots numbered 750, there were **1050 macaws.**

example 66.2   The ratio of the number of wrigglers to the number of squirmers was 13 to 2. When 26 students had the wriggles, how many were squirming?

solution   We begin by writing

$$\frac{W}{S} = \frac{W}{S}$$

Now on the left we put in the ratio numbers, 13 for W and 2 for S.

$$\frac{13}{2} = \frac{W}{S}$$

On the right we put in the given number 26 for W.

$$\frac{13}{2} = \frac{26}{S}$$

Now we cross multiply and solve for S.

$$13S = 2 \cdot 26 \qquad \text{cross multiplied}$$

$$\frac{\cancel{13}S}{\cancel{13}} = \frac{2 \cdot 26}{13} \qquad \text{divided both sides by 13}$$

$$S = 4 \qquad \text{simplified}$$

Thus, when 26 students had the wriggles, **4 students** were squirming.

practice   **a.** The ratio of Holsteins to Charolais in the valley was 22 to 3. If there were 3000 Charolais in the valley, how many Holsteins were gathered in the valley?

problem set 66

1. *(63)* Ephemera was running out of time. She traveled the first 100 leagues in 4 days, but she found that she would have to double her pace in order to avoid disaster. How long would it take her to complete the last 200 leagues at the new pace?

2. *(63)* Tenacious ran 12 miles in 2 hours. Then he ran 36 miles in 3 hours. By how much did his rate increase?

3. *(62)* When Aristotle proclaimed his new theory, 87 responded. If this was only $\frac{3}{5}$ the number of responses expected, how many responses were expected?

4. *(36)* The apothecary could press 104 packages of medicine in 4 hours. How many packages could be pressed in 10 hours?

5. *(66)* The ratio of thespians to mathematicians at the university was 7 to 5. If there were 20 mathematicians at the university, how many thespians were there?

6. *(66)* The ratio of futons to sofas in the showroom was 3 to 2. If there were 15 futons in the showroom, how many sofas were in the showroom?

7. *(55)* Complete the table. Begin by inserting the reference numbers.

Fraction	Decimal	Percent
(a)	(b)	73%

8. *(51)* What decimal part of 450 is 300?

9. *(48)* What fraction of 450 is 300?

10. *(57)* Five and one half of $2\frac{1}{3}$ is what number?

11. *(53)* (a) What is 1% of 2000?

(b) What is 42.1% of 2000?

12. *(60)* The radius of a circle is 12 centimeters.

(a) What is the circumference of the circle?

(b) What is the area of the circle?

13. Find (a) the perimeter and (b) the area of this figure. Dimensions are in millimeters.
(64)

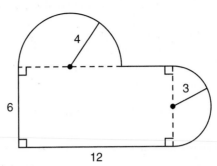

14. Find *m* and *q*.
(65)

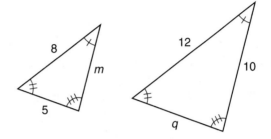

15. The base of a right solid is shown on the left. If the solid is 5 feet tall, what is the volume
(45) of the solid in cubic feet? Dimensions are in feet. All angles are right angles.

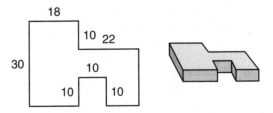

16. (a) Write 0.00392 in scientific notation.
(50)
  (b) Write 6.03×10^{-9} in standard notation.

Solve:

17. $\dfrac{\frac{1}{4}}{\frac{4}{5}} = \dfrac{3}{x}$
(59)

18. $\dfrac{4\frac{3}{4}}{\frac{8}{9}} = \dfrac{2\frac{1}{9}}{x}$
(65)

19. $5\frac{1}{3}x - 3\frac{3}{4} = \dfrac{19}{32}$
(61)

20. $2\frac{1}{2}x - \frac{1}{4} = 2\frac{3}{16}$
(61)

21. $22x - 9 = 57$
(61)

Simplify:

22. $15 + 3[(5-1)(7-2)2 - 4]$
(42)

23. $4^2 + 3^3\left[2(4^2 - 15) - 2\right]$
(44)

24. $\dfrac{1}{5} + 3\frac{1}{2} \cdot \dfrac{2}{7}$
(46)

25. $11\frac{3}{4} - 5\frac{1}{5} + 3\frac{1}{3}$
(35)

26. $\dfrac{1}{2}\left(2\frac{1}{4} + 1\frac{3}{16}\right) - \dfrac{31}{32}$
(52)

27. $2\frac{1}{5} \times 3\frac{1}{4} \div 5\frac{1}{2} \div 6\frac{1}{2}$
(43)

28. Evaluate: $kmx + \sqrt[m]{k} + m^x$ if $k = 64$, $m = 3$, and $x = 4$
(54)

29. Use two unit multipliers to convert 1,000,000 square inches to square feet. Round any
(33) decimal answer to two places.

30. Joanie scored 21, 13, 9, 21, 8, 13, 12, and 15 points in the first eight games. What was
(26) the (a) range, (b) mode, (c) median, and (d) mean of her scores?

LESSON 67   *Using Ratios to Compare*

We can use ratios to determine unit prices. The **unit price** is the price for one item.

example 67.1   If 20 pounds of beans sold for $1.20, what was the price per pound of beans?

solution   We get two ratios from this statement.

$$\text{(a)} \quad \frac{\$1.20}{20 \text{ pounds}} = \frac{\$0.06}{1 \text{ pound}} = \frac{6 \text{ cents}}{1 \text{ pound}} = 6 \text{ cents per pound}$$

$$\text{(b)} \quad \frac{20 \text{ pounds}}{\$1.20} = \frac{1 \text{ pound}}{\$0.06} = \frac{1 \text{ pound}}{6 \text{ cents}} = \frac{1}{6} \text{ pound per cent}$$

We call ratio (a) the unit price because it tells the cost for 1 pound. The unit price will always
have cost as the numerator. Ratio (b) tells us the number of pounds we can buy for 1 cent.
The beans cost **6¢ per pound.** We can buy $\frac{1}{6}$ pound for 1¢.

example 67.2   The big can held 16 ounces and cost 80 cents. The small can held 12 ounces and cost
72 cents. Which can was the better buy?

solution   To tell which price is the best price, we usually compare unit prices. This is the cost for one
item. We compute the cost per ounce for both cans.

$$\text{Big can} = \frac{80 \text{ cents}}{16 \text{ ounces}} \qquad \text{Small can} = \frac{72 \text{ cents}}{12 \text{ ounces}}$$

$$= 5\frac{\text{cents}}{\text{ounce}} \qquad\qquad = 6\frac{\text{cents}}{\text{ounce}}$$

Thus, the **big can** at 5 cents per ounce is a better buy than the small can at 6 cents per ounce.

practice   **a.**   One store sold packages of 1 dozen (12) for $1.44 a package. The other store sold
packages of 3 dozen (36) for $4.68. Use unit prices to tell which price was the best price.

problem set   **1.**   Three fourths of the fans did not carry banners. If 1000 fans attended the game, how
67   (62)   many fans carried banners?

2.   Seven sixteenths of the children smirked when they heard the joke. If 210 children
(62) smirked, how many children heard the joke?

3.   When the score was announced over the PA system, 480 fans were happy. If 3360
(62) fans attended the game, what fraction of the fans were happy when the score
was announced?

4.   The hikers slogged 10 miles through the muck in 5 hours. Then they came to the
(63) pavement and were able to triple their rate. How long would it take them to cover
24 miles on the pavement?

5. At the railroad station the ratio of Hindus to Muslims was 6 to 5. If there were 444
(66) Hindus, how many Muslims were there?

6. Couscous costs $4.50 for a 3 pound bag at the local market. At the Mega-Mart,
(67) couscous costs $14 for an 8 pound bag. Find both unit prices. Which store has the
better buy?

7. Complete the table. Begin by inserting
(55) the reference numbers.

FRACTION	DECIMAL	PERCENT
$\frac{2}{5}$	(a)	(b)

8. What number is $3\frac{3}{5}$ of $2\frac{1}{2}$?
(57)

9. Six tenths of what number is 144?
(51)

10. What fraction of 35 is 21?
(48)

11. What decimal part of 810 is 270?
(51)

12. Find (a) the perimeter and (b) the area
(64) of this figure. Dimensions are in meters.

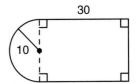

13. Find s and t.
(65)

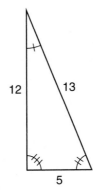
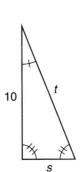

14. The figure shown on the left is the base of a right solid whose sides are 10 centimeters tall.
(45) What is the volume of the solid in cubic centimeters? Dimensions are in centimeters.

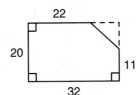

15. Find the least common multiple of 12, 16, and 30.
(20)

Solve:

16. $\dfrac{\frac{1}{4}}{\frac{7}{8}} = \dfrac{6}{x}$
(59)

17. $\dfrac{4\frac{3}{7}}{1\frac{10}{21}} = \dfrac{6}{p}$
(65)

18. $4\frac{1}{7}x - 2\frac{2}{3} = 3\frac{1}{4}$
(61)

19. $4\frac{1}{3}x - \frac{5}{8} = 1\frac{5}{24}$
(61)

20. $18x + 14 = 27$
(61)

Simplify:

21. $13 + 3[(3 - 1)(6 - 4)2 - 1]$
(42)

22. $2^3 + 3\left[3(3^2 - 5) + \sqrt{4}\right]$
(44)

23. $1\dfrac{2}{7} + 3\dfrac{3}{4} \cdot 2\dfrac{1}{3}$
(46)

24. $12\dfrac{4}{5} - 4\dfrac{2}{3} + 11\dfrac{7}{15}$
(35)

25. $9218.98 - 178.621$
(6)

26. $\dfrac{1}{5}\left(2\dfrac{1}{6} - 1\dfrac{1}{4}\right) - \dfrac{1}{30}$
(52)

27. $4\dfrac{3}{4} \times 3\dfrac{7}{12} \div 2\dfrac{1}{3} \times \dfrac{1}{6}$
(43)

28. Use two unit multipliers to convert 144 square feet to square miles. Round any decimal
(33)   answer to two places.

29. (a) Write 1,390,000 in scientific notation.
(50)
         (b) Write 4.26×10^{17} in standard notation.

30. Evaluate: $xyz + y^2 + x^y - xy$ if $x = 6$, $y = 3$, and $z = \dfrac{1}{9}$
(54)

LESSON 68   *Percent Word Problems • Visualizing Percents Less Than 100*

68.A

percent word problems

In Lesson 62, we discussed the following phrase:

A fraction of a number is another number.

This translates into the equation

$$F \cdot A = B$$

since "of" means "·" and "is" means "=". There is a similar phrase for percents.

A percent of a number is another number.

This translates into the equation

$$P \cdot A = B$$

There is one thing to watch out for: **we must change the percent into either a decimal or a fraction before we multiply!**

example 68.1   Sales tax is 5% in Maryland. Joey bought a pair of basketball shoes advertised for $62.00. How much sales tax did he pay?

solution   We put the question into the form of the percent equation, first in English, then in algebra.

A percent of a number is another number.

5% of the cost is the Maryland sales tax.

5% of $62.00 is the sales tax.

We translate this statement into an equation by replacing *of* with "·" and *is* with "=". We change 5% into its decimal form and use the variable *t* for tax.

5% of $62.00 is the sales tax.

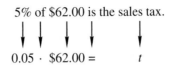

$$0.05 \cdot \$62.00 = \qquad t$$

Finally, we multiply and find that the sales tax was **$3.10.**

example 68.2   The big baby weighed 15 lb. Momma weighed him a week later and he weighed 18 lb! Momma could not believe it—a 3 lb increase! Momma wondered, "What percent increase is this?"

solution   We can restate the problem as:

What percent of 15 lb is 3 lb?

We use the percent equation, substitute, and solve.

$$P \cdot 15 = 3 \qquad \text{equation}$$

$$\frac{P \cdot \cancel{15}}{\cancel{15}} = \frac{3}{15} \qquad \text{divided both sides by 15 to solve for } P$$

$$P = \frac{1}{5} \qquad \text{simplified}$$

So the big baby's weight increased by $\frac{1}{5}$ of its previous weight. That is true, but the question was not what *fraction* increase, but what *percent* increase. We used the variable *P* to remind us to put our answer in the percent form. To change a fraction into a percent, we convert the fraction into a decimal and then multiply by 100 (move the decimal point two places to the right).

$$P = \frac{1}{5} = 0.2 = 20\%$$

The big baby's weight increased by **20%**!

68.B
visualizing percents less than 100

Often it is helpful to draw a diagram when we encounter problems with percents less than 100. A percent less than 100 always indicates that a number is being divided into two parts. To illustrate, we use a two-part diagram to analyze the following statement:

30 percent of 140 is 42

On the left, we show the number 140. This is the "before" diagram and represents 100 percent.

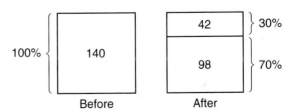

On the right, we show 140 divided into two parts. One of the parts is 42, which is 30 percent. The other part is 98, which is 70 percent. The sum of the numbers 42 and 98 is 140. The sum of 30 percent and 70 percent is 100 percent. **In the diagram, the sum of the two "after" numbers must always equal the "before" number. The sum of the two "after" percents must equal the "before" percent, which is always 100 percent.** We will practice by working percent problems and drawing the two-part diagrams that give us a picture of the solution.

example 68.3 Complete the percent diagram by finding a and b.

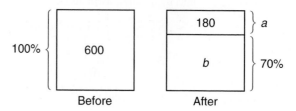

solution The sum of the two "after" percents in the diagram on the right is always equal to 100%, so

$$a + 70\% = 100\%$$
$$a = \mathbf{30\%}$$

The sum of the two "after" numbers on the right must equal the "before" number on the left, so

$$180 + b = 600$$
$$b = \mathbf{420}$$

example 68.4 Ewan was a smart shopper! He got a great kilt for $433.65. It was 30% off the original price. What was the original price?

solution This is a tricky one! We first draw a percent diagram of this problem. On the left, we show the original price which represents 100%. If 30% was taken off the original price, 70% was left. So $433.65 is 70% of the original price. We diagram this on the right.

We see that 70% of the original price is the sale price. We translate this into an algebraic equation.

Seventy percent of the original price is $433.65.

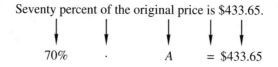

$$70\% \quad \cdot \quad A \quad = \$433.65$$

Now we convert 70% to its decimal form and solve for A.

$$\begin{array}{ll}
0.70 \cdot A = \$433.65 & \text{equation with 70\% as a decimal} \\
\dfrac{\cancel{0.70} \cdot A}{\cancel{0.70}} = \dfrac{\$433.65}{0.70} & \text{divided both sides by 0.70} \\
A = \$619.50 & \text{simplified}
\end{array}$$

The original price was **$619.50.** Now we complete the diagram by subtracting the sale price of $433.65 from $619.50 to find the discount, which is $185.85.

practice

a. Complete the percent diagram by finding *a* and *b*.

100% { 700 | Before

280 } *a*
b } 60% | After

b. Forty percent of all the Eikens in Hannover attended the reunion. If 160 Eikens attended, how many Eikens are in Hannover? Draw a diagram to help solve the problem.

c. Owen placed 700 ice cubes in his cooler. If 280 of the ice cubes melted, what percent did not melt? Draw a diagram to help solve the problem.

problem set 68

1. *(62)* The ancient Sumerians did not have paper. They wrote by pressing wedges into clay. Their writing is called *cuneiform*, which means wedge-shaped. Four fifths of the Sumerians in the town could not read cuneiform. If 16,000 Sumerians were in the town, how many could read cuneiform?

2. *(63)* Monoliths were erected at a rate of 39 every 3 days. However, this was not enough to clear the back orders. If the original rate was quadrupled, how many days would it take to erect 208 monoliths?

3. *(36)* Enrique drove the 240 miles to the park in 4 hours. If his return trip took only 3 hours, what was the difference in his rates?

4. *(66)* The ratio of single-screen theaters to multiple-screen theaters in the metropolitan area is 1 to 15. If there are 9 single-screen theaters, how many multiple-screen theaters are there?

5. *(66)* The ratio of western movies to comedies at the video store was 7 to 9. If there were 210 westerns, how many comedies were there?

6. *(67)* Maria bought three pounds of ground beef for 26 lira. Her husband Mario bought four pounds of ground beef for 33 lira. Who got a better deal?

7. *(68)* Complete the percent diagram by finding *a*, *b*, and *c*.

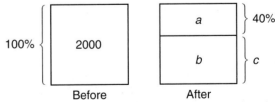

100% { 2000 | Before

a } 40%
b } *c* | After

8. *(68)* Seventy-five percent of all the skateboarders at the competition could execute a kickflip. If 14 could not execute a kickflip, how many skateboarders were at the competition? Draw a diagram to help solve the problem.

9. *(68)* Sixty-eight percent of 360 is what number?

10. *(55)* Complete the table. Begin by inserting the reference numbers.

Fraction	Decimal	Percent
(a)	0.06	(b)

11. *(51)* What decimal part of 930 is 558?

12. What fraction of 930 is 558?
(48)

13. Four and three fifths of $9\frac{1}{2}$ is what number?
(57)

14. Find (a) the perimeter and (b) the area
(64) of this figure. Dimensions are in feet.

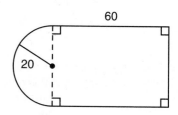

15. The figure shown on the left is the base of a right solid whose sides are 30 meters tall.
(45) What is the volume of the solid in cubic meters? Dimensions are in meters. Remember that volume equals the area of the base times the height. All angles are right angles.

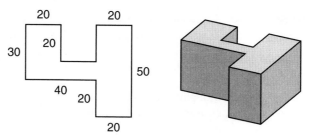

16. Use proportions to find x and y.
(65)

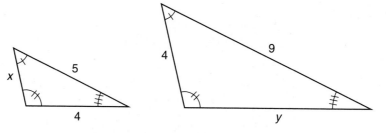

Solve:

17. $\dfrac{2\frac{2}{3}}{\frac{8}{14}} = \dfrac{\frac{1}{2}}{m}$
(65)

18. $\dfrac{2\frac{1}{5}}{m} = \dfrac{1\frac{1}{5}}{\frac{1}{3}}$
(35)

19. $6\frac{1}{2}x - \frac{1}{4} = 2\frac{1}{13}$
(61)

20. $3\frac{1}{5}x - 7\frac{2}{3} = 1\frac{3}{4}$
(35)

21. $35x - 19 = 51$
(61)

Simplify:

22. $11 + 3[(5 - 2)(7 - 3)4 - 36]$
(42)

23. $3^2 + 2\left[2(2^3 - 7) + \sqrt{16}\right]$
(44)

24. $1\frac{2}{3} + 2\frac{1}{2} \cdot 3\frac{1}{5}$
(46)

25. $11\frac{2}{3} - 6\frac{1}{2} + 9\frac{1}{12}$
(35)

26. $\dfrac{230.95}{0.00025}$
(7)

27. $\frac{1}{4}\left(3\frac{1}{3} + 2\frac{1}{2}\right) - \frac{11}{12}$
(52)

28. $6\frac{1}{2} \times 1\frac{3}{5} \div 1\frac{1}{4} \times \frac{7}{10}$
(43)

29. Use two unit multipliers to convert 75,000 centigrams to kilograms.
(33)

30. Evaluate: $mp + \sqrt[p]{x} + p^m$ if $m = 2$, $p = 4$, and $x = 16$
(54)

LESSON 69 *Absolute Value • Adding Signed Numbers*

69.A
absolute value

In Lesson 2 we discussed number lines. Recall that the graph of a positive number is to the right of the origin on a number line. Every positive number has an **opposite** whose graph is the same distance to the left of the origin. We call these numbers the negative numbers.

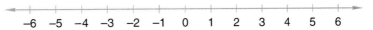

We can see that the graph of +4 is four units to the right of the origin, and −4 is four units to the left of the origin.

We must use a minus sign every time we write a negative number. It is not necessary to use a plus sign to write a positive number.

$$-4 \qquad \text{means negative 4}$$
$$+4 \text{ and } 4 \qquad \text{both mean positive 4}$$

Numbers that have either a plus sign or a minus sign are called **signed numbers.** Signed numbers have two qualities. One of the qualities is designated by the + or − sign. This tells us if the graph of the number is to the left of the origin or to the right of the origin. The other quality is indicated by the numeral and tells us how far the graph of the number is from the origin. We call this quality the **absolute value** of the number. Two vertical lines are used to designate absolute value, as we show here:

$$|-4| = 4 \qquad |4| = 4$$

The absolute value of −4 is four because the graph of −4 is four units from the origin. The absolute value of 4 is also 4 because the graph of 4 is four units from the origin.

69.B
adding signed numbers

There are rules for adding signed numbers. Many textbooks use arrows to help explain these rules. Positive numbers are represented by arrows that point to the right. Negative numbers are represented by arrows that point to the left.

To use these arrows to demonstrate the addition of +2 and −3, we begin at 0 on the number line and draw the +2 arrow. From the head of this arrow, we draw the −3 arrow. The head of the −3 arrow ends over −1 on the number line.

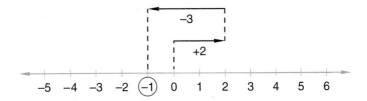

Thus,

$$(+2) + (-3) = -1$$

example 69.1   Use arrows and a number line to add −3 and +1.

solution   Either arrow can be drawn first. We will draw the −3 arrow first.

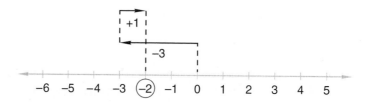

The head of the +1 arrow ends above −2 on the line, so we say that the answer is −2.

$$(-3) + (+1) = -2$$

example 69.2   Use arrows and a number line to determine $(+2) + (+1)$ and $(-2) + (-1)$.

solution   We will use a separate number line for each addition.

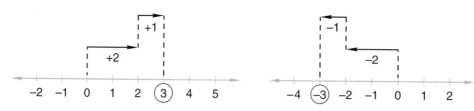

From these diagrams, we see that

$$(+2) + (+1) = +3 \quad \text{and} \quad (-2) + (-1) = -3$$

practice   Quickly sketch four number lines. Then draw arrows to add these numbers.

   a. $(+2) + (-4)$ **b.** $(-2) + (+4)$

   c. $(-2) + (-3)$ **d.** $(+2) + (+3)$

Find the following sums:

   e. $(-14) + (+2)$ **f.** $(41) + (-8)$ **g.** $(-4) + (-15)$

problem set 69

1.
(66)
The ratio of the number of birds to the number of beasts was 3 to 7. How many beasts were there when the birds numbered 750?

2.
(66)
The ratio of the number of smilers to the number of frowners among the students was 13 to 2. When 52 students were smiling, how many were frowning?

3.
(62)
Two thirds of the costumes were polychromatic. If 4800 costumes were polychromatic, how many were not polychromatic?

4.
(63)
Matildabelle traveled the first 100 miles in 4 hours. Then she quadrupled her speed. How long would it take her to travel the next 1400 miles?

5.
(67)
Shanna swam 10 laps in 57 minutes. Jami swam 17 laps in 136 minutes. Who swam faster?

6.
(68)
Bronze is an alloy containing, by weight, 20% tin and 80% copper. Sunnie won the bronze medal in the judo competition. How much did the copper weigh in Sunnie's 14-ounce bronze medal? Draw a diagram to help solve the problem.

7. Complete the table. Begin by inserting
(55) the reference numbers.

FRACTION	DECIMAL	PERCENT
(a)	(b)	25%

8. (a) Write 0.000913 in scientific notation.
(50)
     (b) Write 6.14×10^{-5} in standard notation.

9. Thirty percent of what number is 123?   **10.** What fraction of 36 is 32?
(68)   (48)

11. What decimal part of 360 is 300?
(51)

12. Three and one half of what number is $4\frac{2}{3}$?
(57)

13. Find (a) the perimeter and (b) the area
(64) of this figure. Dimensions are in feet.

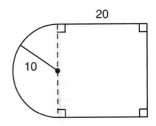

14. The figure shown on the left is the base of a solid whose sides are 3 meters tall. What
(45) is the volume of the solid in cubic centimeters? Dimensions are in centimeters.
     Remember to convert the height to centimeters and to multiply by the area of the base.

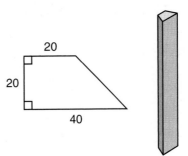

Sketch a number line, and then draw arrows to add:

15. $(-6) + (+2)$ **16.** $(-2) + (+5)$ **17.** $(-4) + (-3)$
(69)   (69)   (69)

Solve:

18. $\dfrac{2\frac{3}{4}}{3\frac{7}{8}} = \dfrac{8}{x}$ **19.** $\dfrac{\frac{6}{7}}{\frac{10}{21}} = \dfrac{9}{x}$ **20.** $5\frac{1}{2}x + 3\frac{1}{3} = 10\frac{1}{7}$
(65)   (59)   (61)

21. $4\frac{6}{7}x - \frac{4}{21} = 11\frac{5}{14}$ **22.** $18x + 14 = 72$
(61)   (61)

Simplify:

23. $3^2 + 3\left[5(3^2 - 2^3) + \sqrt{4}\right]$ **24.** $1\frac{3}{7} + 2\frac{1}{3} \cdot 6\frac{1}{2}$
(44)   (46)

25. $13\frac{4}{5} - 6\frac{1}{8} + 2\frac{3}{40}$ **26.** $\frac{1}{10}\left(2\frac{1}{5} + 7\frac{1}{2}\right) - \frac{3}{10}$
(35)   (52)

27. Sketch a rectangular coordinate system, and graph the points (2, 1) and (3, –2).
(38)

28. (a) What is 1% of 215?
(53)
    (b) What is 14.5% of 215?

29. Evaluate: $xyz + x^t + y^t + z^t$ if $t = 2$, $x = 3$, $y = 3$, and $z = 2$
(54)

30. Find x and y.
(65)

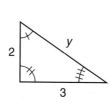 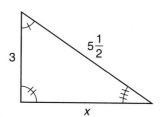

LESSON 70   *Rules for Addition of Signed Numbers*

When we add two numbers that have the same sign, we always get an answer that has the same sign as the sign of the numbers.

RULES FOR ADDITION OF SIGNED NUMBERS

1. The value of the sum of two numbers of the same sign is the sum of the absolute values of the numbers. The sign of the sum is the same as the sign of the numbers.

2. The value of the sum of two numbers of opposite signs is the difference of the absolute values of the numbers. The sign of the sum is the same as the sign of the number with the greater absolute value.

When we add two numbers whose signs are different, sometimes the answer is a positive number and sometimes the answer is a negative number.

$$(-3) + (5) = 2 \qquad (3) + (-5) = -2$$

When we must add more than two signed numbers, we can add from left to right.

example 70.1   Add these signed numbers mentally from left to right.

$$(-4) + (+3) + (-5) + (+7)$$

solution   We add from left to right.

$$(-1) + (-5) + (+7) \qquad \text{added } (-4) \text{ and } (+3)$$
$$(-6) + (+7) \qquad \text{added } (-1) \text{ and } (-5)$$
$$+1 \qquad \text{added } (-6) \text{ and } (+7)$$

example 70.2   Add these signed numbers mentally from left to right.

$$(-4) + (+3) + (-2) + (-6) + (5)$$

solution We begin by adding (−4) and (+3) to get (−1).

$$(-1) + (-2) + (-6) + (5) \qquad \text{added } (-4) \text{ and } (+3)$$
$$(-3) + (-6) + (5) \qquad \text{added } (-1) \text{ and } (-2)$$
$$(-9) + (5) \qquad \text{added } (-3) \text{ and } (-6)$$
$$-4 \qquad \text{added } (-9) \text{ and } (5)$$

In a given problem, it is customary to write all positive numbers with a plus sign, as (+3), or without the plus sign, as (3). In this example we used both notations to emphasize that both notations have the same meaning.

practice Find the following sums by adding mentally from left to right:

a. $(-4) + (-3) + (2) + (-5)$

b. $(-8) + (13) + (-5) + (-8)$

c. $(3) + (-8) + (-9) + (2) + (-4)$

d. $(-5) + (8) + (9) + (-5) + (-7)$

problem set 70

1. (67) The big can held 18 ounces and cost $2.52. The small can held only 12 ounces and cost $1.08. Find both unit prices. Which can was the better buy?

2. (66) The ratio of painted faces to unpainted faces was 3 to 5. If 1800 had painted faces, how many had not painted their faces?

3. (62) Seven eighths of the worker's income was used to pay for necessities. If $5600 was spent on necessities, how much was the worker's income?

4. (55) Complete the table. Begin by inserting the reference numbers.

Fraction	Decimal	Percent
(a)	0.37	(b)

5. (6,50) Round 0.000009153 to the ten-millionths' place, and write the rounded number in scientific notation.

6. (68) There are 130 mountain bikes at Ike's Bikes bicycle shop. If 52 of the mountain bikes have bar ends, what percent of the bikes have bar ends? Draw a diagram to help solve the problem.

7. (51) Four tenths of what number is 216?

8. (48) What fraction of 39 is 24?

9. (68) What percent of 480 is 450?

10. (57) Four and two thirds of what number is $5\frac{4}{5}$?

Refer to the following figures for problems 11 and 12. Dimensions are in inches.

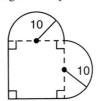

11. (64) Find (a) the perimeter and (b) the area of the figure on the left.

12. (45) What is the volume of a right solid whose base is the figure shown on the left and whose sides are 7 inches tall?

13. Simon Snail slid along at 15 inches per day. Then he got tired and could go only half
(63) that fast. How long would it take Simon to slide 45 inches at the slower rate?

14. Find the surface area of this right
(49) solid. Dimensions are in centimeters.

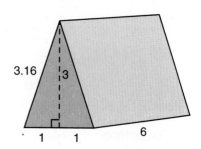

Solve:

15. $\dfrac{3\frac{1}{5}}{2\frac{1}{3}} = \dfrac{4}{x}$
(65)

16. $\dfrac{\frac{3}{4}}{\frac{10}{21}} = \dfrac{8}{x}$
(59)

17. $6\frac{1}{3}x - 4\frac{7}{8} = 3\frac{3}{4}$
(61)

18. $5\frac{6}{7}x - \dfrac{5}{21} = 11\frac{3}{14}$
(61)

Simplify:

19. $(1) + (-2) + (1) + (4) + (-6)$
(70)

20. $(28) + (2) + (-5) + (-10)$
(70)

21. $(9) + (-9) + (2) + (9) + (-7)$
(70)

22. $2^2 + 3\left[2^2\left(2^4 - 3^2\right) - \sqrt{4}\right]$
(44)

23. $2\frac{2}{3} + \dfrac{1}{6} \cdot 2\frac{1}{4}$
(46)

24. $16\frac{11}{12} - 3\frac{5}{6} + 2\frac{7}{18}$
(35)

25. 12.21×0.0017
(7)

26. $11{,}716.181 - 891.7891$
(6)

27. $\dfrac{1}{3}\left(2\frac{1}{3} + 3\frac{1}{4}\right) - \dfrac{13}{36}$
(52)

28. $2\frac{1}{3} \times 12\frac{1}{6} \div 1\frac{5}{12} \div \dfrac{1}{4}$
(43)

29. Evaluate: $xy + xyz - x + y^t$ if $t = 2$, $x = 6$, $y = 8$, and $z = \dfrac{1}{24}$
(54)

30. Find a and b.
(65)

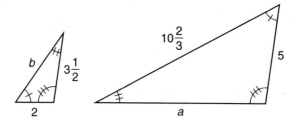

LESSON 71   *Powers of Fractions • Roots of Fractions*

71.A
powers of fractions

We remember that an expression that has an exponent is called an exponential expression. If we write

$$2^3$$

the number 2 is the base, and the number 3 is the exponent. The expression 2^3 means

$$2 \cdot 2 \cdot 2$$

and has a value of 8. Sometimes we use the word *power* to describe the value of the exponential expression. We can say that the third power of 2 is 8. Sometimes the word *power* means the exponent. If we write

$$2^3$$

we say that 2 is raised to the third power. Fractions as well as whole numbers can be used as the base of an exponential expression. We simply perform the multiplication indicated by the power, just as we would with whole numbers.

$$\left(\frac{1}{2}\right)^2 \qquad \text{means} \qquad \frac{1}{2} \cdot \frac{1}{2}$$

$$\left(\frac{1}{2}\right)^3 \qquad \text{means} \qquad \frac{1}{2} \cdot \frac{1}{2} \cdot \frac{1}{2}$$

Notice that when we raise a fraction to a power, we can raise both the numerator and the denominator to that power to simplify the expression.

example 71.1   Simplify: (a) $\left(\frac{2}{3}\right)^2$ (b) $\left(\frac{3}{4}\right)^3$

solution   (a) The exponent 2 tells us to use the base $\frac{2}{3}$ as a factor twice.

$$\left(\frac{2}{3}\right)^2 = \frac{2}{3} \cdot \frac{2}{3} = \frac{4}{9}$$

or

$$\left(\frac{2}{3}\right)^2 = \frac{2^2}{3^2} = \frac{4}{9}$$

(b) The exponent 3 tells us to use the base $\frac{3}{4}$ as a factor 3 times.

$$\left(\frac{3}{4}\right)^3 = \frac{3}{4} \cdot \frac{3}{4} \cdot \frac{3}{4} = \frac{27}{64}$$

or

$$\left(\frac{3}{4}\right)^3 = \frac{3^3}{4^3} = \frac{27}{64}$$

71.B
roots of fractions

When we use the radical

$$\sqrt[3]{\text{number}}$$

we ask a question. The question is, "What number used as a factor three times equals the given number?" The expression

$$\sqrt[3]{\frac{1}{64}}$$

asks us to find the number that used as a factor 3 times equals $\frac{1}{64}$. This number is $\frac{1}{4}$ because

$$\frac{1}{4} \cdot \frac{1}{4} \cdot \frac{1}{4} = \frac{1}{64}$$

Thus, we can write

$$\sqrt[3]{\frac{1}{64}} = \frac{1}{4}$$

Remember that when we raise a fraction to a power, we raise both the numerator and denominator of the fraction to that power to find the answer. Similarly, when we take the root of a fraction, we take the root of the numerator and the root of the denominator to find the result.

example 71.2   Simplify: $\sqrt{\frac{9}{16}}$

solution   This notation asks us to find the number that used as a factor twice gives an answer of $\frac{9}{16}$. The answer is $\frac{3}{4}$ because

$$\frac{3}{4} \cdot \frac{3}{4} = \frac{9}{16}$$

We can find the same result by taking $\sqrt{9}$ and $\sqrt{16}$.

$$\sqrt{\frac{9}{16}} = \frac{\sqrt{9}}{\sqrt{16}} = \frac{3}{4}$$

example 71.3   Simplify: $\sqrt[3]{\frac{8}{27}}$

solution   We find the result by taking $\sqrt[3]{8}$ and $\sqrt[3]{27}$.

$$\sqrt[3]{\frac{8}{27}} = \frac{\sqrt[3]{8}}{\sqrt[3]{27}} = \frac{2}{3}$$

If we use $\frac{2}{3}$ as a factor 3 times, the product is $\frac{8}{27}$.

practice   Simplify:

a. $\left(\frac{1}{3}\right)^3$ b. $\sqrt[3]{\frac{1}{8}}$ c. $\left(\frac{2}{3}\right)^4$ d. $\sqrt{\frac{25}{64}}$

problem set 71

1. The ratio of students who rode horses to school to students who walked to school was
(66) 2 to 9. If 18 students walked to school, how many rode horses to school?

2. Three and one half times as many oceanographers came to the symposium than were
(62) expected. If 840 oceanographers came, how many had been expected?

3. Computer disks can be purchased for $10.90 a dozen or in cases of 60 for $80 a case.
(67) Use unit prices to tell which price is the best deal.

4. Hyunah managed the first 40 miles in 8 hours. If she then doubled her speed, how long
(63) did it take her to manage the next 20 miles?

5. Fifty-five flowers in the garden are snapdragons. If there are 275 flowers in the garden,
(68) what percent of them are snapdragons? Draw a diagram to help solve the problem.

6. Twenty percent of what number is 400?
(68)

7. Find c and d.
(65)

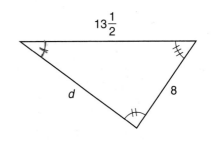
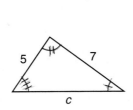

8. Complete the table. Begin by inserting
(55) the reference numbers.

Fraction	Decimal	Percent
(a)	0.3	(b)

9. What decimal part of 300 is 120?
(51)

10. Two and two thirds of what number is $6\frac{1}{7}$?
(57)

Use the following figures for problems 11 and 12. Dimensions are in feet.

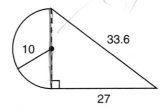
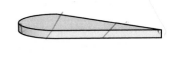

11. Find (a) the perimeter and (b) the area of the figure on the left.
(64)

12. What is the volume of a solid whose base is the figure shown on the left and whose
(45) sides are 2 feet tall?

Solve:

13. $\dfrac{4\frac{1}{3}}{2\frac{6}{7}} = \dfrac{7}{x}$
(65)

14. $\dfrac{\frac{4}{5}}{\frac{16}{15}} = \dfrac{x}{3}$
(59)

15. $7\frac{1}{8}x + 2\frac{3}{10} = 3\frac{2}{5}$
(61)

16. $18x + 7 = 22$
(61)

Simplify:

17. $\left(\dfrac{4}{7}\right)^4$
(71)

18. $\left(\dfrac{1}{9}\right)^2$
(71)

19. $\sqrt{\dfrac{25}{144}}$
(71)

20. $\sqrt[3]{\dfrac{27}{125}}$
(71)

21. $(-8) + (1) + (-3) + (-5)$
(70)

22. $(2) + (1) + (-4) + (-7) + (8)$
(70)

23. $(122) + (5) + (-6) + (-11)$
(70)

24. $(-1) + (6) + (-5) + (-9) + (6)$
(70)

25. $2^3 + 2^2\left[3(2^2 - 1) + \sqrt{16}\right]$ **26.** $6\dfrac{1}{3} + \dfrac{2}{3} \cdot 3\dfrac{3}{4}$
(44)   (46)

27. $17\dfrac{5}{12} - 4\dfrac{5}{6} + 1\dfrac{3}{4}$ **28.** $\dfrac{1}{4}\left(3\dfrac{1}{3} + 2\dfrac{1}{4}\right) - \dfrac{11}{24}$
(35)   (52)

29. $3\dfrac{1}{4} \times 4\dfrac{5}{12} \div 3\dfrac{7}{8} \div \dfrac{1}{4}$
(43)

30. Evaluate: $x^y + y^x + \sqrt[y]{z}$ if $x = 2$, $y = 3$, and $z = 125$
(54)

LESSON 72   *Graphing Inequalities*

In Lesson 2 we used the number line to help us understand how numbers are arranged in order. Before algebra books began using the number line in the 1960s, many students had difficulty understanding how –2 could be greater than –5. Now all books use the number line to help define "greater than," and we can see on the number line why we say that –2 is greater than –5.

One number is greater than another number if its graph on the number line is to the right of the graph of the other number.

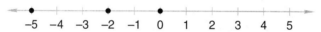

We see that –2 is greater than –5 because the graph of –2 is to the right of the graph of –5. For the same reason, we see that 0 is greater than both –5 and –2. The symbol

$$<$$

is a greater than/less than symbol. The open end is read as "greater than." The closed or pointed end is read as "less than." We read the end we come to first. We do not read the other end. The pointed end points to the smaller number. To read the mathematical expression

$$2 < 4$$

from left to right, we say "2 is less than 4." If we read it from right to left, we say "4 is greater than 2." We can turn the symbol around if we turn the numbers around. The statement

$$4 > 2$$

is read from left to right as "4 is greater than 2" or from right to left as "2 is less than 4."

If we add half an equals sign, we indicate that **equal to** can also be part of the solution. We read

$$-4 \geq -12$$

from left to right as "–4 is greater than or equal to –12" or from right to left as "–12 is less than or equal to –4." This statement

$$4 \geq 2 + 2$$

is read from left to right as "4 is greater than or equal to 2 plus 2." The statement is read from right to left as "2 plus 2 is less than or equal to 4."

An equation states that two quantities are equal, and a **statement of inequality** states that they are not. Some statements of inequality are false.

$$4 > 10 \qquad \text{false}$$

This is a false statement because 4 is not greater than 10. Some statements of inequality are conditional inequalities.

$$x > 2 \qquad \text{conditional}$$

The truth of this inequality depends on the number that is used to replace x. If the replacement number makes the inequality a true inequality, we say the number is a **solution of the inequality.** In the following examples, we show how graphs on the number line can be used to indicate the numbers that satisfy an inequality.

example 72.1   Graph: $x > 2$

solution   We are asked to graph all numbers that are greater than 2.

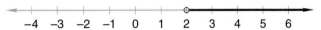

The open circle at 2 tells us that 2 is not a solution because 2 is not greater than 2. The solid arrow means that all numbers to the right of 2 are solutions. For example, 3, 4, 5, and 6, which are marked, are all solutions because they are greater than 2.

example 72.2   Graph: $x \leq 2$

solution   This time we are asked to indicate all numbers that are less than or equal to 2.

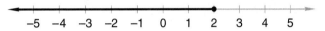

The circle at 2 is a solid circle because 2 is a solution to this inequality as well as all numbers to the left of 2.

practice   Sketch four number lines, then graph each inequality.

    a. $x > -2$ **b.** $x \geq -2$ **c.** $x \leq 4$ **d.** $x < -4$

problem set 72

1. *(36)* Twenty dozen starters cost a total of $5. What was the cost of 1 dozen starters? What would it cost to buy only 10 dozen starters?

2. *(62)* Three fifths of the clowns had solid red noses. If there were 150 clowns in all, how many had solid red noses?

3. *(66)* The ratio of big spenders to the penurious ones was 2 to 5. If 1400 were big spenders, how many were penurious?

4. *(58)* The entourage wended slowly through the forest. If it covered 400 yards in the first 20 minutes, how far did it go in the next hour?

5. *(67)* Health insurance is offered in three plans. One year of coverage costs $762. Three years of coverage costs $1850, and five years of coverage costs $3000. Find the unit cost per year for each plan. Which insurance plan is least expensive?

6. *(68)* Seventy percent of the 420 marathon runners finished the race. How many runners finished the race? Draw a diagram to help solve the problem.

7. *(68)* Thirty percent of what number is 360?

8. What percent of 50 is 12?
(68)

Graph on a number line:

9. $x \leq 5$ **10.** $x > 0$
(72)   (72)

11. Round 216,348,219 to the millions' place, and write the rounded number in scientific
(2,50) notation.

12. What decimal part of 420 is 147?
(51)

Use the following figures for problems 13 and 14. Dimensions are in inches.

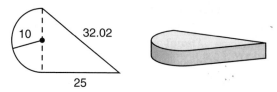

13. Find (a) the perimeter and (b) the area of the figure on the left.
(64)

14. What is the volume of a solid whose base is the figure shown on the left whose sides
(45) are 5 inches tall?

15. Find p.
(65)

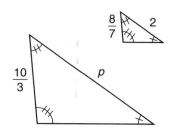

16. $\dfrac{6\frac{1}{4}}{2\frac{1}{3}} = \dfrac{5}{x}$ **17.** $6\frac{2}{3}x - 4\frac{1}{4} = 3\frac{1}{12}$
(65)   (61)

18. $20x + 18 = 132$
(61)

Simplify:

19. $\sqrt[4]{\dfrac{16}{81}}$ **20.** $\left(\dfrac{9}{11}\right)^2$
(71)   (71)

21. $(6) + (-9) + (1) + (-5)$ **22.** $(9) + (-1) + (-7) + (7)$
(70)   (70)

23. $13 + 2\left[2^3(2^2 - 1)(3 - 1) + 1\right]$ **24.** $2^3 + 2^2\left[3(2^2 - 1) + \sqrt{16}\right]$
(44)   (44)

25. $2\dfrac{11}{48} - \dfrac{1}{6} \cdot 3\dfrac{3}{8}$ **26.** $18\dfrac{5}{12} - 12\dfrac{1}{6} + 1\dfrac{3}{4}$
(46)   (35)

27. $6\dfrac{1}{4} \times 2\dfrac{1}{3} \div 1\dfrac{5}{12} \div \dfrac{1}{6}$ **28.** $\dfrac{181.31}{0.005}$
(43)   (7)

29. $\dfrac{1}{5}\left(3\dfrac{1}{4} - 2\dfrac{1}{3}\right) + \dfrac{13}{60}$
(52)

30. Evaluate: $x^x + y^y + x^y + y^x$ if $x = 3$ and $y = 2$
(54)

LESSON 73 *Right Circular Cylinders*

The **right circular cylinder** is important in science because of its structural strength. For example, big steel oil storage tanks are all right circular cylinders. Have you ever noticed that there are no square oil storage tanks or square water towers?

Problems involving right circular cylinders are easy to learn how to work without special formulas. Suppose the base of a right cylinder that is 20 meters tall has a radius of 2 meters. Then the area of the base is $\pi(2 \text{ m})^2$, which is approximately 12.56 m².

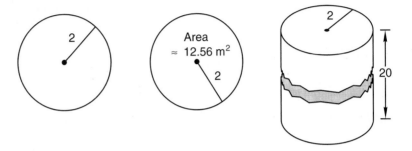

This means that if we crush 12.56 one-meter cubes and pour them into the cylinder, the cylinder will be filled to a depth of 1 meter. Since the cylinder is 20 meters tall, it will take 20×12.56 or 251.2 crushed, one-meter cubes to fill it completely. This leads to our definition of the volume of any right solid. The volume of a right solid equals the area of a base times the height of the solid.

VOLUME OF A RIGHT CIRCULAR CYLINDER

The volume of a right circular cylinder equals the area of a base times the height of the solid.

$$V = Bh = \pi r^2 h$$

B = area of a base h = height r = radius of a base

To find the surface area of a right circular cylinder that is 20 meters tall and has a radius of 3 meters, we treat it like a tin can. First we cut off the top and the bottom. The area of the top equals the area of the bottom. Each area equals $\pi r^2 = \pi(3 \text{ m})^2 = 9\pi \text{ m}^2$.

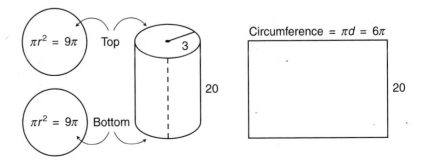

Then we cut the can down the dotted line and unroll it to get a rectangle. The length of the rectangle is the circumference of the circular top. The height of the rectangle is the height of the cylinder. The area of this rectangle is called the **lateral surface area** (the area of the side).

The total surface area of the right circular cylinder is the area of the top plus the area of the bottom plus the lateral surface area.

Surface area = area of top + area of bottom + lateral surface area

$$= 9\pi \text{ m}^2 + 9\pi \text{ m}^2 + (6\pi \text{ m})(20 \text{ m})$$

$$\approx 9(3.14) \text{ m}^2 + 9(3.14) \text{ m}^2 + (6 \text{ m})(3.14)(20 \text{ m}) = 433.32 \text{ m}^2$$

SURFACE AREA OF A RIGHT CIRCULAR CYLINDER

The surface area of a right circular cylinder equals twice the area of a base (that is, the top and bottom) plus the lateral surface area.

$$S.A. = 2B + L.A. = 2\pi r^2 + \pi dh$$

S.A. = surface area r = radius of a base
B = area of a base d = diameter of a base
L.A. = lateral surface area h = height

---

practice

a. Find the volume of a right circular cylinder that has a height of 30 feet and whose base has a radius of 10 feet.

b. Find the surface area of the same cylinder.

problem set 73

1. The result was 5400. This was $2\frac{1}{2}$ times the expected number. What was the expected number?
(57)

2. The ratio of students who took Spanish to students who took German was 15 to 2. If 3000 students took Spanish, how many took German?
(66)

3. Seven thousand, seven hundred biochemists made it on time. If the ratio of those who were on time to those who were late was 7 to 2, how many biochemists were late?
(66)

4. The rate of production of the machine was increased to 1400 bottles per hour. How many bottles could the machine produce if it operated for 8 hours?
(36)

5. A science fiction film earned $85 million during its first four weeks at the box office. The weekly distribution of the earnings is indicated in the pie graph at right. How much money did the film earn in its third week at the box office?
(29)

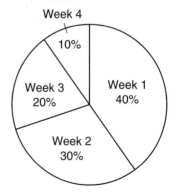

Distribution of Earnings for the First Four Weeks

Week 4 — 10%
Week 1 — 40%
Week 2 — 30%
Week 3 — 20%

6. Eighty percent of 280 is what number?
(68)

Graph on a number line:

7. $x < 6$
(72)

8. $x \geq -22$
(72)

9. Use two unit multipliers to convert 1,000,000 square meters to square centimeters.
(33)

10. Complete the table. Begin by inserting the reference numbers.
(55)

FRACTION	DECIMAL	PERCENT
(a)	(b)	23%

11. Write 6.04×10^{-6} in standard notation.
(50)

12. What decimal part of 600 is 360?
(51)

Use the following figure for problems 13 and 14. Dimensions are in meters. All angles are right angles.

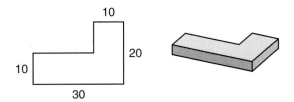

13. Find (a) the perimeter and (b) the area of the figure on the left.
(9,17)

14. What is the volume in cubic meters of the right solid whose base is the figure shown on the left and whose sides are 200 centimeters tall?
(45)

Use the following figure for problems 15 and 16. Dimensions are in inches.

15. Find the volume of the right circular cylinder.
(73)

16. Find the surface area of the right circular cylinder.
(73)

17. Find x.
(65)

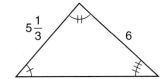

Solve:

18. $\dfrac{\frac{4}{5}}{\frac{8}{25}} = \dfrac{x}{5}$
(59)

19. $5\frac{1}{3}x - 2\frac{1}{4} = 4\frac{7}{12}$
(61)

Simplify:

20. $\left(\dfrac{3}{8}\right)^3$
₍₇₁₎

21. $\sqrt{\dfrac{16}{144}}$
₍₇₁₎

22. $(-8) + (7) + (4) + (-6)$
₍₇₀₎

23. $(21) + (-19) + (8) + (-11)$
₍₇₀₎

24. $\sqrt[3]{8} + \sqrt{4}\left[(2^3 - 4)3 + 1\right]$
₍₄₄₎

25. $3\dfrac{7}{24} - \dfrac{1}{8} \cdot 2\dfrac{5}{6}$
₍₄₆₎

26. $19\dfrac{6}{7} - \dfrac{3}{14} + 1\dfrac{4}{21}$
₍₃₄₎

27. 18.87×0.0032
₍₇₎

28. $\dfrac{1}{4}\left(3\dfrac{1}{5} - 2\dfrac{1}{3}\right) + \dfrac{7}{60}$
₍₅₂₎

29. Four fifths of the hound dogs were shleppers. If there were sixty shleppers, how many
₍₆₂₎ hound dogs were there?

30. Evaluate: $x^y + y^x + \sqrt[y]{x}$ if $x = 8$ and $y = 3$
₍₅₄₎

LESSON 74 *Inserting Parentheses • Order of Addition*

74.A

inserting parentheses

In arithmetic, a minus sign always means to subtract.

$$5 - 3 = 2$$

This expression tells us that 3 is subtracted from 5 resulting in 2. In algebra, this expression means that –3 is added to 5 resulting in 2. It means this:

$$5 + (-3) = 2$$

The result is the same, but the thought process is different. It is important to learn the thought process of **algebra** because it will help us to solve hard problems.

If a problem does not have parentheses, the parentheses can be inserted as the first step. If we have the expression

$$-4 + 3 - 2 - 6$$

we consider that the signs tell if the numbers are positive or negative. We enclose each number and its sign in parentheses and insert plus signs between the parentheses.

$$(-4) + (+3) + (-2) + (-6)$$

Now we simplify by adding the signed numbers.

$$(-1) + (-2) + (-6) \qquad \text{added } (-4) \text{ and } (+3)$$
$$(-3) + (-6) \qquad \text{added } (-1) \text{ and } (-2)$$
$$-9 \qquad \text{added } (-3) \text{ and } (-6)$$

This procedure of inserting parentheses and then adding is called **algebraic addition.** We will use this thought process from now on.

example 74.1   Add: $-2 + 3 - 5 + 7$

solution   First we use parentheses and insert plus signs between the parentheses.

$$(-2) + (+3) + (-5) + (+7)$$

Now we add.

$(+1) + (-5) + (+7)$	added (-2) and $(+3)$
$(-4) + (+7)$	added $(+1)$ and (-5)
$+3$	added (-4) and $(+7)$

example 74.2   Add: $-3 - 2 - 6 + 2 - 7$

solution   First we insert parentheses and plus signs as necessary.

$$(-3) + (-2) + (-6) + (+2) + (-7)$$

Now we add.

$(-5) + (-6) + (+2) + (-7)$	added (-3) and (-2)
$(-11) + (+2) + (-7)$	added (-5) and (-6)
$(-9) + (-7)$	added (-11) and $(+2)$
-16	added (-9) and (-7)

74.B

order of addition   Individual numbers that are enclosed in parentheses can be added in any order. Some people begin by adding the positive numbers together, and then they add the negative numbers together. Finally, they add the two sums.

example 74.3   Add: $-3 - 2 + 3 - 4 + 5$

solution   We begin by inserting the necessary parentheses.

$$(-3) + (-2) + (+3) + (-4) + (+5)$$

Now we add numbers whose signs are the same and get

$(-9) + (+8)$	combined positive numbers and negative numbers
-1	added (-9) and $(+8)$

practice   Use parentheses to enclose each number and its sign. Then insert plus signs between the parentheses. Then add.

a. $-4 + 6 - 1 + 7 - 3 + 2$ **b.** $-2 - 4 - 3 + 2 + 3 + 2 + 4$

problem set 74

1.
(57)   The white cell count was only 980. The patient was in trouble because the count should have been at least $5\frac{1}{2}$ times this number. What was the least the white cell count should have been?

2.
(63)   Doctor Hal and his exploratory scouts traveled 32 miles in 8 hours. The next day they had to travel 49 miles, so they increased their speed by 3 miles per hour. How long did it take them to travel the 49 miles?

3.
(66)   The ratio of winners to losers in the throng was 7 to 2. If 4200 were losers, how many winners were in the throng?

4.
(62)   Three fourths of the bats were in the belfry. If 42 bats were in the belfry, how many bats were there in all?

5. Thirty-five scuba divers succeeded in their lobster quest. If there were 175 scuba divers, what percent succeeded in their lobster quest? Draw a diagram to help solve the problem.
(68)

6. Thirty percent of what number is 123?
(68)

Graph on a number line:

7. $x > -12$
(72)

8. $x \leq 52$
(72)

9. Complete the table. Begin by inserting the reference numbers.
(55)

Fraction	Decimal	Percent
$\frac{37}{100}$	(a)	(b)

10. Round 0.0030796 to the ten-thousandths' place, and write the rounded number in scientific notation.
(6,50)

11. What decimal part of 500 is 125?
(51)

Use the following figures for problems 12 and 13. Dimensions are in meters.

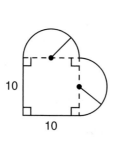
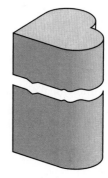

12. Find (a) the perimeter and (b) the area of the figure on the left.
(64)

13. What is the volume of a right solid whose base is the figure shown on the left and whose sides are 50 meters tall?
(45)

14. Find the volume and surface area of the right circular cylinder shown. Dimensions are in decimeters.
(73)

Solve:

15. $\dfrac{4\frac{2}{3}}{1\frac{5}{6}} = \dfrac{8}{x}$
(65)

16. $2\frac{1}{4}x + 4\frac{1}{3} = 5\frac{7}{12}$
(61)

17. Find x.
(65)

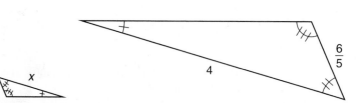

Simplify:

18. $\sqrt[3]{\dfrac{64}{343}} + \left(\dfrac{2}{3}\right)^2$
(71)

19. $\dfrac{1}{5}\left(4\dfrac{2}{5} - 2\dfrac{1}{3}\right) + \dfrac{4}{15}$
(52)

20. $-4 + 5 + -10 + 2$
(74)

21. $-11 + -2 + 20 + -7$
(74)

22. $12 + -7 + -10 + 1$
(74)

23. $-21 + 7 + -2 + 6$
(74)

24. $16\dfrac{7}{8} - 2\dfrac{1}{4} \cdot 1\dfrac{1}{2} + 1\dfrac{7}{16}$
(46)

25. 166.5×0.0024
(7)

26. $19{,}621.81 - 698.971$
(6)

27. $\dfrac{213.19}{0.005}$
(7)

28. $13 + 2\left[2^2\left(3^2 - 2^3\right)\left(2^2 + 1\right) - 15\right]$
(44)

29. Sketch a rectangular coordinate system, and graph the points $(0, 0)$ and $(2, -3)$.
(38)

30. Evaluate: $x^y + y^x - \sqrt[x]{z}$ if $x = 3$, $y = 2$, and $z = 64$
(54)

LESSON 75 *Implied Ratios*

Remember that a ratio is a comparison of two numbers. Ratios are often written in the form of fractions. Remember also that a proportion is a statement that two ratios are equal. These are equal ratios.

$$\frac{3}{4} = \frac{9}{12}$$

The equation is called a proportion. Many ratio word problems do not actually use the word ratio. When we read the problem, we must recognize that the problem is a ratio problem. We must also be able to pick out the **implied ratio.**

example 75.1 It takes $2\frac{1}{2}$ eggs to make 140 cookies. Jenny wants to make 1680 cookies. How many eggs does she need?

solution This problem is a ratio problem about eggs and cookies. We decide to put eggs in the numerator.

$$\frac{E}{C} = \frac{E}{C}$$

The first sentence in the problem gives us the implied ratio. It tells us that the ratio of eggs to cookies is $2\frac{1}{2}$ to 140. We make the substitution.

$$\frac{2\frac{1}{2}}{140} = \frac{E}{C}$$

Jenny wants to make 1680 cookies, so we use 1680 for C and solve for E.

$$\frac{2\frac{1}{2}}{140} = \frac{E}{1680} \qquad \text{substituted}$$

$$\frac{5}{2} \cdot 1680 = 140E \qquad \text{cross multiplied}$$

$$4200 = 140E \qquad \text{simplified}$$

$$30 = E \qquad \text{divided both sides by 140}$$

Jenny needs **30 eggs** to make 1680 cookies.

example 75.2 It takes 3 tons of fertilizer to fertilize 170 acres. Farmer Brown wants to fertilize 1870 acres. How many tons of fertilizer does Farmer Brown need?

solution This problem concerns ratios of tons and acres. We decide to put tons in the numerator.

$$\frac{T}{A} = \frac{T}{A}$$

The first sentence in the problem gives us the implied ratio. It says that the ratio of tons to acres is 3 to 170. We substitute these numbers on the left. On the right we substitute 1870 for A. Then we solve for T.

$$\frac{3}{170} = \frac{T}{1870} \qquad \text{substituted}$$

$$3 \cdot 1870 = 170T \qquad \text{cross multiplied}$$

$$5610 = 170T \qquad \text{simplified}$$

$$33 = T \qquad \text{divided both sides by 170}$$

Farmer Brown needs **33 tons** of fertilizer to fertilize 1870 acres.

practice a. The baker found that it took 4 huge measures of sugar to make 13 confections. The baker needed to make 143 confections. How many huge measures of sugar were needed?

problem set 75

1. (62) The receipts for the day totaled $5200. This was only three fifths of the money needed to pay the bills. How much money was needed to pay the bills?

2. (58) Edsel traveled the 350 miles from the factory to the River Rouge plant in 7 hours. The next day he was in a hurry to return. If he must complete the trip back to the factory in 5 hours, what should be his speed?

3. (66) The ratio of believers to doubters at the meeting was 8 to 3. If 2400 of those in attendance were believers, how many doubters were present?

4. (62) Four fifths of the bees were not in the hive. If 1350 bees were in the hive, how many were not in the hive?

5. (75) Corey needs to develop 5 rolls of film. The machine takes 30 seconds to develop 2 rolls of film. How long will it take Corey to develop the 5 rolls?

6. (75) Jonathon uses 7 sticks of vine charcoal for every 3 drawings he creates. How many drawings can he create with 23 sticks?

7. (68) Twenty-five percent of the apartment complexes in Norman allow pets. If 85 apartment complexes allow pets, how many apartment complexes are there in Norman? Draw a diagram to help solve the problem.

8. Sixty-five is what percent of 325?
(68)

Graph on a number line:

9. $x < -34$
(72)

10. $x \geq 21$
(72)

11. Complete the table. Begin by inserting
(55) the reference numbers.

Fraction	Decimal	Percent
(a)	0.71	(b)

12. Write 26,900,000,000 in scientific notation.
(50)

13. What decimal part of 790 is 474?
(51)

Use the following figures for problems 14 and 15. Dimensions are in yards.

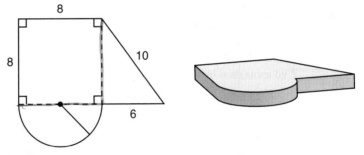

14. Find (a) the perimeter and (b) the area of the figure on the left.
(64)

15. What is the volume in cubic yards of a right solid whose base is the figure shown on
(45) the left and whose sides are 4 feet tall? Round to two decimal places.

16. Find the surface area of a right circular cylinder whose radius is 4 centimeters and
(73) whose height is 9 centimeters.

17. Use two unit multipliers to convert 1,000,000 inches to miles. Round any decimals to
(33) two places.

Simplify:

18. $\left(\dfrac{2}{3}\right)^3$
(71)

19. $\sqrt[3]{\dfrac{8}{27}}$
(71)

20. $\left(\dfrac{1}{5}\right)^3$
(71)

21. $\sqrt[4]{\dfrac{81}{256}}$
(71)

22. $10 + 3\left[3^2\left(1^5 + 2^3\right)\left(3^2 + 1\right)\right]$
(44)

23. $8 + -9 + 6 + -14$
(74)

24. $-30 + 14 + -1 + 17$
(74)

25. $11\dfrac{2}{8} - 5\dfrac{1}{2} \cdot 1\dfrac{2}{3} + 1\dfrac{1}{4}$
(46)

26. $\dfrac{1}{4}\left(3\dfrac{2}{3} - 1\dfrac{1}{4}\right) + \dfrac{6}{7}$
(52)

27. $\dfrac{657.12}{0.0012}$
(7)

Solve:

28. $\quad \dfrac{3\frac{1}{2}}{1\frac{2}{5}} = \dfrac{10}{m}$
(65)

29. $\quad 5\frac{1}{4}y - 2\frac{1}{2} = 4\frac{5}{12}$
(61)

30. Which is a better deal: 3 dingoes for \$57 or 5 dingoes for \$99.50?
(67)

LESSON 76   *Multiplication with Scientific Notation*

To multiply

$$4. \times 1000 \times 100$$

we begin by multiplying 4 by 1000. When we do this, we move the decimal point three places to the right. Now we have

$$4000. \times 100$$

When we do the next multiplication, we move the decimal point two more places to the right and get

$$400,000.$$

Multiplying by 1000 moved the decimal point three places. Multiplying by 100 moved it two more places. We moved the decimal point a total of five places to the right. If we express the problem with 1,000 and 100 as powers of 10, we get

$$4 \times 10^3 \times 10^2$$

We can think of 10^3 and 10^2 as **decimal point movers.** The 10^3 moves the decimal point three places to the right. The 10^2 moves the decimal point two places to the right. This is a total of five places to the right. So this means that

$$4 \times 10^3 \times 10^2 \qquad \text{equals} \qquad 4 \times 10^5$$

This method of multiplication can be directly applied to scientific notation.

> MULTIPLICATION WITH SCIENTIFIC NOTATION
>
> To multiply numbers in scientific notation, we multiply the numbers and add the exponents of the decimal point movers. Then we write the product in scientific notation.

example 76.1   Multiply: $\left(4 \times 10^5\right) \times \left(2 \times 10^{-2}\right)$

solution   As the first step, we put the numbers together and put the decimal point movers together.

$$(4 \times 2) \times \left(10^5 \times 10^{-2}\right)$$

Next we multiply 4 by 2 and get 8.

$$8 \times \left(10^5 \times 10^{-2}\right)$$

Then we add the exponents of the decimal point movers.

$$(+5) + (-2) = 3$$

So our answer in scientific notation is

$$\mathbf{8 \times 10^3}$$

example 76.2 Multiply: $(3 \times 10^8) \times (3 \times 10^3)$

solution First we rearrange the factors and get

$$(3 \times 3) \times (10^8 \times 10^3)$$

Now we multiply the numbers and add the exponents of the decimal point movers.

$$9 \times 10^{11}$$

example 76.3 Multiply: $(4 \times 10^{-6}) \times (6.2 \times 10^4)$

solution We multiply the two numbers. Then we add the exponents of the decimal point movers.

$$24.8 \times 10^{-2}$$

We rewrite this expression in the proper form of scientific notation.

$$(2.48 \times 10^1) \times 10^{-2} = 2.48 \times 10^{-1}$$

practice Multiply and simplify:

a. $(4 \times 10^{-4}) \times (2 \times 10^{14})$

b. $(3 \times 10^6) \times (3 \times 10^{-2})$

c. $(2.1 \times 10^{10}) \times (2 \times 10^3)$

d. $(4 \times 10^{-5}) \times (3 \times 10^{-8})$

problem set 76

1. (62) Rockabilly was old hat, but some of the fans still enjoyed it. There were 29,000 fans at the festival, and 3000 of them were rockabilly fans. What fraction of the fans were rockabilly fans?

2. (62) When the trumpet sounded the charge, seven eighths of the malingerers disappeared. If there were 16,000 malingerers in all, how many disappeared?

3. (63) The stagecoach clattered and rattled but still covered the 40-mile trip in 5 hours. If the speed for the next leg was increased by 4 miles per hour, how long would it take to travel the 36 miles that remained?

4. (66) The ratio of players to onlookers was 7 to 5. If 112 were players, how many were onlookers?

5. (75) The softball complex requires 16 teams for every 2 tournaments. How many teams are needed if they want 6 tournaments?

6. (68) Forty percent of the marsupials at the Australian zoo are wallabies. If there are 22 wallabies at the zoo, how many marsupials are at the zoo? Draw a diagram to help solve the problem.

7. (68) Sixty percent of 480 is what number?

Graph on a number line:

8. (72) $x > -4$

9. (72) $x \le 4$

10. (55) Complete the table. Begin by inserting the reference numbers.

FRACTION	DECIMAL	PERCENT
(a)	0.39	(b)

11. Simplify:
(71)

    (a) $\left(\dfrac{2}{3}\right)^4$ (b) $\sqrt{\dfrac{64}{81}}$

12. Four tenths of what number is 148?
(51)

Use the following figures for problems 13 and 14. Dimensions are in feet.

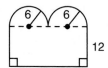 

13. Find (a) the perimeter and (b) the area of the figure on the left.
(64)

14. What is the volume in cubic feet of a solid whose base is the figure shown on the left
(45) and whose sides are 1 yard tall?

15. Find the volume of a right circular cylinder whose radius is 10 meters and whose height
(73) is 11 meters.

16. Find x.
(65)

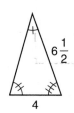 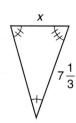

Solve:

17. $\dfrac{\dfrac{3}{7}}{\dfrac{9}{21}} = \dfrac{z}{3}$ **18.** $6\dfrac{1}{2}x + 3\dfrac{1}{4} = 5\dfrac{1}{8}$
(59)   *(61)*

Simplify:

19. $\left(4 \times 10^2\right) \times \left(2 \times 10^8\right)$ **20.** $\left(2 \times 10^7\right) \times \left(3 \times 10^{-4}\right)$
(76)   *(76)*

21. $\left(7 \times 10^{11}\right) \times \left(3 \times 10^{-13}\right)$ **22.** $\left(4.73 \times 10^{-3}\right) \times \left(2 \times 10^{13}\right)$
(76)   *(76)*

23. $-6 + 4 + -10 + 2$ **24.** $-36 + 21 + -6 + -3$
(74)   *(74)*

25. $13\dfrac{3}{4} - 1\dfrac{4}{5} \cdot \dfrac{3}{2} + \dfrac{7}{20}$ **26.** $19{,}611.62 - 687.91$
(46)   *(6)*

27. $\dfrac{218.31}{0.006}$ **28.** $\dfrac{1}{6}\left(2\dfrac{1}{3} \cdot \dfrac{1}{2} - \dfrac{3}{4}\right) + \dfrac{5}{24}$
(7)   *(52)*

29. $4^2 + \sqrt{16}\left[2^2\left(3^2 - 2^2\right)\left(4^2 - 3^2\right) - 10\right]$
(44)

30. Evaluate: $xy + x^2 + y^2 + x^y$ if $x = 4$ and $y = 2$
(54)

LESSON 77   *Percents Greater than 100*

We have learned that percents less than 100 indicate a part of the whole. For example 60% of the 80 parking spaces at the high school were filled on Monday.

$$60\% \times 80 \text{ parking spaces} = 0.6 \times 80 \text{ parking spaces} = 48 \text{ parking spaces}$$

We see that 48 is less than 80. It is a part of the whole. We can say

48 out of 80 parking spaces were filled

$\dfrac{48}{80}$ of the parking spaces were filled

$\dfrac{3}{5}$ of the parking spaces were filled

0.6 of the parking spaces were filled

60% of the parking spaces were filled

A percent equal to 100 means the whole. If on Friday, 80 out of the 80 parking spaces are filled, we can say 100% of them are filled. Now we examine percents greater than 100.

On game day, 120% of the 80 parking spaces are needed. How many spaces are needed?

$$120\% \times 80 \text{ parking spaces} = 1.2 \times 80 \text{ parking spaces} = 96 \text{ parking spaces}$$

Ninety-six parking spaces are needed on game day. Notice that 20% more parking spaces are needed than are available. We observe that 96 is greater than 80. It is not a part of the whole, but rather a number greater than the whole. This concept applies to all percents greater than 100.

example 77.1   (a) Two hundred ten percent of 50 is what number?

(b) What percent of 40 is 60?

(c) One hundred fifty percent of what number is 300?

solution   (a) 210% of 50 is what number?

$210\% \cdot 50 = B$	equation
$2.1 \cdot 50 = B$	equation with 210% as a decimal
$105 = B$	simplified

So 210% of 50 is **105.**

(b) *P* of 40 is 60.

$P \cdot 40 = 60$	equation
$P = \dfrac{60}{40}$	divided both sides by 40
$P = \dfrac{3}{2}$	reduced fraction
$P = 1.5$	converted $\dfrac{3}{2}$ to a decimal
$P = 150\%$	converted 1.5 to a percent

So **150%** of 40 is 60.

(c) 150% of what number is 300?

$$150\% \cdot A = 300 \qquad \text{equation}$$

$$1.5 \cdot A = 300 \qquad \text{equation with 150\% as a decimal}$$

$$A = \frac{300}{1.5} \qquad \text{divide both sides by 1.5}$$

$$A = 200 \qquad \text{simplified}$$

So 150% of **200** is 300.

example 77.2   Jane is mad because today crullers cost 120% of what they did two years ago. What does a cruller that was 60¢ two years ago cost today? Work the problem and then draw a diagram of the problem.

solution   We put the question into the form of the percent equation, first in English, then in algebra.

A percent of a number is another number

120% of 60¢ is today's cost

$$1.20 \cdot 60\text{¢} = B$$

$$72\text{¢} = B$$

The cost today is **72¢.** The two-part percent diagram of this problem is different from all our previous two-part diagrams. The "after" diagram is bigger than the "before" diagram.

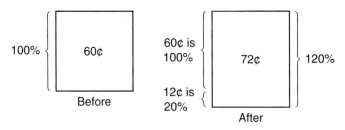

This diagram reveals that the cost of crullers today is 20% (12¢) greater than the cost two years ago.

practice   **a.**   Three hundred percent of 45 is what number?

b.   One hundred forty percent of what number is 364?

c.   The local art supply store sold 20 boxes of crayons last year. This year they sold 80 boxes. This year's sales are what percent of last year's sales? Draw a diagram to help solve the problem.

problem set 77

1.   A harsh law is called a *draconian* law after the Greek law-giver Draco. Two fifths of
(62)   the laws were draconian. If 42 laws were draconian, how many laws were there in all?

2.   A neophyte is a beginner. On the first day of classes, 28,000 students arrived at the
(62)   university campus. If three sevenths were neophytes, how many were not neophytes?

3.   Patton drove his column north and covered 60 miles in 3 hours. By how much did he
(63)   need to increase the column's rate in order to complete the last 200 miles in the remaining 5 hours of daylight?

4.   The ratio of the timorous to the undaunted was 5 to 17. If 200 were timorous, how many
(66)   were undaunted?

5. It takes 5 cups of flour to make 2 loaves of bread. How much flour is needed for
(75) 7 loaves?

6. The coach told the team to give 110% of their previous effort. If their previous effort
(77) was 50 kilojoules, how much effort does the coach want them to give? Draw a diagram
to help solve the problem.

7. What percent of 8.2 is 20.5?
(77)

Graph on a number line:

8. $x > -1$ **9.** $x \le 0$
(72)

10. One hundred forty percent of 310 is what number?
(77)

11. Complete the table. Begin by inserting
(55) the reference numbers.

FRACTION	DECIMAL	PERCENT
$\frac{26}{50}$	(a)	(b)

12. Simplify:
(71)

(a) $\left(\dfrac{3}{4}\right)^3$ (b) $\sqrt[4]{\dfrac{16}{81}}$

13. Sixty-five hundredths of what number is 780?
(51)

14. Find the volume and surface area of
(73) this right circular cylinder. Dimensions are in meters.

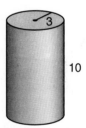

15. Round 1,039,296,119.4 to the nearest ten-millions' place, and write the rounded
(2,50) number in scientific notation.

Solve:

16. $\dfrac{4\frac{1}{4}}{6\frac{4}{5}} = \dfrac{15}{x}$ **17.** $\dfrac{\frac{5}{8}}{\frac{15}{22}} = \dfrac{x}{2}$ **18.** $7\frac{1}{5}x + 2\frac{1}{9} = 4\frac{1}{3}$
(65)   (59)   (61)

Simplify:

19. $(4 \times 10^{23}) \times (3 \times 10^{-14})$ **20.** $(1.8 \times 10^{-3}) \times (2 \times 10^5)$
(76)   (76)

21. $(2.5 \times 10^{60}) \times (3 \times 10^{15})$ **22.** $\dfrac{1}{5}\left(3\frac{1}{2} \cdot \dfrac{4}{7} - \dfrac{11}{14}\right) + \dfrac{3}{28}$
(76)   (52)

23. $-15 + -3 + 14 + 5$ **24.** $-29 + 11 + -5 + -3$
(74)   (74)

25. $10\dfrac{1}{6} - 2\dfrac{5}{6} \cdot \dfrac{5}{4} + \dfrac{11}{12}$
(46)

26. 416.09×0.0011
(7)

27. $15{,}342.16 - 91.091$
(6)

28. $\dfrac{419.42}{0.004}$
(7)

29. $5^2 + \sqrt{64}\left[2^2\left(2 - \sqrt[9]{1}\right)\left(5^2 - 4^2\right) + (+11)\right]$
(44)

30. Evaluate: $\sqrt[m]{p} + \dfrac{x}{\sqrt{p}}$ if $p = 16$, $m = 4$, and $x = 3$
(54)

LESSON 78 *Opposites*

The graph of the number 2 is two units to the right of the origin on a number line. The graph of the number –2 is two units to the left of the origin. Both graphs are the same distance from the origin, but the graphs are on opposite sides of the origin.

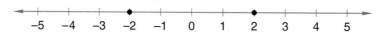

We say that these numbers are a **pair of opposites.** The number –2 is the opposite of 2 and the number 2 is the opposite of –2.

Sometimes it is helpful if we say the words *the opposite of* instead of saying *negative.* If we do this, we read

$$-2$$

as "the opposite of 2." And we would read

$$-(-2)$$

as "the opposite of the opposite of 2."

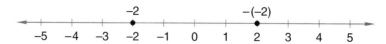

From this diagram we see that –2 is to the left of the origin, and thus the opposite of this is to the right of the origin. Thus,

$$-(-2) = \text{the opposite of}$$

$$\text{the opposite of 2} \qquad \text{which is 2}$$

If we record another minus sign and write $-[-(-2)]$, we move back to the left side of the origin.

$$-[-(-2)] = \text{the opposite of}$$

$$\text{the opposite of}$$

$$\text{the opposite of 2} \qquad \text{which is } –2$$

Every time we record another minus sign, we switch sides again. We can see this in the pattern developed here. In the following expressions and examples, we use braces { }, which are another symbol of inclusion.

EXPRESSION	READ AS	WHICH IS
2	2	2
–2	the opposite of 2	–2
–(–2)	the opposite of the opposite of 2	2
–[–(–2)]	the opposite of the opposite of the opposite of 2	–2
–{–[–(–2)]}	the opposite of the opposite of the opposite of the opposite of 2	2

The expressions in the left-hand column are all equivalent expressions for 2 or for –2. If we look at the right-hand column, we see that every time an additional (–) is included in the left-hand expression, the right-hand expression changes sign. **Therefore, an even number of negative signs indicates a positive number, and an odd number of negative signs indicates a negative number.**

example 78.1   Simplify: $-\left(-\left\{-[-(-7)]\right\}\right)$

solution   There are five (–) signs. Five is an odd number, so

$$-\left(-\left\{-[-(-7)]\right\}\right) = \textbf{–7}$$

example 78.2   Simplify: $-\left\{-[-(-6)]\right\}$

solution   There are four (–) signs. Four is an even number, so

$$-\left\{-[-(-6)]\right\} = \textbf{+6}$$

example 78.3   Simplify: $-\left\{+[-(-4)]\right\}$

solution   There are three (–) signs. Three is an odd number, so

$$-\left\{+[-(-4)]\right\} = \textbf{–4}$$

practice   Simplify:

   a. $-[-(-3)]$ **b.** $-\left\{-[-(-7)]\right\}$

   c. $-(-81)$ **d.** $-\left(+\left\{-[-(+5)]\right\}\right)$

problem set 78

1. Three sevenths of the cherubs had angelic faces. If there were 420,000 cherubs in the firmament, how many did not have angelic faces?
(62)

2. The ratio of chimeras to gargoyles is 2 to 11. If there is a total of 380 chimeras, what is the total number of gargoyles?
(66)

3. Jean traveled the first 100 miles in 5 hours. Then she doubled her speed for the last part of the trip. If the total trip was 300 miles, how many hours did it take Jean to travel the last part?
(63)

4. Four dozen roses cost $24. Homeratho could afford only 6 roses. How much did he pay for them?
(66)

5. Two hundred seventy decorations were displayed last year. If this year's goal is to display 130% of last year's decorations, how many decorations need to be displayed this year? Draw a diagram to help solve the problem.
(77)

6. Sixty is what percent of 300?   **7.** What percent of 8 is 160?
(68)   *(77)*

Graph on a number line:

8. $x \le 3$
(72)

9. $x > -3$
(72)

10. One hundred eighty percent of 620 is what number?
(77)

11. Write 1.03×10^{10} in standard notation.
(50)

12. Two and one fourth of what number is $5\frac{3}{8}$?
(57)

13. Find the volume in cubic inches of a right solid whose base is the figure shown on the
(45) left and whose sides are 1 foot tall. Dimensions are in inches.

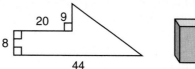
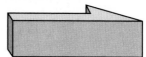

14. What is the surface area of a rectangular solid whose length is 10 feet, whose width is
(49) 5 feet, and whose height is 2 feet?

15. Find the volume and surface area of
(73) this right circular cylinder. Dimensions are in feet.

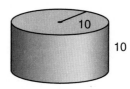

16. Find the least common multiple of 10, 12, and 18.
(20)

Solve:

17. $\dfrac{1\frac{2}{3}}{6\frac{3}{4}} = \dfrac{\frac{3}{4}}{x}$
(65)

18. $\dfrac{\frac{4}{7}}{\frac{8}{28}} = \dfrac{p}{6}$
(59)

19. $5\frac{1}{2}x + 2\frac{1}{3} = 4\frac{5}{6}$
(61)

Simplify:

20. $-\{-[-(-3)]\}$
(78)

21. $-\{+[+(-15)]\}$
(78)

22. $-[+(-22)]$
(78)

23. $(3.16 \times 10^{-7})(3.3 \times 10^{15})$
(76)

24. $-8 + 13 - 6 + 9$
(74)

25. $-4 - 6 + -3 + 1 - 6$
(74)

26. $16\frac{9}{20} - 2\frac{1}{2} \cdot 3\frac{2}{5} + \frac{9}{10}$
(46)

27. $\frac{1}{8}\left(3\frac{1}{2} \cdot \frac{1}{2} - \frac{4}{5}\right) + \frac{9}{40}$
(52)

28. $3^2 + \sqrt{25}\left[2^2(2^2 - 3)(5^2 - 4^2) - 20\right]$
(44)

29. $\left(\frac{3}{4}\right)^3 + \left(\frac{5}{8}\right)^2 - \left(\frac{3}{2}\right)^6$
(71)

30. Evaluate: $\sqrt{x} + x^y + xy$ if $x = 4$ and $y = 3$
(54)

LESSON 79 *Simplifying More Difficult Notations*

When we see an expression such as

$$-4 + 2 - 5 - 7$$

we consider that the signs go with the numbers. We can look at this problem and think

$$(-4) + (+2) + (-5) + (-7)$$

but not physically write down the parentheses. However, there are more difficult notations than these. When we see an expression such as

$$-(-4) + (-2) + [-(-6)]$$

we begin by noting that algebraic addition of three numbers is indicated. We emphasize this by enclosing the numbers that are to be added and writing plus signs between the enclosures.

$$\boxed{-(-4)} + \boxed{+(-2)} + \boxed{+[-(-6)]}$$

The number in the first enclosure is +4, in the second is –2, and in the third is +6. So we can write this as

$$(+4) + (-2) + (+6)$$

example 79.1 Simplify: $-(+4) - (-5) + 5 - (-3) + (-6)$

solution This problem indicates addition of five numbers.

$$\boxed{-(+4)} + \boxed{-(-5)} + \boxed{(+5)} + \boxed{-(-3)} + \boxed{+(-6)}$$

We simplify within each enclosure and add algebraically.

$$(-4) + (+5) + (+5) + (+3) + (-6) = \mathbf{3}$$

example 79.2 Simplify: $-(-3) - [-(-2)] + [-(-3)]$

solution We see three numbers are to be added. We begin by enclosing each number and inserting the necessary plus signs.

$$\boxed{-(-3)} + \boxed{-[-(-2)]} + \boxed{+[-(-3)]}$$

Now we simplify within each enclosure and then add.

$$(+3) + (-2) + (+3) = \mathbf{4}$$

example 79.3 Simplify: $-(-4) + (-2) - [-(-6)]$

solution This time we will picture the enclosures mentally, but we will not write them down. If we do this, we can simplify the given expression as

$$(+4) + (-2) + (-6) = \mathbf{-4}$$

example 79.4 Simplify: $-(+4) - (-5) + 5 - (-3) + (-6)$

solution This time we will not even use parentheses but will write the simplification directly as

$$-4 + 5 + 5 + 3 - 6 = \mathbf{3}$$

It might take a lot of practice to become adept in doing simplifications such as this one. Do not get discouraged if you find these problems troublesome. Instead, work the problems using the procedure in the first two examples.

practice   Use the concept of opposites and algebraic addition to simplify the following. Use additional plus signs and brackets as required.

     a. $-(-3) - (-4)$ **b.** $+(-5) + [-(-6)]$

     c. $-(+6) - (-8) + 7 - (-3) + (-5)$ **d.** $-(-3) - [-(-4)] + [-(-6)]$

problem set   **1.**   The shop uses 65 gallons of oil every 5 weeks. At this rate, how many gallons will the
      79   _(36)_   shop need for 1 year (52 weeks)?

     2.   The recipe for 4 cakes requires 6 eggs. How many eggs will be used to make 86 cakes?
     _(75)_

     3.   The ratio of the number that were mundane to the number that were exotic was 11 to 9.
     _(66)_   If there were 121,000 mundane ones, how many were exotic?

     4.   Five criterion team bikes cost \$11,300. How much would the club have to pay for a
     _(75)_   dozen criterion team bikes?

     5.   Last year, the publisher printed 5000 physics books. If the publisher expects to print
     _(77)_   8000 physics books this year, what percent of the number of books printed last year is
         the number of books to be printed this year? Draw a diagram to help solve
         the problem.

     6.   What is 112% of 250?
     _(77)_

     7.   One thousand six hundred is what percent of 320?
     _(77)_

Graph on a number line:

     8. $x \le -4$ **9.** $x > 0$
     _(72)_   _(72)_

     10.   Find x.
     _(65)_

 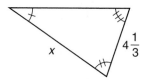

     11.   Sketch a rectangular coordinate system, and graph the points $(4, 1)$ and $(-2, 0)$.
     _(38)_

     12.   Three and one half of what number is 4200?
     _(57)_

     13.   Find the volume, in cubic meters, of a right solid whose base is the figure shown on the
     _(64)_   left and whose sides are 5 meters tall. Dimensions are in meters.

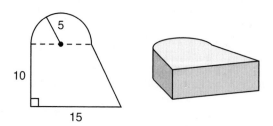

     14.   Find the surface area of a right circular cylinder whose diameter is 4 meters and whose
     _(73)_   height is 10 meters.

Solve:

15. $\dfrac{2\frac{1}{2}}{5\frac{1}{3}} = \dfrac{8}{x}$
(65)

16. $4\frac{1}{8}m + 1\frac{1}{5} = 5\frac{2}{3}$
(61)

Simplify:

17. (a) $-\{+[-(-2)]\}$ (b) $-\big(+\{-[-(+2)]\}\big)$ (c) $+[-(-2)]$
(78)

18. (a) $-\{-[-(-19)]\}$ (b) $+[+(+19)]$ (c) $+[-(+19)]$
(78)

19. $+7 - (-3) + (-2)$
(79)

20. $-3 + (-2) - (-3)$
(79)

21. $-(-3) - [-(-4)] - 2 + 7$
(79)

22. $\dfrac{78.045}{0.06}$
(7)

23. $83{,}041.76 - 76.0915$
(6)

24. $\dfrac{1}{4}\left(2\dfrac{1}{3} \cdot \dfrac{1}{4} + \dfrac{5}{6}\right) + \dfrac{7}{9}$
(52)

25. $\left(\dfrac{3}{4}\right)^4$
(71)

26. $\sqrt{\dfrac{169}{225}}$
(71)

27. $2^3 + \sqrt{25}\left[3^2\left(2 - 1^{11}\right)\left(2^2 - \sqrt[5]{1}\right) + (-9)\right]$
(44)

28. $\left(3 \times 10^{12}\right)\left(15 \times 10^{-2}\right)$
(76)

29. Use one unit multiplier to convert 1,000,000 meters to centimeters, and write the answer in scientific notation.
(24,50)

30. Evaluate: $\sqrt[m]{p} + p^x - x^m$ if $m = 3$, $p = 27$, and $x = 1$
(54)

LESSON 80 *Increases in Percent*

Often we encounter increases in percent. We might hear that the price of peanuts in Beijing went up 10% last year. If the old price was 60 yuan, what is the new price? What is 10% of 60 yuan?

$$0.1 \cdot 60 \text{ yuan} = 6 \text{ yuan}$$

But 6 is not the new price! It is the increase. **To find the new price, we add the increase to the old price:**

$$60 \text{ yuan} + 6 \text{ yuan} = 66 \text{ yuan}$$

example 80.1 To their dismay, the townspeople found that the rodent population had increased 140 percent. If the rodent population had been 400 before, what was the rodent population now?

solution Once again we use the percent equation.

A percent of a number is another number.

140% of 400 is the increase.

$$1.4 \cdot 400 = B$$
$$560 = B$$

The rodents' increase was 560, so the new population is

$$400 + 560 = \textbf{960 rodents}$$

example 80.2   The number of cheering fans increased from 60 to 240. What percent increase was this?

solution   The number was 60 and went up to 240. The increase is the difference:

$$240 - 60 = 180$$

So the increase is 180. What percent of 60 is 180?

$$p \cdot 60 = 180$$
$$p = 3$$
$$p = 300\%$$

It was a **300%** increase.

practice   **a.** The number of acorns on the ground increased 240 percent during the storm. If 5400 acorns were on the ground before the storm, how many were on the ground after the storm?

b. The number increased from 40 to 280. What percent increase was this?

problem set 80

1. Ingrid used 2 eggs to make 153 cookies. How many eggs would she need to make 1071 cookies?
(75)

2. The ratio of noisy ones to quiet ones was 13 to 5. If 3900 were noisy, how many were quiet?
(66)

3. Twain traveled the first 200 miles to Calaveras in 4 hours. Then, for the final 100 miles in the mountains, he slowed to half that speed. How many hours did it take Twain to complete the entire trip?
(63)

4. When the spelunkers entered the cave, four fifths of them got excited. If there were 1650 spelunkers in all, how many did not get excited?
(62)

5. There were 250 students in the 8th grade, and 12% of them loved Beethoven. How many loved Beethoven? Draw a diagram to help solve the problem.
(68)

6. Last month Molly's phone bill was $60, and this month's phone bill is $84. What percent of last month's phone bill is this month's phone bill? Draw a diagram to help solve the problem.
(77)

7. One hundred forty percent of what number is 10,500?
(77)

8. In problem 6, by what percent did last month's phone bill increase?
(80)

9. In 1990, there were 22 pairs of wood thrushes in the park. Thanks to conservation efforts, this year there are 33 pairs of wood thrushes. What percent increase is this?
(80)

10. Marcus' daily caloric intake was 2200 calories. On his birthday, because of Barbara's red velvet cake, his caloric intake increased 35%. How many calories did Marcus consume on his birthday?
(80)

Graph on a number line:

11. $x \geq -2$
(72)

12. Complete the table. Begin by inserting the reference numbers.
(55)

Fraction	Decimal	Percent
(a)	0.28	(b)

13. Use two unit multipliers to convert 90,000 square miles to square feet.
(33)

14. Soapy Suds detergent was $1.89 for the 7 oz box but $2.99 for the super giant-sized
(67) 11 oz box. Which box should the thrifty shopper choose?

15. Find the volume of a right solid whose base is the figure shown on the left and whose
(45) sides are 8 feet tall. Dimensions are in feet.

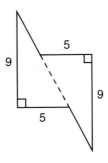
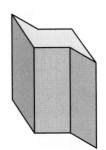

16. Find the volume and surface area of
(73) the right circular cylinder shown.
Dimensions are in inches.

Solve:

17. $\dfrac{\dfrac{4}{7}}{1\dfrac{2}{14}} = \dfrac{m}{\dfrac{2}{9}}$
(65)

18. $11\dfrac{1}{4}x - 3\dfrac{1}{2} = \dfrac{1}{9}$
(61)

Simplify:

19. (a) $-----20$ (b) $-\{-[+(-20)]\}$ (c) $+-+-(+20)$
(78)

20. (a) $-(-3)$ (b) $-\{-[-(+3)]\}$ (c) $+[-(+3)]$
(78)

21. $(4.2 \times 10^4)(3 \times 10^{-2})$
(76)

22. $11,314.091 - 91.3621$
(6)

23. $\left(\dfrac{3}{8}\right)^2$
(71)

24. $\sqrt[5]{\dfrac{1}{32}}$
(71)

25. $-2 - (-3) - \{-[-(-4)]\}$
(79)

26. $-2 - \{-[+(-6)]\}$
(79)

27. 114.09×0.03
(7)

28. $\dfrac{623.89}{0.02}$
(7)

29. $3^2 + \sqrt{121}\left[4^3(5 - 3)(3^2 - 5) + (-400)\right]$
(44)

30. Evaluate: $x^m + xm + \sqrt{m}$ if $x = 2$ and $m = 4$
(54)

LESSON 81   *Multiplication and Division of Signed Numbers*

We can develop the rules for the multiplication and division of signed numbers if we remember that multiplication is shorthand notation for repeated addition. Remember that "2 times 3" means "3 + 3" and that "2 times –3" means "(–3) + (–3)," so

$$2(3) = 6 \quad \text{and} \quad 2(-3) = -6$$

Remember also that division undoes multiplication, so the following must be true:

$$\text{if } 2(3) = 6, \text{ then } \frac{6}{2} = 3 \text{ and } \frac{6}{3} = 2$$

Likewise,

$$\text{if } 2(-3) = -6, \text{ then } \frac{-6}{2} = -3 \text{ and } \frac{-6}{-3} = +2$$

We use these examples to illustrate the fact that when we multiply or divide two positive numbers, the answer is a positive number. On the other hand, when we multiply or divide two numbers whose signs are different, the answer is a negative number. But what happens if we multiply two negative numbers? Since 2 times –3 equals –6

$$2(-3) = -6$$

then the *opposite of* 2 times –3 should equal the *opposite of* –6, which is 6.

$$(-2)(-3) = +6$$

And since division undoes multiplication, the following division examples must also be true:

$$\frac{+6}{-2} = -3 \text{ and } \frac{+6}{-3} = -2$$

These conclusions give us the following rules for multiplication and division of a pair of signed numbers:

1. The answer is a positive number if the signs of the two numbers are alike.

2. The answer is a negative number if the signs of the two numbers are different.

example 81.1   Simplify:

(a) (4)(2)   (b) (–4)(–2)   (c) (–4)(2)   (d) (4)(–2)

solution   The answers to (a) and (b) are both positive because in each multiplication the two numbers have like signs. Note that a negative number times a negative number equals a positive number.

(a) (4)(2) = **+8**   (b) (–4)(–2) = **+8**

The answers to (c) and (d) are both negative because the two numbers being multiplied have different signs.

(c) (–4)(2) = **–8**   (d) (4)(–2) = **–8**

example 81.2   Simplify:

(a) $\dfrac{8}{2}$ (b) $\dfrac{-8}{-2}$ (c) $\dfrac{8}{-2}$ (d) $\dfrac{-8}{2}$

solution   The answers to (a) and (b) are both positive numbers because the two numbers in the problem have like signs. Note that a negative number divided by a negative number equals a positive number.

$$\text{(a) } \dfrac{8}{2} = \mathbf{+4} \qquad \text{(b) } \dfrac{-8}{-2} = \mathbf{+4}$$

The answers to (c) and (d) are both negative numbers because the signs of the two numbers in the problem are different.

$$\text{(c) } \dfrac{8}{-2} = \mathbf{-4} \qquad \text{(d) } \dfrac{-8}{2} = \mathbf{-4}$$

When there are more than two factors in a product, we must count the signs. For example, in the following product there are five (–) signs:

$$(-3)(2)(-1)(-4)(-2)(-1)$$

We may group the numbers in pairs to simplify.

$$[(-3)(2)][(-1)(-4)][(-2)(-1)]$$
$$= (-6)[(4)(2)]$$
$$= (-6)(8)$$
$$= -48$$

Each pair of negative factors results in a positive factor. This illustrates that when there is an odd number of negative factors, the product is negative.

RULE FOR MULTIPLICATION OF SIGNED NUMBERS

When multiplying signed numbers, the product is positive if there is an even number of negative numbers. If there is an odd number of negative numbers, the product is negative.

---

example 81.3   Simplify: $(-3)(-3)(-2)(4)$

solution   There are three negative signs, so the product is negative. We only need one negative sign to indicate this.

$$(-3)(-3)(-2)(4)$$
$$= -(3)(3)(2)(4)$$
$$= -(9)(8)$$
$$= \mathbf{-72}$$

example 81.4   Is the following product positive or negative?

$$(+3)(-3)(2)(-4)(-1001)(-4)(-1)(-10)$$

solution   We simply count the number of negative signs. There are six, which is an even number. Therefore, the product is **positive.** We do not need to multiply this out.

practice   Simplify:

a. (4)(–3)   b. (–3)(4)   c. (–4)(–3)   d. (4)(3)

e. $\dfrac{14}{7}$ f. $\dfrac{-14}{-7}$ g. $\dfrac{-14}{7}$ h. $\dfrac{14}{-7}$

i. (–2)(–3)(–1)(4)(2)   j. (3)(2)(–1)(–2)(–2)(–3)

k. Is the following product positive or negative? (–79)(43)(–203)(–27)(49)(–105)(–21)

problem set
81

1. From her turret the chatelaine could see 440 sheep in the meadow. If she could only see
   (62) four ninths of the sheep, how many sheep were there in all?

2. The ratio of brigands to highway robbers skulking in the shadows was 5 to 7. If 450
   (66) brigands were skulking in the shadows, how many highway robbers were there?

3. Falstaff ate 160 ounces of comestibles and bragged that he could have eaten $3\frac{1}{2}$ times
   (57) that much. How many ounces did Falstaff think he could have eaten?

4. Jana had to travel 480 kilometers before Friday. Her speed would be 20 kilometers per
   (58) hour. How long would the trip take?

5. The fullback rushed for 60% more yards than he did in the last game. During the
   (80) last game he rushed for 90 yards. How many yards rushing did the fullback have
   in the second game?

6. Graph on a number line: $x < 5$
   (72)

7. What percent of 90 is 405?
   (77)

8. Two hundred fifty percent of what number is 80?
   (77)

9. Complete the table. Begin by inserting
   (55,77) the reference numbers.

Fraction	Decimal	Percent
$\frac{7}{5}$	(a)	(b)

10. Use two unit multipliers to convert 12 square miles to square feet.
    (33)

11. Find the volume in cubic feet of a right solid whose base is the figure shown on the left
    (45) and whose sides are 2 yards tall. Dimensions are in feet.

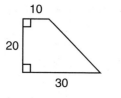

12. What is the surface area of this right
    (49) prism? Dimensions are in feet.

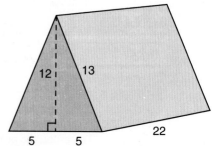

13. If 15 ants could eat 17 cruller crumbs, how many ants would be needed to eat 51
(75) cruller crumbs?

14. Find the least common multiple of 12, 18, and 27.
(20)

Solve:

15. $\dfrac{\frac{5}{6}}{\frac{25}{36}} = \dfrac{p}{12}$
(59)

16. $6\frac{1}{3}x + 1\frac{5}{6} = 7\frac{2}{3}$
(61)

Simplify:

17. (a) $(4.5)(-2)$ (b) $(-4.5)(-2)$ (c) $(-4.5)(2)$
(81)

18. (a) $\dfrac{-5.5}{5}$ (b) $\dfrac{5.5}{-5}$ (c) $\dfrac{-5.5}{-5}$
(81)

19. $2^3 + \sqrt{36}\left[3^2(3^2 - 2^3)(4^2 - 2^4) + 3\right]$
(44)

20. $\sqrt[4]{\dfrac{16}{81}} + \left(\dfrac{4}{5}\right)^2$
(71)

21. $-(+2) - 2 + -3 - (+6) + 3$
(79)

22. $-6 + -3 - 6 - [-(-10)] + 1$
(79)

23. $-\left\{-[-(+2)]\right\}$
(78)

24. $(-1)(-1)(-2)(-1)(-2)$
(81)

25. $17\dfrac{3}{5} - 1\dfrac{3}{5} \cdot \dfrac{1}{2} + 3\dfrac{1}{5}$
(46)

26. 0.1315×0.0012
(7)

27. $(5 \times 10^{-15}) \times (1 \times 10^8)$
(76)

28. $(1 \times 10^{-27}) \times (4 \times 10^{-20})$
(76)

29. Evaluate: $xyz + yz + y^z$ if $x = \dfrac{1}{3}$, $y = 6$, and $z = 2$
(54)

30. Evaluate: $\sqrt[3]{x} + \sqrt{y} + xy$ if $x = 8$ and $y = 16$
(47)

LESSON 82 *Evaluation with Signed Numbers*

The order of operations for simplifying expressions that contain signed numbers is the same as the order of operations for simplifying expressions that contain unsigned numbers. We always do the multiplication before we do the algebraic addition.

example 82.1 Simplify: $2(-4) - 3 - (-6)(-3)$

solution First we will do the multiplication and get

$$-8 - 3 - 18$$

We finish by adding algebraically and get −29 for our answer.

$$-8 - 3 - 18 = \mathbf{-29}$$

example 82.2   Evaluate: $-x - xy$ if $x = -2$ and $y = -4$

solution   Some people find that using parentheses helps prevent making mistakes with signs. We will write parentheses for each variable.

$$-(\ ) - (\ )(\ )$$

Now we insert the proper numbers in the parentheses.

$$-(-2) - (-2)(-4)$$

We multiply before we add, so the final result is -6.

$$2 - 8 = \mathbf{-6}$$

example 82.3   Evaluate: $-a - xa$ if $x = -3$ and $a = 2$

solution   We will use parentheses and write

$$-(2) - (-3)(2)$$

Now we simplify, remembering that we always multiply first.

$$
\begin{array}{ll}
-2 - (-6) & \text{multiplied } (-3) \text{ and } (2) \\
-2 + 6 & \text{simplified } - (-6) \\
\mathbf{4} & \text{added}
\end{array}
$$

practice   Evaluate:

a. $ab - a$ if $a = -2$ and $b = 3$

b. $x - xy$ if $x = -3$ and $y = -2$

c. $-xy - x$ if $x = -3$ and $y = -2$

problem set 82

1.
(75)   The doctor sees 126 patients in 3 days. How many patients could he see in 9 days?

2.
(62)   Chicanery was rampant at the medicine show. If seven eighths of the customers were chicaned and there were 3200 customers, how many were not chicaned?

3.
(62)   The demagogue pandered to five sixths of those who were prejudiced. If he pandered to 1200 who were prejudiced, how many were prejudiced in all?

4.
(63)   After traveling 120 miles in 3 hours, Rebecca reduced the speed of the sled by 10 miles per hour. How long did it take her to travel the next 450 miles?

5.
(80)   After vitamin fortification, Chocolate Marshmallow Crunch has 5.4 more milligrams of niacin. If the cereal had 18 milligrams of niacin before, what is the percent increase of niacin in the cereal?

6.
(72)   Graph on a number line: $x \geq -3$

7.
(77)   Two hundred sixty percent of what number is 143?

8.
(77)   What number is 180 percent of 60?

9.
(68)   There were 300 students in the 9th grade, and 65% of them loved bubble gum. How many loved bubble gum? Draw a diagram to help solve the problem.

10.
(77)   What percent of 80 is 200?

11.
(50)   Write 108,000 in scientific notation.

12. What decimal part of 480 is 360?
(51)

13. Express in cubic centimeters the volume of a right solid whose base is the figure shown
(45) on the left and whose sides are 1 meter tall. Dimensions are in centimeters.

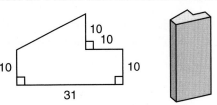

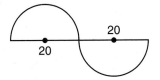

14. Find the perimeter of the figure
(64) shown. Dimensions are in feet.

Solve:

15. $\dfrac{2\frac{6}{7}}{1\frac{1}{14}} = \dfrac{\frac{1}{2}}{y}$
(65)

16. $\dfrac{\frac{6}{5}}{\frac{12}{25}} = \dfrac{5}{p}$
(59)

17. $2\frac{1}{5}x + 2\frac{1}{10} = 6\frac{3}{20}$
(61)

Simplify:

18. $2^4 + \sqrt{25}\left[2^2(3^2 - 2^3)(2^2 + 1) - 1\right]$
(44)

19. (a) $(-6)(-3)$ (b) $(-6)(3)$ (c) $(6)(-3)$
(81)

20. (a) $\dfrac{-6}{-2}$ (b) $\dfrac{6}{-2}$ (c) $\dfrac{-6}{2}$
(81)

21. $(-3)(-1)(-1)(-1)(5)$
(81)

22. $-\{-[-(-5)]\}$
(78)

23. $-6 + -\{+[-(-11)]\} + 3$
(79)

24. $-7 - 31 - -[+(+6)]$
(79)

25. $(7 \times 10^{14}) \times (1 \times 10^{-12})$
(76)

26. 0.1319×0.0014
(7)

27. Four points are graphed on this
(38) rectangular coordinate system. Identify the x- and y-coordinates of each.

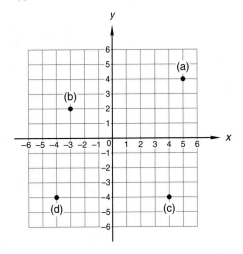

Evaluate:

28. $qrq - r$ if $r = 2$ and $q = -5$
(82)

29. $tv + vt$ if $t = -4$ and $v = 3$
(82)

30. $xy - \dfrac{x}{y}$ if $x = -4$ and $y = 2$
(82)

LESSON 83   *Rate Problems as Proportion Problems*

Remember that a rate is a ratio of two quantities. If seven apples can be purchased for two dollars, we can write two rates or ratios.

(a) $\dfrac{7 \text{ apples}}{2 \text{ dollars}}$ (b) $\dfrac{2 \text{ dollars}}{7 \text{ apples}}$

If we want to know how many apples could be purchased for ten dollars, we would use rate (a) and multiply by ten dollars.

$$\frac{7 \text{ apples}}{2 \text{ dollars}} \times 10 \text{ dollars} = 35 \text{ apples}$$

If we want to know how much ten apples would cost, we would use rate (b) and multiply by ten apples.

$$\frac{2 \text{ dollars}}{7 \text{ apples}} \times 10 \text{ apples} = \frac{20}{7} \text{ dollars}$$

We can also work these problems with proportions. A proportion is a statement that two ratios are equal. The ratios are between *A* for apples and *D* for dollars.

$$\frac{A}{D} = \frac{A}{D}$$

On the left we replace *A* with 7 and *D* with 2.

$$\frac{7}{2} = \frac{A}{D}$$

To find how many apples we could buy with ten dollars, we replace *D* with 10, cross multiply, and solve.

$$\frac{7}{2} = \frac{A}{10} \qquad \text{substituted}$$
$$70 = 2A \qquad \text{cross multiplied}$$
$$35 = A \qquad \text{divided both sides by 2}$$

Thus, we could buy thirty-five apples with ten dollars. To find how much ten apples would cost, we replace *A* with 10 and solve for *D*.

$$\frac{7}{2} = \frac{10}{D} \qquad \text{substituted}$$
$$7D = 20 \qquad \text{cross multiplied}$$
$$D = \frac{20}{7} \qquad \text{divided both sides by 7}$$

Thus, ten apples would cost $\frac{20}{7}$ dollars, or \$2.86. The advantage of this method is that it emphasizes that the problem deals with equal ratios. Both methods should be practiced.

example 83.1   Fourteen bags could be filled in three hours. How many hours would it take to fill eighty-four bags? Work this problem two ways—once as a rate problem and once as a proportion problem.

solution   We get two rates.

(a) $\dfrac{14 \text{ bags}}{3 \text{ hours}}$ (b) $\dfrac{3 \text{ hours}}{14 \text{ bags}}$

We want to know how many hours, so we use rate (b) because it has hours in the numerator.

$$\frac{3 \text{ hours}}{14 \text{ bags}} \times 84 \text{ bags} = \textbf{18 hours}$$

To use the proportion method, we can put either bags or hours in the numerator. We decide to put bags in the numerator this time.

$$\frac{B}{H} = \frac{B}{H}$$

On the left we use 14 for bags and 3 for hours. On the right we use 84 for bags. Then we solve.

$$\frac{14}{3} = \frac{84}{H} \qquad \text{substituted}$$
$$14H = 252 \qquad \text{cross multiplied}$$
$$H = 18 \qquad \text{divided both sides by 14}$$

Thus, it would take **18 hours** to fill eighty-four bags.

practice   **a.** Jimmy could cap 60 bottles in 7 hours. How long would it take to cap 420 bottles? Work the problem once using rates. Then work the problem again using a proportion.

problem set 83

1. The ratio of the bumptious to the gracious was 7 to 3. If 1400 were bumptious, how
(66)   many were gracious?

2. The visiting team attracted only $\frac{3}{11}$ of the fans that the home team attracted. If the
(62)   visitors attracted 2202 fans, how many did the home team attract?

3. Five hours were allotted for the trip. If Apollonia's top speed was 77 miles per hour,
(58)   how far could she go in the time allotted?

4. There was not enough food to go around because gate-crashers swelled the total
(57)   attendance to $2\frac{1}{2}$ times the number of people expected. If 1200 attended, how many
people had been expected?

5. Over Labor Day weekend gas prices increased 20%. If gas was $1.25 per gallon before
(80)   the weekend, how much was it during Labor Day weekend?

6. Li sneezed 23 times in 8 hours. If he keeps this up, how many times will he sneeze in
(83)   24 hours? Use both the rate and proportion methods to solve the problem.

7. Graph on a number line: $x > -2$
(72)

8. Two hundred forty is 240% of what number?
(77)

9. What percent of 60 is 105?
(77)

10. Complete the table. Begin by inserting
(55,77)   the reference numbers.

Fraction	Decimal	Percent
(a)	2.45	(b)

11. Write 9.1×10^{-11} in standard notation.
(50)

12. Find the volume in cubic centimeters of a right solid whose base is shown on the left
(45) and whose sides are 2 meters tall. Dimensions are in centimeters.

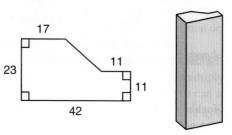

13. What is the surface area of a rectangular solid whose length, width, and height are
(49) 5 meters, 10 meters, and 3 meters respectively?

Solve:

14. $\dfrac{6\frac{1}{4}}{2\frac{1}{3}} = \dfrac{\frac{5}{12}}{x}$
(65)

15. $2\frac{1}{2}x + 2\frac{1}{2} = 6\frac{3}{8}$
(61)

16. Find p.
(65)

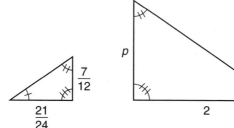

Simplify:

17. $\left(2 \times 10^{-14}\right) \times \left(3 \times 10^{-13}\right)$
(76)

18. $2^3 + \sqrt{36}\left[2^3(2^2 - 1)(5^2 - 22) - 1\right]$
(44)

19. (a) $(3)(-2)$ (b) $(-3)(2)$ (c) $(-3)(-2)$
(81)

20. (a) $\dfrac{12}{-4}$ (b) $\dfrac{-12}{4}$ (c) $\dfrac{-12}{-4}$
(81)

21. $-2 + 3 - 6 + -2 - 5$
(69)

22. $(-2)(-1)(-1)(-1)(3)(-1)(-1)(-4)$
(81)

23. $-\left[-\left(-\left\{-\left[-(-69)\right]\right\}\right)\right]$
(78)

24. 1.218×0.0016
(7)

25. $16\frac{2}{7} - 2\frac{1}{2} \cdot 1\frac{1}{7} + \dfrac{9}{14}$
(46)

26. $\dfrac{1}{3}\left(1\frac{1}{4} \cdot \dfrac{7}{8} - \dfrac{1}{4}\right) + \dfrac{17}{32}$
(52)

Evaluate:

27. $xy + x^y + y^x + \sqrt{x}$ if $x = 4$ and $y = 2$
(54)

28. $ab - a - b$ if $a = 10$ and $b = -2$
(82)

29. $\dfrac{c}{d} + c - d$ if $c = -12$ and $d = -4$
(82)

30. $\dfrac{xz}{y} + y$ if $x = 4$, $y = -6$, and $z = 3$
(82)

LESSON 84 *Formats for the Addition Rule • Negative Coefficients • Properties of Equality*

84.A
formats for the addition rule

The addition rule for equations tells us we can add the same number to both sides of an equation. The number can be a positive number or a negative number.

> ADDITION RULE FOR EQUATIONS
>
> The same quantity can be added to both sides of an equation without changing the solution to the equation.

To solve this equation

$$x + 2 = 6$$

we can add –2 to both sides of the equation.

$$x + 2 + (-2) = 6 + (-2)$$

We have been working problems like this by subtracting 2 from both sides. Now we say that we are adding –2 instead of subtracting +2. We simplify and get

$$x = 4$$

The rule does not say that the –2's have to be on the same line. If we like, we can use another format and write

$$
\begin{array}{ll}
x + 2 = 6 & \text{equation} \\
\underline{-2 \quad -2} & \text{added } -2 \text{ to both sides} \\
x \quad\ = 4 & \text{simplified}
\end{array}
$$

example 84.1 Use the new format and algebraic addition to solve:

$$x + 5 = 7$$

solution We will solve by adding –5 to both sides.

$$
\begin{array}{ll}
x + 5 = 7 & \text{equation} \\
\underline{-5 \quad -5} & \text{added } -5 \text{ to both sides} \\
x \quad\ = \mathbf{2} & \text{simplified}
\end{array}
$$

example 84.2 Solve: $2x + \dfrac{1}{2} = \dfrac{3}{4}$

solution First we add $-\frac{1}{2}$ to both sides.

$$
\begin{array}{ll}
2x + \dfrac{1}{2} = \dfrac{3}{4} & \text{equation} \\[2mm]
\underline{\quad -\dfrac{1}{2} \quad\ -\dfrac{1}{2}\quad} & \text{added } -\dfrac{1}{2} \text{ to both sides} \\[2mm]
2x \quad\ = \dfrac{1}{4} & \text{simplified} \\[2mm]
\dfrac{1}{2} \cdot 2x = \dfrac{1}{4} \cdot \dfrac{1}{2} & \text{multiplied both sides by } \dfrac{1}{2} \\[2mm]
x = \mathbf{\dfrac{1}{8}} & \text{simplified}
\end{array}
$$

84.B

negative coefficients

Often we encounter variables with negative coefficients. In the following equation, the coefficient of x is –2:

$$-2x = 4$$

This equation can be solved by dividing both sides by –2.

$$\frac{-2x}{-2} = \frac{4}{-2}$$
$$x = -2$$

example 84.3 Solve: $-3x = -12$

solution Solve by dividing by –3.

$$\frac{-3x}{-3} = \frac{-12}{-3} \qquad \text{divided both sides by –3}$$
$$x = \mathbf{4} \qquad \text{simplified}$$

example 84.4 Solve: $-3x + 4 = 10$

solution We use the addition rule first. Thus, we begin by adding –4 to both sides.

$$\begin{array}{rl} -3x + 4 = 10 & \text{equation} \\ \underline{-4 \quad -4} & \text{added –4 to both sides} \\ -3x \quad = 6 & \text{simplified} \end{array}$$

Now we divide by –3 and solve.

$$\frac{-3x}{-3} = \frac{6}{-3} \qquad \text{divided both sides by –3}$$
$$x = \mathbf{-2} \qquad \text{simplified}$$

84.C

properties of equality

The properties of equality are rules we use to solve algebraic equations.

PROPERTIES OF EQUALITY
Addition Property of Equality: If $a = b$, then $a + c = b + c$.
Subtraction Property of Equality: If $a = b$, then $a - c = b - c$.
Multiplication Property of Equality: If $a = b$, then $ac = bc$.
Division Property of Equality: If $a = b$, then $\frac{a}{c} = \frac{b}{c}$ (if $c \neq 0$).

These properties say we can add, subtract, multiply, or divide both sides of an equation by any number (except zero, when dividing).

example 84.5 Which property of equality do we use in solving $x - 4 = 9$?

solution We use the **Addition Property of Equality,** since we must add 4 to each side of the equation to solve.

practice Solve:

a. $-2x + 5 = 9$

b. $-3x + \dfrac{1}{2} = \dfrac{3}{8}$

c. Which two properties of equality justify the steps you used to solve problem a. above?

problem set 84

1. Between 1965 and 2003 the number of school-age children will increase 225 percent.
(80) If there were 10,000,000 school-age children in 1965, how many will there be in 2003?

2. The ratio of the loquacious to the taciturn was 9 to 5. If 25,000 were taciturn, how many
(66) were loquacious?

3. Only two thirds of the philosophers were peripatetic. If 49 philosophers were not
(62) peripatetic, how many philosophers were there in all?

4. Thunderheads rolled across the plains at 20 miles per hour. At the beginning of the third
(63) hour, the storm's speed quadrupled. If it covered 600 miles in all, how many hours did
it take for the storm to cover that distance?

5. Graph on a number line: $x \geq -7$
(72)

6. The old man caught 17 fish in three weeks. How many could he be expected to catch
(75) in 24 weeks at the same rate?

7. Ninety is 225 percent of what number?
(77)

8. Six and one fourth of what number is $8\frac{4}{7}$?
(57)

9. Graph the following points on a rectangular coordinate system:
(38)
   (a) $(-1, 5)$ (b) $(5, 2)$ (c) $(-5, -3)$ (d) $(3, -1)$

10. Simplify: $\left(2 \times 10^{-14}\right) \times \left(2 \times 10^{-6}\right)$
(76)

11. Find the volume of a right solid whose base is shown on the left and whose sides are 4
(64) feet tall. Dimensions are in feet.

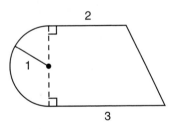
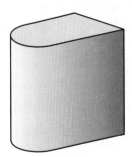

12. Find the volume and surface area of
(73) the right circular cylinder shown.
Dimensions are in centimeters.

Solve:

13. $6a + 15 = 33$
(61)

14. $7\frac{1}{2}m + 2\frac{1}{3} = 9\frac{5}{6}$
(61)

15. $\dfrac{3\frac{1}{2}}{2\frac{1}{5}} = \dfrac{\frac{1}{4}}{p}$
(65)

16. $\dfrac{\frac{2}{3}}{\frac{1}{7}} = \dfrac{s}{21}$
(59)

17. $-5x - 3 = 12$
(84)

18. $-2x + \frac{1}{2} = 8\frac{1}{2}$
(84)

19. Which two properties of equality justify the steps you used to solve problem 18?
(84)

Simplify:

20. $3^3 + \sqrt{144}\left[4^2(3^2 - 8)(5^2 - \sqrt{225}) + (-110)\right]$
(44)

21. (a) $(4)(-5)$ (b) $(-4)(5)$ (c) $(-4)(-5)$
(81)

22. $-(+9) - 12 + 16 - -(-1)$ **23.** $-\left(-\left\{-\left[-(-2.54)\right]\right\}\right)$
(79)   *(78)*

24. $\dfrac{17.658}{0.009}$ **25.** $11\frac{1}{4} - 3\frac{2}{3} \cdot 1\frac{1}{5} + \sqrt{\dfrac{4}{121}}$
(7)   *(46,71)*

26. $\dfrac{1}{4}\left(\dfrac{1}{2} \cdot \dfrac{1}{8} - \dfrac{1}{3}\right) + \dfrac{11}{24}$
(52)

27. What is the mean of $\frac{1}{4}$, $\frac{3}{20}$, $\frac{7}{25}$, and $1\frac{1}{2}$?
(26)

Evaluate:

28. $p^x + \sqrt[m]{x}$ if $m = 3$, $p = 2$, and $x = 8$
(54)

29. $ab - \dfrac{b}{ab}$ if $a = -2$ and $b = 5$
(82)

30. $x - xy + \dfrac{y}{x}$ if $x = -2$ and $y = 6$
(82)

LESSON 85   *Equation of a Line • Graphing a Line*

85.A

equation of a line

If we have an equation with one unknown, the solution to the equation is the value of the variable that will make the equation a true equation. The solution to the equation

$$x + 2 = 5$$

is 3 because if we use 3 for x we get a true equation.

$$(3) + 2 = 5$$
$$5 = 5 \qquad \text{true}$$

If an equation has two variables, the solutions to the equation are pairs of values that make the equation a true equation. The equation

$$y = x + 2$$

is a true equation if we use 5 for y and 3 for x.

$$(5) = (3) + 2$$
$$5 = 5 \qquad \text{true}$$

It is also a true equation if we use 9 for y and 7 for x.

$$(9) = (7) + 2$$
$$9 = 9 \qquad \text{true}$$

There are many pairs of x and y that make this equation a true equation. If we plot these values of x and y on a rectangular coordinate plane, we find that the points they describe form a straight line. When we use points to draw a line, we say we are **graphing** the line.

85.B

graphing a line   It takes only two points to determine a line, but since this is an introduction we will use three points.

example 85.1   Graph the line $y = x - 2$.

solution   To find points that lie on the line we choose values of x and use the equation to find the corresponding values of y. First we make a chart.

x	y

Then we choose values for x and put them in the first column. The numbers 0, 2, and 4 will make calculations easy using the given equation for the line.

x	y
0	
2	
4	

Then we use these values for x in the equation and solve for y.

Using 0 for x: $y = (0) - 2 = -2$
Using 2 for x: $y = (2) - 2 = 0$
Using 4 for x: $y = (4) - 2 = 2$

Now we place the values for y in the second column of the chart.

x	y
0	-2
2	0
4	2

Now we graph the points $(0, -2)$, $(2, 0)$, and $(4, 2)$ and draw a line through the points.

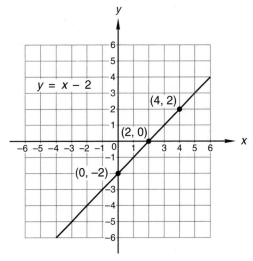

This is the graph of $y = x - 2$.

practice   **a.**   Sketch a rectangular coordinate system, and graph the line $y = x - 3$. Choose 0, 3, and –3 for x-values.

problem set
85

1.   The Braves started the season by hitting 1.375 times their season average for the
(51)   previous year. If their season average for the previous year was .368, what was their beginning average this season?

2.   The website received 102 hits in 3 hours. How many hours will it take for the website
(83)   to receive 612 hits at the same rate? Use both the rate and proportion methods to solve the problem.

3.   For 4 hours Sam traveled at 40 miles per hour. Then he increased his speed to 60 miles
(63)   per hour and drove for another 3 hours. How far did he go in the 7 hours he traveled?

4.   Only a vestige of the original remained. The vestige weighed 14 ounces and
(62)   represented one thirty-fifth $\left(\frac{1}{35}\right)$ of the original. What did the original weigh?

5.   The sales tax in Indiana is 5%. How much sales tax is paid on a $21 shirt?
(68)

6.   Graph on a number line: $x \leq 2$
(72)

7.   What number is 160 percent of 120?
(77)

8.   If 220 is increased by 120 percent, what is the resulting number?
(80)

9.   What percent of 50 is 125?
(77)

10.   What decimal part of 800 is 280?
(51)

11.   Find the volume of a right solid whose
(45)   base is shown on the left and whose sides are 150 centimeters tall. Dimensions are in centimeters.

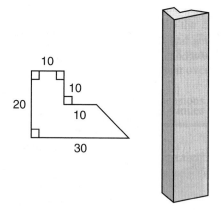

12.   What is the perimeter of the figure
(64)   shown? Dimensions are in yards.

Sketch a rectangular coordinate system, and graph the lines:

13. $y = x + 4$ Let x be –2, –1, and 0.   **14.** $y = 2x - 1$ Let x be –2, 0, and 1.
(85)   (85)

Solve:

15. $\dfrac{7\frac{1}{4}}{2\frac{1}{2}} = \dfrac{\frac{1}{6}}{x}$ **16.** $\dfrac{\frac{3}{4}}{\frac{9}{16}} = \dfrac{z}{6}$
(65)   (59)

17. $3\frac{1}{5}x + 2\frac{1}{3} = 5\frac{2}{5}$
(61)

18. $-5x - 18 = 32$
(84)

19. $5 - 2x = -7$
(84)

20. Which two properties of equality justify the steps you used to solve problem 18?
(84)

Simplify:

21. $3^2 + 2^3\left[\sqrt{36}(2^2 - 3)(2^2 + 1) - 20\right]$
(44)

22. (a) $\dfrac{24}{-6}$ (b) $\dfrac{-24}{6}$ (c) $\dfrac{-24}{-6}$
(81)

23. $-\left(-\left\{-[-(-9)]\right\}\right)$
(78)

24. $-5 - 4 - 2 + 6 + -3$
(69)

25. $-2 - 2 + -4 - 2$
(79)

26. $3\frac{3}{7} - 1\frac{1}{7} \cdot 3\frac{1}{3} + \frac{8}{21}$
(46)

27. $\left(3 \times 10^{26}\right) \times \left(2 \times 10^{-9}\right)$
(76)

Evaluate:

28. $tv + t^v + v^t + v^2$ if $t = 3$ and $v = 3$
(54)

29. $s - sts$ if $s = -3$ and $t = 5$
(82)

30. $qr + r$ if $q = -0.5$ and $r = -6$
(82)

LESSON 86 *Algebraic Phrases*

This book is called *Algebra* $\frac{1}{2}$. What is algebra anyway? Here is the beginning of the answer to that question: algebra is the art of expressing problems with symbols and then solving the problems by manipulating those symbols in accordance with certain rules and techniques.

In algebra, we learn to write equations that have the same meanings as statements made with words. Then we find the solutions to the equations. These solutions give us the answers to the questions asked. When we write the equations, we use algebraic phrases. The algebraic phrases have the same meanings as the word phrases. There are several key words to look for when writing algebraic phrases. The word *sum* means things are added, as do the words *greater than* or *increased by.*

WORD PHRASE	ALGEBRAIC PHRASE
The sum of a number and 7	$N + 7$
The sum of a number and –7	$N + (-7)$
7 greater than a number	$N + 7$
A number increased by 7	$N + 7$

The words *less than* or *decreased by* mean to subtract (add the opposite of).

7 less than a number	$N - 7$
A number decreased by 7	$N - 7$

The word *product* means things are multiplied.

| The product of a number and 7 | $7N$ |

If we use N to represent an unknown number, then we will use $-N$ to represent the opposite of the unknown number. Thus, twice a number and 9 times the opposite of a number could be written as follows:

| Twice a number | $2N$ |
| 9 times the opposite of a number | $9(-N)$ |

Sometimes two or more operations are designated by a single phrase.

| The sum of twice a number and -8 | $2N + (-8)$ |
| 5 times the sum of twice a number and -8 | $5[2N + (-8)]$ |

Cover the answers in the right-hand column below and see if you can write the algebraic phrase that is indicated.

The sum of a number and 9	$N + 9$
A number decreased by 9	$N - 9$
The opposite of a number, decreased by 6	$-N - 6$
The sum of the opposite of a number and -3	$-N + (-3)$
The sum of twice a number and -3	$2N + (-3)$
The product of 5 times a number and 6	$6(5N)$
4 times the sum of twice a number and -3	$4[2N + (-3)]$
The product of -2 and the sum of a number and 5	$-2(N + 5)$

In the previous examples we used the letter N as our variable. Letters at the end of the alphabet, such as x, y, and z, are often used as variables, especially the letter x.

practice   Write the algebraic phrases that correspond to each statement.

a.   The sum of a number and -4

b.   A number reduced by 4

c.   The sum of the opposite of a number and -3

problem set   **1.**   Harry traveled the last 240 miles of the trip at 60 miles per hour. The entire trip covered
86   *(63)*   480 miles and took 10 hours. How fast did Harry travel for the first 240 miles?

2.   Forty tons cost \$20,000. How much would only 12 tons cost?
(75)

3.   The ratio of screaming fans in box seats to screaming fans in bleacher seats was 2 to
(66)   17. If 68,000 screamed in the bleachers, how many screaming fans were in box seats?

4.   One thousand, four hundred stockbrokers remained standing after the crash. If this was
(62)   one seventh of the total, how many stock brokers were no longer standing?

5.   There was a big sale at Insane Irving's Music Emporium! Everything, yes everything,
(68)   was discounted 20% off the already unbelievably low prices. (a) What was the discount
on a boom box that was already an incredibly low \$79? (b) What was the new
insane price?

6.
(86)
Express with an algebraic phrase:

(a) The opposite of one eighth of a number

(b) Seven times the sum of a number and 1

(c) The sum of three tenths of a number and 1

(d) Four less than a number

7.
(72)
Graph on a number line: $x > -1$

8.
(77)
What number is 140 percent of 140?

9.
(80)
If 230 is increased by 160 percent, what is the resulting number?

10.
(77)
What percent of 70 is 98?

11.
(55)
Complete the table. Begin by inserting the reference numbers.

Fraction	Decimal	Percent
$\frac{4}{5}$	(a)	(b)

12.
(51)
Six tenths of what number is 750?

13.
(64)
Find the volume of a right solid whose base is shown on the left and whose sides are 3 inches tall. Dimensions are in inches.

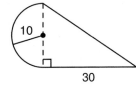

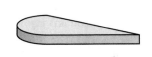

14.
(33)
Use two unit multipliers to convert 4 miles to inches.

15.
(28)
Write $\frac{1357}{12}$ as a mixed number.

16.
(85)
Sketch a coordinate plane, and graph the line $y = x + 4$. Let x be -4, 0, and 2.

Solve:

17.
(65)
$\dfrac{3\frac{3}{4}}{6\frac{3}{8}} = \dfrac{\frac{1}{4}}{x}$

18.
(61)
$2\frac{1}{3}x + 3\frac{1}{2} = 6\frac{1}{6}$

19.
(84)
$-7x + \dfrac{1}{4} = \dfrac{3}{2}$

20.
(84)
$11x - 3 = -58$

21.
(84)
Which two properties of equality justify the steps you used to solve problem 20?

Simplify:

22.
(76)
$(8 \times 10^{10}) \times (1 \times 10^{-10})$

23.
(71)
$3^2 + 2^2 \left[2^3 \left(\sqrt{36} - 2^2 \right) \left(1 + \sqrt{16} \right) - \sqrt[3]{\dfrac{27}{125}} \right]$

24.   (a) 3(–6)   (b) (–2)(–5)   (c) (–1)(+7)
(81)

25.   (–1)(–2)(–3)(–4)(+5)   **26.**   –6 – 3 + (–2) – (–3)
(81)   (79)

27.   Is the following product positive or negative? (–1)(–40)(–5)(44)(7)(–81)(84)(–747)(2)
(81)

Evaluate:

28.   –x – xy   if x = –2 and y = 4
(82)

29.   ay – a – y   if a = –7 and y = –3
(82)

30. $x^y + y^x + 2xy$ if x = 4 and y = 3
(54)

LESSON 87   *Properties of Algebra*

In Lesson 84 we looked at the properties of equality. In this lesson we discuss properties of numbers. The commutative property means that with both addition and multiplication we can change the order of the numbers, and the result is the same.

$$2 + 5 = 7 \qquad \text{and} \qquad 5 + 2 = 7$$
$$2 \cdot 5 = 10 \qquad \text{and} \qquad 5 \cdot 2 = 10$$

COMMUTATIVE PROPERTIES
$a + b = b + a \qquad ab = ba$

The associative property means that when more than two numbers are added or multiplied, we can group (or associate) any two first. So

$$2 + 3 + 4 = (2 + 3) + 4 = 5 + 4 = 9$$
$$\text{and}$$
$$2 + 3 + 4 = 2 + (3 + 4) = 2 + 7 = 9$$

And

$$2 \cdot 3 \cdot 4 = (2 \cdot 3) \cdot 4 = 6 \cdot 4 = 24$$
$$\text{and}$$
$$2 \cdot 3 \cdot 4 = 2 \cdot (3 \cdot 4) = 2 \cdot 12 = 24$$

ASSOCIATIVE PROPERTIES
$(a + b) + c = a + (b + c) \qquad (ab)c = a(bc)$

The reflexive property states the obvious fact that any number is equal to itself!

REFLEXIVE PROPERTY
$a = a$

The symmetric property means that we can change the order of an equation. We usually prefer to write the variable on the left. This property justifies rewriting

$$10 = x \quad \text{as} \quad x = 10$$

SYMMETRIC PROPERTY

If $a = b$, then $b = a$.

The transitive property means that if two things are equal to the same thing, they are equal to each other. If Steve and Sherri are the same age, and Sherri and Brooke are the same age, it is correct to conclude that Steve and Brooke are the same age.

TRANSITIVE PROPERTY

If $a = b$ and $b = c$, then $a = c$.

---

example 87.1 Use the commutative and associative properties to simplify: $87 + 49 + 13 + 51$

solution We notice it is easier to compute the sum $87 + 13$ than the sum $87 + 49$. So we change the order and group these two together. We also group 49 and 51 together.

$87 + 49 + 13 + 51$	problem
$87 + 13 + 49 + 51$	commutative property
$(87 + 13) + (49 + 51)$	associative property
$100 + 100$	simplified
200	simplified

practice **a.** Use the commutative and associative properties to simplify: $5 \cdot 25 \cdot 20 \cdot 4$

problem set 87

1.
(63)
Beatrice traveled the last 220 miles of the trip at 55 miles per hour. The entire trip covered 430 miles and took 7 hours. What was her rate for the first 210 miles?

2.
(75)
Fifty designer dresses cost $15,000. At the same rate, how much would 19 designer dresses cost?

3.
(66)
The ratio of masterpieces in the museum to reproductions in the shop was 2 to 120. If 228,000 reproductions were offered in the shop, how many masterpieces could be viewed in the museum?

4.
(62)
One thousand, one hundred drenched fans awaited the outcome of the final quarter. If this was one twentieth of the total number of fans who had come to the game, how many fans had come to the game?

5.
(83)
Jack could check the chemicals in 25 pools in 7 hours. How long would he take to check the chemicals in 275 pools? Use both the rate and proportion methods to solve the problem.

6.
(68)
A 30% tariff is added to the cost of motorcycles imported to Fredonia. (a) What is the tariff on a $9000 motorcycle? (b) What is the new cost with the added tariff?

7. Graph on a number line: $x \leq 1$
(72)

8. What number is 260 percent of 90?
(77)

9. If 650 is increased by 120 percent, what is the resulting number?
(80)

10. What percent of 90 is 144?
(77)

11. Express with an algebraic phrase:
(86)

(a) Half of a number

(b) Two times a number

(c) The product of a number and its opposite

(d) Two fifths of the square root of a number

12. Write this problem in scientific notation and solve: $20,000 \times 0.000004$
(50,76)

13. Three hundredths of what number is 9.3?
(51)

14. Use two unit multipliers to convert 10,000,000 square inches to square feet.
(33)

15. Find the volume of a right solid whose base is the figure shown on the left and whose
(45) sides are 2 meters tall. The upper and lower sides of the base are parallel. Dimensions are in meters.

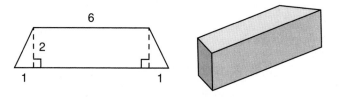

16. Find the volume in cubic yards of a right circular cylinder whose diameter measures
(73) 3 yards and whose height is 3 yards.

17. Sketch a rectangular coordinate system, and graph the line $y = -3x + 2$.
(85) Let x be -1, 0, and 1.

18. Use the commutative and associative properties to simplify: $\dfrac{2}{3} \cdot \dfrac{1}{5} \cdot \dfrac{3}{2} \cdot 5$
(87)

Solve:

19. $-9x + 11 = -92$
(84)

20. $-\dfrac{1}{4}x - 7 = -\dfrac{7}{2}$
(84)

21. $\dfrac{4\frac{1}{5}}{3\frac{1}{2}} = \dfrac{1\frac{1}{8}}{x}$
(65)

22. $\dfrac{\frac{6}{7}}{\frac{54}{42}} = \dfrac{\frac{2}{3}}{x}$
(59)

23. $8\dfrac{3}{14}x + 1\dfrac{1}{5} = 1\dfrac{1}{30}$
(61)

Simplify:

24. $2^3 + 2^2\left[2^1\left(\sqrt{64} - 7\right)\left(1 + 3^2\right) + (-3)\right]$
(44)

25. (a) $\dfrac{27}{-9}$ (b) $\dfrac{-27}{9}$ (c) $\dfrac{-27}{-9}$
(81)

26. $-\left(-\left\{-\left[-(-4)\right]\right\}\right)$
(78)

Evaluate:

27. $x + xy$ if $x = -1$ and $y = -9$
(82)

28. $-m - mx$ if $m = -2$ and $x = -3$
(82)

29. $ap - p + a$ if $a = -4$ and $p = -3$
(82)

30. Use a single unit multiplier to convert 0.6 centimeters to meters.
(24)

LESSON 88   *Surface Area of a Right Solid*

Remember that a right solid is a solid whose sides are perpendicular to the top and bottom. Until now, we have concentrated on finding the surface area of right circular cylinders and right triangular solids. We have also noted that the lateral surface area of a right circular cylinder can be computed by cutting the cylinder lengthwise and unrolling it flat to make a rectangle.

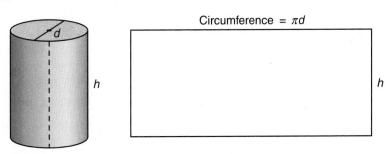

Circumference = πd

The lateral surface area of a right circular cylinder equals the height times the circumference. We can use this procedure to find the lateral surface area of any right solid.

example 88.1 Find the surface area of the right triangular solid shown. Dimensions are in meters.

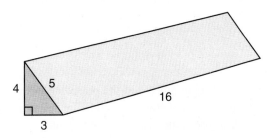

solution The total surface area equals the area of the two triangular ends plus the lateral surface area. **The lateral surface area equals the perimeter of the base times the height of the solid.**

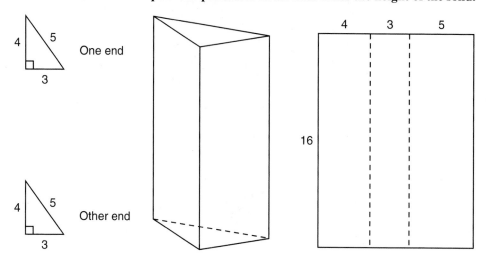

On the right-hand side of the previous diagram we cut the solid down one edge and unfolded it to find that it makes a rectangle. One side is the height, which is 16, and the other side is the perimeter of the base, which is $4 + 3 + 5$, or 12.

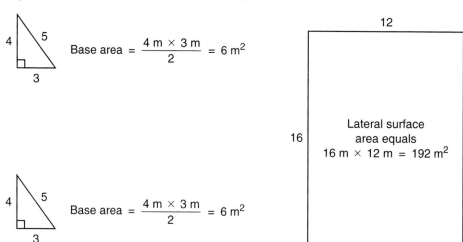

Thus,

$$\text{Total surface area} = 6\text{ m}^2 + 6\text{ m}^2 + 192\text{ m}^2 = \textbf{204 m}^2$$

example 88.2 Find the lateral surface area of a right solid 10 feet tall whose base is the figure shown on the left. Dimensions are in feet.

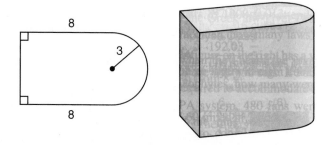

solution The thought process of the preceding example can be extended to help us find the lateral surface area of any right solid. The lateral surface area of a right solid equals the perimeter of the base times the height of the solid.

The perimeter is

$$8 \text{ ft} + 6 \text{ ft} + 8 \text{ ft} + \frac{\pi(6 \text{ ft})}{2} = 22 \text{ ft} + 3\pi \text{ ft}$$

If we use 3.14 for π, the perimeter is

$$22 \text{ ft} + (3 \text{ ft})(3.14) = 31.42 \text{ ft}$$

The lateral surface area equals the height times the perimeter of the base.

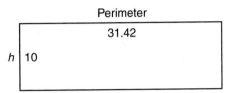

Perimeter

31.42

h | 10

$$\text{Lateral surface area} = 10 \text{ ft}(31.42 \text{ ft}) = \textbf{314.2 ft}^2$$

SURFACE AREA OF A RIGHT SOLID

L.A. = ph
S.A. = L.A. + 2B

L.A. = lateral surface area h = height of the solid
S.A. = total surface area B = area of the base
 p = perimeter of the base

---

practice   **a.** The figure shown on the left is the base of a right solid 40 meters tall. What is the lateral surface area of the right solid? Dimensions are in meters.

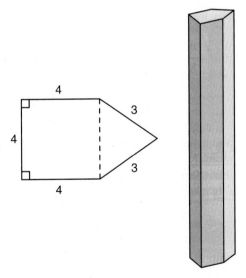

problem set   **1.** Wanataxa peered into the gloom and could positively identify only 2000. If there was
88   (62)   a total of 16,000 in the gloom, what fraction of the total did she identify?

2. The ratio of defective components to nondefective components was 2 to 19. If 380
(66)   components were nondefective, how many were defective?

3. The delegates crowded into the hall until they numbered $1\frac{1}{4}$ times the limit set by the
(57)   fire marshal. If the fire marshal's limit was 800, how many delegates were in the hall?

4. For the first 50 miles, Hannah traveled at 25 miles per hour. Then she doubled her
(63)   speed. If the entire trip was 450 miles, how long did the trip take?

5.
(41)   The average of the first 4 was 19, and the average of the next 9 was 22. What was the overall average, rounded to the nearest hundredth?

6.
(86)   Express with an algebraic phrase:

   (a) An even number

   (b) The next even number

   (c) Three halves of a number

   (d) The sum of $\frac{3}{2}$ of a number and 6

7.
(72)   Graph on a number line: $x \geq -2$

8.
(80)   If 160 is increased by 185 percent, what is the resulting number?

9.
(77)   What percent of 60 is 96?

10.
(55,77)   Complete the table. Begin by inserting the reference numbers.

Fraction	Decimal	Percent
(a)	(b)	250%

11.
(51)   What decimal part of 620 is 217?

12.
(88)   The figure shown on the left is the base of a right solid 7 cm tall. What is the lateral surface area of the right solid? Dimensions are in centimeters.

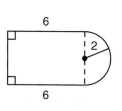 

13.
(88)   Find the total surface area of the right solid in problem 12.

14.
(45)   Express in cubic meters the volume of a solid whose base is shown on the left and whose sides are 10 centimeters tall. Dimensions are in meters.

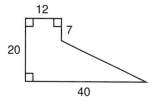 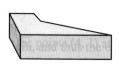

15.
(76)   Simplify: $\left(3 \times 10^{-11}\right) \times \left(2 \times 10^{15}\right)$

16.
(33)   Convert 1385.31 kilometers to centimeters.

17.
(85)   Sketch a rectangular coordinate system, and graph the line $y = -3x - 1$. Let x be -2, 0, and 1.

18.
(87)   Use the commutative and associative properties to simplify: $88 + 75 + 12 + 25$

Solve:

19. $-8x + 4 = 28$
(84)

20. $-2\frac{1}{4}x + \frac{1}{2} = 3\frac{3}{4}$
(84)

21. Find x.
(65)

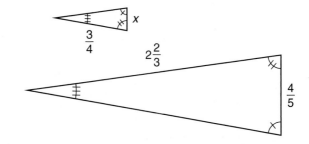

22. Which two of the properties of equality justify the steps you used to solve problem 19?
(84)

Simplify:

23. $2^3 + 2^2\left[2\left(\sqrt{49} - \sqrt{36}\right)\left(1 - \sqrt{9}\right) - \sqrt[3]{\frac{8}{64}}\right]$
(71)

24. $1\frac{3}{4} \cdot 2\frac{1}{3} - \frac{5}{12}$
(46)

25. $\frac{1}{2}\left(1\frac{2}{3} \cdot 1\frac{4}{5} - \frac{1}{2}\right) + \frac{5}{6}$
(52)

26. (a) $(4)(-2)$ (b) $\dfrac{16}{-2}$ (c) $(-6)(-2)$
(81)

27. $-\left(-\left\{-\left[-(5)\right]\right\}\right)$
(78)

28. Is the following product positive or negative? $(-242)(41)(-17)(-22)(4)(-7)(5)(-3)(-3)$
(81)

Evaluate:

29. $xyz + xy$ if $x = -1$, $y = -2$, and $z = -3$
(82)

30. $xy + y^x + x^x$ if $x = 2$ and $y = 3$
(54)

LESSON 89   *Trichotomy • Symbols of Negation*

89.A

trichotomy   We have discussed how we compare numbers by using the words *less than*, *equal to*, or *greater than*. Recall that we use the number line to define what we mean by these words. On this number line we have graphed the numbers -4, -2, 0, and 2.

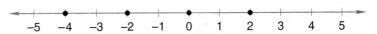

Remember that a number is greater than another number if its graph is to the right of the graph of the other number. By looking at the graphs above, we can verify that all of the following inequalities are true inequalities:

$$0 > -4 \qquad -2 < 0 \qquad 2 > -2 \qquad -4 < 2$$

It is interesting to note that if we have two numbers, then one and only one of the following statements is true:

TRICHOTOMY AXIOM

(a) The first number is greater than the second number. $a > b$

(b) The first number is equal to the second number. $a = b$

(c) The first number is less than the second number. $a < b$

Because there are only three possibilities, this is often called the **trichotomy axiom,** from the Greek word *tricha*, which means "in three parts."

89.B

symbols of negation

The symbols shown here

$$< \qquad > \qquad = \qquad \geq \qquad \leq$$

are used to denote that things are equal or not equal. We can negate each of these symbols by drawing a slash through the symbol. Thus, if we are asked to read the following inequalities:

(a) $4 \not< 1$ (b) $4 \neq 2 + 6$ (c) $7 \not\geq 10$

we can read them from left to right as

(a) $4 \not< 1$	4 is not less than 1	true
(b) $4 \neq 2 + 6$	4 is not equal to $2 + 6$	true
(c) $7 \not\geq 10$	7 is not greater than or equal to 10	true

Negated inequalities can also be false inequalities.

$-4 \not< 10$	-4 is not less than 10	false
$7 \not\geq 3$	7 is not greater than or equal to 3	false

When we graph conditional inequalities, we indicate the numbers that will make them true inequalities.

example 89.1   Graph on a number line: $x \not< 2$

solution   As the first step, we will rewrite the negated inequality. If x is not less than 2, then x must be greater than or equal to 2.

$$x \geq 2$$

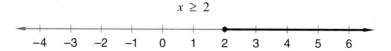

example 89.2   Graph on a number line: $x \not\geq -1$

solution   As the first step, we will rewrite the negated inequality. If x is not greater than or equal to -1, then x must be less than -1.

$$x < -1$$

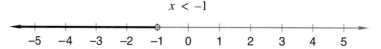

example 89.3   Graph on a number line: $x \not< -2$

solution   If x is not less than -2, then x must be greater than or equal to -2.

$$x \geq -2$$

Note that in this example, we used a solid circle at –2 because of the ≥ sign. In the preceding example, the circle at –1 was not solid because the inequality, <, did not contain part of an equals sign.

practice   Graph on a number line:

    a. $x \nleq -1$ **b.** $x \ngtr 2$ **c.** $x \ngeq 2$

problem set
89

1.
(75) Frances got the first 40 pictures framed for a total of $120. How much would it cost her to get 800 pictures framed at the same rate?

2.
(66) The ratio of roses to snapdragons was 4 to 5. If there were 26,000 roses on the float, how many snapdragons were there?

3.
(57) If $7\frac{4}{5}$ of the total came to 109,200, what was the total?

4.
(58) The last leg of the trip was traveled at 680 miles per hour. If the last leg took 10 hours to travel, what was the length of the last leg?

5.
(86) Write the algebraic phrase that is described:

    (a) The sum of twice a number and –16

    (b) The product of –3 and the sum of a number and 5

    (c) The opposite of a number, decreased by 4

    (d) Five times the sum of twice a number and 6

Graph on a number line:

6.
(89) $x \ngeq -1$

7.
(89) $x \nleq 4$

8.
(77) What number is 190 percent of 340?

9.
(80) If 200 is increased by 160 percent, what is the resulting number?

10.
(77) What percent of 80 is 128?

11.
(87) Use the commutative and associative properties to simplify: $\dfrac{1}{6} + \dfrac{3}{7} + \dfrac{5}{6} + 2\dfrac{4}{7}$

12.
(49) Find the surface area of a cube whose edges measure 0.25 centimeter.

13.
(88) The figure shown on the left is a base of a right solid 10 meters tall. What is the lateral surface area of the right solid? Dimensions are in meters.

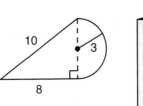 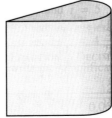

14.
(88) Find the total surface area of the right solid in problem 13.

15. Find the volume of a right solid whose base is shown on the left and whose sides are 2
(45) yards tall. Dimensions are in yards.

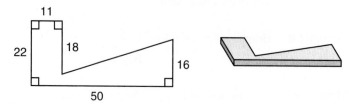

16. Use four unit multipliers to convert 612 square inches to square yards. Round to three
(33) decimal places.

17. There were 30 students in the class. Twenty percent ate the middle of their cookies first,
(68) while one third of the class preferred to dunk their cookies in their milk. How many
more dunkers than middle-eaters were there?

18. Sketch a rectangular coordinate system, and graph the line $y = -x - 2$. You must
(85) choose at least 2 values for x to graph it correctly.

Solve:

19. $-6x - 6 = -3$
(84)

20. $-7x - 3 = 12$
(84)

21. $\dfrac{3\frac{1}{3}}{6\frac{1}{2}} = \dfrac{\frac{4}{13}}{x}$
(65)

22. $-3\frac{1}{3}x + \frac{3}{4} = 2\frac{5}{12}$
(61)

23. Which two properties of equality justify the steps you used to solve problem 19?
(84)

Simplify:

24. $2^2 + 2^3\left[3(\sqrt{49} - \sqrt{36})(\sqrt{16} + \sqrt{4}) - \sqrt{9}\right] + \sqrt{81}$
(44)

25. $2\frac{2}{3} \cdot 3\frac{1}{4} - \frac{5}{12}$
(46)

26. (a) $(3)(-2)$
(81)
(b) $\dfrac{-6}{-3}$
(c) $(-1)(-1)$

27. $-\left(-\left\{-[-(+6)]\right\}\right)$
(78)

28. $-4 - (-3) + [-(-2)] - (+5) - 1$
(79)

Evaluate:

29. $yz - xz$ if $x = -1$, $y = 1$, and $z = 2$
(82)

30. $y^y + x^x + y^x + x^y$ if $x = 2$ and $y = 3$
(54)

LESSON *90*   *Algebraic Sentences*

An **algebraic sentence** is a group of mathematical symbols arranged to form an algebraic relationship. The symbol = functions much like the English verb *is*. Here are some examples of word sentences, and their algebraic translations.

WORD SENTENCE	ALGEBRAIC SENTENCE
A number is three.	$N = 3$
Five more than a number is nine.	$N + 5 = 9$
Twice a number is eleven.	$2N = 11$
One less than thrice a number is fourteen.	$3N - 1 = 14$
Six times a number, increased by five is seventeen.	$6N + 5 = 17$

We can solve algebraic sentences using the Properties of Equality taught in Lesson 84.

example 90.1   The sum of twice a number and 42 is 128. Find the number.

solution   The word *is* means *equals*. Thus, the sum of twice a number and 42 equals 128. We can rewrite this as $2N + 42 = 128$. Now we can solve for N.

$$
\begin{array}{ll}
2N + 42 = 128 & \text{equation} \\
\underline{ -42 \quad -42} & \text{added } -42 \text{ to both sides} \\
2N = 86 & \text{simplified} \\
\dfrac{2N}{2} = \dfrac{86}{2} & \text{divided both sides by 2} \\
N = 43 & \text{simplified}
\end{array}
$$

We will use 43 for N in the original equation to check.

$$
\begin{array}{rcl}
2N + 42 & = & 128 \\
2(43) + 42 & = & 128 \\
86 + 42 & = & 128 \\
128 & = & 128 \quad \text{check}
\end{array}
$$

So the number is **43.**

example 90.2   Twenty-seven less than the product of 3 and a number is 144. What is the number?

solution   If we use N for the number, then the product of 3 and the number is $3N$. We can translate the statement as $3N - 27 = 144$. Now we can solve for N.

$$
\begin{array}{ll}
3N - 27 = 144 & \text{equation} \\
\underline{ +27 \quad +27} & \text{added 27 to both sides} \\
3N = 171 & \text{simplified} \\
\dfrac{3N}{3} = \dfrac{171}{3} & \text{divided both sides by 3} \\
N = 57 & \text{simplified}
\end{array}
$$

We will use 57 for N in the original equation to check.

$$
\begin{array}{rcl}
3N - 27 & = & 144 \\
3(57) - 27 & = & 144 \\
171 - 27 & = & 144 \\
144 & = & 144 \quad \text{check}
\end{array}
$$

So the number is **57.**

example 90.3 Four more than the product of a number and 33 equals –95. What is the number?

solution First we write the equation. Then we solve.

$$33N + 4 = -95 \quad \text{equation}$$
$$\underline{ -4 \quad -4} \quad \text{added } -4 \text{ to both sides}$$
$$33N = -99 \quad \text{simplified}$$
$$N = -3 \quad \text{divided both sides by 33}$$

Now we use –3 for *N* in the original equation to check.

$$33N + 4 = -95$$
$$33(-3) + 4 = -95$$
$$-99 + 4 = -95$$
$$-95 = -95 \quad \text{check}$$

So the number is **–3.**

practice **a.** Express with an algebraic sentence: Five more than the product of six and a number is twenty-one.

b. Four more than the product of 9 and a number is –77. What is the number?

c. Five less than the product of 5 and a number is –55. What is the number?

problem set 90

1. Adrian purchased 20 ballet tickets for a total of $1110. How much would it have cost him for 150 ballet tickets? Solve using both the rate and proportion methods.
(83)

2. The ratio of *Sequoia gigantias* to *Sequoia semivirons* was 6 to 1. If there were 24,600 *Sequoia gigantias* in the forest, how many *Sequoia semivirons* were there?
(66)

3. Business improved by 260 percent this year. If the previous year's receipts totaled $240,000, what was the amount of this year's receipts?
(80)

4. The large aircraft traveled at 1140 miles per hour for the first 2 hours of the flight. For the next 6 hours it traveled at $1\frac{1}{2}$ times the original speed. What was the total distance covered?
(63)

5. Express with an algebraic phrase:
(86)
(a) The sum of 3 times a number and –11
(b) The product of –5 and the sum of a number and the opposite of 2
(c) The product of the opposite of 3 and the difference of a number and 4

6. Twice a number is eleven. What is the number?
(90)

7. One less than the product of three and a number is fourteen. What is the number?
(90)

8. Five more than the product of six and a number is seventeen. What is the number?
(90)

9. Graph on a number line: $x \not> 3$
(89)

10. What number is 270 percent of 250?
(77)

11. If 78 is increased by 150 percent, what is the resulting number?
(80)

12. What percent of 90 is 360?
(77)

13. Find the volume in cubic feet of a right solid whose base is shown on the left and whose
(64) sides are 4 feet tall. Dimensions are in feet.

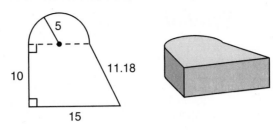

14. Find the lateral surface area of the right solid in problem 13.
(88)

15. Find the total surface area of the right solid in problem 13.
(88)

16. Simplify: $(1 \times 10^{20})(5 \times 10^{24})$
(76)

17. Use two unit multipliers to convert 0.75 square meters to square centimeters.
(33)

18. Seven tenths of what number is 9.1?
(51)

19. Use the commutative and associative properties to simplify: $\dfrac{11}{2} \cdot \dfrac{3}{7} \cdot 4 \cdot \dfrac{2}{11} \cdot \dfrac{7}{4}$
(87)

Solve:

20. $-5x - 4 = 16$
(84)

21. $-11x + 9 = 42$
(84)

22. $\dfrac{5\frac{1}{2}}{\frac{2}{3}} = \dfrac{3}{x}$
(65)

23. $-1\frac{1}{2}x + 2\frac{3}{5} = 4\frac{3}{10}$
(84)

Simplify:

24. $5^2 + 4^2\left[2\left(\sqrt{121} - \sqrt{81}\right)\right]$
(44)

25. $2\frac{1}{5} \cdot 1\frac{1}{2} - \dfrac{7}{10}$
(46)

26. (a) $(-5)(-3)$
(81)   (b) $\dfrac{14}{-2}$ (c) $\dfrac{-8}{-4}$

27. $2 - 5(2) - 4(-2) - 5(-3)$
(82)

Evaluate:

28. $km + m(-k)$ if $k = 3$ and $m = 9$
(82)

29. $-(km) - k(m)$ if $k = 5$ and $m = 3$
(82)

30. $a^b + bax + \sqrt[x]{a}$ if $a = 8$, $b = 2$, and $x = 3$
(54)

LESSON 91 Order of Operations with Signed Numbers and Symbols of Inclusion

If an expression involving signed numbers contains symbols of inclusion, we simplify within these symbols first, always beginning with the innermost symbols of inclusion. Within each pair of inclusion symbols, we always multiply before we add algebraically.

example 91.1 Simplify: $-2(-2 - 3 + 1) - [(-3 - 2) \cdot 4]$

solution We first simplify within the innermost parentheses.

$$-2(-4) - [(-5) \cdot 4]$$

Then we simplify within the brackets.

$$-2(-4) - [-20]$$

Now we multiply.

$$8 - [-20]$$

Then we add.

$$28$$

example 91.2 Simplify: $-2(-2 - 3 \cdot 5) - 2[(3 - 5)2 + 2]$

solution First we simplify within the innermost parentheses.

$$-2(-17) - 2[(-2)2 + 2]$$

Now we simplify within the brackets.

$$-2(-17) - 2[-2]$$

Now we multiply.

$$34 - [-4]$$

Then we add.

$$38$$

practice Simplify:

a. $-2(-3 - 5) - [6(-2 + 8) + 2]$

b. $4(3 - 2) - [3(-8 - 2) + 2]$

problem set 91

1.
(62) The stadium was empty. Then the gates were opened. Three eighths of the seats were filled by 21,000 people. How many seats were in the stadium?

2.
(75) Two computer programs used 230 megabytes of disk space. If all programs required an equal amount of space, how many megabytes of disk space would be required for 5 programs?

3.
(75) Forty of the expensive ones could be purchased for $28,000. What would 72 of the expensive ones cost?

4. After traveling the first 480 miles in 12 hours, the traveler increased her speed by
(63) 20 miles per hour. How long did it take her to travel the last 300 miles?

5. Four times the sum of 3 times a number and −6 is 12. What is the number?
(90)

6. Twenty-five decreased by thrice a number is 7. What is the number?
(90)

7. The difference when 25 is subtracted from the opposite of a number is 0. What is
(90) the number?

Graph on a number line:

8. $x \not< -9$ **9.** $x \not\geq -4$
(89)   (89)

10. If 250 is increased by 170 percent, what is the resulting number?
(80)

11. What percent of 90 is 72?
(68)

12. Convert to scientific notation and simplify: (300,000,000)(0.00000004)
(50,76)

13. Sketch a rectangular coordinate system, and graph the line $y = \frac{2}{3}x + 6$.
(85)

14. Express in cubic centimeters the volume of a right solid whose base is shown on the left
(45) and whose sides are 1 meter tall. Dimensions are in centimeters.

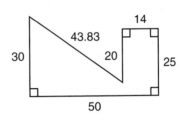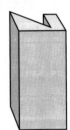

15. Find the lateral surface area of the solid in problem 14.
(88)

16. Use two unit multipliers to convert 2 miles to inches.
(33)

Solve:

17. $-2\frac{1}{3}x - \frac{3}{4} = 3\frac{7}{12}$
(84)

18. $-7x - 7 = -2$
(84)

19. State the properties of equality that justify the steps you used to solve problem 18.
(84)

20. Find x.
(65)

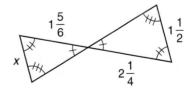

Simplify:

21. $2^3 + 2^2\left[3\left(\sqrt{64} - \sqrt{49}\right)\left(\sqrt[3]{8} + 1\right) - 1\right]$
(44)

22. (a) $2(-3)$ (b) $\dfrac{-12}{-3}$ (c) $(-1)(-2)(3)$
(81)

23. $-2(-3) + 3[(-2)(-4) - (-2)]$
(91)

24. $\frac{1}{2}[(-2)(3) - (-2)(-4)] - 3(-2) - 1$
(91)

25. $(7 - 2 \cdot 2) - 3[(11 - 2) + 3]$
(91)

26. $\frac{1}{2}\left(3\frac{2}{5} \cdot \frac{3}{4} - 1\frac{1}{4}\right)$ **27.** $3\frac{1}{2} \times 2\frac{1}{3} \div \frac{5}{6} \times \frac{1}{3}$
(52)   (43)

Evaluate:

28. $-xy + y$ if $x = -2$ and $y = -3$
(82)

29. $xy + yz + xz$ if $x = -1$, $y = -2$, and $z = -3$
(82)

30. Use the commutative and associative properties to simplify: $6.8 + 4.91 + 5.2 + 1.39$
(87)

LESSON 92 *Estimating Roots*

The roots we have evaluated so far have been whole numbers or ratios of whole numbers, such as

$$\sqrt{9} = 3 \qquad \sqrt{\frac{4}{9}} = \frac{2}{3} \qquad \sqrt[3]{27} = 3 \qquad \sqrt[4]{16} = 2$$

But what about a number like $\sqrt{10}$? It must be a little more than 3, since $3^2 = 9$. It must be less than 4, since $4^2 = 16$. We could write 3 is less than $\sqrt{10}$ which is less than 4 as

$$3 < \sqrt{10} < 4$$

Through trial and error we can better our estimate.

Is $\sqrt{10}$ equal to 3.1?

$$3.1^2 = 9.61 \qquad \text{too low}$$

Is $\sqrt{10}$ equal to 3.2?

$$3.2^2 = 10.24 \qquad \text{too high}$$

So now we know

$$3.1 < \sqrt{10} < 3.2$$

An estimating process like this could go on forever!

When we write "$\sqrt{10}$" we mean "the number that, multiplied by itself, equals 10." We should be able to estimate roots to the nearest integer. Some clever techniques have been devised for efficiently finding more accurate estimates, and all scientific calculators have a key for approximating roots to several decimal places. Your teacher may encourage you to follow such approaches to roots later, but the first step is to be able to determine the consecutive integers that a root is between.

example 92.1   Between which two consecutive integers is $\sqrt{69}$?

solution $8^2 = 64 \qquad 9^2 = 81 \qquad$ So $\mathbf{8 < \sqrt{69} < 9}$

example 92.2   Between which two consecutive integers is $\sqrt[3]{250}$?

solution   We are seeking a number R such that $R \cdot R \cdot R = 250$.

> Let's try 4: $4 \cdot 4 \cdot 4 = 64$ too low
> Let's try 5: $5 \cdot 5 \cdot 5 = 125$ too low
> Let's try 6: $6 \cdot 6 \cdot 6 = 216$ too low
> Let's try 7: $7 \cdot 7 \cdot 7 = 343$ too high

So we know

$$6 < \sqrt[3]{250} < 7$$

example 92.3   Between which two consecutive integers is $\sqrt[4]{123}$?

solution   We are seeking a number R such that $R \cdot R \cdot R \cdot R = 123$.

> Let's try 3: $3^4 = 81$ too low
> Let's try 4: $4^4 = 256$ too high

So we can conclude

$$3 < \sqrt[4]{123} < 4$$

practice   Between which two consecutive integers are the following roots found:

    a. $\sqrt{30}$ **b.** $\sqrt[3]{30}$

problem set 92

1.
(90)   The sum of twice a number and 42 is 126. Find the number.

2.
(90)   Twenty less than thrice a number is 223. What is the number?

3.
(90)   Four more than the product of 33 and a number equals –260. What is the number?

4.
(63)   For the first 20 miles, the stagecoach crawled along at 4 miles per hour. When the robbers were sighted, the speed was quadrupled. How long did it take to travel the last 80 miles at the new speed?

Graph on a number line:

5. $x \nleq 3$
(89)

6. $x \ngtr -2$
(89)

7.
(87)   Simplify using the commutative and associative properties: $11 + 48 + 62 + 109$

8.
(77)   What number is 225 percent of 140?

9.
(92)   Between which two consecutive integers is $\sqrt{56}$?

10.
(92)   Between which two consecutive integers is $\sqrt{108}$?

11.
(80)   There were 20 in the club and 5 more joined. What percent increase is this? What percent of the old membership is the new membership? What percent of the new membership was the old membership?

12.
(67)   Joe's Mack brand was $1.20 for an 8 oz jar, while a 9.5 oz jar of El Primo Deluxe cost $1.52. Which should the thrifty shopper buy?

13.
(85)   Sketch a rectangular coordinate system, and graph the line $y = 2x + 2$.

14. Find the volume in cubic meters of a solid whose base is shown on the left and whose
(64)   sides are 250 centimeters tall. Dimensions are in meters.

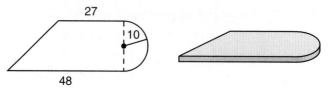

15. Find the volume of a rectangular solid whose length, width, and height measure
(45)   12 inches, 10 inches, and 3 inches respectively.

16. Find the lateral surface area of the rectangular solid in problem 15.
(88)

Solve:

17. $-2x + 6 = 1$
(84)

18. $-3\frac{1}{3}x - \frac{1}{4} = 6\frac{1}{2}$
(84)

19. $\dfrac{3\frac{1}{6}}{2\frac{1}{3}} = \dfrac{\frac{1}{2}}{x}$
(65)

20. Which properties of equality justify the solution of problem 17?
(84)

Simplify:

21. $2^2 + 2\left[\sqrt{9}\left(2^3 - 2 \cdot 3\right)\left(3^2 - 4 \cdot 2\right)\right]$
(44)

22. (a) $3(-2)$ (b) $\dfrac{-18}{3}$ (c) $(-2)(-2)(5)$
(81)

23. $-4[-(-3) - (-4)] + 6 - (-5)$
(91)

24. $-3(-4 - 1) + 2 - 3(6 - 4)$
(91)

25. $-[-(-2)] - (-1) - 5 + \left(\sqrt[3]{\dfrac{64}{27}}\right)$
(71,91)

26. $\dfrac{1}{3}\left(2\frac{1}{4} \cdot 1\frac{1}{5} - \dfrac{17}{20}\right)$
(52)

27. $4\frac{1}{3} \div 1\frac{2}{3} \times 2\frac{3}{4} \div \frac{1}{4}$
(43)

Evaluate:

28. $xy + yz$ if $x = -1$, $y = -2$, and $z = -3$
(82)

29. $zy - zx$ if $x = -2$, $y = -3$, and $z = -1$
(82)

30. $x^2 + y^2 + 2xy$ if $x = 2$ and $y = 3$
(47)

LESSON 93   *Fraction Bars as Symbols of Inclusion*

Let's simplify an order of operations problem that includes division.

$$(5 \cdot 4) \div (2 \cdot 4 + 2)$$

We begin by simplifying within parentheses.

$$(20) \div (8 + 2) \qquad \text{multiplied 5 by 4 and 2 by 4}$$
$$(20) \div (10) \qquad \text{added 8 and 2}$$

We conclude by dividing 20 by 10.

$$(20) \div (10) = 2$$

This problem may be formatted in another way. We can use a fraction bar (division bar) to indicate the division. So

$$(5 \cdot 4) \div (2 \cdot 4 + 2) \quad \text{and} \quad \frac{5 \cdot 4}{2 \cdot 4 + 2}$$

both indicate that $(5 \cdot 4)$ is to be divided by $(2 \cdot 4 + 2)$. Thus, a fraction bar functions as a symbol of inclusion. We simplify above and below the fraction bar before we divide. We follow the order of operations within the symbol of inclusion. As a review, here is the order of operations.

ORDER OF OPERATIONS

1. Simplify within the symbols of inclusion.
2. Simplify exponents and roots.
3. Multiply and divide in order from left to right.
4. Add and subtract in order from left to right.

---

example 93.1   Simplify: $\dfrac{4 - (3 - 7) + 3 \cdot 2 + 6}{2(-4 - 1)}$

solution   We will simplify above and below the fraction bar and will divide as the last step.

$$\frac{4 - (-4) + 3 \cdot 2 + 6}{2(-5)} \qquad \text{simplified within parentheses}$$

$$\frac{4 - (-4) + 6 + 6}{-10} \qquad \text{multiplied}$$

$$\frac{20}{-10} \qquad \text{added}$$

$$-2 \qquad \text{divided}$$

example 93.2   Simplify: $\dfrac{6(-4 + 3) - (-2 - 6)(2)}{3(2 - 4)}$

solution   Again, we simplify above and below the fraction bar.

$$\frac{6(-1) - (-8)(2)}{3(-2)} \qquad \text{simplified within parentheses}$$

$$\frac{-6 - (-16)}{-6} \qquad \text{multiplied}$$

$$\frac{10}{-6} \qquad \text{added}$$

$$-\frac{5}{3} \qquad \text{reduced}$$

We leave the answer as an improper fraction.

practice   a.   Simplify: $\dfrac{6 - (2 - 5) + 4 \cdot 2 + 3}{2(-1 - 1)}$

problem set 93

1. The product of a number and 15 is increased by 4. The result is 49. What is the number?
(90)

2. Fifteen less than the product of 10 and a number is −105. What is the number?
(90)

3.
(90) Hartzler multiplied his magic number by 14. Then he added 8. The result was 50. What was Hartzler's magic number?

4.
(66) The ratio of straights to bents was $2\frac{1}{2}$ to 3. If 300 were bent, how many were straight?

5.
(72) Graph on a number line: $x > 1$

6.
(87) Use the commutative and associative properties to simplify: $\dfrac{2}{3} \cdot 50 \cdot 48 \cdot \dfrac{2}{5}$

7.
(77) What number is 230 percent of 350?

8.
(80) If 200 is increased by 130 percent, what is the resulting number?

9.
(68) There were 1200 cowboys in El Paso. Thirty-six of them were rangy, sixty of them were lanky, and fifty-four were gamey. What percent of the cowboys were rangy, what percent were lanky, and what percent were gamey?

10.
(92) Between which two consecutive integers is $\sqrt[4]{82}$?

11.
(55) Complete the table. Begin by inserting the reference numbers.

Fraction	Decimal	Percent
(a)	0.36	(b)

12.
(73) Find the surface area in square inches of a right circular cylinder with a diameter of 1 foot and a height of 1 foot.

13.
(45) Find the volume of a solid whose base is shown on the left and whose sides are 2 yards tall. Dimensions are in yards.

14.
(88) Find the lateral surface area of the solid in problem 13.

15.
(24) Use one unit multiplier to convert 1234.8792 meters to kilometers.

Solve:

16.
(84) $-3x - 10 = -1$

17.
(65) $\dfrac{3\frac{1}{3}}{2\frac{1}{4}} = \dfrac{1\frac{1}{2}}{x}$

18.
(84) $-3\frac{1}{4}x - \dfrac{3}{8} = 4\frac{1}{2}$

Simplify:

19.
(44) $2^3 + 2^3\left[2^2\left(\sqrt{16} - \sqrt{9}\right)\left(\sqrt{9} + 2^2\right)\right]$

20.
(91) $-2(-2 - 3 \cdot 5) - \left[2(3 - 5) + 2\right]$

21.
(91) $-3(-2 - 6 \cdot 2) - \left[4(2 - 4) - 2\right]$

22.
(93) $\dfrac{5\left[(6 - 3) + 2\right] - 1}{2(5 - 1)}$

23. $\dfrac{2(-1 - 6) + 4(2 - 5)}{3(-1 - 3)}$
$_{(93)}$

24. $\dfrac{(7 + 3)(-7 + 3)}{-3\big[(11 - 2) + 5\big]}$
$_{(93)}$

25. $\dfrac{1}{3}\left(2\dfrac{1}{4} \cdot \dfrac{2}{3} - \dfrac{1}{6} \cdot \dfrac{1}{2}\right)$
$_{(52)}$

26. $2\dfrac{1}{3} \times 1\dfrac{1}{4} \div \dfrac{3}{8} \div \dfrac{1}{2}$
$_{(43)}$

27. Sketch a rectangular coordinate system, and graph the line $y = x + 3$.
$_{(69,85)}$

Evaluate:

28. $yy - xy$ if $x = -1$ and $y = -2$
$_{(82)}$

29. $abc + ab$ if $a = -2$, $b = -1$, and $c = 3$
$_{(82)}$

30. $a^2 + b^2 + c^2 + 2ab$ if $a = 1$, $b = 2$, and $c = 3$
$_{(47)}$

LESSON 94   *Terms • Adding Like Terms, Part 1*

94.A

terms The terms of an algebraic expression are separated by plus and minus signs. This expression has six terms.

$$x + 2y + 3x + 5 - 7y - 2$$

We can simplify this expression by combining the x terms, the y terms, and the numbers. If we do this, we get an expression with three terms.

$$4x - 5y + 3$$

The first term in this expression is $+4x$, and the second term is $-5y$. The third term is $+3$. It is not necessary for a term to have a factor that is a variable. A term that does not contain a variable is often called a **constant term,** because its value does not change.

94.B

adding like terms, part 1 We know that multiplication is shorthand for repeated addition. If we write

$$(5 + 5 + 5 + 5) + (5 + 5 + 5) + 4 + 2$$

we could combine the 5's and write

$$4(\text{fives}) + 3(\text{fives}) + 4(\text{ones}) + 2(\text{ones})$$

We know 4 fives $+ 3$ fives is 7 fives and 4 ones $+ 2$ ones is 6 ones.

$$7(\text{fives}) + 6(\text{ones})$$

We can make no further simplifications by combining like numbers because 5 and 1 are different numbers. Now suppose we write x in place of each 5. We get

$$(x + x + x + x) + (x + x + x) + 4(\text{ones}) + 2(\text{ones})$$

We can combine the x's and get

$$4x + 3x + 4(1) + 2(1)$$

Now we add $4x + 3x$ and $4(1) + 2(1)$.

$$7x + 6$$

We cannot combine $7x$ and 6 because this is a general expression and x could represent any number. We were able to combine the x's because in any given problem every x must represent the same number everywhere within that problem. We say that

$$4x \quad \text{and} \quad 3x$$

are **like terms** because the variable x represents the same number in each expression.

example 94.1   Simplify by adding like terms: $-3x + 2y + 2x + 3 + 7$

solution   We can combine $-3x$ and $2x$ to get $-x$. These terms are like terms because x must represent the same number everywhere it appears in the problem. We can add 3 and 7 to get 10. The $2y$ term cannot be combined with the x's because y could represent some number other than x. The answer is

$$-x + 2y + 10$$

example 94.2   Simplify: $3x + 2m - 14x + 2x - 4m + 4 - 2$

solution   By adding like terms, we can combine 4 and -2. We can also combine the m terms with each other and the x terms with each other. We get

$$-9x - 2m + 2$$

practice   Simplify by adding like terms:

    a. $-4x + 7x + 4 - y - x - 8 + 4y$

    b. $y + 3y - 4 + 10 - 6y + 2m - 6m$

    c. $a + 3b - 6a + 4 - 10 + 7a - 2 + 8b$

problem set 94

1. The product of a number and -4 is increased by 12. The result is 36. What is the number?
(90)

2. Brodsky multiplied his number by 8. Then he added 12. The result was 84. What was Brodsky's original number?
(90)

3. The ratio of the number that were translucent to the number that were opaque was $4\frac{1}{2}$ to 6. If 675 were translucent, how many were opaque?
(66)

4. For the first 4 hours of the tour, the cyclists idled along at 18 miles per hour. If they increased their speed to $1\frac{1}{2}$ times their initial speed and traveled at the new speed for the remaining 4 hours, what was the total distance they traveled?
(63)

5. Karen purchased 40 collectibles at the auction for $5400. If they were of equal value, how many could she have purchased for $13,500?
(75)

6. One prognosticator predicted that from the late 1980s to the late 2010s the number of automobiles will have risen by 215 percent. According to this prediction, how many automobiles will there be in the late 2010s if, in the late 1980s, there were 400,000,000 automobiles?
(80)

7. Graph on a number line: $x \not\le 0$
(89)

8. Between which two consecutive integers is $\sqrt{150}$?
(85)

9. Sketch a rectangular coordinate system, and graph the line $y = \frac{1}{2}x + 1$.
(55)

10. The shares of Joe's Mack Industries, Inc. were a bargain at $90. The investors yelped
(80) with glee when the shares went up 10%! But they howled with disappointment when
the shares went down 10% from there. What was the final price of the shares?

11. What percent of 600 is 2280?
(77)

12. Express in cubic yards the volume of a right solid whose base is shown on the left. Each
(45) side of the base is 1 yard in length, and angles in the base are right angles. The height of
the solid is 3 feet.

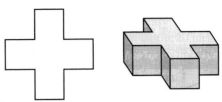

13. Find the lateral surface area in square yards of the solid in problem 12. Remember that
(88) lateral surface area equals the perimeter of the base times the height.

14. Find the volume in cubic meters of a right circular cylinder with a diameter of
(73) 20 meters and a height of 6 meters.

Simplify by adding like terms:

15. $-x + 3y - 2x + y + 4 + 5x - 1$
(94)

16. $5a - 3b + 12 - a + 3 - 14b$
(94)

Solve:

17. $-9x - 4 = 5$
(84)

18. $\dfrac{2\frac{1}{11}}{5\frac{6}{8}} = \dfrac{\frac{1}{11}}{p}$
(65)

19. $-5\frac{2}{3}x - \frac{1}{5} = 4\frac{7}{15}$
(84)

Simplify:

20. $(3 \times 10^{-17}) \times (3 \times 10^{-19})$
(76)

21. $3^2\left[\sqrt{25}(4^2 - 5 \cdot 2)\sqrt{\dfrac{1}{169}}\right]$
(71,91)

22. $5\frac{3}{4} \cdot 1\frac{7}{9} - \dfrac{35}{36}$
(46)

23. $-5(-3 - 4 \cdot 3) - 4 \cdot 6 - (-1)$
(91)

24. $-(-4) - (-9) + 7 + (-9)$
(79)

25. $-[-(+3)] - (-2) - 4 + (-6)$
(79)

26. $\frac{1}{4}\left(3\frac{1}{2} \cdot 5\frac{1}{5} - \dfrac{11}{20}\right)$
(52)

27. $\dfrac{2[(23 - 19) + (6 + 2)3]}{5 - 7 + 6}$
(93)

28. $\dfrac{18 - 3[-1(2 - 4) + 2]}{3(-4 + 2)}$
(93)

Evaluate:

29. $-zm - (-m)(-z)$ if $z = 3$ and $m = 5$
(82)

30. $zp - mp + z^p$ if $z = 2$, $p = 4$, and $m = 5$
(54)

LESSON 95   *Variables on Both Sides*

Some equations have a variable on both sides of the equation. To solve these equations, we first add as necessary to eliminate the variable on one side. Then we add as necessary to place all of the constants on the other side. It may seem strange to add variables to an equation, but this is allowed by the addition property of equality, as long as we add the same variable to both sides.

example 95.1   Solve: $3x + 3 = x - 5$

solution   We can eliminate either the $3x$ or the x. We decide to eliminate the x, so we add $-x$ to both sides.

$$
\begin{array}{ll}
3x + 3 = \ x - 5 & \text{equation} \\
\underline{-x \qquad\quad -x} & \text{added } -x \text{ to both sides} \\
2x + 3 = \qquad -5 &
\end{array}
$$

Now we eliminate the 3 by adding -3 to both sides. Then we divide both sides by 2.

$$
\begin{array}{ll}
2x + 3 = -5 & \\
\underline{\quad -3 \quad -3} & \text{added } -3 \text{ to both sides} \\
2x \quad\ = -8 & \\
\ \ x = -4 & \text{divided both sides by 2}
\end{array}
$$

Check:

$$
\begin{aligned}
3x + 3 &= x - 5 \\
3(-4) + 3 &= (-4) - 5 \\
-12 + 3 &= -9 \\
-9 &= -9 \quad \text{check}
\end{aligned}
$$

Thus, $x = \mathbf{-4}$.

example 95.2   Solve: $4x - 2 = -x$

solution   We will eliminate the $-x$ on the right side of the equation by adding $+x$ to both sides.

$$
\begin{array}{ll}
4x - 2 = -x & \text{equation} \\
\underline{+x \qquad\ +x} & \text{added } +x \text{ to both sides} \\
5x - 2 = \ \ 0 &
\end{array}
$$

Now we add $+2$ to both sides and then divide by 5.

$$
\begin{array}{ll}
5x - 2 = \ \ 0 & \\
\underline{\quad +2 \quad +2} & \text{added } +2 \text{ to both sides} \\
5x \qquad = \ \ 2 & \\
x = \dfrac{2}{5} & \text{divided both sides by 5}
\end{array}
$$

Check:

$$
\begin{aligned}
4x - 2 &= -x \\
4\left(\frac{2}{5}\right) - 2 &= -\left(\frac{2}{5}\right) \\
\frac{8}{5} - \frac{10}{5} &= -\frac{2}{5} \\
-\frac{2}{5} &= -\frac{2}{5} \quad \text{check}
\end{aligned}
$$

So, $x = \dfrac{2}{5}$.

practice   Solve:

 a. $-4x + 3 = 7x - 8$ **b.** $2x - 5 = 6x + 4$

problem set 95

1. A number was multiplied by 4. Then this product was increased by 4. If the result was
(90) 24, what was the number?

2. A number was multiplied by −4. Then this product was increased by −4. If the result
(90) was −24, what was the number?

3. Seventy-five less than the product of 30 and a number is −225. What is the number?
(90)

4. The container overflowed because the kids tried to pour in $3\frac{3}{5}$ times the amount it would
(57) hold. If they tried to pour in 288 gallons, how much would the container hold?

5. Graph on a number line: $x \not< 2$
(89)

6. Use the commutative and associative properties to simplify: $\dfrac{2}{3} + \dfrac{3}{4} + 3\dfrac{1}{3} + 2\dfrac{3}{4}$
(87)

7. What number is 130 percent of 220?
(77)

8. The drought in Fredonia caused the price of bungo beans to skyrocket from 45¢ per lb to
(80) 99¢ per lb. What percent increase is this? The new price is what percent of the old price?

9. Seventy-six is what percent of 95?
(68)

10. Complete the table. Begin by inserting
(55) the reference numbers.

Fraction	Decimal	Percent
(a)	0.53	(b)

11. Between which two consecutive integers is $\sqrt{201}$?
(92)

12. Express in cubic inches the volume of a right solid whose base is shown on the left and
(64) whose sides are 2 feet tall. Dimensions are in inches.

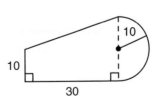
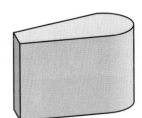
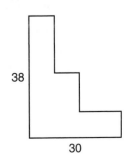

13. Find the perimeter of the figure
(9) shown. Dimensions are in yards. All
 angles are right angles.

14. If the figure in problem 13 was the base of a right solid with a height of 12 yards, what
(88) would its lateral surface area be?

Simplify by adding like terms:

15. $4p - m + 2p + 3m - 5 - 2m$
(94)

16. $-3c + 8 - 2b + c - 4 + 4b - c$
(94)

17. $3a + 4 - 2b + 6 - a - 3b + 1$
(94)

Solve:

18. $-2x - 12 = -2$
(84)

19. $-3x + 6 = 4 - 6x$
(95)

20. $2x - 5 = 9x$
(95)

21. $6x + 6 = -4 + 4x$
(95)

22. $\dfrac{4\frac{1}{5}}{2\frac{1}{3}} = \dfrac{1\frac{1}{2}}{x}$
(65)

Simplify:

23. $3^2 + 2^3\left[2^2\left(\sqrt{16} - \sqrt{9}\right) - \left(\sqrt{25} - \sqrt{4}\right)\right]$
(44)

24. $-2(-6 - 2 \cdot 5) + 2(-2 - 1)$
(91)

25. $\dfrac{5 - (8 - 6) + 3 \cdot 4 + 6}{5(4 - 5)}$
(93)

26. $\dfrac{5 - (4 - 6)2 + 4 \cdot 2}{3(-2 - 1)}$
(93)

27. $\dfrac{1}{4}\left(2\dfrac{1}{3} \cdot \dfrac{1}{4} - \dfrac{5}{6} \cdot \dfrac{1}{2}\right)$
(52)

28. Sketch a rectangular coordinate system, and graph the line $y = -x + 3$.
(69,85)

Evaluate:

29. $-bc - ac$ if $a = -1$, $b = -3$, and $c = -5$
(82)

30. $a^2 + b^2 + c^2 + 2abc + ab$ if $a = 3$, $b = 2$, and $c = 4$
(47)

LESSON 96   *Multiple-Term Equations*

When equations have like terms on either side of the equals sign, the first step in the solution is to combine the like terms.

example 96.1   Solve: $4x + 2 + 3x - 2x = 12$

solution   The first step is to combine the like terms.

$$5x + 2 = 12 \qquad \text{combined like terms}$$

Now we finish by adding -2 to both sides and then dividing both sides by 5.

$$
\begin{array}{rl}
5x + 2 &= 12 \\
\underline{-2 \quad -2} & \qquad \text{added } -2 \text{ to both sides} \\
5x &= 10 \\
x &= 2 \qquad \text{divided both sides by 5}
\end{array}
$$

Check:

$$4x + 2 + 3x - 2x = 12$$
$$4(2) + 2 + 3(2) - 2(2) = 12$$
$$8 + 2 + 6 - 4 = 12$$
$$12 = 12 \quad \text{check}$$

So $x = $ **2.**

example 96.2   Solve: $3x - 3 - x - 4x = 5x + 12 - 2x$

solution   First we simplify both the left and right sides of the equation by adding like terms.

$$-2x - 3 = 3x + 12 \qquad \text{added like terms}$$

Next we decide to eliminate the variable on the left side, so we add $+2x$ to both sides.

$$
\begin{array}{rl}
-2x - 3 = & 3x + 12 \\
+2x \quad\quad & +2x \\
\hline
-3 = & 5x + 12
\end{array}
\qquad \text{added } +2x \text{ to both sides}
$$

Now we finish by adding -12 to both sides and then dividing both sides by 5.

$$
\begin{array}{rl}
-3 = & 5x + 12 \\
-12 \quad\quad & -12 \\
\hline
-15 = & 5x
\end{array}
\qquad \text{added } -12 \text{ to both sides}
$$

$$-3 = x \qquad\qquad \text{divided both sides by 5}$$

Check:

$$3x - 3 - x - 4x = 5x + 12 - 2x$$
$$3(-3) - 3 - (-3) - 4(-3) = 5(-3) + 12 - 2(-3)$$
$$-9 - 3 + 3 + 12 = -15 + 12 + 6$$
$$3 = 3 \quad \text{check}$$

So $x = $ **−3.**

practice   Solve:

a. $4x + 5 + 3x - x = -7x - 8$

b. $12x - 7 + 8x - 3x = -5x + 15$

problem set
96

1.
(90)
A number was multiplied by 6. Then this product was increased by 3. If the result was 33, what was the number?

2.
(90)
Sixty-three less than 15 times a number is 72. What is the number?

3.
(62)
Five eighths of the ranch animals were equine. If 330 ranch animals were not equine, what was the total number of ranch animals?

4.
(66)
The ratio of idle onlookers to serious spectators in the crowd was 2 to 29. If there were 8410 serious spectators, how many idle onlookers were in the crowd?

5.
(57)
The number who attended this year's conference was $2\frac{3}{8}$ times the number who attended the conference last year. If 4180 people attended this year, how many attended last year?

6.
(68)
There were thirty fine chocolates in the box. Papa ate 20% of them. Then Mama ate 25% of those that were left. Then Baby ate 50% of those that remained. Goldi came by and finished off the box. How many fine chocolates did Goldi eat?

7.
(77)
What number is 160 percent of 350?

8.
(80)
If 95 is increased by 40 percent, what is the resulting number?

9. Simplify: $\left(\dfrac{3}{2}\right)^3 - \left(\dfrac{2}{5}\right)^2$
(30,71)

10. Billy Bob was mighty proud because he could eat 30 corn dogs in just 48 minutes. At
(83)   that amazing rate, how long would it take Billy Bob to eat 50 corn dogs? Solve once as
       a rate problem and once as a proportion problem.

11. Find the volume and surface area of a right circular cylinder with a diameter of 200
(73)   centimeters and a height of 100 centimeters.

12. Find the volume of a right solid whose base is shown on the left and whose sides are 5
(45,64) feet tall. Dimensions are in feet.

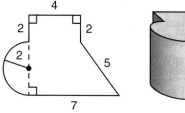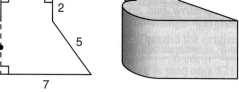

13. Find the lateral surface area of the solid in problem 12.
(88)

Simplify by adding like terms:

14. $-6m + 2m + 8 - p - m$ **15.** $5x + 5 - 11x - 9 + 2x$
(94)   (94)

Solve:

16. $-2x + 3 - 2x = 2 - 5x$ **17.** $2x - 5 = -x + 10x$
(96)   (96)

18. $6x + 6 + 2x = 2x - 4 - 4x$ **19.** $4x + 6 = x - 5$
(96)   (95)

20. $-5x + 9 = 6$ **21.** $\dfrac{2\frac{1}{4}}{5\frac{2}{5}} = \dfrac{x}{4}$
(84)   (65)

Simplify:

22. $\sqrt{81} + 4^3\left[7\left(2^3 - 3^2\right) - \left(\sqrt{4} - 1^{10}\right)\right]$
(44)

23. $-3(-5 - 2 \cdot 3) + 3[5 + 2(-3)]$ **24.** $\dfrac{-6 - (3 - 4)3 + 2(-2)}{3(-2 - 1)}$
(91)   (93)

25. $\dfrac{6 - (2 - 3)3 + 4 \cdot 1}{3(-1 + 2)}$
(93)

26. Sketch a rectangular coordinate system, and graph the line $x = -\frac{y}{2}$.
(85)

Evaluate:

27. $-[bp - (-b)]$ if $b = -3$ and $p = 2$
(82)

28. $a^a b + \sqrt[a]{ab}$ if $a = 2$ and $b = 8$
(54)

29. Write in scientific notation and simplify: $4{,}800{,}000 \times 40{,}000$
(50,76)

30. Between which two consecutive integers is $\sqrt[3]{100}$?
(92)

LESSON **97**   *Two-Step Problems*

Some of the problems that have appeared in the problem sets thus far have required two steps for their solutions. In this lesson we will look at two-step problems that require the solution of an equation as the first step.

example 97.1   If $2x + 4 = 6$, what is the value of $3x - 7$?

solution   We begin by solving the equation to find the value of x that makes it true.

$$
\begin{array}{rll}
2x + 4 &= 6 & \text{equation} \\
\underline{-4 \qquad -4} & & \text{added } -4 \text{ to both sides} \\
2x &= 2 \\
x &= 1 & \text{divided both sides by 2}
\end{array}
$$

Now we use 1 for x to find the value of $3x - 7$.

$$
\begin{array}{rl}
3(1) - 7 & \text{substituted} \\
3 - 7 & \text{multiplied} \\
\mathbf{-4} & \text{added}
\end{array}
$$

example 97.2   If $4x - 2 = 3$, what is the value of $\frac{2}{5}x - \frac{1}{4}$?

solution   As the first step, we solve the equation to find the value of x that makes it true.

$$
\begin{array}{rll}
4x - 2 &= 3 & \text{equation} \\
\underline{+2 \qquad +2} & & \text{added } +2 \text{ to both sides} \\
4x &= 5 \\
x &= \dfrac{5}{4} & \text{divided both sides by 4}
\end{array}
$$

Now we use $\frac{5}{4}$ for x to find the value of $\frac{2}{5}x - \frac{1}{4}$.

$$
\begin{array}{rl}
\dfrac{2}{5}\left(\dfrac{5}{4}\right) - \dfrac{1}{4} & \text{substituted} \\[2mm]
\dfrac{1}{2} - \dfrac{1}{4} & \text{multiplied} \\[2mm]
\mathbf{\dfrac{1}{4}} & \text{added}
\end{array}
$$

example 97.3   If $\frac{4}{3}x - 2 = 4$, what is the value of $6x - \frac{2}{5}$?

solution   We will solve the equation for x.

$$
\begin{array}{rll}
\dfrac{4}{3}x - 2 &= 4 & \text{equation} \\[2mm]
\underline{+2 \qquad +2} & & \text{added } +2 \text{ to both sides} \\[2mm]
\dfrac{4}{3}x &= 6 \\[2mm]
\dfrac{3}{4} \cdot \dfrac{4}{3}x &= 6 \cdot \dfrac{3}{4} & \text{multiplied both sides by } \dfrac{3}{4} \\[2mm]
x &= \dfrac{9}{2} & \text{simplified}
\end{array}
$$

Now we use $\frac{9}{2}$ for x to find the value of $6x - \frac{2}{5}$.

$$6\left(\frac{9}{2}\right) - \frac{2}{5} \qquad \text{substituted}$$

$$27 - \frac{2}{5} \qquad \text{multiplied}$$

$$26\frac{3}{5} \qquad \text{added}$$

practice

a. If $2x - 4 = 6$, what is the value of $3x + 2$?

b. If $5x - 2 = 5$, what is the value of $10x - 3$?

c. If $\frac{1}{5}x = \frac{3}{10}$, what is the value of $15x + 2$?

problem set 97

1. The sum of 7 times a number and 42 is –98. What is the number?
(90)

2. A number was multiplied by –4. Then –6 was added. If the final result was –34, what was the number?
(90)

3. If 140 of the new ones cost $980, what would 200 of the new ones cost?
(75)

4. In an attempt to cut them off at the pass, the posse rode 14 miles in only 2 hours. The horses were tired so they reduced their speed by 2 miles per hour. If it was still 15 miles to the pass, how much longer did it take to get there?
(63)

5. Graph on a number line: $x \not\geq 3$
(89)

6. Simplify by adding like terms: $3x - 4y - 4x + 2x + 5 - y$
(94)

7. Between which two consecutive integers is $\sqrt[3]{40}$?
(92)

8. If 260 is increased by 170 percent, what is the resulting number?
(80)

9. What percent of 80 is 116?
(77)

10. Thirty percent of what number is 180?
(68)

11. Complete the table. Begin by inserting the reference numbers.
(55)

FRACTION	DECIMAL	PERCENT
$\frac{9}{10}$	(a)	(b)

12. Find the volume of a right solid whose base is shown on the left and whose sides are 12 centimeters tall. Dimensions are in centimeters.
(45)

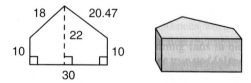

13. Find the lateral surface area of the solid in problem 12.
(88)

14. Use two unit multipliers to convert 1287.321 centimeters to kilometers.
(33)

15. If $3x - 9 = 6$, what is the value of $2x - 6$?
(97)

16. If $6x - 2 = 10$, what is the value of $\frac{1}{2}x + 3$?
(97)

17. If $\frac{3}{4}x - 2 = 1$, what is the value of $3x - 4$?
(97)

Solve:

18. $14x - 1 + 5x = 10 - 2x + 5 + 4x$
(96)

19. $6x + 6 + 2x = 2x - 4 + 4x$
(96)

20. $-4x - 12 = -1$ **21.** $4x + 2 = 2x - 4$
(84)   (95)

22. $-2\frac{1}{3}x + \frac{2}{3} = 1\frac{4}{6}$
(84)

23. Find x.
(65)

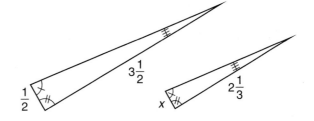

Simplify:

24. $-2(8 - 2 \cdot 3) - 4(3 \cdot 1 - 2)$
(91)

25. $\dfrac{7 - (2 - 4)2 + 5 \cdot 1}{4(-2 + 3)}$ **26.** $\dfrac{8 - (4 - 7)3 + 4 \cdot 2}{5(-3 + 5)}$
(93)   (93)

27. $3^2 + 3\left[2^3\left(\sqrt{49} - 2^2\right)\left(3^2 - 2^3\right) - 2^2\right]$
(44)

28. $3\frac{1}{3} \times 2\frac{1}{5} \div 1\frac{2}{3} \div \frac{1}{4}$
(43)

29. Evaluate: $bcb - ac$ if $a = -1$, $b = -2$, and $c = -5$
(82)

30. Sketch a rectangular coordinate system, and graph the line $y = 2x - 4$. Let x be -1,
(85) 0, 2, and 4.

LESSON 98   *Adjacent Angles • Complementary and Supplementary Angles • Measuring Angles*

98.A

adjacent angles

We can name some angles by using the letter at the vertex. We can name the angles in the triangle below as angle A, angle B, and angle C. We can also use an angle symbol, $\angle$, instead of writing the word *angle*.

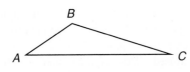

$\angle A$ is read "angle A"
$\angle B$ is read "angle B"
$\angle C$ is read "angle C"

When two or more angles have the same vertex, it is necessary to use three letters to name an angle. The center letter is the vertex and the other two letters name a point on each ray.

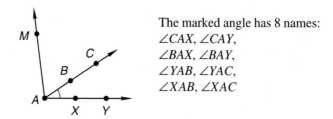

The marked angle has 8 names:
∠CAX, ∠CAY,
∠BAX, ∠BAY,
∠YAB, ∠YAC,
∠XAB, ∠XAC

All eight of the notations shown name the same angle. Notice that the notation ∠A is ambiguous because it could refer to ∠MAB, ∠MAX, or ∠BAX. Yet another way to name an angle is to draw an angle marker inside the angle and then label the arc with a letter.

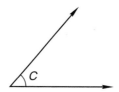

If two angles have the same vertex and share the side between, then the angles are called **adjacent angles.**

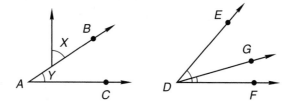

On the left, angles Y and X are not adjacent because they do not have a common vertex. On the right, ∠GDF and ∠FDE both have ray DF as a side, but it is not the side between the angles. Thus, they are not adjacent angles. However, ∠FDG and ∠GDE share ray DG between them and have the same vertex D, so they are adjacent angles.

98.B
complementary and supplementary angles

If the sum of the measures of two angles is 90°, the angles are called **complementary angles.** If the sum of the measures of two angles is 180°, the angles are called **supplementary angles.** Complementary angles and supplementary angles do not have to be next to each other.

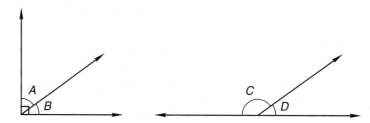

Together angles A and B form a right angle (90° angle), so these angles are complementary angles. Together angles C and D form a straight angle (180° angle), so these angles are supplementary angles. It is easy to get the words complementary and supplementary confused. We can remember which is which if we associate the C in complementary with a picture of a right angle and the *S* in supplementary with two right angles.

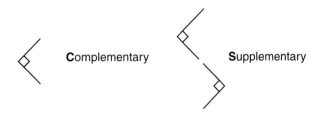

Complementary   Supplementary

example 98.1   What are the measures of (a) ∠*ABC* and (b) ∠*DEF*?

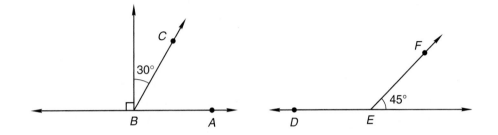

solution   (a)   Angle *ABC*, the 30° angle, and the right angle (90° angle) together make a 180° angle. Thus, ∠*ABC* measures **60°**.

(b)   Angle *DEF* and the 45° angle make a 180° angle. Thus, ∠*DEF* measures **135°**.

98.C

measuring angles

To measure an angle using a **protractor,** we align the baseline of the protractor with one side of the angle and move the protractor left or right as necessary to place the angle vertex under the origin at the center of the baseline. We read the measure of the angle where the other ray passes through the scale.

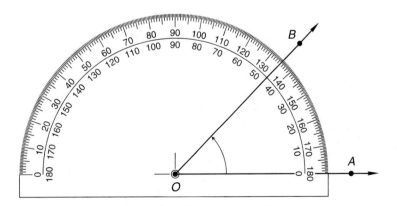

The scale on a protractor has two sets of numbers. One set is for measuring angles starting from the right-hand side, and the other is for measuring angles starting from the left-hand side. The easiest way to be sure we are reading from the correct scale is to decide if the angle we are measuring is acute or obtuse. Looking at ∠*AOB*, we read the numbers 45° and 135°. Since the angle is less than 90° (acute), it must be 45° and not 135°.

practice   **a.**   The supplement of an angle measures 40°. What is the measure of the angle?

b.   The complement of an angle measures 40°. What is the measure of the angle?

Given the angles shown:

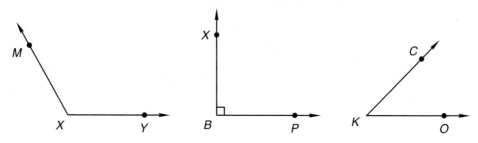

c. Name the obtuse angle.

d. Name the acute angle.

e. Name the right angle.

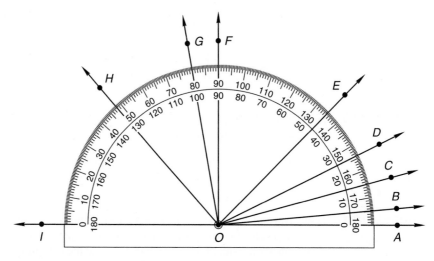

Refer to the figure above to determine the measure of each angle.

f. ∠AOC   **g.** ∠AOD   **h.** ∠AOG   **i.** ∠AOH

j. ∠IOG   **k.** ∠IOF   **l.** ∠IOB   **m.** ∠IOA

problem set 98

1. Six times a number is 14 less than the opposite of the number. What is the number?
(90,95)

2. Seven times a number is 30 greater than the sum of twice the number and 5. What is the number?
(90,95)

3. Graph on a number line: $x \not\leq -1$
(89)

4. The ratio of the number of ratio problems to the number of non-ratio problems is 1 to 29. If there are 3509 non-ratio problems, how many are ratio problems?
(66)

5. The caravan covered the first 90 miles in 15 hours. Then they doubled their pace for the next 180 miles. How long did it take the caravan to travel the total distance of 270 miles?
(63)

6. If 250 is increased by 190 percent, what is the resulting number?
(80)

7. What percent of 90 is 162?
(77)

8. Forty percent of what number is 62?
(68)

9. Find the volume of a solid whose base is shown on the left and whose sides are
(45) 10 centimeters tall. Dimensions are in centimeters.

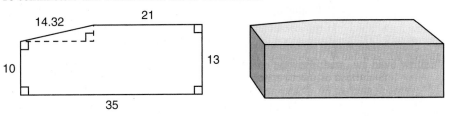

10. Find the lateral surface area of the solid in problem 9.
(88)

11. Angle A and $\angle B$ are supplementary, and $\angle B$ and $\angle C$ are complementary. If $\angle B$
(98) measures 38°, what are the measures of $\angle A$ and $\angle C$?

12. Classify these angles as acute, right, or obtuse, and measure them with a protractor.
(98)

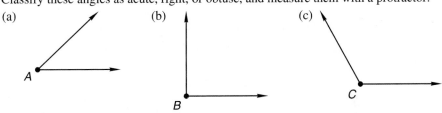

(a) (b) (c)

13. What are three of the four ways to name this angle?
(98)

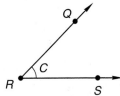

14. Between which two consecutive integers is $\sqrt{17.4}$?
(92)

15. Simplify by adding like terms: $3p - 2q + 5q - 5p + 3 - q$
(94)

16. If $6x - 2 = 16$, what is the value of $x - 3$?
(97)

17. If $\frac{3}{2}x - 3 = 1$, what is the value of $2x + 3$?
(97)

Solve:

18. $-3x + 12 = 1 + 5x + 10 - 6x$
(96)

19. $-2x + 10 - 3x = 5x - 3 - 6x$
(96)

20. $6x + 2 = 3x - 5$
(95)

21. $-6x + 2 = 3x - 6$
(95)

22. $-3\frac{1}{4}x + \frac{3}{4} = 1\frac{3}{8}$
(84)

Simplify:

23. $-2(3 \cdot 2 - 7) - 3(2 \cdot 1 - 5) + \sqrt[4]{\dfrac{16}{81}}$
(71,91)

24. $\dfrac{6 - 3(2 - 1) + 4 \cdot 3}{5(-3 + 6)}$
(93)

25. $\dfrac{8 - 2(3 - 2) + 4 \cdot 2}{4(2 - 3)}$
(93)

26. $2^3 + 3\left[2^2\left(\sqrt{36} + \sqrt{4}\right)\left(\sqrt[3]{8} - 1\right) + 1\right]$
(44)

27. $2\frac{1}{4} \times 3\frac{1}{3} \div 2\frac{1}{3} \times 1\frac{1}{4}$
(43)

28. Sketch a rectangular coordinate system, and graph the line $x - 4 = 2y$.
(85)

Evaluate:

29. $d + c - ac$ if $a = -1$, $c = -1$, and $d = 1$
(82)

30. $abc - a$ if $a = -2$, $b = -1$, and $c = -3$
(82)

LESSON 99   *Exponents and Signed Numbers*

We must be careful when we simplify exponential expressions (powers) whose bases are signed numbers. The exponential expression

$$4^2$$

indicates that 4 is to be used as a factor twice.

$$(4)(4) = 16$$

The notation

$$-4^2$$

indicates "the opposite of (4 squared)." Thus,

$$-4^2 = -(4 \cdot 4) = -16$$

If we wish to indicate that -4 is to be used as a factor twice, we must enclose the -4 in parentheses and write

$$(-4)^2$$

This means -4 times -4, so

$$(-4)^2 = (-4)(-4) = 16$$

example 99.1   Simplify: $-4^2 - (-3)^2 - 3^3$

solution   First we simplify the exponential expressions

$$-16 - 9 - 27$$

and then we add and get

$$\mathbf{-52}$$

example 99.2   Simplify: $(-3)^3 - (-2)^3 - 2^2$

solution   First we simplify the exponential expressions.

$$-27 - (-8) - 4$$

Then we add.

$$-27 + 8 - 4$$
$$\mathbf{-23}$$

practice   Simplify:

     a. $-(-2)^3 - (-2)^2$ **b.** $-2^2 - (-2)^2 - (-2)^3$

problem set   **1.** Five times a number is 35 greater than twice the opposite of the number. What is
99   (90,95)   the number?

2. Seven times the opposite of a number is 50 less than the product of 3 and the number.
(90,95) What is the number?

3. Only $\frac{3}{5}$ of the students in the school came to hear the distinguished scholar. If there were
(62) 1200 students in the school, how many came to hear the distinguished scholar?

4. The ratio of those who stayed awake to those who dozed was $2\frac{1}{2}$ to 7. If 1400 stayed
(66) awake, how many dozed?

5. Graph on a number line: $x \not< -2$
(89)

6. Measure these angles with a protractor, and classify them as acute, right, or obtuse:
(98)

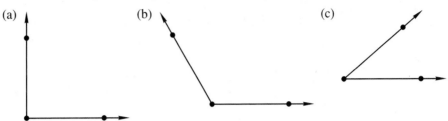

(a)   (b)   (c)

7. What number is 160 percent of 230?
(77)

8. If 180 is increased by 180 percent, what is the resulting number?
(80)

9. Twenty-five percent of what number is 61?
(68)

10. Write 7.34×10^{-5} in standard notation.
(50)

11. Write $\frac{3121}{7}$ as a mixed number.
(28)

12. Simplify: $-\left\{-[-(-3)]\right\} + 3 - [-(-3)]$
(79)

13. Find the volume of a solid whose base is shown on the left and whose sides are 6 feet
(45) tall. Dimensions are in feet.

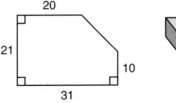
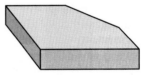

14. Between which two consecutive integers is $\sqrt[5]{40}$?
(92)

15. Simplify by adding like terms: $3x - 4a + 5a - 3x + a$
(94)

16. What is the value of $6x + 12$ when $2x + 10 = 7$?
(97)

17. What is the value of $3 - \frac{4}{3}x$ when $\frac{2}{3}x + 5 = 7$?
(97)

Solve:

18. $-4x + 3 = x + 4$
(95)

19. $3x - 4 = -x + 6 + 11x + 4x - 3$
(96)

20. $-3\frac{1}{3}x - \frac{1}{6} = 1\frac{1}{3}$
(84)

21. $\dfrac{6\frac{1}{2}}{2\frac{1}{3}} = \dfrac{\frac{1}{2}}{x}$
(65)

Simplify:

22. $-2^2 - (-3)^2 - 3^4$
(99)

23. $-3^2 + (-2)^2$
(99)

24. $-2^2(2 \cdot 2 - 3 \cdot 2) - 3(2 \cdot 3 - 2^2)$
(99)

25. $\dfrac{3 - 2(3 - 2) + 3 \cdot 2}{4(-2 + 5)}$
(93)

26. $\dfrac{-3 - 2(3 \cdot 2 - 1) + 2^2}{2^2(-3 - 2^2)}$
(93,99)

27. $3\dfrac{1}{2} \times 2\dfrac{1}{3} \div \dfrac{1}{4} \div \dfrac{1}{6}$
(43)

28. Sketch a rectangular coordinate system, and graph the line $x = 2y$.
(85)

Evaluate:

29. $abc + ab$ if $a = -2$, $b = -3$, and $c = -4$
(82)

30. $-ab + bc$ if $a = 2$, $b = -3$, and $c = -4$
(82)

LESSON 100   *Advanced Ratio Problems*

In this lesson we will consider advanced ratio problems. We begin with an example.

example 100.1   The ratio of nuts to bolts was 11 to 2. If there were 260 nuts and bolts in the pile, how many were bolts?

solution   We begin confidently by writing

$$\frac{N}{B} = \frac{11}{2}$$

Now where does the 260 go? What do we do now? The answer is that this problem is more difficult than the ratio problems we have been working, and we have begun the wrong way. This problem has nuts and bolts but also has the **total.** There is a trick to working these problems. **The trick is to begin by listing the given parts of the ratio, including the ratio total.**

$$\text{Nuts} = 11$$
$$\text{Bolts} = 2$$
$$\text{Ratio Total} = 13$$

There are three ratios hidden here. We can see the ratios if we cover up the lines one at a time with a finger. First we cover the top line. We see that what remains concerns bolts and ratio total. We will use the subscript R to represent ratio values and the subscript A to represent actual values.

$$\text{Bolts} = 2 \quad \longrightarrow \quad \frac{B_R}{T_R} = \frac{2}{13} \qquad \text{(a)}$$
$$\text{Ratio Total} = 13$$

Now we cover the middle line and see that what remains concerns nuts and ratio total.

$$\text{Nuts} = 11$$
$$\longrightarrow \quad \frac{N_R}{T_R} = \frac{11}{13} \qquad \text{(b)}$$
$$\text{Ratio Total} = 13$$

Now we cover the bottom line and see that what remains concerns nuts and bolts.

$$\text{Nuts} = 11$$

$$\text{Bolts} = 2 \quad \longrightarrow \quad \frac{N_R}{B_R} = \frac{11}{2} \qquad \text{(c)}$$

We see that the given information was enough to write three ratios. Ratio (a) is between bolts and ratio total. Ratio (b) is between nuts and ratio total. Ratio (c) is between nuts and bolts. We were told that we had a total of 260 and were asked for the number of bolts. So we want to use Ratio (a).

$$\frac{B_R}{T_R} = \frac{2}{13} \qquad \text{ratio (a)}$$

Ratio (a) is the reduced form of the actual number of bolts to the actual total. Thus we can write a proportion showing that ratio (a) is equal to the ratio of the actual number of bolts to the actual total.

$$\frac{B_A}{T_A} = \frac{B_R}{T_R}$$

Now we can substitute and solve.

$$\frac{B_A}{260} = \frac{2}{13} \qquad \text{replaced } T_A \text{ with 260}$$

$$B_A = \frac{2 \cdot 260}{13} \qquad \text{multiplied both sides by 260}$$

$$B_A = \textbf{40 bolts} \qquad \text{simplified}$$

In ratio problems that discuss the total, it is helpful to begin by writing all three ratios. Then reread the problem to see which ratio should be used.

example 100.2 Farmer Dunncowski wanted to plant his farm with wheat and corn in the ratio of 7 acres to 9 acres. If he had 640 acres, how many should be planted in wheat?

solution First we write down the figures given and the ratio total.

$$W_R = 7$$

$$C_R = 9$$

$$T_R = 16$$

With this information we can write three ratios.

$$\text{(a)} \; \frac{W_R}{C_R} = \frac{7}{9} \qquad \text{(b)} \; \frac{W_R}{T_R} = \frac{7}{16} \qquad \text{(c)} \; \frac{C_R}{T_R} = \frac{9}{16}$$

We were given the total and were asked for wheat, so we will use (b).

$$\frac{W_A}{T_A} = \frac{W_R}{T_R} \qquad \text{proportion}$$

$$\frac{W_A}{640} = \frac{7}{16} \qquad \text{replaced } T_A \text{ with 640}$$

$$16W_A = 7 \cdot 640 \qquad \text{cross multiplied}$$

$$\frac{\cancel{16}W_A}{\cancel{16}} = \frac{7 \cdot 640}{16} \qquad \text{divided both sides by 16}$$

$$W_A = \textbf{280 acres} \qquad \text{simplified}$$

If he plants 280 acres with wheat, then $640 - 280 = 360$ acres will be planted in corn.

example 100.3   When the race began, the ratio of professionals to amateurs was 2 to 17. If 3800 racers were in the race, how many were amateurs?

solution   First we write down the numbers for professionals and amateurs. We add these two numbers to get the ratio total.

$$P_R = 2$$

$$A_R = 17$$

$$T_R = 19$$

Now we can write the three ratios.

(a) $\dfrac{P_R}{A_R} = \dfrac{2}{17}$ (b) $\dfrac{P_R}{T_R} = \dfrac{2}{19}$ (c) $\dfrac{A_R}{T_R} = \dfrac{17}{19}$

We were given a total of 3800 and were asked for the number of amateurs. Thus, we will use ratio (c).

$$\dfrac{A_A}{T_A} = \dfrac{A_R}{T_R} \qquad \text{proportion}$$

$$\dfrac{A_A}{3800} = \dfrac{17}{19} \qquad \text{replaced } T_A \text{ with 3800}$$

$$19A_A = 17 \cdot 3800 \qquad \text{cross multiplied}$$

$$\dfrac{\cancel{19}A_A}{\cancel{19}} = \dfrac{17 \cdot 3800}{19} \qquad \text{divided both sides by 19}$$

$$A_A = \textbf{3400 amateurs} \qquad \text{simplified}$$

If 3400 out of 3800 were amateurs, then 400 must have been professionals.

practice   **a.**   The ratio of big ships to small ships in the harbor was 2 to 9. If there were 242 ships in the harbor, how many were big ships? How many were small ships?

problem set 100   **1.**   Farmer Brown wanted to plant her farm with rye and barley in the ratio of 7 acres to 5
(100)   acres. If she had 240 acres, how many acres should she plant with rye? How many acres should she plant with barley?

2.   The ratio of greens to purples balanced on the ledge was 3 to 17. If there were 400
(100)   greens and purples balanced on the ledge, how many were greens?

3.   Four times a number was 22 greater than twice the same number. What was
(90,95)   the number?

4.   Five sixteenths of the teenies swooned as the star approached the microphone. If 2200
(62)   teenies did not swoon, how many teenies attended the concert?

5.   Graph on a number line: $x > -1$
(72)

6.   What number is 140 percent of 75?
(77)

7.   If 150 is increased by 30 percent, what is the resulting number?
(80)

8.   What percent of 70 is 91?
(77)

9.   Thirty-five is what percent of 140?
(68)

10.   Between which two consecutive integers is $\sqrt[4]{180}$?
(92)

11. Complete the table. Begin by inserting the reference numbers.
<small>(55)</small>

FRACTION	DECIMAL	PERCENT
(a)	(b)	85%

12. Find the volume in cubic feet of a solid whose base is shown on the left and whose sides are 2 yards tall. Dimensions are in feet.
<small>(64)</small>

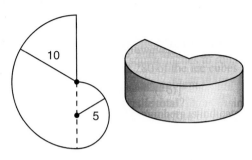

13. Find the total surface area of the solid in problem 12.
<small>(88)</small>

14. Use two unit multipliers to convert 61.131121 kilometers to centimeters.
<small>(33)</small>

15. Simplify by adding like terms: $4x - 3a + 2y - 5x + x + 3a - y - y$
<small>(94)</small>

16. If $\angle B$ measures $47°$, what are the measures of $\angle A$ and $\angle C$, given that $\angle A$ and $\angle B$ are supplementary, and $\angle B$ and $\angle C$ are complementary?
<small>(98)</small>

17. What is the value of $\frac{2}{3}x + 5$ when $6x - 3 = 12$?
<small>(97)</small>

18. What is the value of $22x$ when $7 - 6x = 2x + 13$?
<small>(97)</small>

Solve:

19. $-3x + 6 + 4x = 2x + 1 - 9 + 2x$ **20.** $2x - 4 - 5x = -x + 5 + 7x - 3$
<small>(96)</small>   <small>(96)</small>

21. $-2\frac{1}{2}x - \frac{1}{3} = 2\frac{2}{3}$
<small>(84)</small>

22. Find x.
<small>(65)</small>

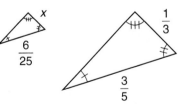

Simplify:

23. $-2^2 - (-2)^3$
<small>(99)</small>

24. $-3^2 - (-3)^2$
<small>(99)</small>

25. $-8(2 \cdot 3 - 4) - 3(8 - 9)$
<small>(91)</small>

26. $\dfrac{4 - 2(6 - 4) + 2^2 \cdot 3}{3(-3 + 5)}$
<small>(93)</small>

27. $\dfrac{-2 + 3(2 \cdot 4 - 3) + 2^2}{3(2^2 - 1)}$
<small>(93)</small>

28. $2\frac{1}{2} \div 3\frac{1}{2} \times \sqrt{\dfrac{9}{16}} \div \dfrac{1}{3}$
<small>(43,71)</small>

Evaluate:

29. $-bc - ab$ if $a = -2$, $b = -2$, and $c = -5$
<small>(82)</small>

30. $ab - ac$ if $a = -1$, $b = -2$, and $c = -1$
<small>(82)</small>

LESSON *101* *Multiplication of Exponential Expressions • Variable Bases*

101.A

multiplication of exponential expressions

Remember that we use exponential notation to indicate how many times a number is to be used as a factor. To review, we consider the notation

$$3^5$$

The base of this exponential expression is 3 and the exponent is 5. This means that 3 is to be used as a factor five times.

$$3^5 = 3 \cdot 3 \cdot 3 \cdot 3 \cdot 3$$

Now we will consider the notation

$$3^5 \cdot 3^2$$

The first part tells us that 3 is a factor five times, and the second part tells us that 3 is a factor twice.

$$(3 \cdot 3 \cdot 3 \cdot 3 \cdot 3)(3 \cdot 3)$$

This means that 3 is a factor seven times, which is written

$$3^7$$

We see from this that the number of times 3 is to be used as a factor can be found by adding the exponents.

$$3^5 \cdot 3^2 = 3^{5+2} = 3^7$$

example 101.1 Simplify: $5^2 \cdot 5^3 \cdot 5^4$

solution This means

$$(5 \cdot 5)(5 \cdot 5 \cdot 5)(5 \cdot 5 \cdot 5 \cdot 5)$$

and 5 is used as a factor nine times. Thus, we can write

$$5^2 \cdot 5^3 \cdot 5^4 = \mathbf{5^9}$$

example 101.2 Simplify: $10^{15} \cdot 10^{17}$

solution The first part has 10 as a factor fifteen times, and the second part has 10 as a factor seventeen times. Thus,

$$10^{15} \cdot 10^{17} = 10^{15+17} = 10^{32}$$

If we use 10 as a factor thirty-two times, we get

$$100,000,000,000,000,000,000,000,000,000,000$$

This numeral is cumbersome and difficult to work with, as it is easy to miscount the number of zeros. Thus, the exponential expression

$$\mathbf{10^{32}}$$

is a better way to write this number and is preferred for most applications.

example 101.3 Simplify: $2^3 \cdot 5^2$

solution If we write the exponential expressions in expanded notation, we get

$$(2 \cdot 2 \cdot 2)(5 \cdot 5)$$

We have 2 as a factor three times and 5 as a factor twice. The expression

$$\mathbf{2^3 \cdot 5^2}$$

cannot be simplified by adding the exponents. The bases are not the same.

101.B

variable bases   Since variables stand for numbers, all the rules for numbers also apply to variables. Thus, if we write

$$x^2 \cdot x^3$$

we mean

$$(x \cdot x)(x \cdot x \cdot x)$$

Here we have x used as a factor 5 times, and we can write this as

$$x^5$$

We call the rule demonstrated by this example the **product rule for exponents.**

PRODUCT RULE FOR EXPONENTS

$$x^m \cdot x^n = x^{m + n}$$

This is a formal way of saying that we multiply exponential expressions that have the same base by adding the exponents.

example 101.4   Simplify: $x \cdot x^2 \cdot y^{17} \cdot x^4 \cdot y^6$

solution   **When we write x, we mean x^1.** We rearrange the expression to place like bases together and get

$$xx^2x^4y^{17}y^6$$

Now we add exponents of like bases and get

$$x^7y^{23}$$

example 101.5   Simplify: $aa^2mm^5a^4m^6$

solution   We will rearrange mentally. Then we add the exponents of like bases and get

$$a^7m^{12}$$

practice   Simplify:

a. $3 \cdot 3^2 \cdot 3^5$ 　　　　　　　　　　　　　　**b.** $xxx^5x^2yy^3$

c. $ab^2ba^3ba^4$ 　　　　　　　　　　　　　　**d.** $yx^2y^3yy^4$

problem set　**1.**   In the very long hallway, the ratio of hats to coats was 2 to 5. If 4900 hats and coats
101　　*(100)*   were stored in the hallway, how many were hats?

　　　　　　2.   Five times the opposite of a number was 56 less than twice the number. What was
　　　(90,95)   the number?

　　　　　　3.   Four hundred diskettes cost $200. What would 140 diskettes cost?
　　　(75)

　　　　　　4.   Wilson bought 60 items for $40 each and 40 items for $150 each. What was the average
　　　(41)   cost of the items?

　　　　　　5.   Graph on a number line: $x \nleq -2$
　　　(89)

　　　　　　6.   What number is 130 percent of 80?
　　　(77)

　　　　　　7.   If 160 is increased by 40 percent, what is the resulting number?
　　　(80)

8. Suzie was surprised to learn that 65% of discriminating gourmets preferred Joe's Mack
(68) Brand Cola to the leading national brands. If 78 chose Joe's Mack Brand, how many
discriminating gourmets were there all together?

9. Forty percent of what number is 240?
(68)

10. Find the volume in cubic centimeters of a right circular cylinder whose radius is
(73) 2 meters and whose height is 1 meter.

11. Find the perimeter of the figure
(9) shown. Dimensions are in inches. All
angles are right angles.

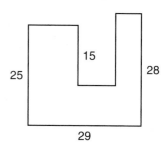

12. Simplify by adding like terms: $-2x + 5 + 4x + 8$
(94)

13. Sketch a rectangular coordinate system, and graph the line $y = -2x + 1$.
(85)

14. Classify these angles as acute, right, or obtuse, and measure them with a protractor:
(98)

(a)

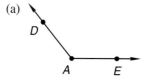

(b)

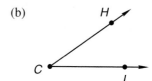

(c)

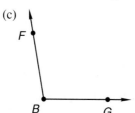

15. If $6x - 5 = 31$, what is the value of $2x - 3$?
(97)

Solve:

16. $-2x + 4 = 3x + 2$
(95)

17. $3x - 2 = -2x + 5 + 4x + 8$
(96)

18. $-3\frac{1}{2}x - \frac{1}{2} = 2\frac{1}{4}$
(84)

19. $\dfrac{-\dfrac{2}{5}}{\dfrac{4}{25}} = \dfrac{-\dfrac{1}{2}}{x}$
(59,81)

Simplify:

20. $-2^3 - (-2)^3$
(99)

21. $-(-3)^2$
(99)

22. $(-3)^2 + (-2)^3$
(99)

23. $x^3 \cdot x^2 \cdot y^{15} \cdot x^6 \cdot y^6$
(101)

24. $5^{15} \cdot 5^{17}$
(101)

25. $aa^3mm^3am^4a^2$
(101)

26. $xx^3x^2yy^5y^6xy^2$
(101)

27. $\dfrac{2^3 - 2(3 - 1)(2^3 - 3)}{2^2(2^2 - 1)}$
(93)

28. $\dfrac{3 - 2^2(2^2 - 1)(2^3 - 1)}{3^2(3^2 - 2^3)}$
(93)

29. $3\frac{1}{2} \div \frac{1}{4} \times 2\frac{1}{3} \div \frac{1}{6}$
(43)

30. Evaluate: $-ab + bc$ if $a = -2$, $b = -1$, and $c = 1$
(82)

LESSON *102*   *Adding Like Terms, Part 2*

Terms can have more than one variable and the variables can be written as indicated multiplications or divisions. The expression

$$4xy + 6yx$$

has two terms. The coefficients are 4 and 6 respectively. To see if

$$4xy \quad\text{and}\quad 6yx$$

are like terms, we consider only the variables, so we discard the coefficients and get

$$xy \quad\text{and}\quad yx$$

If these both represent the same number regardless of the numbers that are used for x and y, we say that the expressions are like terms. To investigate, we let $x = -2$ and $y = 3$. Then

$$xy = (-2)(3) = -6 \quad\text{and}\quad yx = (3)(-2) = -6$$

Since the commutative property states that the order of factors does not affect a product, we see that this will hold true for any numbers that we use for x and y. So we say that $4xy$ and $6yx$ are like terms because xy and yx will have the same value no matter what numbers are used as replacements for the variables. If we have four (-6)'s plus six (-6)'s, we have ten (-6)'s.

$$4(-6) + 6(-6) = 10(-6)$$

This shows why we can add $4xy$ and $6yx$ and get $10xy$.

$$4xy + 6yx = 10xy$$

To add like terms, we add the coefficients of the terms.

example 102.1   Are $2xy^2$ and $3y^2x$ and $7yxy$ like terms?

solution   We first discard the coefficients and get

$$xy^2 \quad\text{and}\quad y^2x \quad\text{and}\quad yxy$$

If we expand these expressions, we get

$$xyy \quad\text{and}\quad yyx \quad\text{and}\quad yxy$$

Each of these has as factors two y's and one x. Since the order of multiplication does not affect the product, these expressions will always represent the same number. To demonstrate we will use -2 for x and 3 for y.

xyy	yyx	yxy
$(-2)(3)(3)$	$(3)(3)(-2)$	$(3)(-2)(3)$
-18	-18	-18

Thus, the terms $2xy^2$ and $3y^2x$ and $7yxy$ are like terms. Since xy^2, y^2x, and yxy are like terms, we can add them by adding the coefficients.

$$2xy^2 + 3y^2x + 7yxy = 12y^2x \quad\text{or}\quad 12xy^2$$

example 102.2   Simplify by adding like terms: $4x + 3 + 6x + 4 + 2xy + 3yx + 2$

solution   We add the constants for a sum of 9.

$$3 + 4 + 2 = 9$$

We add the x terms and get $10x$.

$$4x + 6x = 10x$$

And we add the xy terms and get $5xy$.

$$2xy + 3yx = 5xy$$

So the sum is

$$9 + 10x + 5xy$$

We could write $5yx$ instead, but usually we write the variables in alphabetical order.

example 102.3   Add like terms: $4 + 3x^2 + 2xx + 4x + 7 + 3x$

solution   We add like terms and get

$$11 + 5x^2 + 7x$$

practice   Simplify by adding like terms:

    a. $3yxy + 2xyx - 6xy^2 + 3y^2x$

    b. $xxx + 3x^2x + 4x^3 + 2xy - 3yx$

    c. $y^2xy + x^2yy - 5x^3y$

problem set 102

1.
(100)   The ratio of jacks to marbles in the bowl was 2 to 5. If the bowl contained 350 jacks and marbles, how many were marbles?

2.
(100)   The ratio of flooded land to dry land was 2 to 9. If the plantation consisted of 1210 acres, how many acres were flooded?

3.
(90)   The product of a number and 2 is 20 less than the product of the number and −3. What is the number?

4.
(57)   The tree harvest was followed by seed planting. The forester was amazed because the number of seeds that sprouted was $2\frac{3}{4}$ times the number that had been expected. If 140,000 sprouts had been expected, how many sprouts did the forester get?

5.
(72)   Graph on a number line: $x \geq 1$

6.
(68)   What number is 75 percent of 220?

7.
(80)   If 150 is increased by 60 percent, what is the resulting number?

8.
(55)   Alphonso got 17 out of 20 problems correct on the mathematics test and 21 out of 25 questions correct on the English test. Which was the better score? First express both scores as percents.

9.
(92)   Between which two consecutive integers is $\sqrt{211}$?

10.
(27)   Find the area of the figure shown. Dimensions are in feet.

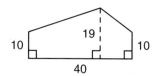

11.
(20)   Find the least common multiple of 12, 30, and 36.

12.
(98)   Two complementary angles have equal measures. What do they measure? Two supplementary angles have equal measures. What do they measure?

13.
(85)   Sketch a rectangular coordinate system, and graph the line $x = \dfrac{y}{3} - 3$.

Solve:

14. $2x - 5 = 5x - 6$
(95)

15. $6x - 2 + 2x - 5 = 2x + 4 + 12 + 3x$
(96)

16. $-4\frac{1}{3}x - \frac{1}{4} = 2\frac{1}{3}$ **17.** $\dfrac{\frac{-1}{4}}{\frac{1}{2}} = \dfrac{\frac{1}{3}}{x}$
(84)   (59,81)

Simplify by adding like terms:

18. $6x + 8 + 6x + 5 + 2xy + 9yx + 2$
(102)

19. $3 + 2ab^2 + 3a + 2abb - 4a$
(102)

20. $6x + 2y + 3xy + 2 + 3x + 4y - xy$
(102)

Simplify:

21. $-2^3 - (-3)^2$ **22.** $-(-3)^2 - [-(-1)]$
(99)   (99)

23. $2^3 - 2[3(2 - 3) + 2(2 - 4)]$ **24.** $aa^3ba^2a^4b^3b^2$
(44,91)   (101)

25. $xxyyx^2y^3x^3y^4$ **26.** $ababa^2b^2a^2b^2a^3b^3$
(101)   (101)

27. $\dfrac{2^4 - 3(2^2 - 1)(3^2 - 2^3)}{2^3(2^2 - 1)}$ **28.** $\dfrac{2^3 - 3^2(2^2 - 1)(3 - 2^2)}{2(3^2 - 2^3)}$
(93)   (93)

29. $3\frac{1}{3} \div \frac{1}{4} \times 2\frac{1}{3} \div \frac{1}{3}$
(43)

30. Evaluate: $p^x + \frac{1}{3}p + \sqrt[x]{p}$ if $p = 9$, and $x = 2$
(54)

LESSON 103   *Distributive Property*

The notation

$$4(2 + 3)$$

tells us to multiply 4 by what is inside the parentheses. There are two ways we can do this.

$$4(2 + 3) \qquad 4(2 + 3)$$
$$4(5) \qquad 4 \cdot 2 + 4 \cdot 3$$
$$20 \qquad 8 + 12$$
$$20$$

On the left we added 2 and 3 to get 5. Then we multiplied 4 by 5 to get 20. On the right we multiplied 4 by 2 to get 8 and multiplied 4 by 3 to get 12. Then we added 8 and 12 to get

20. We got an answer of 20 for both methods. We call this property of numbers the **distributive property.**

DISTRIBUTIVE PROPERTY

$$a(b + c) = ab + ac \qquad \text{or} \qquad (b + c)a = ba + ca$$

This property is especially helpful when we simplify expressions that have variables. If we look at

$$4(x + y)$$

we cannot add x and y and then multiply, because x and y are not like terms. However, we can multiply x by 4 and then multiply y by 4 and then add the two products.

$$4(x + y) = 4x + 4y$$

example 103.1   Use the distributive property to multiply: $4(x + 2y - 8)$

solution   The distributive property also applies to the algebraic sum of three or more terms. We multiply each of the terms in the parentheses by 4.

$$4(x + 2y - 8) = \mathbf{4x + 8y - 32}$$

example 103.2   Use the distributive property to multiply: $3x(y - 2 + 2x)$

solution   We multiply each of the terms in the parentheses by $3x$.

$$3x(y - 2 + 2x) = \mathbf{3xy - 6x + 6x^2}$$

practice   Multiply:

    a. $4\left(3x^2 + 2x\right)$ **b.** $3x(2 + x)$ **c.** $x(y - x - 4)$

problem set 103

1.
(100)
The football coach shuddered when he realized that the ratio of the dextrous to the inept trying to make the team was 3 to 7. If 140 were trying to make the team, how many were dextrous?

2.
(66)
When the score was announced, 420 students were elated and the rest were dejected. If the ratio of elated to dejected was 2 to 9, how many students were there in all?

3.
(63)
When Lafayette led the column, the troops marched 24 miles in 6 hours. Then he left and the troops reduced their speed by 1 mile per hour. How long did it take the troops to march 18 miles without Lafayette?

4.
(90)
Four times a number is 36 greater than the product of the number and –2. What is the number?

5.
(68)
Fifty-six percent of the Trojans secretly thought that Andromache was prettier than Helen. If there were 21,000 Trojans in all, how many held Andromache's beauty in higher esteem than Helen's?

6.
(80)
If 80 is increased by 80 percent, what is the resulting number?

7.
(77)
What percent of 60 is 93?

8.
(20)
Find the least common multiple of 20, 25, and 30.

9. Find the surface area of this right
(88) solid. Dimensions are in centimeters.

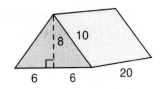

10. Between which two consecutive integers is $\sqrt[3]{155}$?
(92)

Use the distributive property to multiply:

11. $5x(x^2 - 3 + 3x)$
(103)

12. $2ab(a + b)$
(103)

13. Sketch a rectangular coordinate system, and graph the line $y = x + y$.
(85)

Simplify by adding like terms:

14. $3x + 5 + 3y + 2xy + 6x + 5xy$
(102)

15. $a^2 + 5a^2 + 3b^2 + 2a^2 - 5b^2$
(102)

16. $-4yxx + 5xyx + 7x - 6y + 5x$
(102)

Solve:

17. $2x - 6 - 4 = 3x - 4 + 5x$
(96)

18. $6x - 10 = -3 + 2x + 3(5 - 2x)$
(96,103)

19. $-2x + 6 = -4x + 6$
(95)

20. $\dfrac{-\dfrac{2}{3}}{\dfrac{1}{4}} = \dfrac{\dfrac{1}{6}}{x}$
(59)

Simplify:

21. $-3^2 - (-2)^3$
(99)

22. $-[-(-3)] + (-2)^3$
(99)

23. $2^3 - 2^4\left[2(3 - 5) + 2^2\left(3^2 - 2^2\right)\right]$
(44,91)

24. $aa^2ba^3b^2a^2b^3$
(101)

25. $xy^2x^2x^3y^3y^2$
(101)

26. $m^2nn^3m^3n^2n^3$
(101)

27. $\dfrac{2^3 - 2\left(1 - 2^2\right)\left(3 - 2^2\right)}{2\left(2^3 - 3^2\right)}$
(93)

28. $\dfrac{1 - 3\left(2^2 - 3\right) + \left(3^3 - 2 \cdot 3\right)}{6(2 \cdot 3 - 2)}$
(93)

29. $\dfrac{1}{2} + \dfrac{1}{3} + \dfrac{1}{4} + \dfrac{1}{5} + \dfrac{1}{6}$
(30)

30. Measure each angle with a protractor, and classify each angle:
(98)

(a)   (b)   (c)

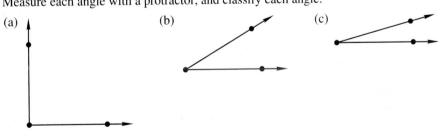

LESSON 104   *Classifying Triangles • Angles in Triangles*

104.A

classifying triangles

We can classify triangles by describing the angles. If one angle is a right angle, the triangle is a **right triangle.** If one angle is an obtuse angle, the triangle is an **obtuse triangle.** If all three angles are acute angles, the triangle is an **acute triangle.**

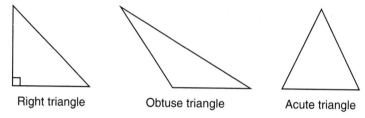

Right triangle   Obtuse triangle   Acute triangle

We can also classify triangles by describing the lengths of the sides. If no two sides have the same length, the triangle is a **scalene triangle.** If two sides have the same length, the triangle is an **isosceles triangle.** If all three sides have equal lengths, the triangle is an **equilateral triangle.** In the drawings, an equal number of tick marks denotes equal lengths.

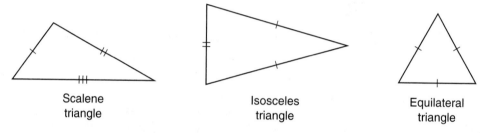

Scalene   Isosceles   Equilateral
triangle   triangle   triangle

If two sides of a triangle have equal lengths, the angles opposite these sides have equal measures. Conversely, if two angles have equal measures, the sides opposite these angles have equal lengths. An equal number of tick marks also denotes equal angle measures.

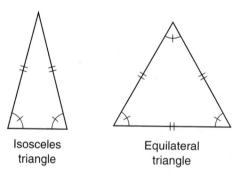

Isosceles   Equilateral
triangle   triangle

104.B

angles in triangles

The sum of the measures of the angles in any triangle is 180°.

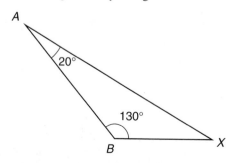

The notation used for naming a triangle is a little triangle (△) followed by the points of the triangle. In △*ABX* the sum of the measures of angles *A* and *B* is 150°. Therefore, the measure of angle *X* must be 30° because

$$130° + 20° + 30° = 180°$$

example 104.1   Find the measure of angle *BCA*.

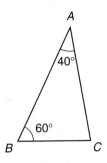

solution   The sum of the measures of the angles must be 180°. The sum of the measures of angles *A* and *B* is 100°. Therefore angle *C*, or angle *BCA*, must have a measure of **80°**.

$$40° + 60° + 80° = 180°$$

We note that angle *BCA* can also be called angle *C* because only one angle has point *C* as its vertex.

example 104.2   What is the measure of angle *B*?

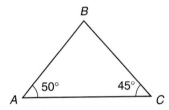

solution   The sum of the measures of the angles of any triangle is 180°. The two given angles are 50° and 45°. Their sum is 95°. Therefore, angle *B* must be an 85° angle because

$$95° + 85° = 180°$$

The measure of angle *B* is **85°**.

example 104.3   Angle *B* measures 110°. What are the measures of angles *A* and *C*?

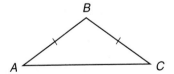

solution   The measures of the three angles must add up to 180°. Angle *B* measures 110°, so the sum of the measures of angles *A* and *C* must be 70° because 180° − 110° = 70°. Angles *A* and *C* must have equal measures because the sides opposite these angles have equal lengths. Since $\frac{70}{2} = 35$, angles *A* and *C* both measure **35°**.

practice   Find the measure of the indicated angles.

a.   Angle *Z*

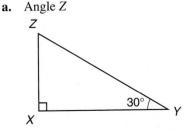

b.   Angle *A*

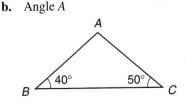

c. Classify $\triangle PQR$ by its sides and angles.

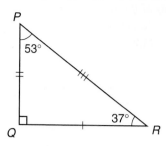

d. Angle M is a 50° angle. Find the measures of angles D and E.

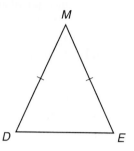

**problem set
104**

1.
(62)
Seven twelfths of the students mispronounced the word *chic*. If 1440 students pronounced *chic* correctly, how many students mispronounced it?

2.
(100)
The ratio of the number who paid the piper to the number who did not pay the piper this month was 12 to 5. If there are 170 in all, how many paid the piper?

3.
(100)
The ratio of sycophants to non-sycophants was 14 to 1. If there were 750 in all, how many were sycophants?

4.
(63)
The Lilliputians marched 500 meters in the first 4 hours. For the next 4 hours, their pace was three times faster. What was the total distance traveled by the Lilliputians in 8 hours?

5.
(90,95)
Three times a number is 12 less than the product of the number and 5. What is the number?

6.
(77)
What number is 170 percent of 120?

7.
(80)
If 80 is increased by 60 percent, what is the resulting number?

8.
(68)
There were thirty students in the class, and 60% of them were in the mathematics club. How many were not in the mathematics club?

9.
(73)
Find the volume in cubic centimeters of a right circular cylinder whose diameter is 4 centimeters and whose height is 1 meter.

10.
(88)
The figure shown on the left is the base of a right solid 100 centimeters tall. Find the total surface area of the solid. Dimensions are in centimeters.

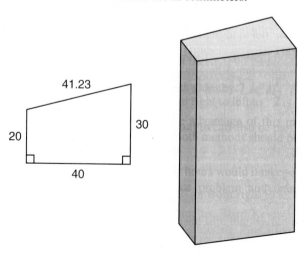

11.
(104)
Sketch a right triangle with a 40° angle. What is the measure of the third angle?

12. If $\angle A$ and $\angle B$ are supplementary and the measure of $\angle A$ is $179\frac{1}{2}°$, what is the measure
(98)   of $\angle B$?

13. Find the measure of $\angle A$, and classify $\triangle ABC$ by its sides and angles.
(104)

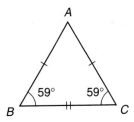

14. Classify $\triangle XYZ$ by its sides and angles.
(104)

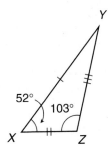

Use the distributive property to multiply:

15. $2bc(a + b + c)$
(103)

16. $ab(a + b + ab)$
(103)

Simplify by adding like terms:

17. $a^3 + 2abb + 3aa^2 + 2ab^2$
(102)

18. $yx^2 + xyx + 3y^2x + 2yxy$
(102)

Solve:

19. $4x - 3 = -x + 6$
(95)

20. $-5x - 2 = -x + 7 + 4(2x - 1)$
(96,103)

21. $7 - 3x + 5 = -2x - 3 + 12x + 2$
(96)

22. $\dfrac{-\frac{1}{3}}{2\frac{1}{3}} = \dfrac{\frac{1}{2}}{x}$
(65,81)

Simplify:

23. $-[-(-6)] + (-2)(-3)$
(91)

24. $2^3 - 2^2\left[2\left(3 - 2^2\right) + 2^2\left(2 \cdot 3 - 2^2\right)\right]$
(44)

25. $aba^2b^2a^3$
(101)

26. $xy^3x^2yy^2x$
(101)

27. $\dfrac{2^2 - 2^3\left(3^2 - 2^2\right) + 2^3}{6\left(5 - 2^2\right)}$
(93)

28. $\dfrac{1}{2} - 0.3$
(15)

Evaluate:

29. $ab^2 + \dfrac{b}{4}$ if $b = 8$ and $a = -2$
(99)

30. $a + b - ab$ if $a = -1$ and $b = -2$
(82)

LESSON 105 *Evaluating Powers of Negative Bases*

Let's examine the following expressions:

$$\text{(a) } x^2 \qquad \text{and} \qquad \text{(b) } -x^2$$

In expression (a) x is squared. If we substitute -2 for x, we must square -2. In algebra this means

$$(-2)^2$$

Notice that we inserted parentheses in this expression to protect the negative sign. Thus, expression (a) tells us to multiply x by x. If $x = -2$,

$$x^2 = (-2)(-2) = +4$$

Expression (b) tells us to find the opposite of the value of x^2. If we substitute -2 for x in (b), we need to find the opposite of $(-2)^2$.

$$-(-2)^2 = -(-2)(-2) = -4$$

There is an easy way to remember if the minus sign is included in the base of the exponent. If the symbol – is not protected by parentheses, cover it with a finger. To simplify

$$-2^4$$

we cover the minus sign with a finger.

 2^4

The value of 2^4 is 16. Now we remove our finger and uncover the minus sign and see that the final result is negative.

$$-16$$

example 105.1 Evaluate: (a) $(-3)^2$ (b) -3^2

solution If we try to cover the minus sign with a finger, we find that the minus sign is protected by the parentheses in (a) but not in (b).

(a)  $(-3)^2$ (b)  3^2

So $(-3)^2$ means $(-3)(-3)$, and -3^2 means $-(3)(3)$.

$$\text{(a) } (-3)^2 = \mathbf{9} \qquad \text{(b) } -3^2 = \mathbf{-9}$$

example 105.2 Evaluate: (a) a^2 (b) $-a^2$ if $a = -4$

solution (a) We first write parentheses where we will insert the value for a.

$$(\quad)^2$$

Then we write -4 inside the parentheses and simplify.

$$(-4)^2 = \mathbf{16}$$

(b) This time we begin by writing

$$-(\quad)^2$$

Then we write -4 inside the parentheses and simplify.

$$-(-4)^2 = \mathbf{-16}$$

example 105.3   Evaluate: $a^2 - ab^2 - b^2$ if $a = -2$ and $b = -3$

solution   Parentheses are not absolutely necessary, but we will use them to help us with the second term. We substitute and get

$$(-2)^2 - (-2)(-3)^2 - (-3)^2$$

We simplify this and get

$$4 - (-2)(-3)^2 - 9 \qquad \text{simplified}$$
$$4 - (-18) - 9 \qquad \text{multiplied}$$
$$4 + 18 - 9 \qquad \text{simplified}$$
$$\mathbf{13} \qquad \text{added}$$

practice   Evaluate:

a. $a^2b - b$ if $a = -2$ and $b = -3$

b. $b^2 - a^2b$ if $a = -2$ and $b = -3$

**problem set
105**

1.
(62)
Six thirteenths of the audiophiles could discriminate between the two products. If 28 of the audiophiles could not discriminate, how many could discriminate?

2.
(62)
Six sevenths of the party delegates were proclaiming their positions. If 1100 were not involved in this behavior, how many delegates were there in all?

3.
(100)
The ratio of the contumacious to the affable was 2 to 17. If there were 7600, all of whom were either contumacious or affable, how many were contumacious and how many were affable?

4.
(100)
Lori studied fruit fly characteristics for her genetics experiment. One in 4 had white eyes; the remainder had red eyes. There were 848 flies in this generation. How many flies had red eyes?

5.
(90,95)
Seven times a number is 9 less than the product of the number and −20. What is the number?

6.
(63)
Gawain and Lancelot drove their horses through the pounding rain and covered 16 miles in 2 hours. When the rain stopped, they slowed to half that pace. How long did it take them to travel the remaining 20 miles?

7.
(68)
Twenty percent chose Plain Vanilla and five percent chose Bubble Gum Delight. If twenty-eight selected Plain Vanilla, how many fancied Bubble Gum Delight?

8.
(80)
If 90 is increased by 80 percent, what is the resulting number?

9.
(77)
What percent of 60 is 78?

10.
(64)
Find the volume of the right solid whose base is shown on the left and whose height is 2 meters. Dimensions are in meters.

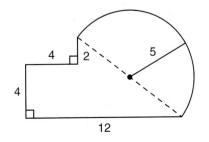
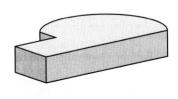

11. Find the lateral surface area of the solid in problem 10.
(88)

12. Between which two consecutive integers is $\sqrt[4]{95}$?
(92)

13. Find the measures of $\angle A$ and $\angle B$, and classify $\triangle ABC$ by its sides and by its angles.
(104)

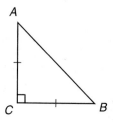

Use the distributive property to multiply:

14. $3px(p + x + 2px)$
(103)

15. $mn^2(m + mny + 3m^2)$
(103)

Simplify by adding like terms:

16. $m^2n^3 + 3nm^2nn - mnmn^2 + 2n^3mm$
(102)

17. $ap^3 + pap^2 - 5p^2ap$
(102)

18. What is the value of $3x \div (10 - x)$ when $2x + 5 = 85$?
(97)

Solve:

19. $5x - 4 = -3x + 20 + 2(x - 1)$
(96,103)

20. $3 - 4x - 3 = -10x + 7 + 2x + 5(1 - x)$
(96,103)

21. $\dfrac{-\dfrac{2}{5}}{2\dfrac{1}{2}} = \dfrac{-\dfrac{11}{13}}{x}$
(65,81)

Simplify:

22. $-\left[-(-6)^2\right] + (-3)(-4)$
(99)

23. $a^3p^2ap^2a^4aa$
(101)

24. $y^8z^2yzyyz^4$
(101)

25. $2\dfrac{1}{4} - 0.315$
(15)

Evaluate:

26. $m^2 + \dfrac{n^2}{m}$ if $m = -8$ and $n = 4$
(105)

27. $p^3 + c^3$ if $p = -3$ and $c = -1$
(105)

28. $\dfrac{a^2}{b^3} - a$ if $a = 4$ and $b = -2$
(105)

29. $p^q + \sqrt[q]{p}$ if $p = 4$ and $q = 2$
(54)

30. Sketch a rectangular coordinate system, and graph the line $y = \frac{1}{2}x - 1$.
(85)

LESSON 106   *Roots of Negative Numbers • Negative Exponents • Zero Exponents*

106.A
roots of negative numbers

Remember that every positive number has a positive square root. Also, every positive number has a negative square root because

$$(2)(2) = 4 \qquad (-2)(-2) = 4$$

When we write

$$\sqrt{4}$$

we indicate the positive square root of 4, which is 2. When we write

$$-\sqrt{4}$$

we indicate the negative square root of 4, which is –2.

Negative numbers **do not have** positive square roots or fourth roots or sixth roots, because the product of an even number of positive or negative numbers is always a positive number.

$$(2)(2) = +4$$
$$(-2)(-2)(-2)(-2) = +16$$
$$(3)(3)(3)(3) = +81$$
$$(-1)(-1)(-1)(-1)(-1)(-1) = +1$$

But negative numbers **do have** negative third roots and fifth roots and seventh roots, because the product of an odd number of negative roots is always a negative number.

$$(-2)(-2)(-2) = -8 \qquad \text{so} \qquad \sqrt[3]{-8} = -2$$
$$(-3)(-3)(-3) = -27 \qquad \text{so} \qquad \sqrt[3]{-27} = -3$$

example 106.1   Find $\sqrt[3]{-64}$.

solution   What number used as a factor 3 times equals –64? The answer is **–4** because

$$(-4)(-4)(-4) = -64$$

example 106.2   Find $\sqrt[5]{-32}$.

solution   What number used as a factor 5 times equals –32? The answer is **–2** because

$$(-2)(-2)(-2)(-2)(-2) = -32$$

106.B
negative exponents

Thus far, we have only encountered negative exponents in scientific notation. We examine further the function of the negative exponent in the following expression:

$$1.5 \times 10^{-3} = 0.0015$$

We see that multiplying 1.5 by 10^{-3} shifted the decimal point three places to the left. Another way to shift the decimal point three places to the left is to divide 1.5 by 1000 or multiply 1.5 by $\frac{1}{1000}$.

$$1.5 \times \frac{1}{1000} = 0.0015$$

Since 10^3 is equal to 1000,

$$1.5 \times \frac{1}{10^3} = 0.0015$$

We can see from this example that

$$\frac{1}{10^3} \text{ must equal } 10^{-3}$$

From this examination we can conclude that 10^{-3} $\left(\text{or } \frac{1}{1000}\right)$ is the reciprocal of 10^3 (or 1000). The same is true when other bases have negative exponents. Whenever we see a negative exponent, we know that the expression is equivalent to its reciprocal with a positive, rather than negative exponent.

$$10^{-5} = \frac{1}{10^5}$$

$$10^{-2} = \frac{1}{10^2}$$

$$3^{-3} = \frac{1}{3^3}$$

$$7^{-8} = \frac{1}{7^8}$$

How about

$$\frac{1}{5^{-2}} \text{ or } \frac{1}{7^{-4}}$$

All expressions with negative exponents are treated the same way. Write the reciprocal of the expression with a positive exponent.

$$\frac{1}{5^{-2}} = 5^2 \qquad \text{and} \qquad \frac{1}{7^{-4}} = 7^4$$

example 106.3   Simplify: $\dfrac{1}{4^{-2}}$

solution   To evaluate a number with a negative exponent, we turn the expression upside down (write the reciprocal) and change the minus sign in the exponent to a plus sign.

$$\frac{1}{4^{-2}} = 4^2 = \mathbf{16}$$

example 106.4   Simplify: $\dfrac{1}{(-2)^{-4}}$

solution   We flip the expression (write the reciprocal) and change the sign of the exponent from $-$ to $+$. **We do not change the sign of the base inside the parentheses.**

$$\frac{1}{(-2)^{-4}} = (-2)^4 = \mathbf{16}$$

example 106.5   Simplify: $-\dfrac{1}{(-3)^{-2}}$

solution   The negative sign outside the fraction is not protected by parentheses, so we cover it with a finger.

Now we remove our finger and simplify.

$$-(-3)^2 = \mathbf{-9}$$

106.C

zero exponents

We know that a nonzero number divided by itself equals 1. For instance

$$1 = \frac{4^2}{4^2}$$

We can simplify this expression by moving the 4^2 in the denominator to the numerator and changing the exponent from 2 to –2. Then we multiply 4^2 by 4^{-2} and get 4^0 by adding the exponents.

$$1 = \frac{4^2}{4^2} = 4^2 \cdot 4^{-2} = 4^0$$

Now, 4^0 must equal 1 because 4^2 divided by 4^2 equals 1. In the same way, we see that any nonzero quantity raised to the zero power must have a value of 1.

$$\left(x + y + z^2\right)^0 = 1 \qquad (pm)^0 = 1 \qquad \left(px^{-4}\right)^0 = 1$$

Each of the above has a value of 1 if the expression in parentheses does not have a value of zero. Zero raised to the zero power has no meaning.

example 106.6   Simplify: (a) 2^0 (b) -2^0 (c) $(-2)^0$

solution   Any expression (except 0) raised to the zero power has a value of 1. Thus, the answer to both (a) and (c) is **1.** The expression in (b) asks for the value of the opposite of 2^0. The answer to (b) is **–1.**

example 106.7   Simplify: $x^2y^5y^{-2}x^{-2}$

solution $x^2y^5y^{-2}x^{-2} = y^3x^0 = \mathbf{y^3}$ $\left(\text{because } x^0 = 1 \text{ if } x \neq 0\right)$

Since we must not use the expression 0^0, it is necessary in problems such as the above to assume that the quantity with the zero exponent is not zero. Further, in the problem sets, we will assume a nonzero value for any quantity that has zero for its exponent.

practice   Find:

a. $\sqrt[3]{-27}$

b. $\sqrt[3]{-343}$

Simplify:

c. 5^{-2}

d. $\dfrac{1}{5^{-2}}$

e. -14^0

f. $x^3y^2x^{-2}y^{-1}$

problem set 106

1.
(90,95) Five times a number is 28 greater than the product of the number and –2. Find the number.

2.
(100) The ratio of ascetics to hedonists visiting the shrine was 4 to 7. If a total of 4400 ascetics and hedonists visited the shrine, how many were ascetics?

3.
(57) Enthusiasm for the new product ran high. There were $2\frac{3}{4}$ as many customers as there were on the previous day. If 2200 customers arrived to inspect the new product, how many were there on the previous day?

4.
(75) Fifty consultations cost $3150. What would 78 consultations cost?

5. It took the DC-9 four hours to go 1600 miles before it encountered a storm. The storm
(63) decreased the plane's speed by 45 miles per hour. How long would it take the plane to
go the remaining 2485 miles at the new rate?

6. Graph on a number line: $x \geq -3$
(72)

7. Twenty-two percent of the students voted for Josh for student council president, and the
(68) others voted for Moe. If there were 900 students in all, how many voted for Moe?

8. If 350 is increased by 90 percent, what is the resulting number?
(80)

9. What percent of 75 is 135?
(77)

10. Find the volume in cubic feet of a right solid whose base is the figure shown on the left
(64) and whose height is 1 yard. Dimensions are in feet.

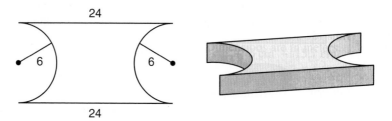

11. Find the total surface area of the solid in problem 10.
(88)

12. What is the mean of $\frac{5}{4}$, $\frac{2}{5}$, and $\frac{3}{10}$?
(26,30)

13. Sketch a rectangular coordinate system, and graph the line $x = \dfrac{y}{2^{-2}}$.
(85,106)

14. Find the measure of $\angle A$.
(98,104)

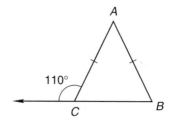

15. Use the distributive property to multiply: $4ax(3a + 3z + 9ax)$
(103)

Evaluate:

16. $m^3 + \dfrac{x}{y} - x^2$ if $m = -3$, $x = -4$, and $y = -2$
(105)

17. $a^3 + b^3 + c^3$ if $a = -1$, $b = -2$, and $c = -3$
(105)

18. $10^a + 10^b + ba$ if $a = 0$ and $b = 3$
(106)

19. Simplify by adding like terms: $3m^2 + 2c^2 - 4cm + 6c^2 - 9m^2$
(102)

Solve:

20. $-7x + 4 = -x - 8 + 5(2 - 3x)$
(96,103)

21. $\dfrac{\dfrac{2}{3}}{-\dfrac{1}{4}} = \dfrac{x}{\dfrac{2}{5}}$
(59,81)

Simplify:

22. $\sqrt[7]{-128}$
(106)

23. $\sqrt[3]{-512}$
(106)

24. (a) 4^{-3}
(106)

(b) $\dfrac{1}{5^{-3}}$

25. $-5^2 - (-3)^3 + \sqrt[3]{-64}$
(106)

26. $-\left[-(-3)^2\right] - (4)^2 - \sqrt[3]{-216}$
(106)

27. $a^3m^3aa^2m^2a$
(101)

28. $\dfrac{4^3 - 2^2(1^5 - 3^2)(3 - 2^2)}{2^2(2^3 - 3^2)}$
(93)

29. $5^{-2} - 0.04$
(106)

30. $3^{-3} + \dfrac{1}{9}$
(106)

LESSON *107* *Roman Numerals*

The Romans did not use the Hindu-Arabic numbers we use today. They used the following seven symbols.

Symbol	I	V	X	L	C	D	M
Value	1	5	10	50	100	500	1000

The Romans did not use place value. They did not have a symbol for zero. The value of a Roman numeral equals the sum of the values of the symbols in the numeral. To write 3, 30, 300, or 3000, they wrote the same symbol 3 times.

III means 3   XXX means 30   CCC means 300   MMM means 3000

Here are the Roman numerals for the numbers from 1 to 50.

1	I	11	XI	21	XXI	31	XXXI	41	XLI
2	II	12	XII	22	XXII	32	XXXII	42	XLII
3	III	13	XIII	23	XXIII	33	XXXIII	43	XLIII
4	IV	14	XIV	24	XXIV	34	XXXIV	44	XLIV
5	V	15	XV	25	XXV	35	XXXV	45	XLV
6	VI	16	XVI	26	XXVI	36	XXXVI	46	XLVI
7	VII	17	XVII	27	XXVII	37	XXXVII	47	XLVII
8	VIII	18	XVIII	28	XXVIII	38	XXXVIII	48	XLVIII
9	IX	19	XIX	29	XXIX	39	XXXIX	49	XLIX
10	X	20	XX	30	XXX	40	XL	50	L

When we look at these numbers, we note that:

1. No symbol appears more than 3 times in a row because the Romans used a trick to write 4, 9, 40, 90, etc.
2. When the symbol with lesser value is written in front of the symbol with greater value, the smaller number is subtracted from the larger. Instead of writing IIII for 4, the Romans wrote IV, which means "5 – 1." Instead of writing VIIII for 9, they wrote IX, which means "10 – 1." Instead of writing XXXX for 40, they wrote XL, which means "50 – 10." Instead of writing LXXXX for 90, they wrote XC, which means "100 – 10."

We can use this technique whenever 4, 9, 40, 90, 400, or 900 appears in a number.

4 = IV	9 = IX	90 = XC	400 = CD	900 = CM
54 = LIV	109 = CIX	590 = DXC	420 = CDXX	1900 = MCM

example 107.1   Write the number 3493 in Roman numerals.

solution   First we write our key.

I	V	X	L	C	D	M
1	5	10	50	100	500	1000

The number 3493 means "3000 + 400 + 90 + 3."

For 3000 we use three M's: MMM
For 400 we use 500 – 100:   CD
For 90 we use 100 – 10:   XC
And we have three 1's on the end: III

MMMCDXCIII

example 107.2   What number is represented by DCCLXIV?

solution   DCCLXIV means 500 + 100 + 100 + 50 + 10 + 4 = **764.**

practice   Write the Roman numeral for:

    a. 4   **b.** 9   **c.** 34

Write the number represented by the Roman numeral:

    d. CCXXXIX   **e.** CXL   **f.** MDXLIX

problem set 107

1. (68) Sixty percent of the populace were iconoclasts; the rest were traditionalists. If 16,000 were traditionalists, how many were iconoclasts?

2. (80) This spring, the number of flowers that could be seen was 360 percent greater than the year before. If 22,000 could be seen the year before, how many flowers could be seen this spring?

3. (57) Originally there were 39,000 employees in the industry. Since the business began, the number of employees has grown to $2\frac{2}{13}$ of the original number. How many people are now employed in the industry?

4. (75) Three hundred new ones cost $2100. What would be the cost of 120 new ones?

5. (100) The ratio of advocates to opponents at the conference was 5 to 7. If 4800 had convened to weigh the issues, how many were advocates and how many were opponents?

6. (90,95) Six times a number is 45 greater than the product of the number and –3. Find the number.

7. Graph on a number line: $x > 0$
(72)

8. What number is 84 percent of 1600?
(68)

9. If 900 is increased by 35 percent, what is the resulting number?
(80)

10. What percent of 89 is 445?
(77)

11. Find the volume in cubic centimeters of a right solid whose base is shown and whose height is 2 meters. Dimensions are in meters.
(45)

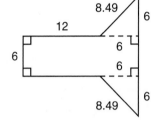

12. Find the lateral surface area in square centimeters of the solid described in problem 11.
(88)

Write the Roman numeral for:

13. 17   **14.** 939
(107)   (107)

Write the number represented by the Roman numeral:

15. VI   **16.** CDXLIV
(107)   (107)

17. Write 13.05 as a mixed number.
(28)

18. If $\angle A$ and $\angle B$ are complementary and the measure of $\angle A$ is 42°, what is $\frac{3}{4}$ of the measure of $\angle B$?
(98)

Use the distributive property to multiply:

19. $5c(3m + 2p + c)$ **20.** $7mp(m + p + x + 2mp)$
(103)   (103)

Simplify by adding like terms:

21. $m^2 + c^3 + 3mm + c^2c$ **22.** $p^2 + 3aam - 2p^2p + a^2m$
(102)   (102)

23. Simplify: $(-5)^2 - 5^2 - (-5)^4 + (-5)^4$
(99)

Solve:

24. $-4x - 3 = -11x + 16$ **25.** $-7x - 4 = 3x + 3$
(95)   (95)

26. Find x.
(65)

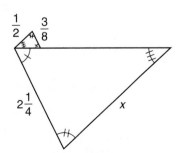

27. Simplify: $-[-(-4)] + (2)^2 - 3^2 + \sqrt[3]{-64} - \sqrt[3]{\dfrac{125}{1000}}$
(106)

28. Find the measure of $\angle A$. What kind of
$_{(104)}$ angle is it?

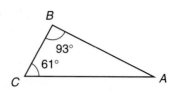

29. Evaluate: $m^2p + p^2$ if $m = -4$ and $p = 5$
$_{(105)}$

30. Simplify: $x^2yx^4y + a^2a^{10} - b^3b^3b + 5^2c(5)$
$_{(101)}$

LESSON 108   *Fractional Percents*

Percents do not have to be whole numbers. They can be decimals or mixed numbers or fractions. To convert fractional percents into decimal numbers, we first convert them to decimal percents, then divide by 100 (move the decimal point two places to the left) to make decimal numbers.

example 108.1   Write each percent as a decimal number:

(a) 4.2%   (b) 0.05%   (c) $4\frac{1}{2}\%$ (d) $\frac{3}{20}\%$

solution   (a) To change a percent to a decimal, we move the decimal point two places to the left.

$$4.2\% = \mathbf{0.042}$$

(b) Similarly,

$$0.05\% = \mathbf{0.0005}$$

(c) We change the mixed number percent to a decimal percent, then move the decimal point to make a decimal number.

$$4\frac{1}{2}\% = 4.5\% = \mathbf{0.045}$$

(d) We divide to get a decimal percent, then move the decimal point to make a decimal number.

$$\frac{3}{20}\% = 0.15\% = \mathbf{0.0015}$$

example 108.2   Four and one half percent of the students did not brush their teeth every day. If there were 1200 students in all, how many did not brush their teeth every day?

solution   We start with the percent equation and then fit our problem into its form.

A percent of a number is another number.

$4\frac{1}{2}\%$ of the 1200 students did not brush their teeth every day.

$$0.045 \cdot 1200 = B$$
$$54 = B$$

So **54 students** did not brush their teeth daily.

practice Complete the table. Begin by inserting the reference numbers.

Fraction	Decimal	Percent
a.	b.	0.04%
c.	d.	$22\frac{1}{2}\%$
e.	f.	$\frac{1}{4}\%$

problem set 108

1. *(80)* Consumption of health food rose 110 percent in the year after the flood. If 500,000 units of health food were consumed the year before the flood, how many units were consumed the year after the flood?

2. *(57)* The number of items recalled at the plant this year was $2\frac{1}{2}$ times the number of items recalled last year. If 8500 items were recalled this year, how many were recalled last year?

3. *(75)* Eleven pedestals cost $74,800. What would be the cost of six pedestals?

4. *(100)* The ratio of bears to pumas in the forest was 7 to 13. If a total of 2600 bears and pumas were in the forest, how many bears and how many pumas were there?

5. *(72)* Graph on a number line: $x \geq 1$

6. *(108)* If 750 is increased by $62\frac{1}{4}$ percent, what is the resulting number?

7. *(77)* What percent of 95 is 228?

8. *(108)* What number is $15\frac{1}{2}$ percent of 9000?

9. *(64)* Find the volume of a right solid whose base is shown and whose height is 2 feet. Dimensions are in feet.

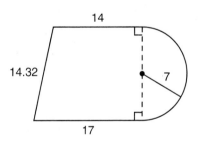

10. *(88)* Find the total surface area of the figure discussed in problem 9.

11. *(107)* Write the Roman numeral for: (a) 19 (b) 1644

12. *(107)* Write the number represented by the Roman numeral: XXVIII + V

13. *(98)* Measure each angle with a protractor:

(a) 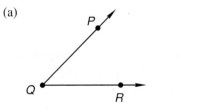 (b)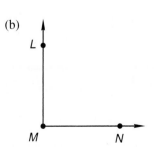

(c)

14. Sketch an isosceles right triangle. What is the measure of each angle?
(104)

15. Simplify: $\left(\dfrac{2}{3}\right)^{-2} + (4)^{-2}$
(106)

Use the distributive property to multiply:

16. $4x(3a + b + ab)$ **17.** $11p(11 + p + 2ab)$
(103)   (103)

Simplify by adding like terms:

18. $mp^2 + mpm + 2a^2b^2 + mp + abab$
(102)

19. $p^2ap + m^2nx + ap^3 + nmxm$
(102)

20. Add: $\dfrac{2}{5} + 0.13 + \dfrac{3}{25}$
(15)

21. Convert $\frac{8}{9}$ to a decimal. Round to the nearest hundredth.
(15)

Write each percent as a decimal number:

22. $9\dfrac{1}{5}\%$ **23.** $86\dfrac{1}{4}\%$
(108)   (108)

Solve:

24. $6x + 3 = x - 22$
(95)

25. $10 - x - 9 = -11x + 91 + 4(3 - x)$
(96,103)

26. $\dfrac{\dfrac{4}{5}}{3\dfrac{1}{2}} = \dfrac{\dfrac{6}{7}}{x}$
(65)

Simplify:

27. $-[-(-4)(-4)] - \left[-(3^2)\right]$
(91)

28. $-[-(6)(3)] + (-9) - [-(-4)] - \sqrt[3]{-27}$
(91,106)

29. $t^3m^{-4}t^{-1}t^{-2}m^{-1}t^5am^5$
(106)

30. Evaluate: $a^2b^2 + b^2 + \dfrac{b}{a}$ if $a = -3$ and $b = -9$
(105)

LESSON 109   *Simple Interest • Compound Interest*

109.A

simple interest   When you put money in a bank, the bank uses your money to make more money. They will pay you for the use of your money. The money they pay is called **interest.** The interest is a fixed percentage of the money you invest.

example 109.1   Jim put $5000 in the bank for 2 years at 8 percent simple interest. How much money did he get when he withdrew his money after 2 years?

solution   The words **simple interest** tell us that Jim will get 8 percent of $5000 every year. We use the percent equation.

> *A percent of a number is another number.*
>
> A percent of the money in the bank is the interest earned each year.
>
> 8% of $5000 is the interest earned each year.
>
> $$0.08 \cdot \$5000 = B$$
> $$\$400 = B$$

The bank paid him $400 in interest for the use of his money *each* year. At the end of 2 years he received

$$\$5000 + \$400 + \$400 = \mathbf{\$5800}$$

example 109.2   Maria deposited $800 at 8 percent simple interest. At the end of 3 years she will have how much money?

solution   She will get 8 percent of $800 each year.

$$0.08 \times \$800 = \$64$$

At the end of 3 years she will have earned

$$3 \times \$64 = \$192 \text{ interest}$$

At the end of 3 years she will have

$$\$800 + \$192 = \mathbf{\$992}$$

109.B
compound interest

At the end of the first year in the preceding example, Maria had earned $64 simple interest, so she had a total of $864. If the bank paid her **compound interest** the second year, they would pay her 8 percent interest on the total amount of $864. Thus, in the second year her interest would be

$$0.08 \times \$864 = \$69.12$$

At the end of the second year she would have

$$
\begin{array}{r}
\$864.00 \\
+ \ \$ \ 69.12 \\
\hline
\$933.12
\end{array}
$$

Her interest the third year at 8 percent compound interest would be

$$0.08 \times \$933.12 = \$74.6496 \approx \$74.65$$

Note that we round to the nearest cent when dealing with money. At the end of the third year she would have

$$
\begin{array}{r}
\$933.12 \\
+ \ \$ \ 74.65 \\
\hline
\$1007.77
\end{array}
$$

Thus, if the bank had paid compound interest, she would have more money in her account than if the bank had paid simple interest.

$$
\begin{array}{ll}
\$1007.77 & \text{3 years' compound interest} \\
- \ \$ \ 992.00 & \text{3 years' simple interest} \\
\hline
\$15.77 & \text{Difference}
\end{array}
$$

You earn more with compound interest because the interest you earn is periodically added to the balance, so when the interest is next calculated, you earn interest on the interest!

example 109.3   How much will $700 be worth in 2 years if the money is deposited at 9 percent interest compounded annually?

solution   The first year's interest would be

$$0.09 \times \$700 = \$63$$

The amount of money at the end of the first year would be

$$\begin{array}{r} \$700 \\ + \ \$ \ 63 \\ \hline \$763 \end{array}$$

The second year's interest would be

$$0.09 \times \$763 = \$68.67$$

The amount of money at the end of the second year would be

$$\begin{array}{ll} \$763.00 & \text{End of first year} \\ + \ \$ \ 68.67 & \text{Second year's interest} \\ \hline \mathbf{\$831.67} & \text{Total} \end{array}$$

practice   **a.**   Elvira put $7000 in the bank at 9 percent simple interest. How much money did she get when she withdrew her money after 2 years?

b.   How much would Elvira's $7000 be worth in 2 years if it had been deposited at 9 percent interest compounded annually?

problem set 109

1.   The ratio of the number of garrulous to the number of reticent at the conference was 2
(100)   to 5. If 4900 people attended the conference, each of whom was either garrulous or reticent, how many were garrulous?

2.   Fertilizer was purchased in large quantities. If 500 tons could be purchased for $3300,
(75)   what would be the cost of 350 tons?

3.   This year the fertile valley produced a harvest 230 percent greater than average. If the
(80)   average harvest produced 11,000,000 bushels, how many bushels were produced this year?

4.   Because the economy is good, $3\frac{3}{4}$ times as many people live on the coast than before.
(57)   If 12,000 people live on the coast now, how many people lived there before?

5.   If Jennifer put $5000 in the bank at 7 percent interest compounded annually, how much
(109)   money would she have at the end of 2 years?

6.   Akeem put $15,000 in the bank at 10 percent simple interest. How much money did he
(109)   get when he withdrew his money after 3 years?

7.   How much would Akeem's $15,000 be worth in 3 years if it had been deposited at 10
(109)   percent interest compounded annually?

8.   Graph on a number line: $x \le -2$
(72)

9.   If 90 is increased by 90% and that number is then decreased by 90%, what is the
(80)   resulting number?

10. What percent of 68 is 170?
(77)

11. What number is $18\frac{1}{20}$ percent of 12,000?
(108)

12. Find the volume in cubic miles of a
(64) right solid whose base is shown and
whose height is 0.5 mile. Dimensions
are in miles. Angles that look like
right angles are right angles.

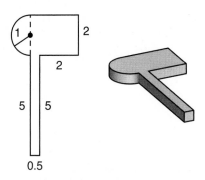

13. Find the volume in cubic feet and the
(73) lateral surface area in square feet of
the right circular cylinder shown.
Dimensions are in feet.

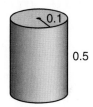

14. Use Roman numerals to write each number: (a) 26   (b) 825
(107)

15. Simplify: $\dfrac{\sqrt[3]{-27}}{\sqrt[5]{-32}} - \left(\dfrac{2}{5}\right)^{-3}$
(106)

16. If one angle of a triangle is $14\frac{3}{4}°$ and another one is 90.31°, what is the measure of the
(104) third angle?

Use the distributive property to multiply:

17. $3c(m + mn + n)$
(103)

18. $a^2(a + ab + b^2)$
(103)

Simplify by adding like terms:

19. $a^3p + mb^2m + apa^2 + m^2bb$
(102)

20. $p^2bc^2 + pbcpc + mx^3 + mp$
(102)

Convert to a decimal:

21. $301\dfrac{1}{40}$
(28)

22. $\dfrac{3}{8}$
(15)

Write each percent as a decimal number:

23. $8\dfrac{1}{5}\%$
(108)

24. $9\dfrac{1}{8}\%$
(108)

Solve:

25. $2x - 11 = -8x + 109$
(95)

26. $6 - x - 4 = -13x - 100 + 3(2 - x)$
(96,103)

27. $\dfrac{\frac{1}{4}}{-3\frac{1}{6}} = \dfrac{-1\frac{1}{2}}{x}$
(65,81)

28. Simplify: $-[-(-3)(2)] - [-(-4)] - (2^2) + \sqrt[3]{-64}$
(106)

Evaluate:

29. $mx^3 + \dfrac{x}{m} + \dfrac{m}{x}$ if $m = -2$ and $x = -4$
(105)

30. $a^c b - a^2 b - a^2 bc$ if $a = -2$, $b = -3$, and $c = 0$
(105,106)

LESSON *110* *Markup and Markdown*

If a merchant is to make a living, goods must be sold for more than the merchant pays for them. The price a merchant pays for goods is called the wholesale price. It is customary to sell goods at a retail price, the wholesale price plus a percentage of the wholesale price. This added price is called **markup.** If the price of an item is reduced for a sale, the amount it is reduced is called **markdown** or discount.

example 110.1 Mr. Franklin bought new dresses for $40 each. He marked each dress up 150 percent. What was the price he charged his customers?

solution As always, we use the percent equation.

> *A percent of a number is another number.*
> A percent of the wholesale price is the markup.
> 150% of $40 is the markup
> $1.50 \cdot \$40 = \$60$

The markup is $60, so he sold the dresses for

$$\$40 + \$60 = \mathbf{\$100}$$

example 110.2 Sybil saw that the coat was marked down 30 percent. If the original price was $80, what was the price of the coat now?

solution First we find out how much the coat was marked down.

> *A percent of a number is another number.*
> A percent of the original price is the markdown or discount.
> 30% of $80 is the markdown or discount
> $0.3 \cdot \$80 = \$24$

The coat was marked down $24. To find the sale price, we subtract.

$$\$80 - \$24 = \$56 \qquad \text{subtracted}$$

Thus, the sale price of the coat was **$56.**

example 110.3 The sale price of the ring was $120. It had been marked down 40 percent for the sale. What was the original price of the ring?

solution   The original price was 100 percent. If the ring was marked down 40 percent, it was selling for 60 percent of the original price.

60% of the original price is the discounted price

$$0.6 \cdot A = \$120 \qquad \text{equation}$$

$$\frac{\cancel{0.6} \cdot A}{\cancel{0.6}} = \frac{\$120}{0.6} \qquad \text{divided both sides by 0.6}$$

$$A = \$200 \qquad \text{simplified}$$

The original price of the ring was **$200.**

practice   **a.**   The wholesale price of the tractor was $8000. If the store owner marked up the price 20 percent, at what price was the store owner selling the tractor?

b.   The suit was marked down 20 percent for the sale, and its sale price was $120. What was the original price of the suit?

problem set 110

1.
(68)   Twenty percent of the little people living in the forest suffered from agoraphobia, and they would not go into the clearing. If 1600 did not suffer from agoraphobia, how many little people lived in the forest?

2.
(100)   The ratio of the reclusive to the gregarious living in the valley was 3 to 14. If 15,300 lived in the valley, and each was either reclusive or gregarious, how many were gregarious?

3.
(90,95)   The product of a number and –2 was increased by 7. This result was 27 greater than the product of the number and 3. What was the number?

4.
(63)   Alfonso traveled 100 miles in 4 hours. Then he increased his speed by 5 miles per hour. How long did it take him to travel the last 120 miles at the new speed?

5.
(110)   The merchant has a standard 60 percent markup on her inventory. She pays $20 a pair for dress shoes. For how much does she sell the dress shoes?

6.
(110)   February is sale month at the clothing store. All items are marked down 20 percent. If the sale price for a purse is $42, what was the price before the markdown?

7.
(92)   Between which two consecutive intergers is $\sqrt[3]{80}$?

8.
(64)   Find the volume of a right solid whose base is shown on the left and whose height is 4 feet. Dimensions are in feet.

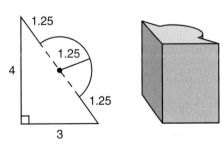

9.
(88)   Find the lateral surface area of the solid in problem 8.

10.
(107)   Write the Roman numeral for 524.

11.
(107)   Write the number represented by the Roman numeral CDXIX?

12. If 120 is increased by 80 percent, what is the resulting number?
$_{(80)}$

13. What percent of 50 is 60?
$_{(77)}$

14. Write each percent as a decimal number: (a) $61\dfrac{3}{5}\%$ (b) $7\dfrac{4}{5}\%$
$_{(108)}$

15. Use two unit multipliers to convert 12 miles to inches.
$_{(33)}$

16. How much simple interest would $200 earn in one year invested at $4\frac{1}{2}\%$ interest?
$_{(109)}$

Use the distributive property to multiply:

17. $2ac(ab + a - b)$
$_{(103)}$

18. $-am\left(a^2 + m - am\right)$
$_{(103)}$

19. Simplify by adding like terms: $3xy^2 - 2xy + 3xyy + 3xy - y^2x$
$_{(102)}$

Solve:

20. $3x + 6 = x + 7$
$_{(95)}$

21. $-2\dfrac{1}{3}x - \dfrac{3}{4} = \dfrac{1}{2}$
$_{(84)}$

22. $\dfrac{-\dfrac{1}{3}}{\dfrac{4}{9}} = \dfrac{\dfrac{1}{4}}{x}$
$_{(59,81)}$

Simplify:

23. $-\left[-(-4)^2\right] + (-3)(4) + (-2)^3 + \sqrt[7]{-128}$
$_{(99,106)}$

24. $2^2 + 2^3\left[-2\left(-3 + 2^2\right)\left(2^2 - 1\right) + 2\right]$
$_{(44,91)}$

25. $6a^2bab^2b^3$
$_{(101)}$

26. $\dfrac{-(-2)^2 + 3^2\left(2^2 - 5\right) + 3}{2\left(2^3 - 4\right)}$
$_{(93)}$

27. $\dfrac{1}{4}\left(2\dfrac{1}{3} \cdot \dfrac{1}{4} - \dfrac{7}{12}\right)$
$_{(52)}$

28. $(-2)^{-2} - \left(\dfrac{1}{3}\right)^{-3} + \sqrt[3]{-64}$
$_{(105,106)}$

Evaluate:

29. $a^a - 2a$ if $a = -2$
$_{(105)}$

30. $a^2 + 3ab^2$ if $a = -1$ and $b = -3$
$_{(105)}$

LESSON *111* *Commission • Profit*

111.A

commission   Many companies pay their sales personnel a basic salary that is low. They also pay them a **commission,** which is a percentage of their sales. With this incentive, many salespersons work hard and make big commissions.

example 111.1   A sales representative was paid a base salary of $300 a month. He was also paid a commission of 10 percent on everything he sold. If he sold $26,000 worth of merchandise in 1 month, what was his paycheck?

solution   His commission was 10% of $26,000.

$$(0.1)(\$26,000) = \$2600$$

To his commission, we add his base salary.

$$
\begin{array}{ll}
\quad \$2600 & \text{Commission} \\
+ \ \$ \ 300 & \text{Base salary} \\
\hline
\quad \$2900 & \text{Paycheck}
\end{array}
$$

His paycheck for the month was **$2900.**

111.B

profit   Markup is not all profit. The store owner must pay overhead: rent, the water bill, the employees' salaries, insurance, and other costs. What the owner has left after all expenses are paid is **profit.**

example 111.2   A store owner marks up her merchandise 40 percent. Her expenses are $5200 a month. If she paid $16,000 for the goods sold in 1 month, what was her profit?

solution   She marked up the merchandise 40 percent, so her markup was

$$(0.4)(\$16,000) = \$6400$$

Her expenses were $5200, so we subtract.

$$
\begin{array}{ll}
\quad \$6400 & \text{Markup} \\
- \ \$5200 & \text{Expenses} \\
\hline
\quad \$1200 & \text{Profit}
\end{array}
$$

Her profit for the month was **$1200.**

practice   **a.** A sales representative receives a base salary of $274 a month and a 7 percent commission on all her sales. If she sold $20,000 worth of merchandise in a month, how much money did she make for the month?

b. A store owner purchased $200,000 worth of merchandise and sold it at a markup of 4 percent. If his expenses totaled $5500, what was his profit?

problem set 111   **1.** The ratio of red marbles to green marbles in the barrel was 2 to 19. If there were 84,000 marbles in the barrel and all were either red or green, how many were red?
(100)

2. Thirty percent of the airplanes in the show were biplanes. If 120 were biplanes, how many were not biplanes?
(68)

3. There were $3\frac{2}{5}$ times as many wet ones as there were dry ones. If there were 8500 dry ones, how many wet ones were there?
(57)

4. A sales representative receives a base salary of $350 a month and is paid 10 percent
(111) commission on all sales. If she sells $45,000 worth of merchandise in a month, how
much money is in her paycheck for the month?

5. A merchant purchased $16,000 worth of merchandise and then sold it at a 60 percent
(111) markup. Her expenses totaled $7000. What was her profit?

6. The sum of $8000 was deposited at 8 percent interest compounded annually. How
(109) much money was in the bank at the end of 2 years?

7. Write $6\frac{1}{4}\%$ as a decimal number.
(108)

8. Write MMMCDXXXIV using Hindu-Arabic numerals.
(107)

9. Use Roman numerals to write 3465.
(107)

10. Forty-five is what percent of 225?
(68)

11. Forty-two percent of what number is 126?
(68)

12. Janie earned 35% commission for her troop on all the cookies she sold. If she sold
(111) $12.50 worth of Mint Delites and $15.50 worth of Mallow Cremes, how much did she
earn for her troop?

13. The children were elated because Joe's Mack brand crullers, their favorite kind, were
(110) on sale for 15% off the regular price. If the discounted price was $4.25 a box, what was
the original price?

14. If $5x = 2\frac{1}{2}$, what is the value of $4x - 12$?
(97)

15. Simplify: $3^{-4} - (-2)^3 + \left(\dfrac{3}{2}\right)^{-5}$
(106)

16. Use the distributive property to multiply: $2ac\left(a + c - ac + a^2\right)$
(103)

17. Simplify by adding like terms: $2xyy + 3xyx - 6xy^2 + 4x^2y$
(102)

18. Classify $\triangle QRS$ by its sides and angles.
(104)

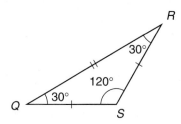

19. Find the volume in cubic meters of a
(50,64) solid whose base is shown on the left
and whose height is 3 centimeters.
Dimensions are in centimeters.
Express your answer in scientific
notation.

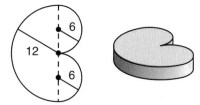

Solve:

20. $5 - 3x + 6 = 2x - 21 + 4(2x - 3)$
(96,103)

21. $-2\dfrac{1}{3}x - \dfrac{5}{6} = \dfrac{1}{3}$
(84)

Simplify:

22.
(106) $\quad -\left[-(-1)^3\right] + (-4) + \sqrt[3]{-125}$

23.
(101) $\quad 2^2 aa^3 ba^2 b^3$

24.
(93) $\quad \dfrac{2^2(2^2 - 2 \cdot 4)}{2^3(3^2 - 2^2)}$

25.
(52) $\quad 2\dfrac{1}{3}\left(2\dfrac{1}{2} \cdot \dfrac{1}{2} - \dfrac{1}{3} \cdot \dfrac{4}{5}\right)$

Evaluate:

26.
(105) $\quad a^2 b + ab^2 \quad$ if $a = -1$ and $b = -2$

27.
(105) $\quad a^2 - b^2 \quad$ if $a = -2$ and $b = -3$

28.
(89) $\quad$ Graph on a number line: $x \not\le 3$

29.
(85) $\quad$ Sketch a rectangular coordinate system, and graph the line $y = -x - 2$.

30.
(6) $\quad$ Round 62,987,134.32 to the nearest ten thousand.

LESSON *112* *Probability, Part 1*

The study of **probability** is based on the study of outcomes that have an equal chance of occurring. If we toss a fair coin many times, it should come up heads as many times as it comes up tails. We say the probability of one toss resulting in a head, $P(H)$, is the number of outcomes that are heads divided by the total number of possible outcomes.

$$P(H) = \frac{\text{number of outcomes that are heads}}{\text{total number of possible outcomes}} = \frac{1}{2}$$

The face of this spinner is divided into four equal parts. If the spinner is spun many times, it should stop on each of the spaces an equal number of times. The probability of getting a 4, $P(4)$, on any one spin is the number of outcomes that are 4 divided by the total number of possible outcomes.

$$P(4) = \frac{\text{number of outcomes that are 4}}{\text{total number of possible outcomes}} = \frac{1}{4}$$

A single die has six faces.

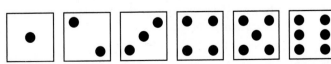

The probability of getting a number greater than 4, $P(>4)$, on one roll of the die is the number of outcomes that are greater than 4 divided by the total number of possible outcomes. There are two possible outcomes that are greater than 4.

$$P(>4) = \frac{\text{number of outcomes greater than 4}}{\text{total number of possible outcomes}} = \frac{2}{6} = \frac{1}{3}$$

example 112.1   A deck of cards contains 52 cards: 13 are spades, 13 are hearts, 13 are clubs, and 13 are diamonds. Jimmy tears up the ace of spades. Then he shuffles the remainder of the deck and draws one card. What is the probability that the card is a spade?

solution   There are 51 cards left, and 12 of them are spades. So

$$P(S) = \frac{12}{51} = \frac{4}{17}$$

example 112.2   One die is red and the other die is green. Both are rolled. What is the probability of getting
(a) a sum of 7?   (b) a sum of 4?

solution   We make a table that shows every possible outcome. The integer values represent the total number of dots displayed on the top face of both dice for each possible combination.

Green Die

	2	3	4	5	6	7
	3	4	5	6	7	8
	4	5	6	7	8	9
	5	6	7	8	9	10
	6	7	8	9	10	11
	7	8	9	10	11	12

Red Die

(a) Six of the possible sums are 7 and there are 36 squares in all. So

$$P(7) = \frac{6}{36} = \frac{1}{6}$$

(b) There are only 3 ways to get a total of 4. Thus, the probability of getting a sum of 4 is

$$P(4) = \frac{3}{36} = \frac{1}{12}$$

practice   a.   There are 16 marbles in a bowl: 3 are red, 6 are black, and 7 are green. Jimmy draws 1 marble from the bowl. What is the probability that the marble is either red or black?

b.   A red die and a green die are rolled at the same time. What is the probability of getting a sum of 11?

problem set 112   **1.**   There are 22 marbles in a bowl: 7 are black, 5 are red, and 10 are blue. Arcelia draws
(112)   a marble from the bowl. What is the probability that the marble is either black or red?

2.   In a standard deck of 52 cards, there are 13 of each suit: spades, hearts, clubs, and
(112)   diamonds. After the deck is fairly shuffled, what is the probability of drawing a diamond?

3.
(112) One die is rolled. What is the probability of getting a (a) 3?   (b) 4?

4.
(68) Forty percent of the airplanes were hydroplanes. If 660 were hydroplanes, how many were not hydroplanes?

5.
(57) There were $2\frac{2}{3}$ times as many that were cordial as those that were aloof. If 3000 were cordial, how many were aloof?

6.
(90,95) Sixteen was added to the product of a number and 3. The result was 5 less than the product of the same number and −4. What was the number?

7.
(109) Find the ending balance in a bank account that began with $3000 and received 9 percent interest compounded annually for 4 years.

8.
(111) Kevin, the pharmaceutical salesman, receives $510 per month base pay plus 6% commission. In 2 months, after touring a metropolitan area, he had sold $260,000 in pharmaceuticals. How much did he make in the two-month period?

9.
(111) A sales representative was paid a base salary of $400 a month. He was also paid a commission of 12 percent on everything he sold. If he sold $550,000 worth of merchandise in 1 year, what was his income for the year? (Remember that he is paid a monthly salary.)

10.
(110) Ari's Pet Shoppe is selling geckoes at $12\frac{1}{2}$% off! If geckoes were originally $20.00 each, what is the sale price?

11.
(107) Write MMMXV as a Hindu-Arabic numeral.

12.
(98) Find the measure of each angle:

(a) ∠*AOB*   (b) ∠*AOC*   (c) ∠*AOD*

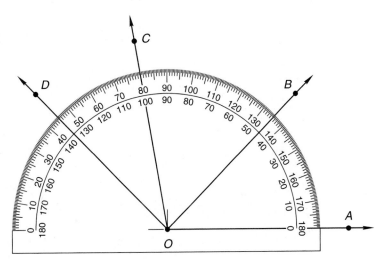

13.
(108) Write each percent as a decimal number:

(a) $5\frac{1}{5}$%   (b) $17\frac{3}{4}$%   (c) $11\frac{3}{8}$%

14.
(73) Find the total surface area of a right circular cylinder whose radius is 10 centimeters and whose height is 7 centimeters.

15. There were about 156 million passenger cars in the United States in 1980. Using the pie
(68) graph below, determine how many commercial vehicles were in the United States
in 1980.

**Vehicles in the U.S.
in 1980**

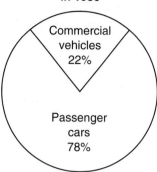

Commercial
vehicles
22%

Passenger
cars
78%

16. Use the distributive property to multiply: $3mp\left(2m + p + \dfrac{m^2}{p} + \dfrac{p^4}{m}\right)$
(103)

17. Simplify by adding like terms: $7d^2z + 7zdz + 7ddz + 7dz^2$
(102)

18. Find the volume of a right solid whose base is the figure shown on the left and whose
(64) height is 0.5 mile. Dimensions are in miles. Angles that look like right angles are
right angles.

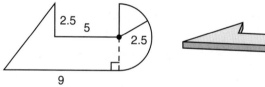
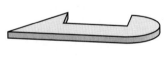
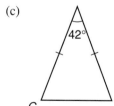

2.5 5 2.5

9

19. Find the surface area of a cube whose edges measure 3 inches.
(49)

Solve:

20. $2 - 5x + 6 = 14x - 32 + 10(2 - x)$
(96,103)

21. $-5\dfrac{5}{6}x - \dfrac{1}{2} = 1\dfrac{1}{4}$
(84)

22. $\dfrac{-\dfrac{5}{6}}{1\dfrac{2}{3}} = \dfrac{\dfrac{3}{4}}{x}$
(65)

23. Find the measures of angles A, B, and C:
(104)

(a) A (b) B (c)

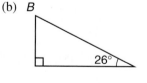

21° 41°

26°

42°

C

24. Graph on a number line: $x \not\geq -1$
(89)

Simplify:

25. $-\left[-(-2)^5\right] + (-9) - \sqrt[5]{-243}$
(106)

26. $3^2 mn^5 mn^2 m^6 (-1)^5$
(101)

27. $\dfrac{-(-3)^2 - 1^9(3^3 - 3 \cdot 2)}{3^3(3^2 - 2^3)}$
(93)

28. $3\dfrac{1}{2}\left(2\dfrac{1}{3} \cdot \dfrac{1}{3} - \dfrac{1}{2} \cdot \dfrac{3}{7}\right)$
(52)

29. (a) 2^{-5} (b) $\dfrac{1}{3^{-3}}$
(106)

Evaluate:

30. $m^3 n^{-2}$ if $m = -2$ and $n = -3$
(105,106)

LESSON 113   *Inch Scale • Metric Scale*

113.A

inch scale We use a ruler to measure lengths. The longest marks note the distance from the left-hand end of the scale in whole inches. On the inch ruler shown here, there are sixteen marks between the inch marks. These marks are $\frac{1}{16}$ inch apart. Two spaces between the shorter marks equal $\frac{1}{8}$ inch. Four spaces between the shorter marks equal $\frac{1}{4}$ inch.

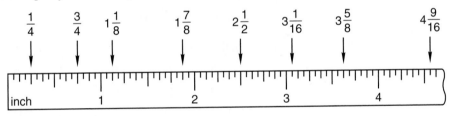

example 113.1 How far is the arrow from the left-hand end of the scale?

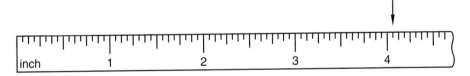

solution The distance between two consecutive marks is $\frac{1}{16}$ inch. The arrow is $4\frac{1}{16}$ **inches** from the left-hand end of the scale.

example 113.2 Use an inch scale to find the length of this line segment.

solution We place the left-hand end of the segment at the left-hand end of an inch scale. Then we read the length on the right-hand end.

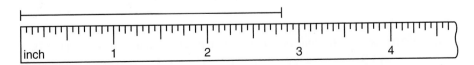

The line segment is about $2\frac{13}{16}$ **inches** long. Since no measurement is exact, this reading is to the nearest sixteenth of an inch.

113.B

metric scale   The longest marks note the distance from the left-hand end of the scale in centimeters. There are nine shorter lines between each pair of the longest lines. The shorter lines are 1 millimeter apart. A millimeter is a tenth of a centimeter. A metric scale is much easier to read than an inch scale.

example 113.3   How far is the arrow from the left-hand end of the scale?

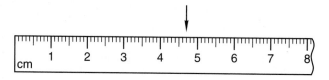

solution   The small spaces are 1 millimeter wide. A millimeter is a tenth of a centimeter. The arrow is about **4.7 centimeters, or 47 millimeters** from the left-hand end of the scale.

example 113.4   Use a metric scale to measure the length of this line segment.

solution   We place the left-hand end of the segment at the left-hand end of the ruler. Then we read the length on the right-hand end.

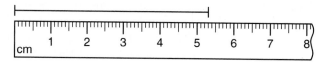

The segment is about **5.3 centimeters** long. This is the same as **53 millimeters.**

practice   Tell how far each of these arrows is from the left-hand end of this inch scale.

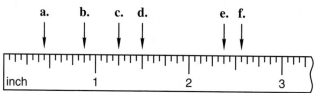

Tell how far each of these arrows is from the left-hand end of this centimeter scale.

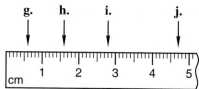

   k.   Use an inch scale and a metric scale to measure the length of this segment.

   l.   Use an inch scale and a centimeter scale to find the approximate length of this line segment.

problem set 113

   1.
(112)
One out of every five pieces of candy is red. What is the probability of choosing a red candy out of 40 pieces?

   2.
(112)
What is the probability of getting a number greater than 2 on one roll of a die?

3. The increase in the turnip crop was 260 percent. If last year's harvest was 230,000 tons,
(80) what was the harvest this year?

4. The ratio of the number who were puissant to the number who were diffident was 2
(100) to 5. If there were 2450 who were either puissant or diffident, how many were
puissant?

5. Find the difference between simple interest and compound interest on $11,000
(109) deposited in an account for 4 years at an annual interest rate of 6 percent.

6. Between which two consecutive integers is $\sqrt[4]{63}$?
(92)

7. Find x and y.
(65)

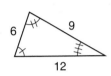 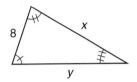

8. Use an inch scale and a centimeter scale to measure the length of this segment.
(113)

9. (a) Use an inch scale to measure the segment to the nearest sixteenth of an inch.
(113)

    (b) Use a metric scale to measure the segment to the nearest millimeter.

10. Find the measures of angles A, B, and C:
(104)

    (a) A (b) B

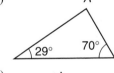 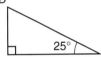

    (c)

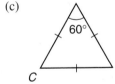

11. Simplify: (a) $2(4^{-2})$ (b) $2\left(\dfrac{1}{4^{-2}}\right)$
(106)

12. Write each percent as a decimal number: (a) $6\dfrac{7}{8}\%$ (b) $132\dfrac{3}{4}\%$
(108)

13. What percent of 90 is 162?
(77)

14. Jeans are marked up 150% at Antoinette's Boutique. Today they are all on sale, 20%
(110) off the usual retail price. If the wholesale price of jeans is $20, how much do they sell
for today?

15. Write MDXCIV in Hindu-Arabic numerals.
(107)

16. A sales representative is paid a base salary of $350 a month. She is also paid a
(111) commission of 20 percent on all sales. If she sells $14,000 worth of merchandise in
1 month, what is her paycheck for the month?

17. Use the distributive property to multiply: $2ac(ab + bc - c)$
(103)

18. Simplify by adding like terms: $2xyx + 3yxy^2 - 3x^2y + 5y^3x - 6yx^2$
(102)

19. Express in cubic feet the volume of a right solid whose base is shown on the left and
(45) whose sides are 2 yards tall. Dimensions are in feet. All angles that look like right angles are right angles.

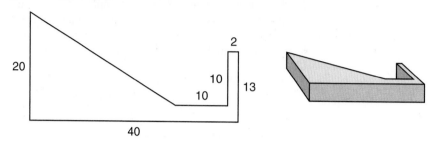

20. Find the surface area of a rectangular solid whose length, width, and height are 4 feet,
(88) 2 feet, and 10 feet respectively.

Solve:

21. $3x - 3 + 2(x - 1) = -8x + 5 + 5(2 - 3x)$
(103)

22. $-\dfrac{1}{4}x + \dfrac{2}{3} = 3\dfrac{5}{12}$
(84)

23. $\dfrac{-\dfrac{2}{3}}{\dfrac{4}{9}} = \dfrac{\dfrac{1}{3}}{x}$
(59,81)

Simplify:

24. $-\left[-(-1)^4\right] + (-3)(-2) - \sqrt[5]{-1}$
(106)

25. $5aba^2b^3a^2$
(101)

26. $3\dfrac{1}{2} \times 2\dfrac{1}{3} \div \dfrac{1}{3} \div \dfrac{1}{2}$
(43)

27. $139.287 - 19.876$
(6)

Evaluate:

28. $-xy + y$ if $x = -2$ and $y = -3$
(82)

29. $ab^2 - a^2b$ if $a = 2$ and $b = -1$
(105)

30. Describe each angle as acute, obtuse, or right:
(98)

(a)

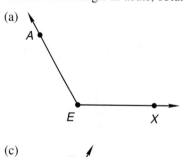

(b)

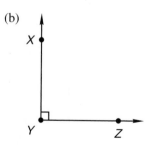

(c)

LESSON 114 Probability, Part 2: Independent Events

We say that events that do not affect one another are **independent events.** If Danny flips a dime and Paul flips a penny, the outcome of Danny's flip does not affect the outcome of Paul's flip. Thus, we say that these events are independent events. **The probability of independent events occurring in a designated order is the product of the probabilities of the individual events.**

A tree diagram can always be used to demonstrate the probability of independent events occurring in a designated order. This diagram shows the possible outcomes if a coin is tossed twice.

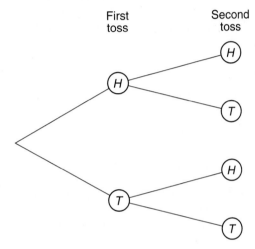

First
toss

Second
toss

On a single toss the probability of getting heads is $\frac{1}{2}$. The probability of getting tails is also $\frac{1}{2}$. There are only four possibilities on two tosses. If the first toss is heads, the second toss can be heads or tails.

$$(H, H) \qquad \text{or} \qquad (H, T)$$

Thus,

$$P(H, H) \ = \ \frac{1}{2} \cdot \frac{1}{2} \ = \ \frac{1}{4} \qquad P(H, T) \ = \ \frac{1}{2} \cdot \frac{1}{2} \ = \ \frac{1}{4}$$

If the first toss is tails, the second toss can be heads or tails.

$$(T, H) \qquad \text{or} \qquad (T, T)$$

Thus,

$$P(T, H) \ = \ \frac{1}{2} \cdot \frac{1}{2} \ = \ \frac{1}{4} \qquad P(T, T) \ = \ \frac{1}{2} \cdot \frac{1}{2} \ = \ \frac{1}{4}$$

There are no other possible outcomes for two tosses. The probability of getting any one of these outcomes is one fourth. The sum of all the probabilities is 1.

example 114.1 A fair coin is tossed 3 times. What is the probability that it will come up heads every time?

solution Coin tosses are independent events because the result of one toss has no effect on the result of the next toss. Since the probability of independent events occurring in a designated order is the product of the individual probabilities, we have

$$P(H, H, H) \ = \ \frac{1}{2} \cdot \frac{1}{2} \cdot \frac{1}{2} \ = \ \frac{1}{8}$$

example 114.2   A fair coin is tossed 4 times and it comes up heads each time. What is the probability that it will come up heads on the next toss?

solution   The results of past coin tosses do not affect the outcome of future coin tosses. Thus, the probability of getting a head on the next toss is $\frac{1}{2}$.

$$P(H) \;=\; \frac{1}{2}$$

practice   **a.**   The spinner is spun 3 times. What is the probability it will stop on 3, 5, and 1 in that order?

b.   The spinner is spun twice. What is the probability it will stop on either 3 or 5 the first time and will stop on 2 the second time?

**problem set
114**

1.
(114)   The first urn contains 6 blue marbles and 1 red marble. The second urn contains 9 blue marbles and 3 red marbles. A marble is picked from each urn. What is the probability that both marbles are red?

2.
(100)   The ratio of the number of philistines to the number of aesthetes was 21 to 2. If 92 philistines and aesthetes were present, how many were aesthetes?

3.
(80)   Objectionable behavior increased by 50 percent during the most recent period. If 3600 incidents of objectionable behavior occurred during the most recent period, how many incidents of objectionable behavior occurred in the previous period?

4.
(90,95)   Seven times a number was 32 greater than the product of the number and –9. What was the number?

5.
(114)   If 1 card is drawn from each of two standard 52-card decks, what is the probability that two black jacks will be drawn? There are 2 black jacks in each deck.

6.
(114)   A fair coin is tossed five times. What is the probability of getting H, H, T, H, H in that order?

7.
(63)   Normally the post office processed letters at a rate of 2500 per hour. During the holiday season the rate tripled. How many hours did it take to process 60,000 letters during the holiday season?

8.
(109)   If $10,000 is deposited in an account at 10 percent interest compounded annually, what will be the amount in the account at the end of 4 years?

9.
(98)   Name
(a) the supplement of 83°.
(b) the complement of 83°.

10.
(65)   Find x and y.

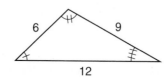

11. Find the measures of angles A, B, and C:
(104)

(a)

(b)

(c)

12. Use a metric scale to measure a 6-inch line segment to the nearest millimeter.
(113)

13. Eighty-seven is what percent of 8.7?
(77)

14. Sixty-one percent of what number is 183?
(68)

15. Use the distributive property to multiply: $4az(z^2 + a - 3a^2z)$
(103)

16. Simplify by adding like terms: $7mpm + 2mpm^2 - 4m^2p + 3pm^3 - 9pm^2$
(102)

17. Find the lateral surface area of a right circular cylinder whose diameter is 2 centimeters
(73) and whose height is 2 centimeters.

18. If Leroy buys crullers wholesale at 30¢ each and sells 325 at 100% markup, what is his
(110) profit if his other expenses are $95.00?

19. Write 1999 in Roman numerals.
(107)

20. Write $79\frac{1}{8}\%$ as a decimal number.
(108)

Solve:

21. $4x - 4 + 5x - 3 = -4x - 46$
(96)

22. $-\frac{1}{3}x + \frac{2}{4} = 1\frac{5}{6}$
(84)

23. $\dfrac{-\dfrac{1}{4}}{\dfrac{7}{11}} = \dfrac{\dfrac{22}{35}}{x}$
(59,81)

Simplify:

24. $(-2)^3(-1) - \sqrt[6]{64}$
(99)

25. $6mp^2m^3p^5m$
(101)

26. $4\frac{1}{5} \times 2\frac{1}{2} \div \frac{1}{5} \div \frac{1}{4}$
(43)

27. $\frac{3}{4} - 0.2 + (2.1)\left(\frac{1}{2}\right)$
(15)

28. Sketch a rectangular coordinate system, and graph the line $y = \frac{3}{2}x - 1$. Let x be -2,
(85) 0, and 2.

Evaluate:

29. $-x^y - y^x$ if $x = -2$ and $y = -3$
(106)

30. $a^2b + \dfrac{b}{a^2}$ if $a = -4$ and $b = 2$
(105)

LESSON 115   *Polygons • Congruence and Transformation*

115.A

polygons   In mathematics we call a flat surface a **plane.** A geometric figure drawn on a flat surface is called a **planar figure.** We remember that all mathematical lines are straight lines that have no ends. A part of a mathematical line is called a line segment. **A polygon is a closed planar geometric figure whose sides are line segments.** If a polygon has an indentation (a "cave"), it is called a **concave polygon.** If it does not have an indentation, it is called a **convex polygon.** Because there are no indentations, any two points in a convex polygon can be connected by a line segment that does not cross the boundary of the polygon.

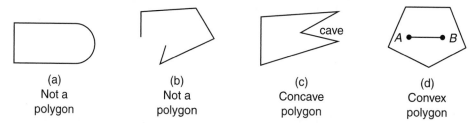

| (a) | (b) | (c) | (d) |
| Not a polygon | Not a polygon | Concave polygon | Convex polygon |

Figure (a) is not a polygon because the curved side is not a line segment. Figure (b) is not a polygon because it is not closed. Figure (c) is a concave polygon. Figure (d) is a convex polygon because no line segment whose endpoints are within the polygon will cross the boundary of the polygon.

The name of a polygon tells how many angles and how many sides the polygon has.

Names of Polygons

Name of Polygon	Number of Sides	Name of Polygon	Number of Sides
Triangle	3	Octagon	8
Quadrilateral	4	Nonagon	9
Pentagon	5	Decagon	10
Hexagon	6	Undecagon	11
Heptagon	7	Dodecagon	12

A polygon with more than twelve sides may be referred to as an *n*-gon, with *n* being the number of sides. Thus, a polygon with fifteen sides is a 15-gon.

Two sides of a polygon meet at a point called the vertex. (The plural of vertex is **vertices.**) A particular polygon may be identified by naming the letters of its vertices in order. Any letter may be first. The rest of the letters can be named clockwise or counterclockwise.

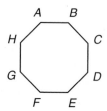

This polygon has sixteen names, which are listed below.

ABCDEFGH	*BCDEFGHA*	*CDEFGHAB*	*DEFGHABC*
EFGHABCD	*FGHABCDE*	*GHABCDEF*	*HABCDEFG*
AHGFEDCB	*HGFEDCBA*	*GFEDCBAH*	*FEDCBAHG*
EDCBAHGF	*DCBAHGFE*	*CBAHGFED*	*BAHGFEDC*

If all angles in a convex polygon have equal measures and all sides have equal lengths, the polygon is called a **regular polygon.** The polygon with the fewest number of sides is the triangle. A regular triangle is called an equilateral triangle. All the angles in an equilateral triangle are 60° angles. A **quadrilateral** has four sides. A regular quadrilateral is called a square.

Regular and Irregular Polygons

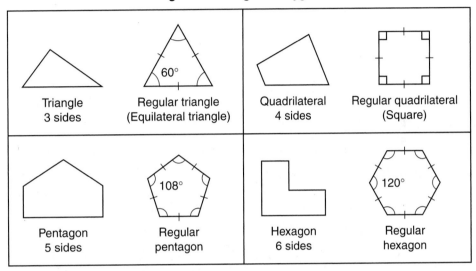

A **diagonal** of a polygon is a line segment that connects two nonconsecutive vertices. We can name a polygon by listing the vertices in order. These polygons are quadrilaterals *MPRQ* and *AXCY*.

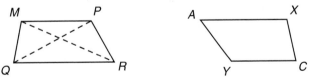

The diagonals of the polygon on the left are $\overline{QP}$ and $\overline{RM}$. We could also call them $\overline{PQ}$ and $\overline{MR}$. If the diagonals of the polygon on the right were drawn in, they could be named $\overline{AC}$ and $\overline{YX}$.

A **trapezoid** is a quadrilateral that has exactly two parallel sides. A **parallelogram** is a quadrilateral that has two pairs of parallel sides. The sides that are parallel in a parallelogram have the same lengths. In these figures equal tick marks denote equal lengths.

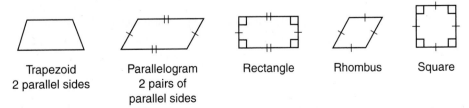

A **rectangle** is a parallelogram in which all angles have a measure of 90 degrees. A **rhombus** is a parallelogram that has four sides of equal length. A **square** is a rhombus in which all angles have a measure of 90°.

115.B

congruence and transformation

Planar figures are **congruent** if they have the same shape and size. This means they are geometrically equal except for position and orientation. If two geometric figures are congruent, then all corresponding measures of the figures are equal. Congruent is a term that is used often in geometry. In trigonometry and in other branches of mathematics, we find it convenient to speak of equal angles and equal segments.

If two figures are congruent, we can place one figure over the other by sliding it over, rotating it, flipping it, or some combination of these actions. If we slide the figure but do not **rotate** it, we call the action **translation.** A flip is called a **reflection** because a flipped figure looks like a mirror image. Translations, rotations, and reflections are called **transformations.** When using transformations to place one figure on another, many combinations of transformations will work. In the problem sets, we will only show one of the possibilities.

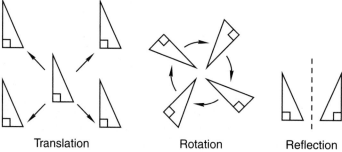

Translation   Rotation   Reflection

practice

All the figures shown below are polygons. Figure (a) is also a quadrilateral, a parallelogram, a rectangle, a rhombus, and a square. Give as many names as you can for each of these figures. Note that arrowheads can be used to indicate parallel lines, as in (c), (d), (e), and (f) below.

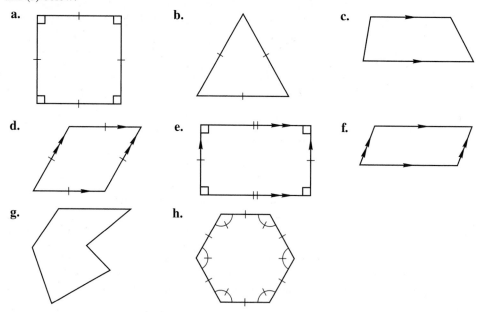

The pairs of figures shown below are congruent. Give a combination of transformations which may be used to place figure *A* exactly on top of figure *B*. Explain the combination you choose.

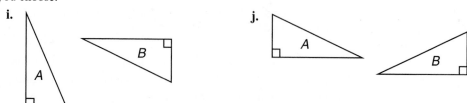

k.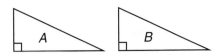

l.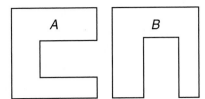

m.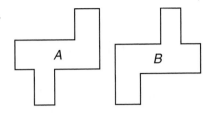

problem set 115

1. The ratio of the number of those who were enthusiastic to the number of those who
(100) were blasé was 8 to 7. If 600 were present, how many were blasé?

2. A fair coin is tossed 6 times. What is the probability of getting *H, H, T, T, H, T* in
(114) that order?

3. The first urn contains 4 blue marbles and 2 white marbles. The second urn contains 4
(114) blue marbles and 11 white marbles. A marble is picked from each of the urns. What is
the probability that both marbles are white?

4. The importation of tulip bulbs increased 350 percent this year over last year. If 900,000
(80) bulbs were imported this year, how many were imported last year?

5. If the product of a number and −25 is decreased by 108, the result is 16 less than the
(90,95) product of the same number and −10. What is the number?

6. There were $2\frac{3}{5}$ times as many that were amorphous as were not. If there were 6500 that
(57) were amorphous, how many were not amorphous?

7. Name
(98)
(a) the supplement of 65°.

(b) the complement of 65°.

8. Find the measures of angles *A*, *B*, and *C*:
(104)
(a)   *A*   (b) *B*   (c)

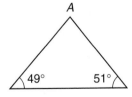 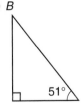

9. Which transformation can be used to place figure *A* exactly on top of figure *B*,
(115) assuming the two are congruent?

(a)   (b)

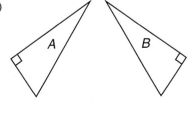   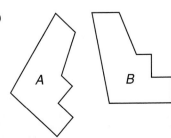

10. Give all the names for each figure:
(115)

(a)    (b)   (c)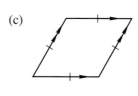

11. Draw a line segment 15 centimeters long. Then use an inch scale to measure the
(113)   segment to the nearest sixteenth of an inch.

12. If Janey earns an $11\frac{1}{2}$% commission on every Thingamabub she manages to sell, what
(108,111)   would she earn on sales of $2350.00 worth of Thingamabubs?

13. How much interest does $550 at $4\frac{1}{4}$% annual interest earn in one year?
(108,109)

14. What percent of 28 is 70?
(77)

15. Write 1984 with Roman numerals.
(107)

16. Use the distributive property to multiply: $2xp\left(x^3 + 4x^2p - 2xp\right)$
(103)

17. Simplify by adding like terms: $3x^2am^4 - xamxmm^2 + 2am^2xmxm$
(102)

18. Find the volume of a right solid whose base is shown on the left and whose height is
(64)   0.6 kilometer. Dimensions are in kilometers.

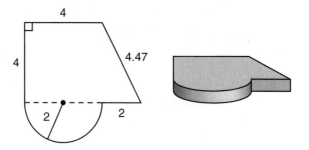

19. Find the lateral surface area of the solid discussed in problem 18.
(88)

Solve:

20. $7x + 4 - 9x = 12x - 48$
(96)

21. $-11\frac{1}{2}x - \frac{1}{4} = 5\frac{1}{2}$
(84)

22. $\dfrac{-\dfrac{1}{5}}{3\dfrac{1}{12}} = \dfrac{x}{\dfrac{1}{2}}$
(65,81)

23. Graph on a number line: $x \nleq 0$
(89)

Simplify:

24. $-\left[-\left(-3^3\right)\right] + \sqrt[3]{-27}$
(99,106)

25. $-6^2mp^5m^2pm^4(-1)^5$
(99,101)

26. $\dfrac{-\left(-4^2\right) - 2^2(3 - 4 \cdot 2)}{2^3\left(2^3 - 3^2\right)}$
(93,99)

27. $2\frac{1}{5}\left(3\frac{1}{2} \cdot \frac{1}{4} - \frac{1}{3} \cdot \frac{3}{5}\right)$
(52)

28. (a) 3^{-3} (b) $\dfrac{1}{3^{-3}}$
(106)

Evaluate:

29. $a^{-3}b^3$ if $a = -2$ and $b = -3$
_(105,106)

30. $ab^2 + ab$ if $a = -3$ and $b = 3$
₍₈₂₎

LESSON 116   Area of Parallelograms and Trapezoids

We have memorized the formulas for the areas of rectangles, triangles, and circles.

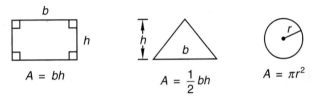

There are formulas for the areas of parallelograms and trapezoids, but formulas are easy to forget. We do not always need to memorize a formula that can be developed quickly from other formulas that we already know. We can find the area of a parallelogram by dividing it into two triangles. We can also find the area of a trapezoid by dividing it into two triangles.

example 116.1   Find the area of this parallelogram. Dimensions are in inches.

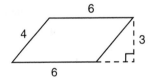

solution   A parallelogram has two diagonals. We can divide the parallelogram into two triangles by drawing either one of the diagonals.

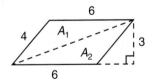

Both triangles in this figure have a base whose length is 6 inches, and their height is 3 inches. The area of each triangle is one half the base times the height.

$$A_1 = \frac{1}{2}(6 \text{ in.})(3 \text{ in.}) = 9 \text{ in.}^2 \qquad A_2 = \frac{1}{2}(6 \text{ in.})(3 \text{ in.}) = 9 \text{ in.}^2$$

The total area is the sum of the two areas.

$$\text{Total area} = A_1 + A_2 = 9 \text{ in.}^2 + 9 \text{ in.}^2 = \textbf{18 in.}^2$$

example 116.2   Two equal sides in this parallelogram are b units long. The other two equal sides are not labeled. Divide this parallelogram into two triangles and find the formula for the area of a parallelogram that uses the letters b and h.

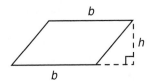

solution   We draw a diagonal to divide the figure into two triangles.

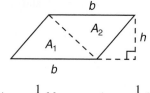

$$A_1 = \frac{1}{2}bh \qquad A_2 = \frac{1}{2}bh$$

$$\text{Total area} = \frac{1}{2}bh + \frac{1}{2}bh = \boldsymbol{bh}$$

The area of a parallelogram equals the base times the height.

$$\boxed{\text{Area of parallelogram} = bh}$$

example 116.3   Find the area of this trapezoid. Dimensions are in feet.

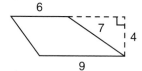

solution   First we draw a diagonal. Either diagonal will do.

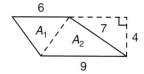

The height of both triangles is 4 ft. The base of one triangle is 6 ft long, and the base of the other triangle is 9 ft long. The area of the trapezoid is the sum of the areas of the two triangles.

$$\text{Total area} = A_1 + A_2$$
$$= \frac{1}{2}b_1h_1 + \frac{1}{2}b_2h_2$$
$$= \frac{1}{2}(6\text{ ft})(4\text{ ft}) + \frac{1}{2}(9\text{ ft})(4\text{ ft})$$
$$= 12\text{ft}^2 + 18\text{ft}^2$$
$$= \boldsymbol{30\text{ ft}^2}$$

example 116.4   Use two triangles to find a general formula for the area of a trapezoid.

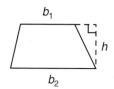

solution   We draw two triangles.

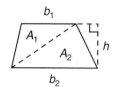

Both triangles have a height of h. One has a base of length b_1, and the other has a base of length b_2.

$$\boxed{\text{Area of trapezoid} = \frac{1}{2}b_1h + \frac{1}{2}b_2h = \frac{1}{2}h(b_1 + b_2)}$$

practice   Find the area of the figures below. Dimensions are in meters.

a.

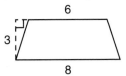

b.

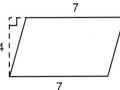

problem set
116

1.
(114)
One card is drawn from a standard 52-card deck and then replaced, and then a second card is drawn. What is the probability that the first card is a red 8 and the second is a black 10?

2.
(100)
The ratio of the number of dissatisfied customers to the number of satisfied customers in a survey was 3 to 2. If 25,000 customers were surveyed, how many were dissatisfied?

3.
(90,95)
Nine times a number, increased by 5, is 16 less than the product of the number and 2. What is the number?

4.
(68)
Aberrations decreased by 92 percent from the first to the second field sample. If only 6 aberrations were noted in the second field sample, how many aberrations were noted in the first field sample?

5.
(108)
Property values appreciated $9\frac{1}{2}$ percent. If 50 acres were originally appraised at $30,000, what was their value after they appreciated?

6.
(113)
(a) Use an inch scale to measure the distance between the marks to the nearest sixteenth of an inch.

(b) Use a metric scale to measure the same length in centimeters.

7.
(111)
Antone is a real estate agent; he earns 6% commission on each house he sells. If he just earned a $6540 commission from one sale, what was the selling price of the house?

8.
(77)
What percent of 90 is 162?

9.
(68)
Thirty-five percent of what number is 2450?

10.
(85)
Sketch a rectangular coordinate system, and graph the line $y = 0$.

11.
(107)
Write MMMCMXCIV in Hindu-Arabic numerals.

12.
(97)
If $7x - 23 = 5$, what is the value of $1.2x + 100$?

13.
(115)
Figures A and B are congruent. Give a combination of transformations which may be used to place figure A exactly on top of figure B. Explain the combination you choose.

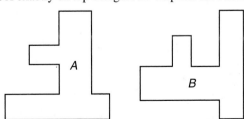

14.
(116)
Find the area of the figures below. Dimensions are in meters.

(a)

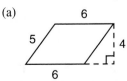

(b)

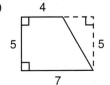

15. (a) Find x.   (b) Find z.
(65,104)

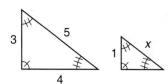   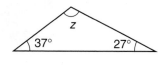

16. Use the distributive property to multiply: $am^2\left(2am + a + \dfrac{m}{b^2}\right)$
(103)

17. Simplify by adding like terms: $4a^3pm^2 + a^2pm^{-1} - 2apma^2m$
(102)

18. Express in cubic inches the volume of a right solid whose base is shown on the left and
(45,116) whose sides are 1 foot tall. Dimensions are in inches. (There is more than one way to find this volume.)

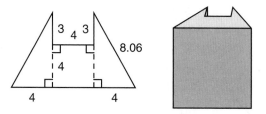

19. Find the perimeter of the figure on the left in problem 18.
(9)

Solve:

20. $16x - 3 + 3x - 5 = -3x - 63$ **21.** $-2\dfrac{1}{2}x + 1\dfrac{1}{16} = \dfrac{1}{8}$
(96)   (84)

22. $\dfrac{\dfrac{1}{5}}{-\dfrac{4}{9}} = \dfrac{\dfrac{3}{10}}{x}$
(59,81)

Simplify:

23. $4(7 - 2 \cdot 6) + \dfrac{1}{3^{-2}} - \left(-3^2\right)$
(106)

24. $3mn^3pn^2p^3m$ **25.** $(-4)^3 + \sqrt[3]{-8}$
(101)   (106)

26. $\dfrac{-\left(-5^2\right) - 2^2(3 - 2 \cdot 3)}{-2\left(\sqrt[3]{-125}\right)}$ **27.** $4\dfrac{1}{2}\left(2\dfrac{1}{3} \cdot 1\dfrac{1}{2} - \dfrac{1}{4} \cdot \dfrac{4}{7}\right)$
(106)   (52)

28. (a) 1^{-11} (b) $\dfrac{2}{2^{-2}}$ (c) $\dfrac{a^2}{a^{-3}}$
(106)

Evaluate:

29. $ab^2 + a^b$ if $a = 2$ and $b = -3$
(106)

30. $\sqrt[a]{-b} - (ab)^{-1}$ if $a = 3$ and $b = 8$
(106)

LESSON *117* *Equations with x² • Pythagorean Theorem • Demonstration of the Pythagorean Theorem*

117.A
equations with x^2

If we consider the equation

$$x^2 = 4$$

we see that there are two solutions that will satisfy the equation. These are +2 and –2.

$$(2)^2 = 4 \qquad \text{check}$$

$$(-2)^2 = 4 \qquad \text{check}$$

From this we conclude that we can solve an equation such as $x^2 = 4$ by taking the square root of both sides. We can use the symbol ± 2 to represent the two solutions to this equation, +2 and –2. It is important to note that the radical symbol, $\sqrt{\quad}$, indicates only the positive or **principal square root.** So $\sqrt{4}$ is +2 only, and does not include –2.

example 117.1 Solve: $p^2 = 16$

solution We take the square root of p^2 and we get p. Then we take the square root of 16.

$$p^2 = 16 \qquad \text{equation}$$

$$p = \pm 4 \qquad \text{square root of both sides}$$

Since $(+4)^2 = 16$ and $(-4)^2 = 16$, the problem has two solutions.

example 117.2 Solve: $p^2 = 42$

solution We take the square root of both sides.

$$p^2 = 42 \qquad \text{equation}$$

$$p = \pm\sqrt{42} \qquad \text{square root of both sides}$$

117.B
Pythagorean theorem

A right triangle is a triangle that has a right angle. The side opposite the right angle is called the **hypotenuse.** The other two sides are called **legs.**

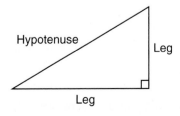

A right triangle has a property that is especially useful. The property is named after a Greek mathematician who was born on the Greek island of Samos in the sixth century B.C. Later he lived in southern Italy in a town called Crotona. His name was Pythagoras. The theorem that bears his name is so simple that it is difficult to appreciate how important it is.

> ### PYTHAGOREAN THEOREM
>
> The area of a square drawn on the hypotenuse of a right triangle equals the sum of the areas of the squares drawn on the other two sides.

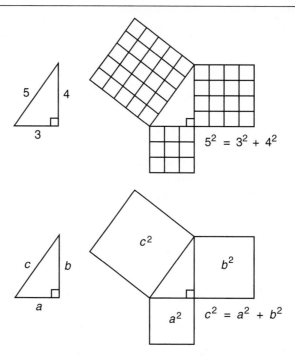

$$5^2 = 3^2 + 4^2$$

$$c^2 = a^2 + b^2$$

In the triangle on the upper left, the area of the square on the hypotenuse is 25. The areas of the squares on the legs are 9 and 16, which add to 25. The area of the square on the hypotenuse in the other triangle is c^2. The areas of the squares on the legs are a^2 and b^2. An algebraic statement of the theorem is

> ### PYTHAGOREAN THEOREM
> $$c^2 = a^2 + b^2$$

where c is the length of the hypotenuse, and a and b are the lengths of the legs.

example 117.3   Given the triangle with the lengths of the sides as shown, use the Pythagorean theorem to find a.

solution   The square of the hypotenuse equals the sum of the squares of the other two sides. Thus,

$$5^2 = 4^2 + a^2 \qquad \text{Pythagorean theorem}$$
$$25 = 16 + a^2 \qquad \text{simplified}$$
$$9 = a^2 \qquad \text{added } -16 \text{ to both sides}$$

We take the square root of each side to finish the solution.

$$a^2 = 9 \qquad \text{equation}$$
$$a = \pm 3 \qquad \text{square root of both sides}$$

While −3 is a solution to the equation $a^2 = 9$, it is not a solution to the problem at hand, because physical lengths are designated by positive numbers. Thus, we reject the negative solution and say that

$$a = 3$$

example 117.4   Find p in the triangle shown.

solution   The square of the hypotenuse equals the sum of the squares of the other two sides.

$$
\begin{aligned}
p^2 &= 5^2 + 4^2 && \text{Pythagorean theorem} \\
p^2 &= 25 + 16 && \text{simplified} \\
p^2 &= 41 && \text{added} \\
p &= \pm\sqrt{41} && \text{square root of both sides}
\end{aligned}
$$

This equation has two answers. They are $+\sqrt{41}$ and $-\sqrt{41}$. But only one of these answers is the length of the hypotenuse because every length is positive.

$$p = \sqrt{\mathbf{41}}$$

Since $6 = \sqrt{36}$ and $7 = \sqrt{49}$, we can conclude $6 < \sqrt{41} < 7$. We can get a numerical approximation with a calculator.

$$p = \sqrt{41} \approx 6.40$$

example 117.5   Find m.

solution   The hypotenuse squared equals the sum of the squares of the other two sides.

$$
\begin{aligned}
9^2 &= 7^2 + m^2 && \text{Pythagorean theorem} \\
81 &= 49 + m^2 && \text{simplified} \\
32 &= m^2 && \text{added } -49 \text{ to both sides} \\
\sqrt{\mathbf{32}} &= m && \text{square root of both sides}
\end{aligned}
$$

117.C
demonstration of the Pythagorean theorem

One way to see why the Pythagorean theorem is true is to consider a large square made up of four shaded right triangles and an inner square.

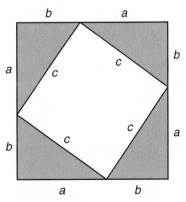

Area of the large square = area of the inner square + area of the 4 right triangles

$$= c^2 + 4\left(\frac{1}{2}ab\right)$$

$$= c^2 + 2ab$$

Now imagine rearranging the four right triangles inside the large square like this.

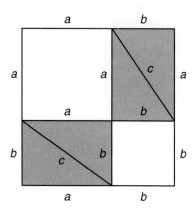

So we can also say,

Area of the large square = area of the two smaller inner squares
                          + area of the 4 right triangles

$$= a^2 + b^2 + 4\left(\frac{1}{2}ab\right)$$

$$= a^2 + b^2 + 2ab$$

The area of the large square is the same in both situations, so we can equate the two expressions we have for its area.

$$c^2 + 2ab = a^2 + b^2 + 2ab \qquad \text{set the area expressions equal to each other}$$
$$c^2 = a^2 + b^2 \qquad \text{subtracted } 2ab \text{ from both sides}$$

A step-by-step demonstration like this is called a **proof** of a theorem. Pythagoras is famous for proving this theorem about right triangles.

practice Solve:

a. $p^2 = 36$

b. $x^2 = 100$

c. Find m.

d. Find p.

problem set 117

1. Bucolic themes dominated the exposition, as 70 percent of the paintings were bucolic
(68) in nature. If 2000 paintings were exhibited, how many were not bucolic?

2. Ninety-six percent of the newcomers caviled every time an event was announced. If
(68) 140 newcomers did not cavil, how many newcomers were there?

3. The ratio of artists to spectators at the art show was 3 to 14. If a total of 1700 artists and
(100) spectators attended the art show, how many were spectators?

4. The sum of a number and 40 is 5 less than the product of the number and 6. What is
(90,95) the number?

5. A fair coin comes up heads twice in a row. If it is flipped again, what is the probability
(114) that it will be heads again?

6. An urn contains 2 white marbles, 3 green marbles, and 5 red marbles. A marble is
(114) drawn and then replaced. Then a second marble is drawn. What is the probability that
the first marble was white and the second was green?

7. Mr. Indecisive, the grocer, just could not make up his mind! His juicy ripe pears were
(110) $1.28 per pound. Then he marked them down 50%; then he marked them up 50%; then
down 50%; then up 50%. What was the final price!?!

8. Mr. Diego deposits $2000 into an account with $4\frac{1}{2}\%$ interest compounded twice per
(109) year. How much money will be in the account in two years?

Find *m* in each triangle.

9.
(117)

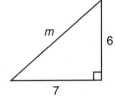

10.
(117)

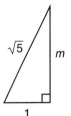

11. Find the perimeter of this figure. Dimensions are in decimeters.
(117)

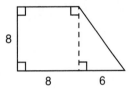

12. Find the area of the trapezoid. Dimensions are in inches.
(116)

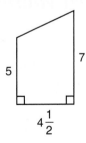

13. If 125 is increased by 60 percent, what is the resulting number?
(80)

14. If 200 is increased by $12\frac{1}{4}$ percent, what is the resulting number?
(110)

15. Draw a $2\frac{1}{4}$-inch line segment. Then use a metric scale to determine the length of the
(113) segment to the nearest millimeter.

16. Use the distributive property to multiply: $3ac(ab + ac + bc)$
(103)

17. Find the complement and supplement of a $22\frac{1}{2}^{\circ}$ angle.
(98)

Simplify by adding like terms:

18. $ab^2 + abb + 2a^2ab + 2abb - baa^2$
(102)

19. $-xy^3 + x^2xyy^2 + x^3y^3 - 3xyy^2$
(102)

Solve:

20. $3x + 4 - 2x - x = 4x - 5$
(96)

21. $3\frac{1}{2}x - 1\frac{3}{4} = -\frac{3}{2}$
(84)

22. $6 + x - 2x + 3x - 4x = 3x + 4$
(96)

23. $\dfrac{-\dfrac{1}{4}}{\dfrac{1}{3}} = \dfrac{\dfrac{16}{9}}{x}$
(59,81)

24. $x^2 = 1$
(117)

Simplify:

25. $aba^2b^2a^3b$
(101)

26. $xy^3x^2xxy^3$
(101)

27. $\dfrac{-(-3)^2 - 2^3(2^3 - 2 \cdot 6) + 3}{2^2(2^3 - 4)}$
(101)

28. $\dfrac{1}{5}\left(2\dfrac{1}{3} \cdot \dfrac{1}{4} - \dfrac{7}{12}\right)$
(93)

Evaluate:

29. $-b^2 + a + b$ if $a = -2$ and $b = -1$
(105)

30. $-b^3 + 2ab$ if $a = -1$ and $b = -2$
(105)

LESSON *118* *English Volume Conversions*

There are many cubic inches in a cubic foot. We can see this clearly by looking at this drawing of a cubic foot.

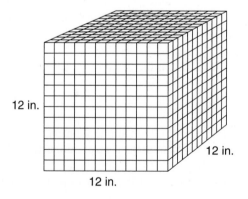

12 in.

12 in.

12 in.

We see that there are $12 \times 12 = 144$ cubes in the front face. The cubes are twelve deep, so there are a total of

$$144 \text{ cubes} \times 12 = 1728 \text{ cubes}$$

Three unit multipliers are needed for every conversion of one English volume measure to another. We will concentrate on the process rather than on numerical answers. Thus, the answers will not be worked out all the way.

example 118.1   Use three unit multipliers to convert 14 cubic feet to cubic inches.

solution   We will write cubic feet (ft^3) as ft · ft · ft so we can see how we use the three unit multipliers.

$$14 \, ft \cdot ft \cdot ft \times \frac{12 \text{ in.}}{1 \, ft} \times \frac{12 \text{ in.}}{1 \, ft} \times \frac{12 \text{ in.}}{1 \, ft} = \mathbf{14(12)(12)(12) \text{ in.}^3}$$

A calculator can be used to do the multiplication if a numerical answer is necessary.

example 118.2   Use six unit multipliers to convert 140 cubic yards (yd^3) to cubic inches $(in.^3)$.

solution   We will go from cubic yards to cubic feet to cubic inches. Three unit multipliers are needed to go from cubic yards to cubic feet, and three more are needed to go from cubic feet to cubic inches.

$$140 \, yd^3 \times \frac{3 \, ft}{1 \, yd} \times \frac{3 \, ft}{1 \, yd} \times \frac{3 \, ft}{1 \, yd} \times \frac{12 \text{ in.}}{1 \, ft} \times \frac{12 \text{ in.}}{1 \, ft} \times \frac{12 \text{ in.}}{1 \, ft}$$
$$= \mathbf{140(3)(3)(3)(12)(12)(12) \text{ in.}^3}$$

example 118.3   Use six unit multipliers to convert 50,163,529 cubic inches to cubic miles (mi^3).

solution   We will go from cubic inches to cubic feet to cubic miles.

$$50,163,529 \, in.^3 \times \frac{1 \, ft}{12 \text{ in.}} \times \frac{1 \, ft}{12 \text{ in.}} \times \frac{1 \, ft}{12 \text{ in.}} \times \frac{1 \text{ mi}}{5280 \, ft} \times \frac{1 \text{ mi}}{5280 \, ft} \times \frac{1 \text{ mi}}{5280 \, ft}$$
$$= \frac{\mathbf{50,163,529}}{\mathbf{(12)(12)(12)(5280)(5280)(5280)}} \text{ mi}^3$$

practice   **a.**   Use six unit multipliers to convert 1,000,000 cubic inches to cubic miles.

problem set 118

1. *(114)*   A single die is rolled twice. What is the probability of getting a 5 and then a 2?

2. *(108)*   The sales tax was $7\frac{1}{2}$ percent. If Moriah's goods cost $40 before tax, how much tax must he pay?

3. *(100)*   The ratio of the number of formidable contestants to the number who were lackluster was 7 to 2. If there were 45,000 contestants who were either formidable or lackluster, how many were formidable?

4. *(90,95)*   The product of a number and −11, increased by 6, is 30 less than the number times 25. What is the number?

5. *(113)*   Draw an 8-cm line segment, and measure its length in inches.

6. *(109)*   Calculate the interest earned in two years on a $2000 deposit at $3\frac{1}{2}\%$ interest compounded annually.

7. *(111)*   The water sprinklers malfunctioned in the shoe store, resulting in considerable damage. The manager, who had purchased the shoes for $61,000, had marked them up 50% but was forced to sell them for half the intended price. His additional expenses for cleanup and repair were $12,000. What was his net profit?

8. *(85)*   Sketch a rectangular coordinate system, and graph the line $y = 3x - 5$.

9. *(108)*   If 160 is increased by $20\frac{1}{2}$ percent, what is the resulting number?

10. Use six unit multipliers to convert 10 cubic miles to cubic inches.
(118)

11. Use six unit multipliers to convert 1000 cubic miles to cubic inches.
(118)

12. Give a combination of transformations that can be used to place the first figure exactly
(115) on top of the other. Explain the combination you chose.

13. Find *m*.
(117)

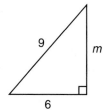

14. (a) Find *k*.
(65,104)

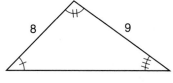

(b) Find the measure of angle Z.

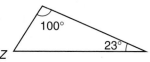

15. Find the area of this trapezoid.
(116) Dimensions are in feet.

16. Find the volume of a right solid whose base is shown on the left and whose height is 10
(64) centimeters. Dimensions are in centimeters.

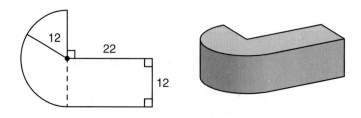
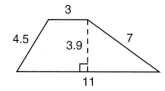

17. Find the lateral surface area of the solid described in problem 16.
(88)

18. Use the distributive property to multiply: $x^2 y^3 (x + yx + 2xy^7)$
(103)

19. Simplify by adding like terms: $4zmn^3 - 2zm^2 + nzmn^2 - mzm$
(102)

Solve:

20. $4x - 9 + x = -3x + 31$
(96)

21. $-1\frac{1}{2}x - \frac{1}{4} = 7\frac{1}{2}$
(84)

22. $\dfrac{-\dfrac{1}{6}}{\dfrac{4}{3}} = \dfrac{x}{-\dfrac{1}{7}}$
$(59,81)$

Simplify:

23. (a) $\dfrac{1}{7^{-2}}$ (b) $(-3)^{-3}$
(106)

24. $-(-3^2) - 4(3 \cdot 2 - 2^2)$
(99)

25. $7mn^4 m^2 bnb^4$
(101)

26. Graph on a number line: $x \geq -2$
(72)

27. Find the least common multiple of 12, 20, and 24.
(20)

28. Find the greatest common factor of 12, 20, and 24.
(13)

Evaluate:

29. $ab^3 + (-ab)^3$ if $a = -2$ and $b = 3$
(105)

30. $\sqrt{pz} + \sqrt[3]{z} + p^z$ if $p = -2$ and $z = -8$
(106)

LESSON *119* *Metric Volume Conversions*

A cubic meter is a relatively large unit of volume which equals approximately 264.17 gallons. A cubic centimeter is a relatively small unit of volume. It takes about 16.39 cubic centimeters to equal a cubic inch. The metric system has a unit of volume that is about the size of a quart—the **liter,** which equals 1000 cubic centimeters. A liter equals about 1.06 quarts. So when we see the word liter, we can think "big quart."

$$1 \text{ liter} \approx 1 \text{ big quart}$$

Because 1000 cubic centimeters makes a liter, we say that a cubic centimeter is a **milliliter,** which is one one-thousandth of a liter.

$$1 \text{ milliliter} = \frac{1}{1000} \text{ liter} = 1 \text{ cubic centimeter}$$

Only one unit multiplier is required to convert between cubic centimeters and liters. At least three unit multipliers are normally required for other volume conversions.

example 119.1   Convert 1,451,600 milliliters (mL) to liters.

solution   Only one unit multiplier is required to make this conversion.

$$1{,}451{,}600 \text{ mL} \times \frac{1 \text{ liter}}{1000 \text{ mL}} = \textbf{1451.6 liters}$$

example 119.2   Convert 40 cubic meters (m^3) to cubic centimeters (cm^3).

solution   We need three unit multipliers.

$$40 \text{ m}^3 \times \frac{100 \text{ cm}}{1 \text{ m}} \times \frac{100 \text{ cm}}{1 \text{ m}} \times \frac{100 \text{ cm}}{1 \text{ m}} = \textbf{40(100)(100)(100) cm}^3$$

example 119.3   Convert 1400 cubic meters to liters.

solution   We will go from m^3 to cm^3 to liters.

$$1400 \text{ m}^3 \times \frac{100 \text{ cm}}{1 \text{ m}} \times \frac{100 \text{ cm}}{1 \text{ m}} \times \frac{100 \text{ cm}}{1 \text{ m}} \times \frac{1 \text{ liter}}{1000 \text{ cm}^3}$$

$$= \frac{1400(100)(100)(100)}{1000} \text{ liters}$$

$$= \textbf{1,400,000 liters}$$

practice   **a.**   Use four unit multipliers to convert 500 cubic meters to milliliters.

b.   Use four unit multipliers to convert 500 liters to cubic meters.

c.   Convert 5,000,000 cubic centimeters to milliliters.

problem set
119

1.
(112)
One die is red and the other die is green. Both are rolled. What is the probability of getting a sum of

(a) 8?   (b) 9?   (c) 10?

2.
(112)
The first three cards dealt from a well-shuffled deck of cards are spades. What is the probability that the next card dealt will be a spade?

3.
(68)
Twenty percent of the flowers in the show were red. If 1400 flowers were not red, how many were red?

4.
(100)
Among the ballplayers, the ratio of ectomorphs to mesomorphs was 3 to 14. If there were 3400 ballplayers that fit in one or the other of these categories, how many were ectomorphs?

5.
(111)
Mr. Fisher marked the cost of his televisions up 60% from the $300 each one cost him. He then put them on sale for 20% off. How much profit does Mr. Fisher make on each television sold at the sale price?

6.
(62)
Only one fourth of those present really believed what the speaker was saying. If 1744 people were present, how many did not believe what the speaker was saying?

7.
(90,95)
Five times a certain number was 6 less than the product of 3 and the same number. What was the number?

8. Find A.
(117)

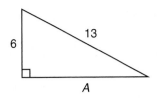

9. Convert 55 cubic inches to cubic feet.
(118)

10. Find the area of the parallelogram. Dimensions are in feet.
(116)

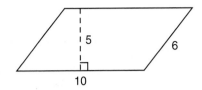

11. Use six unit multipliers to convert 10,000 cubic centimeters to cubic kilometers.
(119)

12. Use four unit multipliers to convert 12 cubic meters to liters.
(119)

13. What percent of 70 is 112?
(77)

14. Sketch a rectangular coordinate system, and graph the line $y = \frac{1}{2}x + 2$.
(85)

15. Use 4 unit multipliers to convert 1320 cubic meters to liters.
(119)

16. Convert 15,321,156 milliliters to liters.
(119)

17. Use the distributive property to multiply: $2ab\left(a + b - ab^2 + a^2b\right)$
(103)

18. Simplify by adding like terms: $2xyy^2 + 3x^2xy - 6yxy^2 + 7xyy^2$
(102)

19. Express in cubic meters the volume of a right solid whose base is shown on the left and whose sides are 3 meters tall. Dimensions are in centimeters.
(45,117)

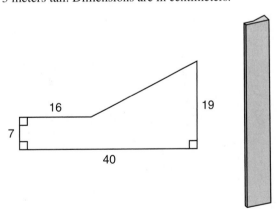

Solve:

20. $5x - 5 = -6x + 2x - 22$
(96)

21. $-\frac{2}{3}x - \frac{1}{5} = 1\frac{5}{6}$
(84)

22. $m^2 = 25$
(117)

Simplify:

23. $-\left[-(-2)^3\right] + (-2)$
(99)

24. $3a^2ba^3b^2b^3$
(101)

25. $\dfrac{-2^3 - 2^2\left(2^2 - 3\right) + 3}{3\left(2^3 - 1\right)}$
(93)

26. $\dfrac{1}{3}\left(2\dfrac{1}{2} \cdot \dfrac{1}{3} - \dfrac{1}{6} \cdot \dfrac{1}{2}\right)$
(52)

27. Evaluate: $xy^2 + 2x^2y$ if $x = 1$ and $y = -2$
(105)

28. Express 444 with Roman numerals.
(107)

29. Draw a $2\frac{3}{4}$-inch line segment, and measure it in centimeters.
(113)

30. Write 621321131.2 in words.
(6)

LESSON 120 *Volume of Pyramids, Cones, and Spheres • Surface Area of Pyramids and Cones*

120.A

volume of pyramids, cones, and spheres

There are formulas for the volumes of cones, pyramids, and spheres, but formulas are hard to learn and easy to forget.

 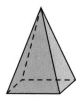  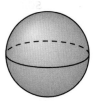

Triangular   Rectangular   Circular   Sphere
pyramid   pyramid   cone

However, there is an easy way to find volumes. The volume of a pyramid or a cone is exactly one third the volume of the right solid that has the same base and the same height. The volume of a sphere is exactly two thirds the volume of the right circular cylinder that has the same radius and the same height as the sphere. The height of the cylinder is equal to the diameter of the sphere.

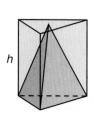 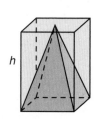 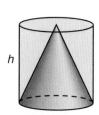 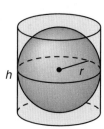

$\frac{1}{3}$ the volume of $\frac{1}{3}$ the volume of $\frac{1}{3}$ the volume of $\frac{2}{3}$ the volume of
a right solid   a right solid   a right solid   a right solid

example 120.1   The base of a triangular pyramid 4 meters tall is shown on the left. Find the volume of the pyramid shown on the right. Dimensions are in meters.

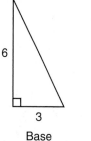 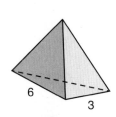

6

3
Base   Right solid   Pyramid

solution   The area of the base of the right solid is the area of the triangle.

$$\text{Area of base} = \frac{1}{2}bh = \frac{1}{2}(3 \text{ m})(6 \text{ m}) = 9 \text{ m}^2$$

The volume of the right solid is the area of the base times the height.

$$\text{Volume of right solid} = bh = (9 \text{ m}^2)(4 \text{ m}) = 36 \text{ m}^3$$

The volume of the pyramid is $\frac{1}{3}$ the volume of the solid.

$$\text{Volume of pyramid} = \frac{1}{3}(36 \text{ m}^3) = \mathbf{12 \text{ m}^3}$$

example 120.2   Find the volume of a circular cone 4 cm tall whose radius is 10 cm.

Base   Right solid   Cone

solution   First we find the area of the base.

$$\text{Area of base} = \pi r^2 \approx (3.14)(10 \text{ cm})^2 = 314 \text{ cm}^2$$

The volume of the right solid is the area of the base times the height.

$$\text{Volume of right solid} = bh \approx (314 \text{ cm}^2)(4 \text{ cm}) = 1256 \text{ cm}^3$$

The volume of the cone is $\frac{1}{3}$ the volume of the solid.

$$\text{Volume of cone} \approx \frac{1}{3}(1256 \text{ cm}^3) = \mathbf{418\frac{2}{3} \text{ cm}^3}$$

example 120.3   Find the volume of a sphere whose radius is 10 cm.

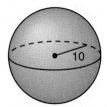

solution   A sphere is perfectly round. Every point on the sphere is the same distance from the center of the sphere. We could fit this sphere into a circular cylinder 20 cm tall whose radius is 10 cm.

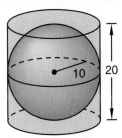

The volume of the cylinder is the area of the base times the height.

$$\text{Volume of cylinder} = \text{area of base} \times \text{height}$$
$$\approx 3.14(10 \text{ cm})^2(20 \text{ cm})$$
$$\approx 6280 \text{ cm}^3$$

The volume of the sphere is $\frac{2}{3}$ the volume of the cylinder.

$$\text{Volume of sphere} \approx \frac{2}{3}(6280 \text{ cm}^3) \approx \mathbf{4186.67 \text{ cm}^3}$$

120.B

surface area of pyramids and cones

Remember that the lateral surface area of a right solid is the perimeter of the base times its height. The base of a pyramid may be a triangle, a square, a rectangle or the shape of any polygon. Because a pyramid is pointed, all the faces are triangular. The surface area of a pyramid equals the area of the base plus the sum of the areas of the triangular faces. The surface area of a cone equals the area of the base plus the lateral surface area. In this book, we will consider only the surface area of right circular cones.

Lateral surface area of a right circular cone $= \pi rl$

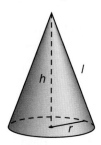

The *l* in this formula is the **slant height** of the cone. The slant height of a cone is the hypotenuse of the right triangle whose one leg is the radius of the base and whose other leg is the height of the cone.

example 120.4   The base of a pyramid is a square whose sides are 4 meters long. The height of each triangular face of the pyramid is 3 meters. Find the surface area of the pyramid.

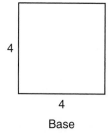 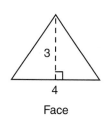 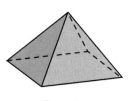

          Base   Face   Pyramid

solution   The area of the base is $4\,\text{m} \times 4\,\text{m} = 16\,\text{m}^2$. The area of each triangular face is

$$\text{Area of face} = \frac{1}{2}bh = \frac{1}{2}(4\text{m})(3\text{m}) = 6\,\text{m}^2$$

There are four triangular faces, so the total surface area is

$$\text{Surface area} = 16\,\text{m}^2 + 6\,\text{m}^2 + 6\,\text{m}^2 + 6\,\text{m}^2 + 6\,\text{m}^2 = \mathbf{40\,m^2}$$

example 120.5   Find the surface area of a right circular cone whose slant height is 6 meters and whose radius is 5 meters.

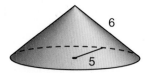

solution   The surface area equals the area of the base plus the lateral surface area.

$$\text{Area of the base} = \pi r^2 \approx (3.14)(5\,\text{m})^2 = 78.5\,\text{m}^2$$

$$\text{Lateral surface area} = \pi rl \approx (3.14)(5\,\text{m})(6\,\text{m}) = 94.2\,\text{m}^2$$

The total surface area is approximately

$$78.5\,\text{m}^2 + 94.2\,\text{m}^2 = \mathbf{172.7\,m^2}$$

practice   **a.** Find the volume of a pyramid 4 meters tall if the base is a square whose sides are 6 meters long.

b. Find the volume of a right circular cone 6 meters tall if the radius of the base is 2 meters.

c. Find the volume of a sphere whose radius is 6 centimeters.

d. Find the surface area of a pyramid whose base is a 5 ft × 5 ft square and whose triangular faces each have a height of 10 ft.

problem set   **1.** A fair coin is tossed 4 times. What is the probability that all 4 tosses will be tails?
120   *(114)*

2. A red die and a green die are rolled. There are 36 possible combinations. What is the
(112)   probability that the sum on the dice will equal 8?

3. The number of grant recipients increased 200 percent this year over last year. If 1200
(80)   people received grants this year, how many received grants last year?

4. The ratio of azure to teal stones was 9 to 7. If there were a total of 1600 stones that were
(100)   either azure or teal, how many were teal?

5. Graph the points on a rectangular coordinate system:
(38)

(a) (−3, 3)   (b) (1, 1)   (c) (2, −3)

6. Find the surface area of a right circular cone whose slant height is 5 meters and whose
(120)   base has a radius of 2 meters.

7. Find the volume of a right circular cone whose base has a radius of $2\sqrt{2}$ meters and
(120)   whose height is 2 meters. Round to two decimal places.

8. Find the volume of a right pyramid whose square base has sides 6 meters long and
(120)   whose height is 4 meters.

9. Find the surface area of the pyramid in problem 8 if the triangular faces have a height
(120)   of 5 meters.

10. Find the volume of a sphere with a radius of 3 m.
(120)

11. Find *m*.
(65)

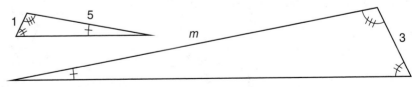

12. Measure and classify the angle:
(98)

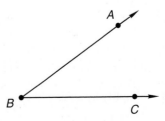

13. Find the measure of angle Z.
(104)

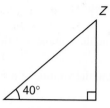

14. Find b.
(117)

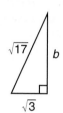

15. Find the area of the trapezoid. Dimensions are in feet.
(116)

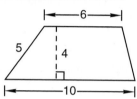

16. What number is $16\frac{1}{2}$ percent of 1100?
(108)

17. Between which two consecutive integers is $\sqrt{57}$?
(92)

18. Use four unit multipliers to convert 70,000,000 milliliters to cubic meters.
(119)

19. Use six unit multipliers to convert 60 cubic inches to cubic miles.
(118)

Solve:

20. $5x + 4 - x = 3x + 2$
(96)

21. $-4\frac{1}{3}x + \frac{1}{4} = -3\frac{1}{12}$
(84)

22. $\dfrac{-\dfrac{1}{6}}{\dfrac{2}{5}} = \dfrac{x}{\dfrac{1}{3}}$
(59,81)

Simplify:

23. (a) $\dfrac{1}{9^{-2}}$ (b) 4^{-3}
(106)

24. $\dfrac{(-2)^3 - 3(-1^5 - 3 \cdot 2)}{2(3^3 - \sqrt[5]{-243})}$
(93,106)

25. $6b^3ab^2a^5b$
(101)

26. $\dfrac{1}{4}\left(2\dfrac{1}{2} \cdot \dfrac{1}{3} - \dfrac{1}{6} \cdot \dfrac{1}{5}\right)$
(52)

Evaluate:

27. $ab^3 - b$ if $a = 3$ and $b = -3$
(105)

28. $cx^2 - c^5x$ if $c = -1$ and $x = -2$
(105)

29. If $8000 is deposited in an account that pays 10 percent interest compounded annually,
(109) how much money will be in the account in 4 years?

30. Simplify by adding like terms: $2abab - 4ba^2b + 7ab^2a + 3a^2b$
(102)

LESSON 121 *Forming Solids • Symmetry*

121.A

forming solids   Visualizing solids that can be formed by folding patterns is interesting and useful.

example 121.1   What is the volume of the geometric solid formed by folding the shape along the dashed lines? Dimensions are in inches.

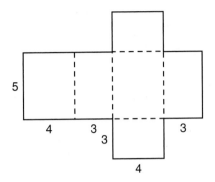

solution   The shape will form the box shown.

Volume = 3 in. × 4 in. × 5 in. = **60 in.³**

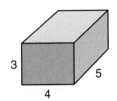

example 121.2   What is the volume of the geometric solid formed by folding this shape along the dashed lines? Dimensions are in centimeters.

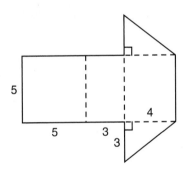

solution   The solid will be a triangular prism. The volume is the area of the triangle times the length.

$$\text{Volume} = \left(\frac{1}{2}bh\right)(l)$$

$$= \frac{1}{2}(4\text{ cm})(3\text{ cm})(5\text{ cm}) = \textbf{30 cm}^3$$

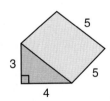

121.B

symmetry   A figure is **symmetric about a line** if one side of the figure is a mirror image of the other side of the figure. This quadrilateral is symmetric about line *r*.

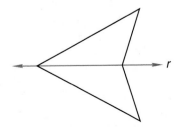

Figures are symmetric about a line if the perpendicular distance from any point on the line to the figure is equal to the perpendicular distance from the same point to a corresponding point in the figure that is on the other side of the line. To demonstrate, we have picked three points on line r. The arrows point to corresponding points on the figure. The arrows above the line are the same length as the arrows below the line.

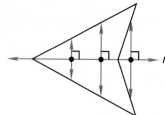

A figure can have more than one line of symmetry. The equilateral triangle has three lines of symmetry, and the square has four lines of symmetry.

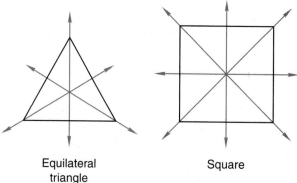

Equilateral
triangle   Square

Figures can also be symmetric about a point. This figure is symmetric about the point shown.

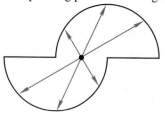

A figure is **symmetric about a point** if, for any line drawn through the point, it is the same distance in both directions to corresponding points on the figure. We show three such lines.

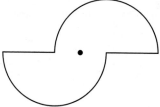

Sometimes we can use symmetry to help us solve problems.

example 121.3   Find the area of this symmetric figure. Dimensions are in yards.

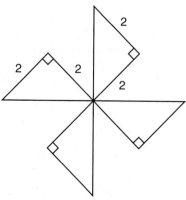

solution   We label the pieces of the figure and indicate the point of symmetry.

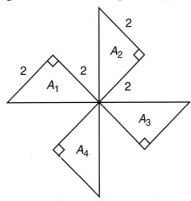

The figure is symmetric about its central point. Since it is symmetric about a point, pieces on opposite sides of the point of symmetry have the same area. Thus,

$$A_1 = A_3 \quad \text{and} \quad A_2 = A_4$$

In this case, all four pieces have the same area because A_1 and A_2 are determined by the same dimensions. Therefore, the total area is four times the area of one of the triangles.

$$\text{Total area} = 4\left(\frac{1}{2}\right)(2 \text{ yd})(2 \text{ yd})$$
$$= 8 \text{ yd}^2$$

practice   Find the volume of the solid formed when each figure is folded along the dashed lines. Dimensions are in inches.

a.

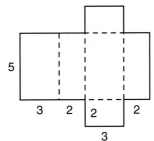

b.

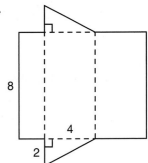

Quickly sketch each figure, and draw in the lines of symmetry.

c.

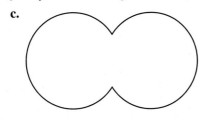

d.

Are these figures symmetric about a point, a line, or both?

e.

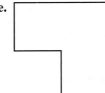

f.

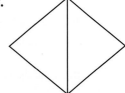

Use symmetry to find the areas of these symmetric figures. Dimensions are in meters.

g.

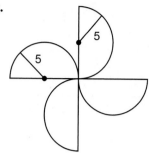

h.

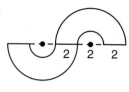

**problem set
121**

1.
(114)
The urn contained 34 marbles: 18 were black, 9 were red, and 7 were green. One marble was drawn and then put back. Then a second marble was drawn. What is the probability that both marbles were red?

2.
(90,95)
If the product of a number and –17 is decreased by 5, the result is 3 greater than the product of the number and –9. What is the number?

3.
(68)
Thirty percent of those present were not able to produce a likeness of the subject. If 1260 could produce a likeness, how many were present?

4.
(100)
The ratio of the number of audiophiles to the number of nonaudiophiles was 2 to 3. If there were 325 in all, what was the number of audiophiles?

5.
(38)
Graph the following points on a rectangular coordinate system:

(a) (2, 3)   (b) (–1, 4)   (c) (2, –2)

6.
(116)
Find the area of the parallelogram. Dimensions are in inches.

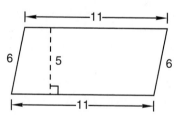

7.
(121)
Find the volume of the solid formed when this figure is folded along the dashed lines. Dimensions are in inches.

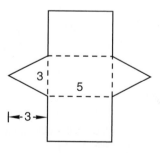

8.
(120)
Find the surface area of a pyramid whose base is a 6 ft × 6 ft square and whose triangular faces each have a height of 5 ft.

9.
(120)
Find the volume of a sphere with a radius of 9 ft.

10. Find the volume of a right circular cone with a radius of 10 m and a height of 2 m. Round
(120) to two decimal places.

11. Find:
(104,117)

(a) z

(b) m

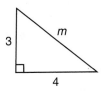

12. Find m.
(65)

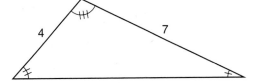

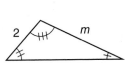

13. Sketch the figures and draw any lines of symmetry. Which figure is symmetric about
(121) a point?

(a)   (b)

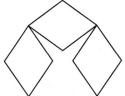

14. Find the area of the shaded portion of this symmetric figure. Dimensions are in inches.
(121)

15. If Billy Bob earns $11\frac{3}{4}\%$ commission on every Diggity Dawg he sells, and in May he
(111) sells four Diggity Dawgs for $2500 each, what is his commission for May?

16. Sketch a rectangular coordinate system, and graph the line $y = -\frac{1}{2}x + 3$.
(85)

17. Nine and one half percent of what number is 9500?
(108)

18. Use six unit multipliers to convert 100,000 cubic centimeters to cubic kilometers.
(119)

19. Use six unit multipliers to convert 20 cubic miles to cubic inches.
(118)

20. Use the distributive property to multiply: $ab^2(ac + 3ab^2 - b)$
(103)

21. Simplify by adding like terms: $2mp^2 - 3m^2p - 4pmp + 5mpm$
(102)

Solve:

22. $4x - 6x - 6 = 3x + 14$
(96)

23. $\dfrac{-\dfrac{1}{5}}{\dfrac{7}{8}} = \dfrac{-\dfrac{1}{20}}{x}$
(59,81)

Simplify:

24. (a) $(-4)^{-3}$ (b) $\dfrac{1}{-4^{-2}}$

$\quad$ **(106)**

25. $-3^3 + (2)^3 - 3(2^3 - 3^2)$

$\quad$ **(99)**

26. $6m^3n^2bm^4n$

$\quad$ **(101)**

27. $\dfrac{1}{6}\left(2\dfrac{1}{2} \cdot \dfrac{2}{5} - \dfrac{1}{5} \cdot \dfrac{1}{4}\right)$

$\quad$ **(52)**

Evaluate:

28. $x^y - y^x$ if $x = -2$ and $y = -3$

$\quad$ **(105)**

29. $\sqrt[a]{b} + \sqrt{b} + a^2$ if $a = 3$ and $b = 64$

$\quad$ **(54)**

30. Graph on a number line: $x \nleq -4$

$\quad$ **(89)**

LESSON 122 *Permutations*

There are six ways we can arrange the letters A, B, and C in order. If we put A first, there are two ways:

| A | B | C | and | A | C | B |

If we put B first, there are two ways:

| B | A | C | and | B | C | A |

If we put C first, there are two ways:

| C | A | B | and | C | B | A |

We could put any one of the **three** letters in the first box. Then there are **two** letters left that could be put in the second box. Then the last letter is forced into the last box because it is the only letter left. There are

$$3 \cdot 2 \cdot 1 = 6$$

ways these three letters could be arranged in order. Each of these ways is called a **permutation.** If there are five objects, any of the five could go in the first place.

| 5 | | | | |

Now any one of the four remaining could go in the second place.

| 5 | 4 | | | |

Then, any one of the three remaining could go in the next place and two in the place after, leaving just one possibility for the last place.

| 5 | 4 | 3 | 2 | 1 |

$$5 \times 4 \times 3 \times 2 \times 1 = 120$$

There are 120 ways five objects can be arranged in order.

There is an easier way to write

$$5 \times 4 \times 3 \times 2 \times 1$$

All we do is write 5 and follow it with an exclamation point.

$$5! \quad \text{means} \quad 5 \times 4 \times 3 \times 2 \times 1$$

The notation 5! is read as "5 factorial."

If we have ten objects and want to find how many ways we can arrange four of them in a row, we think literally:

> Any one of ten could be in first place.
> Any one of the nine remaining could be in second place.
> Any one of the eight remaining could be in third place.
> Any one of the seven remaining could be in fourth place.

There are $10 \cdot 9 \cdot 8 \cdot 7$ ways ten objects can be arranged four at a time:

$$10 \cdot 9 \cdot 8 \cdot 7 = 5040$$

There are 5040 permutations of ten objects taken four at a time.

example 122.1 Mary has eight different objects. How many permutations are possible?

solution There are 8! possible permutations.

$$8! = 8 \cdot 7 \cdot 6 \cdot 5 \cdot 4 \cdot 3 \cdot 2 \cdot 1 = \textbf{40,320 permutations}$$

example 122.2 If Mary chose three objects at a time from her eight, in how many different orders could they be arranged in a row?

solution Any one of eight can go into the first box, any one of the seven remaining can go into the second box, and any one of the six remaining can go into the third box.

$$\boxed{8 \quad 7 \quad 6} = 8 \cdot 7 \cdot 6 = 336$$

There are **336 ways** eight objects can be arranged in a row three at a time.

practice **a.** In how many different orders can 9 objects be arranged in a row?

b. In how many different orders can 5 of the 9 objects be arranged in a row?

problem set 122

1.
(114) One card is pulled from a standard deck of 52 cards and then replaced. Then a second card is drawn. What is the probability of getting a black 2 and then a red 9?

2.
(112) Two dice are rolled. What is the probability that the sum will be 12?

3.
(109) If \$10,000 is deposited in an account that receives $9\frac{1}{2}$ percent interest compounded annually, how much money will be in the account in 3 years?

4.
(100) The ratio of philatelists to archivists was 2 to 8. If there were 1110 philatelists and archivists in all, how many were philatelists and how many were archivists?

5.
(38) Graph each point on a rectangular coordinate system:
(a) (4, 2)   (b) (0, –1)   (c) (–1, 0)

6.
(122) In how many different orders can 5 objects be arranged in a row?

7.
(122) (a) In how many different orders can 7 objects be arranged in a row?
(b) In how many different orders can 3 of the 7 objects be arranged in a row?

8.
(118) Convert 5 cubic miles to cubic feet.

9. Find the volume of a right pyramid that has a height of 30 meters and a square base
(120) whose sides measure 10 meters each.

10. Sketch a rectangular coordinate system, and graph the line $y = 2x + 1$.
(85)

11. What percent of 60 is 84?
(77)

12. Seventy percent of what number is 651?
(68)

13. Use six unit multipliers to convert 1,000,000 cubic centimeters to cubic kilometers.
(119)

14. Use four unit multipliers to convert 10,500 cubic meters to milliliters.
(119)

15. Find the volume of the solid formed
(121) when this figure is folded along the
dashed lines. Dimensions are in feet.
(*Note:* The height of the right solid is
not 5 feet.)

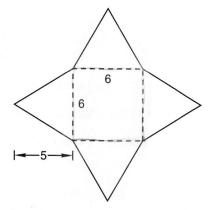

16. Sketch the figures, and draw any lines of symmetry. Which figure is symmetric about
(121) a point?

(a)   (b)

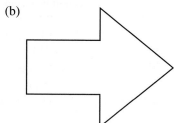

17. Find:
(104,117)
(a) z

(b) m

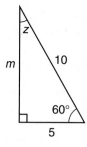

18. Find m.
(65)

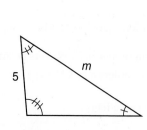
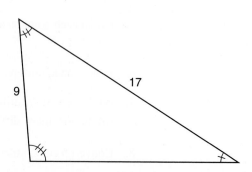

19. Find the area of each figure. Dimensions are in meters.
(116)

(a)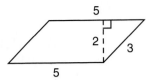

(b)

Solve:

20. $7x + 3 + 2x = -4 - 2x + 3 - x$
(96)

21. $-1\frac{4}{5}x + 2\frac{1}{2} = -\frac{1}{15}$
(84)

22. $\dfrac{\frac{1}{9}}{\frac{4}{7}} = \dfrac{x}{\frac{3}{14}}$
(59)

Simplify:

23. (a) $\dfrac{1}{-2^{-6}}$ (b) $(-2)^{-6}$
(106)

24. $\dfrac{(-1)^7 - 2(3^2 - 2 \cdot 4)}{3(\sqrt[3]{-216} + 2^3)}$
(93,106)

25. $m^5 p^6 m^2 pmz$
(101)

26. $\dfrac{2}{5}\left(3\frac{1}{4} \cdot \frac{1}{6} - \frac{1}{2} \cdot \frac{1}{4}\right)$
(52)

Evaluate:

27. $a^2 z - z^2$ if $a = -5$ and $z = -3$
(105)

28. $\sqrt[p]{m} + p^z$ if $m = -8$, $p = 3$, and $z = -2$
(106)

29. The sales tax in Rome was VIII percent. How much tax did Caesar pay on a toga that
(107) cost CXXV denarii?

30. Simplify: $\dfrac{1}{2} - 0.2(\sqrt{36}) + 5^{-2} \div 1\frac{1}{5} + 1\frac{3}{4}$
(44,106)

LESSON 123   *Numerals and Numbers • The Subsets of the Real Numbers*

123.A

numerals and numbers

A *number* is an idea. A *numeral* is the symbol we write to make us think of the idea. The three people below have the quality of threeness, as do the three pencils. The items on the right have this same quality of threeness even though they are all different.

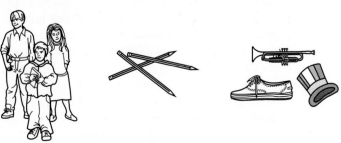

Three   ι Three   Three

When we want to express the **idea** of three, we often write the following symbol:

$$3$$

This symbol is not a number but is a numeral that makes us think of the number 3. The ancient Romans used the numeral

$$\text{III}$$

when they wanted to symbolize the number 3. There are many numerals for 3. All the following numerals have the value of 3.

$$\frac{30}{10} \qquad 2 + 1 \qquad \frac{15}{5} \qquad 6 \div 2 \qquad 14 - 11 \qquad 1 + 1 + 1$$

Each of these groups of numerals can also be called a **numerical expression.** We see that the value of a numerical expression is the number that the expression represents. Since all these expressions represent the number 3, we say that each of them has a value of 3.

The distinction between a numeral and a number is often helpful. For instance, we cannot add the fractions

$$\frac{1}{4} + \frac{1}{2}$$

in their present form because the denominators are not the same. But we can add the fractions if we change the numeral for the second number to a numeral whose denominator is 4.

$$\frac{1}{4} + \frac{2}{4} = \frac{3}{4}$$

We did not change the number. We changed the numeral used to represent the number. We could do this because both

$$\frac{1}{2} \qquad \text{and} \qquad \frac{2}{4}$$

have the same value and represent the same number.

From this we see the distinction between a number and a numeral:

A number is an idea and a numeral is a symbol.

123.B
the subsets of the real numbers

To count the members of your family or the desks in your classroom, you use the numbers

$$1, 2, 3, 4, 5, \ldots$$

These are the **natural** or **counting numbers** or positive integers. But if you measure the length of your pencil, you might find it is $5\frac{1}{2}$ inches or 12.2 cm. Whole numbers are not enough if we wish to express fractional quantities or parts of numbers. Any number that can be expressed as $\frac{\text{integer}}{\text{integer}}$ is called a **rational number.** For example, $5\frac{1}{2} = \frac{11}{2}$, $12.2 = \frac{122}{10}$, and $5 = \frac{5}{1}$ are all rational numbers. It may be difficult to imagine, but some numbers cannot be expressed as $\frac{\text{integer}}{\text{integer}}$, so they are not rational numbers. Examples are π, the ratio of the circumference to the diameter of a circle, and many of the roots you have encountered, such as $\sqrt{2}$. Such numbers are called **irrational** because they cannot be expressed as a ratio of integers. To express no quantity, we use zero, which is an integer. We also have negative numbers, which we use for temperatures below zero or money owed in a bank balance. Integers, rational, and irrational numbers can all be negative, while whole numbers and natural numbers cannot. These five number sets together are called the **real numbers.**

This diagram shows the relationship between these sets of numbers.

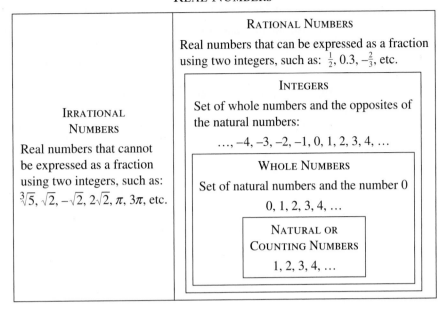

REAL NUMBERS

Note that this diagram shows the relationship between the sets of numbers, but not their relative sizes. A discussion of the sizes of these sets is beyond the scope of this course.

A set included in another set is called a **subset.** So we can say that the integers are a subset of the rational numbers and that counting numbers are a subset of integers. All the different sets of numbers are subsets of the real numbers.

example 123.1   To which number sets discussed in this lesson do (a) −3 and (b) $\frac{2}{3}$ belong?

solution   (a) Negative three is an **integer,** a **rational number** $\left(-\frac{3}{1}\right)$, and a **real number.**

(b) Two-thirds is a **rational number** and a **real number.**

practice   To which number sets discussed in this lesson do (a) 3 and (b) π belong?

problem set 123

1.
(114)   A fair coin is tossed 7 times. What is the probability that all tosses will be tails?

2.
(80)   Reminiscences increased 110 percent. If the previous number of reminiscences was 840, what was the new number of reminiscences?

3.
(100)   The ratio of the number of ratio problems to the number of non-ratio problems is 1 to 29. If there are 3930 problems, how many are ratio problems?

4.
(90,95)   The product of a number and 21 is decreased by 102. The result is equal to the product of the number and 11, increased by 8. What is the number?

5.
(63)   The caravan covered the first 90 miles in 15 hours. Then it doubled its pace to travel the next 180 miles. How long did it take the caravan to travel the total distance of 270 miles?

6.
(26)   The governor of Minnesota gave Steve 14 assignments the first week, 17 the next week, and 23 the week after that. What was the average number of assignments given per week?

7.
(110)
Donnie bought a 360 cubic-inch motor that was marked down 25 percent. If the original price was $1500, how much did Donnie pay?

8.
(122)
(a) In how many different orders can 10 objects be arranged in a row?

(b) In how many different orders can 4 of the 10 objects be arranged in a row?

9.
(123)
To which number sets discussed in this lesson does π belong?

10.
(123)
To which number sets discussed in this lesson do (a) $\frac{2}{9}$ and (b) 10 belong?

11.
(121)
Find the volume in cubic feet of the solid formed when this figure is folded along the dashed lines. Dimensions are in meters.

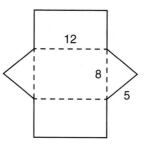

12.
(116)
Find the area of this trapezoid. Dimensions are in inches.

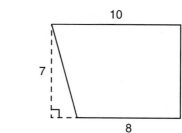

13.
(104,117)
Find:

(a) z

(b) m

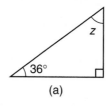

(a)

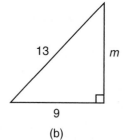

(b)

14.
(65)
Find m.

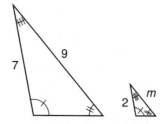

15.
(85)
Sketch a rectangular coordinate system, and graph the line $y = 3x - 2$.

16.
(108)
Eleven and one-fourth percent of what number is 562.5?

17.
(77)
What percent of 90 is 148.5?

18. Use four unit multipliers to convert 1000 milliliters to cubic meters.
(119)

19. Use six unit multipliers to convert 11,000,000 cubic miles to cubic inches.
(118)

20. Use the distributive property to multiply: $m^2b(m^3 + b^2 + cm)$.
(103)

21. Simplify by adding like terms: $2abab - 4ba^2b + 7ab^2a + 3a^2b$.
(102)

22. Find the volume in cubic meters of a right circular cylinder with a diameter of $4\sqrt{2}$
(73)   meters and a height of 2 meters.

23. Find the volume in cubic meters of a right pyramid whose square base has sides 6
(120)   meters long and whose height is 4 meters.

24. Find the surface area in square meters of the pyramid discussed in problem 23 if the
(120)   four faces each have a height of 5 meters.

Solve:

25. $5x - 4 + 2x - 1 = 3x + 6 + 2x + 1$
(96)

26. $\dfrac{-\dfrac{1}{4}}{\dfrac{2}{7}} = \dfrac{x}{\dfrac{1}{3}}$
(59,81)

Simplify:

27. $5!$ **28.** $(-3)^{-2}$
(122)   (106)

29. Evaluate: $-a^{-2} + b^{-3}$ if $a = 3$ and $b = -5$
(105,106)

30. Graph on a number line: $x \geq 0$
(72)

Appendix
Additional Topics

TOPIC A *Geometric Constructions*

You have used a ruler to draw segments of certain lengths and a protractor to draw angles with certain measures. The ancient Greeks **constructed** many geometric figures using only two instruments, a **straightedge** and a **compass.** (The Greeks did not have a modern metal compass like we have. We think they may have used a forked stick or a piece of string instead. In any case, what they used functioned like our compass.) In this lesson you will learn some of their ingenious techniques for geometric constructions. The items needed for the constructions are unlined paper, a straightedge, and a compass. No other items are needed.

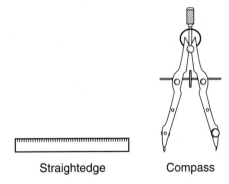

Straightedge   Compass

If the only straightedge you have is a ruler, you may use it; however, you must ignore its markings. You may also use lined paper if that is all that is available; however, you must not use the lines on the paper to draw your own lines.

Construction A: angle copies

We can copy an angle in six steps by using a straightedge and a compass. We begin with angle *A*.

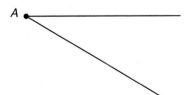

1. Draw a ray to create one side of the copied angle.

A' •—————————————

2. Use a compass to draw an arc on the original angle.

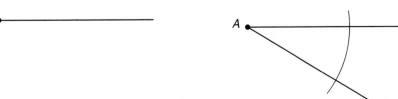

3. Draw an arc of the same radius centered at the vertex of the future copy.

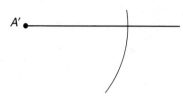

4. On the given angle, use the compass to measure the distance between the points on the arc where the arc intercepts the sides of the angle.

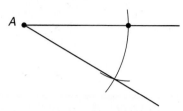

5. On the future copy, draw an arc of the same radius centered at the intersection of the first arc and first side. Be sure the arc you draw intercepts the first arc.

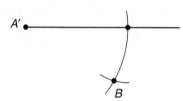

6. To complete the copy, draw a ray from the vertex through the intersection of the two arcs.

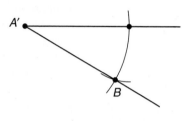

Construction B:
angle bisectors

An angle bisector is a ray that divides an angle into two equal parts. To bisect the angle PMN below,

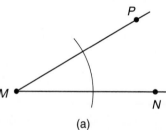

(a)

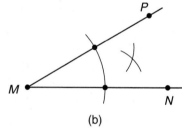

(b)

we first draw an arc that intersects both rays, as shown in (a). Then we draw arcs of equal radii from each of the points of intersection, as shown in (b). The point where these arcs cross, K, lies on the angle bisector, which we draw in (c).

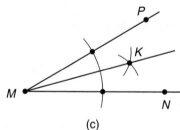

(c)

$$\text{m}\angle NMK = \frac{1}{2}\text{m}\angle NMP \quad \text{and} \quad \text{m}\angle PMK = \frac{1}{2}\text{m}\angle PMN$$

practice   1. Copy $\angle A$.

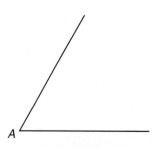

2. Copy ∠B and then bisect the copy.

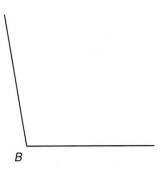

3. Draw a segment and label its endpoints A and B. Draw a circle centered at A whose radius is the length of segment AB; then draw a second circle centered at B with the same radius. Label one of the points where the circles intersect C. Then draw $\overline{AC}$ and $\overline{BC}$. What kind of triangle is △ABC?

4. Construct a 60° angle and a 30° angle. (*Hint:* An equilateral triangle is also equiangular. If the sides have the same length, the angles have the same measure. Since the sum of the interior angles in a triangle is 180°, each angle of an equilateral triangle is 60°.)

5. Draw an acute triangle, △ABC. Construct a triangle, △DEF, that is congruent to △ABC.

6. Construct a 120° angle.

7. Construct a 15° angle.

8. Construct a 45°angle.

Construction C: perpendicular bisectors

A perpendicular bisector of a segment is the line that is perpendicular to the segment at its midpoint. To construct the perpendicular bisector of $\overline{MN}$, we first use the compass to draw two arcs of equal radius centered at point M. Their radius should be a little longer than half of the length of the line segment, as shown in (a). Then we draw arcs of the same radius centered at point N, as shown in (b).

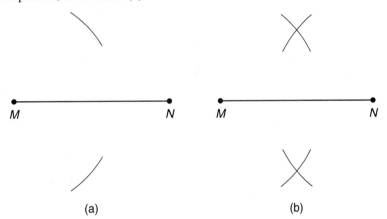

(a)   (b)

The points where the arcs cross are **equidistant** (the same distance) from points M and N. **Any point on the line that connects these intersections will also be equidistant from points M and N.** A line drawn through these points is the perpendicular bisector of $\overline{MN}$.

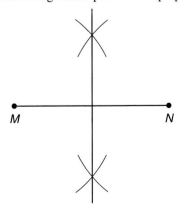

Construction D:
perpendiculars
to lines, 1

We want to draw a line, perpendicular to a given line, that passes through a designated point that is not on the given line. We begin with a drawing and call the point P.

$P \bullet$

———————————

Next we swing an arc from P that intercepts the line at two points. We label the points where this arc intercepts the line A and B, as shown in (a). Then we construct the perpendicular bisector of $\overline{AB}$, as shown in (b).

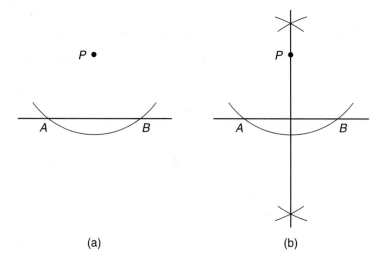

(a)   (b)

Construction E:
perpendiculars
to lines, 2

Now we want to draw a line, perpendicular to a given line, that passes through a specified point on the given line. To begin, we draw line m with point P on it.

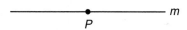

We put the pin of the compass on P and draw arcs of the same radius that intercept the line on each side. We label the points of intersection A and B.

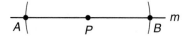

Now we construct the perpendicular bisector of $\overline{AB}$.

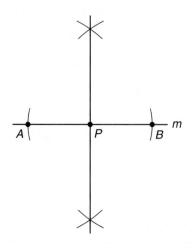

practice For problems 9–11, begin by drawing a figure similar to the one shown but larger.

9. Construct the perpendicular bisector of $\overline{WV}$.

10. Construct the perpendicular line to $\overline{CZ}$ from J.

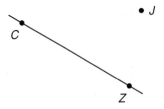

11. Construct the line perpendicular to line j at point Q.

12. Construct a right triangle.

13. Construct a 30°-60°-90° triangle.

14. Construct a 45°-45°-90° triangle.

15. Construct a square.

16. Construct a rectangle with lengths x and y.

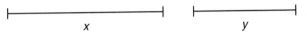

17. Construct a right triangle with legs of lengths 1 and 2.

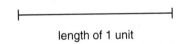

length of 1 unit

TOPIC B *Representing Data*

In Lesson 29, we learned to read graphs. We use graphs to help us understand and analyze quantitative information. In this lesson, we will explore other methods of representing data.

stem-and-leaf plots To discuss **stem-and-leaf plots,** we begin with the following data. The data could represent many things, but you may suppose that the data represents the scores of 30 students in a mathematics class.

82, 75, 69, 56, 99, 62, 75, 82, 91, 75,
65, 70, 80, 96, 82, 87, 94, 58, 96, 89,
91, 82, 82, 94, 87, 89, 96, 75, 87, 84

To analyze the data, we organize the scores using a stem-and-leaf plot. Noticing that the scores range from a low of 56 to a high of 99, we choose the initial digits of 50, 60, 70, 80, and 90 to serve as stem digits.

Stem

```
5 |
6 |
7 |
8 |
9 |
```

Then we use the ones' place digits of the scores as the leaves.

Stem	Leaf
5	6 8
6	9 2 5
7	5 5 5 0 5
8	2 2 0 2 7 9 2 2 7 9 7 4
9	9 1 6 4 6 1 4 6

6 | 2 represents
a score of 62

A key is included to the left to help readers interpret the plot. (The top row of leaves indicates the scores 56 and 58.) To facilitate data analysis the leaves may be rearranged. Below we show the same information as before, but with the leaves in each row arranged in ascending order.

Stem	Leaf
5	6 8
6	2 5 9
7	0 5 5 5 5
8	0 2 2 2 2 2 4 7 7 7 9 9
9	1 1 4 4 6 6 6 9

6 | 2 represents
a score of 62

Now it is much easier to discuss the mean (average), median, mode, and range of the data.

example B.1   Create a stem-and-leaf plot for the following data:

$$21, \ 33, \ 23, \ 49, \ 11, \ 19, \ 28,$$
$$19, \ 37, \ 42, \ 23, \ 44, \ 20, \ 35,$$
$$23, \ 41, \ 15, \ 43, \ 26, \ 23, \ 16$$

Then determine the mean, median, mode, and range of the data.

solution   The lowest number is 11 and the highest is 49, so we use the initial digits of 10, 20, 30, and 40 as our stems. The leaves are determined by the ones' place digit in each number.

Stem	Leaf
1	1 9 9 5 6
2	1 3 8 3 0 3 6 3
3	3 7 5
4	9 2 4 1 3

Next we rearrange the plot and include a key.

Stem	Leaf
1	1 5 6 9 9
2	0 1 3 3 3 3 6 8
3	3 5 7
4	1 2 3 4 9

2 | 3 represents
the number 23

Now we analyze the data.

$$\text{Mean} = \frac{\text{sum of the numbers}}{\text{quantity of numbers}} = \frac{591}{21} \approx \mathbf{28.14}$$

$$\text{Median} = \text{middle number} = \mathbf{23}$$

$$\text{Mode} = \text{most frequent number} = \mathbf{23}$$

$$\text{Range} = \text{greatest} - \text{least} = 49 - 11 = \mathbf{38}$$

practice   Create a stem-and-leaf plot for each data set given. Organize each row of leaves in ascending order.

1. 30, 40, 51, 62, 35, 45, 54, 61, 39, 49,
   32, 43, 54, 65, 33, 42, 55, 64, 31, 49,
   31, 49, 58, 68, 37, 49, 59, 67, 30, 40

2. 85, 55, 63, 72, 54, 64, 74, 84, 61, 70,
   73, 81, 50, 64, 87, 58, 63, 77, 59, 66,
   63, 74, 85, 56, 78, 88, 53, 69, 89, 59

3. The following data represents points scored by a basketball team in its twenty-four-game season.

   49, 49, 53, 72, 66, 65, 42, 77, 56, 66, 71, 58,
   60, 68, 48, 73, 59, 62, 49, 70, 75, 65, 49, 74

   (a) Create a stem-and-leaf plot of the scores.
   (b) Determine the mode of the scores.
   (c) Determine the range of the scores.
   (d) Determine the median of the scores.
   (e) Determine the mean of the scores.

box-and-whisker plots   We can begin with a stem-and-leaf plot and create another data representation tool, called a **box-and-whisker plot**. For demonstration, we shall begin with the same stem-and-leaf plot discussed in the previous section.

Stem	Leaf
5	6 8
6	2 5 9
7	0 5 5 5 5
8	0 2 2 2 2 2 4 7 7 7 9 9
9	1 1 4 4 6 6 6 9

6 | 2 represents a score of 62

Box-and-whisker plots are based on points called quartiles and on extreme values. The middle number of the upper half of the scores is the **upper quartile** or **third quartile**. The middle number of the lower half of the scores is the **lower quartile** or **first quartile**. The **second quartile** is the median of the complete data. We indicate the particular values of the quartiles for this data below.

Stem	Leaf
5	6 8
6	2 5 9
7	0 5 5 5 5
8	0 2 2 2 2 2 4 7 7 7 9 9
9	1 1 4 4 6 6 6 9

6 | 2 represents a score of 62

lower quartile

upper quartile   median

The box-and-whisker plot **of this data shows the location of these values compared to a number line. The five dots on a box-and-whisker plot show the extremes** of the scores—the lowest score and highest score—as well as the lower quartile, median, and upper quartile. A "box" divided by the median shows the location of the **middle half** of the scores. The "whiskers" show the extents of the scores below the first quartile and above the third quartile.

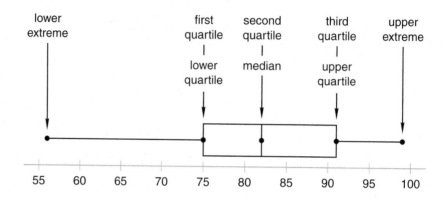

example B.2   Create a box-and-whisker plot from the data given below:

15, 26, 26, 27, 28, 29, 30, 31, 35, 35, 36, 37, 37, 38, 38, 40,
42, 42, 43, 45, 46, 47, 47, 49, 49, 49, 49, 52, 54, 55, 57, 58

solution   The numbers are already in order, so we do not need to create a stem-and-leaf plot first. We simply need to determine the median, lower quartile, and upper quartile. There are thirty-two entries, so the median is the average of the 16th and 17th entries.

$$\text{Median} = \frac{40 + 42}{2} = 41$$

The lower quartile is the middle of the lower sixteen entries, and the upper quartile is the middle of the upper sixteen entries. Since neither of these have a true middle, the lower quartile is the average of the 8th and 9th entries and the upper quartile is the average of the 24th and 25th entries.

$$\text{Lower quartile} = \frac{31 + 35}{2} = 33$$

$$\text{Upper quartile} = \frac{49 + 49}{2} = 49$$

Now we create the box-and-whisker plot.

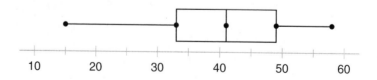

practice   Create a box-and-whisker plot for each of the following data sets.

4.   30, 40, 51, 62, 35, 45, 54, 61, 39, 49,
        32, 43, 54, 65, 33, 42, 55, 64, 31, 49,
        31, 49, 58, 68, 37, 49, 59, 67, 30, 40

5. 40, 41, 41, 41, 43, 47, 48, 50, 50, 51,
    53, 57, 59, 63, 63, 68, 69, 70, 72, 77,
    77, 78, 79, 79, 79, 80, 82, 83, 83, 85

6. 25, 33, 45, 36, 29, 34, 26, 31, 42, 43,
    35, 39, 28, 38, 27, 30, 41, 32, 40, 37,
    44, 27, 42, 25, 45, 36, 40, 27, 39, 42

histograms   Again we begin with data. The following may be thought of as final grades for a class of thirty algebra students:

92, 75, 69, 56, 88, 62, 75, 82, 90, 74,
65, 70, 80, 96, 81, 87, 95, 58, 96, 89,
91, 81, 83, 94, 86, 88, 93, 74, 87, 85

We can quickly create a stem-and-leaf plot of this data, as seen below.

	Stem	Leaf
	5	6 8
8 | 2 represents	6	9 2 5
a score of 82	7	5 5 4 0 4
	8	8 2 0 1 7 9 1 3 6 8 7 5
	9	2 0 6 5 6 1 4 5

The data from our stem-and-leaf plot of the final grades show us that there were two scores in the 50s, three scores in the 60s, five scores in the 70s, twelve scores in the 80s, and eight scores in the 90s. If we turn the stem-and-leaf plot on its side, we get the figure on the left-hand below.

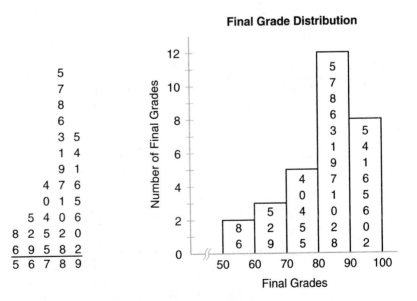

Final Grade Distribution

On the right-hand above, we show the same data within a figure called a **histogram,** which is a bar graph of a **frequency distribution.** This graph shows us that there were two scores in the 50s, three scores in the 60s, five scores in the 70s, twelve scores in the 80s, and eight scores in the 90s. The data itself is not actually part of the histogram. Thus, histograms do not give us precise information but do give us a good idea of how data is distributed.

example B.3   Each member of the twenty-person squad kicked the ball in the air. The distances the ball was kicked (measured in yards) were as follows:

$$41, \ 52, \ 63, \ 35, \ 43, \ 51, \ 54, \ 48, \ 65, \ 38,$$
$$31, \ 45, \ 47, \ 54, \ 53, \ 62, \ 59, \ 42, \ 40, \ 39$$

Create a histogram to show the frequency distribution of this data.

solution   We begin by counting the number of measurements in the 30s, 40s, 50s, and 60s. There are four measurements in the 30s, seven measurements in the 40s, six measurements in the 50s, and three measurements in the 60s. Thus, we have the following histogram.

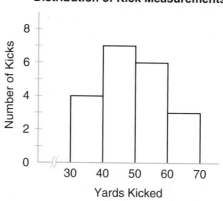

Distribution of Kick Measurements

practice   **7.** In a recent tournament, three teams averaged in the 30's, seven teams averaged in the 40's, four teams averaged in the 50's, and two teams averaged in the 60's. Create a histogram that represents this frequency distribution.

8. The following data represents daily traveling miles for a salesperson over a three week period. (Days off are not included.)

$$99, \ 110, \ 82, \ 94, \ 103, \ 97, \ 89, \ 81,$$
$$92, \ 108, \ 119, \ 88, \ 95, \ 112, \ 80$$

Create a histogram to show a frequency distribution of this data.

TOPIC C *Arithmetic in Base 2*

base 2   The system of numbers that we normally use is the Hindu-Arabic system. This system is a base 10 system and uses the ten digits

$$0, 1, 2, 3, 4, 5, 6, 7, 8, \text{ and } 9$$

Whole numbers in this system have values equal to the sums of the products of the digits and their place values. The place values in this system are as shown here:

BASE 10 PLACE VALUES

	10,000	1,000	100	10	1
...					

Thus, the number 2001 has the value of

	10,000	1,000	100	10	1
...		2	0	0	1

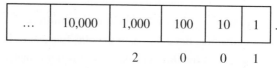

2 times 1000, plus 0 times 100, plus 0 times 10, plus 1 times 1

and the number 4327 has the value of

...	10,000	1,000	100	10	1

                           4   3   2   7

4 times 1000, plus 3 times 100, plus 2 times 10, plus 7 times 1

Not all systems use ten digits. Some systems use fewer than ten digits, and some use more than ten digits. Each system uses the same number of digits as the base of the system. The base 9 system uses nine digits, the base 6 system uses six digits, the base 4 system uses four digits, etc. Any whole number greater than 1 can be used as a base of a number system.

In this lesson, we will investigate the base 2 number system, which uses the two digits

                             0   and   1

Another name for this system is the **binary number system.** The place values in the base 2 system are shown here as base 10 numbers.

BASE 2 PLACE VALUES

...	128	64	32	16	8	4	2	1

The first place to the left of the decimal point has a value of 1. To get the next value, we multiply 1 by 2 and get 2. To get the next value, we multiply 2 by 2 and get 4. To get the next value, we multiply 4 by 2 and get 8, etc. Each place has a value that is twice the value of the place to its right.

example C.1 What is the base 10 value of 10101 (base 2)?

solution We begin by making a table of base 2 place values. We use base 10 numerals to write the place values. Then we write the digits of the base 2 numeral under their place values.

BASE 2 PLACE VALUES

64	32	16	8	4	2	1

                      1   0   1   0   1

We see that we have one 16, one 4, and one 1.

$$16 + 4 + 1 = 21$$

Since the sum of these numbers is 21, the base 10 value of 10101 (base 2) is 21 (base 10).

    10101 (base 2)   equals   **21 (base 10)**

example C.2 What base 10 number does 110101 (base 2) represent?

solution We make a table of place values and write each digit of the base 2 numeral beneath its proper place.

BASE 2 PLACE VALUES

64	32	16	8	4	2	1

                1   1   0   1   0   1

We see that we have one 32, one 16, no 8's, one 4, no 2's, and one 1.

$$32 + 16 + 4 + 1 = 53$$

so

    110101 (base 2)   equals   **53 (base 10)**

example C.3   Write 43 (base 10) using base 2 numerals.

solution   We always begin by making a table of place values.

BASE 2 PLACE VALUES

64	32	16	8	4	2	1

There are no 64's in 43, but there is one 32 in 43. So we put a 1 under the thirty-twos' place and subtract 32 from 43.

64	32	16	8	4	2	1
	1					

$$\begin{array}{r} 43 \\ -\ 32 \\ \hline 11 \end{array}$$

There are no 16's in 11, so we put a 0 under the sixteens' place and subtract 0 from 11.

64	32	16	8	4	2	1
	1	0				

$$\begin{array}{r} 11 \\ -\ 0 \\ \hline 11 \end{array}$$

Since there is one 8 in 11, we put a 1 under the eights' place and subtract 8 from 11.

64	32	16	8	4	2	1
	1	0	1			

$$\begin{array}{r} 11 \\ -\ 8 \\ \hline 3 \end{array}$$

There are no 4's in 3. Thus, we put a 0 under the fours' place and subtract 0 from 3.

64	32	16	8	4	2	1
	1	0	1	0		

$$\begin{array}{r} 3 \\ -\ 0 \\ \hline 3 \end{array}$$

Since there is one 2 in 3, we put a 1 under the twos' place and subtract 2 from 3.

64	32	16	8	4	2	1
	1	0	1	0	1	

$$\begin{array}{r} 3 \\ -\ 2 \\ \hline 1 \end{array}$$

There is a single 1 in 1, so we put a 1 under the units' place.

64	32	16	8	4	2	1
	1	0	1	0	1	1

The number 43 has one 32, one 8, one 2, and one 1, so

$$43 \text{ (base 10)} = \mathbf{101011 \text{ (base 2)}}$$

example C.4   Write 102 (base 10), using base 2 numerals.

solution   We always begin by writing a table of place values.

BASE 2 PLACE VALUES

64	32	16	8	4	2	1

We can abbreviate the steps used in the preceding example.

BASE 2 PLACE VALUES

64	32	16	8	4	2	1

| 1 | 1 | 0 | 0 | 1 | 1 | 0 |

$$\begin{array}{r} 102 \\ -\ 64 \\ \hline 38 \\ -\ 32 \\ \hline 6 \end{array} \qquad \begin{array}{r} 6 \\ -\ 4 \\ \hline 2 \\ -\ 2 \\ \hline 0 \end{array}$$

Thus, we see that we can write 102 (base 10) as **1100110 (base 2)**.

practice

1. What is the base 10 value of 1100100 (base 2)?

2. What is the base 2 value of 107 (base 10)?

3. What base 10 number does 101001 (base 2) represent?

4. What base 10 number does 11111 (base 2) represent?

5. Write 74 (base 10) using base 2 numerals.

6. What base 10 number does 10111 (base 2) represent?

7. Write 96 (base 10) using base 2 numerals.

8. Convert 111110 (base 2) to base 10.

9. Convert 1000101 (base 2) to base 10.

10. Convert 10001 (base 2) to base 10.

adding in base 2

We review our procedure for adding in base 10 by noting that we split the sum of a column into two parts. One part is a whole number times the base, and the other part is the remainder. We record the remainder and carry the whole number to the next column.

$$\begin{array}{r} 5\ 3\ 9 \\ 8\ 4\ 4 \\ +\ 6\ 3\ 8 \\ \hline \textcircled{21} \end{array} \qquad 21 = 2(10) + 1 \qquad \begin{array}{r} 5\ \overset{2}{3}\ 9 \\ 8\ 4\ 4 \\ +\ 6\ 3\ 8 \\ \hline 1 \end{array}$$

In the problem above, the sum of the first column is 21. This is 2 times the base (10) with 1 left over. We record the 1 and carry the 2 to the second column, as we see on the right-hand above.

$$\begin{array}{r} 5\ \overset{2}{3}\ 9 \\ 8\ 4\ 4 \\ +\ 6\ 3\ 8 \\ \hline \textcircled{12}\,1 \end{array} \qquad 12 = 1(10) + 2 \qquad \begin{array}{r} \overset{1}{5}\ \overset{2}{3}\ 9 \\ 8\ 4\ 4 \\ +\ 6\ 3\ 8 \\ \hline 2\ 1 \end{array}$$

When we find the sum of the digits in the second column, we get 12. This is 1 times the base (10) with 2 left over. We record the 2 and carry the 1 to the next column.

$$\begin{array}{r} \overset{1}{5}\ \overset{2}{3}\ 9 \\ 8\ 4\ 4 \\ +\ 6\ 3\ 8 \\ \hline \textcircled{20}\,2\ 1 \end{array} \qquad 20 = 2(10) + 0 \qquad \begin{array}{r} \overset{2}{5}\ \overset{1}{3}\ \overset{2}{9} \\ 8\ 4\ 4 \\ +\ 6\ 3\ 8 \\ \hline 2\ 0\ 2\ 1 \end{array}$$

The total of the third column is 20. This is 2 times the base, with 0 left over. We record the 0 and carry the 2. The total in the fourth column is 2, which is 0 times the base (10) with 2 left over.

We will use the same procedure to add in base 2. We split the sum of a column into two parts. One part is a whole number times the base, and the other part is the remainder. We record the remainder and carry the whole number.

example C.5   Add: 1111 (base 2) + 1011 (base 2) + 1101 (base 2) + 1101 (base 2)

solution   We record the numbers vertically and add the first column. We express the sum as a whole number times the base, plus a remainder.

$$
\begin{array}{r}
1\ 1\ 1\ 1 \\
1\ 0\ 1\ 1 \\
1\ 1\ 0\ 1 \\
+\ 1\ 1\ 0\ 1 \\
\hline
④
\end{array}
\qquad 4 = 2(2) + 0
$$

The sum of the first column in base 10 is 4. This is 2 times the base (2), with a remainder of 0. We record the 0 and carry 2 to the next column and add this column.

$$
\begin{array}{r}
1\ 1\ \overset{2}{1}\ 1 \\
1\ 0\ 1\ 1 \\
1\ 1\ 0\ 1 \\
+\ 1\ 1\ 0\ 1 \\
\hline
④0
\end{array}
\qquad 4 = 2(2) + 0
$$

This sum is 2 times the base, with a remainder of 0. We record 0 and carry 2. Then we add the third column.

$$
\begin{array}{r}
1\ \overset{2}{1}\ \overset{2}{1}\ 1 \\
1\ 0\ 1\ 1 \\
1\ 1\ 0\ 1 \\
+\ 1\ 1\ 0\ 1 \\
\hline
⑤0\ 0
\end{array}
\qquad 5 = 2(2) + 1
$$

We get 5, which is 2 times the base, with a remainder of 1. We record 1, carry the 2, and add the next column.

$$
\begin{array}{r}
\overset{2}{1}\ \overset{2}{1}\ \overset{2}{1}\ 1 \\
1\ 0\ 1\ 1 \\
1\ 1\ 0\ 1 \\
+\ 1\ 1\ 0\ 1 \\
\hline
⑥1\ 0\ 0
\end{array}
\qquad 6 = 3(2) + 0
$$

The number 6 is 3 times the base, with a remainder of 0.

$$
\begin{array}{r}
\overset{3}{1}\ \overset{2}{1}\ \overset{2}{1}\ \overset{2}{1} \\
1\ 0\ 1\ 1 \\
1\ 1\ 0\ 1 \\
+\ 1\ 1\ 0\ 1 \\
\hline
③0\ 1\ 0\ 0
\end{array}
\qquad 3 = 1(2) + 1
$$

But 3 is 1 times the base, with a remainder of 1.

$$
\begin{array}{r}
\overset{3}{1}\ \overset{2}{1}\ \overset{2}{1}\ \overset{2}{1} \\
1\ 0\ 1\ 1 \\
1\ 1\ 0\ 1 \\
+\ 1\ 1\ 0\ 1 \\
\hline
1\ 1\ 0\ 1\ 0\ 0
\end{array}
$$

So our final sum in base 2 is **110100.**

As a check, we can convert everything to base 10 and compare the results. The addends are 15, 11, 13 and 13 in base 10. So 110100 (base 2) should equal 15 + 11 + 13 + 13 (base 10), which is 52. We use the place value chart to verify this.

64	32	16	8	4	2	1
	1	1	0	1	0	0

We see that 110100 (base 2) equals 32 + 16 + 4 (base 10), which also equals 52. So our addition was correct.

practice   In problems 11–16, express the sum in base 2. Check your answer by converting everything to base 10.

11.   1101 (base 2) + 1011 (base 2)

12.   1111 (base 2) + 100001 (base 2)

13.   101101 (base 2) + 100011 (base 2)

14.   11000 (base 2) + 10000 (base 2)

15.   1001 (base 2) + 1111 (base 2) + 1001 (base 2) + 1000 (base 2)

16.   1110 (base 2) + 111101 (base 2)

binary fractions   In base 10, the notation 102.37 expands to equal

$$
1(100) + 0(10) + 2(1) + 3\left(\frac{1}{10}\right) + 7\left(\frac{1}{100}\right)
$$

Said another way,

$$
102.37 = 1(10^2) + 0(10^1) + 2(10^0) + 3(10^{-1}) + 7(10^{-2})
$$

The value of a number is determined by multiplying the digit in each place by the appropriate power of 10.

The base 10 value of a number in base 2 can be found by multiplying the digit in each place by the appropriate power of 2. For example,

10110.101
$$
= 1(2^4) + 0(2^3) + 1(2^2) + 1(2^1) + 0(2^0) + 1(2^{-1}) + 0(2^{-2}) + 1(2^{-3}) \text{ (base 10)}
$$

$$
= 16 + 0 + 4 + 2 + 0 + \frac{1}{2} + 0 + \frac{1}{8} \text{ (base 10)}
$$

$$
= 22\frac{5}{8} \text{ (base 10)} = 22.625 \text{ (base 10)}
$$

As with whole binary numbers, we add binary fractions by lining up the numbers by place value.

example C.6   Find 10101.1 (base 2) + 100.01 (base 2) + 111.101 (base 2). Express the answer in base 2, but check the answer using base 10.

solution   We begin by expressing the sum in a vertical format with place values aligned vertically.

$$
\begin{array}{r}
{\scriptstyle 1\ \ 1\ \ 2\ \ 1\ \ 1\ \ 1} \\
1\ 0\ 1\ 0\ 1.1 \\
1\ 0\ 0.0\ 1 \\
+\quad 1\ 1\ 1.1\ 0\ 1 \\
\hline
\mathbf{1\ 0\ 0\ 0\ 0\ 1.0\ 1\ 1}
\end{array}
$$

Now we convert the addends to base 10 to check the answer.

$$10101.1 \text{ (base 2)} = 1\left(2^4\right) + 1\left(2^2\right) + 1\left(2^0\right) + 1\left(2^{-1}\right) \text{ (base 10)}$$
$$= 21.5 \text{ (base 10)}$$

$$100.01 \text{ (base 2)} = 1\left(2^2\right) + 1\left(2^{-2}\right) \text{ (base 10)}$$
$$= 4.25 \text{ (base 10)}$$

$$111.101 \text{ (base 2)} = 1\left(2^2\right) + 1\left(2^1\right) + 1\left(2^0\right) + 1\left(2^{-1}\right) + 1\left(2^{-3}\right) \text{ (base 10)}$$
$$= 7.625 \text{ (base 10)}$$

Thus, the sum in base 10 should be 21.5 + 4.25 + 7.625 = 33.375. We check this by converting our answer to base 10.

$$100001.011 \text{ (base 2)} = 1\left(2^5\right) + 1\left(2^0\right) + 1\left(2^{-2}\right) + 1\left(2^{-3}\right) \text{ (base 10)}$$
$$= 33.375 \text{ (base 10)}$$

Thus, the solution is correct.

practice   For problems 17–20, the addends in each sum are base 2 numbers. Express the sum in base 2, but check your answers using base 10.

17.   10.11 + 101.011   **18.**   111.011 + 110.1 + 11.011

19.   111011.01 + 1011.11   **20.**   11.01 + 111.101 + 10000.01

multiplication in base 2   Multiplication in base 2 is easy because there are only two digits in the multiplication table. Also, even in base 2,

$$0 \cdot \text{(any number)} = 0 \qquad \text{and} \qquad 1 \cdot \text{(any number)} = \text{the number}$$

Thus, the base 2 times table is as follows:

$$
\begin{array}{c|c|c}
\times & 0 & 1 \\
\hline
0 & 0 & 0 \\
\hline
1 & 0 & 1 \\
\end{array}
$$

example C.7   Multiply in base 2: 1011 × 110

solution   To find the product, we write the problem in the traditional multiplication format and use the traditional algorithm. The only difficulty is remembering to add in base 2.[†]

$$
\begin{array}{r}
1\ 0\ 1\ 1 \\
\times\quad 1\ 1\ 0 \\
\hline
0\ 0\ 0\ 0 \\
1\ 0\ 1\ 1 \\
1\ 0\ 1\ 1 \\
\hline
\mathbf{1\ 0\ 0\ 0\ 0\ 1\ 0}
\end{array}
$$

[†]Note: We are multiplying in base 2 as well. However, there is no difficulty since the products are the same as if it were base 10.

We check our answer with base 10 conversions:

$$1011 \text{ (base 2)} = 1(2^3) + 1(2^1) + 1(2^0) \text{ (base 10)} = 11 \text{ (base 10)}$$
$$110 \text{ (base 2)} = 1(2^2) + 1(2^1) \text{ (base 10)} = 6 \text{ (base 10)}$$

So our answer should convert to 11×6, or 66.

$$1000010 \text{ (base 2)} = 1(2^6) + 1(2^1) \text{ (base 10)} = 66 \text{ (base 10)}$$

So our base 2 multiplication was correct.

example C.8   Multiply in base 2: 11.01×1.101

solution   We use the traditional multiplication format and algorithm, but we use the multiplication and addition rules of base 2. We insert the "binary point" five places from the right of the last nonzero digit since there are five places to the right of the "binary points" in the problem.

$$
\begin{array}{r}
1\,1.0\,1 \\
\times\ 1.1\,0\,1 \\
\hline
1\,1\,0\,1 \\
0\,0\,0\,0 \\
1\,1\,0\,1 \\
1\,1\,0\,1 \\
\hline
1\,0\,1.0\,1\,0\,0\,1
\end{array}
$$

Again we check in base 10.

$$11.01 \text{ (base 2)} = 1(2^1) + 1(2^0) + 1(2^{-2}) \text{ (base 10)} = 3.25 \text{ (base 10)}$$
$$1.101 \text{ (base 2)} = 1(2^0) + 1(2^{-1}) + 1(2^{-3}) \text{ (base 10)} = 1.625 \text{ (base 10)}$$

So our answer should convert to $3.25 \cdot 1.625$, or 5.28125.

$$101.01001 \text{ (base 2)} = 1(2^2) + 1(2^0) + 1(2^{-2}) + 1(2^{-5}) \text{ (base 10)}$$
$$= 5.28125 \text{ (base 10)}$$

practice   For problems 21–27, the factors in each indicated product are base 2 numbers. Express the product as a base 2 number, but check your answer using base 10.

21. 1101×11 | **22.** 10101×1011

23. 11×11 | **24.** 11010×11.1

25. 1.001×0.11 | **26.** 1.01×1.01

27. 11.001×101.01

TOPIC D   *Theorems About Angles and Circular Arcs*

angles formed by parallel lines and a transversal

Parallel lines are lines in a plane that do not intersect. A **transversal** is a line that intersects two or more lines at different points. When a transversal intersects a pair of parallel lines, angles of equal measure are formed.

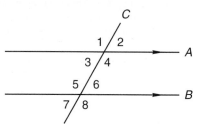

Lines *A* and *B* are parallel lines and this is shown by the arrowheads. Line *C* is a transversal. Angles 3, 4, 5, and 6 are called **interior angles** because they are between the parallel lines. Angles 3 and 6 are a pair of **alternate interior angles,** as are angles 4 and 5. Angles in corresponding positions relative to the two parallel lines and the transversal are called **corresponding angles.** The following are pairs of corresponding angles:

$\angle 1$ and $\angle 5$ $\angle 2$ and $\angle 6$

$\angle 3$ and $\angle 7$ $\angle 4$ and $\angle 8$

The measure of $\angle 1$ is denoted $m\angle 1$. When parallel lines are cut by a transversal, the measures of corresponding angles are equal, and so are the measures of alternate interior angles. The angles marked in each figure have the same measure.

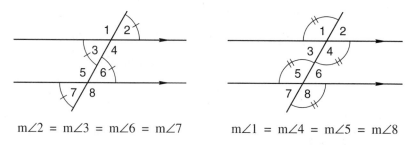

$m\angle 2 = m\angle 3 = m\angle 6 = m\angle 7$ $m\angle 1 = m\angle 4 = m\angle 5 = m\angle 8$

When two adjacent angles combine to form a straight angle, as with *x* and *y* below,

the sum of their measures is 180°. Thus, all the adjacent angles in the figures above are supplementary. The pairs of supplementary angles are:

$\angle 1$ and $\angle 2$ $\angle 5$ and $\angle 6$

$\angle 1$ and $\angle 3$ $\angle 5$ and $\angle 7$

$\angle 2$ and $\angle 4$ $\angle 6$ and $\angle 8$

$\angle 3$ and $\angle 4$ $\angle 7$ and $\angle 8$

Noncorresponding angles on the same side of the transversal are also supplementary. The following are pairs of supplementary angles:

$\angle 1$ and $\angle 7$ $\angle 2$ and $\angle 8$

$\angle 3$ and $\angle 5$ $\angle 4$ and $\angle 6$

example D.1 Find x and y.

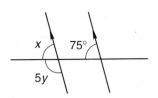

solution Corresponding angles have equal measure, so $x = 75°$. Since x and $5y$ are the measures of a supplementary pair of angles, their sum must be $180°$.

$$x + 5y = 180° \qquad \text{supplementary angles}$$
$$75° + 5y = 180° \qquad \text{substituted}$$
$$5y = 105° \qquad \text{subtracted } 75° \text{ from both sides}$$
$$y = \mathbf{21°} \qquad \text{divided both sides by 5}$$

practice **1.** Find $a, b, c, d, e, f,$ and g.

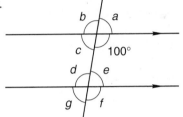

2. Find x and y.

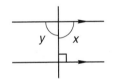

3. Find m and n.

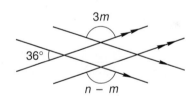

4. Find p and q.

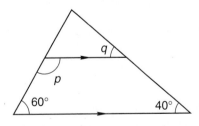

5. Find a and b.

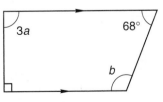

6. Find c and d.

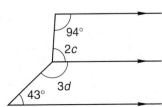

**arcs formed by
central angles
and inscribed
angles**

When the vertex of an angle is at the center of a circle, we say the angle is a **central angle.** In the figure below,

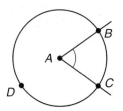

the piece of the circle from B to C is called a **minor arc,** which we denote $\overset{\frown}{BC}$. The rest of the circle is called a **major arc,** denoted $\overset{\frown}{BDC}$. We use three letters to designate a major arc. A central angle has the same measure as the minor arc it intercepts. In the figure above, $m\angle BAC = m\overset{\frown}{BC}$.

An angle in a circle whose vertex is on the circle is called an **inscribed angle.** Its measure is exactly half that of the arc it intercepts. In the figure below, $m\angle EFG = \frac{1}{2}m\overset{\frown}{EG}$.

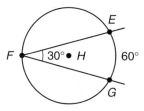

example D.2   Find p and q.

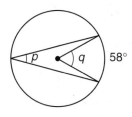

solution   A central angle has the same measure as the minor arc it intercepts, so $q = \mathbf{58°}$. An inscribed angle has half the measure of the arc it intercepts, so $p = \frac{1}{2} \cdot 58°$ or $p = \mathbf{29°}$.

practice   Find the measure of the indicated angle or arc.

7.   Find x and y.

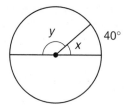

8.   Find x and y.

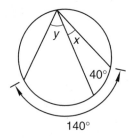

9.   Find the measures of $\overset{\frown}{BC}$, $\overset{\frown}{CD}$, and $\overset{\frown}{BD}$.

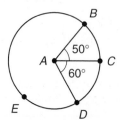

10.   Find the measures of $\overset{\frown}{WZ}$, $\angle XYW$, and $\overset{\frown}{XW}$.

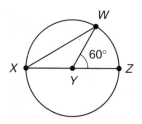

11. Find the measures of $\overset{\frown}{AC}$ and $\angle ECB$.

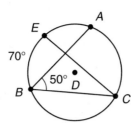

12. Find the measure of $\angle BDC$.

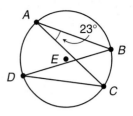

13. Find x and y.

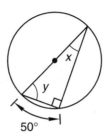

14. Find the measures of $\angle ABC$ and $\angle BCA$.

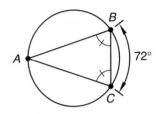

TOPIC E Approximating Roots

In Lesson 92 we learned about estimating roots. To estimate $\sqrt{21}$, we think of the nearest perfect squares to 21, $16 = 4^2$ and $25 = 5^2$, and conclude

$$4 < \sqrt{21} < 5$$

But how can we estimate roots more accurately? A simple answer is "with a calculator." But how does a calculator do it? Mathematicians have developed many techniques to estimate roots. Before calculators became widely available, students were taught these techniques in school. Now we teach students these techniques to increase their understanding of roots, to improve their arithmetic skills, and most of all, to expand their understanding of other mathematical concepts.

square roots The technique we use in this section is sometimes loosely called Newton's method.[†] To calculate square roots, we begin with a guess. (Choosing any positive number will work eventually. For convenience, choose the closest integer value to the actual square root.) To get a better estimate, we use the following formula:

$$(\text{A better estimate}) = \frac{(\text{the guess})^2 + \left(\begin{array}{c}\text{the number whose} \\ \text{square root we seek}\end{array}\right)}{2 \cdot (\text{the guess})}$$

For demonstration, we consider $\sqrt{15}$. What is its value? A good initial guess is 4. To get a better estimate, we use the formula.

$$\text{A better estimate} = \frac{4^2 + 15}{2 \cdot 4} = \frac{31}{8} = 3\frac{7}{8} = 3.875$$

We check this by squaring the estimate.

$$3.875^2 = 15.015625$$

[†] Newton's method is actually much more complicated than this. It is a topic usually reserved for a course in calculus. The formula we use is a consequence of applying Newton's method to a specific situation.

This is a good approximation. It is noticeably close to 15. To get an even better approximation, we can use the same formula again!

$$(\text{An even better estimate}) = \frac{(\text{the second estimate})^2 + \left(\begin{array}{c}\text{the number whose} \\ \text{square root we seek}\end{array}\right)}{2 \cdot (\text{the second estimate})}$$

$$= \frac{\left(\dfrac{31}{8}\right)^2 + 15}{2 \cdot \dfrac{31}{8}} = \frac{\dfrac{961}{64} + 15}{\dfrac{31}{4}} = \frac{\dfrac{961}{64} + \dfrac{960}{64}}{\dfrac{31}{4}}$$

$$= \frac{1921}{64} \cdot \frac{4}{31} = \frac{1921}{16 \cdot 31} = \frac{1921}{496} = 3\frac{433}{496}$$

$$\approx 3.8729839$$

To check, we see

$$\left(\frac{1921}{496}\right)^2 \approx 15.000004$$

Wow! These steps can be repeated again and again, each time usually adding two decimal places of accuracy to the approximation. Below we summarize what we calculated.

Estimate	As Fraction	As Mixed Number	As Decimal	Estimate Squared
x_1	4	4	4	16
x_2	$\dfrac{31}{8}$	$3\dfrac{7}{8}$	3.875	15.015625
x_3	$\dfrac{1921}{496}$	$3\dfrac{433}{496}$	≈ 3.8729839	≈ 15.000004

A more compact way of writing the formula is as follows:

$$x_{n+1} = \frac{x_n^2 + c}{2x_n}$$

where

$$x_n = \text{an estimate}$$

$$x_{n+1} = \text{the next estimate}$$

$$c = \text{the number whose square root we seek}$$

example E.1   Approximate the value of $\sqrt{99}$ to the nearest hundredth without using the square root feature of a calculator.

solution   A good initial guess is $x_1 = 10$, since $10^2 = 100$. A better estimate can be found using the formula.

$$x_2 = \frac{(x_1)^2 + 99}{2x_1}$$

$$x_2 = \frac{10^2 + 99}{2(10)}$$

$$x_2 = \frac{199}{20}$$

$$x_2 = 9.95$$

To be certain we are accurate to two decimal places, we must repeat the process. Once the digits in the first three places immediately to the right of the decimal point stop changing, we can be assured of the accuracy we desire.

$$x_3 = \frac{(x_2)^2 + 99}{2x_2}$$

$$x_3 = \frac{9.95^2 + 99}{2 \cdot 9.95}$$

$$x_3 = 9.94987\ldots$$

The first three values to the right of the decimal point were not stable, so we continue. We may use 9.94987 for x_3 rather than its fully expanded value, since this method simply corrects estimates. It is preferable to use at least three extra digits when attempting to round to a specific place value.

$$x_4 = \frac{(x_3)^2 + 99}{2x_3}$$

$$x_4 = \frac{9.94987^2 + 99}{2 \cdot 9.94987}$$

$$x_4 = 9.94987\ldots$$

The digits in the first three places to the right of the decimal point did not change. Thus, we may round x_4 to two decimal places without losing accuracy.

$$\sqrt{99} \approx \mathbf{9.95}$$

For confirmation we check the answer with a calculator, which tells us $\sqrt{99} \approx 9.949874371$. Thus, our estimate was correct to the nearest hundredth.

practice   Approximate the following roots to the nearest hundredth. Use the method prescribed in the previous section rather than using a calculator. Show all your work.

1. $\sqrt{2}$ **2.** $\sqrt{3}$ **3.** $\sqrt{5}$ **4.** $\sqrt{10}$

5. $\sqrt{90}$ **6.** $\sqrt{27}$ **7.** $\sqrt{28}$ **8.** $\sqrt{105}$

Approximate the following roots to the nearest ten-thousandth. Use the method prescribed in the previous section rather than using a calculator. Show all your work.

9. $\sqrt{6}$ **10.** $\sqrt{7}$ **11.** $\sqrt{11}$ **12.** $\sqrt{12}$

13. $\sqrt{24}$ **14.** $\sqrt{29}$

higher order roots   The method just used works for finding square roots. The method explained in this section works for all roots. Let us work through an example, an approximation of $\sqrt[3]{25}$. Since the index of the root is 3, we seek a number x such that

$$x \cdot x \cdot x = 25$$

As in the previous section, we must begin with a guess. For convenience, we always begin with the nearest integer. Since $3 \cdot 3 \cdot 3 = 27$, we use $x_1 = 3$ as our initial guess. We now need to find a number a_1 such that $3 \cdot 3 \cdot a_1 = 25$.

$$3 \cdot 3 \cdot a_1 = 25 \qquad \text{equation}$$

$$a_1 = \frac{25}{9} \qquad \text{solved for } a_1$$

Finally, we calculate the average of two 3's and one a_1.

$$x_2 = \frac{3 + 3 + \dfrac{25}{9}}{3} = \frac{\dfrac{79}{9}}{3} = \frac{79}{27} = 2\frac{25}{27} = 2.\overline{925}$$

Notice that x_2 is a good approximation of $\sqrt[3]{25}$ since

$$\left(\frac{79}{27}\right)^3 = 25.0489\ldots$$

To improve the approximation, we repeat the process.

First we find a_2 such that $\frac{79}{27} \cdot \frac{79}{27} \cdot a_2 = 25$.

$$\frac{79}{27} \cdot \frac{79}{27} \cdot a_2 = 25 \qquad\qquad \text{equation}$$

$$\frac{6241}{729} \cdot a_2 = 25 \qquad\qquad \text{multiplied}$$

$$a_2 = \frac{18{,}225}{6241} \qquad\qquad \text{divided}$$

$$a_2 \approx 2.920 \qquad\qquad \text{estimated } a_2$$

Then we calculate the average of two x_2's and one a_2. Without loss of rigor, x_2 and a_2 may be rounded for simplicity.

$$x_3 = \frac{2.926 + 2.926 + 2.920}{3} = \frac{8.772}{3} = 2.924$$

This is an even better approximation of $\sqrt[3]{25}$ since

$$(2.924)^3 = 24.9995\ldots$$

This process can be used for calculating any root. The only difference in calculating another root is that the number of factors in the initial equation and the number of terms in the sum of the average equals the index of the root.

example E.2   Approximate $\sqrt[5]{50}$ to the nearest thousandth. You may not use a root or power function of the calculator to determine the answer.

solution   We begin with the initial guess $x_1 = 2$, since $2^5 = 32$. There is no other integer whose fifth power is as close to fifty. Since the index of the root is 5, we look for the number a_1 such that $x_1 \cdot x_1 \cdot x_1 \cdot x_1 \cdot a_1 = 50$.

$$x_1 \cdot x_1 \cdot x_1 \cdot x_1 \cdot a_1 = 50$$

$$2 \cdot 2 \cdot 2 \cdot 2 \cdot a_1 = 50$$

$$a_1 = \frac{50}{16} = \frac{25}{8}$$

$$a_1 = 3.125$$

To calculate the next estimate, x_2, we find the average of four x_1's and one a_1.

$$x_2 = \frac{x_1 + x_1 + x_1 + x_1 + a_1}{5}$$

$$= \frac{2 + 2 + 2 + 2 + 3.125}{5}$$

$$= 2.225$$

We desire three decimal places of accuracy. Thus, we must repeat this process until the four digits immediately to the right of the decimal point become stable. To determine the next estimate, x_3, we look for the number a_2 such that the product of four x_2's and one a_2 is 50.

$$x_2 \cdot x_2 \cdot x_2 \cdot x_2 \cdot a_2 = 50 \qquad \text{equation}$$

$$(2.225)(2.225)(2.225)(2.225)a_2 = 50 \qquad \text{substituted}$$

$$a_2 = 2.0400928\ldots \qquad \text{solved}$$

The next estimate, x_3, is the average of four x_2's and one a_2.

$$x_3 = \frac{x_2 + x_2 + x_2 + x_2 + a_2}{5}$$

$$= \frac{2.225 + 2.225 + 2.225 + 2.225 + 2.040093}{5}$$

$$= 2.1880186$$

The first four digits to the right of the decimal point changed, so we must find a better estimate, x_4. We look for a_3 such that $x_3 \cdot x_3 \cdot x_3 \cdot x_3 \cdot a_3 = 50$.

$$x_3 \cdot x_3 \cdot x_3 \cdot x_3 \cdot a_3 = 50 \qquad \text{equation}$$

$$(2.1880186)(2.1880186)(2.1880186)(2.1880186)a_3 = 50 \qquad \text{substituted}$$

$$a_3 = 2.1815539\ldots \qquad \text{solved}$$

The next estimate is determined using an average.

$$x_4 = \frac{x_3 + x_3 + x_3 + x_3 + a_3}{5}$$

$$= \frac{4(2.1880186) + 2.1815539}{5}$$

$$= 2.186725\ldots$$

The first four digits to the right of the decimal point were not stable. Thus, we continue the process.

$$x_4 \cdot x_4 \cdot x_4 \cdot x_4 \cdot a_4 = 50 \qquad \text{equation}$$

$$(2.186725)(2.186725)(2.186725)(2.186725)a_4 = 50 \qquad \text{substituted}$$

$$a_4 = 2.186720\ldots \qquad \text{solved}$$

Now determine the average.

$$x_5 = \frac{x_4 + x_4 + x_4 + x_4 + a_4}{5}$$

$$= \frac{4(2.186725) + 2.186720}{5}$$

$$= 2.186724$$

Finally, the digits in the necessary places remain the same. Thus, we round x_5 to the nearest thousandth and achieve the desired accuracy.

$$\sqrt[5]{50} \approx \mathbf{2.187}$$

For confirmation, we check the answer using a calculator. According to the calculator, $\sqrt[5]{50} \approx 2.186724148\ldots$. We see that our estimation was correct to the nearest thousandth.

practice Approximate the following roots to the nearest hundredth using the method prescribed in the previous section. Show all your work.

15. $\sqrt[3]{12}$ **16.** $\sqrt[3]{5}$ **17.** $\sqrt[3]{100}$

18. $\sqrt[3]{120}$ **19.** $\sqrt[4]{6}$ **20.** $\sqrt[4]{25}$

21. $\sqrt[4]{109}$ **22.** $\sqrt[5]{15}$ **23.** $\sqrt[5]{155}$

24. $\sqrt[5]{200}$ **25.** $\sqrt[6]{85}$

TOPIC F *Polynomials*

Consider the following expressions:

(a) $\dfrac{x^{-3} + m}{x}$ (b) $\dfrac{2y}{x^3}$ (c) $4a^{-2}x + m^3$

(d) rtn^{-2} (e) 4 (f) $-4a^2$

(g) $7x^2 + 2$ (h) $4x^2y$ (i) $7y^3 + 3y + 2$

All of these expressions are called **algebraic expressions** or **mathematical expressions** and are individual terms or indicated sums of terms. The more complicated algebraic expressions shown in (a) through (d) have no special names and are just called **terms** or **algebraic expressions.** The simple algebraic expressions shown in (e) through (i) occur so often and are so useful that we give these algebraic expressions a special name: **polynomial.** It is unfortunate that we use such an intimidating word to describe the simplest kind of algebraic expression. We should think "simplenomial" when we see the word *polynomial.*

A **polynomial in one variable** is one term or a sum of individual terms each of which has the form

$$ax^n$$

where **a is a real number, x is a variable,** and **n is a whole number,** such as the following:

(a) $4x^2$ (b) $-x^3$ (c) $-1.414x^{32}$

(d) $2x^4$ (e) $-7x$ (f) -7

The last polynomial shown, -7, can be thought of as being $-7x^0$, which is the same as -7 if x has a value other than zero. Remember that **any nonzero quantity raised to the zero power has a value of 1!**

A **polynomial of one term** is called a **monomial,** so algebraic expressions (a) through (f) can be called both polynomials and monomials.

A **polynomial of two terms** is called a **binomial,** and a **polynomial of three terms** is called a **trinomial.** Thus, each of the following can be described by using either the word *polynomial* or the word *binomial*:

$$4 + x \qquad p^{15} - 4p \qquad -y^{10} + 3y$$

The following algebraic expressions can be called either polynomials or trinomials:

$$x^2 + 2x + 4 \qquad y^{14} - 1.6y^2 + 4 \qquad m^4 + 2m - 1.6$$

Sums of more than three monomial terms have no special names and are just called polynomials. Thus, we can call any of the following algebraic expressions a polynomial:

(g) -14.2 (h) $\dfrac{7}{2}$ (i) $4x^2$ (j) $6x^2 + 4$

(k) $x^4 - 3x^2 + 2x$ (l) $-7x^{15} + 2x^3 - 5x^2 + 6x + 4$

Algebraic expressions (g) and (h) are polynomials because the exponent of the understood variable is the number zero.

$$\text{(g) } -14.2m^0 = -14.2 \qquad \text{(h) } \frac{7}{2}y^0 = \frac{7}{2}$$

Although algebraic expressions (i), (j), and (k) are all polynomials, they can also be called a monomial, a binomial, and a trinomial respectively. The last algebraic expression, (l), is a polynomial because each term in the sum is a monomial. This algebraic expression does not have a more restrictive name.

DEFINITION OF A POLYNOMIAL IN ONE UNKNOWN

A polynomial in one unknown is an algebraic expression with a form similar to the following:

$$4x^{15} + 2x^{14} - 3x^{10} + \cdots + 2x + 2$$

Here the coefficients are real numbers, x is a variable, and the exponents are whole numbers.

Thus, none of the following algebraic expressions is a polynomial.

$$\text{(a) } 4x^{-3} \qquad \text{(b) } \frac{-6x + y}{z} \qquad \text{(c) } -15y^{-5}$$

The algebraic expressions (a) and (c) have real number coefficients, but the exponent of each variable is not a whole number. Algebraic expression (b) is not a polynomial because it is not in the required form ax^n.

DEFINITION OF A POLYNOMIAL IN ONE OR MORE UNKNOWNS

A polynomial in one or more unkowns is an algebraic expression having only terms in the form $ax^n y^m z^p \ldots$, where the coefficient a is a real number; x, y, z, $\ldots$, are variables; and the exponents n, m, p, $\ldots$, are whole numbers.

Thus, the general definition of a polynomial has the same restrictions that are given by the definition of a polynomial in one unknown, namely:

1. The numerical coefficients of the individual terms must be **real numbers.**

2. The exponents of the variables must be **whole numbers.**

The following can therefore be called polynomials in more than one variable:

$$xyz^2m \qquad 4x^{15}ym^3 + pq^5 \qquad -11x^2p^4 + 2$$

Polynomials are usually written in descending powers of one of the variables. The polynomials

$$x^5 - 3x^4 + 2x^2 - x + 5$$
$$x^4m + x^3m^2 - 2xm^5 - 6$$
$$-2xm^5 + x^3m^2 + x^4m - 6$$

are written in descending powers of a particular variable. The first two polynomials are written in descending powers of x. The third polynomial is the same polynomial as the second, but it is written in descending powers of m instead of descending powers of x.

The **degree of a term** of a polynomial is the sum of the exponents of the variables in the term.

$$4x^3, 6xym, 2x^2y \qquad \text{are third-degree terms}$$

$$4x^2m^3, 3y^5, 2xypmz \qquad \text{are fifth-degree terms}$$

The **degree of a polynomial** is the same as the degree of its highest-degree term.

$3x^2 + xyz + m$ is a third-degree polynomial because the degree of its highest-degree term (xyz) is 3

$4x^5 + yx^3 + 2x^2 + 2$ is a fifth-degree polynomial because the degree of its highest-degree term $(4x^5)$ is 5

addition   Since polynomials are composed of individual terms, the rule for adding polynomials is the same rule that we use for adding terms: **like terms may be added.**

example F.1   Add. Write the answer in descending powers of the variable.

$$\left(x^3 + 3x^2 + 2\right) + \left(2x^3 + 4\right)$$

solution   Remember that we can discard parentheses preceded by a plus sign without changing the signs of the terms therein.

$$\left(x^3 + 3x^2 + 2\right) + \left(2x^3 + 4\right) = x^3 + 3x^2 + 2 + 2x^3 + 4$$
$$= \mathbf{3x^3 + 3x^2 + 6}$$

example F.2   Add. Write the answer in descending powers of the variable.

$$\left(3x^4 - 2x^2 + 3\right) - \left(x^4 - 2x^3 + x^2\right)$$

solution   When we discard the parentheses in this problem, we remember to **change the sign of every term in the second set of parentheses,** because the second set of parentheses is preceded by a minus sign.

$$\left(3x^4 - 2x^2 + 3\right) - \left(x^4 - 2x^3 + x^2\right) = 3x^4 - 2x^2 + 3 - x^4 + 2x^3 - x^2$$
$$= \mathbf{2x^4 + 2x^3 - 3x^2 + 3}$$

practice   Add. Write the answers in descending powers of the variable x or k.

1. $\left(3x^3 + 2x^2 - x + 4\right) - \left(x^2 - 7x - 5\right)$

2. $-\left(3x^5 + 6x^4 - 7x^3 - 5\right) + \left(x^5 - x^4 + 3x^2 - 2x - 8\right)$

3. $\left(3x^2 + x^4 - 6x + 2\right) - \left(15x^4 + 2x^3 - 6x^2 + 5x - 3\right)$

4. $\left(6k^7 - 5k^5 + 3k^3 - k\right) + \left(5k^6 + 4k^4 + 2k^3 + 3k^2\right)$

5. $\left(5k^4 + 3k^3 - 2k^2 - 1\right) - \left(4k^4 + 2k^3 - 3k^2 - k - 2\right)$

6. $\left(2x^3 + 5x^2 - 7\right) + \left(2x^2 - 4x + 1\right) - \left(3x^4 + 4x^2 - 2x\right)$

7. $\left(x^4 - 3x^3 + x^2 + 2\right) - \left(3x^2 + 7x - 2\right) + \left(-x^3 + 2x^2 - 4\right)$

8. $\left(3x^3y - 4x^2y + 2xy - y\right) + \left(-x^3y - 5x^2y - 6xy - 3y\right)$

multiplication   Multiplying monomials is simple. We just have to remember the commutative property and the rules for exponents.

$$\left(3xy^2\right)\left(5x^2y^4\right) = 3 \cdot 5 \cdot x \cdot x \cdot x \cdot y \cdot y \cdot y \cdot y \cdot y \cdot y$$
$$= 15x^3y^6$$

All we have to do is multiply the coefficients and add the exponents of like variables.

$$(3xy^2)(5x^2y^4) = 3 \cdot 5x^{1+2}y^{2+4}$$
$$= 15x^3y^6$$

The answer is the same either way.

example F.3   Multiply: $(3x^2y)(5x^3z)$

solution   The product of the coefficients is 15. The sum of the exponents of x is $2 + 3$, or 5. Therefore,

$$(3x^2y)(5x^3z) = \mathbf{15x^5yz}$$

example F.4   Multiply. Write the answer in descending powers of the variable.

$$4x(x^2 - 2)$$

solution   To multiply a monomial by a binomial, we must use the distributive property. Remember that

$$a(b + c) = ab + ac$$

The expression on the outside of the parentheses is multiplied by both terms inside the parentheses. Thus, we must multiply $4x$ by x^2 and by -2. Then we sum the products.

$$4x(x^2 - 2) = 4x(x^2) + 4x(-2) = \mathbf{4x^3 - 8x}$$

To develop a general procedure for multiplying two polynomials, we will use the distributive property to multiply

$$(a + b)(c + d)$$

The notation $(a + b)(c + d)$ tells us that $(a + b)$ is to be multiplied by c, that $(a + b)$ is also to be multiplied by d, and that the two products are to be summed.

$$(a + b)(c + d) = (a + b)c + (a + b)d$$

Now we use the distributive property again to multiply $(a + b)$ by c

$$(a + b)c = ac + bc$$

and to multiply $(a + b)$ by d

$$(a + b)d = ad + bd$$

and to sum the products.

$$(a + b)(c + d) = (a + b)c + (a + b)d$$
$$= ac + bc + ad + bd$$

This has been a rather involved illustration of the following rule:

RULE FOR MULTIPLYING POLYNOMIALS

To multiply one polynomial by a second polynomial, each term of the first polynomial is multiplied by each term of the second polynomial and then the products are summed.

---

example F.5   Multiply. Write the answer in descending powers of the variable.

$$(4x + 5)(3x - 2)$$

solution   The notation indicates that $4x$ is to be multiplied by both $3x$ and -2

$$4x(3x - 2) = 12x^2 - 8x$$

and that $+5$ is to be multiplied by both $3x$ and -2

$$+5(3x - 2) = 15x - 10$$

and that the products are to be added algebraically.

$$(4x + 5)(3x - 2) = 12x^2 - 8x + 15x - 10 = \mathbf{12x^2 + 7x - 10}$$

practice   Multiply. Express all polynomials in descending powers of one of the variables.

    9. $(7xyz)(3wy^2z)$ **10.** $(2x^2y^2)(4xy^5z^3)(-3x^5y^{10}z^{19})$

    11. $(4x + 2)(x - 5)$ **12.** $(4x + 2)(3x - 5)$

    13. $(3x + 2)^2$ **14.** $(x - 27y)(3x - 3y)$

    15. $4x^2(3x - y + 5x^2y)$ **16.** $(5x)(3y)(5x - 3y)$

    17. $abc(abc - def)$ **18.** $12n^2(2n - 3n^2)$

simple division   The simplest type of polynomial division is the division of a polynomial by a monomial. The desired result can be obtained by dividing each term of the polynomial by the monomial, as shown in the following examples.

example F.6   Divide $3x^3 + 7x^2 - x$ by x.

solution   We will divide each of the three terms by x.

$$\frac{3x^3}{x} + \frac{7x^2}{x} - \frac{x}{x} = 3x^2 + 7x - 1$$

example F.7   Divide $12x^{12} - 8x^8 + 4x^6$ by $4x^4$.

solution   We will divide every term by $4x^4$.

$$\frac{12x^{12}}{4x^4} - \frac{8x^8}{4x^4} + \frac{4x^6}{4x^4} = 3x^8 - 2x^4 + x^2$$

example F.8   Divide $4xy^2 - 100x^2y^3z + 22x^5y^4$ by $2xy$.

solution   We will divide every term by $2xy$.

$$\frac{4xy^2}{2xy} - \frac{100x^2y^3z}{2xy} + \frac{22x^5y^4}{2xy} = 2y - 50xy^2z + 11x^4y^3$$

We choose to simplify the answer by expressing it in descending powers of y.

$$11x^4y^3 - 50xy^2z + 2y$$

practice   Divide. Express all sums in descending powers of a variable.

    19. $\dfrac{140x^2}{7x}$ **20.** $\dfrac{88x^{10}y}{11xy}$

    21. $\dfrac{90m^4n^3}{6mn^3}$ **22.** $\dfrac{200m^3n^{10}q}{10m^2n}$

    23. $\dfrac{200m^3 - 10m}{5m}$ **24.** $\dfrac{6x^3 - 3x^2 + 9x}{3x}$

    25. $\dfrac{80x^5 - 40x^2yz + 8x}{8x}$ **26.** $\dfrac{40a - 4a^3 + 8a^2b}{4a}$

    27. $\dfrac{12c^3 + 20c^2d - 400cd}{4c}$ **28.** $\dfrac{90y^3 + 18xy^2 - 45y}{9y}$

TOPIC G *Transformational Geometry*

In geometry, a **mapping** is a correspondence between two sets of points. The input points are called **preimages,** and they are mapped to **images.** We call a mapping a **transformation** if each preimage is mapped to exactly one image. An example of a transformation is

$$T: (x, y) \longrightarrow (-x, -2y)$$

The notation indicates that the name of the transformation is T, and that T maps the preimage point (x, y) to the image point $(-x, -2y)$. So T applied to $(0, 0)$ is $(0, 0)$, and T applied to $(-2, -1)$ is $(2, 2)$.

A transformation that maps any figure to a congruent figure is called an **isometry.** In this activity we examine three kinds of isometries—translations, reflections, and rotations.

translations A **translation** is a transformation that slides figures. For example, the transformation $T: (x, y) \longrightarrow (x - 1, y - 3)$ is a translation. It transforms the triangle whose vertices are $A(-2, 6)$, $B(4, 1)$, and $C(-2, 1)$ to the triangle whose vertices are $A'(-3, 3)$, $B'(3, -2)$, and $C'(3, -2)$.

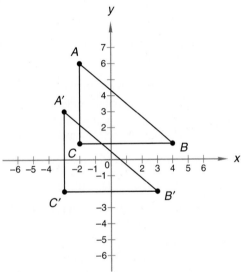

It appears that T slides $\triangle ABC$ to $\triangle A'B'C'$. Notice that the two figures are congruent.

example G.1 (a) Graph the points $A(1, 2)$, $B(-2, 0)$, and $C(4, -1)$, and draw $\triangle ABC$.
(b) Find the images A', B', and C' under the transformation $T: (x, y) \longrightarrow (x + 2, y + 1)$.
(c) Graph A', B', and C', and draw $\triangle A'B'C'$.

solution (a) First we sketch axes. Then we graph the points and draw $\triangle ABC$.

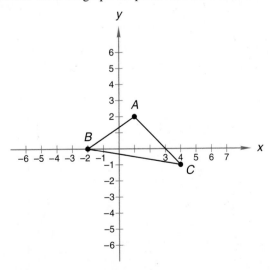

(b) The transformation T tells us to add two to the x-coordinate and one to the y-coordinate.

$$T:\ (x, y) \longrightarrow (x + 2,\ y + 1)$$
$$T:\ (1, 2) \longrightarrow (3, 3) \qquad \text{so } A' \text{ is } (3, 3)$$
$$T:\ (-2, 0) \longrightarrow (0, 1) \qquad \text{so } B' \text{ is } (0, 1)$$
$$T:\ (4, -1) \longrightarrow (6, 0) \qquad \text{so } C' \text{ is } (6, 0)$$

(c) Now we graph the image points A', B', and C' and draw the image $\triangle A'B'C'$. We use the same coordinate plane as above.

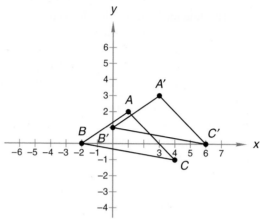

practice   For problems 1–3:

(a) Graph the preimage points indicated, and draw the preimage polygon.

(b) Find the image points under the indicated transformation.

(c) Graph the image points and the image polygon.

  1. $A(1, 1), B(0, 2), C(-2, -3) \qquad T:\ (x, y) \longrightarrow (x + 3,\ y + 2)$

  2. $A(-2, 0), B(-2, -2), C(0, -2), D(0, 0) \qquad T:\ (x, y) \longrightarrow (x - 1,\ y + 4)$

  3. $A(-4, -2), B(-2, 1), C(0, 0) \qquad T:\ (x, y) \longrightarrow (x + 4,\ y)$

  4. Graph $A(-5, -3)$, $B(-4, 1)$, and $C(-1, -1)$, and draw $\triangle ABC$. Find A', B', and C' under the transformation $R:\ (x, y) \longrightarrow (x + 8,\ y - 1)$. Graph A', B', and C' and draw $\triangle A'B'C'$. Then using A', B', and C' as the preimage points, find A'', B'', and C'' under the transformation $S:\ (x, y) \longrightarrow (x - 1,\ y + 4)$. Graph A'', B'', and C'' and draw $\triangle A''B''C''$. Finally, find the transformation T that maps A, B, and C to A'', B'', and C''.

reflections   A **reflection** across a line is a transformation that produces a mirror image. A reflection is always an isometry since the figures do not change size or shape. In the next two examples we show a reflection in the y-axis and then a reflection in the x-axis.

example G.2   Graph $P(-3, 2)$ and $Q(-1, -3)$ and draw $\overline{PQ}$. Then find the image points P' and Q' under the transformation $R:\ (x, y) \longrightarrow (-x, y)$. Finally, graph P' and Q' and draw $\overline{P'Q'}$.

solution   First we sketch a coordinate system and graph the preimage.

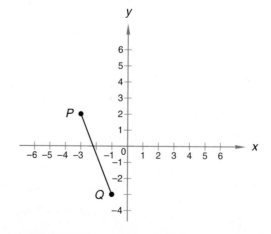

Then we find P' and Q'.

$$R: (x, y) \longrightarrow (-x, y)$$

$$R: (-3, 2) \longrightarrow (3, 2) \qquad \text{so } P' \text{ is } (3, 2)$$

$$R: (-1, -3) \longrightarrow (1, -3) \qquad \text{so } Q' \text{ is } (1, -3)$$

Finally, we graph P' and Q' and draw $\overline{P'Q'}$.

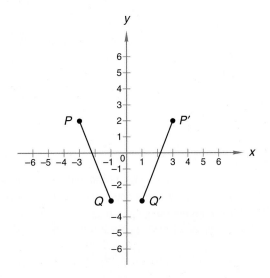

example G.3   Graph $E(-2, 3)$, $F(2, 0)$, and $G(3, 2)$, and draw $\triangle EFG$. Then find the image points E', F', and G' under the transformation $R: (x, y) \longrightarrow (x, -y)$. Graph the image points and draw $\triangle E'F'G'$.

solution   First we sketch a coordinate system and graph the preimage.

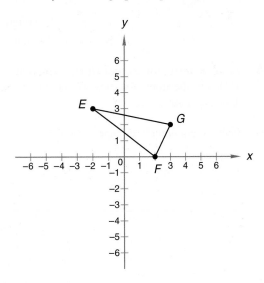

Then we find E', F', and G'.

$$R: (x, y) \longrightarrow (x, -y)$$

$$R: (-2, 3) \longrightarrow (-2, -3) \qquad \text{so } E' \text{ is } (-2, -3)$$

$$R: (2, 0) \longrightarrow (2, 0) \qquad \text{so } F' \text{ is } (2, 0)$$

$$R: (3, 2) \longrightarrow (3, -2) \qquad \text{so } G' \text{ is } (3, -2)$$

Finally, we graph E', F', and G' and draw $\triangle E'F'G'$.

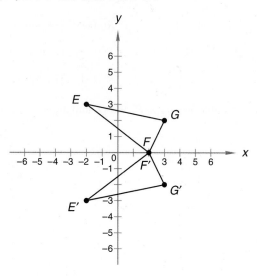

practice
For problems 5–7:

(a) Graph the preimage points indicated, and draw the preimage polygon.

(b) Find the image points under the transformation indicated.

(c) Graph the image points and draw the image polygon.

   5. $A(-1, 4)$, $B(2, 1)$, $C(4, 3)$ R: $(x, y) \longrightarrow (x, -y)$

   6. $A(-1, 4)$, $B(2, 1)$, $C(4, 3)$ S: $(x, y) \longrightarrow (-x, y)$

   7. $D(-3, -1)$, $E(-4, 3)$, $F(3, 4)$, $G(4, 1)$ T: $(x, y) \longrightarrow (x, -y)$

   8. Apply T from problem 7 to D', E', F', and G' from problem 7. What are the image points? What does this mean about reflections in a line?

rotations   A third isometry is **rotation** around the origin. The two rotational transformations we will use now are

U: $(x, y) \longrightarrow (-x, -y)$ 180° rotation around the origin
V: $(x, y) \longrightarrow (-y, x)$ 90° counterclockwise rotation around the origin

example G.4   Graph $K(1, 0)$, $L(4, 2)$, and $M(3, 4)$, and draw $\triangle KLM$. Then find the image points K', L', and M' using the transformation U: $(x, y) \longrightarrow (-x, -y)$. Finally, graph the image points and draw $\triangle K'L'M'$.

solution   First we graph the preimage.

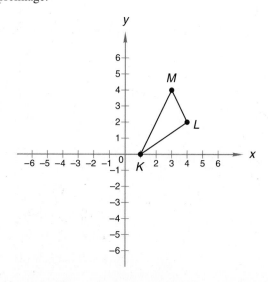

Then we calculate the image points.

$$U: (x, y) \longrightarrow (-x, -y)$$
$$U: (1, 0) \longrightarrow (-1, 0) \qquad \text{so } K' \text{ is } (-1, 0)$$
$$U: (4, 2) \longrightarrow (-4, -2) \qquad \text{so } L' \text{ is } (-4, -2)$$
$$U: (3, 4) \longrightarrow (-3, -4) \qquad \text{so } M' \text{ is } (-3, -4)$$

Finally, we graph the image points and draw $\triangle K'L'M'$.

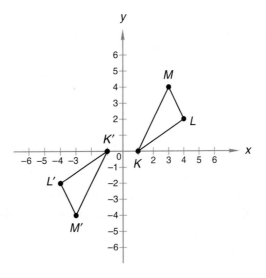

example G.5 Graph $N(0, 0)$, $P(4, -1)$, and $Q(4, 2)$, and draw $\triangle NPQ$. Then find the points N', P', and Q' using the transformation $V: (x, y) \longrightarrow (-y, x)$. Finally, graph the image points and draw $\triangle N'P'Q'$.

solution First we graph the preimage.

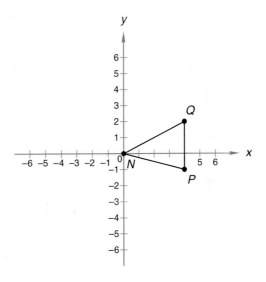

Then we calculate the image points.

$$V: (x, y) \longrightarrow (-y, x)$$
$$V: (0, 0) \longrightarrow (0, 0) \qquad \text{so } N' \text{ is } (0, 0)$$
$$V: (4, -1) \longrightarrow (1, 4) \qquad \text{so } P' \text{ is } (1, 4)$$
$$V: (4, 2) \longrightarrow (-2, 4) \qquad \text{so } Q' \text{ is } (-2, 4)$$

Finally, we graph the image points and draw the image polygon.

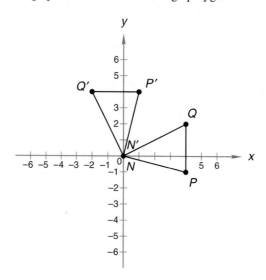

practice   For problems 9–11:

(a)   Graph the preimage points indicated, and draw the preimage polygon.

(b)   Find the image points under the indicated transformation.

(c)   Graph the image points and draw the image polygon.

9. $A(0, 0)$, $B(-1, -3)$, $C(1, -2)$ R: $(x, y) \longrightarrow (-y, x)$

10. $D(-1, 0)$, $E(-4, 1)$, $F(-3, 3)$, $G(0, 4)$ S: $(x, y) \longrightarrow (-x, -y)$

11. $H(-1, 0)$, $I(-3, 0)$, $J(-2, 3)$ T: $(x, y) \longrightarrow (y, -x)$

12.   For the points $A(0, 1)$, $B(-1, -3)$, and $C(-3, 2)$:

(a)   Find the images of A, B, and C under the 90° rotation R: $(x, y) \longrightarrow (-y, x)$. Call the images A', B', and C' respectively.

(b)   Find the images of A', B', and C' under the transformation R. Call the images A'', B'', and C'' respectively.

(c)   Find the images of A, B, and C under the 180° rotation S: $(x, y) \longrightarrow (-x, -y)$. Call the images A''', B''', and C''' respectively.

(d)   How do A'', B'', and C'' compare with A''', B''', and C''' respectively?

13.   For the points $D(-1, 0)$, $E(-4, 1)$, $F(-3, 3)$, and $G(0, 4)$:

(a)   Apply the y-axis reflection T: $(x, y) \longrightarrow (-x, y)$ to D, E, F, and G. Call the images D', E', F', and G' respectively.

(b)   Apply the x-axis reflection W: $(x, y) \longrightarrow (x, -y)$ to D', E', F', and G'. Call the images D'', E'', F'', and G'' respectively.

(c)   Apply the 180° rotation S: $(x, y) \longrightarrow (-x, -y)$ to D, E, F, and G. Call the images D''', E''', F''', and G''' respectively.

(d)   How do D'', E'', F'', and G'' compare with D''', E''', F''', and G''' respectively?

TOPIC H Advanced Graphing

Previously in the text, we evaluated expressions with exponents. For example:

Evaluate: $5x - y^2$ when $x = 2$ and $y = 3$

Solution: $5(2) - 3^2 = 10 - 9 = 1$

We also performed operations with variables that have exponents. For example:

Simplify: $5x^2(3 - 2x + x^2)$

Solution: $5x^2(3 - 2x + x^2) = 15x^2 - 10x^3 + 5x^4$

However, we have only graphed equations like $y = 2x - 1$, where the x has no exponent (that is, unless we write x as x^1). Such equations are called linear equations because their graph is a line.

We can also graph equations when the x-variable is raised to the second power. These equations are called **quadratic equations,** and their graph is *not* a line.

example H.1   Graph: $y = x^2$

solution   As with linear equations, we make a chart, choose x-values, calculate corresponding y-values, plot the points, and connect the points to form the curve. We will choose all the integers from -3 to 3 for x, so that we can get a good idea of the shape of the curve.

x	y
-3	
-2	
-1	
0	
1	
2	
3	

Now we calculate the corresponding y-values.

x	y
-3	$(-3)^2 = 9$
-2	$(-2)^2 = 4$
-1	$(-1)^2 = 1$
0	$0^2 = 0$
1	$1^2 = 1$
2	$2^2 = 4$
3	$3^2 = 9$

So, we plot the points (–3, 9), (–2, 4), (–1, 1), (0, 0), (1, 1), (2, 4), and (3, 9).

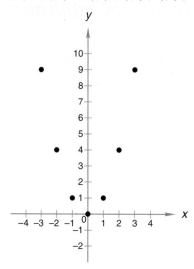

Now we connect the points to form a curve. The graph seems to bend upward on either side of the y-axis with increasing steepness. If we let x be 4 and –4, we would get the points (4, 16) and (–4, 15), which are well above the top of our sketched coordinate system. Thus, we connect the points, not with line segments, but with a curve that increases in steepness as x gets farther from zero.

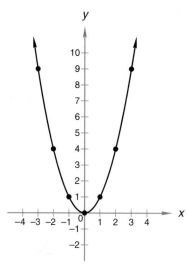

This curve is called a **parabola.**

practice   1.   Graph $y = 2x^2$. (Use $x = -2, -1, 0, 1, 2$.)

2.   Graph $y = \dfrac{1}{2}x^2$. (Use $x = -4, -2, 0, 2, 4$.)

3.   Graph $y = 3x^2$.   4.   Graph $y = \dfrac{1}{4}x^2$.

5.   Graph $y = 5x^2$.

6.   Describe how a large or small coefficient changes the shape of the parabola.

7.   Graph $y = -x^2$.   8.   Graph $y = -3x^2$.

9.   Graph $y = 4x^2$. $\left(\text{Use } x = -2, -1, 0, \tfrac{1}{2}, 1, \tfrac{3}{2}, 2.\right)$

10. Graph $y = -2x^2$.

11. Graph $y = -\dfrac{1}{2}x^2$.

12. Describe how a negative coefficient changes the orientation of the parabola.

13. Graph $y = x^2 + 1$.

14. Graph $y = x^2 - 2$.

15. Graph $y = x^2 + 4$.

16. Graph $y = x^2 - 5$.

17. Describe how adding or subtracting from the x^2 term changes the position of the parabola.

18. Graph $y = 2x^2 - 6$.

19. Graph $y = 4x^2 - 10$. (Use $x = -2, -1, 0, 1, 2$.)

20. Graph $y = -\dfrac{1}{2}x^2 + 5$.

TOPIC I *Slope*

finding the slope of a line using points

When we talk about the slope of a hill, we are speaking of how steeply it goes up or down. Lines and other curves also have slope, and their slope is a measure of going up or going down. The mathematical definition of slope is

$$\text{slope} = \frac{\text{change in } y}{\text{change in } x}$$

For example, the slope of the line through $(-4, 2)$ and $(1, 3)$ is $\frac{1}{5}$.

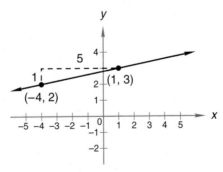

To go from the left point to the right point we count 1 up and 5 across. So

$$\text{slope} = \frac{\text{change in } y}{\text{change in } x} = \frac{1}{5}$$

This means that as we change one unit in the y-direction we change five units in the x-direction. Equivalently, for every five-unit increase in x, the graph goes up one unit.

The formula for calculating the slope between two points looks more complicated than it really is. If we designate the two points as (x_1, y_1) and (x_2, y_2), then the slope of the line through them can be calculated as follows:

$$\text{slope} = \frac{y_2 - y_1}{x_2 - x_1}$$

The subscripted 1's and 2's just tell us which point the x- and y-coordinates come from. So the formula means

$$\text{slope} = \frac{\text{the difference of the } y\text{-coordinates}}{\text{the difference of the } x\text{-coordinates}}$$

This is a rephrasing of the first definition of slope. In the next example we will use the formula to recalculate the slope previously determined by inspection.

example I.1   Find the slope of the line through $(-4, 2)$ and $(1, 3)$.

   solution   We use the slope formula.

$$\text{slope} = \frac{y_2 - y_1}{x_2 - x_1}$$

$$= \frac{3 - 2}{1 - (-4)}$$

$$= \frac{1}{5}$$

The slope is the same whichever point we call "point 1" or "point 2." If we say $(1, 3)$ is (x_1, y_1) instead, we calculate

$$\text{slope} = \frac{y_2 - y_1}{x_2 - x_1} = \frac{2 - 3}{-4 - 1} = \frac{-1}{-5} = \frac{1}{5}$$

It does matter that both coordinates of one point come first in the subtractions, and that the y-coordinates are in the numerator—be careful!

When we have the graph of a line and we need to find its slope, we can pick *any* two points on the line to calculate the slope with the formula.

example I.2   What is the slope of this line?

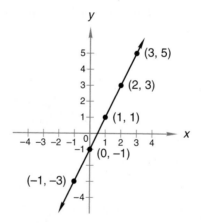

   solution   We pick $(2, 3)$ and $(3, 5)$ and use the slope formula.

$$\text{slope} = \frac{y_2 - y_1}{x_2 - x_1} = \frac{5 - 3}{3 - 2} = \frac{2}{1} = 2$$

Any two other points on the graphed line will yield the same answer. Also, we might have noticed that from point to point, x increases by one unit and y by two units, which means the slope is 2.

When points are not so clearly indicated on the graph, we need to estimate the coordinates. Our answer will be an approximate slope.

example I.3 What is the slope of this line?

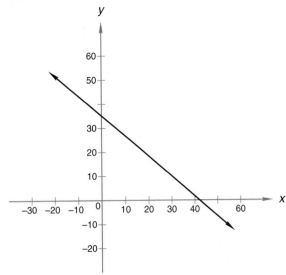

solution Two estimated points are (30, 10) and (0, 35). The slope can be approximated using the same formula.

$$\text{slope} = \frac{y_2 - y_1}{x_2 - x_1} \approx \frac{35 - 10}{0 - 30} = \frac{25}{-30} = -\frac{5}{6}$$

The slope is **about** $-\frac{5}{6}$.

practice Sketch the points and the line they determine; then calculate the slope of the line.

1. (3, 1) and (5, 5)   **2.** (−2, 0) and (4, 2)

3. (5, 6) and (−10, 6)   **4.** (−1, 1) and (4, 7)

5. (2, 3) and (4, −1)

What is the slope of the graphed lines?

6.
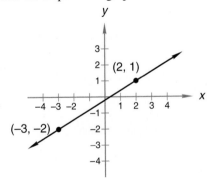

7.
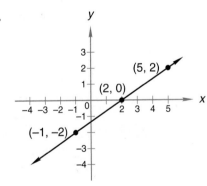

8.
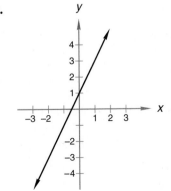

9.
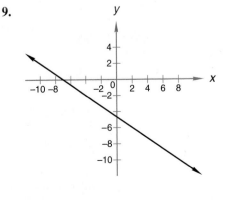

finding the slope of a line using its equation

If we have the equation of a line, we can quickly calculate the slope by finding any two points on the line and then using the slope formula.

example I.4   Find the slope of $y = 3x - 4$.

solution   We let x be 0 and 2. Then we will find the corresponding y-coordinates. With those two points, we can graph the line and calculate the slope.

x	y
0	$3(0) - 4 = -4$
2	$3(2) - 4 = 2$

The points are $(0, -4)$ and $(2, 2)$, which leads to the following graph:

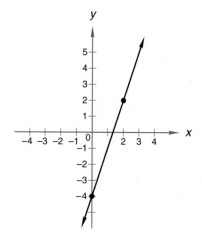

We now use the slope formula:

$$\text{slope} = \frac{y_2 - y_1}{x_2 - x_1} = \frac{2 - (-4)}{2 - 0} = \frac{6}{2} = \mathbf{3}$$

Any two x-coordinates will produce the same graph and slope, so try to choose x-coordinates that make the calculations easy.

practice   For each equation, find two ordered pairs, sketch the graph of the line, and calculate the slope of the line.

10. $y = 2x + 1$

11. $y = -5x + 6$

12. $y = 4x$

13. $y = -3x + 2$

14. $y = \frac{1}{2}x - 3$ (*Hint*: use an even number for x.)

TOPIC J *Basic Trigonometry*

**trigonometric
ratios**
The sides and angles of a right triangle can be used to define relationships called **trigonometric ratios.** These ratios are called **sine, cosine,** and **tangent.** In the right triangle below,

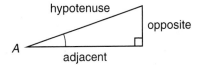

the *sine of angle A* (or sin A) is the ratio of the length of the side opposite angle A to the length of the hypotenuse.

$$\sin A = \frac{\text{opposite}}{\text{hypotenuse}}$$

The *cosine of angle A* (or cos A) is the ratio of the length of the side adjacent to angle A to the length of the hypotenuse.

$$\cos A = \frac{\text{adjacent}}{\text{hypotenuse}}$$

The *tangent of angle A* (or tan A) is the ratio of the length of the side opposite angle A to the length of the side adjacent to angle A.

$$\tan A = \frac{\text{opposite}}{\text{adjacent}}$$

example J.1   In the triangle below, what is the cosine of angle A? What is the cosine of angle B?

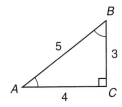

solution   The cosine of angle A is the ratio of the length of the side adjacent to angle A to the length of the hypotenuse.

$$\cos A = \frac{\text{length of side adjacent to angle } A}{\text{length of hypotenuse}}$$

The hypotenuse is $\overline{AB}$, and $\overline{AC}$ is the side that is adjacent to angle A. Thus,

$$\cos A = \frac{AC}{AB} = \frac{4}{5}$$

The cosine of angle B is the ratio of the length of the side adjacent to angle B to the length of the hypotenuse.

$$\cos B = \frac{\text{length of side adjacent to angle } B}{\text{length of hypotenuse}}$$

The side adjacent to angle B is different from the side adjacent to angle A. Segment $\overline{BC}$ is the side adjacent to angle B.

$$\cos B = \frac{BC}{AB} = \frac{3}{5}$$

example J.2   Refer to the right triangle below to calculate the values for the sine, cosine, and tangent of angle A.

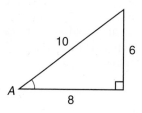

solution   The length of the hypotenuse is 10 units, the side adjacent to angle A has a length of 8 units, and the side opposite angle A is 6 units long. We simply put this information into the ratios to find the values for the sine, cosine, and tangent of angle A.

$$\sin A = \frac{\text{opposite}}{\text{hypotenuse}} \qquad \cos A = \frac{\text{adjacent}}{\text{hypotenuse}} \qquad \tan A = \frac{\text{opposite}}{\text{adjacent}}$$

$$\sin A = \frac{6}{10} \qquad\qquad \cos A = \frac{8}{10} \qquad\qquad \tan A = \frac{6}{8}$$

$$\mathbf{\sin A = \frac{3}{5}} \qquad\qquad \mathbf{\cos A = \frac{4}{5}} \qquad\qquad \mathbf{\tan A = \frac{3}{4}}$$

practice   Use the triangles below to determine the values indicated in problems 1–12.

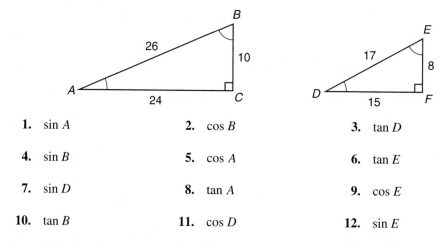

1. $\sin A$	**2.** $\cos B$	**3.** $\tan D$
4. $\sin B$	**5.** $\cos A$	**6.** $\tan E$
7. $\sin D$	**8.** $\tan A$	**9.** $\cos E$
10. $\tan B$	**11.** $\cos D$	**12.** $\sin E$

trigonometric tables   The triangles below are similar.

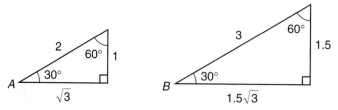

The measures of angles A and B are equal. Notice also that $\sin A = \sin B$.

$$\sin A = \frac{\text{opposite}}{\text{hypotenuse}} \qquad\qquad \sin B = \frac{\text{opposite}}{\text{hypotenuse}}$$

$$\sin A = \frac{1}{2} \qquad\qquad\qquad \sin B = \frac{1.5}{3}$$

$$\sin A = 0.5 \qquad\qquad\qquad \sin B = 0.5$$

Even though the sides of the triangles have different lengths, the ratios of the lengths of corresponding sides are equal. This information is not new—it was previously discussed in

Lesson 65 in the section on similar triangles. We review it here to demonstrate that **the values of the sine, cosine, and tangent of an angle do not depend on the size of a triangle—they only depend on the measure of the angle.** For this reason, we can make tables of the values of the sine, cosine, and tangent of various angles.[†]

example J.3   Use the following table to find the approximate values of (a) sin 35°, (b) tan 30°, (c) cos 45°, and (d) tan 40°.

DEGREES	SINE	COSINE	TANGENT
30	0.5	0.8660	0.5774
35	0.5736	0.8192	0.7002
40	0.6428	0.7660	0.8391
45	0.7071	0.7071	1

solution   (a) To approximate sin 35°, we look for the number in the same row as 35 and the same column as sine. This number is 0.5736. Thus, sin 35° ≈ **0.5736.**

The other answers are found similarly.

(b) tan 30° ≈ **0.5774**   (c) cos 45° ≈ **0.7071**   (d) tan 40° ≈ **0.8391**

example J.4   Use the table in example J.3 to find an angle measure whose cosine is approximately 0.8660.

solution   First, we find 0.8660 in the cosine column. Then we look for the degree measure in the same row. The measure is **30°**, which is our answer.

practice   For problems 13–28, refer to the following table:

DEGREES	SINE	COSINE	TANGENT
10	0.1736	0.9848	0.1763
15	0.2588	0.9659	0.2679
20	0.3420	0.9397	0.3640
25	0.4226	0.9063	0.4663
30	0.5	0.8660	0.5774
35	0.5736	0.8192	0.7002
40	0.6428	0.7660	0.8391
45	0.7071	0.7071	1

Approximate the values indicated in problems 13–24.

13. tan 15°   **14.** cos 30°   **15.** tan 35°

16. sin 10°   **17.** sin 25°   **18.** tan 10°

19. cos 15°   **20.** sin 45°   **21.** cos 20°

22. tan 45°   **23.** cos 10°   **24.** sin 30°

[†]Most of the time, we approximate the values in the tables to four decimal places since many of the values are actually nonterminating, nonrepeating decimals.

25. Find an angle measure whose tangent is approximately 0.4663.

26. Find an angle measure whose sine is approximately 0.2588.

27. Find an angle measure whose cosine is approximately 0.8192.

28. Find an angle measure whose sine and cosine are equal.

applications We can use the trigonometric ratios to find unknown lengths in right triangles, as we show in the following example.

example J.5 Find a and b.

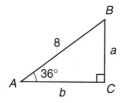

Use the information below as necessary.

Degrees	Sine	Cosine	Tangent
36	0.5878	0.8090	0.7265

solution We know that the sine of angle A is the ratio of the length of the side opposite angle A to the length of the hypotenuse. Thus,

$$\sin A = \frac{a}{8}$$

Since angle A is a $36°$ angle, we can use the table to say

$$\sin A \approx 0.5878$$

Now we combine these two pieces of information and solve for a.

$$\frac{a}{8} \approx 0.5878$$

$$8 \cdot \frac{a}{8} \approx 0.5878 \cdot 8$$

$$a \approx \mathbf{4.7024}$$

Similarly, we see that the cosine of angle A can be expressed as a ratio using the triangle and as a numerical value using the table.

$$\cos A = \frac{b}{8} \qquad \cos A \approx 0.8090$$

So we combine the two pieces of information. This time we solve for b.

$$\frac{b}{8} \approx 0.8090$$

$$8 \cdot \frac{b}{8} \approx 0.8090 \cdot 8$$

$$b \approx \mathbf{6.4720}$$

We now use this technique to solve a real-world problem.

example J.6   An airplane is 8000 feet above the ground. The plane is at a 16° angle of elevation from a ground-level observer, as shown below.

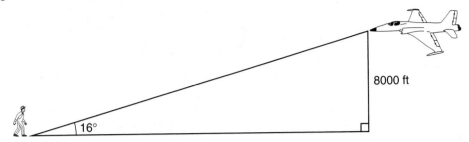

8000 ft

16°

To the nearest hundred feet, what is the direct-line distance from the plane to the observer? Use the table below as necessary.

DEGREES	SINE	COSINE	TANGENT
16	0.2756	0.9612	0.2867

solution   We redraw the triangle and use x to label the length in question.

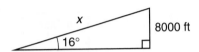

x

8000 ft

16°

We have a 16° angle, the length of the side opposite the angle, and an unknown length for the hypotenuse. Thus, we use sine. Using ratios we can say

$$\sin 16° = \frac{8000 \text{ ft}}{x}$$

The table gives us a value to substitute for sin 16°, which we use to solve for x.

$\sin 16° = \dfrac{8000 \text{ ft}}{x}$	from triangle
$0.2756 \approx \dfrac{8000 \text{ ft}}{x}$	substituted from table
$x \cdot 0.2756 \approx \dfrac{8000 \text{ ft}}{x} \cdot x$	multiplied by x
$\dfrac{0.2756x}{0.2756} \approx \dfrac{8000 \text{ ft}}{0.2756}$	divided by 0.2756
$x \approx \dfrac{8000}{0.2756} \text{ ft}$	simplified

After some quick long division, we see that x is about **29,000 ft.**

practice   **29.**   Find a.

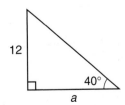

12

40°

a

Use the following table as necessary:

DEGREES	SINE	COSINE	TANGENT
40	0.6428	0.7660	0.8391

30. Find *y*.

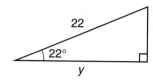

Use the following table as necessary:

DEGREES	SINE	COSINE	TANGENT
22	0.3746	0.9272	0.4040

31. The bed of a trailer is 75 centimeters above the ground. A ramp is inclined 13° for use when loading the trailer, as seen in the diagram below.

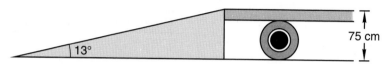

To the nearest centimeter, find the length of the loading ramp. Use the following table as necessary:

DEGREES	SINE	COSINE	TANGENT
13	0.2250	0.9744	0.2309

Glossary

absolute value   The quality of a number that equals the distance of the graph of the number from the origin. Since the graphs of –3 and +3 are both 3 units from the origin, the absolute value of both numbers is +3.

acute angle   An angle whose degree measure is between 0° and 90°.

acute triangle   A triangle in which all three angles are acute angles.

addend   One of two or more numbers that are to be added to find a sum.

adjacent angles   Two angles that have a common side and a common vertex. The angles lie on opposite sides of their common side.

algebraic addition   The combining of positive and/or negative numbers to form a sum.

algorithm   A particular process for solving a certain type of problem. Often the process is repetitive, as in the long division algorithm.

altitude   The perpendicular distance from the base of a figure to the opposite vertex, side, or face of the figure. The altitude can also be called the *height* of the figure.

angle   In geometry, the figure formed by two rays that have a common endpoint.

angle bisector   A ray from the vertex of an angle that divides the angle into two angles whose measures are equal.

arc   A segment or a piece of a curve.

average   The sum of a set of quantities divided by the number of quantities in the set.

axis   A number line used to reference points.

base   (1) A designated side (or face) of a geometric figure. (2) The lower number in an exponential expression. In the exponential expression 2^5, 2 is the base and 5 is the exponent.

bisect   To divide or separate into two equal parts.

chord   A segment that connects two points on a circle.

circle   A two-dimensional figure that is the set of all points that are an equal distance from a center point.

circumference   The perimeter of a circle.

coefficient   A factor of an indicated product. In the product $4x$, 4 is the coefficient of x and x is the coefficient of 4.

common factor   A number that is a factor of every number in a list of two or more numbers.

complementary angles   Two angles whose sum is 90°.

composite number   A counting number that is the product of two counting numbers, neither of which is the number 1.

compound fraction   A fraction whose numerator or denominator (or both) is also a fraction.

concave polygon   A polygon in which at least one interior angle has a measure that is greater than 180°.

conditional equation   An equation whose truth or falsity depends on the number or numbers used to replace one or more variables.

congruent polygons   Two polygons in which the corresponding sides have equal lengths and the corresponding angles have equal measures.

convex polygon   A polygon in which all interior angles have a measure that is less than 180°.

coordinate   The number on a number line associated with a point.

coordinate plane   A plane with two intersecting number lines, which are used to designate the position of any point in the plane.

corresponding sides   Sides of similar polygons that occupy corresponding positions. Corresponding sides are always opposite angles whose measures are equal.

counting numbers   Sometimes called the *natural numbers*, these numbers are 1, 2, 3, 4, 5, ….

curve   An endless connection of mathematical points.

decimal fraction   A decimal number.

decimal number   A number designated by a horizontal arrangement of digits using a decimal point to define the place values of the digits.

decimal point   A dot placed in a decimal number to use as a place value reference point. The place to the left of the decimal point is always the units place.

denominate number   A combination of a number and a descriptor that designates units. Examples are 4 ft, 16 tons, 42 miles per hour.

denominator   The bottom number in a fraction.

diagonal   A line segment connecting two nonconsecutive vertices in a geometric figure.

diameter   A chord that passes through the center of a circle; the length of the chord.

difference   The result of subtraction.

digit   In the base 10 system, any of the symbols 0, 1, 2, 3, 4, 5, 6, 7, 8, or 9.

dividend   The number being divided in a division problem. In the expression $10 \div 2$, the dividend is 10 and the divisor is 2.

divisible   If one whole number is divided by another whole number and the quotient is a whole number (the remainder is zero), we say that the first whole number is divisible by the second whole number.

divisor   The number that divides in a division problem. In the expression $10 \div 2$, the divisor is 2 and the dividend is 10.

equidistant   The same distance. If points A and B are the same distance from point C, we say that A and B are equidistant from C.

equilateral triangle   A triangle whose sides all have the same length.

equivalent fractions   Fractions that have the same value.

expanded form   A way of writing a number as the sum of the products of each digit and its place value.

expanded fraction   A fraction of equal value whose denominator is greater than the denominator of the original fraction.

exponent   The upper number in an exponential expression. In the expression 2^5, 5 is the exponent and 2 is the base.

exponential expression   An expression that indicates that one number is to be used as a factor a given number of times. The expression 4^3 tells us that 4 is to be used as a factor 3 times.

exponential notation   A notation that uses an exponential expression to designate a number.

factor   (1) A counting number that divides a second counting number without remainder is a factor of the second number. The factors of 12 are 1, 2, 3, 4, 6, and 12. (2) To write as a product of factors. The number 6 can be factored by writing it as 2×3.

factorial   A counting number followed by an exclamation point. The value of a factorial expression is the product of the counting number and all lesser counting numbers. We write 6 factorial as 6!, which means $6 \cdot 5 \cdot 4 \cdot 3 \cdot 2 \cdot 1$.

fraction bar   The line segment that separates the numerator and the denominator of a fraction.

geometric solid   A three-dimensional geometric figure. Spheres, cones, and right solids are examples of geometric solids.

graph   (1) The mark(s) made on a number line or coordinate plane to indicate the location of a point or a set of points. (2) A tool used to display data.

greater than   One number is said to be greater than a second number if the graph of the number on a number line is to the right of the graph of the second number.

height   See *altitude*.

hypotenuse   The side of a right triangle that is opposite the right angle.

improper fraction   A fraction whose numerator is equal to or greater than the denominator.

independent events   Two events are said to be independent if the outcome of one event does not affect the probability of the other event. If a dime is tossed twice, the outcome (heads or tails) of the first toss does not affect the probability of heads or tails on the second toss.

integers   The numbers ..., –3, –2, –1, 0, 1, 2, 3, ...

inverse operation   Two operations are inverse operations if one operation will "undo" the other operation. If we begin with 3 and multiply by 2, the product is 6. If we divide 6 by 2, we will undo the multiplication by 2, and the answer will be 3, the original number.

invert   To turn upside down.

irrational number   The numbers whose decimal part is nonrepeating and nonterminating.

isosceles triangle   A triangle in which at least two sides have equal lengths.

lateral surface area   The sum of the areas of an object's sides.

least common denominator (LCD)   Of two or more fractions, a denominator that is the least common multiple of the denominators of the fractions.

least common multiple (LCM)   The smallest whole number that every member of a set of whole numbers will divide evenly.

less than   One number is said to be less than a second number if the graph of the number on a number line is to the left of the graph of the second number.

like terms   Terms whose variable components have the same values regardless of the numbers used as replacements for the variables. The terms $14xy$ and $10yx$ are like terms because xy and yx have equal values.

line   A straight curve.

line segment   A part of a line.

liter   The basic unit of volume in the metric system.

lowest terms   The numerator and denominator of a fraction are in lowest terms when their only common factor is one.

mean   The average of a set of numbers.

median   The middle number when a set of numbers is arranged in order from the least to the greatest.

meter   The basic unit of length in the metric system.

midpoint   A point that is equidistant from two designated points.

milliliter   One-thousandth of a liter.

mixed number   A numerical expression composed of a whole number and a fraction.

mode   The number that appears most often in a set of numbers.

multiple   A product of one counting number and any other counting number.

multiplier   One of two numbers that are to be multiplied. A factor.

natural numbers   See *counting numbers.*

numeral   Symbol or group of symbols used to represent a number.

numerator   The top number in a fraction.

numerical expression   A numeral.

obtuse angle   An angle whose measure is greater than 90° and less than 180°.

obtuse triangle   A triangle that contains an obtuse angle.

opposites   A positive number and a negative number whose absolute values are equal. The numbers −3 and +3 are a pair of opposites.

origin   (1) The point on a number line with which the number zero is associated. (2) The point where the axes of the coordinate plane intersect. The coordinates of this point are (0, 0).

parallel lines   Lines in a plane that never intersect.

parallelogram   A quadrilateral that has two pairs of parallel sides.

percent   Hundredth. Forty percent is forty hundredths.

perimeter   Of a flat geometric figure, the distance around the figure.

permutation   The number of different ways a set of objects can be arranged in a row.

perpendicular bisector   A line that is perpendicular to a given line segment at the midpoint of the segment.

planar figure   A figure drawn on a flat surface.

plane   A mathematical point has no size. A mathematical line has no ends. A mathematical plane is a "flat surface" that has no boundaries.

point   A location on a line or in space. A mathematical point has no size. The dot we make to indicate the location of the mathematical point is called the graph of the point.

polygon   A closed, planar geometric figure whose sides are line segments.

power   The value of an exponential expression. The expression 2^4 is read as "2 to the fourth power" and has a value of 16. Thus, 16 is the fourth power of 2. The word *power* is also used to describe the exponent.

prime factor   A factor that is a prime number.

prime number   A whole number greater than 1 whose only whole number divisors are 1 and the number itself.

probability   For a given event, a number between 0 and 1 (inclusive) that indicates the likelihood of the event occurring. A probability of 0 means the event cannot occur, while a probability of 1 means that it will occur.

product   The result of multiplication.

proper fraction   A fraction whose numerator is a smaller number than the denominator.

proportion   An equation that equates two ratios.

quadrant   Any one of the four sectors of a rectangular coordinate system that is formed by two perpendicular number lines that intersect at the origins of both number lines.

quadrilateral   A four-sided polygon.

quotient   The result of division.

radical expression   An expression that contains radical signs, such as $\sqrt{x}$, $\sqrt[3]{16}$, $\sqrt[4]{xy}$, which indicate roots of a number.

radicand   The number under the radical sign.

radius   The distance from the center of a circle to a point on the circle.

rate   Speed.

ratio   A comparison of the magnitudes of two numbers. The ratio of a to b is $\frac{a}{b}$.

rational numbers   The numbers that can be expressed as $\frac{a}{b}$, where a and b are integers and $b \neq 0$.

ray   A half-line. A ray begins at one point and continues without end on a straight path through another point.

reciprocal   Of a fraction, the inverted form of the fraction. The reciprocal of $\frac{4}{3}$ is $\frac{3}{4}$.

rectangle   A parallelogram that has four right angles.

reflection   Flipping a geometric figure to produce a mirror image of the original copy.

regular polygon   A polygon in which all sides have equal lengths and all angles have equal measures.

rhombus   A parallelogram that has four sides whose lengths are equal.

right angle   One of the angles formed at the intersection of two perpendicular lines. A right angle has a measure of 90°.

right solid   A solid whose sides are perpendicular to both bases.

right triangle   A triangle that contains a right angle.

Roman numerals   Numerals used by the ancient Romans.

root   (1) The value of a radical expression. (2) The solution to an equation.

rotation   The turning of a figure about a point.

scalene triangle   A triangle that has no two sides whose lengths are equal.

scientific notation   A method of writing a number as the product of a decimal number and a power of 10.

semicircle   A half circle.

signed numbers   Numbers that are either positive numbers or negative numbers.

similar triangles   Two triangles that have the same angles.

sphere   A geometric solid whose surface is the set of all points that are an equal distance from a center point.

square   A rhombus in which all angles are right angles.

straight angle   An angle whose measure is 180°.

sum   The result of addition.

supplementary angles   Two angles whose measures sum to 180°.

surface area   The total outside area of a geometric solid.

translation   The sliding of a geometric figure without rotation.

trapezoid   A quadrilateral having exactly one pair of parallel sides.

triangle   A three-sided polygon.

unit conversion   The process of changing a denominate number to an equivalent denominate number that has different units.

unit multiplier   A fraction of denominate numbers whose value is 1.

unity   The state of being 1.

variable   A letter used to represent a number that has not been designated.

vertex   The point where the rays of an angle intersect.

vinculum   A bar drawn over digits in a decimal number to indicate that the digits repeat endlessly. The vinculum in 43.3$\overline{256}$ means that the digits 256 repeat without end as 43.3256256256256….

volume   The space occupied by a geometric solid.

whole numbers   The numbers 0, 1, 2, 3, 4, ….

Index

A

Absolute value, 219

Acute angles, 36

Acute triangles, 322

Addends, 4, 11

Addition
  addends, 4, 11
  algebraic, 234–235, 249–250, 257–258, 286
  algebraic phrases for, 269
  associative property of, 272
  commutative property of, 272
  decimal points in, 5
  in base 2, 411–413
  in order of operations, 104–105, 139–140, 146, 152, 222, 234–235, 257, 286, 291
  inverse operation, 11
  of decimals, 24–25
  of fractions, 100–102
  of like terms, 293–294, 317–318
  of mixed numbers, 112–113
  of money, 5
  of polynomials, 426
  of signed numbers, 219–220, 222–223, 234
  of whole numbers, 4–5
  pattern, 11–12, 20–21
  repeated, 15
  sums, 4, 74, 269
  word problems, 20–21

Addition Property of Equality, 127, 264

Addition rule for equations, 263

Addition-subtraction rule for equations, 127–129, 195

Adjacent angles, 303–304, 416

Advanced graphing, 435–437

Algebra
  algebraic addition
      order of operations for, 234–235, 257–258, 286
      rules for, 234–235, 249–250
  algebraic expressions
      polynomials, 424–428
      terms, 293, 424
  algebraic phrases, 269–270
  algebraic sentences, 283–284
  definition of, 269
  multiplication, designation of, 67
  properties of (*see* Properties of numbers)

Algorithms, 16

Alternate interior angles, 416

Altitude of triangles, 90

Angles
  acute, 36
  adjacent, 303–304, 416
  alternate interior, 416
  bisectors of, 400
  central, 418
  complementary, 304–305
  copying, 399–400
  corresponding, 416
  cosine of, 441–444
  defined, 36
  geometric constructions of, 399–400
  inscribed, 418
  interior, 416
  measuring, 305
  naming, 303

Angles (cont.)
  obtuse, 36
  right, 36
  sine of, 441–444
  straight, 36
  sum of measures of, in triangles, 322–323
  supplementary, 304–305, 416–417
  tangent of, 441–444
  theorems about, 416–417
  trigonometric ratios, 441–442
  trigonometric tables, 442–444
  vertices of, 36

Arcs, major and minor, 418

Arc length of semicircles, 203

Area
  as difference, 84–85
  definition of, 61
  of circles, 192, 363
  of parallelograms, 363–364
  of rectangles, 61–62, 84–85, 148, 363
  of right circular cylinders, 231
  of semicircles, 203
  of trapezoids, 363–364
  of triangles, 90, 363
  units of, 62, 110
  See also Surface area

Arithmetic. *See* Addition; Division; Multiplication; Subtraction

Arrow, 8, 25, 28, 219, 429

Arrowhead, 416

Associative properties, 272

Average (mean)
  in word problems, 88
  of sets, 74–75, 87–88
  overall average, 136–137

Answers to Odd-Numbered Problems

practice   **a.** 2000   **c.** $(8 \times 10{,}000) + (5 \times 1000) + (2 \times 10)$ **e.** Thirty-six million, twenty-five thousand, one hundred three

problem set 1

1. (a) 60,000 (b) 900 (c) 3   **3.** 3,666,766   **5.** 41,000,200,520
7. 407,000,090,742,072   **9.** Five hundred seventeen million, two hundred thirty-six thousand, four hundred twenty-eight   **11.** Thirty-two billion, six hundred fifty-two
13. Six million, forty thousand   **15.** 304,020   **17.** 9405
19. $(5 \times 1000) + (2 \times 100) + (8 \times 10)$ **21.** $(7 \times 10{,}000) + (6 \times 100)$
23. $(4 \times 1000) + (5 \times 1)$ **25.** 294   **27.** \$106.36   **29.** 2942

practice   **a.**

c. 914,470,000

problem set 2

1.

3. 249, 294, 429, 924, 942

5. 83,722,000   **7.** 777,727,757   **9.** 107,047,020   **11.** Seven hundred thirty-one million, two hundred eighty-four thousand, six   **13.** Nine billion, three million, one thousand, two hundred fifty-six   **15.** 70,654   **17.** 9609
19. $(6 \times 10{,}000) + (8 \times 1000) + (3 \times 100) + (1 \times 10) + (2 \times 1)$
21. \$228.58   **23.** 219,258   **25.** 213,820   **27.** 1036   **29.** \$17.32

practice   **a.** \$27.17   **c.** 399   **e.** 369

problem set 3

1. 225,223   **3.** 4,144,444   **5.** 500,000,465,182
7. $(7 \times 10{,}000) + (9 \times 1000) + (3 \times 1)$ **9.** 377   **11.** 1410   **13.** \$10.51   **15.** 521
17. 476   **19.** 85,325   **21.** 320,907   **23.** 2083   **25.** 255,945   **27.** 720,000,000
29.

practice   **a.** \$375.00   **c.** 8 r 21   **e.** 12   **g.** 4

problem set 4

1. 7333   **3.** 47,000,014   **5.** 716,000,000   **7.** $(7 \times 1000) + (6 \times 100) + (5 \times 10)$
9. \$2.79   **11.** 1115 r 42   **13.** 104 r 5   **15.** 91,485   **17.** 163,840   **19.** 210,000
21. 669   **23.** 3182   **25.** 25   **27.** 2,026,416   **29.** 6781

practice　　**a.** 1176 knights

problem set　**1.** 870 people　**3.** 175,000,000 people　**5.** 86,838,887　**7.** 1328 r 4　**9.** 2607 r 13
5　　**11.** 13,662　**13.** 963　**15.** 412　**17.** 469　**19.** 7　**21.** 22
　　　23. $(2 \times 1000) + (1 \times 100) + (9 \times 1)$　**25.** 14,000,042,755　**27.** Five thousand,
　　　twenty-one　**29.** 1,324,261

practice　　**a.** 5000.0742　**c.** Seven thousand and sixty-five thousandths　**e.** 43.8738　**g.** 416.04274

problem set　**1.** 18,819,491　**3.** 4580 runners　**5.** 372,333　**7.** 926.97　**9.** $0.75　**11.** 81 r 2
6　　**13.** 1812 r 26　**15.** 14.11932　**17.** Five hundred four thousand, three hundred twenty-seven
　　　and one million, five hundred ten thousand, five hundred twelve billionths　**19.** 0.000029
　　　21. 722　**23.** $6.25　**25.** 21　**27.** 79.2253　**29.** 94,579

practice　　**a.** ~80; 95.46968　**c.** 1601.48

problem set　**1.** 2806 heroic acts　**3.** 32,600 delegates　**5.** 1.3992　**7.** 36.44　**9.** ~9; 12.067836
7　　**11.** $3.92　**13.** 1129.09　**15.** 91.6486　**17.** −13, −10, −2, 0, 6, 12　**19.** 702.00942
　　　21. Nine thousand, one and three hundred twenty-one thousandths　**23.** 678　**25.** 23　**27.** 9
　　　29. 4407.314

practice　　**a.** 416,200　**c.** 734,260　**e.**

problem set　**1.** 18,014,390 light-years　**3.** 413.6268　**5.** 9.31521　**7.** 0.0165164　**9.** 0.00200304
8　　**11.** 388.086　**13.** 15.5　**15.** 73.2　**17.** 12　**19.** 7.43　**21.** 1463.64　**23.** 31.64
　　　25. 1003.04742　**27.** Four million, sixty-two and thirteen thousandths　**29.** 7371.752

practice　　**a.** $\overleftrightarrow{AB}$ or $\overleftrightarrow{BA}$; $\overrightarrow{AB}$, $\overrightarrow{BA}$; $\overline{AB}$ or $\overline{BA}$　**c.** See student work.

problem set　**1.** 15,237 musicians　**3.** 31.64215　**5.** 417.3652　**7.** 0.07584　**9.** 7.3107
9　　**11.** 2.855　**13.** 92 in.　**15.** 0.05　**17.** 5950　**19.** 433.68515　**21.** 0.0001748
　　　23. Twenty-seven million, three hundred sixteen and eighty-one thousandths　**25.** 1633.343
　　　27. 164.96　**29.** 4.68

practice　　**a.** 45,285, 305,961, 235,725, 84,603, 72,840　**c.** 72,840

problem set　**1.** 1,081,307 people　**3.** 762,000,442.12792　**5.** 118 m　**7.** 0.078848　**9.** 1255.42
10　　**11.** 0.799　**13.** 1.365　**15.** 28　**17.** 0.1　**19.** 503.64　**21.** (a) 300, 4888, 9132,
　　　72,654　(b) 300, 9132, 72,654　(c) 235, 300　(d) 300　**23.** 478.644　**25.** 40,265
　　　27. Four hundred seventy-two and fifty-eight thousandths　**29.** 3.57 cm

practice　　**a.** 1400 kids　**c.** 4 spaces will have 18 kids; 4 spaces will have 19 kids

problem set　**1.** 750 players　**3.** 43.5369 in.　**5.** 112 in.　**7.** 13.2116　**9.** 0.1236　**11.** 36.4011
11　　**13.** 61.8088　**15.** 1.079　**17.** 6.74　**19.** 3.56　**21.** 1600
　　　23. One hundred twenty-three and nine thousand, six hundred twenty-one ten-thousandths
　　　25. 1168.23　**27.** 3.2 cm　**29.** 389.7

practice   **a.** $2 \cdot 2 \cdot 2 \cdot 3 \cdot 5$ **c.** $2 \cdot 2 \cdot 2 \cdot 3 \cdot 3 \cdot 5 \cdot 7$

problem set 12

1. 10,979.04098 in.   **3.** 148 containers   **5.** (a) 302, 9172, 3132, 62,120   (b) 3132
(c) 625, 62,120   (d) 62,120   **7.** 112 ft   **9.** 36,821.1   **11.** 77   **13.** 0.28124
15. 162.1207   **17.** $51.22   **19.** 620.992   **21.** 1087.7   **23.** 4700
25. 961,313,000,025   **27.** Sixteen and five hundred sixty-two ten-thousandths   **29.** 2185.16

practice   **a.** 1, 2, 3, 6   **c.** $22.68

problem set 13

1. 2,076,464 points   **3.** 260 bags   **5.** 210   **7.** 112 cm   **9.** 31.621   **11.** 5036.31
13. (a) $2 \cdot 2 \cdot 2 \cdot 3 \cdot 3 \cdot 5$ (b) $2 \cdot 2 \cdot 2 \cdot 2 \cdot 3 \cdot 3 \cdot 5$
(c) $2 \cdot 2 \cdot 2 \cdot 2 \cdot 2 \cdot 3 \cdot 3 \cdot 5$ **15.** 1, 3, 9   **17.** $385.99   **19.** 25   **21.** 25
23. 2003.23   **25.** 321,617,212.231   **27.** One hundred sixty-one and sixteen thousandths
29. 653.43

practice   **a.** $\frac{54}{18}$ **c.** $\frac{8}{18}$ **e.** $\frac{1}{2}$

problem set 14

1. 440 family meals   **3.** 0.00001197 m   **5.** 45,000.011805 ft   **7.** 150 km
9. (a) $\frac{3}{4}$ (b) $\frac{2}{5}$ (c) $\frac{4}{11}$ (d) $\frac{1}{5}$ **11.** 0.012361   **13.** 1.017
15. (a) $2 \cdot 2 \cdot 2 \cdot 3 \cdot 3 \cdot 5 \cdot 5$ (b) $2 \cdot 3 \cdot 3 \cdot 5 \cdot 5$ (c) $2 \cdot 3 \cdot 3 \cdot 5 \cdot 5$
17. 175.482   **19.** $184.99   **21.** 20   **23.** 814.82   **25.** 1612.3163
27. Three and one hundred twenty-one thousandths   **29.** 2121.2516

practice   **a.** 4.613614   **c.** $0.\overline{3}$ **e.** $\frac{31}{10,000}$

problem set 15

1. 14,907,987 hungry locusts   **3.** 452 bunches with 2 not in a bunch   **5.** 109
7. $0.\overline{5}$ **9.** $\frac{9}{42}$ **11.** 16.9211   **13.** 5539.941   **15.** (a) $2 \cdot 2 \cdot 2 \cdot 2 \cdot 3 \cdot 3 \cdot 5 \cdot 5$
(b) $2 \cdot 3 \cdot 3 \cdot 5 \cdot 5$ (c) $2 \cdot 2 \cdot 3 \cdot 3 \cdot 5 \cdot 5 \cdot 5$ **17.** 186.359   **19.** 0.9719
21. 17   **23.** 2.52   **25.** 4017.336336   **27.** $\frac{17}{20}$ **29.** 7842

practice   **a.** 64   **c.** 625

problem set 16

1. 272 spaces   **3.** 79,027 genes   **5.** (a) 650, 625, 15, 20, 30   (b) 650, 20, 30
7. 162 yd   **9.** 0.57   **11.** $\frac{3}{5}$ **13.** 0.25   **15.** 970.393   **17.** 181,129.6324
19. 1, 2, 5, 10   **21.** $2^5 \cdot 3^2$ **23.** $2^4 \cdot 3^3 \cdot 5^2$ **25.** 437.00621622   **27.** 1495.80
29. 92,679.969

practice   **a.** 12 ft^2 **c.** 84 ft^2

problem set 17

1. 982 mi   **3.** 103,173 ants   **5.** 238   **7.** 78 cm^2 **9.** $0.\overline{1764705882352941}$ or 0.18
11. 0.014 or 0.01   **13.** $2 \cdot 3 \cdot 5$ **15.** 36   **17.** $\frac{3}{4}$ **19.** 484.614   **21.** 168.0448
23. 26.64   **25.** 3.1415927   **27.** $\frac{67}{500}$ **29.** 0.512

practice   **a.** 20   **c.** $\frac{15}{7}$

problem set 18

1. 71,266 peaches   **3.** 44,102,079 rocks   **5.** 29, 31, 37, 41, 43, 47   **7.** 570 cm^2
9. $\frac{12}{25}$ **11.** $\frac{5}{7}$ **13.** 0.941   **15.** 0.846   **17.** $\frac{84}{90}$ **19.** 0.06211378   **21.** 169
23. 10   **25.** 60   **27.** 0.0999   **29.** $\frac{19}{200}$

practice   **a.** $\frac{1}{9}$ **c.** $\frac{2}{5}$

problem set 19

1. Charles's guess: 975.2157 kg; Mary's guess: 975.0137 kg; Mary's guess was closer.
3. 13,292 Romans   **5.** 37   **7.** $\frac{5}{12}$ **9.** $\frac{27}{56}$ **11.** 700 yd^2 **13.** $\frac{2}{3}$ **15.** $\frac{16}{45}$
17. 0.29   **19.** $2^5 \cdot 3^2 \cdot 5 \cdot 7$ **21.** 1.44   **23.** 61   **25.** 28.3057576   **27.** 60
29. 1903.441

practice   **a.** 7, 14, 21, 28, 35, 42, 49   **c.** 2250

problem set 20

1. 36,825 volksmarchers   **3.** 114,012 ragweed plants   **5.** 4, 8, 12, 16, 20, 24, 28, 32, 36, 40
7. $\frac{5}{24}$ **9.** $\frac{1}{4}$ **11.** 484 m^2 **13.** $\frac{3}{4}$ **15.** $\frac{49}{169}$ **17.** 0.46
19. 0.0049, 0.0096, 0.04, 0.1   **21.** 0.33   **23.** 24,200   **25.** $\frac{2}{3125}$
27. One hundred eleven million, five hundred forty-six thousand, four hundred thirty-five   **29.** $\frac{63}{2}$

practice   **a.** $89.\overline{3}$ **c.** $8.74

problem set 21

1. 1,527,474,973.0173   **3.** 1713 times   **5.** 31, 37, 41, 43, 47   **7.** $1357.55   **9.** $\frac{3}{8}$
11. $\frac{1}{5}$ **13.** 380 cm^2 **15.** $\frac{5}{6}$ **17.** 0.65   **19.** $2^3 \cdot 3^2 \cdot 5 \cdot 7$ **21.** 112.404
23. $\frac{19}{20}$ **25.** $\frac{5}{24}$ **27.** 19.27   **29.** 5

practice   **a.** $\frac{2}{35}$ **c.** $\frac{1}{3}$

problem set 22

1. 3,576,999.998662   **3.** 52.4 s   **5.** $1189.\overline{3}$ **7.** $\frac{21}{44}$ **9.** 4   **11.** 357 ft^2 **13.** 5
15. 0.27   **17.** $\frac{3}{8}$ **19.** $\frac{6}{7}$ **21.** 0.064   **23.** 6852.449   **25.** 64   **27.** 1617.29
29. 36

practice   **a.** $\frac{412}{3}$ yd   **c.** 4944 in.   **e.** 20 tons

problem set 23

1. 27,049.4995 cm   **3.** 79 work periods   **5.** (a) 61, 67 (b) 63   **7.** 10 ft   **9.** 21 lb
11. $\frac{6}{5}$ **13.** 170 yd   **15.** $2^6 \cdot 3^2 \cdot 5$ **17.** 0.68   **19.** $\frac{45}{64}$ **21.** $\frac{1}{4}$ **23.** 691.04
25. 60, 120, 180   **27.** $23,937.\overline{6}$ **29.** 70.3489

practice   **a.** 5800 cm   **c.** 48 g

problem set 24

1. 6065 items   **3.** 43 slots   **5.** (a) 23, 29 (b) 24, 28   **7.** 8.59 m   **9.** 17 ft
11. 500 g   **13.** 1   **15.** 104 ft   **17.** 15, 30, 45   **19.** 0.21   **21.** 0.6   **23.** $\frac{3}{4}$
25. $\frac{7}{200}$ **27.** (a) $\frac{9}{42}$ (b) $\frac{24}{42}$ (c) $\frac{11}{42}$ **29.** 900

practice   **a.** 56 cm^2

problem set 25

1. 54,285 students   **3.** 3284 monkeys   **5.** (a) 41, 43, 47 (b) 42, 45, 48   **7.** 4631 cm
9. 0.416 kg   **11.** 1   **13.** $\frac{3}{2}$ **15.** 4 m^2 **17.** $2 \cdot 3^2 \cdot 5 \cdot 7$ **19.** 0.35   **21.** $\frac{1}{2}$
23. 21   **25.** 28   **27.** $\frac{7}{24}$ **29.** 3403.5

practice   **a.** (a) 7 (b) 4 (c) 5 (d) 5.43

problem set 26

1. 4020 lb   **3.** 9.625   **5.** 1525 beanbags   **7.** 1.3615 m   **9.** 1.899 km   **11.** 1
13. 575 m^2 **15.** $\frac{512}{27}$ **17.** 0.54   **19.** $\frac{6}{7}$ **21.** $\frac{9}{16}$ **23.** 48   **25.** 711.999
27. 181.15   **29.** 7.792

practice   **a.** 6 ft^2 **c.** 40 ft^2

problem set   **1.** 2095 units   **3.** 296,002   **5.** 1229   **7.** 720 oz   **9.** 489,900 cm   **11.** 2
27   **13.** 140 ft   **15.** 400 ft^2 **17.** $2^2 \cdot 3^6$ **19.** 0.54   **21.** $\frac{3}{5}$ **23.** $\frac{1}{8}$ **25.** 120
  27. 15,283   **29.** 350

practice   **a.** $\frac{17}{3}$ **c.** $4\frac{2}{3}$ **e.** 157.17

problem set   **1.** 0.03753   **3.** Thirty-three million, seven hundred forty-five thousand, twenty-six   **5.** $1\frac{8}{9}$
28   **7.** ▨▨▨ ▨▨▨ ▨□□   **9.** $\frac{60}{7}$ **11.** 1.9272 m   **13.** $\frac{1}{6}$ **15.** $\frac{4}{3}$
  ▨▨▨ ▨▨▨
  17. 1000 cm   **19.** 5.7   **21.** $\frac{6}{7}$ **23.** $\frac{5}{7}$ **25.** 180   **27.** 260,376.67
  29. (a) 28   (b) 85   (c) 85.5   (d) 87.375

practice   **a.** 30,000 cars

problem set   **1.**   **3.** 164,802 visitors   **5.** 24 trucks   **7.** 40   **9.** $2\frac{1}{7}$
29   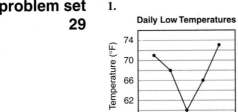   **11.** ▨▨▨ ▨▨▨ ▨□□   **13.** $\frac{20}{3}$
  15. 19.962 g   **17.** $\frac{3}{2}$ **19.** 1050 m^2 **21.** 8.64
  23. $\frac{61}{90}$ **25.** 0.0375   **27.** 52.593
  29. (a) 5   (b) 7, 9   (c) 7   (d) 7

practice   **a.** $\frac{7}{20}$ **c.** $\frac{3}{8}$

problem set   **1.** 200 cars   **3.** 21 elephants   **5.** 46,710 marbles   **7.** $\frac{63}{4}$ **9.** $2\frac{1}{8}$
30   **11.** ▨▨▨ ▨▨▨   **13.** $\frac{55}{7}$ **15.** $\frac{13}{24}$ **17.** $\frac{49}{24}$ **19.** 192.62 m
  ▨▨▨ ▨□□   **21.** $\frac{2}{3}$ **23.** 9.6 m   **25.** $\frac{16}{45}$ **27.** 2.53   **29.** $301\frac{1}{125}$

practice   **a.** 16

problem set   **1.** $50   **3.** 17 hr   **5.** (a) $\frac{20 \text{ kursh}}{1 \text{ riyal}}, \frac{1 \text{ riyal}}{20 \text{ kursh}}$ (b) 800 riyals   **7.** 121   **9.** $3\frac{1}{4}$
31   **11.** 98,700   **13.** $\frac{47}{3}$ **15.** $\frac{1}{9}$ **17.** $\frac{31}{18}$ **19.** $\frac{13}{27}$ **21.** 52   **23.** 16
  25. 4,200,000 cm^2 **27.** $\frac{15}{17}$ **29.** 1.6

practice   **a.** 16

problem set   **1.** $40.09   **3.** (a) 8700   (b) None   (c) 11,200   (d) 11,283.33   **5.** 68,969 fans
32   **7.** 1100   **9.** $5\frac{6}{7}$ **11.** 80   **13.** $\frac{7}{31}$ **15.** $\frac{2}{35}$ **17.** $\frac{4}{5}$ **19.** 0.0024081   **21.** $16\frac{4}{25}$
  23. 425 ft^2 **25.** $\frac{52}{61}$ **27.** 0.74   **29.** $\frac{1}{4}$

practice   **a.** 6(5280)(12) in. = 380,160 in.

problem set   **1.** 6475 tickets   **3.** 94   **5.** $91.60   **7.** 140   **9.** $5\frac{5}{7}$ **11.** 15   **13.** $\frac{39}{40}$ **15.** 40
33   **17.** 10   **19.** $\frac{1}{6}$ **21.** $50\frac{1}{20}$ **23.** 90(3)(12) in. = 3240 in.   **25.** $\frac{450}{(3)(3)}$ yd^2 = 50 yd^2
  27. $2^6 \cdot 5 \cdot 13$ **29.** 4.25

practice   **a.** $5\frac{3}{10}$ **c.** 8 yd per s, $\frac{1}{8}$ s per yd

problem set 34

1. 311 boxes   3. 150 cars   5. 8 ft per s, $\frac{1}{8}$ s per ft   7. 0.825   9. $12\frac{1}{3}$ 11. 840
13. $\frac{15}{16}$ 15. 16   17. 14,300   19. $11\frac{1}{3}$ 21. $15\frac{3}{20}$
23. $132(100)(100)$ cm^2 = 1,320,000 cm^2 25. 90   27. 345 ft^2 29. 4.6

practice   **a.** $2\frac{8}{15}$

problem set 35

1. The second measurement was larger by 0.0033 m.   3. 20 parades   5. $\frac{1}{16}$ 7. $42\frac{4}{5}$
9. 1800   11. $\frac{2}{3}$ 13. 2   15. $72\frac{1}{24}$ 17. $5\frac{3}{7}$ 19. $\frac{17}{3}$ 21. 4
23. $\frac{100}{9}$ yd = $11\frac{1}{9}$ yd   25. $4(5280)(5280)$ ft^2 = 111,513,600 ft^2 27. 740 cm^2 29. 12.875

practice   **a.** $\frac{40 \text{ cents}}{2 \text{ ounces}}, \frac{2 \text{ ounces}}{40 \text{ cents}}$ **c.** \$10

problem set 36

1. 214 lb   3. \$997.80   5. (a) $\frac{40 \text{ skins}}{8 \text{ liras}}, \frac{8 \text{ liras}}{40 \text{ skins}}$ (b) 1000 skins   (c) 40 liras   7. 0.8917
9. $5\frac{1}{4}$ 11. 1400   13. $\frac{13}{20}$ 15. 30   17. $8591\frac{7}{15}$ 19. $2\frac{19}{28}$ 21. 89,525
23. $40\frac{1}{25}$ 25. 24   27. $\frac{187,625.8}{(100)(1000)}$ kg = 1.876258 kg   29. 114 cm

practice   **a.** 6   **c.** 20

problem set 37

1. (a) $\frac{180 \text{ dollars}}{10 \text{ items}}, \frac{10 \text{ items}}{180 \text{ dollars}}$ (b) \$450   (c) 50 items   3. \$10,000,000   5. 10   7. 6
9. $\frac{3}{7}$ 11. $13\frac{2}{7}$ 13. $\frac{5}{8}$ 15. $10\frac{7}{8}$ 17. $751\frac{1}{3}$ 19. $517\frac{11}{16}$ 21. 575.2782
23. $\frac{1}{6}$ 25. 19   27. $10(5280)12$ in. = 633,600 in.   29. 0.85

practice

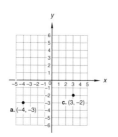

problem set 38

1. $\frac{56 \text{ dollars}}{7 \text{ hours}}, \frac{7 \text{ hours}}{56 \text{ dollars}}$; \$320   3. 435,204 points   5. 4   7. $\frac{1}{5}$ 9. $173\frac{2}{3}$ 11. $\frac{14}{17}$
13. 14   15. $5\frac{13}{40}$ 17. $27\frac{1}{8}$ 19. 272.4   21. 2, 3, 5, 10   23. 18
25. $\frac{400}{(12)(12)}$ ft^2 ≈ 2.78 ft^2 27. 146 yd   29.

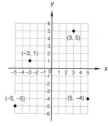

practice   **a.** 2   **c.** $\frac{1}{4}$

problem set 39

1. 16 hiding places   3. (a) 0.5 m   (b) 5.6 m   (c) 5.5 m   (d) 5.47 m   5. 24   7. $85\frac{3}{5}$
9. $\frac{11}{15}$ 11. 9   13. $9\frac{5}{21}$ 15. $31\frac{4}{7}$ 17. 3.72832   19. $\frac{3}{2}$ 21. 19   23. 7.5
25. 9   27. 566.5 ft^2 29. $14\frac{29}{200}$

practice   **a.** $\frac{77}{5}$ **c.** 15

problem set 40 **1.** 473 skiers **3.** 608 buses **5.** $13\frac{2}{3}$ **7.** 3780 **9.** $5\frac{1}{3}$ **11.** 9 **13.** $660\frac{7}{10}$
15. $395\frac{7}{8}$ **17.** 28,600 **19.** 4 **21.** 17 **23.** $\frac{11}{14}$ **25.** 5 **27.** $51\frac{157}{200}$
29. 722 in.^{2}

practice **a.** $64

problem set 41 **1.** 2.6 in. **3.** 60 compartments **5.** 33.1 lb **7.** $16\frac{2}{5}$ **9.** 840 **11.** $\frac{4}{3}$ **13.** 60
15. 35 **17.** 19 **19.** 286 **21.** 6601.91 **23.** $9\frac{29}{45}$ **25.** 44 **27.** 291 m^2
29. 0.79

practice **a.** 3 **c.** 13

problem set 42 **1.** 600 units per hour **3.** $37,000 **5.** **7.** $13\frac{3}{7}$ **9.** $\frac{1}{16}$
11. 4 **13.** 9 **15.** $\frac{1}{12}$ **17.** 178
19. 9232.51 **21.** $9\frac{1}{18}$ **23.** 47
25. 23 **27.** 4 **29.** 1135 ft^2

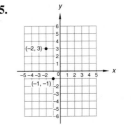

practice **a.** $\frac{34}{9}$ **c.** $\frac{65}{44}$

problem set 43 **1.** The second guess was greater by 0.066268. **3.** $\frac{40 \text{ dollars}}{1 \text{ bunch}}, \frac{1 \text{ bunch}}{40 \text{ dollars}}$; $4000 **5.** 200 astronauts
7. $18\frac{1}{15}$ **9.** $\frac{9}{2}$ **11.** 300 **13.** $\frac{3}{8}$ **15.** $46\frac{2}{15}$ **17.** 2172.93 **19.** 1 **21.** 54
23. $\frac{2}{3}$ **25.** $\frac{75}{46}$ **27.** 61 **29.** 140 cm

practice **a.** 5 **c.** 9

problem set 44 **1.** $\frac{78 \text{ pots}}{312 \text{ dollars}}, \frac{312 \text{ dollars}}{78 \text{ pots}}$; $1600 **3.** 7,134,108 rabbits **5.** **7.** 294
9. 20 **11.** $\frac{15}{14}$ **13.** 49 **15.** 6 **17.** $\frac{66}{7}$
19. $\frac{49}{75}$ **21.** $1\frac{1}{2}$ **23.** 5.549 **25.** 33
27. 3(5280)(12) in. = 190,080 in. **29.** 6

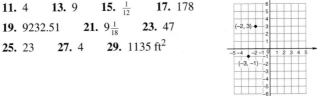

practice **a.** 240 cubes **c.** 70 m^3

problem set 45 **1.** 176 teachers **3.** $\frac{1 \text{ avocado}}{79 \text{ cents}}, \frac{79 \text{ cents}}{1 \text{ avocado}}$; 30 avocados **5.** **7.** 756 ft^3
9. 18 **11.** $\frac{41}{100}$ **13.** 15 **15.** $\frac{91}{15}$ **17.** $\frac{49}{69}$
19. $1\frac{9}{16}$ **21.** $22\frac{61}{90}$ **23.** 16,105,000
25. 17(1000)(100) cm = 1,700,000 cm **27.** 8
29. 120(5280)(5280) ft^2 = 3,345,408,000 ft^2

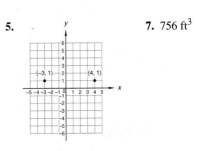

practice **a.** $\frac{3}{14}$

problem set 46 **1.** $\frac{4 \text{ large ones}}{40 \text{ dollars}}, \frac{40 \text{ dollars}}{4 \text{ large ones}}$; $1200 **3.** 29.6 min **5.** 3150 **7.** $\frac{1}{2}$ **9.** 9 **11.** 3
13. $7\frac{5}{6}$ **15.** 74 **17.** 44,830 **19.** $\frac{243}{50}$ **21.** $\frac{1}{5}$ **23.** $\frac{11}{50}$ **25.** 72
27. 1850 cm^3 **29.** 10 × 10 × 10 × 10 × 10 × 10 × 10 × 10 × 10

practice   **a.** 16   **c.** 3

problem set 47

1. 132   **3.** 420 frogs   **5.** 84 in.^{3} **7.** 144   **9.** 6   **11.** 47   **13.** 34   **15.** $476\frac{5}{8}$
17. 663.019   **19.** 12   **21.** $\frac{152}{115}$ **23.** $\frac{4}{15}$ **25.** 216   **27.** 0.0625   **29.** $\frac{7}{2000}$

practice   **a.** $\frac{7}{1}$ **c.** 10

problem set 48

1. 40 boxes   **3.** $\frac{14\text{ games}}{70\text{ dollars}}$, $\frac{70\text{ dollars}}{14\text{ games}}$; 40 games   **5.** 25   **7.** 186   **9.** $12\frac{16}{25}$ **11.** 21
13. 45   **15.** 12   **17.** $\frac{46}{35}$ **19.** 5   **21.** $105\frac{3}{10}$ **23.** $\frac{124}{47}$ **25.** 3   **27.** $10\frac{1}{4}$
29. 340 cm^3

practice   **a.** 40 ft^2

problem set 49

1. $\frac{40\text{ pecks}}{640\text{ dollars}}$, $\frac{640\text{ dollars}}{40\text{ pecks}}$; \$1600   **3.** 62,640 flowers   **5.** 512.9 ft^2 **7.** $\frac{5}{2}$ **9.** $26\frac{5}{8}$ **11.** 16
13. $\frac{87}{40}$ **15.** 27   **17.** $\frac{1}{16}$ **19.** $7\frac{3}{16}$ **21.** 2.5296   **23.** $\frac{81}{95}$ **25.** 243   **27.** 9
29. $\frac{250,001}{(100)(1000)}$ km = 2.50001 km

practice   **a.** 4.76×10^5 **c.** 3.056×10^7 **e.** 406,000

problem set 50

1. 1600 certificates   **3.** $\frac{40\text{ good ones}}{12\text{ dollars}}$, $\frac{12\text{ dollars}}{40\text{ good ones}}$; 11 good ones   **5.** $\frac{49}{15}$ **7.** 120
9. (a) 4.203742×10^6 (b) 5.6305×10^{-3} **11.** 18   **13.** 32   **15.** $\frac{3}{4}$ **17.** $121\frac{9}{14}$
19. 8   **21.** 1,222,240   **23.** 17   **25.** 3   **27.** 2200 ft^2 **29.** $24\frac{221}{360}$

practice   **a.** 0.2   **c.** 0.42

problem set 51

1. 85,251   **3.** 250 tons   **5.** 1350 m^2 **7.** 105   **9.** $\frac{26}{5}$ **11.** 33   **13.** $23\frac{6}{7}$
15. $2\frac{9}{10}$ **17.** 46   **19.** $\frac{11}{12}$ **21.** $3\frac{19}{30}$ **23.** 36.981   **25.** $\frac{46}{17}$ **27.** 8
29. (a) 9.8213×10^7 (b) 0.00003207

practice   **a.** $\frac{3}{5}$

problem set 52

1. 5643 attendees   **3.** $\frac{15}{\$315}$, $\frac{\$315}{15}$; \$2940   **5.** 276 ft^3 **7.** $2\frac{3}{20}$ **9.** $\frac{7}{8}$ **11.** 200
13. $2\frac{5}{6}$ **15.** 61   **17.** $\frac{8}{7}$ **19.** 33   **21.** $\frac{32}{9}$ **23.** $3\frac{7}{20}$ **25.** $\frac{308}{51}$ **27.** 35
29. $\frac{2162.18}{(100)(1000)}$ kg = 0.0216218 kg

practice   **a.** 0.64   **c.** 0.05

problem set 53

1. 0.008825 in.   **3.** 84.4 points   **5.** 4200 yd^3 **7.** 68   **9.** 6000
11. (a) 0.24   (b) 13.44   **13.** $\frac{157}{22}$ **15.** $\frac{45}{22}$ **17.** 17   **19.** $1\frac{3}{4}$ **21.** $\frac{19}{18}$ **23.** $11\frac{1}{2}$
25. $\frac{203}{48}$ **27.** 72   **29.** $625(3)(3)(12)(12)$ in.^{2} = 810,000 in.^{2}

practice   **a.** $\frac{8}{7}$ **c.** 16

problem set 54

1. 155,982,014   **3.** 7700 troops   **5.** $0.1\overline{6}$ **7.** 660 m^3 **9.** $\frac{3}{8}$ **11.** (a) 0.772
(b) 386   **13.** 91   **15.** $\frac{9}{4}$ **17.** 42   **19.** $7\frac{5}{7}$ **21.** 0   **23.** $303,501.\overline{6}$ **25.** $\frac{65}{138}$
27. 216   **29.** 5

practice   **a.** 0.125   **c.** $\frac{11}{50}$

problem set 55
1. $\frac{70 \text{ items}}{\$3500}, \frac{\$3500}{70 \text{ items}}$; $36,000   3. 698,042 crones and curmudgeons   5. 0.125
7. (a) 0.37   (b) 48.82   9. 5200 cm^3 11. 84   13. 65   15. $\frac{45}{14}$ 17. 12
19. $\frac{32}{15}$ 21. 12   23. 6202.903   25. $\frac{35}{44}$ 27. $\frac{23}{32}$ 29. 6

practice
a. $\frac{34}{9}$

problem set 56
1. (a) $\frac{\$780}{10 \text{ tires}}, \frac{10 \text{ tires}}{\$780}$ (b) $4524   (c) 2 tires   3. 1052 lb   5. (a) 0.375   (b) 37.5%
(c) $\frac{19}{50}$ (d) 0.38   7. 80   9. $\frac{15}{19}$ 11. 44   13. $\frac{118}{17}$ 15. $\frac{15}{2}$ 17. $\frac{21}{10}$
19. 31   21. 14   23. 18,188.318   25. $\frac{39}{8}$ 27. $\frac{7}{8}$ 29. 26

practice
a. $\frac{175}{8}$ c. $\frac{395}{136}$

problem set 57
1. $\frac{80 \text{ trees}}{\$3520}, \frac{\$3520}{80 \text{ trees}}$; $440   3. 1072   5. (a) $\frac{19}{25}$ (b) 0.76   (c) $\frac{3}{5}$ (d) 60%
7. $\frac{10,000}{(12)(12)}$ ft$^2 \approx$ 69.44 ft^2 9. $\frac{4}{5}$ 11. 3   13. 1040 ft^3 15.
17. $\frac{10}{3}$ 19. $\frac{27}{28}$ 21. 28   23. $4\frac{9}{40}$ 25. 9156.949
27. $\frac{22}{15}$ 29. (a) 13   (b) 3.92×10^{-2}

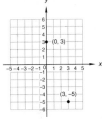

practice
a. 40 mph

problem set 58
1. 27,000.00666   3. $\frac{53 \text{ new ones}}{\$742}, \frac{\$742}{53 \text{ new ones}}$; $350   5. (a) 65 mph   (b) 8 hr
7. (a) 1.06×10^8 (b) 0.0000000413   9. $\frac{8}{9}$ 11. $\frac{136}{7}$ 13. 900 in.^{3} 15. 12
17. $3\frac{11}{42}$ 19. 53   21. $4\frac{1}{5}$ 23. 0.21866   25. $\frac{1}{10}$ 27. $\frac{4}{7}$ 29. 25

practice
a. $\frac{1}{30}$ c. $\frac{1}{2}$

problem set 59
1. 21   3. 7245 lb   5. (a) $\frac{4}{25}$ (b) 0.16   (c) 0.8   (d) 80%   7. 80   9. 0.7
11. $\frac{65}{6}$ 13. (a) 1.92   (b) 86.4   15. $\frac{9}{8}$ 17. $\frac{15}{4}$ 19. 47   21. $6\frac{2}{3}$ 23. 1.2012
25. $20,383.\overline{6}$ 27. $2\frac{9}{10}$ 29. $\frac{675}{22}$

practice
a. 200 m   c. $10,000\pi$ m$^2 \approx$ 31,400 m^2

problem set 60
1. $\frac{560 \text{ red ones}}{7 \text{ pesos}}, \frac{7 \text{ pesos}}{560 \text{ red ones}}$; 4800 red ones   3. 2 mph   5. (a) $\frac{18}{25}$ (b) 72%   (c) 0.6   (d) 60%
7. 700   9. $0.58\overline{3}$ 11. $\frac{21}{4}$ 13. (a) 0.053   (b) 1.325   15. $\frac{128}{5}$ 17. $\frac{25}{14}$
19. 48   21. $\frac{85}{12}$ 23. 11.1924   25. $2602.\overline{142857}$ 27. $\frac{5}{48}$
29. (a) $(-2, -1)$ (b) $(-4, 2)$ (c) $(2, 0)$

practice
a. 1   c. $\frac{56}{75}$

problem set 61
1. $\frac{6900 \text{ ft}}{230 \text{ s}}, \frac{230 \text{ s}}{6900 \text{ ft}}$; $\frac{10,000}{3}$ s   3. 20 hr   5. (a) $\frac{11}{50}$ (b) 22%   (c) 0.84   (d) 84%   7. 120
9. 0.83   11. $\frac{147}{40}$ 13. 184 in.^{2} 15. $\frac{18}{5}$ 17. $\frac{49}{4}$ 19. $\frac{13}{7}$ 21. 7.9443
23. $10\frac{19}{20}$ 25. $\frac{5}{3}$ 27. $\frac{26}{35}$ 29. (a) 0.312   (b) 15.6

practice
a. 1150 racers

problem set 62
1. $\frac{14 \text{ big ones}}{9 \text{ crowns}}, \frac{9 \text{ crowns}}{14 \text{ big ones}}$; 560 big ones   3. $\frac{1}{5}$ 5. 70 students   7. (a) $\frac{3}{25}$ (b) 12%   (c) $0.8\overline{3}$
(d) $83.\overline{3}$%   9. 790   11. 0.875   13. $\frac{77}{20}$ 15. 28π ft $\approx$ 87.92 ft;

196π ft^2 ≈ 615.44 ft^2 **17.** $\frac{36}{5}$ **19.** $\frac{21}{23}$ **21.** $\frac{45}{49}$ **23.** 46   **25.** $10\frac{9}{10}$ **27.** $\frac{5}{16}$

29. (a) 0.0000309   (b) 1.9×10^4

practice   **a.** 2.4 hr

problem set 63

1. 70 min   **3.** 10 hr   **5.** 80 e-mail messages   **7.** (a) 0.000309   (b) 6.103×10^6

9. $\frac{3}{25}$ **11.** $\frac{24}{5}$ **13.** 2200 in.^{3} **15.** $\frac{16}{5}$ **17.** $\frac{7}{24}$ **19.** $\frac{22}{3}$ **21.** 32   **23.** $10\frac{17}{30}$

25. 2.6939   **27.** $\frac{13}{4}$ **29.** 252

practice   **a.** 29.7 cm

problem set 64

1. 64 mi   **3.** 124 mi   **5.** 2 kielbasas   **7.** (a) 1.03×10^4 (b) 601,900,000   **9.** $\frac{1}{16}$

11. (a) 14π ft ≈ 43.96 ft   (b) 49π ft^2 ≈ 153.86 ft^2 **13.** 304 ft^3 **15.** $\frac{15}{2}$ **17.** $\frac{11}{18}$

19. 6   **21.** $\frac{58}{21}$ **23.** $\frac{35}{48}$ **25.** 38,522   **27.**   **29.** 46

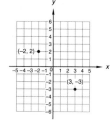

practice   **a.** 2   **c.** $m = \frac{36}{5}$, $p = \frac{28}{5}$

problem set 65

1. 1050 pixies   **3.** 1600 jigsaw puzzles   **5.** (a) $\frac{9}{50}$ (b) 18%   **7.** $0.8\overline{3}$ **9.** $\frac{91}{12}$

11. (a) 75.4 dkm   (b) 397 dkm^2 **13.** 1536 in.^{2} **15.** $\frac{9}{5}$ **17.** $\frac{15}{13}$ **19.** $\frac{31}{17}$ **21.** $\frac{61}{42}$

23. 2.3556   **25.** $250.8\overline{714285}$ **27.** $\frac{75}{17}$ **29.** (a) 0.403   (b) 48.36

practice   **a.** 22,000 Holsteins

problem set 66

1. 4 days   **3.** 145 responses   **5.** 28 thespians   **7.** (a) $\frac{73}{100}$ (b) 0.73   **9.** $\frac{2}{3}$

11. (a) 20   (b) 842   **13.** (a) 43.98 mm   (b) 111.25 mm^2 **15.** 4400 ft^3 **17.** $\frac{48}{5}$

19. $\frac{417}{512}$ **21.** 3   **23.** 16   **25.** $9\frac{53}{60}$ **27.** $\frac{1}{5}$ **29.** $\frac{1,000,000}{(12)(12)}$ ft^2 ≈ 6944.44 ft^2

practice   **a.** $1.44 per dozen

problem set 67

1. 250 fans   **3.** $\frac{1}{7}$ **5.** 370 Muslims   **7.** (a) 0.4   (b) 40%   **9.** 240   **11.** $0.\overline{3}$

13. $s = \frac{25}{6}$, $t = \frac{65}{6}$ **15.** 240   **17.** 2   **19.** $\frac{11}{26}$ **21.** 34   **23.** $\frac{281}{28}$ **25.** 9040.359

27. $\frac{817}{672}$ **29.** (a) 1.39×10^6 (b) 426,000,000,000,000,000

practice   **a.** $a = 40\%$, $b = 420$ **c.**

problem set 68

1. 3200 Sumerians **3.** 20 mph **5.** 270 comedies **7.** $a = 800$, $b = 1200$, $c = 60\%$
9. 244.8 **11.** 0.6 **13.** $\frac{437}{10}$ **15.** 54,000 m^3 **17.** $\frac{3}{28}$ **19.** $\frac{121}{338}$ **21.** 2
23. 21 **25.** $14\frac{1}{4}$ **27.** $\frac{13}{24}$ **29.** $\frac{75{,}000}{(100)(1000)}$ kg = 0.75 kg

practice **a.**  -2 **c.** 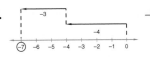 -5 **e.** -12 **g.** -19

problem set 69

1. 1750 beasts **3.** 2400 costumes **5.** Shanna **7.** (a) $\frac{1}{4}$ (b) 0.25 **9.** 410
11. $0.8\overline{3}$ **13.** (a) 91.4 ft (b) 557 ft^2
15. -4 **17.** 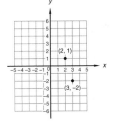 -7
19. 5 **21.** $\frac{485}{204}$ **23.** 30 **25.** $9\frac{3}{4}$ **27.**   **29.** 40

practice **a.** -10 **c.** -16

problem set 70

1. $0.14 per oz, $0.09 per oz; small can **3.** $6400 **5.** 9.2×10^{-6} **7.** 540
9. 93.75% **11.** (a) 102.8 in. (b) 714 in.^{2} **13.** 6 days **15.** $\frac{35}{12}$ **17.** $\frac{207}{152}$ **19.** -2
21. 4 **23.** $\frac{73}{24}$ **25.** 0.020757 **27.** $\frac{3}{2}$ **29.** 108

practice **a.** $\frac{1}{27}$ **c.** $\frac{16}{81}$

problem set 71

1. 4 students **3.** $10.90 per dozen **5.** 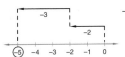 20% **7.** $c = 8\frac{7}{16}$, $d = 11\frac{1}{5}$
9. 0.4 **11.** (a) 92 ft (b) 427 ft^2
13. $\frac{60}{13}$ **15.** $\frac{44}{285}$ **17.** $\frac{256}{2401}$
19. $\frac{5}{12}$ **21.** -15 **23.** 110
25. 60 **27.** $14\frac{1}{3}$ **29.** $\frac{1378}{93}$

practice **a.** 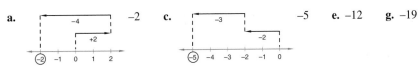 **c.**

problem set 72

1. 25¢, $2.50 **3.** 3500 **5.** $762 per year, $616.67 per year, $600 per year; Five years of coverage for $3000 is the least expensive insurance plan. **7.** 1200
9. 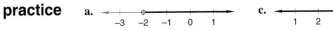 **11.** 2.16×10^8 **13.** (a) 88.42 in. (b) 407 in.^{2}
15. $5\frac{5}{6}$ **17.** $\frac{11}{10}$ **19.** $\frac{2}{3}$ **21.** -7 **23.** 111 **25.** $\frac{5}{3}$ **27.** $\frac{1050}{17}$ **29.** $\frac{2}{5}$

practice   a. 9420 ft³

problem set 73

1. 2160   3. 2200 biochemists   5. $17 million   7. ●————|————|————|————○————→
                                                         3   4   5   6   7

9. 1,000,000(100)(100) cm² = 10,000,000,000 cm²   11. 0.00000604

13. (a) 100 m (b) 400 m²   15. 62.8 in.³   17. $3\frac{9}{16}$ 19. $\frac{41}{32}$ 21. $\frac{1}{3}$ 23. −1

25. $\frac{47}{16}$ 27. 0.060384   29. 75 hound dogs

practice   a. +7

problem set 74

1. 5390   3. 14,700 winners   5.

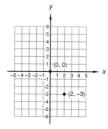

7. ←————○————|————|————|————→
       −13 −12 −11 −10 −9

9. (a) 0.37 (b) 37%

11. 0.25   13. 8925 m³

15. $\frac{22}{7}$ 17. 1   19. $\frac{17}{25}$ 21. 0   23. −10   25. 0.3996   27. 42,638

29.

y
6
5
4
3
2
1 (0, 0)
———————————————— x
−5 −4 −3 −2 −1   1 2 3 4 5
−1
−2
−3 ● (2, −3)
−4
−5
−6

practice   a. 44 huge measures

problem set 75

1. $8666.67   3. 900 doubters   5. 75 s

7.   25% { 85 allow pets }
                                        340 apartment complexes
      75% { 255 do not allow pets }   { 340 apartment complexes } 100%

      Parts of Total   Total

9. ←————|————|————○————|————→   11. (a) $\frac{71}{100}$ (b) 71%   13. 0.6   15. 150.83 yd³
       −37 −36 −35 −34 −33

17. $\frac{1,000,000}{(12)(5280)}$ mi ≈ 15.78 mi   19. $\frac{2}{3}$ 21. $\frac{3}{4}$ 23. −9   25. $\frac{10}{3}$ 27. 547,600

29. $\frac{83}{63}$

practice   a. 8 × 10¹⁰   c. 4.2 × 10¹³

problem set 76

1. $\frac{3}{29}$ 3. 3 hr   5. 48 teams   7. 288   9. ←————|————|————|————●————|————→
                                                              1   2   3   4   5

11. (a) $\frac{16}{81}$ (b) $\frac{8}{9}$ 13. (a) 85.68 ft (b) 401.04 ft²   15. 3454 m³   17. 3

19. 8 × 10¹⁰   21. 2.1 × 10⁻¹   23. −10   25. $\frac{57}{5}$ 27. 36,385   29. 536

practice   a. 135   c.

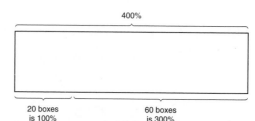

problem set 77

1. 105 laws   **3.** 20 mph   **5.** $\frac{35}{2}$ cups of flour   **7.** 250%

9.   **11.** (a) 0.52 (b) 52%   **13.** 1200   **15.** 1.04×10^9

17. $\frac{11}{6}$ **19.** 1.2×10^{10} **21.** 7.5×10^{75} **23.** 1   **25.** $\frac{181}{24}$ **27.** 15,251.069

29. 401

practice   **a.** –3   **c.** 81

problem set 78

1. 240,000 cherubs   **3.** 5 hr   **5.** 351 decorations

7. 2000%

9. (number line from –4 to 0)

11. 10,300,000,000   **13.** 4368 in.^{3}

15. 3140 ft^3, 1256 ft^2 **17.** $\frac{243}{80}$

19. $\frac{5}{11}$ **21.** 15

23. 1.0428×10^9 **25.** –18

27. $\frac{11}{32}$ **29.** $-\frac{677}{64}$

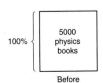

practice   **a.** 7   **c.** 7

problem set 79

1. 676 gal   **3.** 99,000 exotic ones   **5.** 160%   **7.** 500%

9. (number line from –1 to 3)

11.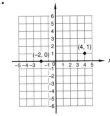

13. 821.25 m^3 **15.** $\frac{256}{15}$

17. (a) –2 (b) –2 (c) 2   **19.** 8

21. 4   **23.** 82,965.6685   **25.** $\frac{81}{256}$ **27.** 98   **29.** 1.0×10^8 cm

practice   **a.** 18,360 acorns

problem set 80

1. 14 eggs   **3.** 8 hr   **5.** 30 students   **7.** 7500

9. 50%

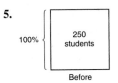

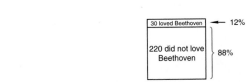

11. (number line from –3 to 1)   **13.** $90,000(5280)(5280)$ ft$^2 = 2,509,056,000,000$ ft^2

15. 360 ft^3 **17.** $\frac{1}{9}$ **19.** (a) –20 (b) –20 (c) 20   **21.** 1.26 × 10^3 **23.** $\frac{9}{64}$
25. 5   **27.** 3.4227   **29.** 1241

practice   **a.** –12   **c.** 12   **e.** 2   **g.** –2   **i.** –48   **k.** negative

problem set 81

1. 990 sheep   **3.** 560 oz   **5.** 144 yd   **7.** 450%   **9.** (a) 1.4 (b) 140%
11. 2400 ft^3 **13.** 45 ants   **15.** $\frac{72}{5}$ **17.** (a) –9 (b) 9 (c) –9   **19.** 26
21. –10   **23.** –2   **25.** 20   **27.** 5 × 10^{-7} **29.** 52

practice   **a.** –4   **c.** –3

problem set 82

1. 378 patients   **3.** 1440 were prejudiced.   **5.** 30%   **7.** 55
9.

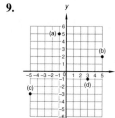

$\left. \begin{array}{c} \text{105 did not love bubble gum} \end{array} \right\}$ 35%   195 students

$\left. \begin{array}{c} \text{195 students loved bubble gum} \end{array} \right\}$ 65%

100% { 300 students }   Before   After

11. 1.08 × 10^5
13. 41,500 cm^3
15. $\frac{3}{16}$ **17.** $\frac{81}{44}$
19. (a) 18 (b) –18 (c) –18

21. 15   **23.** –14   **25.** 7 × 10^2 **27.** (a) $x = 5$, $y = 4$ (b) $x = -3$, $y = 2$
(c) $x = 4$, $y = -4$ (d) $x = -4$, $y = -4$ **29.** –24

practice   **a.** 49 hr

problem set 83

1. 600   **3.** 385 mi   **5.** $1.50 per gal   **7.** ⟨———○———→ –3 –2 –1 0 1   **9.** 175%
11. 0.000000000091   **13.** 190 m^2 **15.** $\frac{31}{20}$ **17.** 6 × 10^{-27}
19. (a) –6 (b) –6 (c) 6   **21.** –12   **23.** 69   **25.** $\frac{197}{14}$ **27.** 42   **29.** –5

practice   **a.** –2   **c.** Answers may vary. See student work.

problem set 84

1. 32,500,000 school-age children   **3.** 147 philosophers   **5.** ←——●———→ –8 –7 –6 –5 –4
7. 40   **9.**

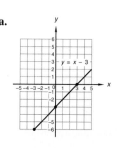

11. 26.28 ft^3 **13.** 3   **15.** $\frac{11}{70}$ **17.** –3
19. Answers may vary. See student work.
21. (a) –20 (b) –20 (c) 20   **23.** –2.54
25. $\frac{1547}{220}$ **27.** $\frac{109}{200}$ **29.** $-9\frac{1}{2}$

practice   **a.**

$y = x - 3$

problem set 85

1. .506 **3.** 340 mi **5.** $1.05 **7.** 192 **9.** 250% **11.** 52,500 cm^3

13.
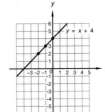

15. $\frac{5}{87}$ **17.** $\frac{23}{24}$ **19.** 6 **21.** 89 **23.** –9 **25.** –10

27. 6×10^{17} **29.** –48

practice **a.** $x + (-4)$ **c.** $-x + (-3)$

problem set 86

1. 40 mph **3.** 8000 screaming fans **5.** (a) $15.80 (b) $63.20

7.

9. 598 **11.** (a) 0.8 (b) 80% **13.** 1371 in.^{3}

15. $113\frac{1}{12}$ **17.** $\frac{17}{40}$ **19.** $-\frac{5}{28}$ **21.** Answers may vary. See student work. **23.** $\frac{1633}{5}$

25. 120 **27.** negative **29.** 31

practice **a.** 10,000

problem set 87

1. 70 mph **3.** 3800 masterpieces **5.** 77 hr **7.**

9. 1430 **11.** (a) $\frac{1}{2}N$ (b) $2x$ (c) $(x)(-x)$ (d) $\frac{2}{5}\sqrt{x}$ **13.** 310 **15.** 28 m^3

17.
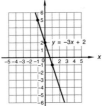

19. $\frac{103}{9}$ **21.** $\frac{15}{16}$ **23.** $-\frac{7}{345}$ **25.** (a) –3 (b) –3 (c) 3

27. 8 **29.** 11

practice **a.** 720 m^2

problem set 88

1. $\frac{1}{8}$ **3.** 1000 delegates **5.** 21.08 **7.**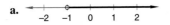

9. 160% **11.** 0.35 **13.** 216.52 cm^2 **15.** 6×10^4 **17.**

19. –3 **21.** $\frac{9}{40}$ **23.** –10 **25.** $\frac{25}{12}$ **27.** 5 **29.** –4

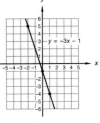

practice **a.**  **c.**

problem set 89

1. $2400 **3.** 14,000 **5.** (a) $2N - 16$ (b) $-3(N + 5)$ (c) $-N - 4$ (d) $5(2N + 6)$

7.

9. 520 **11.** 4 **13.** 274.2 m^2 **15.** 1264 yd^3

17. 4 more dunkers **19.** $-\frac{1}{2}$ **21.** $\frac{3}{5}$ **23.** Answers may vary. See student work.

25. $\frac{33}{4}$ **27.** 6 **29.** 4

practice   **a.** $6x + 5 = 21$ **c.** -10

problem set 90

1. $8325   **3.** $864,000   **5.** (a) $3N - 11$ (b) $-5(N - 2)$ (c) $-3(N - 4)$ **7.** 5

9.
0. 1 2 3 4   **11.** 195   **13.** 657 ft^3 **15.** 536.02 ft^2 **17.** 7500 cm^2

19. 3   **21.** -3 **23.** $-\frac{17}{15}$ **25.** $\frac{13}{5}$ **27.** 15   **29.** -30

practice   **a.** -22

problem set 91

1. 56,000 seats   **3.** $50,400   **5.** 3   **7.** -25

9. ←———————→
  -7 -6 -5 -4 -3 **11.** 80%   **13.**

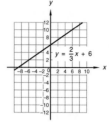

15. 18,283 cm^2 **17.** $-\frac{13}{7}$

19. Answers may vary. See student work.

21. 40   **23.** 36   **25.** -33 **27.** $\frac{49}{15}$

29. 11

practice   **a.** $5 < \sqrt{30} < 6$

problem set 92

1. 42   **3.** -8 **5.** ←———○———→
              2 3 4 5 6   **7.** 230   **9.** $7 < \sqrt{56} < 8$

11. 25%, 125%, 80%   **13.**

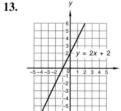

15. 360 in.^{3} **17.** $\frac{5}{2}$

19. $\frac{7}{19}$ **21.** 16

23. -17 **25.** $-\frac{14}{3}$

27. $\frac{143}{5}$ **29.** 1

practice   **a.** -5

problem set 93

1. 3   **3.** 3   **5.** ←——○————→
              0 1 2 3 4   **7.** 805   **9.** 3%, 5%, 4.5%

11. (a) $\frac{9}{25}$ (b) 36%   **13.** 1042 yd^3 **15.** 1.2348792 km   **17.** $\frac{81}{80}$ **19.** 232

21. 52   **23.** $\frac{13}{6}$ **25.** $\frac{17}{36}$ **27.**

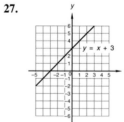

29. 8

practice   **a.** $2x + 3y - 4$ **c.** $2a + 11b - 8$

problem set 94

1. -6 **3.** 900 were opaque.   **5.** 100 collectibles   **7.** ←————○————→
                                                              -1 0 1 2 3

9.

   **11.** 380%   **13.** 12 yd^2 **15.** $2x + 4y + 3$ **17.** -1

19. $-\frac{14}{17}$ **21.** $\frac{270}{13}$ **23.** 52   **25.** -5 **27.** 14

29. -30

practice   **a.** 1

problem set 95   **1.** 5   **3.** –5   **5.** 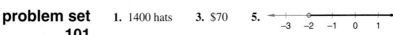   **7.** 286   **9.** 80%

11. $14 < \sqrt{201} < 15$ **13.** 136 yd   **15.** $6p - 5$ **17.** $2a - 5b + 11$ **19.** $-\frac{2}{3}$

21. –5   **23.** 17   **25.** $-\frac{21}{5}$ **27.** $\frac{1}{24}$ **29.** –20

practice   **a.** –1

problem set 96   **1.** 5   **3.** 880 ranch animals   **5.** 1760 people   **7.** 560   **9.** $\frac{643}{200}$

11. 3,140,000 cm³, 125,600 cm²   **13.** 131.4 ft²   **15.** $-4x - 4$ **17.** $-\frac{5}{7}$ **19.** $-\frac{11}{3}$

21. $\frac{5}{3}$ **23.** 30   **25.** $\frac{13}{3}$ **27.** 9   **29.** 1.92×10^{11}

practice   **a.** 17   **c.** $\frac{49}{2}$

problem set 97   **1.** –20   **3.** $1400   **5.** 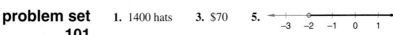   **7.** $3 < \sqrt[3]{40} < 4$

9. 145%   **11.** (a) 0.9 (b) 90%   **13.** 1061.64 cm²   **15.** 4   **17.** 8

19. –5   **21.** –3   **23.** $\frac{1}{3}$ **25.** 4   **27.** 69   **29.** –25

practice   **a.** 140°   **c.** $\angle MXY$ **e.** $\angle XBP$ **g.** 26°   **i.** 132°   **k.** 90°   **m.** 180°

problem set 98   **1.** –2   **3.** 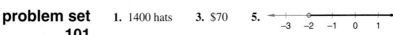   **5.** 30 hr   **7.** 180%   **9.** 4340 cm³

11. 142°, 52°   **13.** $\angle R, \angle C, \angle QRS,$ or $\angle SRQ$ **15.** $-2p + 2q + 3$ **17.** $\frac{25}{3}$

19. $\frac{13}{4}$ **21.** $\frac{8}{9}$ **23.** $11\frac{2}{3}$ **25.** $-\frac{7}{2}$ **27.** $\frac{225}{56}$ **29.** –1

practice   **a.** 4

problem set 99   **1.** 5   **3.** 720 students   **5.** 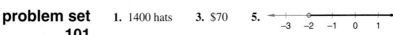   **7.** 368   **9.** 244

11. $445\frac{6}{7}$ **13.** 3543 ft³   **15.** $2a$ **17.** –1   **19.** $-\frac{7}{11}$ **21.** $\frac{7}{39}$ **23.** –5

25. $\frac{7}{12}$ **27.** 196   **29.** –18

practice   **a.** 44 big ships, 198 small ships

problem set 100   **1.** 140 acres, 100 acres   **3.** 11   **5.** 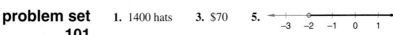   **7.** 195   **9.** 25%

11. (a) $\frac{17}{20}$ (b) 0.85   **13.** 735.1 ft²   **15.** 0   **17.** $6\frac{2}{3}$ **19.** $\frac{14}{3}$ **21.** $-\frac{6}{5}$

23. 4   **25.** –13   **27.** $\frac{17}{9}$ **29.** –14

practice   **a.** 3^8 **c.** $a^8 b^4$

problem set 101   **1.** 1400 hats   **3.** $70   **5.** 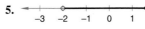   **7.** 224   **9.** 600

11. 144 in.   **13.** 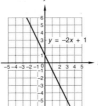   **15.** 9   **17.** 15   **19.** $\frac{1}{5}$ **21.** –9

23. $x^{11} y^{21}$

25. $a^7 m^8$

27. –1

29. 196

practice   **a.** $2x^2y$ **c.** $xy^3 + x^2y^2 - 5x^3y$

problem set
102

1. 250 marbles   **3.** −4   **5.**   **7.** 240

9. $14 < \sqrt{211} < 15$ **11.** 180   **13.** 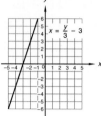   **15.** $\frac{23}{3}$ **17.** $-\frac{2}{3}$

19. $4ab^2 - a + 3$ **21.** −17

23. 22   **25.** x^7y^9 **27.** $\frac{7}{24}$

29. $\frac{280}{3}$

practice   **a.** $12x^2 + 8x$ **c.** $xy - x^2 - 4x$

problem set
103

1. 42 players   **3.** 6 hr   **5.** 11,760 Trojans   **7.** 155%   **9.** 736 cm^2

11. $5x^3 + 15x^2 - 15x$ **13.** 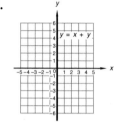   **15.** $8a^2 - 2b^2$ **17.** −1

19. 0   **21.** −1

23. −248   **25.** x^6y^7

27. −1   **29.** $1\frac{9}{20}$

practice   **a.** 60°   **c.** scalene and right

problem set
104

1. 2016 students   **3.** 700 sycophants   **5.** 6   **7.** 128   **9.** 1256 cm^3

11. 50°   **13.** 62°, isosceles, acute   **15.** $2abc + 2b^2c + 2bc^2$

17. $4a^3 + 4ab^2$ **19.** $\frac{9}{5}$ **21.** 1   **23.** 0   **25.** a^6b^3

27. $-\frac{14}{3}$ **29.** −126

practice   **a.** −9

problem set
105

1. 24 audiophiles   **3.** 800 contumacious, 6800 affable   **5.** $-\frac{1}{3}$ **7.** 7   **9.** 130%

11. 75.4 m^2 **13.** 45°, 45°, isoceles, right   **15.** $3m^3n^2 + m^2n^3y + m^2n^2$ **17.** $-3ap^3$

19. $\frac{11}{3}$ **21.** $\frac{275}{52}$ **23.** $a^{10}p^4$ **25.** 1.935   **27.** −28   **29.** 18

practice   **a.** −3   **c.** $\frac{1}{25}$ **e.** −1

problem set
106

1. 4   **3.** 800 customers   **5.** 7 hr   **7.** 702 students   **9.** 180%   **11.** 606.96 ft

13.   **15.** $36a^2x^2 + 12a^2x + 12axz$ **17.** −36

19. $-6m^2 + 8c^2 - 4cm$ **21.** $-\frac{16}{15}$ **23.** −8   **25.** −2

27. a^7m^5 **29.** 0

practice   **a.** IV   **c.** XXXIV   **e.** 140

problem set
107

1. 24,000 iconoclasts   **3.** 84,000 people   **5.** 2000 advocates, 2800 opponents

7.   **9.** 1215   **11.** 288,000,000 cm^3 **13.** XVII   **15.** 6

17. $13\frac{1}{20}$ **19.** $5c^2 + 15cm + 10cp$ **21.** $4m^2 + 2c^3$ **23.** 0   **25.** $-\frac{7}{10}$ **27.** $-13\frac{1}{2}$

29. 105

practice   **a.** $\frac{1}{2500}$ **c.** $\frac{9}{40}$ **e.** $\frac{1}{400}$

problem set 108

1. 1,050,000 units   **3.** $40,800

5. (number line from 0 to 4 with point between 1 and 2)

7. 240%   **9.** 587.86 ft^3 **11.** (a) XIX   (b) MDCXLIV

13. (a) 45°   (b) 90°   (c) 170°   **15.** $\frac{37}{16}$ **17.** $11p^2 + 121p + 22pab$

19. $2ap^3 + 2m^2nx$ **21.** 0.89   **23.** 0.8625   **25.** $7\frac{2}{7}$ **27.** 25   **29.** at^5

practice   **a.** $8260

problem set 109

1. 1400 people   **3.** 36,300,000 bushels   **5.** $5724.50   **7.** $19,965   **9.** 17.1

11. 2166   **13.** 0.0157 ft^3, 0.314 ft^2 **15.** $-14\frac{1}{8}$ **17.** $3cm + 3cmn + 3cn$

19. $2a^3p + 2m^2b^2$ **21.** 301.025   **23.** 0.082   **25.** 12   **27.** 19   **29.** $130\frac{1}{2}$

practice   **a.** $9600

problem set 110

1. 2000 little people   **3.** −4   **5.** $32   **7.** $4 < \sqrt[3]{80} < 5$ **9.** 53.7 ft   **11.** 419

13. 120%   **15.** 760,320 in.   **17.** $2a^2bc + 2a^2c - 2abc$ **19.** $5xy^2 + xy$

21. $-\frac{15}{28}$ **23.** −6   **25.** $6a^3b^6$ **27.** 0   **29.** $4\frac{1}{4}$

practice   **a.** $1674

problem set 111

1. 8000 red marbles   **3.** 28,900 wet ones   **5.** $2600   **7.** 0.0625   **9.** MMMCDLXV

11. 300   **13.** $5.00   **15.** $8\frac{35}{243}$ **17.** $-4xy^2 + 7x^2y$ **19.** 1.01736×10^{-3} m^3

21. $-\frac{1}{2}$ **23.** $4a^6b^4$ **25.** $\frac{413}{180}$ **27.** −5   **29.**

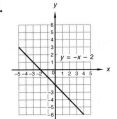

$y = -x - 2$

practice   **a.** $\frac{9}{16}$

problem set 112

1. $\frac{6}{11}$ **3.** (a) $\frac{1}{6}$ (b) $\frac{1}{6}$ **5.** 1125 were aloof.   **7.** $4234.75   **9.** $70,800

11. 3015   **13.** (a) 0.052   (b) 0.1775   (c) 0.11375   **15.** 44 million commercial vehicles

17. $14d^2z + 14dz^2$ **19.** 54 in.^{2} **21.** $-\frac{3}{10}$ **23.** (a) 118°   (b) 64°   (c) 69°

25. −38   **27.** $-\frac{10}{9}$ **29.** (a) $\frac{1}{32}$ (b) 27

practice   **a.** $\frac{7}{16}$ in.   **c.** $1\frac{1}{4}$ in.   **e.** $2\frac{3}{8}$ in.   **g.** 0.6 cm   **i.** 2.8 cm   **k.** $2\frac{3}{4}$ in., 7 cm

problem set 113

1. $\frac{1}{5}$ **3.** 828,000 tons   **5.** $247.25   **7.** $x = 12, y = 16$ **9.** (a) $1\frac{1}{2}$ in.   (b) 47 mm

11. (a) $\frac{1}{8}$ (b) 32   **13.** 180%   **15.** 1594   **17.** $2a^2bc + 2abc^2 - 2ac^2$

19. 2268 ft^3 **21.** $\frac{5}{7}$ **23.** $-\frac{2}{9}$ **25.** $5a^5b^4$ **27.** 119.411   **29.** 6

practice   **a.** $\frac{1}{512}$

problem set 114

1. $\frac{1}{28}$ **3.** 2400 incidents   **5.** $\frac{1}{676}$ **7.** 8 hr   **9.** (a) 97°   (b) 7°

11. (a) 141°   (b) 46°   (c) 65°   **13.** 1000%   **15.** $4az^3 + 4a^2z - 12a^3z^2$ **17.** 12.56 cm

19. MCMXCIX   **21.** −3   **23.** $-\frac{8}{5}$ **25.** $6m^5p^7$ **27.** 1.6   **29.** $\frac{1}{72}$

practice **a.** convex polygon, regular quadrilateral, rectangle, rhombus, square, parallelogram

c. convex polygon, trapezoid, quadrilateral

e. convex polygon, rectangle, quadrilateral, parallelogram

g. concave polygon, hexagon

i.–m. Answers may vary. See student work.

problem set 115

1. 280   **3.** $\frac{11}{45}$ **5.** $-\frac{92}{15}$ **7.** (a) 115° (b) 25°   **9.** (a) reflection (b) rotation   **11.** $5\frac{7}{8}$ in.   **13.** \$23.38   **15.** MCMLXXXIV   **17.** $4x^2am^4$ **19.** 12.45 km²   **21.** $-\frac{1}{2}$ **23.** [number line from −1 to 3, open circle at 0]   **25.** $36m^7p^6$ **27.** $\frac{297}{200}$ **29.** $\frac{27}{8}$

practice **a.** 21 m²

problem set 116

1. $\frac{1}{676}$ **3.** −3   **5.** \$32,850   **7.** \$109,000   **9.** 7000   **11.** 3994   **13.** Answers may vary. See student work.   **15.** (a) $\frac{5}{3}$ (b) 116°   **17.** $2a^3pm^2 + a^2pm^{-1}$ **19.** 38.12 in.   **21.** $\frac{3}{8}$ **23.** −2   **25.** −66   **27.** $\frac{423}{28}$ **29.** $18\frac{1}{8}$

practice **a.** ±6   **c.** $\sqrt{13}$

problem set 117

1. 600 paintings   **3.** 1400 spectators   **5.** $\frac{1}{2}$ **7.** 72¢ per lb   **9.** $\sqrt{85}$ **11.** 40 dm   **13.** 200   **15.** 57 mm   **17.** $67\frac{1}{2}°$, $157\frac{1}{2}°$ **19.** $2x^3y^3 - 4xy^3$ **21.** $\frac{1}{14}$ **23.** $-\frac{64}{27}$ **25.** a^6b^4 **27.** $\frac{13}{8}$ **29.** −4

practice **a.** $\frac{1,000,000}{(12)(12)(12)(5280)(5280)(5280)}$ mi³ $\approx 3.93 \times 10^{-9}$ mi³

problem set 118

1. $\frac{1}{36}$ **3.** 35,000 contestants   **5.** $3\frac{1}{8}$ in.   **7.** −\$27,250   **9.** 192.8   **11.** $1000(5280)(5280)(5280)(12)(12)(12)$ in.³ $\approx 2.54 \times 10^{17}$ in.³   **13.** $\sqrt{45}$ **15.** 27.3 ft²   **17.** 1056.8 cm²   **19.** $5zmn^3 - 3zm^2$ **21.** $-\frac{31}{6}$ **23.** (a) 49 (b) $-\frac{1}{27}$ **25.** $7m^3n^5b^5$ **27.** 120   **29.** 162

practice **a.** 500(100)(100)(100) mL = 500,000,000 mL   **c.** 5,000,000 mL

problem set 119

1. (a) $\frac{5}{36}$ (b) $\frac{1}{9}$ (c) $\frac{1}{12}$ **3.** 350 flowers   **5.** \$84.00   **7.** −3   **9.** $\frac{55}{(12)(12)(12)}$ ft³ ≈ 0.032 ft³   **11.** $\frac{10,000}{(100)(100)(100)(1000)(1000)(1000)}$ km³ $= 1 \times 10^{-11}$ km³   **13.** 160%   **15.** $\frac{(1320)(100)(100)(100)}{1000}$ L = 1,320,000 L   **17.** $2a^2b + 2ab^2 - 2a^2b^3 + 2a^3b^2$ **19.** 0.1272 m³   **21.** $-\frac{61}{20}$ **23.** −10   **25.** $-\frac{3}{7}$ **27.** 0   **29.** 7 cm

practice **a.** 48 m³   **c.** 904.32 cm³

problem set 120

1. $\frac{1}{16}$ **3.** 400 people   **5.**   **7.** 16.75 m³   **9.** 96 m²   **11.** 15   **13.** 50°   **15.** 32 ft²   **17.** $7 < \sqrt{57} < 8$

19. $\frac{60}{(12)(12)(12)(5280)(5280)(5280)}$ mi³ $\approx 2.36 \times 10^{-13}$ mi³   **21.** $\frac{10}{13}$ **23.** (a) 81 (b) $\frac{1}{64}$ **25.** $6a^6b^6$ **27.** −78   **29.** \$11,712.80

practice **a.** 30 in.^{3} **c.**    **e.** line   **g.** 157 m^2

problem set 121

1. $\frac{81}{1156}$ **3.** 1800   **5.** 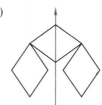   **7.** 22.5 in.^{3} **9.** 3052.08 ft^3

11. (a) 42° (b) 5   **13.** (a) 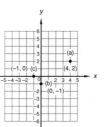 (b)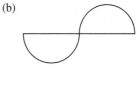

15. $1175   **17.** 100,000   **19.** 20(5280)(5280)(5280)(12)(12)(12) in.^{3} ≈ 5.09 × 10^{15} in.^{3}

21. $-2mp^2 + 2m^2p$ **23.** $\frac{7}{32}$ **25.** −16   **27.** $\frac{19}{120}$ **29.** 21

practice **a.** 362,880

problem set 122

1. $\frac{1}{676}$ **3.** $13,129.32   **5.** 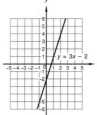   **7.** (a) 5040 (b) 210   **9.** 1000 m^3

11. 140%   **13.** $\frac{1,000,000}{(100)(100)(100)(1000)(1000)(1000)}$ km^3 = 1 × 10^{-9} km^3 **15.** 48 ft^3

17. (a) 30° (b) $\sqrt{75}$ **19.** (a) 17.53 m^2 (b) 10 m^2 **21.** $\frac{77}{54}$ **23.** (a) −64 (b) $\frac{1}{64}$

25. m^8p^7z **27.** −84   **29.** X denarii

practice **a.** counting numbers, whole numbers, integers, rational numbers, real numbers

problem set 123

1. $\frac{1}{128}$ **3.** 131   **5.** 30 hr   **7.** $1125   **9.** irrational numbers, real numbers

11. 144 m^3 **13.** (a) 54° (b) $\sqrt{88}$ **15.**   **17.** 165%

19. 11,000,000(5280)(5280)(5280)(12)(12)(12) in.^{3} ≈ 2.8 × 10^{21} in.^{3} **21.** $5a^2b^2 + 3a^2b^3$

23. 48 m^3 **25.** 6   **27.** 120   **29.** $-\frac{134}{1125}$

Topic A practice

1. Students should use the steps in Construction A to copy the angle.

3. equilateral

5. Students should use the compass to measure the length of one side of $\triangle ABC$ and then construct the corresponding side of $\triangle DEF$ with the same length. Then students should copy the adjacent angles on $\triangle ABC$ to their corresponding angles on $\triangle DEF$.

7. Students should use the steps in Construction A to copy the 30° angle constructed in practice problem 3. Then they should bisect that copy using the steps in Construction B.

9. Students should use the steps in Construction C.

11. Students should use the steps in Construction E.

13. Answers may vary. Students may construct a right angle first, then construct a copy of the 60° angle on one of the sides adjacent to the right angle.

15. Answers may vary.   17. Answers may vary.

Topic B practice

1.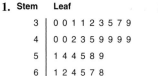

Stem	Leaf
3	0 0 1 1 2 3 5 7 9
4	0 0 2 3 5 9 9 9 9
5	1 4 4 5 8 9
6	1 2 4 5 7 8

3. (a)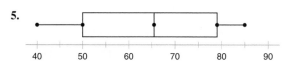

Stem	Leaf
4	2 8 9 9 9 9
5	3 6 8 9
6	0 2 5 5 6 6 8
7	0 1 2 3 4 5 7

(b) 49   (c) 35   (d) 63.5

(e) 61.5

5.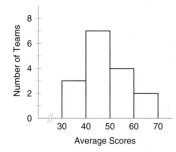

7.

Distribution of Teams' Average Scores

(histogram: Number of Teams vs. Average Scores)

Topic C practice

1. 100   3. 41   5. 1001010 (base 2)   7. 1100000 (base 2)   9. 69

11. 11000 (base 2)   13. 1010000 (base 2)   15. 101001 (base 2)   17. 1000.001

19. 1000111   21. 100111   23. 1001   25. 0.11011   27. 10000.01101

Topic D practice

1. $b = d = f = 100°$, $a = c = g = e = 80°$ 3. $m = 48°$, $n = 192°$

5. $a = 30°$, $b = 112°$ 7. $x = 40°$, $y = 140°$

9. $m\widehat{BC} = 50°$, $m\widehat{CD} = 60°$, $m\widehat{BD} = 110°$ 11. $m\widehat{AC} = 100°$, $m\angle ECB = 35°$

13. $x = 25°$, $y = 65°$

Topic E practice

1. 1.41   3. 2.24   5. 9.49   7. 5.29   9. 2.4495   11. 3.3166   13. 4.8990

15. 2.29   17. 4.64   19. 1.57   21. 3.23   23. 2.74   25. 2.10

Topic F practice

1. $3x^3 + x^2 + 6x + 9$ 3. $-14x^4 - 2x^3 + 9x^2 - 11x + 5$ 5. $k^4 + k^3 + k^2 + k + 1$

7. $x^4 - 4x^3 - 7x$ 9. $21wxy^3z^2$ 11. $4x^2 - 18x - 10$ 13. $9x^2 + 12x + 4$

15. $20x^4y + 12x^3 - 4x^2y$ 17. $a^2b^2c^2 - abcdef$ 19. $20x$ 21. $15m^3$ 23. $40m^2 - 2$

25. $10x^4 - 5xyz + 1$ 27. $3c^2 + 5cd - 100d$

Topic G practice

1. (a–c)

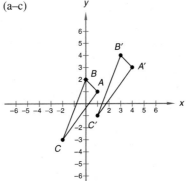

3. (a–c)

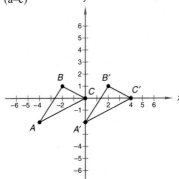

5. (a–c)

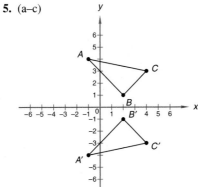

7. (a–c)

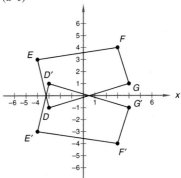

9. (a–c)

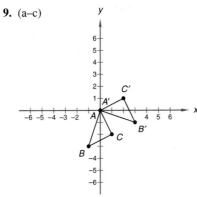

11. (a–c)

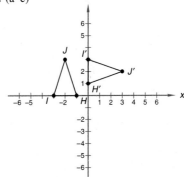

13. (a) $D'(1, 0)$, $E'(4, 1)$, $F'(3, 3)$, $G'(0, 4)$

(b) $D''(1, 0)$, $E''(4, -1)$, $F''(3, -3)$, $G''(0, -4)$

(c) $D'''(1, 0)$, $E'''(4, -1)$, $F'''(3, -3)$, $G'''(0, -4)$

(d) They are the same points.

Topic H practice

1.

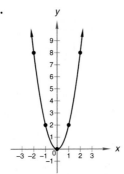

3.

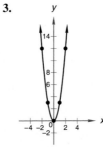

5.

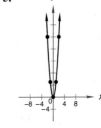

7.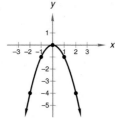

9.

11.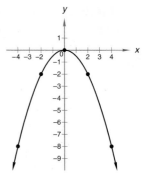

13.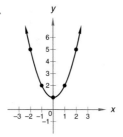

15.

17. Adding a number to the x^2 term shifts (or slides or translates) the parabola up that many units, and subtracting a number from the term shifts (or slides or translates) the parabola down that many units.

19.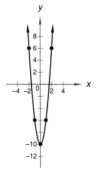

Topic I practice

1. slope = 2

3. 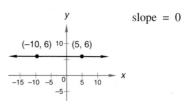 slope = 0

5. 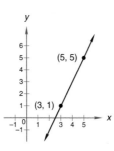 slope = −2

7. slope = $\frac{2}{3}$

9. slope $\approx \frac{-2-2}{-4-(-10)} = \frac{-4}{6} = -\frac{2}{3}$

11.

x	y
0	6
1	1

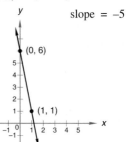 slope = −5

13.

x	y
0	2
1	−1

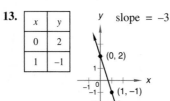 slope = −3

Topic J   **1.** $\frac{5}{13}$ **3.** $\frac{8}{15}$ **5.** $\frac{12}{13}$ **7.** $\frac{8}{17}$ **9.** $\frac{8}{17}$ **11.** $\frac{15}{17}$ **13.** 0.2679   **15.** 0.7002

17. 0.4226   **19.** 0.9659   **21.** 0.9397   **23.** 0.9848   **25.** 25°   **27.** 35°

practice   **29.** ~14.30   **31.** 333 cm